SPECIAL EDITION
USING
Solaris 9

LANCE

3 The Solaris Interactive Installation 31
4 Installing Software Packages and Patches 51
5 Booting and Shutting Down the System 69

Part II 83

6 GUI in Solaris 85
7 The Shell Environment 109

Part III 125

8 Understanding the Solaris File System 127
9 The Network File System (NFS) 151
10 CacheFS 165

Part IV 177

11 Managing Users and Groups 179
12 Disk and Storage Administration 203
13 Managing Serial Devices 219
14 Managing Printing 237
15 Backup and Recovery 259
16 Process Management 277
17 Administering Remote Systems 293
18 Administering TCP/IP in Solaris OE 309

Part V 335

19 DNS 337
20 Network Information Service (NIS) 355
21 Network Information Service + (NIS+ and FNS) 371
22 Lightweight Directory Access Protocol (LDAP) 389

Part VI 403

23 Mailing Service 405
24 Implementing Security 421
25 Enhanced Security Features 441
26 Performance Monitoring 489

Part VII 515

A What's New in Solaris 9.0 517
B NVRAM Parameters 525
C Solaris Management Tools 531
D Troubleshooting 537
E Solaris Tunable Parameters 559
F Glossary 567
Index 595

Radhika Girisan

Tanuj Jain

201 W. 103rd Street
Indianapolis, Indiana 46290

SPECIAL EDITION USING SOLARIS 9.0

Copyright © 2003 by Que Publishing

International Standard Book Number: 0-7897-2605-5

Library of Congress Catalog Card Number: 2002105209

Printed in the United States of America

First Printing: September 2002

04   04   03   02   4   3   2   1

Trademarks

All terms mentioned in this book that are known to be trademarks or service marks have been appropriately capitalized. Que cannot attest to the accuracy of this information. Use of a term in this book should not be regarded as affecting the validity of any trademark or service mark.

Warning and Disclaimer

Publisher
David Culverwell

Executive Editor
Candace Hall

Acquisitions Editor
Jenny Watson

Development Editor
Howard Andrew Jones

Managing Editor
Thomas Hayes

Project Editor
Sheila Schroeder

Copy Editor
Margo Catts

Indexer
Mandie Frank

Proofreader
Jody Larsen

Technical Editor
Edgar Danielyan

Team Coordinator
Cindy Teeters

Interior Designer
Anne Jones

Cover Designer
Anne Jones

Page Layout
Michelle Mitchell
Brad Lenser

TABLE OF CONTENTS

Introduction   1

I   Introducing Solaris

1   Introducing Solaris 9   9

Solaris—An Overview   10
  Solaris Features   10
  Applications Supported by Solaris   11
  Networking Services   12

What's New in Solaris 9?   12

Solaris Architecture   14
  The Kernel   15
  The Shell   15
  File System   16

SPARC Architecture   17
  Sun Fire   19

Summary   19

2   The OpenBoot PROM   21

OpenBoot Firmware—An Overview   22
  Components of the Solaris Firmware   22
  Boot Prom Versions   22
  Boot PROM   22
  The NVRAM   23

Configuring NVRAM Parameters   24

Booting the System from OpenBoot   26
  Testing Hardware from the OpenBoot   28

Interrupting Processing   29

Summary   30

3   The Solaris Interactive Installation   31

Solaris 9 Installation—An Overview   32
  Planning Your Installation   33

The Solaris WebStart Installation Method   38
  Automating the Pre-Installation Tasks   38
  Installing Solaris Using the WebStart Method   41

JumpStart Installation   42
  The Custom JumpStart Installation   42
  Factory JumpStart   45

The Solaris SunInstall Installation   45

WebStart Flash Installation   46
  Pre-Installation Tasks   46

Live Upgrade   48
  Disk Space Requirements   48
  Packages Required   49
  Installing the Live Upgrade Software   49

Summary   50

4   Installing Software Packages and Patches   51

Packages in Solaris   52

Managing Packages   52
  Installing Packages   53
  Removing Packages   60

Patches—Fixing Bugs   61
  Downloading Patches   62
  Installing Patches   64
  Removing Patches   66

Summary   67

5 **Booting and Shutting Down the System 69**

The Boot Process for a SPARC System
70
   The OBP Phase   71
   The Boot Program Phase   71
   Kernel Initialization Phase   71
   The init Phase   74

The Shutdown Process   78
   The init Command   78
   The shutdown Command   79
   The reboot Command   81
   The poweroff Command   81
   The halt Command   81
   Run Control Scripts for Shutdown
   81

Summary   82

II Working with Solaris

6 **GUI in Solaris   85**

Introduction and Brief History of X
Windows   86

Window Managers for Solaris   86

Common Desktop Environment   88
   Front Panel   89

Configuring CDE   96
   The Login Manager   96
   The Session Manager   99

The Workspace Manager   101
   Customizing the Front Panel   103
   Customizing the Workspace   103

GNOMEs   104
   Planning GNOME Installation   104
   Installing GNOME 1.4   105

Universal Language Coverage   107

Summary   108

7 **The Shell Environment   109**

Understanding the Shell   110
   Features of the Shell   110
   How the Shell Functions   112
   Types of Shells in Solaris   113

Customizing the Shell Environment
115
   Initialization Files   115
   Changing Shells   117

Shell Variables and the Environment
117

Template Initialization Files   120

Aliases   122

Summary   124

III File Systems in Solaris

8 **Understanding the Solaris File System 127**

An Overview of File Systems   128
   Disk-Based File Systems   128
   Memory-Based File Systems   129
   Network File Systems (NFS)   129

Solaris File System Structure   129
   Boot Block   130
   Super Block   130
   Inode Block   131
   Data Block   132
   Vnode   132

Links   132

Solaris File Systems and Their Functions
133
   Mounting File Systems   134
   Unmounting File Systems   136
   /etc/vfstab File   136
   Finding Information About the
   Mounted File Systems   138

Restricting the File Size and Disk Space Usage   139
    ulimit Command   139
    Disk Quota   140

Default File System for the Local and Remote Systems   140

Checking and Repairing File Systems   141
    fsck Command   141
    Recovering Damaged Super Blocks   143

Monitoring Disk Usage   144
    df Command   144
    du Command   146
    quot Command   147

Other Solaris Commands Related to File Systems   147
    devnm Command   147
    fstyp Command   147
    fuser Command   148
    clri Command   148

Summary   148

9 Network File System (NFS)   151

Overview of NFS   152
    Evolution of NFS in Solaris   152

NFS Daemons   154
    Mountd   154
    Nfsd   154
    Lockd   155
    Statd   155

Mounting a File System   156
    Mount an NFS File System Through a Firewall   157
    Use an NFS URL to Mount an NFS File System   157

Automatic File-System Sharing   158
    Large Files on an NFS Server   158
    NFS Files   159

Securing the NFS System   159
    DES   159
    DH Authentication   161

Troubleshooting NFS   161

WebNFS Access   163

Summary   164

10 CacheFS   165

Defining CacheFS   166

Using cfsadmin to Manage a Cached File System   166
    Creating the Cached File System   167
    Modifying Space and Files of the Cache   167
    Specifying File Systems to be Mounted in the Cache   168
    Clearing the Cache   170

Administering Cached File System Using cachefspack   170
    Packing Files in the Cache   171
    Packing Lists   171
    Displaying Packed Files Information   172
    Unpacking Files   173

Maintaining the Cache   173
    Checking Consistency on a Cached File System   173
    Checking Cached File System Integrity   174
    Tuning CacheFS   174
    Sizing the Cache   175

Summary   175

IV Solaris Administration

11 Managing Users and Groups   179

Overview of the User Environment in
Solaris   180
  User Accounts   180
  User Account Database   181

Managing Users   183
  Adding Users with the useradd
  Command   183
  Assigning Passwords   185
  Modifying a User Account   186
  Deleting a User Account   186

Managing Groups   187
  Group Accounts Database   188
  Adding a Group   188
  Deleting a Group   190
  Modifying a Group Definition   190
  User Monitor Commands   190
  User Limiting Commands   194

Using SMC to Manage Users and Groups
194
  Managing Users and Groups Using
  SMC   195

Summary   201

12 Disk and Storage Administration   203

Introducing Disk and Storage
Administration   204

Disk Slices   205
  Format Utility   206

Adding and Configuring a New Disk   210
  cfgadm Utility   211
  RAID Levels   212

Volume Manager   212

SVM   213
  Configuring SVM   213
  Accessing the SVM   215
  Increasing the Number of Default

Volumes   215
  Expanding the File Systems   216
  Sun StorEdge (Veritas) Volume
  Manager   216

Summary   216

13 Managing Serial Devices   219

Modems and Terminals   220

Managing Modems and Terminals   221
  SAF   221
  Port Service   227
  SMC   228

Connecting Modems and Terminals   231

Troubleshooting Modems and Terminals
235

Summary   236

14 Managing Printing   237

Solaris Printing Services   238
  Printer Environment Design
  Considerations   239

LP Print Service   240
  lp commands   241
  Configuration Files   242
  The Scheduler   242
  Interface and Filter Files   243
  The terminfo Database   243
  Log Files   243
  The Printing Process   244

Solaris Print Manager   246
  Configuring Print Server and Print
  Client   248
  Migrating Configuration Information
  248

Printer Administration Using lp
Commands   249
  Configuring Printers   249
  Setting Printer Definitions   252
  Administering Print Requests   256

Summary   257

15 Backup and Recovery   259

Introducing Backup   260

Solaris Backup Mechanisms   261
Backup Frequency and Components
262
Backup Media   263
Types of Backup   265

Creating and Restoring Backups   266
Other Backup Utilities   268
Third Party Backup Utilities   273

Summary   275

16 Process Management   277

Processes—An Overview   278
Monitoring Processes   278
Terminating Processes   282
The pkill Command   283

The CDE Process Manager   283

Process Scheduling   286
The crontab Command   286
The at command   288
nice and renice Command   289
The priocntl command   290
Truss   291

Summary   292

17 Administering Remote Systems   293

Remote Login Services   294
The Telnet Utility   294
The rlogin Command   295
The Solaris Secure Shell   301

Transferring Files Across Remote Systems
304
Remote Copy   305
The ftp Command   306

Summary   307

18 Administering TCP/IP   309

TCP/IP—An Overview   310
Components of Solaris Network   311
Planning a Network   312
Configuring TCP/IP   314

Configuring Routers   316

DHCP   316
Configuring a DHCP Server   317
Configuring the DHCP Client   327

Introducing Internet Protocol Version 6
(IPv6)   328
IPv6 Addressing   328
Enabling IPv6 Addresses on Your Host
329

Troubleshooting Solaris Networks   330

Summary   333

V Configuring Network and Naming Services

19 DNS   337

Naming Services—An Overview   338
Solaris Naming Services   342
Name Switch File (nsswitch.conf)   343

DNS   347
Name Resolution Process   348
Setting Up DNS Clients   349
Setting Up DNS Servers   350
Setting Up Slave Servers   351
Adding and Deleting Clients   352

Summary   353

20 Network Information Service (NIS)   355

Introducing NIS   356
NIS Architecture   356
NIS Databases, Daemons, and Utilities
357
How NIS Works   358

Planning the NIS Domain   359
    Configuring NIS   360
    Setting Up NIS Slave Servers   364
    Setting Up NIS Clients   365
    Adding Users to the NIS Domain   366
    Creating NIS Maps   367
    Propagating NIS Maps   368

Summary   368

21 Network Information Service Plus and Federated Naming System (NIS+ and FNS)   371

Getting Started with NIS+   372
    Difference Between NIS and NIS+   373
    Transition from NIS to NIS+   377
    Preparing the NIS+ Namespace   378
    Populating the NIS+ Tables   379

Configuring the Master and Slave Servers   381
    Setting Up the Master NIS+ Server   382
    Setting Up the NIS+ Slave Server/Client   383
    Configuring the Root Domain   384

Federated Naming Service (FNS)   386
    Advantages of Using FNS   386
    Administering FNS   387

Summary   387

22 Lightweight Directory Access Protocol (LDAP)   389

Directory Services—An Overview   390
    LDAP   390

Setting Up LDAP   393
    Setting Up the iPlanet 5.1 Directory Server   393
    Setting Up LDAP Clients   399

Summary   401

VI   Advanced Solaris Administration

23 Mailing Service   405

Email   406
    Components of a Mail System   406
    Mail Transfer Protocols   408
    Sendmail   410

Implementing a Mail System   411
    Setting Up a Mail System   413
    Setting Up a Mail Host   415
    Setting Up a Mail Server   415
    Setting Up a Mail Client   416
    Testing the Mail Configuration   417

Administering Mail Services   417
    Mail Queue   417
    Mail Aliases   418

Summary   419

24 Implementing Security   421

Solaris 9 and Security Considerations   422

Securing Your OpenBoot PROM (OBP)   423
    Password Recovery Procedure   424
    Preventing Unauthorized OBP Password Changes   425

File System Security   426
    Understanding File System Permission Levels   426
    Methods for Setting File and Directory Permissions   427
    Using chmod and chown to Set Files and Directory Permissions   429
    umask   431
    Default File Permissions and umask   432
    Default Directory Permissions and umask   432

Monitoring User Login   432
    Using syslog   435
    Monitoring Superuser Account Usage   437

Log Files Used to Monitor Usage of the Superuser Account 438

Summary 439

25 Enhanced Security Features 441

Solaris Security Features—An Overview 442

SSH 442
SSH Authentication 442

Understanding, Planning, and Implementing SEAM 445
How SEAM Works 445
Installing SEAM 448

Using Kerberos with Solaris 9 451
Setting Administrative Access Controls 453
Synchronizing Server Clocks 453
Kerberos Options 453
Kerberos Client Applications 454

GSS-API 455

Role-Based Access Control (RBAC) 456
Rights Profiles in RBAC 457
Setting Up RBAC 457

ASET 468
ASET Security Levels 468
Configuring ASET 469

TCP Wrappers 471
Using TCP Wrappers to Prevent IP Spoofing Attacks and for Early Warning 472

IPSec 472
IPSec Modes 473
IPSec Security Protocols 473

Internet Key Exchange (IKE) 476
The in.iked Daemon 477
IKE Configuration Files 479

Firewalls 480
SunScreen Administration 481
Security Considerations 483
FireWall-1 487

Summary 488

26 Performance Monitoring 489

An Overview of Performance Monitoring 490

Monitoring CPU Usage 490
The mpstat command 490
The prstat command 492

Monitoring Virtual Memory 493
The vmstat Command 494
The swap Command 495
The pmap command 496

Monitoring Disk Utilization 499
The iostat command 499
The df command 500

Monitoring Network Activity 501
The ifconfig command 501
The netstat command 502
The ping command 503
The traceroute command 503
The nfsstat command 504
The snoop command 505

Using sar to Monitor Systems 505

Using the Solaris Management Console (SMC) for Performance Monitoring 508

Summary 513

VII Appendixes

A What's New in Solaris 9 517

New Features for System Administrators 518

New Features for Desktop Users 523

B NVRAM Parameters   525

C Solaris Management Tools   531

Solaris Management Commands   534

D Troubleshooting   537

Troubleshooting Installation of Software
Packages   538

Troubleshooting File System-Related
Problems   539
   Problems Related to File Access on the
   Local System   539
   Problems Related to Accessing Files
   over the Network   540
   Problems Related to Search Paths   540
   Using fsck to Audit and Repair File
   System Inconsistencies   541

Troubleshooting Printing-Related
Problems   550
   Problems Related to Hardware   551
   Problems Related to Network
   Connections   551
   Problems Related to Incorrect Printer
   Configuration   552

   Steps to Delete a Printer and Deny
   Access to Remote Printers   553
   Steps to Examine the Status of Printers
   554

Troubleshooting System Crash   554
   Information Obtained from Crashed
   Systems   555
   Steps to Display the Current System's
   Crash Dump Configuration   556
   Steps to Scrutinize Crash Dump
   Information   556
   Steps to Modify a Crash Dump
   Configuration   556
   Steps to Recover from a Full Crash
   Dump Directory   557
   Steps to Disable or Enable Saving Crash
   Dump Information   557
   Examining System Messages   557

E Solaris Tunable Parameters   559

F Glossary   567

Index 595

About the Authors

Radhika Girisan is an instructional designer and a technical writer by profession. She has been in the content development industry for over six years developing books, white papers, instructor-led training programs, and e-learning material on various technologies for Sun Microsystems, Microsoft, Computer Associates, Pearson Technology Groups, PeopleSoft, Hitachi Data Systems, and NETg.

Tanuj Jain has over seven years of experience with designing, setting, and maintaining enterprise-wide solutions based on different architectures. His main focus has been on enterprise systems architecture, system performance monitoring and tuning, and OS technology. Tanuj has worked on different flavors of Unix such as Solaris, SCO, Linux, and HP-UX. He has provided security solutions and also designed and implemented mass storage solutions for various clients such as ITE Singapore, Vizzavi Europe Ltd., Sun Microsystems, NTT, RPG group, and NIIT Ltd. Tanuj is a Microsoft Certified Professional and a Certified Novell administrator.

DEDICATION

To Ma and Pa

—Radhika Girisan

To my parents (Archana and Ravi)

—Tanuj Jain

ACKNOWLEDGMENTS

We wish to thank the following people, who were more than help in the successful completion of this book:

Ramadas Shanmugam, Vijay Shriram, Uma M V, Aamer Ali, and Siddhartha Mukherjee, who made the journey extremely pleasant by providing their invaluable inputs.

Naveen K. Siromani for using his artistic skills to create the graphics for the book.

Our family, friends, and co-workers, who encouraged us all the way.

TELL US WHAT YOU THINK!

As the reader of this book, *you* are our most important critic and commentator. We value your opinion and want to know what we're doing right, what we could do better, what areas you'd like to see us publish in, and any other words of wisdom you're willing to pass our way.

As an Executive Editor for Que, I welcome your comments. You can fax, e-mail, or write me directly to let me know what you did or didn't like about this book—as well as what we can do to make our books stronger.

Please note that I cannot help you with technical problems related to the topic of this book, and that due to the high volume of mail I receive, I might not be able to reply to every message.

When you write, please be sure to include this book's title and author, as well as your name and phone or fax number. I will carefully review your comments and share them with the author and editors who worked on the book.

Fax: 317-581-4666

E-mail: feedback@quepublishing.com

Mail: Candace Hall
         Que
         201 West 103rd Street
         Indianapolis, IN 46290 USA

INTRODUCTION

In this chapter

This Book Is for You   2

How This Book Is Organized   2

Conventions Used in This Book   4

Designed and created to enable high performance, Solaris provides services suited to the requirements of evolving business needs. Solaris, being a Unix-based system, incorporates all the power of Unix, reinforced with the expertise of Sun to render it as one of the most stable operating systems. The stability of Solaris is well established through an analysis of the uptimes for various running Solaris servers, which span years of non-stop and trouble-free performance.

Solaris 9.0 Operating Environment is the latest version of Solaris. It provides a wide range of administration tools that assist both user and system administration tasks. Solaris 9 offers several enhanced and new features. For example, it includes significant security enhancements. In addition, it improves functionality for allocating, monitoring, and controlling system resources. The multithreaded kernel in Solaris 9 increases performance for core system functions and enterprise applications. The Solaris 9 operating environment is better by design and supports a high-level infrastructure that organizations need to support both enterprise and Internet-based services.

THIS BOOK IS FOR YOU

If you are looking at getting to know enhanced and new features added to Solaris OE, even if you are a beginner or a skilled administrator, this book is for you. The scope of the book is wide, with the topics ranging from basic evolution of Solaris to advanced topics such as implementing security. This book covers key administration topics, such as device administration, storage administration, managing users and groups, managing file systems, and performance monitoring. This is a must-buy book for prospective Solaris administrators and will act as a comprehensive guide for experienced administrators and Solaris desktop users.

HOW THIS BOOK IS ORGANIZED

This book covers the following topics:

- Chapter 1, "Introducing Solaris 9," introduces the Solaris 9 operating system and describes the new features that have been included in it.
- Chapter 2, "The OpenBoot PROM," introduces you to the OpenBoot system in the SPARC architecture.
- Chapter 3, "The Solaris Interactive Installation," describes the various installation procedures, such as WebStart, Custom JumpStart, Solaris SunInstall, WebStart Flash, Factory JumpStart, and Live Upgrade, in the Solaris 9 operating environment.
- Chapter 4, "Installing Software Packages and Patches," describes the tools and command line utilities you can use to install and uninstall software packages and patches.
- Chapter 5, "Booting and Shutting Down the System," details the booting and shutting down process for SPARC systems.
- Chapter 6, "GUI in Solaris," describes the desktop environments available in the Solaris operating environment: CDE and GNOME.

- Chapter 7, "The Shell Environment," gives you an insight into the different types of shells in Solaris.

- Chapters 8, " Understanding the Solaris File System " describes the file system in Solaris.

- Chapter 9, "The Network File System (NFS)" explores how NFS enables computers with different operating systems and architectures to access, share, and mount file systems across a network.

- Chapter 10, "CacheFS" describes CacheFS, which enables data caching on the local system.

- Chapter 11, "Managing Users and Groups" describes the commands and tools you can use to manage a single user or a group of users in a Solaris Operating Environment.

- Chapter 12, "Disk and Storage Administration" details the disk administration tasks, such as adding and configuring new disks and formatting and repairing the disk drives. The chapter also details the storage management solutions provided by Solaris, such as Solaris Volume Manager (SVM).

- Chapter 13, " Managing Serial Devices" describes modems, terminals, and ports, including the method to connect asynchronous modems and terminals to a SPARC workstation/server.

- Chapter 14, "Managing Printing," analyzes the requirements that must be complied with in the design of a Solaris printing environment. In addition, it deals with the intricacies of the Print Manager and the LP Print Service components.

- Chapter 15, "Backup and Recovery," delves into the various causes for data loss and the preventive measures you can take to prevent such losses.

- Chapter 16, "Process Management," looks at what processes are and how to manage these processes in a Solaris environment.

- Chapter 17, "Administering Remote Systems" explains the commands that are used to perform the most common tasks on remote systems. In addition, it details the parameters supplied with the commands in detail.

- Chapter 18, "Administering TCP/IP in Solaris OE," defines how to set up, administer, and expand a local area network (LAN) that will run the Solaris implementation of TCP/IP.

- Chapter 19, "DNS," describes the basic concept of naming services and the procedure to implement Domain Name Service (DNS).

- Chapter 20, "Network Information Service (NIS)," describes the role of NIS as a naming service.

- In Chapter 21, "Network Information Service Plus and Federated Naming System (NIS+ and FNS)," you will learn about the two naming services: NIS+ and FNS. NIS+ enables you to store system information, user information, security information, and information about the available network services. FNS provides a set of common names that can be used over different naming services.

- Chapter 22, "Lightweight Directory Access Protocol (LDAP)," explores LDAP directory services.

- Chapter 23, "Mailing Service," details the concepts you need to understand to set up mailing services, as well as how to implement them.

- Chapter 24, "Implementing Security," details the method to implement security at the system level. You will learn how to monitor incorrect logins, set up permissions to secure file systems, secure OpenBoot PROM, monitor logged-in users, recover lost passwords, and so on.

- Chapter 25, "Enhanced Security Features," delves into the various security protocols, mechanisms, and products that are available for Solaris 9.

- Chapter 26, " Performance Monitoring," describes the tools used to monitor the performance of a Solaris operating environment. This will enable you to analyze performance and avoid potential problems, which can lead to downtime.

The appendixes in this book contain a quick reference to

- What's New in Solaris 9
- NVRAM Parameters
- Solaris Management Tools
- Troubleshooting
- Solaris Tunable Parameters
- Glossary

CONVENTIONS USED IN THIS BOOK

This book uses various stylistic and typographic conventions to make it easier to use.

Code snippets and commands that run utilities are specified within a syntax. For example, to show how the `Ping` command must be used, the following code snippet can be provided within syntax:

```
ping xxx.xxx.xxx.xxx
```

The monospace font is used within the syntax to represent code in a different font. When commands or terms appearing in syntax are specified in normal text, they are represented in monospace. For example, the `Ping` command is represented in monospace to ensure that the command is not confused with other terms in normal text.

NOTE

> When you see a note in this book, it indicates additional information that can help you better understand a topic or avoid problems related to the subject at hand.

TIP

> Tips introduce techniques applied by experienced developers to simplify a task or to produce a better design. The goal of a tip is to help you apply standard practices that lead to robust and maintainable applications.

CAUTION

> Cautions warn you of hazardous procedures (for example, actions that have the potential to compromise the security of a system).

Cross-references are used throughout the book to help you quickly access related information in other chapters.

➔ To see a detailed list of different security features, **see** "Implementing Security," **p.421**, and "Enhanced Security Features," **p.441**.

## PART I

INTRODUCING SOLARIS

1 Introducing Solaris 9.0 9

2 The OpenBoot PROM 21

3 The Solaris Interactive Installation 31

4 Installing Software Packages and Patches 51

5 Booting and Shutting Down the System 69

INTRODUCING SOLARIS 9

In this chapter

Solaris—An Overview   10

What's New in Solaris 9?   12

Solaris Architecture   14

SPARC Architecture   17

Summary   19

SOLARIS—AN OVERVIEW

The Solaris OS was originally designed with the intranet and the Internet in mind. Solaris, being a Unix system, incorporates all the power of Unix, reinforced with the expertise of Sun, which render it one of the most stable operating systems. Starting from the original SunOS, all subsequent versions of Solaris continued to incorporate additional features and at the same time maintained a considerable backward compatibility with their previous versions.

Solaris 9.0 Operating Environment is the latest version of Solaris. Sun Microsystems offers its Solaris 9 Operating Environment—the Customer Early Access Program—for use through its Free Binary Software Evaluation Agreement, without requiring users to pay a license fee at the time this book was written. You can use this software on any number of computers, each having a capacity of eight or fewer CPUs, for only the cost of media and shipping. Even cost-conscious organizations can migrate to the Solaris operating environment to reap its benefits.

SOLARIS FEATURES

Although each version of Solaris is released with enhanced features, some features are common to most versions of Solaris. Some of these common features are:

- **Multitasking**—Solaris OE supports multitasking, which allows users to perform several tasks at a time. This means that some tasks execute in the background while the user continues to work in the foreground. The non-interactive tasks are the ones that are usually executed in the background.

- **Multiuser**—Solaris supports thousands of users at a time. In other words, multiple users can log on and simultaneously use the system. They can work on the same application/file concurrently. In this way, system resources, such as files and applications, and network resources, such as printers, can be shared, allowing optimum use of these resources.

- **Scalability**—Solaris is scalable from a single processor to a 64-processor system, such as the E10000 server. It functions and performs as required when upgraded or expanded in response to user demands.

- **Portability**—The Solaris kernel, its graphical interfaces, and the underlying utilities are portable to all the platforms that are currently supported by Solaris. The platform-dependent code of the Solaris operating environment is less than 5% of the core code. Therefore, it is very easy to port Solaris applications to systems with different instruction sets and processors.

- **Security**—Solaris enables you to set up security at the PROM level. This restricts users from starting the system. Solaris, like any other Unix OS, provides an authentication mechanism that requires users to authenticate themselves by entering a password when they attempt to log in to a server. However, it is entirely at the administrator's discretion to assign passwords to users. You can set up security at the file/system level by setting permissions to the files and directories that you own and deciding the users who

1

can access them. Solaris also provides encryption through various encryption methodologies, such as DES, md5, DH, and blowfish.

■ **POSIX Compliance**—Solaris is Portable Operating System Interface for Computer Environments (POSIX) compliant. Solaris is compliant with both the POSIX.1 and POSIX.2 standards.

■ **Common Desktop Environment** (CDE)—Solaris supports two types of desktops: CDE and Getworking Model Environment (GNOME). The CDE, an advanced Motif-based desktop with an easy-to-use interface, delivers a consistent look and feel across various Unix platforms. The other desktop environment, GNOME, provides the user with a user-friendly desktop environment and easy access to the Internet.

NOTE

In addition to Sun, several IT giants, such as IBM, Hewlett-Packard, and others, acquired the Unix source code. Consequently, the POSIX standards were formulated to minimize the differences between the various versions they developed.

■ **Time Sharing**—Solaris supports time-sharing. The central processing unit allocates each program a specific amount of time for execution.

■ **Virtual Memory**—The amount of RAM or the physical memory might not meet the memory requirement in systems that run complex programs and multiple applications. In this case, a portion of the hard disk is used as a swap space or as a temporary storage area to facilitate effective processing.

■ **Shell Programming**—Shells in Solaris offer various programming constructs that can be used to automate complex tasks.

■ **Multithreading**—In Solaris, a process can be separated into multiple executable threads; these threads have the capabilities to run simultaneously. A single thread of control manages all the separated threads pertaining to a single process.

■ **Java Application Development**—Solaris provides support for Java application development. Java programs run on most operating systems and are widely used for application development.

APPLICATIONS SUPPORTED BY SOLARIS

The main application areas supported by Solaris are as follows:

■ **Relative Database Management Systems (RDBMSs)**—The database management systems Solaris supports are Oracle, Sybase, Informix, MySQL, PostgreSQL, and others.

■ **Web Servers**—Apache 1.3.22 (Unix) is shipped along with the Solaris 9 distribution pack.

NETWORKING SERVICES

Solaris supports a wide range of networking protocols and services. The most important ones are as follows:

- **TCP/IP**—Enables Solaris users to unleash the full potential of the Internet.
- **DHCP**—Enables dynamic IP address configuration of clients.
- **Naming Services**—Facilitates network and system object management. Solaris supports naming services such as the DNS, NIS, and NIS+.
- **NFS**—Enables users to share file systems across heterogeneous systems.
- **LDAP**—Provides directory services.

WHAT'S NEW IN SOLARIS 9?

Solaris 9 comes with many new features, as compared to its predecessors. The recent enhancements in Solaris version 9 are discussed in this section. Let us look at what is new in Solaris 9 for each category of users, such as system/network administrators, software developers, and desktop users.

The following list describes the features that will benefit system/network administrators.

- **System Management Tools**—Solaris 9 provides several administrative tools, such as Solaris 9 Resource Manager, Solaris Volume Manager, Patch Manager, and Solaris WBEM Services 2.5, which provide improved functionality.
- **Solaris 9 Resource Manager**—The Solaris 9 Resource Manager provides enhanced features, such as allocating and monitoring of computing resources. In addition, a new fair share scheduler has been added to the Resource Manager, which enables the sharing of CPU resources. Solaris 9 also includes a Fixed-Priority (FX) scheduler that provides a scheduling policy to prioritize processes that require user attention.
- **Solaris Volume Manager**—This tool supports several kinds of management functionality, such as active disk monitoring, common management interface for storage devices, and disk partitioning on a single drive.
- **Patch Manager**—The new version of Solaris now includes a Patch Manager that allows you to install, add, and remove patches. You can download patches from SunSolve Online™service.
- **WBEM Services 2.5**—Solaris 9 also provides support to the World Wide Web. The Solaris WBEM Services 2.5 is an Internet management technology that unifies the management of enterprise computing management. Note that in Solaris 9, the WBEM includes an SNMP adapter that allows system administrators to access system management information.
- **Security**—Solaris 9 includes new and enhanced security features. Administrators can make use of these features for secured management of systems locally as well as remotely. Examples of security management features in Solaris 9 are Internet Key Exchange (IKE) Protocol, Solaris Secure Shell, and Kerberos.

➔ To see a detailed list of different security features, **see** "Implementing Security," **p.421**, and "Enhanced Security Fearures" **p.441**.

- **IKE**—This tool automates the key management for the IP Security Architecture (IPsec). This way an administrator need not be concerned about manual key management because the IKE protocol dynamically generates and manages keys for IPsec.

- **Solaris Secure Shell**—With the introduction of the Secure Shell (SSH), users no longer need to bother about accessing data over an unsecured network. The Secure Shell acts as a secured tunnel that allows data transfer, data access, and interactive user sessions in encrypted and compressed format. This feature provides fast and secure data transaction.

- **Kerberos**—This feature in Solaris 9 includes a centralized server for local and remote management of users and security policies.

- **Installation**—Solaris 9 can be installed with minimal packages because several features are grouped into logical packages. Also, Solaris 9 offers some new features, such as increased time zone selections and simplified administration of the installation procedure with Solaris Web Start Wizard.

- **Networking**—The networking features in Solaris 9 are iPlanet Directory Service integration, Sendmail, mobile IP Agent, and X11 support for IPV6.

- **iPlanet Directory Service integration**—Solaris 9 integrates the iPlanet directory service that helps manage users and resources in an enterprise-wide environment. The ipConsole is used to manage the Directory Server. Management activities, such as granting and revoking file access permissions, replicating data, and managing databases, can be performed with ipConsole.

- **Sendmail**—The features of Sendmail have been enhanced in Solaris 9. Some of the new features are new command line options, new defined macros, new compile and delivery agent flags, and new queue features.

➔ To learn more about Sendmail, **see** "Sendmail," **p.410**.

- **Mobile IP Agent**—The mobile IP agent enables the exchange of information between two mobile hosts, such as laptops and wireless devices. This agent allows a mobile computer to be accessible at a fixed IP address (called its *home address*), regardless of its current point of attachment to the Internet. Transport layer connections are maintained across different locations and this is accomplished without host-specific routes being propagated throughout the Internet routing fabric.

- **X11 Support for Internet Protocol Version 6 (IPV6) on Solaris**—The Solaris X Window System servers and client libraries support the IPv6 and the IPv4. This extension enables you to use IPv6 addresses and connections when displaying X applications across the network.

Software developers can benefit from several new and enhanced features in Solaris 9. Some of these features are as follows:

- **Extended File Attributes**—File systems in Solaris 9 now contain some extended file attributes. Application developers can use the file attributes to associate specific attributes to the relevant files. For example, a programmer developing an inventory control system can associate the application with a display icon.

- **Audio Enhancements**—Solaris 9 has enhanced audio support. Note that application header files are stored in `/usr/include/audio`. The `/usr/share/audio` stores miscellaneous audio files. In addition, a symbolic link from `/usr/demo/SOUNDS/sounds` to `/usr/share/audio/samples/au` is created to enable applications to run without failure.

- **Modular Debugger(mdb)**—Debugging is one of the primary concerns for application developers. Solaris 9 comes with an enhanced debugging utility, mdb(1). This utility provides debugging support to the Solaris kernel.

- **Improved Multithreading Library**—Solaris 9 has a new, improved, and faster multi-threading library.

- **Solaris Providers**—Developers can use the Solaris Providers to create managed resources. These resources help procure data about managed devices in a Common Information Model (CIM) environment. Five new Solaris Providers are available in the Solaris 9 software: WBEM Solaris Device/System Performance Monitor Provider, WBEM Product Registry Provider, WBEM SNMP Provider, WBEM EEprom Provider, and WBEM System Availability Provider.

In addition to system/network administrators and software developers, desktop users can also benefit from the following features in Solaris 9:

- **Xterm Terminal Emulator**—The Xterm terminal emulator supports multibyte character sets. This feature enables the use of xterm windows in UTF-8 and other multibyte locales. UTF-8 is a standard font format with the new X-term support. It is available for many new locales that are discussed in Chapter 6. The Xterm command line and resources incorporate new options to specify X font sets.

- **Universal Language Coverage**—The Solaris 9 operating environment supports 39 languages.

- **Xsun Server**—The Xsun Server can be used as a display device without keyboard and mouse support. You can use alternative devices, rather than the keyboard or mouse, to use the server.

→ To learn more about the new features of Solaris, **see** "Appendix A," **p.518**.

SOLARIS ARCHITECTURE

The Solaris operating system, which retains the basic structure of Unix, contains three main parts: the kernel, the shells, and the file systems (see Figure 1.1). Each is discussed within this section.

Figure 1.1
The Solaris operating system has three main parts: the kernel, the shells, and the file systems.

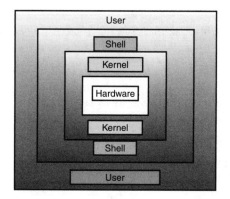

THE KERNEL

The kernel forms the core of an OS, providing basic services to all parts of the OS.

It is responsible for managing the system resources, such as devices, memory, CPU, and so on.

It allocates memory and time for various users and processes running on the system and assigns priorities for the processes. The kernel includes an interrupt handler, scheduler, and a supervisor to control the following functions:

- Memory management
- I/O services
- Process management
- System accounting
- Interrupt and error handling
- File management and security

The OS or an application program requests the services of the kernel through a specified set of program interfaces called the system calls.

THE SHELL

The shell is the layer above the kernel. The kernel starts a separate process that interacts with users, which is known as the *shell*. In a multiuser environment, such as Solaris, the shell must isolate the user interface from the kernel. This enables the kernel to allocate the system resources efficiently to all the users working on the operating system.

The shell acts as an interface between the user and the kernel. It interprets the commands executed by the user. No task is allowed to take direct control of the operating system in Solaris. Instead, each user gets a copy of the shell to interact with the kernel. The shell communicates with the kernel through system calls.

1

NOTE

System calls are a set of routines that allow an application to access the kernel services.

SHELLS IN SOLARIS

The features of the shells present in Solaris are as follows:

- **Wild Card Patterns**—Files that match a particular wild card pattern can be grouped together and actions can be performed on them.

- **Interactive Processing**—Communication between the system and the user takes the form of an interactive dialogue with the shell. This is known as *interactive processing*.

- **Shell Scripts**—These files contain a sequence of commands to be performed. This feature enables system administrators to perform their administrative tasks effectively by writing programs in the shell language.

- **Background Processing**—Some processes are time-consuming and are not interactive in nature. Such processes are done in the background while you continue using the system to do other tasks.

- **Shell Variables**—By storing data in variables, you control the behavior of shells as well as that of some programs and utilities.

  For example, the PATH variable stores the path names of all the directories to be searched for an executable file. The user controls the search process by specifying the alternate search path.

- **Input/Output Redirection**—Programs are instructed to obtain the input from a file other than the standard input device, which is the keyboard. This is called *input redirection*. Programs are instructed to send the output to a file rather than to the standard output, which is the visual display unit. This is called *output redirection*.

- **Programming Language Constructs**—The shell has features that enable it to be used as a programming language. Through the use of programming features, complex shells are built to perform complex operations.

- **Pipes**—Pipes can be used to develop simple programs that do complex operations with minimum effort. This reduces the necessity of writing new programs for the complex operations.

FILE SYSTEM

The file system in Solaris is hierarchical in nature, resembling a tree-like structure, with the root directory at the top of the file system hierarchy. The root directory forms the base directory, which holds the core of the operating system—the kernel. The root directory contains the following directories:

- **/usr**—Contains system files and directories that are shared with other users. The /usr/bin directory, a subdirectory of /usr, contains executable utilities.

- **/etc**—Stores the system-related data that is used for obtaining the system configuration data and for administration purposes. It contains important files, such as /etc/password and /etc/hosts.

- **/kernel**—Contains important kernel files, loadable modules, and device drivers. The kernel is portable across hardware platforms.

- **/export/home**—Stores the home directories of the various users.

- **/opt**—Stores the application software, which may accompany the OS, the bundled software, as well as software obtained from the third parties.

- **/var**—Stores system log files, such as /var/adm/messages, and user mail directories.

- **/dev**—Contains device-related files, such as the device drivers for the system hardware.

- **/bin**—Contains the essential system binaries.

Figure 1.2 depicts the Solaris file system.

Figure 1.2
The file system in
Solaris.

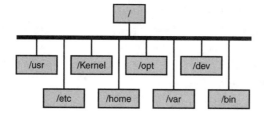

Solaris supports three types of file systems: disk-based, network-based, and virtual.

The file systems stored on physical media such as hard disks and CD-ROMs are referred to as *disk-based* file systems. They facilitate constant storage and management of the data present in different physical storage media. The Unix file system (UFS), PC file system (PCFS), CD file system (ISO 9660), and DVD Universal Disk Format (UDF) are some of the available formats in which disk-based file systems can be written.

Network-based file systems store files on a remote server. Although the files are stored in a remote location, they can be accessed as easily as local files.

Virtual file systems are special memory-based systems. By providing access to kernel-related information, they enable efficient system management.

SPARC ARCHITECTURE

The Solaris operating system runs on SPARC systems. SPARC—Scalable Processor Architecture—is a 32- and 64-bit microprocessor architecture from Sun Microsystems that is based on Reduced Instruction Set Computing (RISC) architecture. SPARC has become a widely used architecture for hardware used with Unix-based operating systems, including Sun's Solaris systems. SPARC is an open architecture that is available for licensing to microprocessor manufacturers through SPARC International.

1

NOTE

> RISC—Reduced Instruction Set Computing—is based on the fact that a complex instruction in a conventional computer can be reduced to a series of simpler operations, requiring a simpler architecture and a more compact and faster microprocessor.

The SPARC architecture was aimed to achieve the following:

- Reduce the number of instructions that need to be processed.
- Reduce the types of memory addresses that the processor needs to handle.
- Provide language compilers that optimize the code for a SPARC processor.

The SPARC platform has the OpenBoot PROM, which is used to perform extensive diagnosis and hardware testing and to select the boot device.

NOTE

> Sun Microsystems ships both workstation- as well as server-class computers. Sun currently provides support for the following hardware:
>
> - SPARCclassic™
> - SPARCstation LX
> - SPARCstation 4
> - SPARCstation 5
> - SPARCstation 5 Model 170
> - SPARCstation 10
> - SPARCstation 10SX
> - SPARCstation 20
> - SPARCstation 20 Model HS11, HS12, HS14, HS21, HS22, 151, and 152
> - Ultra™ 1 Model 140, 170
> - Ultra 1 Creator Model 140E, 170E, 200E
> - Ultra 1 Creator3D Model 140E, 170E, 200E
> - Sun Enterprise™ 1 Model 140, 170, 170E
> - Ultra 2 Creator Model 1170, 2170, 1200, 2200, 1300, 2300
> - Ultra 2 Creator3D Model 1170, 2170, 1200, 2200
> - Ultra 5
> - Ultra 10
> - Ultra 30
> - Ultra 60
> - Ultra 450
> - Sun Enterprise 2 Model 1170, 2170, 1200, 2200, 1300, 2300
> - Sun Enterprise 150
> - Sun Enterprise 250

- Sun Enterprise 450
- Sun Enterprise 3000
- Sun Enterprise 4000
- Sun Enterprise 5000
- Sun Enterprise 6000
- Sun Enterprise 3500
- Sun Enterprise 4500
- Sun Enterprise 5500
- Sun Enterprise 6500
- Sun Enterprise 10000
- SPARCserver™ 1000 and 1000E
- SPARCcenter 2000 and 2000E

SUN FIRE

The Sun Fire is the new generation hardware platform that runs Solaris 8 and 9. It enables the users partition up to four separate servers in one box. Sun Fire also provides the ability to do "hot" or on-the fly CPU upgrades and kernel patching, as well as full hardware redundancy and fault-isolated Dynamic System Domains.

SUMMARY

Solaris 9 has several features common to the previous versions of Solaris OE, such as multitasking, multithreading, multiprocessing, and so on. However, Solaris 9 comes with several new features useful for the different categories of users. Solaris 9 provides several administrative tools, such as Solaris 9 Resource Manager, Solaris Volume Manager, Patch Manager, and Solaris WBEM Services 2.5. In addition, Solaris 9 supports enhanced security components, such as Internet Key Exchange (IKE) Protocol, Solaris Secure Shell, and Kerberos.

The Solaris architecture includes the kernel, the shell, and the file system. The kernel is the core of the operating system and is responsible for managing the system resources. The shell enables the kernel to allocate the system resources efficiently. The types of shell in Solaris are Bourne, Korn, C, Bash, and Zee. The file system in Solaris is a tree-like structure with the root directory holding the core of the Kernel. The directories in the root directory are /kernel, /usr, /exporbt/home, /etc, /sbin, /dev, and /opt.

CHAPTER **2**

THE OpenBoot PROM

In this chapter

OpenBoot Firmware—An Overview 22

Configuring NVRAM Parameters 24

Booting the System from OpenBoot 26

Interrupting Processing 29

Summary 30

OpenBoot FIRMWARE—AN OVERVIEW

The OpenBoot system in SPARC architecture provides a significant enhancement in functionality when compared to the proprietary systems of the past. This architecture was first implemented by Sun Microsystems on SPARC systems. OpenBoot performs the following tasks:

- Testing and initializing the hardware.
- Providing access to a set of tools to program and to debug it.
- Starting the operating system.

OpenBoot is the standard firmware for the Sun systems and is unique to the SPARC platform. The firmware state is an operating state of the computer between the time the computer is turned on and the loading of the boot program. In the firmware state, a small program in non-volatile memory runs on the system and allows the user to perform certain system operations, which may not be available after the operating system is loaded. The two kinds of firmware operations are running firmware commands and running bootable programs.

Firmware commands include commands for displaying the device table, performing a system memory dump, displaying the firmware version, and so on. Bootable programs include the operating system and other bootable programs such as hardware monitors and debuggers. When a bootable program is requested to be loaded, the firmware loads and executes the program, passing control of the system to the bootable program.

COMPONENTS OF THE SOLARIS FIRMWARE

The firmware of SPARC systems has two hardware elements: the Boot PROM and the Non-Volatile Random Access Memory (NVRAM). The Boot PROM provides a user interface, which enables users to manipulate the configuration variables. The NVRAM stores various configuration variables.

BOOT PROM VERSIONS

All SPARC systems have this resident firmware that is soldered with the system motherboard. The various versions of Boot PROM are 1.x, 2.x, and 3.x. The current version used by SPARC systems is 3.x. Some older systems still use Version 2.x. Version 1.x is not supported nowadays.

BOOT PROM

The Boot PROM has a command line interface (CLI), which supports two modes: the restricted monitor and the Forth monitor.

The restricted monitor has a > prompt. It is the default prompt in older SPARC systems. You can use the restricted monitor to perform the following:

- Boot the operating system with options.
- Resume the execution of a halted program.
- Switch to the ok prompt (Forth monitor prompt).

The newer models of SPARC, such as the SunFire, use the Forth monitor as the default, which displays an ok prompt. The newer models support the restricted monitor also. Several OpenBoot commands can be issued at the ok prompt to perform the following functions:

- Hardware testing and initialization.
- Boot from the network, mass storage device, or from a wide range of devices, such as the hard disk drive, tape drive, and so on.
- Determine the system's hardware configuration and identify the system.
- Modify the boot parameters that are stored in the NVRAM.
- Perform extensive diagnosis for debugging operations.

To enter the OpenBoot environment, use one of the following methods:

- Shut down the system.
- Press the Stop+A key (should be used with caution).
- Power cycle the system.

NOTE

You can switch between the > prompt and the ok prompt with the following commands.
- To switch to the ok prompt, type **n** at the > prompt.
- To enter the restricted monitor, type **old-mode** at the ok prompt.

NOTE

The help command provides help to users on OpenBoot commands. This command without any parameter displays the instructions for using the help system and lists the available help categories. The help command, with the name of a help category, displays help on all the commands of that category. If a command name is supplied with the help command, it displays help on that command. For example, to know the usage of the boot command, type **help boot** at the ok prompt.

→ To know more about the OpenBoot commands and variables, **see** "NVRAM Parameters," **p.525**.

THE NVRAM

The NVRAM is a removable chip with a unique host ID. The uniqueness of the host ID is important in software licensing and hence, whenever a new motherboard is installed, this chip must be retained to maintain the uniqueness of the host ID. The NVRAM chip also has the ethernet address, time-of-day clock, and an eeprom section. The eeprom section stores the configuration parameters of the system.

Figure 2.1 represents a schematic diagram of the OpenBoot PROM and the NVRAM on the system motherboard.

Figure 2.1
OpenBoot PROM and NVRAM on the system motherboard.

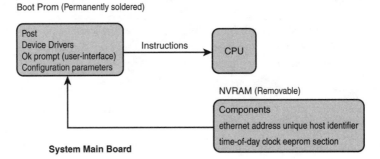

CONFIGURING NVRAM PARAMETERS

You use the OpenBoot commands to display and modify the configuration parameters stored in the NVRAM. The printenv and eeprom commands display the configuration parameters. The printenv command is used at the OpenBoot prompt, whereas the eeprom command is used at the operating system prompt. The printenv command lists the NVRAM configuration parameters with their current settings and default values. Listing 2.1 shows a sample output of the printenv command:

LISTING 2.1   A SAMPLE OUTPUT OF THE *printenv* COMMAND

```
ok printenv
Variable Name          Value                      Default Value
tpe-link-test?         true                       true
scsi-initiator-id      7                          7
keyboard-click?        false                      false
keymap
ttyb-rts-dtr-off       false                      false
ttyb-ignore-cd         true                       true
ttya-rts-dtr-off       false                      false
ttya-ignore-cd         true                       true
ttyb-mode              9600,8,n,1,-               9600,8,n,1,-
ttya-mode              9600,8,n,1,-               9600,8,n,1,-
pcia-probe-list        1,2,3,4                    1,2,3,4
pcib-probe-list        1,2,3                      1,2,3
mfg-mode               off                        off
diag-level             max                        max
#power-cycles          321
system-board-serial#
system-board-date
fcode-debug?           false                      false
output-device          screen                     screen
input-device           keyboard                   keyboard
load-base              16384                      16384
boot-command           boot                       boot
auto-boot?             true                       true
```

```
watchdog-reboot?        false                        false
diag-file
diag-device             net                          net
boot-file
boot-device             disk net                     disk net
local-mac-address?      false                        false
ansi-terminal?          true                         true
screen-#columns         80                           80
screen-#rows            34                           34
silent-mode?            false                        false
use-nvramrc?            false                        false
nvramrc
security-mode           none
security-password       security-#badlogins    0
oem-logo
oem-logo?               false                        false
oem-banner              abc
oem-banner?             false                        false
hardware-revision
last-hardware-update
diag-switch?            false                        false
ok
```

To modify the NVRAM parameters, you have to issue the setenv command at the ok prompt. For example, the following syntax sets the auto-boot parameter—the NVRAM parameter to configure automatic booting—to false:

```
ok setenv auto-boot false
ok reset
```

The reset command in the preceding syntax is to make the changes permanent. To restore the default values of the NVRAM parameters, issue the set-defaults command at the ok prompt. The following syntax restores the default values for all NVRAM parameters that have default values.

```
ok set-defaults
```

The eeprom command is used to display and modify the configuration parameters at the operating system prompt (#). The eeprom command does not need a subsequent reset command because it makes the necessary updates automatically. Listing 2.2 shows a sample output of the eeprom command.

LISTING 2.2   A SAMPLE OUTPUT OF THE *eeprom* **COMMAND**

```
# eeprom
tpe-link-test?=true
scsi-initiator-id=7
keyboard-click?=false
keymap: data not available.
ttyb-rts-dtr-off=false
ttyb-ignore-cd=true
```

continues

2

LISTING 2.2 CONTINUED

```
ttya-rts-dtr-off=false
ttya-ignore-cd=true
ttyb-mode=9600,8,n,1,-
ttya-mode=9600,8,n,1,-
pcia-probe-list=1,2,3,4
pcib-probe-list=1,2,3
mfg-mode=off
diag-level=max
#power-cycles=98
system-board-serial#: data not available.
system-board-date: data not available.
fcode-debug?=false
output-device=screen
input-device=keyboard
load-base=16384
boot-command=boot
auto-boot?=true
watchdog-reboot?=false
diag-file: data not available.
diag-device=net
boot-file: data not available.
boot-device=disk net
local-mac-address?=false
ansi-terminal?=true
screen-#columns=80
screen-#rows=34
silent-mode?=false
use-nvramrc?=true
nvramrc: data not available.
security-mode=none
security-password: data not available.
security-#badlogins=0
oem-logo: data not available.
oem-logo?=false
oem-banner: data not available.
oem-banner?=false
hardware-revision: data not available.
last-hardware-update: data not available.
diag-switch?=false
#
```

BOOTING THE SYSTEM FROM OpenBoot

The boot process of the system is controlled by certain boot parameters, which the administrator can configure at the OpenBoot prompt before booting the system. The parameters to be configured depend on the kind of problems faced during booting or the configuration changes that are required for booting. For example, if the administrator needs to boot from a different boot device, the boot-device parameter is used. Table 2.2 describes the OpenBoot parameters that control booting and their functions.

TABLE 2.2 OpenBoot PARAMETERS USED IN BOOTING

Variable	Description	Default Value
auto-boot?	If true, boot automatically after power-on or reset.	True
diag-switch?	If true, boot in diagnostic mode.	True
diag-device	Diagnostic boot source device.	Net
diag-file	File used for booting in diagnostic mode.	empty string
boot-command	The boot command to be executed if auto-boot? is true.	Boot
boot-device	The device to be used for booting. This parameter can contain zero or more device specifiers separated by spaces.	disk net
boot-file	File to boot (an empty string lets the secondary booter choose default).	empty string

NOTE

The eeprom parameters with a trailing question mark (?) need to be enclosed in double quotation marks (" ") or preceded by the backslash character to mask the special meaning of ? (wildcard) from the shell.

After configuring the boot parameters, boot the system using the boot command. The following is the syntax for the boot command:

```
ok boot [options] [device-specifier]
```

If the device specifier is not provided, the boot process loads and executes the program from the default boot device.

The following are the device-specifier names for various boot devices:

- **Disk**—Hard disk
- **cdrom**—CD-ROM Drive
- **Net**—Ethernet Card
- **Tape**—SCSI Tape

The following syntax gives the command to boot from the primary disk:

```
ok boot disk
```

The option used with the boot command determines the kind of booting. Table 2.3 describes the various boot options.

TABLE 2.3   BOOT OPTIONS

Options	Description
A	Performs an interactive boot that prompts for root and swap devices and the location of other important system files.
R	Performs a reconfiguration boot where the system scans all attached devices and creates entries in the /devices and /dev directories. This also updates the /etc/path_to_inst file.
S	Brings the system to run level S (single–user mode). It is used for troubleshooting and system maintenance.
V	Displays detailed startup messages. The messages displayed with this option are helpful in understanding the boot problems and troubleshooting.

→ To learn more about the boot command, **see** "Booting and Shutting Down the System," **p.69**.

TESTING HARDWARE FROM THE OpenBoot

The OpenBoot is used to perform extensive hardware testing. Table 2.4 lists the OpenBoot commands used for hardware testing.

TABLE 2.4   OpenBoot COMMANDS USED IN HARDWARE TESTING

Command	Description
Banner	Displays CPU data.
module-info	Displays the clock speed of the bus, frequency rate of the processors, and the amount of cache.
pcia-probe-list	Tests PCI on computers that have a PCI bus.
probe-scsi	Tests the built-in SCSI for connected devices.
probe-scsi all	Tests all SCSI buses.
show-devs	Displays all installed and probed devices.
test-all	Tests a group of installed devices.
test floppy	Tests the disk drive.
test memory	Tests the system memory.
test net	Tests the on-board ethernet interface.
Version	Displays version and date of the startup PROM.
watch-aui	Tests the AUI ethernet link; it displays "." for good packets and "X" for bad packets.
watch-clock	Monitors the system clock.
watch-net	Monitors the network connection.

To display the current hardware setup, use the `banner` command. Figure 2.2 shows a sample output of the `banner` command.

Figure 2.2
A sample output of the *banner* command. Type **probe-scsi** to check the devices attached to the `scsi` bus.

```
ok banner
           Sun Ultra 5/10 UPA/PCI (UltraSPARC-IIi 360Mhz), Keyboard Present
           OpenBoot 3.19, 384 MB (50 ns) memory installed, Serial #12654238.
           Ethernet address 8:0:20:c1:16:9e, Host ID: 80c1169e.

ok ▮
```

The `probe- pci` command performs the same activity as the `probe-scsi` command, but checks with the devices connected to the `pci` bus.

Typing **watch-clock** at the `ok` prompt tests the clock function. The following syntax shows the output of the `watch-clock` command.

```
ok watch-clock
Watching the 'seconds' register of the real time clock chip.
It should be 'ticking' once a second.
Type any key to stop.
3
ok
```

INTERRUPTING PROCESSING

The SPARC firmware has some keys programmed in it to interrupt processing in case of emergency. The keyboard interrupt keys are Stop+A, Stop+D, Stop+N, and the Stop keys.

The Stop+A key interrupts any running programs and processes and displays the `ok` prompt. It is normally used to enter the `ok` prompt by interrupting a hung system. This key can be used for diagnostic purposes. Note that any Forth monitor command can be issued at the `ok` prompt.

NOTE

> It is always advisable to write the memory buffers to the disk when the Stop+A key is used. To flush the buffer, issue the `sync` command at the `ok` prompt. However, STOP+A should not be used on running production systems.

The system enters the diagnostic mode when the `Stop+D` keys are pressed. It is used to run extensive POST diagnostics.

The NVRAM contents are reset to default values when the `Stop+N` keys are pressed. This helps to rectify problems in cases where the NVRAM contents are corrupt and it renders the system unbootable.

Pressing the STOP key and powering on the system bypasses POST and displays the `ok` prompt.

SUMMARY

The OpenBoot firmware for the Sun systems is processor-independent and provides enhanced functionality as compared to the proprietary systems in the past. The two kinds of firmware operations are running firmware commands and running bootable programs. Firmware commands include commands for displaying the device table, performing a system memory dump, displaying the firmware version, and so on. Bootable programs include the operating system and other bootable programs. When a bootable program is requested from firmware, the firmware loads and executes the program, passing control of the system to the bootable program.

The firmware of SPARC systems has two hardware elements: the Boot PROM and the NVRAM. The Boot PROM enables users to manipulate the configuration variables by providing a user interface. The NVRAM stores various configuration variables.

## CHAPTER 3

THE SOLARIS INTERACTIVE INSTALLATION

In this chapter

Solaris 9 Installation—An Overview   32

The Solaris WebStart Installation Method   38

JumpStart Installation   42

The Solaris SunInstall Installation   45

WebStart Flash Installation   46

Live Upgrade   48

Summary   50

SOLARIS 9 INSTALLATION—AN OVERVIEW

The Solaris 9 OE offers a variety of installation procedures, such as WebStart, Custom JumpStart, Solaris SunInstall, WebStart Flash, Factory JumpStart, and Live Upgrade.

- **WebStart**—The WebStart installation bundles all necessary software components as a single entity, enabling network administrators to use a familiar Web interface to install Solaris.

- **Custom JumpStart**—Use CLI to run the Custom JumpStart installation method. By using this method, you can install many systems simultaneously. This method requires you to have the knowledge of shell scripting and the JumpStart system. You can write scripts to perform installation tasks. You can create profiles for all the systems on which you want to install/upgrade Solaris. The profiles define specific software installation requirements. This method is not suitable for installing one or two systems, in terms of time and feasibility. It is effective only in mass rollouts.

- **Factory JumpStart**—The Factory JumpStart installation method installs software components based on the configuration of your system. You are not prompted for any information. It starts the installation procedure as soon as you insert the Solaris 9 DVD or the Solaris 1 of 2 CD.

- **Solaris SunInstall**—Use CLI to run the Solaris SunInstall installation program. This installation program guides you step by step through installing or upgrading to Solaris 9.

- **WebStart Flash**—The WebStart Flash installation helps you use the same software and configuration to install several systems simultaneously. The installation is based on the configuration of the master system that the WebStart Flash installation uses.

- **Live Upgrade**—This method is used for upgrading and not for installation. You can upgrade a running version of Solaris without halting your system in most cases. This method saves downtime for production servers.

Each installation procedure has different features that are designed for specific installation requirements and environments.

The following are the new features introduced in the Solaris 9 installation package:

- **Solaris WebStart Enhanced Installation CD**—The Solaris 9 Installation CD provides a graphical, wizard-based software application to install Solaris. Following are the new features introduced in Solaris WebStart installation method.
  - Solaris WebStart is modified to use the sysidcfg file.
  - You have the option to automatically reboot the system after the installation is complete.
  - You can preserve your existing file system during upgrade.
  - The new WebStart Wizard SDK 3.0.1 can be installed using the WebStart installation program. This wizard simplifies the installation tasks and the administration

of native Solaris, Java, and the new Java applications. In addition, developers can use this wizard to co-package both Solaris and MS Window versions of their applications.

- **Custom JumpStart**—This installation program has the following new and enhanced features.
  - Provides options to specify the location of the configuration used to perform the installation.
  - The NOWIN option can be used to specify that the Custom JumpStart program does not use the X Window System, which shortens the time for installation.
  - You can upgrade mirrors with JumpStart that you must have created earlier with Solaris Volume Manager.
  - The installation program attempts to find your default router.
  - Attempts to automatically find LDAP server in addition to NIS, NIS+, and DNS server.

- **Option to Duplicate Current Running Boot Environment**—As the original boot environment continues to run, you can upgrade your ODS on the duplicated boot environment. After the reboot, your new upgrade boot environment becomes your active boot partition.

- **DNS Support in System Identification**—DNS is added to the list of name services that are configured through the system identification utilities.

- **IPv6 Support**—Solaris supports IPv6, which provides increased IP address space, among other additions and improvements over Ipv4. IPv6 improves Internet security by using a simplified header format and enhances the authentication mechanism. The installation program allows you to configure both IPv6 and IPv4.

PLANNING YOUR INSTALLATION

Before installing Solaris, determine whether you are going to perform a fresh installation or upgrade from an existing version. Based on what your objective is, you should plan your installation accordingly. The following sections present the key planning tips.

DISK SPACE

Plan your disk space in advance. This should be in accordance with your installation need. Check what extra software you will install. The following are some important things to keep in mind while planning your disk space:

- If you plan to install any third-party software, check the disk space requirement for all the software that you plan to install.
- Plan your swap space partition. It should be at least 512MB and is usually the double of RAM. Please note that this can be larger depending on your requirements.
- If you plan to support printing, mail, and crash dump features, then you should double the space allocation for your /var file system.

- Consider how much space you would allocate to the users' home directory. For example, if there are 10 users and you plan to give 300MB to each user, then you should provide an additional 3GB disk space to the /export file system.

- For any extra language support, plan to add additional disk space.

- Determine the minimum requirement for the software group that you plan to install. Table 3.1 provides information on disk space requirements for each software group.

TABLE 3.1 DISK SPACE REQUIREMENTS FOR VARIOUS SOFTWARE GROUPS

Software Group	Minimum Requirement
Entire Solaris Software Group Plus OEM Support	2.4 GB
Entire Solaris Software Group	2.3 GB
Developer Solaris Software Group	1.9 GB
End User Solaris Software Group	1.6 GB

- You can install Solaris from a local media or from the network. Choose how you would carry out your installation/upgrade. If you plan to install from the network, ensure that the remote server is accessible over the network and that enough bandwidth is available (at least 10Mbps).

PRE-INSTALLATION INFORMATION

Ensure the availability of resources and decide on the following pre-installation information. Note that the following options appear during the installation procedure. It is advisable that you be ready with all the necessary information before you perform the installation.

- **Network Support**—Determine the network support for your Solaris system. Solaris can be installed in a network environment or as a standalone system.

- **DHCP**—Verify whether there is a DHCP server on the network, which would automatically configure the IP Address and netmask for your system.

- **Hostname**—Determine the hostname for the system. The hostname uniquely identifies a host on a local area network.

- **IP Address**—If you do not have a DHCP server, you need to specify an IP address. An IP address is a unique 32-bit number assigned to a computer on the network.

- **The Subnet Mask**—Ensure that the network in which the Solaris system will participate is in a Class A, Class B, or Class C network. In addition, determine whether the network is subnetted. In this case, you would be required to calculate the netmask for that subnet.

- **IPv6**—Determine whether the Solaris system will support only Ipv4 or Ipv4 and Ipv6. IPv6 is a recent version of the Internet protocol.

- **Kerberos Security**—Kerberos is a network authentication system. The Kerberos authentication option may be used with many network services, such as NFS. If you choose to enable Kerberos security, then you also need to input values for the following components.
  - Default realm
  - Abdministration Server
  - First KDC (Kerberos server)
  - Additional KDCs (optional)
- **Name Service**—Determine which naming service your system will use. The available options are
  - LDAP
  - NIS+
  - NIS
  - DNS
  - None

→ To learn more about all the above naming services, **see** "Configuring Network and Naming Services," **p.335**.

- **Domain Name**—The domain name is the name given to a domain, which typically encompasses a group of hosts. You need to decide whether your system uses the domain name service or not. If a domain name service is used, determine the type of name service for the environment.
- **NIS+ and NIS**—The installation program gives you the option of specifying the NIS/NIS+ servers or finding these servers for you. If you choose to specify this information yourself, you would be required to key in the server's IP address and the server hostname.
- **DNS**—Specify the IP address for the DNS server. You have to enter at least one IP address. Note that the installation program lets you enter three DNS addresses. In addition, you can also choose the sequence in which your search query should do a name lookup.
- **LDAP**—To configure the LDAP settings you need to specify the following settings for your LDAP profile:
  - Profile NAME
  - Profile Server
  - IP Address of Profile Server
- **Default Router**—Specify the IP address of the gateway your system will be using. The installation program can find it for you. However, if you choose to specify it manually, you are required to key in the IP address for your default router.
- **Time Zone**—In the Time Zone option, specify the time zone settings based on the geographic location. You can also select the Offset from GMT option or specify a time zone file (if there are any on your network). The purpose for all three options is the

3

same. It just depends on what method you choose. For example, if you specify a time zone in the time zone file for a mass rollout, you can avoid setting the timezone for each machine.

- **Locales**—Based on your geographic location, you can specify support for the appropriate locale. You can choose your local language, which can be used for user interaction during installation.

→ To learn more about the languages supported by Solaris, **see** "GUI in Solaris," **p.85**.

- **Power Management**—You can preconfigure Power Management depending upon the type of installation that you are performing. For example, if you use a custom JumpStart installation, you can preconfigure the Power Management information by using a finish script to create an /autoshutdown or /noautoshutdown file on the system. When the system reboots, the /autoshutdown file enables Power Management and the /noautoshutdown file disables Power Management.

- **Proxy Server Configuration**—During the installation procedure, you may have to configure your proxy server. Note that this choice would appear only if you were using the Solaris WebStart program. When this choice appears, you need to specify whether your system is directly connected to the Internet or you will be using a proxy server to connect to the Internet. If you choose to use the proxy server, then you have to specify your proxy server's hostname and port number. Note that unless a port is assigned a specific number, the port number is normally 80.

- **Automatic Reboot**—You have the option to specify the mode, automatic or manual, in which you want your system to reboot after the installation is complete.

- **Eject Installation CD/DVD**—The Eject installation option enables you to specify whether the CD/DVD ROM drive should eject automatically after the installation is complete or you would eject it manually.

- **Software Group**—Solaris 9 is shipped with different software groups. During the installation, you need to specify which software group you want to install. The choices of software groups are as follows:

  - **Entire Plus OEM**—Installs all the components plus the OEM support. It requires maximum hard disk capacity.

  - **Entire**—Installs all the components barring the OEM support.

  - **Developer**—Installs core components, as well as end user and the developer system support.

  - **End User**—Installs core components and the end user system support.

  - **Core**—This is also known as minimum installation. It installs minimal components necessary to run the OS only.

- **Custom Package Installation**—Solaris installation program lets you customize your package installation. You can add and remove additional packages according to your specifications. Before you remove any package, you must ensure that no other package is dependent on this package to run. Removing package requires you to have thorough knowledge of Solaris software functionalities.

- **64-bit support**—Specify whether you want to install support to run 64-bit applications.

- **Choose Installation Disk**—Here you are required to specify the target disk where your installation files are to reside.

- **Preserve Existing Data**—Because you might have some data existing already on your target disk, the installation program asks whether you want to preserve your data or not. If you choose to preserve it, then the installation program does not overwrite your existing data.

- **Auto File Systems**—Here you are asked to specify whether you want the installation program to lay an auto file system on your disk or you want to set it up manually. If you choose to set up the file system manually, you are required to provide file system configuration. Table 3.2 depicts the partitions in a typical Solaris file system.

TABLE 3.2   DIRECTORIES IN THE SOLARIS FILE SYSTEM

Directories	Functions
/	Contains the kernel and device drivers.
/usr	Contains the commands and programs for system-level usage and administration.
/var	Contains system log files and spooling files.
/export/home	Contains users' home directories.
/opt	Contains optional third-party software and applications.
/swap	Contains virtual memory space that improves performance by moving the unused segments of programs (or data) from memory to disk.
/proc	Contains information on all active processes.
/tmp	Contains temporary files that are deleted on booting the system.

- **Mounting Remote File System**—The installation program asks you to specify whether you want to mount a remote file system. If you choose to mount the remote file system, you are required to specify the IP address of the remote host, name of the remote file system you want to mount, and the local mount point.

NOTE

This pre-installation information is specific to the Solaris `SunInstall` installation program. Don't use it as a guideline for installing other programs.

THE SOLARIS WebStart INSTALLATION METHOD

As discussed earlier, the Solaris WebStart installation provides both GUI and CLI (Command Line Interface).

Table 3.3 describes hardware requirements for each interface type:

TABLE 3.3 HARDWARE REQUIREMENTS FOR GUI AND CLI		
Requirements	**GUI**	**CLI**
DVD/CD-ROM Drive	Local/Remote	Local/Remote
Network Connection	Yes (for remote DVD/CD-ROM Drive)	Yes (for remote DVD/CD-ROM Drive)
Disk Space	Refer to table for software group.	Refer to table for soft ware group.
Video Adapter	Yes	Yes
Keyboard	Yes	Yes
Monitor	Yes	Yes
Ram	Min—96Mb Recommended—128Mb or above. (For high-end servers, sizing should be done accordingly)	Min –96Mb Recommended—128Mb or above (For high-end servers, sizing should be done accordingly)

The software requirements for the Solaris WebStart GUI and CLI are as follows:

- If you have a DVD ROM drive on you system, you require the Solaris 9 SPARC Platform Edition DVD.
- If you have a CD-ROM drive on your system, then you require the following:
  - Solaris 9 Installation SPARC Platform Edition CD
  - Solaris 9 Software 1 of 2 and 2 of 2 SPARC Platform Edition CD
  - Solaris 9 Languages SPARC Platform Edition (For Language Support)

AUTOMATING THE PRE-INSTALLATION TASKS

You can automate the installation program to enable it to provide information such as IP address, subnet mask, time zone, and so on, dynamically. To automate the installation program, provide all the relevant information in the sysidcfg file or in the Name Server Database. The installation program reads information first from the sysidcfg file and then from the Name Server Database before prompting you for information.

NOTE

> You can automate the installation for SunInstall and Custom `JumpStart` using the `sysid-cfg` file or the Name Server database.

The following are the advantages of automating the installation program:

- Saves time
- Simplifies the installation process
- Enables unattended hands-free installation
- Minimizes the system administration tasks
- Reduces the overall cost of ownership

USING `sysidcfg` FILE

You must create `sysidcfg` files based on your need for pre-configuring different systems. You have the option of using a single `sysidcfg` file for all the systems you configure. However, you may want to avoid entering information such as hostname, IP address, subnet mask, or root password each time you perform installation. Therefore, it is advisable to use a unique `sysidcfg` file for different systems.

You can place the `sysidcfg` file in one of the following:

- **NFS file system**—If you put the `sysidcfg` file in a shared NFS file system, then use the following command while booting from the network:

  `Ok>add_install_client -p`

  The `-p` flag specifies the location of the `sysidcfg` file when you install the Solaris 9 software.

- **UFS or PCFS (FAT) disk**—Place the `sysidcfg` file in the root (/) directory on the disk.

Remember the following rules while creating the `sysidcfg` file:

- Keywords are not case-sensitive.
- You can list the keywords in any order.
- There are two types of keywords that you can use in sysidcfg file: dependent and independent. The dependent keywords are defined within the independent keywords. Note that dependent keywords are unique within the independent keywords. The dependent keywords should be enclosed within curly braces.

You can provide the following information in the `sysidcfg` file:

- Name service
- Domain name
- Name server

3

- Network interface
- Hostname
- IP address
- Netmask
- DHCP
- IPv6
- Root password
- Security policy
- Locale
- Time zone
- Date and time
- Terminal type
- Power management

A sample `sysidcfg` file follows:

```
system_locale= de_DE.UTF-9
timezone=wet
terminal=sun-cmd
timeserver=localhost
name_service=NIS {domain_name=corp.mydomain..com
➥name_server=myserver(172.17.20.50)}
network_interface=primary {protocol_ipv6=no netmask=255.255.255.129}
security_policy=none
 root_password=expre$$
```

> **NOTE**
> To create the `sysidcfg` file, use any text editor, input the required values, and save it as the `sysidcfg` file.

USING NAME DATABASE SERVER

Perform the following steps to preconfigure settings using the Name Database Server:

1. Log in as superuser on your NIS server.
2. Add a local map to your `/var/yp/makefile`.
3. The `/var/yp/makefile` comprises various procedures. Look for the `variable.time` procedure. Below this procedure, create a `local.time` procedure.

> **NOTE**
> If you are new to shell scripting, a template procedure is available at `http://docs.sun.com`.

4. Within the `/var/yp/makefile` look for a string `all`. The string `all` is preceded by variables such as `passwd group host` and so on. At the end of these variables, add a string `locale`. It should look like this:

```
all:passwd group host ethers ............auto.home locale
```

5. Add the line `local:local.time` at the end of the file.

6. Create a file called `/etc/locale` and create an entry for each domain or system. If your domain name is mycomp.com, your `/etc/locale` file should look like this:

```
Locale mycomp.com
```

The default locale for the domain `mycomp.com` is Greek. If your system name is `mysys`, then `/etc/locale` should look like this:

```
el.sun_eu_greek mysys
```

This means Greek is the default locale for system `mysys`.

7. Make the maps, using the `make` command.

```
#make /var/yp
```

> **NOTE**
>
> If you have an NIS+ domain, use `nistbladm` to create a locale and add entries to it. For options, use the `man` command, `# man nistbladm`.

INSTALLING SOLARIS USING THE WebStart METHOD

The `WebStart` installation is an interactive installation program, which provides a GUI. It installs Solaris and all co-packaged software by default. However, the user can customize the installation by selecting the desired co-packaged software. The main advantage of the `WebStart` installation is that it installs additional software in one session. It is simple to use because of its enhanced user interface.

> **NOTE**
>
> Co-packaged software refers to the software packages that are distributed with Solaris. For example, Netscape and StarOffice, which are not part of the OS and distributed with Solaris, are referred to as co-packaged software.

The `WebStart` installation procedure is as follows:

1. Boot the system using the following commands.

   If you are installing from the network, type the command:
   ```
   ok boot net
   ```
   If you have a local DVD/CD-ROM, type the command:
   ```
   ok boot cdrom
   ```

2. You are prompted to enter system configuration. If you did not preconfigure any information in the `sysidcfg` file or the Name Server Database, then you are required to provide all the configuration information at this prompt.

3. If you opt for GUI, after you have provided the correct system configuration information, the Solaris WebStart Installation Kiosk and Welcome to Solaris dialog box appears. If your system has insufficient memory, Kiosk does not display.

4. Click Next on the Welcome screen to proceed with the installation. The Installer screen appears, prompting you for information. At this point, decide whether you want to reboot the system and eject the disc automatically after the installation is complete.

5. The Select Media screen appears next. Select the media you will be using to install Solaris, such as CD or DVD, Network, HTTP, or local tape. After selecting the appropriate device, click Next.

6. Specify whether the installation is a fresh installation or an upgrade to Solaris 9. The Solaris WebStart program checks for the following conditions to check whether your system meets the minimum requirements needed to upgrade. You must have a Solaris root (/) file system partition available. Also, if you are upgrading using the Solaris 9 Installation CD, then you must have a 512-MB slice.

7. The installation program provides the relevant instructions on the screen for you to install the Solaris software and any additional software for your system. After the installation is complete, WebStart installation program reboots your system automatically or prompts you to reboot manually.

8. After the installation is done, you can verify installation by viewing the installation logs in the following directories:

```
/var/sadm/system/logs
/var/sadm/install/logs
```

JumpStart INSTALLATION

The JumpStart installation helps you to automate the installation of the Solaris software on new SPARC systems. This installation uses a default profile to determine the software that needs to be installed. You cannot manually select the software to be installed. The default profile is selected considering the system model and hard disk capacity. The JumpStart installation is used in places, such as training centers and corporate organizations, where you need to install Solaris on a large number of systems that are configured identically. The recent versions of SPARC systems have a pre-installed JumpStart boot image. For JumpStart installation on older SPARC systems, use the re-preinstall command. The re-preinstall command copies the boot image to the system on which Solaris need to be installed.

THE CUSTOM JumpStart INSTALLATION

The Custom JumpStart installation automatically installs from the Solaris 9 distribution CD in the local CD-ROM drive. A custom profile determines the software that needs to be installed. The Custom JumpStart installation requires a rule file and a profile for systems of each group or platform. A *group* refers to a set of systems having similar attributes. The *rule file* is a text file that contains platform-specific or group-specific rules for systems of similar requirements. The rule file distinguishes the systems, based on one or more system attributes, such as the platform name and disk size.

The *profile* is a text file that contains instructions on how the Solaris software is to be installed on systems of each group or platform. It contains keywords and associated values, which guide the installation process. Keywords are system parameters, such as boot disk, disk size, and so on.

The advantages of JumpStart are as follows:

- It enables you to automate the installation process.
- Installation can be performed identically on several systems.
- Patches can be applied automatically.

JumpStart has some limitations:

- It is complex when compared with the WebStart and the interactive methods.
- It does not install diskless clients.
- It requires a boot server on the local network or subnet.
- It requires additional administrative steps. For example, it needs a script to assign the root password. Also, the IP addresses are assigned manually by the administrator.

SET UP THE JumpStart SERVER

The following section lists the steps for setting up the JumpStart server.

1. Copy the files from the Solaris distribution CDs to the /JumpStart directory. The following script is supplied when Solaris copies files.
   ```
   # cd /cdrom/cdrom0/s0/Solaris_9/Tools
   # mkdir /JumpStart/sol9
   # ./setup_install_server /JumpStart/sol9
   ```

2. Next, share the directory where the files are copied. You can share the directory by adding the following syntax to /etc/dfs/dfstab:
   ```
   share -F nfs -o ro,anon=0 -d "JumpStart" /JumpStart
   ```

3. After making the directory shareable, you need to run the shareall script for the changes to take affect. Please note that you will run shareall, only if the machine is an NFS server. If your machine does not have NFS server processes running in it, run the following command:
   ```
   "/etc/init.d/nfs.server start"
   ```

4. Ensure tftp in inetd.conf is enabled. You can do this by checking whether the following statement exists in inetd.conf and is uncommented:
   ```
   tftp    dgram    udp6    wait    root    /usr/sbin/in.tftpd
   ➥        in.tftpd -s /tftpboot
   ```

5. Set up the new client's name in whatever database you use for naming (NIS/NIS+/hosts) on the JumpStart server:
   ```
   # cd /JumpStart/sol9/Solaris_9/Tools
   # ./add_install_client -e 8:0:20:22:33:44 clientname sun4u
   ```

The -e command represents the MAC address of the client machine, which can be obtained by using the banner command at the ok prompt. The clientname command represents the client's hostname, which can be sun4m (SS4/5/10/20), sun4d (SS1000/2000), or sun4u (any Ultra machines).

6. You can now boot your client, using the boot net command:

```
<#0> ok boot net
Boot device: /iommu/sbus/ledma@f,400010/le@f,c00000  File and args:
20800
SunOS Release 5.9 Version Generic_108528-07 32-bit
Copyright 1983-2001 Sun Microsystems, Inc.  All rights reserved.
[..etc..]
```

CONFIGURE THE JumpStart SERVER

After setting up the server, the next step is to configure the server. You can automate the configuration process by setting up the sysidcfg file.

1. Set up the client once again to use the sysidcfg file by using the following command:

```
# cd /JumpStart/sol9/Solaris_9/Tools
# ./add_install_client -e 8:0:20:22:33:44 -p
servername:/JumpStart/sol9/conf/server/sysidcfg27
➥ clientname sun4m
```

2. Set up a profile for the JumpStart server. To do this, create the files, profiles, rules, and config in the /JumpStart/sol9/conf/server directory.

The sample profile directs JumpStart to install the complete software in addition to the OEM. The specifications for each partition include a 2000Mb root partition on slice 0, a 1100Mb swap on slice 1, an unused 4Mb partition on slice 3, and a 1100Mb partition on slice 4 for /var.

```
/JumpStart/sol9/conf/server/server_js1A
install_type initial_install
system_type server
cluster SUNWCXall
partitioning explicit
filesys rootdisk.s0 2000 /
filesys rootdisk.s1 1100 swap
filesys rootdisk.s3 4 unnamed
filesys rootdisk.s4 1100 /var
```

The Rules file defines the profile to be used for each server. During the server configuration stage, this file needs only a single entry, listing the name of the client to install and the profile to use. The syntax to create the Rules file is defined as follows:

```
/JumpStart/sol9/conf/server/rules
hostname clientname                 -      server_ js1a_           -
```

Note that the JumpStart server does not use the Rules file. Instead, it uses the processed version of the Rules file called rules. Please note that to create this file, you need the check script supplied with JumpStart. Copy this file into the /JumpStart/sol9/conf/server/ directory using the following command:

```
# cp /JumpStart/sol9/Solaris_9/Misc/JumpStart_sample/check
➥ /JumpStart/sol9/conf/server/
```

3. Use the check script to confirm that the profile is set up correctly and to create the rules file:

```
# ./check
```

4. With the profile set up on the server, point the client config to the `rules` file by running `add_install_client`:

```
# cd /JumpStart/sol9/Solaris_9/Tools
# ./add_install_client -e 8:0:20:21:45:e0  \
      -c servername:/JumpStart/sol9/conf/server  \
      -p servername:/JumpStart/sol9/conf/server/sysidcfg27  \
      clientname sun4u
```

This should complete the install without any manual intervention. During the install you should see output similar to the following:

```
Searching for JumpStart directory...
Using rules.ok from xx.xx.xx.xx:/JumpStart/sol9/conf/server.
Checking rules.ok file...
Using profile: server_ js1A_
```

This output confirms that your install is using the correct setup files.

FACTORY JumpStart

The Factory JumpStart installation automatically installs itself on a SPARC system when you insert the Solaris 9 DVD or Solaris 9 Software 1 of 2 CD into the drive and switch on the system.

Based on the model and the disk size of the SPARC system, a default profile is created. Note that you are not prompted for the system configuration information required for all other types of installations. Therefore, you cannot select the software you want installed on your system.

THE SOLARIS SunInstall INSTALLATION

SunInstall is an installation program that supports various Sun architectures. It can be installed on any standalone workstation.

This installation program facilitates `installation/upgrade` with either of the following:

- CD-ROM drive
- Net installation image

NOTE

Using Net Installation server requires you to have a boot server.

Steps to carry out the SunInstall installation are as follows:

1. Boot using the installation media, CD-ROM, or Network Install server.

   To install from a CD-ROM drive, type the following command at the ok prompt:

   ok boot cdrom

   To install from an install server, type the following command:

   ok boot net

> **NOTE**
>
> If you preconfigured the system using the sysidcfg file or the name server database, the Solaris SunInstall program does not prompt you to enter configuration information.

2. The installation program guides you step by step through the installation. Follow the instructions on the screen to install Solaris 9.

3. After the installation is complete, the system reboots automatically or asks for your instruction to reboot manually.

4. Verify the installation by viewing the logs in the following directories:

   ```
   /var/sadm/system/logs
   /var/sadm/install/logs
   ```

WebStart FLASH INSTALLATION

The WebStart Flash method of installation creates the archives of the installation information. This information is used during the Solaris installation. The WebStart Flash contains four archive sections: Archive Cookie Section, Archive Identification Section, User-Defined Sections, and Archive Files Section.

- **Archive Cookie Section**—This section contains a cookie that identifies the information file as a WebStart Flash archive.

- **Archive Identification Section**—This section contains keywords with values that provide identification information about the archive.

- **User-Defined Sections**—This section enables you to define and insert archive sections. Note that the WebStart Flash archive does not use user-defined archive sections.

- **Archive Files Section**—The Archive Files Section contains the files that were saved from the master system.

PRE-INSTALLATION TASKS

Perform the following pre-installation tasks before you start installation with the WebStart Flash Archive:

1. Create the WebStart Flash archive on a master system that has Solaris installed. This archive will contain all the files on the master system.

2. Install the WebStart Flash archive on clone systems. The clone system is the system that has the same installation configuration as the master system.

You can install WebStart Flash archive with any one of the following installation types:

- Solaris WebStart installation
- Solaris SunInstall program
- Custom JumpStart installation

SOLARIS WebStart

The steps to install WebStart Flash archive with Solaris WebStart follow:

1. Install Solaris 9 using the WebStart installation method.
2. Select the media you want to use for installing WebStart Flash archive from the Specify Media panel. The options available are DVD/CD-ROM drive, NFS, HTTP, and Local Tape.
3. If the media from which you want to install is DVD/CD-ROM or the NFS server, the Select Flash Archives panel displays. Select one or more archives to install from this panel and click Next. Confirm your selection(s) in the Flash Archives Summary panel.
4. The Additional Flash Archives panel enables you to install additional archives. If you do not want to install these archives, select None and click Next to continue with the installation.

SunInstall

The steps to install WebStart Flash archive with the SunInstall method are follows:

1. Install the SunInstall program.
2. On the Flash Archive Retrieval Method screen, select the location of the WebStart Flash archive. Select the media you want to use. The options to choose from are HTTP Server, Local Tape, Local File, and Local Device. The Solaris SunInstall program installation prompts you to proceed depending on the media you selected.
3. On the Flash Archive Selection screen, you can select to install layered WebStart Flash archives by selecting New. If you do not want to install additional archives, click Continue to complete the installation.

CUSTOM JumpStart

To use the JumpStart method for installing the WebStart Flash archive, create the custom JumpStart rules and the profiles file on the Install server. Use the steps to create the JumpStart rules as described earlier. To create the profile file, perform the following steps:

1. Set the value of the keyword `install_type` as `flash_install`.
2. Use the new `archive_location` keyword to add the path to the `WebStart` Flash archive.
3. Specify the file system configuration.

NOTE

> To install layered `WebStart` Flash archives on the clone systems, add one `archive_location` line for each archive that you want to install.

Examples follow that show profiles that can be used to install a `WebStart` Flash archive with the custom `JumpStart` installation method.

In the following example, the profile indicates that the Custom `JumpStart` program retrieves the `WebStart` Flash archive from an HTTP server.

```
install_type  flash_install
archive_location http installserver /flasharchive/S8u3.Xall.alllc.64bit.4u
partitioning explicit
filesys c0t1d0s0 4000 /
filesys c0t1d0s1 512 swap
filesys c0t1d0s7 free /export/home
```

In the following example, the profile indicates that the Custom `JumpStart` program retrieves the `WebStart` Flash archive from an NFS server.

```
install_type  flash_install
archive_location nfs installserver:/export/solaris/flasharchive
➥/S8u3.Xall.alllc.64bit.4u
partitioning explicit
filesys rootdisk.s0 6000 /
filesys rootdisk.s1 512 swap
filesys rootdisk.s7 free /export/home
```

LIVE UPGRADE

Solaris Live Upgrade is a feature introduced in Solaris 9 OE. This feature enables you to upgrade to a newer release of Solaris OE. However, if you use a previous version of Solaris OE, such as Solaris 2.6 or Solaris 7 or 8, then you would be required to install Solaris Live Upgrade packages on your current operating system. You can install the Solaris Live Upgrade packages from the Solaris 9 DVD or Solaris 9 Software 2 of 2 CD.

When upgrading from Solaris 2.6 to Solaris 9, you can use the `WebStart`, `SunInstall`, and the `JumpStart` upgrade methodologies. For Solaris 7 and 8, you can use Live Upgrade to upgrade, in addition to `WebStart`, `SunInstall`, and `JumpStart`.

DISK SPACE REQUIREMENTS

Live Upgrade requires you to create a boot environment on your system. Each boot environment may require a minimum of 350Mb to a maximum of 800Mb of disk space, depending on your system software requirements.

You need to estimate the size of the file system to create the boot environment. To do so, start the process of creating a new boot environment. The process automatically calculates the size of the file system. When you find the size, terminate the process.

To create a boot environment, all you need is a disk that can serve as a boot device.

PACKAGES REQUIRED

If you are upgrading from Solaris 2.6, you require the following packages:

- SUNWadmap
- SUNWadmfw
- SUNWadmc
- SUNWmfrun
- SUNWloc

Use the following packages if you are upgrading from Solaris 7:

- SUNWadmap
- SUNWadmc
- SUNWlibC

If upgrading from Solaris 8, use the following packages:

- SUNWadmap
- SUNWadmc
- SUNWlibC
- SUNWbzip

NOTE

> While you are creating an inactive boot environment, you will have to create a slice to which the root (/) system files are copied. This partition should be on the slice from where the system can boot.

INSTALLING THE LIVE UPGRADE SOFTWARE

You can install the Live Upgrade software from the Solaris 9 DVD or Solaris 9 Software 2 of 2 CD.

1. When you insert the CD, the command prompt displays. At the command prompt, type the following command to run the installer:
   `$./installer`
2. A Select panel appears. Click Custom in this panel.

3. The Product Selection panel displays. From the choices available in this panel, click the type of installation you want for Solaris Live Upgrade.

   Follow the directions on the Solaris `WebStart` installer panel to install the software.

To start the live upgrade, perform the following steps:

1. Log in to the system as root.

2. At the command prompt, issue the following command:

   `$/usr/bin/lu`

3. The Solaris Live Upgrade main menu displays. Choose the option to upgrade.

4. To abort the Live Upgrade program, press F6.

NOTE

> For steps to creating a boot environment and upgrading with Solaris Live Upgrade, refer to http://docs.sun.com.

SUMMARY

Based upon your requirements, you can install Solaris 9 OE using any of the six installation procedures, such as `WebStart`, Custom `JumpStart`, Factory `JumpStart`, Solaris `SunInstall`, `WebStart` Flash, and Live Upgrade. `WebStart` packages all software components as a single entity. Custom `JumpStart` allows you to customize the Solaris installation. It is specifically useful for mass rollouts. Factory `JumpStart` does not prompt you for any information. It starts the installation procedure as soon as the installation CDs are inserted in the CD-ROM drive. The `WebStart` Flash installation provides both GUI and CLI. It helps simultaneously install several systems that use the same software and configuration. The Live Upgrade method is used to upgrade from the previous versions of Solaris to the next.

CHAPTER 4

INSTALLING SOFTWARE PACKAGES AND PATCHES

In this chapter

Packages in Solaris   52

Managing Packages   52

Patches—Fixing Bugs   61

Summary   67

PACKAGES IN SOLARIS

Packages are sets of independent products that are licensed as a single product. When a product is developed, vendors define packages in the license certificate and not in the software product. This allows vendors to change the components of a package until the time they ship the license.

Packages are collections of files that are required to run an application. The files are grouped together logically, as packages, to facilitate administration. An example of a package is SUNWman, which is the package for the online manual pages. Sun packages always begin with the prefix SUNW, as in SUNWniscr, SUNWnisu, and SUNWaudio. Third-party packages usually begin with a prefix that corresponds to the company's stock symbol or name.

MANAGING PACKAGES

When you install Solaris, a few default packages are installed, depending on the configuration cluster that you choose for installation. After Solaris installation, you can install, maintain, and remove other packages in two ways: from the command line and using Admintool. You can also spool a package from the CD-ROM onto the local hard disk and install it later. If you are a hard-core CLI user, you will probably be more comfortable operating from the command line.

Solaris stores the information on all the installed packages in the `/var/sadm/install/contents` file. Listing 4.1 shows a sample `/var/sadm/install/contents` file.

LISTING 4.1 A SAMPLE `/var/sadm/install/contents` FILE

```
/dev d none 0755 root sys SUNWcsr SUNWcsd
/dev/allkmem=../devices/pseudo/mm@0:allkmem s none SUNWcsd
/dev/arp=../devices/pseudo/arp@0:arp s none SUNWcsd
/dev/conslog=../devices/pseudo/log@0:conslog s none SUNWcsd
/dev/console=../devices/pseudo/cn@0:console s none SUNWcsd
/dev/dsk d none 0755 root sys SUNWcsd
/dev/eri=../devices/pseudo/clone@0:eri s none SUNWcsd
/dev/fd d none 0555 root root SUNWcsd
/dev/hme=../devices/pseudo/clone@0:hme s none SUNWcsd
/dev/icmp=../devices/pseudo/icmp@0:icmp s none SUNWcsd
/dev/icmp6=../devices/pseudo/icmp6@0:icmp6 s none SUNWcsd
/dev/ip=../devices/pseudo/ip@0:ip s none SUNWcsd
/dev/ip6=../devices/pseudo/ip6@0:ip6 s none SUNWcsd
/dev/ipsecah=../devices/pseudo/ipsecah@0:ipsecah s none SUNWcsd
/dev/ipsecesp=../devices/pseudo/ipsecesp@0:ipsecesp s none SUNWcsd
/dev/keysock=../devices/pseudo/keysock@0:keysock s none SUNWcsd
/dev/kmem=../devices/pseudo/mm@0:kmem s none SUNWcsd
/dev/ksyms=../devices/pseudo/ksyms@0:ksyms s none SUNWcsd
/dev/le=../devices/pseudo/clone@0:le s none SUNWcsd
/dev/log=../devices/pseudo/log@0:log s none SUNWcsd
/dev/mem=../devices/pseudo/mm@0:mem s none SUNWcsd
/dev/msglog=../devices/pseudo/sysmsg@0:msglog s none SUNWcsd
/etc d none 0755 root sys SUNWcsr SUNWocfr SUNWnfscr SUNWnfssr SUNWnisr SUNWmdr
```

```
➥SUNWntpr SUNWsckmr SUNWsfdrr SUNWuxflr SUNWpcmci SUNWpcr SUNWdtlog SUNWpiclr SUN
Wpmr SUNWpmowr SUNWscpr SUNWbsr SUNWpsr SUNWrcmdr SUNWgssc SUNWadmr SUNWsacom SU
NWslpr SUNWafbr SUNWsndmr SUNWsolnm SUNWatfsr SUNWtnetr SUNWusb SUNWvolr SUNWefc
r SUNWftpr SUNWgfbr SUNWcvcr SUNWifbr SUNWkrbr SUNWllcr IPLTdsr SUNWwbcor SUNWlv
mr SUNWwrsmx SUNWplowr SUNWpppdr SUNWdhcsr SUNWrtvc:base SUNWGtkr SUNWaccr SUNWa
➥pchr SUNWsmbar SUNWlur SUNWsshdr SUNWsshr SUNWbnur SUNWwgetr SUNWdial SUNWypr SU
NWfnsx5 SUNWkcsrr SUNWkdcr SUNWlpmsg SUNWmipr SUNWncar
/etc/.login e renamenew 0644 root sys 524 39191 1009930584 SUNWcsr
/etc/TIMEZONE=./default/init s none SUNWcsr
/etc/acct d none 0755 adm adm SUNWaccr
/etc/acct/holidays e preserve 0644 root bin 289 22044 1009929784 SUNWaccr
/etc/aliases=./mail/aliases s none SUNWsndmr
/etc/apache d none 0755 root bin SUNWapchr
/etc/apache/README.Solaris f none 0644 root bin 2541 6653 1010133897 SUNWapchr
/etc/apache/access.conf e renamenew 0644 root bin 348 30403 1010133894 SUNWapchr
/etc/apache/httpd.conf-example f none 0644 root bin 37327 56610 1010133898 SUNWa
pchr
/etc/apache/jserv.conf e renamenew 0644 root bin 6376 20736 1010133896 SUNWapchr
/etc/apache/jserv.properties e renamenew 0644 root bin 13137 27716 1010133896 SU
Nwapchr
/var/uucp/.Sequence d none 0755 uucp uucp SUNWbnur
/var/uucp/.Status d none 0755 uucp uucp SUNWbnur
/var/yp d none 0755 root bin SUNWnisr SUNWypr
/var/yp/Makefile e renameold 0555 root bin 18268 29931 1009931595 SUNWypr
/var/yp/aliases e preserve 0555 root bin 153 12266 1009931595 SUNWnisr
/var/yp/binding d none 0755 root bin SUNWnisr SUNWypr
/var/yp/nicknames e ypnicknames 0644 root bin 226 22121 1009931595 SUNWnisr
/var/yp/updaters f none 0500 root bin 870 2119 1009931595 SUNWypr
# Last modified by pkgadd for SUNWdtad package
```

INSTALLING PACKAGES

Depending on the installation type you choose, Solaris automatically installs a few default packages. Other packages need to be installed separately. The steps to install the packages are as follows:

1. Double-click the Admintool icon to invoke Admintool from the CDE application manager. Figure 4.1 displays the Admintool window.

Figure 4.1
The Admintool window.

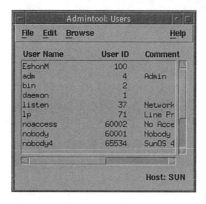

2. Choose the Browse menu and then the Software submenu to display the Admintool:Software window. The Admintool:Software window displays a list of existing software packages in the system, as shown in Figure 4.2. This window has a list box that displays three software categories:

Figure 4.2
The Admintool:Software window.

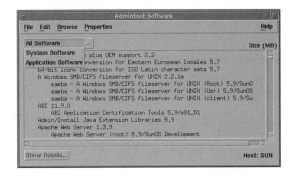

- **All software**—Displays all the software packages present in the system.
- **System software** —Controls the hardware resources of the computer by translating the high-level language instructions to machine-level binary code.
- **Application software** —Displays the programs used for various applications such as database management systems, word processors, text editors, multimedia utilities, and others.

You can choose to display specific packages or all packages by using the check box in the Admintool: Software window.

3. Choose Edit, Add to display the Admintool:Set Source Media window, as shown in Figure 4.3.

Figure 4.3
Admintool:Set Source Media window.

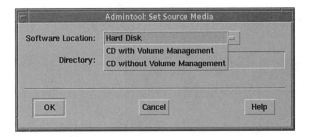

The Software Location list box displays three locations. Select any one location from the three locations listed.

- Hard Disk
- CD with Volume Management
- CD without Volume Management

If the package that you want to install exists on the hard disk, select Hard Disk and type the absolute path of the package in the Directory text box. If you want to install the software from the CD-ROM, choose CD-ROM with Volume Management or CD-ROM without Volume Management, depending on whether the volume management software is running. If volume management is running, type the path of the CD-ROM in the CDPath text box, or type the mount point directory in the MountPoint text box. For a Solaris CD, the default CD path is /cdrom/cdrom0/s2 on x86-based systems and /cdrom/cdrom0/s0 on SPARC systems. For a product CD, the default CD path is /cdrom/cdrom0 on both x86 and SPARC systems. By default, Admintool assumes the /export/install as the mount point for the CD-ROM. If the CD is mounted on a different location, you can specify that path. By default, the CD-ROM with Volume Management option is displayed.

NOTE

> The Solaris environment gives users and software developers a standard interface for dealing with disks and CDs, termed volume management. This interface provides three major benefits:
> - By automatically mounting disks and CDs, it simplifies their use.
> - It enables you to access disks and CDs without having to become a superuser.
> - It allows you to give other systems on the network automatic access to any disks and CDs you insert into your system.

→ To know more about volume management, **see** "Disk and Storage Administration," **p.204**.

4. If the specified source path contains any packages, the Admintool:Add Software window is displayed. If Admintool does not find the software package in any of these locations, it displays an error message, as shown in Figure 4.4.

Figure 4.4
Admintool:Error
Window–Displaying
the error.

5. The Admintool:Add software window displays a list of software packages present in the device selected. Select the packages to be installed from the software section and click the Add button. In this example, the Kerberos Version 5 support (kernel) 1.00 is selected. Click the Space Meter button if you want to check the free space available in each partition. Figure 4.5 shows the Space Meter window.

Figure 4.5
The Space Meter shows the available free space in the various disk partitions.

6. To customize the selected software, click the Customize button. The Admintool:Customize Installation window is displayed, as shown in Figure 4.6, where you can customize the package installation by selecting the individual components of a package. The description text box shows descriptive information about the selected package, such as the name, vendor, and the disk space required for installation. The Installation Directory text box displays the default installation location of the selected product. If you want to install the software in a different location, specify an alternate location in this text box. The Unresolved Dependencies text box displays other software products required for the selected package to work properly. Select the required software components or click the Select All button to select all the components. Click OK to continue.

Figure 4.6
Customizing the installation by selecting the individual components of a particular package.

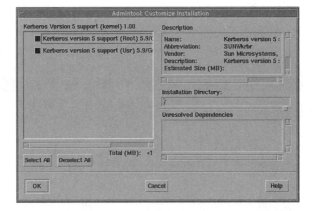

Click the Add button to add the selected package. A new interactive window is displayed where you are asked, "Do you want to continue installation of <package name>?" for the package and all its dependent packages.

To install a package from the command line, use the `pkgadd` command. A package can be directly installed from a CD-ROM, a network, or from a spool directory. Before installing a package you might consider checking whether the package is already installed, in which case you can use the `pkginfo` command.

The `pkginfo` command obtains information about the software packages. Every software package comes with a file named `pkginfo`, which contains the information about the package, such as the package instance name, name, category, architecture, version number, base directory, vendor information, a short description of the package, the package stamp, the status, and the size in 512-byte blocks.

NOTE

> *Package instance name* refersto the file name for the package, whereas *name* refers to the name of the package. For example, SUNWypr is the package instance name for NIS Server, and NIS Server for Solaris is the name of the package.

The command syntax is

```
pkginfo <option> <package name>.
```

The `pkginfo` command without any arguments displays a list of packages installed in the system, such as the following:

```
system       FJSVhea       SunOS Header Files
system       FJSVmdb       Fujitsu Platform Modular Debugger
system       FJSVmdbx      Fujitsu Platform Modular Debugger (64-bit)
system       IPLTadcon     Administration Server Console
system       IPLTadman     Administration Server Documentation
system       IPLTadmin     Administration Server
system       IPLTcons      Console Client Base
system       IPLTdscon     Directory Server Console
system       IPLTdsman     Directory Server Documentation
system       IPLTdsr       Directory Server (root)
system       IPLTdsu       Directory Server (usr)
system       IPLTjss       Network Security Services for Java
system       IPLTnls       Nationalization Languages and Localization Support
system       IPLTnspr      Portable Runtime Interface
system       IPLTpldap     PerLDAP
application  NSCPcom       Netscape Communicator
system       SMEvplr       SME platform links
system       SMEvplu       SME usr/platform links
system       SUNW1251f     Russian 1251 fonts
system       SUNW1394h     Sun IEEE1394 Framework Header Files
system       SUNW1394x     Sun IEEE1394 Framework (64-bit)
```

The `pkginfo` command, followed by the name of the package without any option, displays very limited information about the specified package. The package information for the SUNWman package is shown here:

```
# pkginfo SUNWman
system       SUNWman       On-Line Manual Pages
```

Even though the preceding output suggests that the SUNWman package is installed, it does not state the version/release of the package that is installed. If you want to check the version of the package, use the `-1` option of the `pkginfo` command.

```
   PKGINST:  SUNWaadm
      NAME:  Solaris 9 Beta System Administrator Collection - HTML
  CATEGORY:  application
```

```
      ARCH:  all
   VERSION:  900.0.0,REV=4
   BASEDIR:  /opt
    VENDOR:  Sun Microsystems, Inc.
      DESC:  Solaris HTML Documentation
    PSTAMP:  thoreau20010711174555
  INSTDATE:  Feb 25 2002 11:47
   HOTLINE:  Please contact your local service provider
    STATUS:  completely installed
     FILES:      1993 installed pathnames
#
```

Table 4.1 describes the other options of the pkginfo command.

TABLE 4.1 OPTIONS OF THE *pkginfo* COMMAND

Option	Description
-d	Specifies the device or the path for the packages.
-l	Lists information about a particular package in the long format.
-p	Displays information about partially installed packages.
-I	Displays information about fully installed packages.
-a arch	Specifies the package architecture as arch.
-r	Lists the installation base for relocatable packages.
-R root_path	Specifies the path to the package to be checked.
-v version	Specifies the version of the package.

To install or spool a package from the command line, use the pkgadd command. The syntax is

```
pkgadd <option> package name
```

> **NOTE**
>
> You cannot use admintool to spool a package.

You can specify an alternative location if the disk space is inadequate. Specify the location of the package with the –d option and specify the directory where you want to spool the package with the –s option. For example, the following syntax spools the package SUNWgzip to the /pkg directory:

```
# pkgadd -d /cdrom/sol_9_ia_2/Solaris_8/Product -s /pkg SUNWgzip
Transferring <SUNWgzip> package instance
#
```

To install a package from the default spool directory, use the `pkgadd` command followed by the package name. The `-d` option can be used to install from any other spool directory. The following syntax installs the SUNWxwman package from the default spool directory:

```
# pkgadd -d
```

To install a package directly from the CD-ROM, specify the location of the package in the CD-ROM. The following example shows how to install the SUNWwebnfs package from the location `/cdrom/sol_9_ia_2/Solaris_9/Product`.

```
# pkgadd -d /cdrom/asian_sol_9_doc/Solaris_9_Doc/common/Product
```

After you have installed a package, you might want to verify whether the package is installed properly. You can use the `pkgchk` command to verify the accuracy of the package installation. The following is the syntax of the `pkgchk` command:

```
pkgchk <options> package name
```

The `pkgchk` command verifies the package attributes by comparing their values in the `/var/sadm/install/contents` file. Error messages are displayed if a mismatch is found.

The following command checks the SUNWman package for proper installation.

```
# pkgcheck SUNWman
#
```

Table 4.2 lists the various available options for the `pkgchk` command and their descriptions.

TABLE 4.2   OPTIONS OF THE *pkgchk* COMMAND AND THEIR DESCRIPTIONS

Options	Description
`-a`	Audits only the file permissions and not the file contents.
`-c`	Audits only the file contents and not the file permissions.
`-v`	Displays file names as the `pkgchk` command processes them.
`-d spooldir`	Specifies the absolute path of the spool directory.

The `pkgchk -v <package name>` command determines whether there are any errors. If there are no errors it returns a list of installed files. Otherwise, it displays the error messages. The following example checks the package SUNWgzip for errors.

```
# pkgchk -v SUNWgzip
/usr
/usr/bin
/usr/bin/gunzip
/usr/bin/gzcat
/usr/bin/gzcmp
/usr/bin/gzdiff
```

4

```
/usr/bin/gzexe
/usr/bin/gzforce
/usr/bin/gzgrep
/usr/bin/gzip
/usr/bin/gzmore
/usr/bin/gznew
/usr/share
/usr/share/man
/usr/share/man/man1
/usr/share/man/man1/gunzip.1
/usr/share/man/man1/gzcat.1
/usr/share/man/man1/gzcmp.1
/usr/share/man/man1/gzdiff.1
/usr/share/man/man1/gzexe.1
/usr/share/man/man1/gzforce.1
/usr/share/man/man1/gzgrep.1
/usr/share/man/man1/gzip. 1
/usr/share/man/man1/gzmore.1
/usr/share/man/man1/gznew.1
```

The following command checks the SUNWxwman package, which is spooled in the /var/spool/pkg directory.

```
# pkgchk -d /var/spool/pkg SUNWxwman
Checking uninstalled directory format package <SUNWxwman> from </var/spool/pkg>
## Checking control scripts.
## Checking package objects.
NOTE: some pathnames are in private formats that cannot be verified
## Checking is complete.
```

REMOVING PACKAGES

When you no longer require a package or when you want to install a higher version of that package, you can use the Admintool in Solaris 9 to remove it. The steps to remove a package are as follows:

1. Invoke Admintool. Select the package to be deleted from the list of packages.

2. Choose Edit, Delete to display the Admintool:Warning dialog box as shown in Figure 4.7.

Figure 4.7
Warning dialog box.

3. Click the Delete button to delete the package. To retain the package, click Cancel.

4. On clicking the Delete button, the Admintool:Delete Software window appears, which displays interactive messages during deletion. After removing the package, the status of the delete operation—success or failure—is displayed.

To uninstall the packages from the command line, use the `pkgrm` command. To remove a package from the command line, specify the name of the package to be removed as an argument to the `pkgrm` command. The command syntax is as follows:

```
pkgrm <package-name>
```

The system warns you about the removal and proceeds only after confirming it.

The `pkgrm` command, without any arguments, displays the packages installed on the system and displays more packages if you press the Return key. You identify the packages to be removed from the list.

CAUTION

> If the package is dependent on any other packages or files, the dependencies are displayed as a warning.

If you try to remove a package that is spooled but not installed on the system, the following error message is displayed:

```
# pkgrm SUNWypr
pkgrm: ERROR: no package associated with <SUNWypr>
#
```

NOTE

> The Admintool utility works only if the GUI mode is available. It does not work with Telnet and some remote login sessions. However, it does work with X Windows terminals or terminal emulation software, such as Xmanager.

PATCHES—FIXING BUGS

Sun Microsystems delivers certain files, known as patches, that are used to fix any defects (bugs) in the system source code. Patches contain the files that replace or update the existing files that prevent the proper execution of the software. A patch is a collection of files and directories that contains the actual program used to fix the bugs, along with some other files and directories related to the patch.

Sometimes patches might cause some problems. For example, when the patch intended for fixing the bugs for one version is applied on a different version of the OS, it results in some unpredictable incompatibility problems. In such cases, remove the patch and install the new patch for the correct version.

A unique eight-digit number identifies the patches. The first six digits represent the base patch code and the last two digits represent the patch revision number. The base patch code and the patch revision number are separated by a hyphen.

N O T E

Only the superuser has the privileges to install or remove patches.

DOWNLOADING PATCHES

The patches for Solaris are available on the Web site http://sunsolve.sun.com. You can either download the patches from the web site or use FTP.

The pub/patches directory on the Web site has patches available for various versions of Solaris. This site provides Patch Report Update report, which list the patches released and the unbundled software. This report is updated twice a month and is available to customers. The Patch Report Update report has the following sections:

- The Quick Reference Section provides a listing of all new patches released, existing patch revision changes, obsolete patches, security patches, and a listing of the current recommended patches.

- The Recommended Patches Section contains the most important patches needed to avoid critical system, user, or security related bugs that have been reported and fixed.

- Unbundled Product Patches contains a reference to specific Solaris releases, which are included in the Complete Listing of Released Patches section in this report.

Not everyone can download every available patch from this site. Users who have a service contract with Sun Microsystems can obtain an extended set of patches. Other users can download only a restricted set of patches.

Users with service contracts are assigned a password they can use to download the patches. They also receive the SunSolve CD-ROM on a periodic basis (every 4-6 weeks), which includes patch updates on Solaris.

N O T E

You can also access publicly available patches using the URL http://metalab.unc.edu/pub/sun-info/sun-patches/.

You can download patches using either the Solaris Management Console (SMC) or the FTP. SMC is a graphical user interface that enables the administrator to perform system administration effectively by avoiding the complexities of the command line. SMC is used for

- managing patches.
- managing hosts.
- administering users and groups.
- editing and updating user information.
- setting up printer, modems, terminals, and other devices.

To download patches using SMC, select Patches, Action, Download Patches, as shown in Figure 4.8.

Figure 4.8
Downloading patches using SMC.

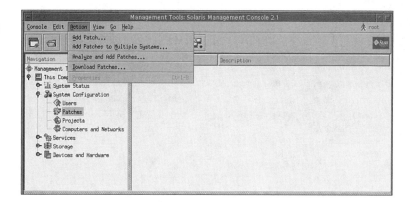

The Download Patches wizard guides you through the remaining steps necessary to download patches.

For downloading using FTP, connect to ftp.sun.sunsolve.com. You can log in as anonymous, or if you are a Sun customer you will already have a username and password supplied to you. Switch to the directory where you want to download the patch on your local machine and follow the steps provided to you. For example, if you want to download the patches to the /patchload directory of your system, follow these steps:

1. Change the working directory to /patchload.
2. FTP to sunsolve.sun.com, type **anonymous** when prompted for a login name, and use your email address as the password. If you have a login and password supplied by Sun you can use that to log in.
3. Most FTP programs allow you to select Binary, ASCII, or Auto as file transfer methods. This determines the language the client and server use to make the transfer. You can use binary mode to download files. Type **binary** at the FTP prompt.
4. Change the current working directory to the /pub/patches directory.
5. Search for the required patch using wild card characters. The following command lists the patches that have a base patch code 109168.
   ```
   ftp> ls  109168*
   ```
6. To download a patch, identify the patch release that you want to install and use the mget command. For example, the following syntax downloads all the releases of this patch. This is helpful if you need different releases for different client systems.
   ```
   ftp>mget  109168*
   ```

Patches can be in the compressed or the uncompressed forms. You can uncompress a patch by using the unzip command. The following example uncompresses the patch 109168-01.zip.

```
# unzip 109168-01.zip
```

The patch files for the SPARC platform are compressed using either the gzip utility or the tar utility. The files compressed using the gzip utility have an extension .gz.

The files compressed using the tar utility have an extension .tar.z. The following syntax uncompresses the file 109168-01.tar.z using the tar command and extracts the content of the 109168-01.tar file to a new subdirectory with the patch name under the current working directory:

```
# uncompress   109168-01.tar.z
# tar  -xvf  109168-01 .tar
```

INSTALLING PATCHES

You can install/add patches to single or multiple systems running the Solaris 9 or a compatible operating environment. To add patches using SMC, choose Action, Add Patches. If you want to install packages in multiple systems, choose Action, Add Patches to Multiple Systems. The Add Patches and Add Patches to Multiple Systems wizards guide you through the remaining steps to add patches. When installing one or more patches in multiple systems, ensure the following:

- Target systems must run Solaris 9.
- The directory where the patches will be installed is shared.
- The patch server and the machines in which you are installing the patches are running nfsd, mountd, and automountd.

To install the extracted patch using the command line, change the working directory to the directory that stores all the extracted files and use the patchadd command.

During installation, the patch subdirectories are created in the /var/sadm/patch directory. The patch subdirectories contain scripts that are required to install and remove the patch and replace the original files.

> **NOTE**   Before installing a patch, carefully read the README file provided along with the patch.

The following command displays a list of patches that are currently applied to the system:

```
# patchadd -p
```

The following syntax installs a new patch on the local system:

```
# patchadd /var/spool/patch/108529-09
```

The -R option installs the patch on a client system from the server. For example, the following syntax installs a patch on a client system, client1, from the server's console:

```
# patchadd -R  /export/root/client1/var/spool/patch/104945-02
```

The -M option is used to install multiple patches with a single command. The following syntax installs three patches from the /var/spool/patch directory.

```
# patchadd  -M  /var/spool/patch/108529-30 108653-02 108976-04
```

The following syntax installs multiple patches on a client:

```
# patchadd  /var/spool/patch -R /export/root/client  108529-30 108653-02 108976-
04
```

The patchadd command also creates a backup of the files that are changed during installation in the default backup directory—the /var/sadm/pkg directory. You can specify an alternate location for backup by using the -B option with the patchadd command. The following example installs multiple patches to a client and saves the backup data to the patchbackup directory.

```
# patchadd  /var/spool/patch -R /export/root/client1 -B /export/patchbackup
➥   108529-30 108653-02 108976-04.
```

If you experience a patch mismatch, you can remove the patch and bring the system back to the pre-patched state by using the backup directory.

If you choose not to create a backup, then use the -d option with the patchadd command, as shown in the following line. However, remember that such patches cannot be removed and if installed incorrectly may result in unusable system.

```
# patchadd  -d  /var/spool/patch/108529-09
```

CAUTION

Never use the -d option. Using this option makes it difficult to remove patches that become obsolete.

Table 4.3 lists the options of the patchadd command.

TABLE 4.3   THE *patchadd* **COMMAND OPTIONS AND THEIR DESCRIPTIONS**

Option	Description
-d	Installs without a backup of the updated files.
-p	Displays a list of the patches currently applied.
-R	Specifies the client system where the patch has to be installed.
-M	Installs multiple patches.
-B backout_directory	Saves backout data to a directory other than the package database. Specifies the absolute pathname of the backout directory.

The patchadd command fails to install a patch under the following conditions:

- A package being patched is not installed or is not completely installed on the host.
- The patch requires another patch that is not installed.
- The patch is incompatible with another patch already installed.
- The current version or a higher version of the patch is already installed.

REMOVING PATCHES

Sometimes you need to remove patches. For example, if you are planning to add a new update of a patch, the corresponding older patch or patches have to be removed. This is how you avoid incompatibility problems with the newer patches.

To use the SMC to delete one or more patches, select the patches on the right pane of the SMC and select Edit, Delete.

The patchrm command is used to remove patches installed on a Solaris system.

The following example removes a patch from a standalone system:

```
# patchrm   108529-09
```

The following example removes a patch that is from a client's system from the server's console:

```
# patchrm -R /export/root/client1 108529-09
```

Table 4.4 summarizes the options of the patchrm command.

TABLE 4.4   THE _patchrm_ COMMAND OPTIONS AND THEIR DESCRIPTIONS

Options	Description
-f	Forcibly removes the patch.
-R	Removes the patch from a client's system. (To be specified on the server)
-B backout_directory	Removes a patch whose backout data has been saved to a directory other than the package database. This option is needed only if the original backout directory, supplied to the patchadd command at installation time, has been moved.

When a patch is removed using the patchrm command, the patchrm command restores all files modified by that patch. However, restoring files is not possible under the following conditions:

- The patch was installed with the patchadd -d option and hence backup does not exist.
- The patch is required by another patch.

SUMMARY

A package is a collection of files, grouped together logically, and is required to run an application. The logical grouping of packages facilitates easy administration. You can install and remove packages using the command line or the Admintool.

Patches are collections of files and directories that are used to fix any source code bugs in the system. You can download patches from the Web site `http://sunsolve.sun.com`. To install patches, use the `patchadd` command. To remove packages, use the `patchrm` command.

4

BOOTING AND SHUTTING DOWN THE SYSTEM

In this chapter

The Boot Process for a SPARC System   70

The Shutdown Process   78

Summary   82

THE BOOT PROCESS FOR A SPARC SYSTEM

In SPARC systems, the OpenBoot PROM (OBP) controls the system before the kernel is loaded. The SPARC boot process consists of the OBP phase, boot program phase, kernel initialization phase, and the init phase. The following list outlines the SPARC boot process:

1. When you power on the system, the system firmware executes the power on self test (POST). The system initializes and PROM displays the system identification information. It runs the self-diagnostics. The bootstrap procedure in PROM loads the primary boot program, `bootblk`.

2. The primary boot program `bootblk` finds and executes the secondary boot program, `ufsboot`.

3. The secondary boot program, `ufsboot`, loads the kernel and transfers the control to it.

4. The kernel initializes itself and loads the kernel modules by using `ufsboot`. After loading the necessary modules, the kernel starts the init program.

5. The parent process init starts the other processes based on the information from the `/etc/inittab` file.

6. The init program executes the run control scripts that are used to set up the various system services.

Figure 5.1 depicts the SPARC booting process.

Figure 5.1
The boot process.

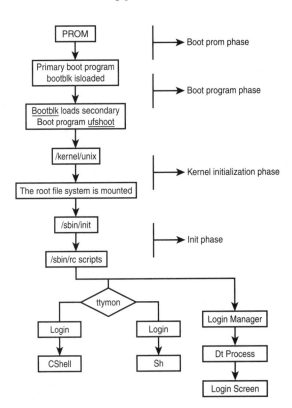

THE OBP PHASE

As discussed in Chapter 4, "Installing Software Packages and Patches," the OBP is unique to the SPARC architecture. The OBP performs various diagnostics and runs a quick POST procedure, to verify the system's hardware and memory. The PROM monitor is used to control the system activities before the kernel is loaded. The primary boot program, the bootblk, contains a UFS file system reader that is responsible for loading the secondary boot program, the ufsboot, from the default boot device. The system proceeds with the boot program phase if the auto-boot parameter is set to true. If the auto-boot parameter is set to false, the ok prompt is displayed, where you can boot with the desired options.

The system can boot in the single-user mode or the multi-user mode. Multi-user mode enables more than one user to log on and work on the system. The boot command without any options causes the system to boot in the multi-user mode. The single-user mode is preferred for system maintenance. To boot the system in the single-user mode, type boot -s at the ok prompt.

If you have added any device to the system recently, use the reconfiguration boot. This boot type configures any new device(s) added to the system. To perform a reconfiguration boot, type **boot –r** at the ok prompt.

You can boot a Solaris system from various devices, such as a hard disk, CD-ROM, and so on. In systems with multiple hard disks, if you want to boot from a specific hard disk among a number of hard disks, type **boot <HD name>** at the ok prompt. If you choose to boot the system from the CDROM, type **boot cdrom** at the ok prompt.

The system proceeds with the boot program phase when you type the **boot** command.

THE BOOT PROGRAM PHASE

The primary boot program, bootblk, finds the secondary boot program and loads it into memory. The ufsboot program has device drivers for the device that contains the Solaris operating system kernel. The secondary boot program then loads the kernel. By default, all versions above Solaris 6 (that is, Solaris 7 and Solaris 8) boot a 64-bit kernel on UltraSPARC systems.

KERNEL INITIALIZATION PHASE

The kernel is a set of software programs made up of the core image files (composed of unix and genunix files). The kernel modules are loaded on demand. The kernel comprises two parts: platform-specific and generic. The file genunix is the platform-independent component of the base kernel.

The kernel initializes itself and begins loading modules using the /platform/'uname -m'/ ufsboot program to read the files. After loading the modules required to mount the root file system, it unloads the /platform/'uname -m'/ufsboot program from memory and starts the system initialization, using the kernel modules. In this phase, the kernel initializes the memory and hardware and checks for the devices attached, such as disk drives, tape drives, floppy drives, ethernet cards, display cards, and controllers. The kernel modules, such as software

5

components or device drivers, are hardware-specific. The kernel loads the necessary kernel modules on demand. For example, if the kernel detects a hardware device, such as a CD-ROM drive, it loads the necessary device driver into the memory, whenever the drive is accessed.

Table 5.1 describes the modules in the `/kernel`, `/platform/platform-name/kernel`, `/platform/hardware-class-name/kernel`, and `/usr/kernel` directories.

NOTE

> The kernel loads from the `/platform/sun4u/kernel/unix`. The boot program reads the kernel configuration from the file `/etc/system` and loads the required kernel modules. Simultaneously, the init (PID 1) process is created. Based on the `/etc/default/init` file, this process sets environment variables. It then consults the `/etc/inittab` file and executes the commands defined for the chosen run level.

TABLE 5.1 MODULE TYPES AND THEIR DESCRIPTIONS

Module Type	Description
Drv	Loadable device drivers
Exec	The modules that execute programs stored in various file formats
Fs	File system modules
Misc	Miscellaneous system-related modules
sched	Operating system schedulers
Strmod	System V STREAMS loadable modules
Sys	Loadable system calls

You can modify the kernel configuration process by using the `/etc/system` file. The `/etc/system` file is read by the kernel during the Auto Configuration phase. Listing 5.1 shows a sample `/etc/system` file.

LISTING 5.1 THE `/etc/system` FILE

```
*ident "@(#)system   1.18   97/06/27 SMI" /* SVR4 1.5 */
*
* SYSTEM SPECIFICATION FILE
*

* moddir:
*
*     Set the search path for modules.  This has a format similar to the
*     csh path variable. If the module isn't found in the first directory
*     it tries the second and so on. The default is /kernel /usr/kernel
*
*     Example:
*          moddir: /kernel /usr/kernel /other/modules
```

```
* root device and root filesystem configuration:
*
*       The following may be used to override the defaults provided by
*       the boot program:
*
*       rootfs:     Set the filesystem type of the root.
*
*       rootdev:    Set the root device.  This should be a fully
*                   expanded physical pathname.  The default is the
*                   physical pathname of the device where the boot
*                   program resides.  The physical pathname is
*                   highly platform and configuration dependent.
*
*       Example:
*           rootfs:ufs
*           rootdev:/sbus@1,f8000000/esp@0,800000/sd@3,0:a
*
*       (Swap device configuration should be specified in /etc/vfstab.)


* exclude:
*
*       Modules appearing in the moddir path which are NOT to be loaded,
*       even if referenced. Note that 'exclude' accepts either a module name,
*       or a filename which includes the directory.
*
*       Examples:
*           exclude: win
exclude: sys/shmsys
* forceload:
*
*       Cause these modules to be loaded at boot time, (just before mounting
*       the root filesystem) rather than at first reference. Note that
*       forceload expects a filename which includes the directory. Also
*       note that loading a module does not necessarily imply that it will
*       be installed.
*
*       Example:
*           forceload: drv/foo


* set:
*
*       Set an integer variable in the kernel or a module to a new value.
*       This facility should be used with caution.  See system (4).
*
*       Examples:
*           forceload: drv/foo


* set:
*
*       Set an integer variable in the kernel or a module to a new value.
*       This facility should be used with caution.  See system(4).
*
```

continues

LISTING 5.1 CONTINUED

```
*      Examples:
*
*      To set variables in 'unix':
*
*          set nautopush=32
*          set maxusers=40
*
*      To set a variable named 'debug' in the module named 'test_module'
*
*          set test_module:debug = 0x13
set rlim_fd_max=8182
set rlim_fd_cur=8192
```

The `/etc/system` file contains variables, such as `moddir`, `exclude`, `forceload`, `rootfs`, `rootdev`, and `set`. By default, this file contains only comment entries, which explain these variables. The `moddir` variable sets the search path for the system modules. The default value of `moddir` is `/kernel/usrkernel`. The kernel module is searched in all the directories listed in the path, in the same sequence, until it is found. The `exclude` variable defines the modules in the `moddir` path that are not to be loaded. The `forceload` variable loads the specified modules at boot time, just before mounting the root file system. The `rootfs` variable sets the file system type of the root. The `rootdev` variable specifies the root device. The default value for the `rootdev` variable is the physical device name of the device where the boot program resides. The `set` keyword is used to modify the default kernel parameters. For example, to configure the maximum number of users to 75, the following command entry is added to the `/etc/system` file:

```
set maxusers=75
```

CAUTION

The `/etc/system` file has a great impact over the kernel as it is read by the kernel during the auto configuration process. Any changes to this file need to be made with utmost caution.

The kernel mounts the necessary file systems and starts a process known as the swapper process with a process ID of 0. The swapper is the parent process for all other processes on the system. It starts the first process, init, which has a process ID of 1.

THE INIT PHASE

The init is the parent process for all other processes and is created by the kernel. It starts the other processes by reading the information stored in the `/etc/inittab` file. The init process is invoked in the init phase. It reads the `/etc/default/init` file to set the environment variables and then searches for the `init default` entry in the `/etc/inittab` file. The `init default` signifies the initial run level of the system. If the `init` process does not exist in `/etc/inittab`, it prompts the user to enter a run level from the system console. A `run level`, also called the init state, is a system state defined by a set of system services or processes. It is a software configuration, which consists of a selected group of processes. Solaris has eight run levels, each having a defined set of services, processes, and resources available to the users.

THE /etc/inittab FILE

The /etc/inittab file controls the behavior of the init process. The init process refers to the /etc/inittab file, and it starts, stops, respawns, and modifies the processes based on that. The respawn option specifies that whenever a process such as getty is terminated by itself, it is restarted automatically.

Listing 5.2 shows a sample /etc/inittab file.

LISTING 5.2   THE /etc/inittab FILE

```
ap::sysinit:/sbin/autopush -f /etc/iu.ap
ap::sysinit:/sbin/soconfig -f /etc/sock2path
fs::sysinit:/sbin/rcS sysinit              >/dev/msglog 2<>/dev/msglog </dev/consol
e
is:3:initdefault:
p3:s1234:powerfail:/usr/sbin/shutdown -y -i5 -g0 >/dev/msglog 2<>/dev/msglog
sS:s:wait:/sbin/rcS                        >/dev/msglog 2<>/dev/msglog </dev/consol
e
s0:0:wait:/sbin/rc0                        >/dev/msglog 2<>/dev/msglog </dev/consol
e
s1:1:respawn:/sbin/rc1                     >/dev/msglog 2<>/dev/msglog </dev/consol
e
s2:23:wait:/sbin/rc2                       >/dev/msglog 2<>/dev/msglog </dev/consol
e
s3:3:wait:/sbin/rc3                        >/dev/msglog 2<>/dev/msglog </dev/consol
e
s5:5:wait:/sbin/rc5                        >/dev/msglog 2<>/dev/msglog </dev/consol
e
s6:6:wait:/sbin/rc6                        >/dev/msglog 2<>/dev/msglog </dev/consol
e
fw:0:wait:/sbin/uadmin 2 0                 >/dev/msglog 2<>/dev/msglog </dev/consol
e
of:5:wait:/sbin/uadmin 2 6                 >/dev/msglog 2<>/dev/msglog </dev/consol
rb:6:wait:/sbin/uadmin 2 1                 >/dev/msglog 2<>/dev/msglog </dev/consol
e
sc:234:respawn:/usr/lib/saf/sac -t 300
co:234:respawn:/usr/lib/saf/ttymon -g -h -p "'uname -n' console login: " -T sun
-d /dev/console -l console -m ldterm,ttcompat
```

The /etc/inittab file has the following record structure:

```
    id: run level: action: process
```

The ID field contains a unique value for every entry in the inittab file. The run level field specifies the run level at which the process is executed. If this field is blank, the init program executes the process at all run levels. If you specify more than one run level in this field, the process is executed at each of the mentioned run levels. The process field contains a command that is to be executed. Keywords in the action field define the action to be taken on the process specified in the process field.

All processes that have a sysinit entry in the action field of the inittab file start whenever the system is first booted. Table 5.2 describes the possible values in the action field.

TABLE 5.2   *Action* KEYWORDS AND THEIR DESCRIPTIONS

Keyword	Description
`init default`	Identifies the default run level. For Sun systems, the default run level is 3.
`respawn`	Starts the process and restarts it when it dies.
`powerfail`	Starts the process when the init receives a power fail signal.
`sysinit`	Starts the process before trying to access the console and waits for the completion before continuing further. That is, entries of this type are executed before the `Console Login:` prompt is displayed.
`wait`	Starts the process and waits for it to complete, before executing the next entry for this run state.

NOTE

You can determine the system's current run level using the `who -r` command.

RUN CONTROL SCRIPTS

The `rc` scripts are Bourne shell scripts written to stop and start system services and processes. These scripts are stored in the `/sbin` directory with links pointing to them from the `/etc` directory. The exact services and processes that run at each init level are determined by the scripts in the `/etc/rc#.d` directories.

Whenever a system enters a new run level, it executes the associated run control script. For example, when the system enters run level 2, the script `/etc/rc2` is executed.

Figure 5.2 shows a section of the `ls -la` output, which displays the run control scripts and the `rcx.d` directories in the `/etc` directory.

Figure 5.2
Output of the
`ls-la` command—
depicting the links.

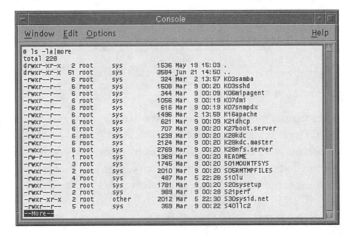

The link value of 1 for the rcx files of the /etc directory indicates a symbolic link. The rcx files in the /etc directory are linked to the rcx files in the /sbin directory.

Files in the rcx.d directories beginning with S are start scripts, which are used to start the processes and services, whereas files beginning with K are stop scripts, which are used to kill the processes. Consider, for example, the cron utility, which is used to automatically execute commands. You need to start the cron utility at run level 2 and stop at run levels 0, 1, 5, 6, and S. So the cron script exists as S75cron in the /etc/rc2.d directory and as K40cron in the respective /etc/rcx.d directories for the run levels 0, 1, 5, 6, and S.

The significance of the naming convention for rc scripts is that when the system enters that run level, the scripts with lower numbers are given priority for execution over those with higher numbers. For example, when the system enters run level 2, it executes all the scripts starting with S in the /etc/rc2.d directory. These scripts are executed in the increasing order of their numbers; that is, the system starts with S01MOUNTFSYS and ends with S99dtlogin. Figure 5.3 lists the contents of the /etc/rc2 directory.

Figure 5.3
The start and stop scripts in the /etc/rc2/ directory.

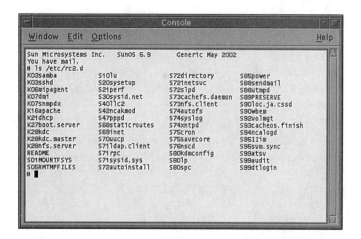

Copies of the run control scripts are also located in the /etc/init.d directory. The advantage of storing a copy in the /etc/init.d directory is that a system service can be started or stopped without changing the current run level. The system services can be started and stopped only by the superuser.

The following syntax depicts how to stop and start a service.

```
# /etc/init.d/<filename> stop
# /etc/init.d/<filename> start
```

For example, to stop the Network File System server service, type **/etc/init.d/nfs.server stop**. To start the Network File System server service, type **/etc/init.d/nfs.server start** at the # prompt.

THE SHUTDOWN PROCESS

A system might have to be shut down for various reasons:

- To prevent the system from an anticipated power failure
- To perform maintenance tasks, such as backup and recovery
- To perform a reconfiguration boot when new hardware devices are added or removed
- To force a crash dump when the system hangs
- To repair a damaged file system
- To boot the system using the kernel debugger
- To perform an installation

A system can be shut down with any one of the following commands: `init`, `shutdown`, `reboot`, `poweroff`, or `halt`. The administrator should choose the method of shutdown depending on the reason behind the shutdown. The rest of this section discusses which command is appropriate for each kind of shutdown. The `shutdown` and the `init` commands are the preferred means of shutting down the system. The `halt` and the `poweroff` commands are not advisable because they do not run the `rc` scripts.

> **NOTE**
>
> All the shutdown-related commands are located in the `/usr/sbin` directory.

THE init COMMAND

The `init` command is used to change the system run levels and is associated with process control and initialization. Table 5.3 describes the various run levels in Solaris.

TABLE 5.3   VARIOUS RUN LEVELS AND THEIR DESCRIPTIONS

Run level	Init state	Description
0	Power down	The system shuts down. All the users are forced to log off the system and operating system services are stopped in an orderly manner. The system returns to the open boot mode. It is safe to turn off the power to the system and peripherals.
S or s	Single user	Enables the system to prepare for maintenance. Users log out of the system. All services, except the core operating system, are stopped in an orderly manner. Mounted file systems remain mounted. A command line interface (with superuser privileges) is started and associated with the system console. This allows the system administrator to perform maintenance tasks, such as system backup, without interruptions from users or applications.

5

Run level	Init state	Description
1	Administrative	Currently logged on users are not affected. Multiple users can log on and use available system resources. All services, except the core operating system service, are stopped in an orderly manner. All mounted file systems remain mounted. A command line interface (with superuser privileges) is started and associated with the system console. This allows the system administrator to perform system maintenance while users are working on the system.
2	Multi-user	The system is set up for normal operations. Multiple users can log on and use the system resources. All services, except the network file system (NFS) service, are started. All default file systems are mounted.
3	Multi-user with NFS	The system is set up for normal operations. This is the default system state. Multiple users can access the system resources. All services, including the network file system (NFS) are started. All default file systems are mounted.
4	Alternative Multi-user	Is available to be defined as an alternative multi-user environment configuration. It is not necessary for system operation and is usually not used.
5	Power Down	The system is shut down. All users are logged off the system. All operating system services are stopped in an orderly manner. When complete, it is safe to turn off the power to the system a nd peripherals. If supported by the system hardware, the power to the system is automatically turned off.
6	Reboot	The system is shut down (run level 0) and then restarted, and brought back up to the default run level defined in the `inittab` file.

The `init` command requires superuser privileges. The `init` command executes the commands in the `/etc/inittab` file. The appropriate `rc` scripts for each run level specified in the `/etc/inittab` file are run to stop and start the processes.

The `init 6` command brings the system down to run level 0 and then back to the default run level. To bring the system to the single-user mode, issue the `init s` command. All user logins are disabled and the file systems relevant to the single-user mode are mounted.

THE shutdown COMMAND

The `shutdown` command is normally used to shut down a system in multi-user mode. The `shutdown` command writes the data in memory to the disk and brings the system to the specified run level. It stops all processes, dismounts the file systems, and dumps the contents of the memory to disk. The `shutdown` command also notifies the `syslog` daemon about the shutdown.

Only users with superuser privileges can issue the shutdown command. The advantage of the shutdown command over the init command is that it notifies the users that the system is being shut down.

The shutdown command is mainly used to perform three tasks:

- Halting the system
- Rebooting the system
- Switching to single-user mode

The shutdown command has the following syntax:

```
shutdown [-I init-state] [-g seconds] [-y] [message]
```

Table 5.4 describes the options of the shutdown command.

TABLE 5.4   OPTIONS OF THE *shutdown* COMMAND AND THEIR DESCRIPTIONS

Option	Description
[-I init-state]	Brings the system to the specified run level (init-state). The possible run levels are 0, 1, 2, S, and 6. The default run level for the shutdown command is run level S.
[-g]	Waits for a specified grace period before the system is shut down. The default time limit is 60 seconds.
[-y]	Executes the shutdown command without intervention.
[message]	Sends a warning message to users logged on to the system. Messages are enclosed within quotes.

Without any argument, the shutdown command brings the system to the single-user mode and displays the # prompt. The default grace period for users to log out is 60 seconds, after which the system terminates all user sessions and shuts down.

The following syntax brings the system to the single-user mode with a grace period of 2 minutes:

```
# shutdown -g120 -y
```

The following syntax brings the system to run level 0 with a grace period of 3 minutes and displays the ok prompt:

```
# shutdown -i0 -g180 -y
```

NOTE

A grace period of 15 minutes for the users to log off after saving their files is considered a good practice.

THE reboot COMMAND

The reboot command changes the run level to the default run level specified in the /etc/inittab file. It requires superuser privileges for execution. It synchronizes the data in memory to the disk, logs to the syslog daemon, and reboots to the default run level. Even though the functionality is similar to the init 6 command, the reboot command does not execute the shutdown scripts in the /etc/rcX.d directory.

During the shutdown process, the rc script stored in the /sbin/rcX directory executes all /etc/rcX.d/K* and /etc/rcX.d/S* scripts. Simultaneously, the init process (PID 1) executes the /etc/rc0 script. This script in turn executes all /etc/rc0.d/K* and /etc/rc0.d/S* scripts and then kills all processes and dies.

NOTE

> The reboot command supports all valid boot options. The options are specified with the "--" option.

THE poweroff COMMAND

The poweroff command brings the system to run level 5. When it is used, the system is powered off. The poweroff command is functionally equivalent to the init 5 command, but it does not execute the rc0 script. The poweroff command writes any pending information to the disk and halts the processor. It logs the shutdown to the syslog daemon and writes a shutdown record in the /var/adm/wtmp file, which is the system login accounting file. Table 5.5 describes the options of the poweroff command.

TABLE 5.5   OPTIONS OF THE poweroff COMMAND AND THEIR DESCRIPTIONS

Options	Description
-n	Prevents the sync program from writing out any pending information to the disk.
-l	Prevents logging the shutdown to the syslogd daemon.
-y	Halts the system, even from a dialup terminal.

THE halt COMMAND

The halt command brings the system to run level 0. The halt command writes any pending information to the disk and halts the processor. It logs the shutdown to the syslog daemon and writes a shutdown record in the /var/adm/wtmp file. The init 0 command is preferred to the halt command because it performs a proper shutdown and brings the system to the ok prompt. The halt command does not run the rc0 scripts.

RUN CONTROL SCRIPTS FOR SHUTDOWN

The init process (PID 1) executes the /etc/rc0 script. This script executes all /etc/rc0.d/K* and /etc/rc0.d/S* scripts and then kills all processes and dies.

SUMMARY

The SPARC boot process has four main phases: OBP, boot program, kernel initialization, and init. The OBP phase performs various diagnostics and runs a quick POST procedure, to verify the system's hardware and memory. In the boot program phase, the primary boot program, bootblk, finds the secondary boot program and loads it into memory. The next phase is the kernel initialization phase, where the kernel initializes itself and begins loading modules using the /platform/'uname -m'/ufsboot program to read the files. Init is the parent process for all other processes and is created by the kernel. It starts the other processes by reading the information stored in the /etc/inittab file.

A system can be shut down with any one of these commands: init, shutdown, reboot, poweroff, or halt. The shutdown command is used normally to shut down a system in multi-user mode. The reboot command changes the run level to the default run level specified in the /etc/inittab file. The poweroff command brings the system to run level 5 and the system is powered off. The halt command brings the system to run level 0.

5

WORKING WITH SOLARIS

6   GUI in Solaris   85

7   The Shell Environment   109

## CHAPTER 6

GUI IN SOLARIS

In this chapter

Introduction and Brief History of X Windows   86

Window Managers for Solaris   86

Common Desktop Environment   88

Configuring CDE   96

The Workspace Manager   101

GNOMEs   104

Universal Language Coverage   107

Summary   108

INTRODUCTION AND BRIEF HISTORY OF X WINDOWS

The common complaint against Unix-based operating systems is that they are not user friendly. Graphical user interfaces make user interaction with the OS easy so that even novices feel comfortable. In recent years, this aspect, long ignored by Unix developers, is being given its rightful importance. Imagine a user using the drag-and-drop feature of the File Manager utility to move files across directories and receiving instant gratification. This is better than dealing with a cumbersome command line interface where commands need to be memorized and are often invalidated by typographical errors.

To improve the user interface, many Unix vendors began working on their own versions of GUIs and only in recent years they have come together to develop a common GUI to be used across various Unix platforms. This section briefly traces the history of Unix GUIs and explains the essential terms you need to be familiar with before proceeding to Solaris GUIs.

The first widely accepted and available standard of Unix windowing systems or GUIs (graphical user interfaces), X Windows, took shape at the Massachusetts Institute of Technology (MIT). The project, undertaken in the year 1984 and supported by IBM and Digital Equipment Corporation, was a precursor to further research and development on X Windows. In fact, this project became so popular that it was used on Windows 95, 98, NT, and Macintosh.

Solaris uses X Windows as the default windowing system. A windowing system is a set of software libraries used to control and manage a system's graphical capabilities.

The special feature of X Windows that sets it apart from other GUIs is that right from its conception and initial developmental stages, it was targeted for the client/server environment. It follows a client-server architecture where a client requests a server for some service, such as display of client data, and the server responds to it.

NOTE

> X Windows is a hardware-independent network-based window platform. There have been numerous versions of the X Windows System, but it was not until the eleventh version, known simply as X11. Since then there have been many further releases that added extra functionality while attempting to remain largely backward compatible. The current release is the sixth one, and is known as X11R6.4 or simply R6.

6

WINDOW MANAGERS FOR SOLARIS

A Window Manager is a program that controls the features of the GUI. The windowing system uses the Window Manager to keep track of the location of each window on the desktop. Operations such as opening, closing, moving, resizing, and positioning of windows and handling windowing sessions are handled by Window Managers. X Windows uses many Window Managers to manage the various desktop environments.

A popularly known Window Manager is Motif Window Manager (mwm). Motif is the industry standard GUI, which conforms to the IEEE 1295 standard. It is used on more than 200 hardware and software platforms. It provides application developers and system vendors with the industry's most widely used environment for standardizing application presentations on a wide range of platforms. Motif is the most popular user interface for Unix-based operating systems. But Motif Window Manager is not included with Solaris.

The desktop environment is a user interface that runs on the Window Manager. The CDE and GNOME are the desktop environments available in Solaris 9. Other popular desktop environments are HP-VUE (Hewlett Packard Visual User Environment) for HP/Unix and the KDE (K Desktop Environment) for all popular Unix flavors. The desktop environment provides a GUI, which provides a collection of utilities also known as the X utilities.

The difference between a Window Manager and the desktop environment is that the Window Manager manages the location and the look of the window, but it does not provide the utilities for the X Windows. You can customize your desktop by using the Window Manager, and you can use the utilities provided by the desktop environment to suit your needs. The CDE is an industry standard in the GUI area because all major developers of Unix have adopted this GUI. Sun Microsystems ships Solaris with Desktop Window Manager (DTWM) for CDE.

NOTE

> Major vendors, such as IBM, Novell, HP, SunSoft, and later Hitachi, Digital, and Fujitsu were part of the combined effort christened the Common Open Software Environment (COSE) started in 1993. The goal was to develop a common windowing standard across Unix platforms. The fruit of their efforts is a product known as Common Desktop Environment (CDE).

CDE is a user-friendly desktop environment that maintains a consistent look across all Unix platforms. Users can use CDE to customize their workstations. It has an extended front panel that can be used to manage files and print jobs, send mail, administer network services, and provide online help.

To start the Solaris GUI, follow these steps:

1. After the boot process occurs as discussed in Chapter 5, "Booting and Shutting Down the System," the Login Manager displays the login screen, authenticates the user, and passes control to the session manager, which manages the user session.

2. To log on, type the login name in the Please Enter Your User Name text box and click OK. To erase the login name, click the StartOver button. The Options drop-down list has the Language, Session, and Return to Local Host options.

   The Language option displays the default language option, which is C—the POSIX standard. The Sessions option allows you to choose the desktop environment. The sessions available are CDE, User's Last Desktop, and Failsafe Session. You can select the CDE session to work with the GUI. If you select the User's Last Desktop, you are logged on to the environment that was running when you last logged off. The Failsafe Session runs with a single terminal window and minimum options. This session can be used to rectify the errors in the windowing environment, such as misconfiguration of the CDE files, so that the user can log on without any problem the next time. When the user selects the FailSafe Session from the Session submenu option of the login screen Options menu, the login server runs the Xfailsafe script. This script executes commands to start a minimal windowing environment, which is usually a Terminal window and an optional window manager.

NOTE

> To switch back to the login screen from the command line prompt, you can use the following command:
>
> # /usr/dt/bin/dtlogin -daemon

3. When you exit a login session, control is passed back to the Login Manager, which displays the login screen again. The Login Manager can accept requests from the hosts on the network to display a login screen on a particular terminal, which can be either a local or a network terminal. For local login, the Login Manager starts an X server automatically and displays a login screen. For remote login, the Login Manager accepts or rejects network/logon requests with the help of the X Display Manager Control Protocol (XDMCP).

COMMON DESKTOP ENVIRONMENT

Common Desktop Environment (CDE) is a user interface that runs on the Window Manager and provides a number of utilities known as X utilities.

CDE provides four independent workspaces for users. Users can switch between these workspaces. For example, an administrator can perform user administration tasks in one workspace, work with application files in another, use backup tools in the third workspace, and monitor system performance in the fourth workspace.

Figure 6.1 shows a CDE workspace with several utility windows open. The window that appears across the bottom of the workspace is the Front Panel. You can use the subpanels in the Front Panel to open the applications or utility windows.

Figure 6.1
A CDE workspace with several utility windows open.

FRONT PANEL

The Front Panel is divided into two areas, namely the box and the workspace switch. The workspace switch is present at the center of the panel and the panel areas to the left and right constitute the box. Figure 6.2 shows the Front Panel.

Figure 6.2
The CDE Front Panel with the Links and the Hosts subpanels displayed.

The Front Panel has various subpanels that have submenus. To add an application to a subpanel, drag the corresponding icon to the Install Icon control of the subpanel.

LINKS

The Links subpanel contains the Web applications you use frequently. Refer to Figure 6.2, which displays the Links subpanel. The following are the default Web applications in this panel:

- **Web Browser**—Starts the default web browser. Hot Java Web Browser is the user's personal interface to the wide realm of the Internet and is the default Web browser in Solaris. It can also accept NFS URLs from remote hosts and the local network.

- **Personal Bookmarks**—Opens the Personal Bookmarks folder and displays bookmarks. The bookmarks are stored in the $HOME/.dt/bookmarks directory.

- **Find Web Page**—Starts an Internet search application.

CARDS

Use the Cards subpanel for personal applications you use frequently. Figure 6.3 displays the Cards subpanel. The following is the list of default personal applications found on this panel.

- **Calendar Manager**—Can be used to schedule appointments, to allocate tasks with the To Do List, and to date and time displays.

- **Address Manager**—Manages the email address book. It can be used to compose emails.

6

Figure 6.3
The Cards subpanel.

FILES

Use the Files subpanel for file management applications you use frequently. Figure 6.4 displays the Files subpanel. The following is the list of default file management applications in this panel.

Figure 6.4
The Files subpanel.

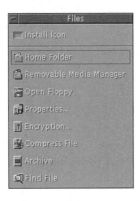

- **Home Folder**—Displays the File Manager.
- **Open Floppy**—Displays the contents of the floppy disk in the floppy disk drive.
- **Open CD-ROM**—Displays the contents of the CD-ROM.
- **Properties**—Displays the permissions of the selected file or folder.
- **Encryption**—Encrypts files with a specified key.
- **Compress File**—Compresses the selected files.
- **Archive**—Opens a dialog box that enables you to archive or restore a file.
- **Find File**—Searches files based on the arguments supplied.

The File Manager is one of the most useful and powerful utilities on the CDE desktop. It supports almost all operations with files, such as creating, renaming, moving, copying, deleting, creating bookmarks, and changing permissions. Figure 6.5 shows the File Manager dialog box.

6

Figure 6.5
The File Manager
dialog box.

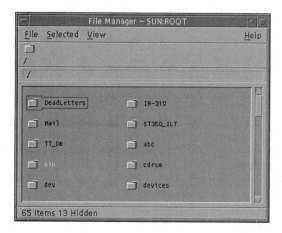

APPLICATIONS

Use the Applications subpanel to access applications you use frequently. Figure 6.6 displays the Applications subpanel. The following list explains the various options of the Applications subpanel.

Figure 6.6
The Applications
subpanel.

- **Text Note** —Opens the Text Note application.
- **Text Editor** —Opens the Text Editor application, which has useful features such as spell check, word finder, margin alignment, and so on.
- **Applications** —Opens the Application Manager window (see Figure 6.7).

Figure 6.7
The Application
Manager window.

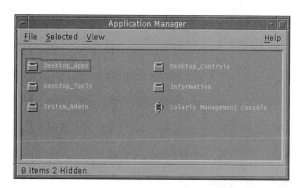

6

MAIL

Use the Mail subpanel to store frequently used mail addresses. Figure 6.8 displays the Mail subpanel, which includes the following items:

- **Mail Manager**—Manages a user's mail. It supports mailing lists, templates, and mail folders.
- **Suggestion Box**—Opens a Mailer Compose window preaddressed to Sun Microsystems, Inc.

Figure 6.8
The Mail subpanel.

PERSONAL PRINTERS

Use the Personal Printers subpanel to access printers you use frequently. Figure 6.9 displays the Printers subpanel. The following list explains the various options of the Personal Printers subpanel.

- **Default**—Drag and drop files to be printed to this icon to start printing. The Printer Manager assigns the job to the default printer.
- **Print Manager**—Manages the system printers. It helps to monitor and reschedule tasks in the printer queue of specific printers.

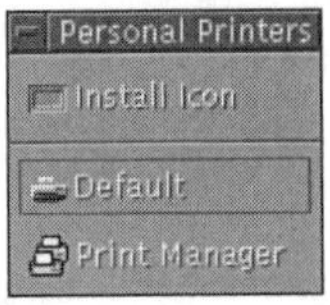

Figure 6.9
Personal Printers subpanel.

TOOLS

To access tools and applications you use frequently, use the Tools subpanel. Figure 6.10 displays the Tools subpanel.

Figure 6.10
The Tools subpanel.

6

The following list explains the default tools under the Tools subpanel.

- **Desktop Controls**—The Style Manager is used to customize the window features, color, font, background, keyboard, mouse, beep, screen, window, and startup of the CDE display. Figure 6.11 shows the Style Manager dialog box.

Figure 6.11
The Style Manager dialog box.

- **Solaris Management Console**—This is a powerful new suite of GUI-based system administration tools, which can be used to perform efficient system administration tasks. In support of Solaris WebStart and Solaris WebStart Wizards software, Solaris Management Console performs the following tasks:
  - Installation of Solaris and other applications.
  - Configuration of services, such as DHCP and DNS, on Solaris servers.
- **CDE Error Log**—Displays logged CDE display-related errors.
- **Customize Workspace Menu**—Helps to customize the workspace by enabling you to drag and drop icons in a File Manager Window.
- **Add Item To Menu**—Helps you add new menu items to the Workspace menu. By default, the new item occupies the first position in the Workspace menu.
- **Find Process**—Helps you view system processes based on several parameters, such as process ID, parent process ID, process name, owner, and so on. It can be used to trace system calls, daemons, and child processes, to look up the owner of processes, and so on. The entire data of system processes, thus sampled, can even be logged to any file.
- **Hotkey Editor**—Helps you accomplish tasks quickly by assigning a series of commands to a function key.

HOSTS

Use the Hosts subpanel to access terminal-specific applications, such as system console, system details, CPU performance, and so forth. Figure 6.12 displays the Hosts subpanel.

Figure 6.12
The Hosts subpanel.

The following list explains the various options of the Hosts subpanel.

- **Performance meter**—Provides a graphical representation of CPU and hard disk performance.

6

- **This Host**—Opens a default terminal emulator (dtterm).

- **System Info**—Displays system details, such as User Name, Workstation Name, Internet (IP) Address, Virtual Memory, Domain Name and so on.

- **Console**—Opens the default console for the user.

- **Find Host**—Has utilities to measure performance of the system while a certain program or application is running. You can open the console through this utility by clicking on the Console icon. The Find Host icon can be used to find a remote host present somewhere on the network.

HELP

Use the Help subpanel to obtain help both online and offline. Figure 6.13 displays the Help subpanel. The following are the various Help features.

Figure 6.13
The Help subpanel.

- **Help Manager**—Opens Help viewer.

- **SunSolve Online**—Opens the Hot Java Web Browser and connects to the SunSolve URL.

- **Solaris Support**—Opens a browser for the Sun Microsystems download site for patches and technical support.

- **Information**—Opens the Information folder in Application Manager.

- **Desktop Introduction**—Opens Help viewer for a Desktop Introduction module for new CDE users.

- **Front Panel Help**—Opens Help viewer for a Front Panel Introduction module for new CDE users.

- **On Item Help**—Displays a question mark icon, which can be dragged and dropped onto any object on the workspace for which you need help.

- **Answerbook2**—Solaris Answer Book documentation.

TRASH CAN

The Trash Can is a special File Manager container that contains the objects you have deleted. Figure 6.14 displays the Trash subpanel. The following list explains the various options of the Trash subpanel.

Figure 6.14
The Trash subpanel.

- **Trash**—Discards unwanted files, directories, and applications dragged and dropped from any other CDE utility. Files that are accidentally trashed can be recovered from the Trash Can.

- **Empty Trash Can**—Clears the contents of the Trash Can. The Trash Can files cannot be recovered after the Trash Can has been cleared.

WORKSPACE BUTTONS

Workspace buttons are used to change workspaces. The user can modify the default names of the workspaces present on the buttons.

LOCK BUTTON

The Lock button is used to lock the user's desktop and displays a default screen saver. Locking prevents any unauthorized usage during periods of inactivity during a user's session. The desktop can be unlocked only by typing the correct password. Figure 6.15 shows the Lock Screen button.

This is the Lock Button

Figure 6.15
Lock button.

6

THE EXIT BUTTON

Pressing the Exit button exits the CDE session, logging out the user, and displays the login screen. Figure 6.16 shows the Exit button.

Figure 6.16
Exit button.

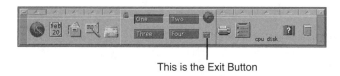

This is the Exit Button

CONFIGURING CDE

You can configure the CDE to control its appearance and functionality by using the configuration files. The CDE has three configurable components:

- **Login Manager**—Displays the login screen, authenticates users, and passes control to the Session Manager.
- **Session Manager**—Starts, maintains, and tracks the user sessions. A session is a group of settings, applications, and resources on the user's desktop.
- **Workspace Manager**—Controls the appearance and behavior of the windows in various workspaces.

CDE can be configured in three ways: default configuration, system-wide configuration, and user-specific configuration. The default configuration files exist in the /usr/dt/config directory; the system-wide configuration files exist in the /etc/dt/config directory; and the user-specific configuration files are in the user's home directory. The system-wide and user-specific configuration files do not exist by default; you need to create them. The user-specific configuration overrides the system-wide configuration, which in turn overrides the default configuration.

However, regular users cannot configure the login server-related files discussed in Table 6.1. User-specific configuration applies only to files that are specific to the Session Manager and Workspace Manager. For system-wide customization, it is strongly recommended that the superuser copy the files from the /usr/dt/config directory to the /etc/dt/config directory and change the copied files rather than the original files. This will preserve the default configuration. In addition, /etc/dt/config files can also be used for system upgrade. If the Solaris version is upgraded, the contents of the files in the /usr/dt/config directory will be changed and changes made during customization, if any, will be lost.

THE LOGIN MANAGER

The Login Manager displays the login screen and starts a session for the authenticated user. The Login Manager is also referred to as *Login Server*.

A system administrator can stop the GUI login process when the system is running by typing

```
# /etc/init.d/dtlogin stop
```

or restart it by typing

```
# /etc/init.d/dtlogin start
```

Alternately, the permanent removal of the startup script in the run level 2 directory (/etc/rc2.d) prevents automatic startup of the GUI mode.

To disable automatic starting of the GUI mode during system startup, type

```
# /usr/dt/bin/dtconfig -d
done
desktop auto-start disabled.
#
```

or type

```
# /usr/dt/bin/dtconfig -e
done
desktop auto-start enabled.
#
```

to enable it.

Table 6.1 lists the configuration files that control the Login Manager.

TABLE 6.1   LOGIN MANAGER CONFIGURATION FILES

File Name	Function
/usr/dt/bin/dtlogin	Login Manager.
/usr/dt/config/Xconfig	Is the default Login Manager configuration file.
/usr/dt/config/Xaccess	Controls remote host access to Login Server.
/usr/dt/config/Xservers	Configures local and network displays.
/usr/dt/config/Xresources	Controls the display of the login screen.
/var/dt/Xpid	Stores the process ID of the Login Manager.
/var/dt/Xerrors	Records the errors regarding the Login Manager.
/usr/dt/config/Xsetup	Runs commands before displaying the login screen.
/usr/dt/config/Xstartup	Runs commands before starting the session.
/usr/dt/config/Xfailsafe	Starts a failsafe session.
/usr/dt/config/Xreset	Runs commands after exiting from a session.
/usr/dt/bin/dtchooser	Displays a chooser screen for a display.
/usr/dt/bin/dtgreet	Displays a login screen.

NOTE

A chooser screen enables users to display login screens from other login servers on the network.

6

The characteristics of the Login Manager can be controlled and customized with the following configuration files:

- Xconfig
- Xservers
- Xaccess
- Xresources

THE Xconfig FILE

The Xconfig file controls the entire logon process. This file contains information that controls the behavior of the Login Manager. It stores the name and location of all the configuration files used in the logon process in the GUI mode, and the default values for several configuration variables. Table 6.2 displays the default entries in the Xconfig file and their values.

TABLE 6.2   THE XCONFIG FILE DEFAULT ENTRIES AND THEIR   VALUES

Keywords	Default Values	Description
Dtlogin.errorLogFile:	/var/dt/Xerrors	Stores the logged errors.
Dtlogin.pidFile:	/var/dt/Xpid	Stores the login server process ID.
Dtlogin.accessFile:	Xaccess	Controls the login server access.
Dtlogin.servers:	Xservers	Manages local and network displays.
Dtlogin*resources:	%L/Xresources	Stores the configuration of the login screen.
Dtlogin*startup:	Xstartup	Stores the session startup details.
Dtlogin*reset:	Xreset	Stores the commands to be executed after the session ends.
Dtlogin*setup:	Xsetup	Establishes the display setup.
Dtlogin*failsafeClient:	Xfailsafe	Controls the failsafe session.
Dtlogin*terminateServer:	True	Stores the commands to terminate and restart the Xserver at user logout.

By default, the /var/dt/Xpid file stores the process ID of the Login Server. For example, to change the file that stores the process ID of the login process to /var/dt/newpid file, modify the value of the Dtlogin.pidFile variable in the Xconfig file to /var/dt/newpid. The following syntax illustrates this.

```
Dtlogin.pidFile:    /var/dt/newpid
```

THE Xaccess FILE

The Xaccess file controls access privileges to the login server for hosts on the network. You can allow or restrict logon for any host on the network.

The Xaccess file contains one hostname per line. It can contain either the names of only those hosts that are granted access privileges or all hosts with a ! symbol preceding the names of hosts that are denied access.

NOTE

The default location of the Xaccess, Xconfig, and Xservers files is the /usr/dt/config directory. To make modifications, copy the respective files to the /etc/dt/config directory and modify them.

When a remote terminal requests logon, the Login Manager checks the Xaccess file to determine whether service should be granted or denied.

THE Xservers FILE

The Xservers file controls the display of local and network logins and the starting up of Xservers. It provides the names of terminals where the Xservers need to be started. This file specifies whether the locations are local or remote. The Login Manager reads this file and starts the Xservers as needed.

THE Xresources FILE

The Xresources file configures the display of the login screen. Keywords in this file determine the functionality and appearance of the login screen. The default location of the Xresources file is the /usr/dt/config/en_US.UTF-8 directory. To make modifications, copy the respective files to the /etc/dt/config/en_US.UTF-8 directory and modify them.

NOTE

> The location en_US.UTF-8 for the Xresources file is applicable only if the language you are using in your system is U.S. English. When you configure language or local support during the installation of Solaris, the directory /usr/dt/app-defaults lists the default language you have chosen at the time of installation. However, you can change the default language setting at the login screen by selecting the Options menu and then selecting the Languages option.

The following list shows the functions of the variables declared in this file.

- **Dtlogin*logo*bitmapFile**—Determines the bitmap logo (normally the Sun logo).
- **Dtlogin*greeting*LabelString and Dtlogin*greeting*fontList**—Defines the welcome message and its font.
- **Dtlogin*greeting*persLabelString**—Defines the personalized welcome message on the login screen that prompts users to specify a password.
- **Dtlogin*foreground and Dtlogin*background**—Defines the foreground and background colors.

THE SESSION MANAGER

A session is a group of settings, applications, and resources that are present on a user's desktop. The Session Manager, which exists as an executable file Xsession in the location /usr/dt/bin, controls the user sessions.

There are three types of user sessions: current, initial, and home.

- **Current**—The session is said to be current as long as the user is logged on. The current user session can be saved and restored when the user logs on again.

6

- **Initial** —The default session that is started the first time the user logs on after the user's account is created is called the initial session. It displays the File Manager and a Help dialog box called Introduction to the Desktop.

- **Home** —Users can customize a session according to their preferences. Such a session is called a home session.

> **NOTE**
>
> To execute any user-defined profiles automatically, update the .dtprofile file in the user's home directory. The DTSOURCEPROFILE variable in this file determines automatic execution of user profiles. If the value of this variable is set to true, the user profiles are executed. If the value is set to false, the profiles are not executed. By default, the value is true.

The Session Manager executes the following sequence of tasks:

1. **Traces the .dtprofile script in the user's home directory**—The .dtprofile is a script that configures the environmental variables for the user's session. When a user logs in for the first time, the Session Manager copies the default desktop profile file /usr/dt/config/sys.dtprofile to the user's home directory as the .dtprofile file.

2. **Traces the Xsession.d scripts**—The script files in the /usr/dt/config/Xsession.d directory start the optional daemons and set up additional environment variables for the user session.

3. **Displays a welcome message on the user's console**—The welcome messages are stored in a variable named dtstart_hello[0]. To turn off the message, a script file can be created in the /etc/dt/config/Xsession.d directory with the dtstart_hello[0] variable set as follows :
   dtstart_hello[0]="".

   To display user-specific welcome messages, configure the variable dtstart_hello[0] in the $HOME/.dtprofile file.

4. **Sets up desktop search paths**.

5. **Loads applications**.

6. **Optionally reads the .profile file in the user's home directory**—The .profile and .login files are stored (for Bourne & Korn shells and the .cshrc file for C shell) in the user's home directory and executed only if the value of the DTSOURCEPROFILE variable in the .dtprofile file is set to true.

7. **Starts Tooltalk messaging system**—Independent applications communicate with each other with the help of the Tooltalk messaging daemon. The working of this messaging system can be customized on a system-wide basis if you alter the variable dtstart_ttsession in any executable file in the /etc/dt/config/Xsession.d directory.

8. **Loads the session resources**—The session resources are specified in the following files:

   - `$HOME/.Xdefaults`—User-specific
   - `/etc/dt/config/C/sys.resources`—System-wide
   - `/usr/dt/config/C/sys.resources`—Default

9. **Starts Color Server**—The color server manages the background and foreground colors.

10. **Starts Workspace Manager**—The default Workspace Manager `/usr/dt/bin/dtwm` is started. Any other system-wide Workspace Manager can be specified by altering the value of the `Dtsession*wmStartup` command variable in the `/etc/dt/config/C/sys.resources` file. Similarly, users may change their Workspace Manager by changing the value of this variable in the `$HOME/.Xdefaults` directory.

11. **Starts applications**—All applications defined in the `/etc/dt/config/C/sys.session` file are started. Table 6.3 explains the functions of the Session Manager configuration files.

TABLE 6.3   SESSION MANAGER CONFIGURATION FILES AND THEIR FUNCTIONS

File Name	Function
`/usr/dt/config/C/sys.resources`	Stores the system-wide default session resources.
`/usr/dt/bin/Xsession`	The Session Manager executable file.
`$HOME/.dt/sessions/current/dt.session`	Contains active window names, sizes, positioning, workspace details, startup file locations.
`$HOME/.dt/sessions/current/dt.resources`	Contains details of resources such as language, color, fonts, and so on.
`$HOME/.dt/sessions/current/dt.settings`	Contains details of all Session Manager settings.
`$HOME/.dt/sessions/home`	Directory for saving the user's customized session.
`/etc/dt/config/Xsession.d`	Contains scripts to set additional environment variables and execute commands.
`/etc/dt/config/C/sys.session`	Defines system-wide session applications.
`$HOME/.dt/sessions/sessionetc`	Contains commands to be automatically executed on session startup.
`$HOME/.dt/sessions/current`	Directory for saving the user's current session.
`$HOME/.dt/sessions/sessionexit`	Contains commands to be automatically executed on session exit.

THE WORKSPACE MANAGER

The Front Panel and the applications started by the user together constitute the workspace. Figure 6.17 shows the various workspace buttons in the Front Panel. Click on a button to switch to that workspace. The Workspace Manager is the program that controls the workspace features, such as workspace and window menus, window behavior, window appearance, key and button bindings, and so on.

Various Workspaces in the Front Panel

Figure 6.17
Various workspaces
in the Front Panel.

The Workspace Manager uses any one of the following configuration files::

- **User-specific**—$HOME/.dt/dtwmrc
- **System-wide** —/etc/dt/config/C/sys.dtwmrc
- **Default** —/usr/dt/config/C/sys.dtwmrc

The system-wide and user-specific configuration files do not exist by default. They need to be created.

The Workspace Manager consists of following three menus by default:

- **Workspace**—This menu, also called *root menu*, is displayed when the user clicks the right mouse button on the workspace backdrop.
- **Window**—This menu is displayed when the user clicks the left or right mouse buttons on the windows in the workspace.
- **Front Panel**—This menu is displayed when the user clicks the left or right mouse button over the upper-left corner of the Front Panel.

Table 6.4 lists the files used to configure the Workspace and the Front Panel.

TABLE 6.4 WORKSPACE MANAGER CONFIGURATION FILES

File	Function
/usr/dt/config/C/sys.dtwmrc	Default configuration File
/etc/dt/config/C/sys.dtwmrc	System-wide configuration File
$HOME/.dt/dtwmrc	User-specific configuration File
/usr/dt/appconfig/types/C/dtwm.fp	Default Front Panel configuration file
$HOME/.dt/types/dtwm.fp	User-specific Front Panel configuration file
$HOME/.dt/types/fp_dynamic	Directory used for user customizations made from Front Panel

Choose the Restart Workspace Manager option to restart the Workspace Manager after updating the configuration files. The four default workspace buttons constitute the workspace switch. The workspace switch can also be customized.

You can change workspaces according to your needs. For example, if you are opening a few files of a similar category, each in a separate window, and you want to open another category of files, you can create them in a different workspace. This helps to avoid the clutter of too many windows on the same workspace. To change the number of workspaces, modify the file /usr/dt/app-defaults/C/Dtwm. This file, apart from customizing the workspaces, can be used to set various Window Manager-related defaults. This file has the following two default entries for workspace count:

```
Dtwm*0*workspaceCount:4
Dtwm*workspaceCount:1
```

These variables are set so that multiple workspaces can exist on screen 0 and a single workspace on other screens. To alter the default number of workspaces, change the value of the Dtwm*0*workspace count variable and save the file.

The following syntax changes the system-wide workspace names:

```
Dtwm*ws0title: One
Dtwm*ws1title: Two
Dtwm*ws2title: Three
Dtwm*ws3title: Four
```

CUSTOMIZING THE FRONT PANEL

The Front Panel contains the main panel and several subpanels. The large rectangular window in the bottom of the display is the main panel. The subpanels are the menus that pop up when a button on the main panel is selected. The switch, panel, subpanel, and controls within the subpanel are all objects with different properties. The container for a control is a subpanel and the container for the subpanel is the panel. The default Front Panel is defined in the /usr/dt/appconfig/types/C/dtwm.fp file. To customize, copy this file to the /etc/dt/appconfig/types/C directory and modify it. Note that customization is need-dependent. For example, if a certain task is performed frequently, you may want to create it as an action and add it to one of the panels, rather than follow a long procedure to do the task every time.

NOTE

> User customizations of the Front Panel objects done from the pop-up menus and the Install Icon control are written to the $HOME/.dt/types/fp_dynamic directory. Another file, $HOME/.dt/sessions/dtwmfp.session is used to save and restore the state of the customized Front Panel for each session. These directories and files are automatically created by the Front Panel and should not be altered.

6

CUSTOMIZING THE WORKSPACE

To customize the user workspace, so that the user gets the same workspace each time after logon, you should save the workspace settings after customizing. You can do this by choosing Workspace, Utilities, Save Workspace.

> **NOTE**
>
> The custom workspace details of users are stored in two files: $HOME/.openwin-init and $HOME/.Owdefaults. The OpenLook Window Manager creates these files automatically.

GNOMEs

The objective for developing GNOME was to enable user-friendly applications, easy access to global information, and an easy-to-use desktop. It is designed to help users locate information and launch applications easily.

> **NOTE**
>
> GNOME runs on many Unix platforms, including Solaris.

GNOME has three major components: desktop, development platform, and office. The GNOME desktop contains a windows-based environment for users. The GNOME development platform provides tools that enable users to develop powerful applications on Unix. The GNOME office contains office productivity tools, such as word processing tools, spreadsheet programs, presentation tools, a Web browser, and an email program.

Sun has packaged GNOME 1.4 in the Solaris platform with several new client software applications, such as Nautilus, GNOME Virtual File System (VFS), Bonobo, and GConf.

- Nautilus is the file manager that makes viewing, organizing, and managing files an easy task.
- GNOME VFS acts as an abstract file system that enables applications to access the real file systems. GNOME VFS ensures that an application or component will be usable by Nautilus or other GNOME VFS applications for handling the display of data from various URIs.
- Bonobo creates reusable software components and custom applications.
- GConf is a configuration data storage mechanism.

> **NOTE**
>
> GNOME is free software that enables users to use, create, and distribute the software for no cost. If you create any application using the GNOME software, you have the rights to distribute modified versions to anybody.

PLANNING GNOME INSTALLATION

Before you start GNOME 1.4 installation, you must know that GNOME 1.4 is an unsupported release. It is recommended that this software be installed only on test machines that are used to test prerelease products.

CAUTION

> Although the installation of GNOME should not interfere with your system software, it is advisable that you back up any system software before the installation.

GNOME can be installed in Solaris 8 and higher versions. When planning to install GNOME, ensure the availability of at least 275MB of free hard disk space and 128MB of system memory. Also, there should be a graphics card that supports the 24-bit true color graphics mode. The graphics cards that can be used are Sun Creator3D™, Sun Elite3D™, Sun Expert3D™, PGX32, and Mach_64.

INSTALLING GNOME 1.4

You have the option of installing GNOME by downloading it or by using the software from the GNOME 1.4 CDs. Also, note that you can download the GNOME as one large file or as a group of smaller files that must be downloaded separately.

To download the one large file, execute the following command from the download directory using the Terminal window.

```
gunzip -c gnome-1_4-solaris-sparc.tar.gz | tar xvf
```

However, if you prefer to download the smaller files, execute the following command:

```
sh gnome-1_4-solaris-sparc-011.bin
```

After these steps are performed, the install image is stored in a subdirectory called gnome-install. You can now begin installing GNOME 1.4.

Note that the key applications displayed in Table 6.4 are installed with GNOME:

TABLE 6.4   KEY APPLICATIONS INSTALLED WITH GNOME

Application	Description
CD Player	Music playback utility
Eye of Gnome	Image viewer
Gedit	Text editor
GNOME Ghostview	PostScript file viewer
GNOME terminal	Command-line interface to GNOME
Nautilus	File management system
Simple Calculator	Basic calculator
Time tracking tool	Time-management software

Apart from the preceding applications, you have the option of installing additional applications that are available after the GNOME is installed. You can install these extra applications from the GNOME footprint menu. The additional applications that you can install are given in Table 6.5.

TABLE 6.5 ADDITIONAL APPLICATIONS THAT CAN BE INSTALLED WITH GNOME

Applications	Description
Address Book	Basic address book tool
Calendar	Basic calendar tool
Dia	Flowcharting tool
Gfax	Fax program
Glade	User interface design tool for GNOME
Gmc	Midnight Commander file manager
GNOME-DB	Database access client
Sodipodi	Vector-based drawing program
The GIMP	Image manipulation program
X-Chat	Internet Relay Chat (IRC) client

NOTE

> GNOME 1.4 requires Solaris patch #108827-08 (SPARC). If this patch is not present on your system, the GNOME installer will add it to your system.

To install GNOME 1.4, perform the following steps:

1. If you are installing GNOME from the download version, go to the subdirectory `gnome-install` and execute the command `./install`.

   Alternatively, if you are installing GNOME from the CD, move to the root directory of the CD-ROM and execute the command `./install`.

2. You can install GNOME using the typical install or the custom install. Typical install launches all the default applications in your system. Custom install enables you to make your choice for installing the additional applications available.

3. Next, set your graphics card to run in default 24-bit (if it is not set already). To find out which graphics cards you have installed, issue the following command from a terminal window:

   `/usr/sbin/fbconfig -list`

   You must log out and log in again before the command will take effect. To distinguish between an old and a new Creator3D card, issue the following command:

   `/usr/sbin/ffbconfig -propt`.

   If the output contains the phrase `Gamma Correction`, the card is a new Creator3D card.

   If the installer indicates that it changed your shared memory kernel settings to suit GNOME, you must reboot after the install to ensure that the new settings can take effect. The changes are made and clearly commented in the `/etc/system` file. The old `/etc/system` file is copied to `/etc/system.pre_gnome-1.4`.

If you installed from a downloaded install image directory, remove the install image with a `rm -R gnome-install` command.

REMOVING GNOME 1.4

To remove GNOME 1.4, execute the following two commands (as superuser) from a terminal window:

```
cd /var/sadm/prod
```

```
java uninstall_gnome_1_4
```

UNIVERSAL LANGUAGE COVERAGE

To provide a wider scope and audience for Solaris, the Solaris 9 operating system has been designed to include support for 133 locales that cover 39 languages. The locale is the software behavior that is based on a particular language, custom, or cultural environment. For example, desktop text or error messages should appear in the locale's specified language. Some of the locale support in Solaris 9 includes Asian, Japanese, and European. Table 6.5 describes the different locales supported by Solaris 9.

TABLE 6.5 LOCALE SUPPORT	
Locales	**Description**
GB18030-2000 Character Set-	Supports Chinese, Tibetan, Wei, Yi, and Mongolian character sets. Provides backward compatibility to Chinese codesets (GBK and GB2312).
Chinese and Korean Collation Locales	Supports collation algorithm to sort data. This algorithm uses collation APIs that provide an interface between the collation algorithms and the locale. This helps end-users and applications sort data.
Wordbreaker Modules for Thai	Formats the Thai text within Motif.
Asian UTF-8 (Unicode) Locales	Contains character sets for the Asian and European languages for Solaris Locales. For example: ■ th_TH.UTF-8—Unicode locale for Thailand. ■ hi_IN.UTF-8—Unicode locale for India.
New Thai Input Method	Supports the Thai input standard, called the WIT.
New Chinese input methods	More popular and powerful input methods in the Traditional Chinese and Simplified Chinese locales have been added for new character sets and new locales: New Chuyin IM for Traditional Chinese locales Cantonese IM for all Chinese locales English-Chinese IM for all Chinese locales

continues

TABLE 6.5 CONTINUED

Locales	Description
iconv Modules	Allows conversion between native encoded data and Unicode. To support new character sets, the following new iconv modules are added: UTF-8 <---> HKSCS UTF-8 <---> Hindi UTF-8 <---> GB18030 UTF-8 <---> ISO8859-11
zh_CN.GB18030 Locale Enhanced From zh_CN.GBK	Supports the GB18030 standard encoding that is required by Chinese law.
zh_HK.BIG5HK Locale	Supports the Hong Kong Supplementary Character Set (HKSCS).
Japanese iconv Modules	Provides the conversion feature between Solaris Japanese locale codesets and Japanese mainframe codesets.
Unicode (UTF-8) Locales for Europe and the Middle East	Supports UTF-8 locales for Turkey, Egypt, Brazil, Finland, and Belgium-Walloon. The locale names are as follows: ca_ES.ISO8859-1 and ca_ES.ISO8859-15—Spain (Catalan) pl_PL.UTF-8—Poland ru_RU.UTF-8—Russia. tr_TR.UTF-8—Turkey. ar_EG.UTF-8—Egypt pt_BR.UTF-8—Brazil. fi_FI.UTF-8—Finland. fr_BE.UTF-8—Belgium-Walloon.

SUMMARY

X Windows is the first widely-accepted standard of Unix windowing systems. X Windows follows a client/server architecture where the client requests the server for some service and the server responds to the client's requests. To manage the various desktop environments, X Windows uses many Window Managers.

The Window Manager is a program that controls the features of the GUI, such as opening, closing, moving, resizing, and positioning of windows.

The desktop environments available in the Solaris operating environment are CDE and GNOME. CDE is a user interface that runs on the Window Manager and provides utilities known as X utilities. The GNOME interface helps users to locate information and launch applications easily.

CHAPTER 7

THE SHELL ENVIRONMENT

In this chapter

Understanding the Shell   110

Customizing the Shell Environment   115

Shell Variables and the Environment   117

Template Initialization Files   120

Aliases   122

Summary   124

UNDERSTANDING THE SHELL

The shell acts as an intermediary between the user and the system kernel. It interprets the commands that are typed at the terminal and translates them into system calls that are performed by the kernel or other programs. The shell thus acts as a cover around the kernel and eliminates any need for the user to have direct interaction with the kernel.

The shell is a utility program and, like other Solaris utilities, exists as individual files, such as /bin/sh for the Bourne shell, /bin/csh for the C shell, and /bin/ksh for the Korn shell. It can be considered a master utility program, which enables a user to gain access to all the other utilities and resources of the computer. A shell reads the first word of a command line and tries to identify whether it is an alias, a function, or an internal command. An alias is a pseudonym or shorthand for a command or series of commands. To execute a command, the shells search through the directories specified in the path for the command file and then execute the command.

FEATURES OF THE SHELL

The shell is an intermediary between the kernel and the users, and includes various features. The key features of a shell are as follows:

- **Interactive Processing**—Communication between the users and the system takes the form of an interactive dialogue with the shell.

- **Background Processing** —Time-consuming, non-interactive tasks can proceed while the user continues with other processing. Therefore, the system can perform many different tasks at the same time on behalf of a single user.

  For example, to start a process in the background, your command should be followed by an ampersand (&) symbol.

  ```
  #/usr/bin/admintool &
  7268
  #
  ```

  This command starts admintool as a background process. 7268 is the process ID for this process.

- **Input/Output Redirection**—This is a feature of the shell that can be used to read and write data from and to a file, device file, or a pipe. Instead of printing the contents on a default destination, such as the monitor, you can use redirectors to send data to another destination, such as a file. For example, the ps -ef command lists all the currently running processes. You can use the redirectors to send data to a file, rather than the monitor, which can record the output. This will help you to analyze the output at a later time.

- **Pipes**—Programs that perform simple functions can easily be connected to perform more complex functions. This helps minimize the need to develop new programs.

  For example, the pipe command used in the following syntax prints the number of filenames in the directory /etc that contains the string host.

7

```
#   ls -l /etc | grep host | wc -l
 6
```

The output suggests that 6 files in the /etc directory contain the string hosts.

■ **Shell Scripts**—A frequently used set of shell commands can be stored in a file. The file can later be used to execute the stored commands with a single command.

For example, the following script, which is placed in /etc/rc2.d, sets up routes whenever the system boots and also enables IP forwarding:

```
#/usr/bin/sh
ndd -set /dev/ip ip_forwarding 1
route add  default 172.17.24.1
route add -net 172.17.0.0 172.17.24.1
route add -net 172.16.0.0 172.16.96.100
```

■ **Shell Variables**—A user can control the behavior of the shell, as well as other programs and utilities, by storing data in variables that are significant to the shell. For example, the PATH variable stores the path names of all the directories to be searched for an executable file. In the following syntax, the environment variable PATH has been assigned the values /usr/ucb and /usr/bin for the current shell. When you export the environment variable, the variable PATH will contain these values for all subsequent shells.

```
#PATH=/usr/bin:/usr/ucb
#export PATH
```

■ **Programming Language Constructs**—The shell includes features that allow it to be used as a programming language. These features can be used to build shell scripts that perform complex operations.

For example, constructs such as while, if then else, case, and for are available.

■ **Command History**—The shell maintains a history of all the commands that you have used, which enables you to check your command history not only for the current session but also for the previous one. The history command displays a list of the most recent commands that are available in the command history.

For example, if you are using bash shell (acronym for Bourne Again Shell), then you can use the up arrow key to browse through the history of commands.

■ **Command Alias** —The shell allows you to create alternative names for commonly used commands. These aliases are abbreviations of the actual commands. You can also have a combination of commands denoted by one alias. You can use alias commands to perform aliasing.

For example, the following command creates an alias l for the ls -la command:

```
SUN#alias l "ls -la"
```

The next time you want to see the listing of files with la option, you just need to type **l** at the command line.

You can undo aliasing by using the unalias command. The syntax to do this would be something like this:

```
SUN#unalias l "ls -la"
```

7

> **NOTE**
>
> Aliasing/unaliasing is done differently for different shells.

HOW THE SHELL FUNCTIONS

After the users log on to the system, their contact with the system takes the form of an interactive dialogue with the shell. The shell interprets commands by following this process:

1. The shell waits for the user to type a command.

2. The user types a command at the command line prompt.

3. The shell reads the command. It then locates the file with the specified name in the directories that contain utilities. It loads the utility into memory and executes the utility.

4. After execution, the shell displays the output and displays the prompt again. This means that it is ready to process any further commands.

Figure 7.1 depicts the command interpretation process of the shell.

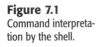

Figure 7.1
Command interpretation by the shell.

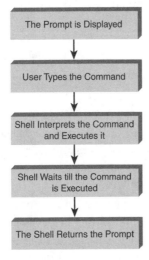

When a user sends a request to the shell, the shell executes the user request and returns the output. In this case, there is only one shell and the user's request is run in the same shell. The best example for this is the set command, which does not require a new shell. Figure 7.2 illustrates this case.

Figure 7.2
The shell processes the user commands and returns the output.

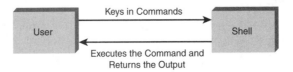

Most of the time, when a utility is to be executed, the shell forks another shell and passes on the name of the utility to the new shell—the child shell—for execution. This ensures that the environment of the current shell is not affected. The child shell is a temporary shell and is terminated after the execution of the called utility. This process is illustrated in Figure 7.3.

Figure 7.3
The shell forks another shell called the child shell for the execution of a utility.

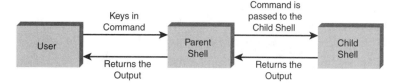

When the command issued by the user requires interaction with the system hardware, the shell requests the kernel to interact with the hardware. For example, if you want to read a file from any device, the shell forwards its request to the kernel. Figure 7.4 illustrates this scenario.

Figure 7.4
When hardware interaction is required, the shell sends a request to the kernel.

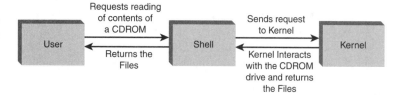

TYPES OF SHELLS IN SOLARIS

Various shells are available for use with Solaris. The basic shells available for Solaris are the Bourne, C, and Korn shells.

- **Bourne Shell**—The Bourne shell is the default shell for Solaris. The Bourne shell is the original command processor developed at AT&T and named after its developer, Stephen R. Bourne. This shell is officially distributed with all Unix systems. The Bourne shell is the fastest Unix command processor available and is available on all Unix systems. The sh is the executable file for the Bourne shell and is located in /bin directory. The Bourne shell does not have the best of features in the interactive mode as compared to other shells, but is widely used for shell scripts. It is available on all Unix systems, which is one of the reasons it is the most widely used shell at present for Unix systems.

- **C Shell** —The C shell is another command processor, developed by William Joy and others at the University of California at Berkeley. It got its name from its programming language, which resembles the C programming language in syntax. The C shell was developed to provide a programming interface similar to the C programming language. However, it was not appropriate for writing sophisticated shell scripts. The C shell is not compatible with the Bourne shell. The C shell became popular because it

7

was among the first shells to introduce the feature of command history. The C shell's executable file is named csh.

■ **Korn Shell** —The Korn shell was developed by David Korn and is a product of AT&T. It combines the best features of both the Bourne and the C shells. The Korn shell's executable file is named ksh.

The other freeware shells that are included with Solaris 9 are the Bourne-Again shell (bash), the Tom's C shell (tcsh), Zsh shell, and the desktop kornshell (dktsh).

■ **Bash**—Bash is an enhancement to the Bourne shell. The bash shell is the default shell for most Linux systems.

■ **Tcsh**— Tcsh stands for Tom's C shell, also known as the TC shell, and it is an enhancement of the C shell. The tcsh can be used as an interactive login shell and a shell script command processor.

■ **Zsh** —The zee shell (zsh) is a command interpreter. It is an interactive shell that has many useful features of bash, ksh, and tcsh.

■ **dtksh**— Based on the powerful ksh-93 that supports the standard set of kshell programming commands, the desktop kornshell was designed to enable easy access to Xt and Motif functions.

Table 7.1 compares the three basic shells and the three freeware shells.

TABLE 7.1   A COMPARISON OF THE THREE BASIC SHELLS AND OTHER FREEWARE SHELLS AND THEIR FEATURES

Features	Bourne	Korn	C	Bash	Tcsh	Zsh
Background processing	Yes	Yes	Yes	Yes	Yes	Yes
Command history	No	Yes	Yes	Yes	Yes	Yes
Input/Output redirection	Yes	Yes	Yes	Yes	Yes	Yes
Shell scripts	Yes	Yes	Yes	Yes	Yes	Yes
Command alias	No	Yes	Yes	Yes	Yes	Yes
Protect files from overwriting (noclobber)	No	Yes	Yes	Yes	Yes	Yes
Command line editing	No	Yes	Yes	Yes	Yes	Yes

The restricted shell is used when you need to restrict users' activities on the system. This shell allows you to assign a guest login privilege, which has read-only access to a single directory.

The user who is assigned a restricted shell has the following limitations:

■ The user cannot change directory.

■ The user cannot specify the absolute path—path starting with / —either in a filename or in a command.

7

- The user cannot redirect output.
- The user cannot change the PATH variable.

→ To learn more about guest logins with restricted access, **see** "Implementing Security," **p.421**, Chapter 24.

CUSTOMIZING THE SHELL ENVIRONMENT

As discussed earlier, every user who logs on to the server is assigned a default profile. The profile defines the environment in which the user works and can be customized based on user preferences. The profiles of the users are stored as initialization files. These initialization files are executed automatically when a user logs on.

INITIALIZATION FILES

The initialization files can be classified into two types: system-wide initialization files and user-level initialization files.

The system-wide profile decides the environment for all users logging on for the first time and users who do not have a customized profile. The system-wide profiles for Bourne and Korn shells are stored in /etc/profile and for the C shell in /etc/.login.

Listing 7.1 shows a sample /etc/profile file.

LISTING 7.1   A SAMPLE /etc/profile **FILE**

```
#ident  "@(#)profile    1.19    01/03/13 SMI"   /* SVr4.0 1.3    */

# The profile that all logins get before using their own .profile.

trap "" 2 3
export LOGNAME PATH

if [ "$TERM" = "" ]
then
        if /bin/i386
        then
                TERM=sun-color
        else
                TERM=sun
        fi
        export TERM
fi

#       Login and -su shells get /etc/profile services.
#       -rsh is given its environment in its .profile.

case "$0" in
-sh | -ksh | -jsh | -bash)
```

continues

7

Listing 7.1   Continued

```
            if [ ! -f .hushlogin ]
            then
                    /usr/sbin/quota
                    #       Allow the user to break the Message-Of-The-Day only.
                    trap "trap " 2"  2
                    /bin/cat -s /etc/motd
                    trap "" 2

                    /bin/mail -E
                    case $? in
                    0)
                            echo "You have new mail."
                            ;;
                    2)
                            echo "You have mail."
                            ;;
                    esac
            fi
esac
umask 022
trap  2 3
```

The user-level initialization files are shell scripts located in the user's home directory. These files customize the work environment for the users when they log on to the system.

The user-level initialization files vary from shell to shell. The user-level initialization file for the Bourne shell is the .profile file.

The Korn shell has two user-level initialization files: .profile and .Ksh_env. The .profile file cannot include many commands that are designed to work only with the Korn shell. Hence, Korn shell-specific commands can be included in the .Ksh_env file. When a user logs on, the .profile file is read first, followed by the .Ksh_env file. The .Ksh_env file also configures the environment whenever the user starts a Korn shell from the command line.

The .Ksh_env file is read only if the ENV variable is set for it and exported. The following syntax configures and exports the environment variables for the .Ksh_env file:

```
$ENV= $HOME/.Ksh_env; export ENV
$
```

To define the name and location of .Ksh_env, configure the ENV variable in your .profile file; otherwise the .Ksh_env file might not be located when you log on.

The C shell has two user-level initialization files: .login and .cshrc. The .login file is read first on logon. The .cshrc file is read only if the user starts the C shell from the command line.

After making any modifications to the initialization file, you should execute it for your changes to take effect in the current shell. For example, the following syntax executes the initialization file for the Bourne shell:

```
$ . ./.profile
```

When a user logs on to the system, the default profile, depending on the default shell, configures the user environment. For users with a custom profile, the custom profile customizes the environment based on user preferences.

CHANGING SHELLS

The default shell for a user is defined in the /etc/passwd file. The user can use the other shells from the command line without modifying the /etc/passwd file. To change to a different shell, type the executable file name of the shell and press the return key. The ps command without any arguments can be used to verify the shells currently in use along with their process IDs and the terminal types.

The following example shows how to change the shell to the Korn shell.

```
$ Ksh
$ ps
    PID TTY      TIME CMD
    548 pts/5    0:00 Ksh
    539 pts/5    0:00 sh
$
```

NOTE

You can change the default prompts for any shell by using the PS1 variable.

When you want to return to the original shell after completing the work with the newly created shell, type exit to quit the current shell.

SHELL VARIABLES AND THE ENVIRONMENT

The shell has different types of variables: user-defined variables and environment (or predefined) variables. As the name suggests, users create the user-defined variables. Solaris uses environmental variables that determine the work environment of a user. These variables are assigned default values in the system-wide initialization files. If users want to customize their environments, then they can configure these variables according to their preferences. The environment variables have some variables, which are pre-defined, such as HOME, PATH, and so forth. Only the particular shell in which you are working recognizes the environment variables.

The following list explains some standard shell environment variables:

- **HOME**—This is used to set the path name for your home directory.
- **LOGNAME**— This is used to specify the user's login name.

7

- **PATH**—This sets the search path for the commands you type. Whenever a command is typed, the system searches for that command in the directories that are specified with the PATH variable. You can specify more than one directory by using a colon. The directories are searched according to their specified order. For example, the PATH variable set in your system by default is:

```
# echo $PATH
/usr/sbin:/usr/bin:/usr/dt/bin:/usr/openwin/bin:/bin:/usr/ucb
```

  If you type the command admintool, the search is first performed in your current working directory. If the command is not found, then it searches the directories specified with the PATH variable. The search is performed in the order specified in the command. In the preceding example, the search is performed on the subsequent /usr/sbin directories. The command is executed when it is found in the relevant directory.

- **PS1**—Defines any symbol to represent your command prompt. Normally, the prompt will be a # for the superuser and $ for the normal user.

- **PS2**—Provides continuation of a command in a new line. Note that while specifying a command, if you want to continue in the next line, you use the backslash(\) before pressing the Enter key. A different prompt (>) appears at the next line. You set this by using the PS2 variable. The following syntax specifies the usage of (\) for providing command or comment continuation.

```
$ echo "able was I ere I\"
>saw alba
able was I ere I saw elba
```

- **CDPATH**—Specifies the directories to be searched when a unique directory name is typed without a full path name.

- **TZ**—Defines the time zone for your system clock.

- **LPDEST**—Defines your default printer.

- **HISTORY**—Sets the number of commands available to the history command (for the C shell only).

- **LANG**—Specifies the local language. Appropriate values are French, German, Italian, Japanese, and Swedish.

- **TERM**—Defines the terminal you are currently using. When you run an editor, the system searches for a file with the same name as the definition of this variable. It first searches the path (if any) referenced by the TERMINFO variable, and then the default directory, /usrshare/lib/terminfo, to determine the characteristics of the terminal. If a definition is not found in either location, the terminal is identified as dumb.

- **TERMINFO**—Specifies the path name for an unsupported terminal that has been added to the terminfo database. You do not need to set this variable for default terminals in this database.

- **MAIL**—Notifies of the arrival of new mails.

- **MANSECTS**—Sets the available sections of online man pages.

7

The `set` command displays the values of all the environmental variables. The following is a sample output of the C shell environmental variables for the user root.

```
argv    ()
cwd     /
home    /
path    (/usr/sbin /usr/bin)
prompt  sun#
shell   /bin/csh
status  0
term    ansi
user    root
```

The system-defined variables are automatically included in the user's environment. However, the user-defined variables need to be exported to shells other than the login shell. You can transfer the user-defined variables to the child shells by using the `export` command. The `export` command provides a copy of the parent shells' variables to the child shells. The `export` command exports the value of any variable to a child shell. The `export` command without any argument displays the list of all variables that are already exported. The syntax for defining an environment variable differs with shells. The following syntax defines a variable in the Bourne or Korn shell:

```
VARIABLE=value;export VARIABLE
Example
EDITOR=vi; export EDITOR
```

The following example shows how to create a simple user-defined variable. It creates a variable called `month` and its value at this instance is `august`. You can verify the value of the shell variable by using the `echo` command.

```
$ month=august;
$echo $month
august
$
```

You can also export multiple variables with a single command as follows:

```
export PATH MAIL LPDEST
```

To find the value of any environmental variable, use the `echo` command. For example, the following syntax displays the value of the `PATH` variable.

```
echo $PATH
```

The C shell uses the `setenv` command to define an environment variable. For example, the following syntax declares a variable `month` and assigns a value `august` to it.

```
setenv month august
```

Users can display the environment variables currently set by using the `env` command. A sample output for the `env` command for a user using the C shell is shown here.

```
PWD=/
TZ=Asia/Calcutta
HZ=100
HOSTNAME=sun
```

7

```
MACHTYPE=sparc-sun-solaris2.9
MAIL=/var/mail/root
LOGNAME=root
SHLVL=1
SHELL=/sbin/sh
HOSTTYPE=sparc
OSTYPE=solaris2.9
HOME=/
TERM=ansi
PATH=/usr/sbin:/usr/bin
_=/usr/bin/csh
USER=root
```

TEMPLATE INITIALIZATION FILES

Template initialization files store the templates of user-level initialization files. Users can customize their environments by copying these template files to their home directories and modifying them.

The /etc/skel directory contains the following template files for the user-level initialization files:

- local.profile

- local.login

- local.cshrc

The local.profile is copied to the .profile file in the home directory of the Bourne and the Korn shell users. Listing 7.2 shows a sample local.profile file in the /etc/skel directory.

LISTING 7.2   A SAMPLE /etc/skel/profile FILE

```
# ident "@(#)local.profile     1.10    01/06/23 SMI"
stty istrip
PATH=/usr/bin:/usr/ucb:/etc:.
export PATH


#
# If possible, start the windows system
#
if [ "'tty'" = "/dev/console" ] ; then
        if [ "$TERM" = "sun" -o "$TERM" = "sun-color" -o "$TERM" = "AT386" ]
        then

                if [ ${OPENWINHOME:-""} = "" ] ; then
                        OPENWINHOME=/usr/openwin
                        export OPENWINHOME
                fi

                echo ""
                echo "Starting OpenWindows in 5 seconds
```

7

```
➥ (type Control-C to interrupt)"
                sleep 5
                echo ""
                $OPENWINHOME/bin/openwin

                clear           # get rid of annoying cursor rectangle
                exit            # logout after leaving windows system


        fi
fi

#
```

The local.login and local.cshrc files are copied to the .login and .cshrc files, respectively, in the home directory of users whose login shell is the C shell. The .login file should be customized with necessary variables that need to be configured while user login sessions. Listing 7.3 shows the default local.login file present in the /etc/skel directory.

LISTING 7.3   A SAMPLE /etc/skel/local.login **FILE**

```
# ident "@(#)local.login        1.7      01/06/23 SMI"
stty -istrip
# setenv TERM 'tset -Q -'

#
# if possible, start the windows system.  Give user a chance to bail out
#
if ( "'tty'" == "/dev/console" ) then

        if ( "$TERM" == "sun" || "$TERM" == "sun-color" || "$TERM" == "AT386" )
then

                if ( ${?OPENWINHOME} == 0 ) then
                        setenv OPENWINHOME /usr/openwin
                endif

                echo ""
                echo -n "Starting OpenWindows in 5 seconds➥
  (type Control-C to interrupt)"
                sleep 5
                echo ""
                $OPENWINHOME/bin/openwin
                clear           # get rid of annoying cursor rectangle
                logout          # logout after leaving windows system

        endif

endif
#
```

The .cshrc file contains the commands and the defined variables that have to be executed whenever you run a shell, whereas the .login file is read only at login. Listing 7.4 shows the default local.cshrc file present in the /etc.skel directory.

LISTING 7.4   A SAMPLE /etc/skel/local.cshrc FILE

```
#ident   "@(#)local.cshrc        1.2      00/05/01 SMI"
umask 022
set path=(/bin /usr/bin /usr/ucb /etc .)
if ( $?prompt ) then
        set history=32
endif
```

ALIASES

Aliases are pseudonyms that are used to represent the corresponding commands for which they are set. The need for aliases arises when you want to set a shortcut for frequently used commands that are lengthy. For example, you can just type c rather than clear to clear the terminal screen, if you have set an alias for the clear command to c. An alias defined in a parent shell is available to all its child shells.

If the alias name consists of spaces, then it should be enclosed in quotes. The alias feature is not available in the default Bourne shell, but the C shell and the Korn shell support this feature.

To display the existing aliases, use the alias command, as follows:

```
# alias
autoload='typeset -fu'
command='command'
functions='typeset -f'
history='fc -l'
integer='typeset -I'
local=typeset
nohup='nohup'
r='fc -e -'
stop='kill -STOP'
suspend='kill -STOP $$'
#
```

To create an alias in the Korn shell, the following syntax is used:

```
$ alias aliasname=command
```

Table 7.2 lists the various default aliases for the *Korn* shell and their default values.

TABLE 7.2   THE VARIOUS DEFAULT ALIASES FOR THE *Korn* SHELL AND THEIR DEFAULT VALUES.

Alias	Value	Definition
Autoload	Typeset -fu	Defines an autoloading function.
False	Let -0	Returns a nonzero status. Often used to generate infinite until loops.
Functions	Typeset -f	Displays a list of functions.

Alias	Value	Definition
Hash	Alias -t-	Displays a list of tracked aliases.
History	Fc -1	List commands from the history file.
Integer	Typeset -1	Declares integer variable.
Nohup	Nohup	Keep jobs running even if you log out.
R	Fc -e-	Executes the previous command again.
Stop	Kill -STOP	Suspends job.
Suspend	Kill -STOP	Suspends job.
True	:	Returns a zero exit status.
Type	Whence -v	Displays information about commands.

For example, the ifconfig -a command is used to obtain network-related information. The ifconfig command will not work without any options. To create an alias for the ifconfig -a command to ifconfig for the Korn shell, type the following command and verify whether the alias is set by issuing the alias name.

```
# alias ifconfig="ifconfig -a"
# ifconfig
lo0: flags=0700849<UP,LOOPBACK,RUNNING,MULTICAST,IPv4> mtu 8232 index 1
        inet 127.0.0.1 netmask ff000000
cnft0: flags=1000843<UP,BROADCAST,RUNNING,MULTICAST,IPv4> mtu 1500 index 2
        inet 192.168.100.185 netmask ffffff00 broadcast 192.168.100.255
        ether 0:8:c7:b1:8e:64
#
```

The C shell does not contain any pre-defined aliases. To create an alias in the C shell, use the following syntax:

```
alias aliasname commands
```

The following syntax creates an alias for the history command to his and also verifies creation of the alias.

```
ganzkart% alias his history
ganzkart% his
1       umask
2       umask -s
3       umask -S
4       alias
5       csh
6       alias
7       csh
8       alias his history
9       alias his=history
10      his
```

7

The unalias utility removes the definition for each alias name specified. The aliases are removed from the current shell execution environment.

SUMMARY

The shell is a utility program that translates the commands typed by the user into commands that are interpreted by the kernel. Some of the features of shells include interactive and background processing, input/output redirection, command alias support, and command history maintenance.

The different types of shells in Solaris are Bourne, C, Korn, Bash, Tcsh, and Zsh. The Bourne shell is the default shell, and it is used for shell scripts. The C shell provides a programming interface that is similar to the C programming language. The korn shell combines the features of both the Bourne and the C shells. The bash shell is an enhancement to the Bourne shell and is the default shell for most Linux systems. The tcsh shell provides an interactive login shell and a shell script command processor. Zsh combines the features of tcsh and korn shells.

Users can customize the shell environment according to their requirements. Each user is assigned a profile and these profiles are stored as initialization files. The two types of initialization files are system-wide initialization files and user-level initialization files. The system-wide profile decides the environment for users. The user-level initialization customizes the work environment for users when they log on to the system.

The two types of variables in the shell environment are user-defined and environment variables. The user defines the user-defined variables and the environment variable defines the work environment of the user. Users can customize their environment by copying the template initialization files to their home directory and modifying them.

7

FILE SYSTEMS IN SOLARIS

8   Understanding the Solaris File System   127

9   The Network File System (NFS)   151

10   CacheFS   165

## CHAPTER 8

UNDERSTANDING THE SOLARIS FILE SYSTEM

In this chapter

An Overview of File Systems   128

Solaris File System Structure   129

Links   132

Solaris File Systems and Their Functions   133

Restricting the File Size and Disk Space Usage   139

Default File System for the Local and Remote Systems   140

Checking and Repairing File Systems   141

Monitoring Disk Usage   144

Other Solaris Commands Related to File Systems   147

Summary   148

AN OVERVIEW OF FILE SYSTEMS

8

The file system is one of the basic building blocks of an operating system. The structure and the features of the file system make Unix a powerful and stable operating system (OS).

A file system can be a structure of directories used to organize and store files. It can also be a logical grouping of files and directories in a partition. The term "file system" is used in various contexts. Some of these contexts are described in the following list.

- A particular type of file system, such as disk-based, network-based, virtual, and so forth.
- The data structure of a disk slice or other media storage device.
- A portion of a hierarchical tree structure that is attached to a mount point on the main file tree so that it is accessible.
- The entire file system hierarchy starting from the root directory at the top.

Unix has a directory structure that contains a single root or an inverted tree. The name "root" given to the primary directory and the file system is derived from this analogy. In an inverted tree structure, the branches and leaves originate from the root.

Figure 8.1 displays various directories, such as usr, var, and opt, which lie beneath the root directory. These directories contain several sub-directories. These file systems can be stored in separate physical media, such as hard disk, floppy disk, or CD-ROM. They can be attached to the main tree whenever desired.

Figure 8.1
Various directories, such as *usr*, *var*, and *opt* lie beneath the root directory.

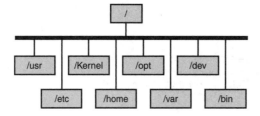

NOTE

> A file system can span multiple disks with the help of advanced features, such as meta devices. A *meta device* is a virtual disk that is a collection of one or more physical disk partitions. To create it, you use disk management products, such as Solaris Volume Manager, Veritas Volume Manager, and so on.

Solaris supports several file system types. The file systems supported by Solaris are disk-based, memory-based, and network-based.

DISK-BASED FILE SYSTEMS

The file types that can be applied over and reside on the physical disks, such as the local disks, CD-ROMs, and diskettes, are disk-based files systems.

- **Unix File System (UFS)**—The default file system for the Solaris Operating Environment.
- **System V File System (S5)**—An old type of hard disk file system.
- **PC File System (PCFS)**—The standard file system for DOS-formatted diskettes.
- **High Sierra File System (HSFS)**—The standard file system for CD-ROMs.
- **Universal Disk Format File System (UDF)**—An industry-standard file system format was introduced with Solaris 8 for storing information on DVDs. It has the advantages of flexibility in exchange for information across platforms and access to industry-standard DVD-ROM media containing the UDF file system, as well as improved audio/video quality. UDF does not support re-writeable CDs, DVD RAM, or incremental recording.

MEMORY-BASED FILE SYSTEMS

Memory-based file systems are virtual file systems that provide access to special kernel information and facilities.

- **Process file system (procfs)**—The procfs is not a regular file system. It does not physically exist on the disk. It is rather a depiction of the kernel state and system memory through processes represented as directories. Only the kernel and the debugging system utilities use the procfs.
- **Temporary file system (tmpfs)**—The tmpfs stores all the active processes running in the system. All files in tmpfs are deleted when the system is shut down or re-booted. The command to mount a tmpfs file system follows:

```
# mount -F tmpfs swap /tmp
```
- **Cache file system (cachefs)**—When a file system is cached, the data read from the file system is stored in a cache on the local system. Solaris uses the cachefs to access data from the cache. This is useful with a remote file system or CD-ROM where access speed can be considerably improved.

NETWORK FILE SYSTEMS (NFS)

The NFS is the default Solaris file system for sharing file systems among remote systems. The server shares the file system by exporting it. Clients who have access to the file system can mount it on their local systems to access the shared resources.

→ For a complete understanding of NFS, **see** "Network File System," **p.151**.

SOLARIS FILE SYSTEM STRUCTURE

A file system consists of blocks of data. The number of bytes constituting a block varies depending on the OS. The internal physical structure of a hard disk consists of cylinders. The hard disk is divided into groups of cylinders known as *cylinder groups*, further divided into blocks.

8

The file system is comprised of five main blocks:

- Boot block
- Super block
- Inode block
- Data block
- Vnodes

BOOT BLOCK

The boot block is part of the disk label that contains a loader used to boot the operating system.

SUPER BLOCK

All partitions within the Unix filing system usually contain a special block called the *super block*. The super block contains the basic information about the entire file system. It stores the following details about the file system:

- The size of the file system
- The status of the file system
- The date and time of the last update
- The pathname of the last mount point
- Cylinder group size
- The name of the partition
- The modification time of the file system
- The number of data blocks
- The list of free and allocated blocks

A super block plays an important role during the system boot up and shutdown process. When the system boots, the details in the super block are loaded into the memory to improve the speed of processing. The super block is then updated at regular time intervals from the data in the memory. During system shutdown, a program called sync writes the updated data in the memory back to the super block. This process is very crucial because an inaccurate super block might even lead to an unusable file system. This is precisely why the proper shutdown of a Solaris system is essential.

Because of the critical nature of the super block, it is replicated at the beginning of every cylinder group. These blocks are known as *surrogate super blocks*. A damaged or corrupted super block is recovered from one of the surrogate super blocks.

Inode BLOCK

Inode is a kernel structure that contains a pointer to the disk blocks that store data. This pointer points to information such as file type, permission type, owner and group information, file size, file modification time, and so on. Note that the inode does not contain the filename as part of the information. The filename is listed in a directory that contains a list of filenames and related inodes associated with the file. When a user attempts to access a given file by name, the name is looked up in the directory where the corresponding inode is found.

Inode stores the following information about every file:

- The type of the file
- The owner
- The group
- The size of the file
- The time and date of creation
- The time and date of last modification
- The time and date of last access
- An array of 15 disk block addresses

Each inode has a unique number associated with it, called the inode number. The -li option of the ls command displays the inode number of a file, as shown in Listing 8.1.

LISTING 8.1   A SAMPLE OUTPUT OF THE *ls -li* OPTION

```
# ls -li
total 290
        63 lrwxrwxrwx   1 root     root          9 Dec  7 16:48 bin -> ./usr/bin
    218322 drwxr-xr-x   2 root     nobody      512 Jan 23 12:46 cdrom
    325183 drwx------   2 root     other       512 Feb 27 11:25 DeadLetters
    185981 drwxr-xr-x  15 root     sys        3584 Mar 11 19:34 dev
    122236 drwxr-xr-x   4 root     sys         512 Dec  7 17:05 devices
    201856 drwxr-xr-x  39 root     sys        3584 Mar 11 19:34 etc
     10624 drwxr-xr-x   4 root     sys         512 Dec  7 16:45 export
     74607 dr-xr-xr-x   1 root     root          1 Mar 11 19:33 home
    297486 drwxr-xr-x   9 root     sys         512 Dec  7 16:48 kernel
        67 lrwxrwxrwx   1 root     root          9 Dec  7 16:48 lib -> ./usr/lib
         3 drwx------  18 root     root       8192 Dec  7 16:45 lost+found
     42841 drwx------   2 root     other       512 Dec 26 15:16 Mail
        68 drwxr-xr-x   2 root     sys         512 Dec  7 16:48 mnt
    314054 dr-xr-xr-x   1 root     root          1 Mar 11 19:33 net
    244717 drwx------   2 root     other       512 Dec 10 09:11 nsmail
      5331 drwxrwxr-x  11 root     sys         512 Feb 18 20:43 opt
     42496 drwxr-xr-x  29 root     sys        1536 Dec  7 17:04 platform
     10653 dr-xr-xr-x  71 root     root      94656 Mar 11 20:16 proc
     15968 drwxr-xr-x   2 root     sys        1024 Dec  7 16:50 sbin
    139252 drwxrwxrwt  10 root     sys       17920 Mar 11 19:48 tmp
    122795 drwxr-xr-x   2 root     root        512 Dec 10 08:56 TT_DB
```

continues

8

LISTING 8.1   CONTINUED

```
 31872 drwxr-xr-x  32 root      sys          1024 Dec  7 17:43 usr
  5312 drwxr-xr-x  32 root      sys           512 Dec 10 08:56 var
106722 dr-xr-xr-x   6 root      root          512 Mar 11 19:34 vol
 53766 dr-xr-xr-x   1 root      root            1 Mar 11 19:33 xfn
#
```

Listing 8.1 shows a long listing of the directory with the numbers in the first column representing the inodes. The second column lists the read, write, and execute permissions assigned to the owner, group, and others. The third column is the number of links for the file. The concept of links is explained later in this chapter.

Inodes are allotted when a file is created in a file system and released when the file is deleted. For example, if a file, file1, is created in directory1 and is allotted the inode 465, and at the same time another file, file2, is created in directory2 in the same file system, the inode allotted to file2 will be 466.

DATA BLOCK

The data block is the storage unit of data in the Solaris file system. The default size of a data block in the Solaris file system is 8192 bytes. After a block is full, the file is allotted another block. The addresses of these blocks are stored as an array in the Inode.

The first 12 pointers in the array are direct addresses of the file; that is, they point to the first 12 data blocks where the file contents are stored. If the file grows larger than these 12 blocks, then a 13th block is added, which does not contain data. This block, called an *indirect block*, contains pointers to the addresses of the next set of direct blocks.

If the file grows still larger, then a 14th block is added, which contains pointers to the addresses of a set of indirect blocks. This block is called the *double indirect block*. If the file grows still larger, then a 15th block is added, which contains pointers to the addresses of a set of double indirect blocks. This block is called the *triple indirect block*.

Vnode

A Virtual Node or vnode is a data structure that represents an open file, directory, or device that appears in the file system namespace. A vnode does not render the physical file system it implements. The vnode interface allows high-level operating system modules to perform uniform operations on vnodes.

LINKS

Links are a special feature of all -Unix-based operating systems. A link is a reference entry in a directory to a file stored in another directory. There might be several links—references—to a file. Links eliminate redundancy because you do not need to store multiple copies of a file.

Links are of two types: hard and soft (also known as symbolic). A hard link is a pointer to a file and is indistinguishable from the original directory entry. Any changes to a file are independent of the name used to reference the file. Hard links may not span file systems and may not refer to directories. The ln command by default creates hard links.

A soft link is an indirect pointer to a file; its directory entry contains the name of the file to which it is linked. Soft links can span across file systems and refer to directories. In other words, a soft link is a file that contains the name of another file. With soft links, you can link both directories as well as files. Unlike hard links, soft links exist across file systems.

To create a soft link, you must use the -s option with the ln command. Files that are soft linked contain an l symbol at the first bit of the access permission bits displayed by the ls -l command, whereas those that are hard linked do not contain the l symbol. A directory is symbolically linked to a file. However, it cannot be hard linked. Therefore, it is obvious that no file exists with a link count less than one. You might have used the relative pathname . or .. to refer to other files and directories from the current directory. These are nothing but links for the current directory and its parent directory. Hence, the current directory can also be represented by a dot '.' and the parent directory by a double dot '..'. These are present in every directory. They are listed by the ls -lia option. A directory must have a minimum of two links. The number of links increases as the number of sub-directories increase.

So what does a directory contain? When you use the ls command to list the contents of a directory, it gives a list of files and their attributes with the -l option. These files and their file names are not stored in the directory, but their inode numbers are stored.

A directory stores the two links ., .. and the Inode numbers of the files. As a result, whenever you issue a command to list the file attributes, it refers to the Inode block with the Inode number and the corresponding data is retrieved.

When a user creates a file in the directory or modifies it, the following events occur:

- The Inode of the file is stored in the Inode block of the file system.
- The file contents are stored in the allocated data blocks referenced by the Inode.
- The Inode number is stored in the directory.

SOLARIS FILE SYSTEMS AND THEIR FUNCTIONS

Each file system used in Solaris is intended for a specific purpose.

The root file system is at the top of an inverted tree structure (refer to Figure 8.1). It is the first file system that the kernel mounts during booting. It contains the kernel and device drivers. The / directory is also called the *mount point directory* of the file system. All references in the file system are relative to this directory. The entire file system structure is attached to the main system tree at the root directory during the process of mounting, and hence the name. During the creation of the file system, a lost + found directory is created within the mount point directory. This directory is used to dump into the file system any unredeemed

8

files that were found during the customary file system check, which you do with the fsck command.

Table 8.1 lists the various Solaris file systems and their functions.

TABLE 8.1   SOLARIS FILE SYSTEMS AND THEIR FUNCTIONS

File System	Components and Functions
/ (root)	The directory located at the top of the Unix file system. It is represented by the "/" (forward slash) character.
/usr	Contains commands and programs for system-level usage and administration.
/var	Contains system log files and spooling files, which grow in size with system usage.
/home	Contains user home directories.
/opt	Contains optional third-party software and applications.
/tmp	Contains temporary files, which are cleared each time the system is booted.
/proc	Contains information about all active processes.

You create file systems with the newfs command. The newfs command accepts only logical raw device names. The syntax is as follows:

```
newfs [ -v ] [ mkfs-options ] raw-special-device
```

For example, to create a file system on the disk slice c0t3d0s4, the following command is used:

```
# newfs -v /dev/rdsk/c0t3d0s4
```

The -v option prints the actions in verbose mode. The newfs command calls the mkfs command to create a file system. You can invoke the mkfs command directly by specifying a -F option followed by the type of file system.

MOUNTING FILE SYSTEMS

Mounting file systems is the next logical step to creating file systems. *Mounting* refers to naming the file system and attaching it to the inverted tree structure. This enables access from any point in the structure. A file system can be mounted during booting, manually from the command line, or automatically if you have enabled the automount feature.

With remote file systems, the server shares the file system over the network and the client mounts it.

→ To know more about the Network File System (NFS) **see** "Network File System (NFS)" **p.151**.

The / and /usr file systems, as mentioned earlier, are mounted during booting. To mount a file system, attach it to a directory anywhere in the main inverted tree structure shown in Figure 8.1. This directory is known as the *mount point*. The syntax of the mount command is as follows:

```
# mount <logical block device name>   <mount point>
```

The following steps mount a file system c0t2d0s7 on the /export/home directory:

```
# mkdir /export/home
# mount  /dev/dsk/c0t2d0s7 /export/home
```

You can verify the mounting by using the mount command, which lists all the mounted file systems.

NOTE

> If the mount point directory has any content prior to the mounting operation, it is hidden and remains inaccessible until the file system is unmounted.

Data is stored and retrieved from the physical disk where the file system is mounted.

Although there are no defined specifications for creating the file systems on the physical disk, Table 8.2 lists the recommended conventions.

TABLE 8.2   SLICES AND FILE SYSTEMS

Slices	File Systems
0	Root or /—Files and directories of the OS.
1	Swap—Virtual memory space.
2	Refers to the entire disk.
3	/export—Different OS versions.
4	/export/swap—Unused. Left to user's choice.
5	/opt—Application software added to a system.
6	/usr—OS commands by users.
7	/home—Files created by users.

The slices shown in Table 8.2 pertain to a single disk. However, there is no restriction that all file systems need to be located on a single disk. They can also span across multiple disks. Slice 2 refers to the entire disk. Hence, if you want to allocate an entire disk for a file system, you can do so by creating it on slice 2. The mount command supports a variety of useful options. They are listed in Table 8.3.

8

TABLE 8.3 *Mount* **COMMAND OPTIONS**

Option	Description
-o largefiles	Files larger than 2GB are supported in the file system.
-o nolargefiles	Does not mount file systems with files larger than 2GB.
-o rw	File system is mounted with read and write permissions.
-o ro	File system is mounted with read-only permission.
-o bg	Repeats mount attempts in the background. Used with non-critical file systems.
-o fg	Repeats mount attempts in the foreground. Used with critical file systems.
-p	Prints the list of mounted file systems in /etc/vfstab format.
-m	Mounts without making an entry in /etc/mnt /etc/tab file.
-O	Performs an Overlay mount. Mounts over an existing mount point.

The mountall command mounts all file systems that have the mount at boot field in the /etc/vfstab file set to yes. It can also be used anytime after booting.

UNMOUNTING FILE SYSTEMS

A file system can be unmounted with the umount command. The following is the syntax for umount:

umount <mount-point or logical block device name >

File systems cannot be unmounted when they are in use or when the umount command is issued from any subdirectory within the file system mount point.

NOTE

> A file system can be unmounted forcibly if you use the -f option of the umount command. Please refer to the man page to learn about the use of these options.

The umountall command is used to unmount a group of file systems. The umountall command unmounts all file systems in the /etc/mnttab file except the /, /usr, /var, and /proc file systems. If you want to unmount all the file systems from a specified host, use the -h option. If you want to unmount all the file systems mounted from remote hosts, use the -r option.

/etc/vfstab FILE

The /etc/vfstab (Virtual File System Table) file plays a very important role in system operations. This file contains one record for every device that has to be automatically mounted when the system enters run level 2. The vfstab file has seven fields that are explained in Table 8.4.

TABLE 8.4 STRUCTURE OF THE `/etc/vfstab` FILE

Column Name	Description
device to mount	The logical block name of the device to be mounted. It can also be a remote resource name for NFS.
device to fsck	The logical raw device name to be subjected to the `fsck` check during booting. It is not applicable for read-only file systems, such as High Sierra File System (HSFS) and network File systems such as NFS.
Mount point	The mount point directory.
FS type	The type of the file system.
fsck pass	The number used by fsck to decide whether the file system is to be checked. 0—File system is not checked. 1—File system is checked sequentially. 2—File system is checked simultaneously along with other file systems where this field is set to 2.
Mount at boot	The file system to be mounted by the `mount all` command at boot time is determined by this field. The options are either yes or no.
Mount options	The mount options to be supported by the `mount` command while the particular file system is mounted.

In Listing 8.2, the first two lines contain the column headings. Though the sixth column is titled Mount at Boot, it essentially means "mount while entering run level 2." Note the no values in this field for the root, /usr, and /var file systems. These are mounted by default. The fd field refers to the floppy disk and the swap field refers to the tmpfs in the /tmp directory.

A sample vfstab file looks like Listing 8.2:

LISTING 8.2 A SAMPLE `vfstab` FILE

```
#device          device          mount       FS     fsck   mount    mount
#to mount        to fsck         point       type   pass   at boot  options
#
fd       -       /dev/fd fd      -     no     -
/proc    -       /proc   proc    -     no     -
/dev/dsk/c0t0d0s4         -           -     swap   -      no       -
/dev/dsk/c0t0d0s0         /dev/rdsk/c0t0d0s0     /      ufs    1      no
-
/dev/dsk/c0t0d0s6         /dev/rdsk/c0t0d0s6     /usr   ufs    1      no
-
/dev/dsk/c0t0d0s3         /dev/rdsk/c0t0d0s3     /var   ufs    1      no
-
/dev/dsk/c0t0d0s7         /dev/rdsk/c0t0d0s7     /export/home   ufs    2
```

continues

LISTING 8.2   CONTINUED

```
yes      -
/dev/dsk/c0t0d0s5        /dev/rdsk/c0t0d0s5        /opt    ufs    2    yes
-
/dev/dsk/c0t0d0s1        /dev/rdsk/c0t0d0s1        /usr/openwin    ufs   2 yes  -
swap     -   /tmp    tmpfs   -       yes     -
```

FINDING INFORMATION ABOUT THE MOUNTED FILE SYSTEMS

The /etc/mnttab file comprises a table that defines which partitions and/or disks are currently mounted by the system.

The /etc/mnttab file contains the following details about each mounted file system:

- The file system name
- The mount point directory
- The file system type
- The mount command options
- A number denoting the time of the mounted file system

A sample mnttab file is given in Listing 8.3.

LISTING 8.3   A SAMPLE *mnttab* FILE

```
/dev/dsk/c0t0d0s0       /       ufs     rw,intr,largefiles,xattr,onerror=panic,s
uid,dev=2200000 1014366934
/dev/dsk/c0t0d0s6       /usr    ufs     rw,intr,largefiles,xattr,onerror=panic,s
uid,dev=2200006 1014366934
/proc    /proc   proc    dev=4300000     1014366933
mnttab   /etc/mnttab      mntfs   dev=43c0000     1014366933
fd       /dev/fd fd      rw,suid,dev=4400000     1014366935
/dev/dsk/c0t0d0s3       /var    ufs     rw,intr,largefiles,xattr,onerror=panic,s
uid,dev=2200003 1014366937
swap     /var/run        tmpfs   xattr,dev=1     1014366937
swap     /tmp    tmpfs   xattr,dev=2     1014366939
/dev/dsk/c0t0d0s5       /opt    ufs     rw,intr,largefiles,xattr,onerror=panic,s
uid,dev=2200005 1014366939
/dev/dsk/c0t0d0s7       /export/home    ufs     rw,intr,largefiles,xattr,onerror
=panic,suid,dev=2200007 1014366939
/dev/dsk/c0t0d0s1       /usr/openwin    ufs     rw,intr,largefiles,xattr,onerror
=panic,suid,dev=2200001 1014366939
-hosts   /net    autofs  indirect,nosuid,ignore,nobrowse,dev=4580001     10143669
44
auto_home        /home   autofs  indirect,ignore,nobrowse,dev=4580002    10143669
44
-xfn     /xfn    autofs  indirect,ignore,dev=4580003     1014366944
sun:vold(pid295)        /vol    nfs     ignore,dev=4540001      1014366950
#
```

RESTRICTING THE FILE SIZE AND DISK SPACE USAGE

Some applications and processes create temporary files that occupy a lot of hard disk space. As a result, it is necessary to impose a restriction on the size of the files that are created.

Solaris provides tools to control the storage. They are:

- The `ulimit` command
- Disk quotas

ulimit COMMAND

The `ulimit` command is a built-in shell command, which displays the current file size limit. The default value for the maximum file size, set inside the kernel, is 1500 blocks. The following syntax displays the current limit:

```
$ ulimit -a
time(seconds) unlimited
file(blocks) unlimited
data(kbytes) unlimited
stack(kbytes) 8192
coredump(blocks) unlimited
nofiles(descriptors) 256
memory(kbytes) unlimited
```

If the limit is not set, it reports as `unlimited`.

The system administrator and the individual users change this value to set the file size at the system level and at the user level, respectively. The following is the syntax of the `ulimit` command:

```
ulimit <value>
```

For example, the following syntax sets the file size limit to 1600 blocks:

```
# ulimit  1600

# ulimit -a
time(seconds) unlimited
file(blocks) 1600
data(kbytes) unlimited
stack(kbytes) 8192
coredump(blocks) unlimited
nofiles(descriptors) 256
memory(kbytes) unlimited
#
```

The file size can be limited at the system level or the user level. To set it at the system level, change the value of the `ulimit` variable in the `/etc/profile` file. To set it at the user level, change the value in the `.profile` file present in the user's home directory. The user-level setting always takes precedence over the system-level setting. It is the user's profile file that sets the working environment.

8

NOTE

The `ulimit` values set at the user level and system level cannot exceed the default `ulimit` value set in the kernel.

DISK QUOTA

Disk quota refers to an individual user's share of hard disk space. This helps in imposing a restriction on the hard disk space a user can use. The two kinds of limits that can be imposed are a soft limit and a hard limit.

The hard limit is more than the soft limit. When the user exceeds the soft limit, a timer is activated. The user is allowed to exceed the soft limit but restricted from exceeding the hard limit. If the user exceeds the hard limit, the user is not allowed to store data in the disk until the user frees some disk space and drops below the soft limit. Several commands are used to allot quotas, turn quotas on, check quotas, and so on. Table 8.5 describes the various commands regarding disk quotas.

TABLE 8.5   A DESCRIPTION OF VARIOUS COMMANDS REGARDING DISK QUOTAS

Quotas	Description
Edquota	Allocates disk space for a user and changes quota settings.
Quotacheck	Checks consistency between the quotas and current disk usage.
Quotaon	Enforces the quota.
Quotaoff	Turns the quota off.
Quota	Displays a user's quota and checks for exceeded quotas.
Repquota	Reports all quotas for the file system.

DEFAULT FILE SYSTEM FOR THE LOCAL AND REMOTE SYSTEMS

The `/etc/default/fs` file contains the default local file system. All commands that require the file system type to be specified should use the `-F` option. All commands search the `-F` option in the command line to identify the file system. If the file system is not specified in the command line with the `–F` option, the command searches the `/etc/vfstab` file for the file system type. If it cannot determine the file system type, it checks the `/etc/default/fs` file to determine the default local file system. The default local file system used in Solaris is UFS.

Change the entry `LOCAL=ufs` in the `/etc/default/fs` file to change the default local file system.

```
#vi /etc/dafault/fs
LOCAL=ufs
```

The /etc/dfs/fstypes file contains the default remote file system. Almost all commands relating to remote file systems need to mention the type of the file system along with the -F option. If the command does not use the -F option, the /etc/dfs/fstypes file is checked to determine the default remote file system. The first line of this file specifies the default remote file system type. Listing 8.4 shows a sample /etc/dfs/fstypes file.

LISTING 8.4   A SAMPLE /etc/dfs/fstypes

```
#vi /etc/dfs/fstypes
nfs NFS Utilities
autofs AUTOFS Utilities
cachefs CACHEFS Utilities
~
```

Alter the contents of this file to change the default remote file system.

CHECKING AND REPAIRING FILE SYSTEMS

In some cases an improper shutdown might cause damage to the file systems. The fsck command checks the file systems for consistency on booting. In addition, the fsck command also performs automatic and interactive correction of the problems detected during booting. The S01Mountfsys script in the /etc/rc2.d directory calls the mountall command and runs fsck on all file systems with fsck pass field in the /etc/vfstab file set above zero. This is one of the several startup scripts the system executes on booting prior to entering the multi-user state.

> **NOTE**
>
> The mountall command used during booting invokes the fsck command to check and repair the file systems. However, two file systems on the same disk are not checked simultaneously because doing so increases the load on the head of the hard disk drive.

fsck COMMAND

The fsck command without any arguments checks all the file systems that have the fsck pass field set to yes. The syntax of the fsck command is as follows:

```
fsck <logical raw device name>
```

Only logical raw device names, and not logical block device names, should be supplied as arguments to the fsck command. For example, the following command performs file system checks on /dev/rdsk/c0t0d0s4:

```
# fsck /dev/rdsk/c0t0d0s4
```

Table 8.6 describes the various options of the fsck command.

TABLE 8.6   OPTIONS OF THE *fsck* COMMAND

Option	Description
-m	Checks whether a file system is mountable. It displays a short message and an exit status. Does not repair errors if any.
-n or –N	Assumes a negative response to any questions that may be generated by fsck.
-y or –Y	Assumes a positive response to any questions that may be generated by fsck.
-V	Displays the action to be taken without executing it.
-o	Supports a variety of sub options: **b=<block number>**—Uses the block number specified as the super block. Such alternate super blocks may be used in case of bad super blocks. **c**—Converts the file system to a compatible version **f**—Forces the checking of the file system regardless of the state of the file system's super block clean tag. **p**—Attempts automatic repair of any error that is encountered. Quits if user intervention is required. **W**—Checks the file systems that have write permissions.

CAUTION

> A file system should not be checked while it is being mounted because it causes irreparable damage to the file system. In such cases, it is recommended that you stop the command operation by pressing the Ctrl+C key combination or the Stop+A key combination.

The general structures of the file system, the inodes, and the super blocks, are verified for consistency by the fsck command in five stages. Additional stages are run depending on the number of errors fsck detects. These stages are explained in the following sections.

PHASE 1: CHECKS BLOCKS AND SIZES

In the first phase of fsck, every inode in the file system is checked for invalid entries. If any invalid entry is found, it prompts the user for action. The following list is a sample of the queries generated by fsck:

- PARTIALLY TRUNCATED INODE I=4578 (SALVAGE)?
- UNKNOWN FILE TYPE I=33785 (CLEAR)?
- INCORRECT BLOCK COUNT I=2878 (should be 2) CORRECT?

Generally it is recommended that you respond in the positive to all these queries by entering y at each prompt.

PHASE 2: CHECKS PATHNAMES

In the second phase, directory entries are removed from all the bad inodes found in Phase 1. Further, fsck checks for inode pointers that are out of range or pointing to bad inodes and the directories holding these pointers. The errors detected in this phase include usage of unallocated inodes in directories, reference to an inode with a bad or duplicate block number, bad inode number, and so on. For each error detected, the superuser is prompted to choose between Yes and No to correct these errors. The types of messages a superuser is likely to encounter in this phase in case of errors are as follows:

- ROOT INODE NOT A DRECTORY (FIX)?
- I=OUT OF RANGE I=42335 NAME=projects.txt (REMOVE)?

PHASE 3: CHECKS CONNECTIVITY

In the third phase, all directories that are not referenced by any other directory in the file system are placed in the lost + found sub-directory in the root file system. Status messages are printed on the monitor for all directories placed in the lost + found directory.

PHASE 4: CHECKS REFERENCE COUNTS

In the fourth phase, the data gathered from phases 2 and 3 are used to check for unreferenced files and incorrect link counts on files and directories.

PHASE 5: CHECKS CYLINDER GROUPS

In the fifth phase, fsck compares the free blocks and the unused inodes. If they do not match, they are fixed automatically.

NOTE

> The fsck command should be run only on an unmounted file system. It is recommended to run the fsck command on file systems when the system is in single user mode.

RECOVERING DAMAGED SUPER BLOCKS

In a situation where the super block might be damaged or corrupted, rendering the file system unusable, the following steps are to be considered:

1. Determine the logical raw device name for the file system from the /etc/vfstab table.

2. Supply the logical raw device name as an argument to the newfs command. A list of alternate super blocks in the file system is displayed. Make a note of at least three of them. The command syntax is as follows:

   ```
   # newfs -N <logical raw device name>
   ```

3. Supply any one of the alternate (or surrogate) super block numbers found in step 2 as an argument to the fsck command:

   ```
   # fsck -F <FS type> -o b=<alternate super block no.> < logical raw device
   name>
   ```

8

The errors are detected and rectified by the fsck utility. The user must answer some of the queries generated by the errors.

4. Mount the file system and use it.

MONITORING DISK USAGE

Solaris provides very useful tools to monitor the use of disk space by individual file systems, such as /, /usr, /var, and so on. These tools are very handy in diagnosing problems relating to file systems. The following commands are used to monitor a file system's usage:

- df

- du

- quot

These three commands report the disk space usage from different perspectives. The df command reports the used and unused disk space in terms of the number of blocks and kilobytes for all file systems. The du command reports the disk usage for files and directories. The quot command reports disk usage for users.

df COMMAND

The df command reports details, such as the mount point directory, the logical block device name, the number of free blocks (the size of which is 512 bytes), and the number of files created for each mounted file system. The df command without any options lists details about all file systems. A sample output of the df command is displayed in Listing 8.5.

LISTING 8.5 A SAMPLE OUTPUT OF THE *df* COMMAND

```
# df
/                 (/dev/dsk/c0t0d0s0 ):  338962 blocks   273608 files
/proc             (/proc            ):       0 blocks     5845 files
/dev/fd           (fd               ):       0 blocks        0 files
/etc/mnttab       (mnttab           ):       0 blocks        0 files
/var              (/dev/dsk/c0t0d0s3 ):  287246 blocks   240484 files
/var/run          (swap             ): 1521472 blocks    40320 files
/tmp              (/dev/dsk/c0t0d0s4 ):  548086 blocks   237039 files
/export/home      (/dev/dsk/c0t0d0s7 ): 7897584 blocks   642304 files
/export/home0     (/dev/dsk/c0t1d0s7 ):11789698 blocks  1077890 files
#
```

Note that the details of all file system types are reported in the listing. For example, in the preceding output, /dev/fd refers to the floppy disk (PCFS) and /tmp refers to TMPFS. You can display details about file systems of a particular type by using the -F option. The df -F ufs command, when used to display the remaining disk space in all UFS file systems, displays the output as shown in Listing 8.6.

8

LISTING 8.6 **THE** df -F ufs -a **COMMAND**

```
# df -F ufs -a
/                  (/dev/dsk/c0t0d0s0 ):   338962 blocks    273608 files
/var               (/dev/dsk/c0t0d0s3 ):   287246 blocks    240484 files
/tmp               (/dev/dsk/c0t0d0s4 ):   548086 blocks    237039 files
/export/home       (/dev/dsk/c0t0d0s7 ):  7897584 blocks    642304 files
/export/home0      (/dev/dsk/c0t1d0s7 ):11789698 blocks   1077890 files
#
```

You can display the details about a single file system by supplying the mount point directory as an argument to the df command.

```
$ df  /opt
/opt        (/dev/dsk/c0d0s5):      923608 blocks   294516  files
```

The -k option of the df command is preferred for monitoring file systems because it displays the total disk space, available disk space, and used disk space along with the percentage of utilization. The output is also well formatted with headers. A sample output of the df -k command is shown in Listing 8.7.

LISTING 8.7 **SAMPLE OUTPUT OF THE** df -k **COMMAND**

```
# df -k
Filesystem            kbytes     used    avail capacity  Mounted on
/dev/dsk/c0t0d0s0    2052750  1883269   107899    95%    /
/proc                      0        0        0     0%    /proc
fd                         0        0        0     0%    /dev/fd
mnttab                     0        0        0     0%    /etc/mnttab
/dev/dsk/c0t0d0s3     492422   348799    94381    79%    /var
swap                  770496        0   770496     0%    /var/run
/dev/dsk/c0t0d0s4     471223   197180   226921    47%    /tmp
/dev/dsk/c0t0d0s7    5159318  1210526  3897199    24%    /export/home
/dev/dsk/c0t1d0s7    8759116  2864267  5807258    34%    /export/home0
```

The mount point directory as an argument to the df -k command displays the details about a single file system. The options supported by the df command are displayed in Table 8.7.

TABLE 8.7 **OPTIONS FOR THE** df **COMMAND**

Option	Description
-a	Reports usage details for all file systems.
-k	Reports usage details in terms of kilobytes (that is, 1024 bytes rather than 512-byte blocks) with a neat header.
-l	Reports usage details for local file systems only.

du COMMAND

The du command reports the disk space usage in terms of 512-byte blocks for the files and sub-directories of the current working directory. A sample output of the du command is given in Listing 8.8.

LISTING 8.8 SAMPLE OUTPUT OF THE du COMMAND

```
# du
2           ./lost+found/#298011
2           ./lost+found/#292553
2           ./lost+found/#281763
2           ./lost+found/#276758
2           ./lost+found/#223645
2           ./lost+found/#218348
2           ./lost+found/#191821
2           ./lost+found/#175870
2           ./lost+found/#032291
2           ./lost+found/#117520
2           ./lost+found/#026560
2           ./lost+found/#325184
2           ./lost+found/#314058
2           ./lost+found/#282240
2           ./lost+found/#234877
2           ./lost+found/#314060
48          ./lost+found
2           ./var/lost+found/#151087
2           ./var/lost+found/#143545
2           ./var/lost+found/#109563
2           ./var/lost+found/#060469
2           ./var/lost+found/#117117
2           ./var/lost+found/#109565
2           ./var/lost+found/#173755
```

The last line in the output shown in Listing 8.8 contains the total blocks consumed by the files and the sub–directories of the current directory. The options supported by the du command are displayed in Table 8.8.

TABLE 8.8 OPTIONS FOR THE du COMMAND

Option	Description
-a	Reports usage details for all files.
-k	Reports usage details in terms of kilobytes (that is, 1024 bytes rather than 512-byte blocks).
-d	Reports usage details only for files that are in the same file system.
-r	Displays error messages, if any.
-s	Displays summarized directory-wide information.

quot COMMAND

The quot command reports the number of blocks owned by each user in the file system. Unlike the df and du commands, it reports usage in terms of kilobytes or 1024-byte blocks. The syntax of the quot command is as follows:

```
quot [options] <file system name>
```

An example of quot command follows:

```
$ quot      /export/home
/dev/rdsk/c0d0s7:
987         jack
271         root
43 bin
```

Table 8.9 describes the options supported by the quot command:

TABLE 8.9   OPTIONS FOR THE *quot* COMMAND

Option	Description
-a	Displays information on all mounted file systems.
-v	Displays a verbose report.
-c	Displays file sizes in sorted order of blocks used.
-f	Displays the number of files.

OTHER SOLARIS COMMANDS RELATED TO FILE SYSTEMS

Solaris provides some commands to obtain other file system-related details. The most useful commands are covered in this section.

devnm COMMAND

Use the devnm (device name) command to find the logical device name of a file system by supplying the mount point as an argument. The syntax of the devnm command is as follows:

```
devnm   <mount-point directory>
```

In the following example, the /usr file system is mounted on the device /dev/dsk/c0t6d0s0.

```
$ devnm /usr
/dev/dsk/c0t6d0s0   /usr
```

fstyp COMMAND

You can use the fstyp (file system type) command to find the type of a file system by supplying the logical block device name as an argument. The syntax of the fstyp command follows:

```
fstyp   <logical block device name>
```

8

In the following example, the file system type is UFS.

```
$ fstyp  /dev/dsk/c0d0s6
ufs
```

fuser COMMAND

The fuser command is used to display the processes owned by each user. Along with the –u and –c options, it displays the processes owned by each user in a file system. The syntax follows:

```
fuser -uc <mount-point directory>
```

The -u option displays user login name and the -c option displays all the active processes currently using/accessing the file system.

```
$ fuser   -uc    /export/home
/export/home:   586c(jack)    549co(jack)   547c(jack)   546c(jack)   532c(jack)
530c(jack)   511c(jack)   505o(jack)   504c(jack)   503c(jack)   488c(jack)
487co(jack)   484co(jack)   448co(jack)   438co(jack)   419c(root)
```

The preceding output shows that as many as 15 active processes owned by the user Jack exist in the /export/home file system. The superuser owns the process ID (PID) 419c. The -c suffix to the PID indicates that the process is using the mountpoint because it is the current directory.

clri COMMAND

The clri command is used to clear inodes. It has a symbolic link called dcopy. It is used to remove unreferenced files. The inode numbers of unreferenced files are obtained by the fsck or the ls -I command. The syntax of the command follows:

```
clri      <I-node number>   or
dcopy      < I-node number>
```

CAUTION

> The devnm, fstype, fuser, and clri commands are to be used with utmost caution. They are meant only for experienced system administrators. Wrong usage of these commands may cause irreparable damage to the file system.

SUMMARY

A file system is a directory that organizes files in a logical order and stores them in separate physical media, such as hard disk, floppy disk, or CD-ROM. The file system in Solaris has a directory structure with a single root. The root is the primary directory of the file system. The three types of file systems that Solaris supports are disk-based, memory-based, and network-based. Disk-based file types can be applied over physical disks. Memory-based file systems are virtual file systems. Network-based file systems enable file sharing across a network.

8

The Solaris file system consists of five blocks: boot block, super block, inode block, data block, and vnodes. The boot block helps to load the operating system. The super block contains all necessary information about the entire file system. Inode is a pointer to the disk blocks that contain information about files. The data block is the storage unit of data. The vnode is a data structure that represents an open file.

The files in a directory use links to reference each other. There are two kinds of links: hard links and soft links. A hard link is a pointer to a file, and the soft link is a symbolic link that can be used to link directories and file systems. Each file system in Solaris has specific significance. For example, the root file system contains the kernel and device drivers, and the home file system contains the home directories.

Data from the file systems are retrieved from the physical disks where the file systems are mounted. The mountall command is used to mount all file systems that have the mount at boot field. To unmount a file system, use the umount command. Examples of Solaris file systems are /etc/vfstab and /etc/mnttab. The /etc/vfstab contains one record for every device that has to be automatically mounted when the system enters run-level 2. The /etc/mnttab file contains information about the mounted file system.

Solaris provides commands to control storage, troubleshoot the file system, and monitor the use of disk space. The commands to control storage are ulimit and disk quotas. The fsck command is used to perform interactive correction of the problems detected during booting. The commands to monitor the use of disk space are df, du, and quot.

Network File System (NFS)

In this chapter

Overview of NFS   152

NFS Daemons   154

Mounting a File System   156

Automatic File-System Sharing   158

Securing the NFS System   159

Troubleshooting NFS   161

WebNFS Access   163

Summary   164

OVERVIEW OF NFS

The Network File System (NFS) service enables computers with different operating systems and architectures to access, share, and mount file systems across a network. The objects that can be shared are directories. Note that in an NFS environment, a computer cannot share a file hierarchy that overlaps the one that is already shared. NFS can be implemented in different operating systems because it defines a portable file system model instead of an OS or platform-dependent file system specification. This allows computers, without respect to which OS they use, to access files as if they were stored locally.

NFS provides the following benefits:

- **Reduced storage costs**—You can store file(s) in a single location on the network and share them with other computers on the network. This saves you from storing the copies of the file(s) in each computer on the network, thus helping you save storage space and reduce storage costs.

- **Sharing and mounting files**—If you are trying to access files from a remote location, NFS provides specific commands, such as automount, that automatically mount specified files and directories.

- **Heterogeneous environment supported**—NFS can scale the enterprise, providing unparalleled breadth of access. Users can navigate through an NFS environment as though they were browsing through the local directory structure. In addition, users on different operating systems can access files across a network. PC users can mount files on a mainframe at a different location.

- **Easy network administration**—The automounter and the enterprise naming support NFS networking. This enables easy and efficient administration of NFS where you can add, delete, and modify resources. The changes are automatically reflected in all the computers on the network.

EVOLUTION OF NFS IN SOLARIS

NFS version 2 was the first version of the NFS protocol introduced in SunOS. This version of NFS is widely used and has been around for several years. NFS version 2 uses User Datagram Protocol (UDP) to provide stateless network connection between the client and the server. This type of connection helps in reducing network traffic.

NFS version 3 was the next version of NFS and was a new feature in Solaris 2.5. It had several enhanced performance features. However, to take advantage of these features, NFS v3 should be used on both the server and the client. Features such as safe asynchronous writes on the server, improved file access permissions, enhanced data transfer size rate, access control list support, and support for TCP were implemented in NFS version 3. The features of NFS version 3 are as follows:

- **Asynchronous writes on the server**—This feature enables the server to cache client requests in memory. This process improves the server's response time because the client need not wait for the server to commit the changes to disk. In addition, the server can batch the requests, which improves the response time on the server.

- **File access permissions**—In NFS version 2, if an unauthorized user tries to access a file on a remote system, an error is generated. In NFS version 3 there are checks for permissions before the user can access a file on a remote system.

- **Data transfer size rate**—The Solaris 2.5 implementation of NFS version 3 allows 32KB transfer size, unlike version 2, which allows only 8KB transfer size.

- **Access control list (ACL) support**—In Solaris 2.5 ACL support was added to enable an enhanced mechanism to set file access that is available in Unix file permissions.

- **TCP support**—To improve performance on slow networks, the default transport protocol for NFS was changed to the Transmission Control Protocol (TCP) from the User Datagram Protocol (UDP). TCP helps to improve performance on slow networks and wide area networks.

The NFS version 3 was further enhanced for the Solaris 2.6 release. Solaris 2.6 support for NFS version 3 provides the following features:

- **File manipulation**—This version provides support for file manipulation for files larger than 2GB. This is not possible in NFS version 2 and NFS version 3 for Solaris 2.5.

- **Dynamic failover**—The NFS version 3 implementation for Solaris 2.5 provides support for dynamic failover of read-only file systems. This support ensures the availability of read-only resources, such as man pages and shared binaries.

- **Inclusion of Kerberos V4 clients**—The support for Kerberos V4 clients was included in the Solaris 2.0 release. In Solaris release 2.6, the mount and share commands were modified to support NFS mounts using Kerberos V5 authentication. Also, the share command was changed to allow for multiple authentication features to different clients.

- **WebNFS support**—A file system can be accessed through the Internet, even through the firewalls, by someone using an extension protocol. The WebNFS implementation reduces the time required to access a file by providing greater throughput for HyperText Transfer Protocol (HTTP) access to a Web server. In addition, this implementation provides the features to share files without the administration overhead.

The Solaris 7 implementation of NFS provides greater security as compared to its earlier versions. In Solaris 7, the RPCSEC_GSS Command RPC has been modified based on the Generic Security Standard API (GSS-API). This modification removes restrictions of a single security mechanism for the NFS services. To improve security, a new networking layer, GSS-API, has been added that offers two additional security services: integrity and privacy.

Solaris 7 also includes support for the WebNFS software development kit. This kit provides support for remote file access for Java applications that use WebNFS. Note that this kit does not require the NFS support on the host system because it implements the NFS protocol directly.

9

The NFS implementation in Solaris 8 provides logging support that contains a record of file operations performed on a file system. In addition, IPV6 support has been added for NFS and RPC. This enables NFS and RPCs to run over IPV6 without updating their commands. However, some advanced RPC applications with transport knowledge might require updates.

Another feature that has been added to the NFS version in Solaris 8 is the JavaBeans component. This component uses the XFileChooser class that enables Java 2 applications to display a file chooser. This file chooser enables users to access files on a local disk or on an NFS server through the NFS URL.

In Solaris 9, the UFS, NFS, and TMPFS file systems have been enhanced to include extended file attributes, which enable application developers to associate specific attributes to a file.

NFS DAEMONS

To provide NFS services to other hosts in the network, you run NFS daemons on your machine. The daemons and their related services are generally started at boot time by the system boot scripts. They are started when a system is in the multiuser mode. The boot script that starts NFS daemons in Solaris is `Solaris-/etc/init.d/nfs.server`, `/etc/init.d/nfs.client`.

The NFS servers run `Mountd` and `Nfsd`, whereas the NFS clients support the `Lockd` and `Statd` daemons.

Mountd

`Mountd` is an RPC server that enables remote systems to mount file systems. The `share` command creates a table of shared local resources to enable mounting. In the table, a line for each shared resource contains the pathname of the resource, the resource being shared, the file system type, options specifying how the resource is being shared, and a description of the resource `/etc/dfs/sharetab` directory. `Mountd` assesses this directory to determine the file systems that the remote systems can access and mount. You can use two options for remote mounting with `Mountd`: `-v` and `-r`. The `-v` option runs in verbose mode. This means that the command prints a list of clients that can access the file systems remotely on the console. To disable the remote systems from future access to the file systems, use the `-r` option. Please note that the `-r` option does not remove access to the clients that already have access to the file systems.

Nfsd

The `Nfsd` daemon handles requests for other file systems. The current version of `Nfsd` on Solaris 9 does not generate multiple copies to manage client requests. This daemon uses several options to perform its tasks. Table 9.1 lists some of the options that are used with `Nfsd`, along with their descriptions.

TABLE 9.1   THE *Nfsd* OPTIONS AND THEIR DESCRIPTIONS

Options	Description
-l	Sets the connection queue length for the NFS/TCP over connection-oriented transports. The default value is 32 entries.
-c	Selects the maximum number of connections per connection-oriented transport. The default value for #_conn is unlimited.
nsservers	Defines the maximum number of simultaneous requests that a server can handle. The default value is 1.

Lockd

The Lockd daemon is the client-side daemon that supports record-locking operations on NFS files. Three options can be used with record locking: -g, -t, and nthreads. Table 9.2 describes each of these options.

TABLE 9.2   THE Lockd OPTIONS AND THEIR DESCRIPTIONS

Options	Description
-g	Defines the grace period when clients can retrieve locks after the NFS server reboots. The default grace period time is 45 seconds. During this time, clients can retrieve only old locks. The NFS server does not service any other requests.
-t	Specifies the time that the server must wait before re-transmitting the lock request to the remote server. The default timeout value is 15 seconds. Note that you have the option to reduce the default value. This may improve the response time, but at the cost of additional server loads because of increasing lock requests.
nthreads	Specifies the maximum number of concurrent threads the server handles per connection. The default value is 20 seconds. This means that each TCP client that uses a single connection with the NFS server can utilize up to 20 threads per connection. You have the option of increasing the number of threads. However, the downside of it is that when the threads are used, more memory is used on the NFS server. On the other hand, if threads are never used then increasing the number of threads will have no effect.

Statd

The Statd daemon works in tandem with the Lockd daemon. It enables lock and recovery functions for the lock manager. This daemon is stored in the NFS client and the NFS server. When a server crashes, the server Statd informs the client Statd of the same. The client Statd then attempts to recover all locks from the server. In the same manner, if the client crashes, the client Statd reports to the server to enable the server Statd clear client locks.

9

MOUNTING A FILE SYSTEM

When a client needs to mount a file system from a server, it must obtain from the server a file handle that corresponds to the file system. This process requires several transactions to occur between the client and the server.

File systems shared through the NFS service can be mounted with automatic mounting. Autofs is a client-side service, which enables automatic mounting. This service performs the task of automatically mounting and unmounting file systems, without the user's intervention, during boot time.

The `automount` command used by the Autofs service, starts the `automountd daemon`, which runs continuously and mounts and unmounts file systems on an as-needed basis. Previous releases would mount an entire file system in a hierarchy. The Autofs service mounts only the top file system. The rest in the hierarchy are mounted only when the users demand them. Also, users can mount directories of their choice without mounting each file system. A `-nobrowse` option is added to the Autofs maps, so that large file systems, such as `/net` and `/home`, are not automatically browsable. Also, you can turn off the browsing option in Autofs on each client by using the `-n` option with `automount`.

There are three methods to mount files:

- **Automatic mounting**—You can set the relevant commands to mount file systems in the `/etc/vfstab` file. This enables mounting during boot time. However, please note that the procedure to set commands in the `vfstab` file is recommended only for local file systems. If you set commands for the remote file system, you have to complete the task for every client.

- **Command line**—You can mount from the command line for temporary viewing of the file system. Note that to mount a file system from the command line, you must be logged on as the superuser.

- **Automounter**—Automounter provides the mounting facility for all users. You do not need the superuser facility if you are using Automounter to mount files. Automounter mounts files only on an as-needed basis. After a user finishes viewing a file, it is unmounted automatically.

For the sake of an example, pretend that there are two servers, DB1 and DB2. Server DB1 has a partition named vol1 that needs to be mounted on server DB2 over the network. To complete this task, perform the following steps:

1. Log in as root on DB1.

2. Check whether NFS services is started. If not, then start the NFS services by typing the following command on the command line.
   ```
   #/etc/init.d/nfs.server start
   ```

3. Enter the following command in the `/etc/dfs/dfstab` file. Note that you have the option to type this command in the command line.
   ```
   share -F nfs -o rw /vol1
   ```

4. Log in as root on DB2.

5. Ensure NFS services are started.

6. Create a mount point, vol1, on this server by using the following command:
   ```
   #mkdir vol1
   ```

7. To automount at boot, edit the /etc/vfstab file to insert the following command:
   ```
   DB1:/vol1 - /vol1 nfs -yes rw
   ```

   To mount from the command line, issue the following command at the command prompt:
   ```
   #mount -F nfs -o rw DB1:\vol1 \vol1
   ```

8. Use df -k to verify that vol1 is mounted on DB2, or run the following command to verify that vol1 is mounted with all correct options:
   ```
   #nfsstat -m
   ```

   The -m option used with the nfsstat command displays the statistical information for each NFS mounted file system. It displays the server name and address, mount flags, current read and write, and so on.

The preceding steps mount the partition from DB1 to the server DB2 over the network.

MOUNT AN NFS FILE SYSTEM THROUGH A FIREWALL

To mount an NFS file system through a firewall requires that the file system on the NFS server be shared using the public option and any firewalls between the client and the server allow TCP connections on port 2049. Starting with the 2.6 release, all file systems that are shared allow for public file handle access.

In the following example, the file system /export/home/data is mounted manually on the local client using the public file handle. An NFS URL can be used instead of the standard pathname. If the server bee does not support the public file handle, the mount operation will fail.

1. Become a superuser.

2. Manually mount the file system, using a command like:
   ```
   # mount -F nfs -o public server1:/export/home/data /mnt
   ```

USE AN NFS URL TO MOUNT AN NFS FILE SYSTEM

In the following example, the /export/home/data file system is being mounted from the server called server1 via NFS port number 3050. The standard NFS port number of 2049 is the default port used unless the user defines otherwise. In this example, the port value defined is 3050.

1. Become a superuser.

2. Manually mount the file system, using a command like:
   ```
   # mount -F nfs nfs://server1:3050/export/home/data /mnt
   ```

AUTOMATIC FILE-SYSTEM SHARING

Servers in the NFS environment share file systems with the share command, located in the /usr/bin, or with entries in the /etc/dfs/dfstab file. Each entry in the dfstab file contains a share command that is the same as the one you type in the command line. The file systems that have entries in the dfstab file are shared automatically when you start the NFS server operation.

The following steps set up automatic file-system sharing:

1. Add the following syntax in the /etc/dfs/dfstab file. This syntax should be added for each file system you want shared.

   ```
   share [-F fstype] [ -o options] [-d "<text>"] <pathname> [resource]
   share –F nfs –o ro /export/home/data
   ```

2. Check to ensure that the NFS service is running on the server. If the service is not running, run the following commands to kill all processes and re-run the service:

   ```
   # /etc/init.d/nfs.server stop
   # /etc/init.d/nfs.server start
   ```

Using the share command makes a resource available for mounting. You use the -F option with the share command to specify the file system type. In the preceding example, the file system type used is NFS. If you do not use the -F option, the first file system type listed in /etc/dfs/fstypes is used as default.

LARGE FILES ON AN NFS SERVER

All releases starting from Solaris 2.6 support access to files that are over 2GB. The UFS file systems can be mounted manually using the -largefiles option. This option enables the access of files larger than 2GB. Therefore, no changes need to occur on a Solaris 2.6 if an NFS client is trying to access a large file. However, note that clients that do not support NFS 3 protocol with the large files extension cannot access large files.

If there are clients on the NFS environment that do not support large file access, you have the option to unmount or change the location of these files. Following is a list of steps that locates large files and unmounts or moves them to another file system.

1. Use the following command to locate large files:

   ```
   # cd /export/home1
   # find . -xdev -size +2000000 -exec ls -l {} \;
   ```

2. If large files are found, you can unmount or move these files to another file system, as follows:

   ```
   # umount /export/home1
   ```

3. If the file systems that were unmounted use the -largefiles option, it is important to reset the file system state. The fsck command is used to reset the file system state:

   ```
   # fsck /export/home1
   ```

4. To ensure that no large files are in the system, mount the file system by using the
   -nolargefiles option:

   ```
   # mount -F ufs -o nolargefiles /export/home1
   ```

5. To ensure that this option is permanent, add the following entry in the /etc/vfstab:

   ```
   /dev/dsk/c0t3d0s1 /dev/rdsk/c0t3d0s1 /export/home1 ufs 2 yes nolargefiles
   ```

NFS FILES

Several configuration files are required to support NFS activities. These files define commands that enable local and remote mounting of file systems, the local and remote resources that can be shared, and so on. Table 9.3 lists these files and their functions.

TABLE 9.3 NFS ASCII FILES

File Name	Function
/etc/vfstab	Defines file systems to be mounted locally.
/etc/mnttab	Lists file systems that are currently mounted, including the auto-mounted directories.
/etc/rmtab	Lists file systems remotely mounted by NFS clients.
/etc/default/fs	Lists the default file system type for local file systems.
/etc/dfs/dfstab	Lists the local resources to be shared.
/etc/dfs/fstypes	Lists the default file system types for remote file systems.
/etc/dfs/sharetab	Lists the resources (local and remote) that are shared.

SECURING THE NFS SYSTEM

Using the NFS environment is a convenient way to share file systems over the network. However, at the same time, file sharing in the NFS environment poses security risks. The NFS server authenticates a computer making a file request. However, it does not authenticate users using the Unix authentication. Users in a Unix environment all have unique IDs within a domain. However, they may not have unique IDs across domains. Therefore, any user can become the superuser of a computer and can make file requests. By using Data Encryption System (DES), NFS server makes this kind of impersonation harder.

DES

Users can protect the privacy of sensitive information by encrypting data that goes over the network. DES authentication uses DES, a standard encryption mechanism, and Diffie-Hellman (DH), a public key cryptography algorithm, to authenticate users and computers. The DH keys provide a secure method for authenticating users. These keys are generated when the administrator runs either the newkey or the nisaddcred programs.

9

DES encrypts the current time at the server end. The client decrypts this time and compares against its own clock. In this case, it is important that the server and the client agree on the same time stamp and use the same encryption key.

When the server and the client agree on the time stamp, they generate a conversation key. The conversation key is used to encrypt and decrypt the client's time stamp. If the time stamps for the server and the client do not agree, then synchronize the two by using the synchronization program of the network or by using the server's time. If the server's time is used to compute the time, the client clock computes the difference, if any. The difference is used to offset the client's clock when computing time stamps. If the server time and client time are out of sync, the DES resynchronizes the server. This ensures that the server does not reject the client requests.

Let us now look at how this DES mechanism operates in the NFS environment in more detail.

When a user logs into the system, the login password is compared with the RPC password. If the two are different, then the user has to log in and then use the keylogin separately. The keylogin is a program that authenticates the user based on the secure RPC password. It uses the password to decrypt the secret key.

If the passwords are the same, the decrypted secret key is passed to the key server (running the keyserv daemon), which saves the key and waits for the user to initiate a secure RPC transaction with a server.

> **NOTE** If the passwords are required to be different and the keylogin program must be run each time the user logs in, include the keylogin program in the user's environment configuration file. This automates the running of the keylogin program every time the user logs in.

After the user logs in and initiates the transaction with the server, the keyserver generates the conversation key. This key is used to encrypt the client's time stamp. The keyserver then uses the client's secret key and the server's public key, found in the public database of the keyserver, to create a common key. The keyserver encrypts the conversation key with the common key.

Next, a transmission that contains a credential and a verifier, including the conversation key and the client's encrypted time stamps, is sent to the server. The credential contains the client's net name, the conversation key, and the window, encrypted with the conversation key. The client defines the window that specifies the time difference between the server clock and the client's time stamp. Note that if the difference between the server's clock and the time stamp is greater than the window, the server rejects the client's request. The verifier is composed of an encrypted time stamp and an encrypted verifier of the specified window, decremented by 1.

When the server receives the transmission from the client, the keyserver verifies the client's public key in the publickey database. The keyserver uses the client's public key and the server's secret key to compute the common key. This common key is used to decrypt the conversation key. Note that the kernel uses the keyserver to decrypt the client's time stamp with the decrypted conversation key. Next, the server stores the client's computer name, conversation key, window, and the client's time stamp in the credential table. Finally, it returns a verifier to the client, which contains the credential cache and the client's time stamp. The client receives the verifier and authenticates the server. The client knows that only the server can send the verifier, because only the server knows what time stamp the client sent.

DH AUTHENTICATION

In DH authentication, the user, the client, and the server have their own respective private keys. They use the private key along with the public key to create a common key. The client and the server use this common key to communicate with each other. The key encryption and decryption of keys is done using an encryption/decryption function such as DES.

> **NOTE** The public and private keys are stored in an NIS or NIS+ database.

In the NFS environment, authentication is implemented at the RPC level. The RPC system enables security at all levels, including the NFS system. When NFS uses secure RPC, it is known as secure NFS.

You can set up a secure NFS environment with DH authentication. Perform the following steps to enable the DH authentication mechanism:

1. Run the `newkey` or `nisaddcred` command to generate the public keys and secret keys for users. Store these keys in the server's `publickey` database.
2. If you are running NIS+, verify whether the name service is responding by typing the following command:
   `# nisping -u`
3. To verify whether the `keyserver` is running, type the following command:
   `# ps -ef | grep keyserv`
4. If the daemon is not running, start it by using the following command:
   `# /usr/sbin/keyserv`
5. Run `keylogin` to decrypt and store the secret key.

TROUBLESHOOTING NFS

When tracking errors in the NFS environment, analyze all the components of NFS. The errors could be occurring in the server, the client, or the network. Check for the following to determine where exactly the fault lies:

- Connectivity between the client and the server
- NFS service running on the server

Table 9.4 describes the various commands that can be used to check for connectivity and the working of NFS services. You can use these commands to check and troubleshoot NFS.

TABLE 9.4   THE COMMANDS USED TO CHECK CONNECTIVITY AND THE WORKING OF NFS SERVICES

Commands	Descriptions
`% /usr/sbin/ping bee`	Verifies the connectivity between the NFS server and the client.
`% /usr/lib/nis/nisping -u`	Checks to make sure that the local name service is running in NIS.
`% /usr/bin/getent hosts bee`	Ensures that the client has received the correct host information if the name service is running.
`% rpcinfo -s bee|egrep 'nfs|Mountd'`	Determines whether the NFS services have started on the NFS server.
`# /etc/init.d/nfs.server stop` `# /etc/init.d/nfs.server start`	Enables daemons without rebooting.
`% rpcinfo -s bee|egrep 'nfs|Mountd'`	Checks whether the NFS services have started on the NFS server.
`% /usr/bin/rpcinfo -u bee nfs`	Checks whether the server's `Nfsd` processes are responding.
`% /usr/bin/rpcinfo -u bee Mountd`	Checks whether the server's `Mountd` is responding.
`-t option`	Tests the TCP connection.
`% cd /net/wasp`	Verifies the use of the local autofs service.
`# /etc/init.d/autofs stop` `# /etc/init.d/autofs start`	Restarts the Autofs service. You can use this command when you choose a `/net` or `/home` mount point that you know should work properly. If this doesn't work, then as root on the client, type the relevant command to restart the Autofs service.
`% /usr/sbin/showmount -e bee`	Verifies that the file system is shared as expected on the NFS server remotely.
`# rpcinfo -u localhost nfs`	Checks whether the `Nfsd` daemon is running. `# ps -ef | grep Nfsd`
`# /usr/bin/rpcinfo -u localhost Mountd` `# ps -ef | grep Mountd`	Determines whether the `Mountd` daemon is running.

Commands	Descriptions
`# /usr/bin/rpcinfo -u localhost rpcbind`	Checks whether the `rpcbind` daemon is running.
`Nfsstat -m`	Runs the `nfsstat` command with the `-m` option to gather current NFS information.

WEBNFS ACCESS

To enable the WebNFS functionality, you must have an application that can access NFS URLs. In addition, you must select the file system that can be exported for WebNFS access. File systems that are already open to the public, such as the top directory in an FTP archive or the main URL directory for a Web site, are good candidates for export.

In the WebNFS environment, the public file handle of the NFS server is associated with a directory in the root file system. The path to the NFS URL is evaluated with this directory. If the directory is in an exported file system, then the server provides access. You have the option to associate the public file handle to a specific exported directory (if it is not already) by using the `-public` option. Note that users who have mount privileges can use the `-public` option to access files in the WebNFS environment regardless of the file system being exported. When the file systems are chosen, establish relevant access permissions. For most sites, 755 permissions for directories and 644 permissions for files provide the correct level of access.

NOTE

> To enable WebNFS access for clients through a firewall, configure the firewall to allow a TCP connection on port 2049.

Following are the steps to export the file system using the `-public` option, for users who do not have the mount privileges.

1. Edit the `/etc/dfs/dfstab` file. Add the following entry to the file for the file system that you want to share automatically:
   ```
   share -F nfs -o ro,public,welcome=welcome.html /export/ftp
   ```
2. Determine whether the NFS service is running on the server. If it is not running, restart the daemon.
3. Share the file system either by rebooting or by using the shareall command:
   ```
   # shareall
   ```
4. Verify whether the information is correct by running the share command:
   ```
   # share
   ```

SUMMARY

The NFS service enables computers with different architectures and operating systems to access, share, and mount file systems. This enables computers to store files in a single location, thus saving storage costs and space. In addition NFS provides easy installation and administration features.

The four NFS daemons that implement NFS are Mountd, Nfsd, Lockd, and Statd. Mountd enables remote systems to mount file systems. The Nfsd daemon handles other file system requests. Lockd and Statd are client-side daemons. Lockd supports record-locking operations on NFS files, and Statd supports lock and recovery functions for the lock manager.

The mounting of the file systems in the NFS environments can be automated if you use the Autofs service. You can also mount files using the command line or the Automounter. The command line utility is useful if you are mounting files for temporary viewing. The Automounter is beneficial when you want files to be mounted only on an as-needed basis. To mount an NFS file system through a firewall, share the NFS server by using the public option.

You can share file systems in the NFS environment with the share command, located in the /usr/bin, or with entries in the /etc/dfs/dfstab file. The -largefiles option allows sharing of file systems that are larger than 2GB.

## CHAPTER 10

CacheFS

In this chapter

Defining CacheFS   166

Using cfsadmin to Manage a Cached File System   166

Administering Cached File System Using cachefspack   170

Maintaining the Cache   173

Summary   175

DEFINING CacheFS

Available in Solaris 2.3 and later, the Cache File System (CacheFS) is a layered file system where a file system is cached on another file system. CacheFS supports a caching mechanism that improves the performance and scalability of NFS servers or CD-ROM/DVD drives by caching data. When a data read is performed the first time, CacheFS caches this data in its local cache system. The first data read may take a little longer than the normal time frame because the data read is being performed across the network. However, after this data is stored in the local cache system, the subsequent reads to the same data are done from the local cache instead of across the network. This reduces the server and network overheads.

Figure 10.1 provides an example of how this mechanism works.

Figure 10.1
Working of the
CacheFS.

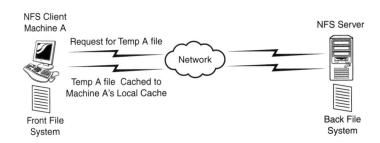

This figure represents an NFS environment. Note that there are two file systems: the back file system and the front file system. The back file system is the original data source and the front file system is the local file system on which cached data is mounted.

Within this NFS environment, Machine A requests for data from the file Temp A that is stored in the server's back file system. This request travels across the network to the server. When the file Temp A is read, the data is subsequently cached in the local cache of Machine A. The next time Machine A requests the same file, the request does not need to travel across the network and can be retrieved from the local cache of Machine A. This shifts part of the server burden to the local machine.

NOTE

> The use of CacheFS should be restricted to read-only or mostly read-only file systems.

USING cfsadmin TO MANAGE A CACHED FILE SYSTEM

The cfsadmin command is used to administer the cached file system. Table 10.1 describes the options used with the cfsadmin command to perform various administration tasks.

TABLE 10.1   OPTIONS USED WITH *cfsadmin* **COMMAND ALONG WITH THEIR CORRESPONDING ADMINISTRATION TASKS**

Options	Administration Tasks
`cfsadmin -c [ -o cachefs_parameters ] cache_directory`	Creates a cached file system.
`cfsadmin -u[ -o cachefs_parameters ] cache_directory`	Updates the resource parameters for unmounted cached file systems.
`cfsadmin -l cache_directory`	Lists the contents of the cache.
`cfsadmin -d [cache_ID	all] cache_directory`	Deletes the cached file system.

CREATING THE CACHED FILE SYSTEM

You create the cache with the `cfsadmin` command. You also specify the local cache directory and the resource parameters to use for the cache.

Use `cfsadmin` to create a cached file system and set the cache file system parameters. Log in as a superuser on the client computer and use the following command:

```
# cfsadmin -c cache-directory
# cfsadmin -c -o maxblocks=80,minblocks=25,threshblocks=60 /export/cache
```

`Cache-directory` is the name of the directory where the cache resides.

CAUTION

After creating the cache, do not perform any operations within the cache directory.

MODIFYING SPACE AND FILES OF THE CACHE

The default values for the cache parameters are for a cache that uses the entire front file system for caching. You can modify the space and files allocated for a cache in the front file system by modifying the default parameter values with the following command. You can only increase the cache size. To decrease it you need to remove and re-create the cache.

```
# cfsadmin -u -o maxblocks=80,minblocks=30,threshblocks=60 /export/cache
```

NOTE

For the values to take effect, it is important for the file systems to be mounted and remounted.

Table 10.2 defines the various cache parameters and the default values. These default values are expressed in percentages.

TABLE 10.2   CACHE PARAMETERS AND THE CORRESPONDING DEFAULT VALUES

Cache Parameters	Default Values
maxblocks	90%
threshblocks	85%
minblocks	75%
maxfiles	90%
threshfiles	85%
minfiles	75%

The maxblocks parameter is relative to the total number of blocks in the front file system. It defines the maximum amount of cache it is allowed to claim within the front file system. The minblocks parameter sets the minimum number of blocks available to CacheFS. CacheFS allows the cache to grow to the maximum size specified if you have not reduced available resources by using part of the front file system for other storage purposes. When the maximum number of blocks or files is reached, CacheFS removes cached files to stay within the established percentage.

NOTE

> These parameters do not guarantee that the space allocated is limited to CacheFS. If you allow the front file system to be used for purposes other than CacheFS, there may be fewer blocks or files available to CacheFS than you intend.

The maxfiles parameter sets the maximum percentage of available inodes CacheFS can claim. The minfiles parameter defines, in percentage, the total number of inodes in the front file system that CacheFS can use without limitation. Currently, CacheFS ignores the maxfiles parameter. Changing its value has no effect.

The threshblocks parameter sets the high water mark for disk usage. It defines the threshold value for the inodes that CacheFS can access after it reaches its usage level specified by the minfiles parameter.

SPECIFYING FILE SYSTEMS TO BE MOUNTED IN THE CACHE

You specify file systems to be mounted in the cache to enable users to locally access files in the file system. The files are not physically placed in the cache until the user accesses the files.

Files can be mounted by using the mount command, autofs, or by editing the /etc/vfstab file. Note that if you use the mount command to mount files, you have to perform the task of mounting the file system each time the system reboots. Editing the /etc/vfstab file or using the autofs command saves you from this task, because after the /etc/vfstab file is edited, it remains unchanged even after the system reboots. The same is true for autofs. You can mount a file system in a cache with autofs by specifying the -fstype=cachefs mount option in your automount map. These maps do not change on system reboots. You can choose the type of mounting based upon your requirements.

To use the mount command to mount file systems, log in as the superuser and create a mount point. The *mount point* is the directory where the system is mounted. Mount the file system using the following command. Each option in this command is described in Table 10.3.

```
# mount -F cachefs -o backfstype=fstype,cachedir=cache-directory[, options]
➥    back-filesystem mount-point
```

TABLE 10.3   MOUNT COMMAND OPTIONS

Mount Command Options	Descriptions
fstype	Indicates the file system type of the back file system. The file system can be either NFS or HSFS.
cache-directory	Specifies the directory where the cache resides.
options	Provides other mount options that you include when mounting a file system in a cache.
back-filesystem	Specifies the mount point of the back file system to the cache.
mount-point	Indicates the directory where the file system is mounted.

Use the cachefsstat command to verify that the cache you created was actually mounted. The cachefsstat command specifies statistical information, such as consistency checking and cache hits and misses, about the cached file system mounted on path:

```
    # cachefsstat mount-point
```

If you choose to mount file systems using the /etc/vfstab file, make the following entry in the file to specify the file systems to be mounted:

```
    # device    device mount   FS   fsck   mount   mount
    # to mount  to fsck point   type pass   at boot options
    /dev/dsk/c0t1d0s0 /dev/rdsk/c0t1d0s0  /usr/local cachefs   2   yes-
```

Mounting a file system using autofs enables you to mount and unmount file systems on an as-needed basis. To use autofs for mounting file systems, specify the -fstype=CacheFS mount option in the auto_direct map.

```
/mount-point -fstype=CacheFS,cachedir=/directory,backfstype=nfs
server:/file-system
```

Use an editor to add the following line to the `auto_master` map. This entry is a pointer to check the auto-direct map.

```
/-
```

CLEARING THE CACHE

If you are not using the entire cache space, it is advisable to free up the cache by purging files and directories. Reducing the cache size helps improve the performance of the cache. To clear the cache, unmount the `mount-point`:

```
# umount mount-point
# umount /cache
```

In the preceding command, the `mount-point` option specifies the cached file system that you want to delete.

Next, use the `cfsadmin -l` command to list the contents of the cache and determine the cache ID you want to delete. Listing 10.1 displays the cache ID in the output of the `cfsadmin -l` command. Cache ID specifies the name of the cached file system.

LISTING 10.1   OUTPUT OF THE `cfsadmin -l` COMMAND

```
bash-2.03# cfsadmin -l /export/cache
cfsadmin: list cache FS information
    maxblocks       80%
    minblocks       20%
    threshblocks    60%
    maxfiles        90%
    minfiles         0%
    threshfiles     85%
    maxfilesize      3MB
bash-2.03#
```

To delete the specified cache ID, use the `-d` option with the `cfsadmin` command and specify the cache ID and the cache directory. Note that to delete all the cached file systems in a cache, you use the option `all` rather than the cache ID.

```
# cfsadmin -d cache-id cache-directory
```

ADMINISTERING CACHED FILE SYSTEM USING `cachefspack`

The packing functionality in `CacheFS` enables automatic updates of the file systems. The command used to pack files in the `CacheFS` is the `cachefspack`. In addition, you can also pack a list of files and directories in the cache.

Table 10.4 describes the various options that can be used with the `cachefspack` command.

TABLE 10.4   cachefspack **COMMAND**

Options	Descriptions
-p	Packs the selected files individually.
-f	Packs a list of files or directories.
-u	Unpacks specific file(s) from the cache. You must specify a filename(s) with this option.
-U	Unpacks all filenames in the directory.

PACKING FILES IN THE CACHE

The packing feature enables you to specify files and directories to be loaded in the cache. It ensures that the cache maintains the latest copies of the file systems.

Issue the following command to pack files in the cache:

```
$ cachefspack -p filename
```

The -p option specifies the file(s) you want packed. It is the default option used with cachefspack. Filename specifies the names of the files or directories to pack.

In the following example, the cachefspack command specifies the file Employee to be packed in the cache.

```
$ cachefspack -p Employee
```

You also can specify multiple files to be packed simultaneously. The following command packs the files Employee, Department, and Stock:

```
$ cachefspack -p Employee Department Stock
```

If you want a directory of files to be packed in the cache, provide the path to the directory in the cachefspack command.

In the following example, the directory books, stored in /usr/mydir, is packed using the cachefspack command.

```
$ cachefspack -p /usr/mydir/books
```

PACKING LISTS

Imagine having to pack a huge list of files or directories in the cache. Using the -p option to specify each file can be time-consuming. Instead, you can use the packing list feature of the cachefspack command. This command enables you to create a list of files or directories that need to be packed. Note that if a directory is in the packing list, all its subdirectories and files are also packed.

Before packing the list, use any editor to create a packing list file. Listing 10.2 defines a packing list file in an editor.

10

LISTING 10.2   CREATING A PACKING LIST

```
BASE /home/EmpDept
LIST Employees
LIST Department
IGNORE *.tif
```

The BASE command specifies the path to the directory that has files to be packed. In Listing 10.2, the directory to be packed is called EmpDept. The LIST commands specify the files within the directory that need to be packed. The IGNORE command is optional. This command lets you ignore specific file types that you want to exclude from the packing list. In this example, the files of type .tif are ignored.

To pack files in the cache as specified in the packing list, use the cachefspack -f command. The -f option used with the cachefspack command specifies that you want to pack files specified in the packing list, and the packing_list option specifies the name of this list.

```
$ cachefspack -f packing_list
```

You can specify the packing lists to be packed as a regular expression instead of the literal file names by using the -r option along with the -f option of the cachefspack command. In this command, the packing_list option indicates the name of the packing list that contains the LIST command with the file or files you want treated as regular expressions.

```
$ cachefspack -rf packing_list
```

PACKING FILES FROM A SHARED DIRECTORY

Defining the LIST command within the packing list file enables you to pack files from a shared directory. In this LIST command, you specify files owned by a specific user. The following syntax is used in the packing list file to specify packing files from a shared directory:

```
LIST !find . -user user_name -print
```

Replace the user_name option with the name of the user who owns the files to be packed.

To pack this packing list in the cache, use the following command:

```
$ cachefspack -f packing_list
```

DISPLAYING PACKED FILES INFORMATION

After packing the required files in the cache, you may want to view information about the file(s) you have packed and their current packing status in the cache. To display this status, use the -i option with the cachefspack command. The -i option specifies the information you want to view about your packed file(s). The cached-filename-or-directory option is where you specify the file or directory for which to display information.

```
$ cachefspack -i[v] cached-filename-or-directory
```

UNPACKING FILES

It is advisable to constantly monitor your cache for files that are no longer in use and can be unpacked to ensure the efficient use of the cache. To unpack a file from the cache, use the -u option with the `cachefspack` command. Specify a filename to be unpacked with the -u option. Note that if you specify the -U option, all files in the cache will be unpacked.

NOTE

> You can unpack only files that are mounted in the cache.

The following example displays the command to unpack a specific file from the cache.

```
$ cachefspack -u Employee
```

The preceding command unpacks the `Employee` file from the cache. To unpack more than one file from the cache, list the filenames along with the -u option, as displayed in the following command.

```
$ cachefspack -u Employee, Department, Admin
```

However, if you want to unpack an entire packing list from the cache, use the following command:

```
$ cachefspack -U /export/cache
```

MAINTAINING THE CACHE

To ensure efficient use of the cache, it is important to continuously maintain it. For example, to ensure that the cached files and directories are kept up to date, you must perform a consistency check of the files stored in the cache. Some of the maintenance tasks include:

- Checking for cache consistency
- Checking cached file system integrity
- Tuning the CacheFS
- Sizing the cache

CHECKING CONSISTENCY ON A CACHED FILE SYSTEM

Consistency checking is important so that you periodically update the file systems. To check consistency, CacheFS compares the current modification time to the pervious modification time. In case of any difference, data from files and directories is cleared and new data is retrieved from the back file system. Then a comparison is done between the retrieved data and the current modification time. You can check for the consistency using the `cfsadmin -s` command. The `demandconst` option verifies consistency only when requested. This option eliminates default consistency checking.

```
# mount -F CacheFS -o backfstype=nfs,cachedir=/directory,demandconst server:
➥/file-system /mount-point
```

To start consistency checking on a specific cached file system, use the `cfsadmin -s` command as follows:

```
# cfsadmin -s /mount-point
```

CHECKING CACHED FILE SYSTEM INTEGRITY

The `fsck` command is used to check the integrity of the cached file system. It reports any inconsistencies in the file systems. In case of any inconsistencies, it prompts for permission to repair the relevant file system. The CacheFS version of `fsck` automatically corrects problems without requiring user interaction. However, if you want to perform a manual check, run the following command. Note that you must run the command before the file system is mounted. The `fsck` command does not repair mounted file systems.

```
# fsck-d CacheFS[-m -o noclean] cache-directory
```

The `-m` option performs an integrity check but does not repair the mounted file system. It also checks whether the file system is appropriate for mounting. The `-o` option is followed by the `noclean` option. This option checks the cached file systems without making any repairs.

`Fsck` is also used to generate reports on the number of files used and the number of used and free blocks.

TUNING CacheFS

Constant tuning of CacheFS ensures improved and faster performance of read/write requests to the cache. The CacheFS tunable parameters, such as `cachefs_maxthreads`, `cachefs_readahead`, `fileheader_cache_size`, `replacement_timeout`, are used to tune CacheFS. These parameters keep track of processes, files, and system activity. They are stored in the `var/sysgen/mtune/CacheFS` file. The key parameters to tune CacheFS are described in the following list:

- `cachefs_maxthreads`—This parameter specifies the maximum number of asynchronous I/O daemons that can be run per CacheFS mount. Asynchronous I/O daemons are used for only asynchronous I/O requests issued against file systems. Note that the range that is set to define the number of I/O daemons is from 1 through 10. The default value is 5. Increasing the number of asynchronous I/O daemons allows the client to double buffer with lower CPU overhead.

- `cachefs_readahead`—This parameter defines the number of blocks that are to be read asynchronously ahead of the current read block. The default value that is specified by this parameter for the number of blocks is 1. The minimum value is 0 and the maximum value is 10.

- `fileheader_cache_size`—This parameter defines the size of the in-memory cache of file header information in 512-byte units. This number indicates the number of such headers retained after other internal system data for a file has been released. File-header caching can be monitored using `cfsstat -b`. Note that the `cfsstat` command displays and reinitializes statistics about CacheFS. It must be used as the superuser.

- `replacement_timeout`—This parameter controls the time between successive cache reconstructions made by the replacement daemon (`cachefs_replacement`). If no replacement requests are made by the kernel within this time limit, the daemon times out and reconstructs the list.

SIZING THE CACHE

The amount of cache size needed for each file system mounted in the cache can be determined by using the `cachefswssize` command. This command displays the cache size determined from the log file. Generated by the `cachefslog` command, this log file contains data that includes data for the cache space needed for each filesystem and the total cache space. The log file is stored in the `cachelogs` directory. The `cachefslog` command also displays where the CacheFS statistics are being logged.

The following command creates a cache log called `/var/cachelogs/data.log`. This log is created for CacheFS and is called `/data`:

```
# cachefslog -f /var/cachelogs/data.log /data/var/cachelogs/data.log: /data
```

You have the option to change this log by issuing the following command:

```
/var/cachelogs/data_new.log:
# cachefslog -f /var/cachelogs/data_new_newdata.log /data/var/cachelogs/
    data_newdata.log: /data
```

You also can determine the current log file at any time. The following is a sample command that describes the procedure:

```
# cachefslog /data/var/cachelogs/data_new_062100.log: /data
```

You can verify logging by using the following commands:

```
# cachefslog -h /data
# cachefslog /data
```

After you enable logging, you can check the size of the cache by using the following command:

```
# cachefswssize /var/cachelogs/data.log
total for cache
initial size: 4256k
end size: 511k
high water size: 511k
```

SUMMARY

CacheFS makes it possible to cache data on the local system. When there is a read request for the same data, it is read from the local cache, which improves server performance. You can use the `cfsadmin` command to create CacheFS. Combined with options such as `-l`, `-d`, `-u`, this command can also be used to perform administration tasks, such as list, update, and delete cache content. Before you perform add or delete tasks on the cached file systems, it is important to mount them. You can mount the cached file system, using the mount command, edit the /etc/vfstab file, or use the autofs mechanism. To enhance the performance of CacheFS, it is important to constantly maintain it. The maintenance tasks include checking for consistencies, correcting the cached file system errors, updating CacheFS, tuning CacheFS, and sizing the cache.

10

## PART IV

SOLARIS ADMINISTRATION

11   Managing Users and Groups   179

12   Disk and Storage Administration   203

13   Managing Serial Devices   219

14   Managing Printing   237

15   Backup and Recovery   259

16   Process Management   277

17   Administering Remote Systems   293

18   Administering TCP/IP in Solaris OE   309

## CHAPTER 11

MANAGING USERS AND GROUPS

In this chapter

Overview of the User Environment in Solaris   180

Managing Users   183

Managing Groups   187

Using SMC to Manage Users and Groups   194

Summary   201

OVERVIEW OF THE USER ENVIRONMENT IN SOLARIS

Solaris is a multi-user operating environment that allows thousands of users to operate in a single system. Managing such a large client base can become a challenging task for the Solaris administrator. Therefore, it becomes necessary to lay out an effective user policy to avoid security breeches and maintain smooth workflow.

Some of the most important user administration tasks include maintaining unused disk space, finding disk I/O bottlenecks, answering user queries, and adding and removing users.

In a multi-user environment, such as Solaris, multiple users log on to the system simultaneously. These users are categorized as:

- Guest Users
- Application Users
- System Administrators or Superusers

The guest users have restricted access to the system and its resources. They can access the server to only upload or download a file to or from a particular directory or subdirectories within that directory, or use a specific, predefined application. However, these users may not be able to run commands related to altering system configuration files or viewing contents of files, or even browsing through the file system.

The application users of a system have more privileges than guest users. These users can run applications or create application-level scripts related to their applications. For example, if there is a server that runs Oracle database server and also runs iPlanet application server, then there would be two separate user logins, such as "oracle" and "iplanet." A user maintaining the Oracle database would log in as user "oracle," and a user deploying applications that use Iplanet application server logs in as user "iplanet." System administrators grant privileges to access the resources of the application based on the requirements.

System administrators have complete control over the system, including the applications installed on it. They have superuser/root access to the system.

USER ACCOUNTS

Every user who needs to access the server or workstation needs a user account. Every user account has a unique user identification number (UID). Any processes or files created by the user account are owned by this user. The maximum number of UIDs available is 2147483647. UIDs ranging from 0 to 99 are reserved for use by system accounts, such as root, bin, sys, and so on. The root account is assigned a UID of 0. Any user account with a UID 0 has all the privileges of the root account. The daemon account is assigned a UID of 2. The regular users ideally fall within the range of 100–60,000. The UID 60,001 is assigned to the anonymous account. The UID 60,002 is the no-access account, which is assigned to any user or process that needs access to a system through some application without actually logging in.

CAUTION

> Versions earlier than Solaris 2.5.1 support users up to only 60,000. Therefore, to avoid compatibility problems with earlier versions, avoid using UIDs over 60,000.

Table 11.1 describes the reserved UIDs for various user accounts.

TABLE 11.1   RESERVED UIDs FOR VARIOUS USER ACCOUNTS AND THEIR DESCRIPTIONS

UIDs	Login Account	Description
0	Root	Root account
1	Daemon	Daemon account
2	Bin	Pseudo user bin account
3-99	sys, uucp logins, who, tty, and ttytype	System accounts
100-60,000	Regular users	General-purpose accounts
60,001	Nobody	Unauthenticated users or anonymous users
60,002	no access	Non-trusted users
60,003-2147483647	Regular users	General purpose accounts

USER ACCOUNT DATABASE

Solaris stores all user account information in the files /etc/passwd and /etc/shadow.

The /etc/passwd file is an ASCII file. The default access permission of this file is read-only. This is to ensure system security. Every line in the /etc/passwd file defines a user account and has seven colon-separated fields. The following list describes all the fields in the /etc/passwd file.

- The first field contains the login name, which is a unique name assigned to each user. The login name should be eight characters or fewer in length. Spaces and underscores are not allowed. Numerals can be used but at least one lowercase letter should be present. The first letter alone can be an uppercase letter. However, using only lowercase letters and numerals is recommended to maintain compatibility with previous releases of Solaris and older application software that may expect lowercase login names.

- The second field contains an entry x. This is a placeholder for the encrypted passwords that are stored in the /etc/shadow file. Disabled accounts have an asterisk (*). In early Unix versions (before 3.2), the password field contained the fully encrypted passwd. Now, these encrypted passwords are stored in the /etc/shadow file because it could be a severe security threat if anyone who was able to access the /etc/passwd file tried some decryption tools on the encrypted passwords.

11

- The third field contains the UID provided to the users. The root account has a UID of 0, the system accounts have UIDs less than 100, and the UID for ordinary user accounts begins at 100.

- The fourth field contains a unique group identification number (GID) provided to each group. Groups are defined in the /etc/group file.

- The fifth field is a comment field. This field normally contains the full names of the users. Other information such as e-mail address and phone number can also be mentioned here.

- The sixth field specifies the full path name of the user's home directory. It is the directory where the user is located initially after logging in to a system.

- The seventh field specifies a program that the system automatically executes when the user logs in. This is known as the login shell, which may be /bin/sh for the Bourne shell, /bin/ksh for the Korn shell, or /bin/csh for the C shell. The sh is the default shell. If the last field is empty, the sh shell is invoked. This field should not necessarily be a shell. It can be any other program.

NOTE

> A user can belong to more than one group. All groups to which the user belongs are specified in the /etc/group file. Every user can have 1 primary group and up to 11 secondary groups.

The /etc/shadow file has one entry corresponding to an entry in the /etc/passwd file. The password after encryption appears as a series of numerals and uppercase and lowercase letters, which make it look unrelated to the original password. The /etc/shadow file consists of nine colon-separated fields as displayed in the syntax. The following list provides a brief description of all nine fields in the /etc/shadow file.

```
uid:password:lastchange:min:max:warning:inactive:expire:flag
```

- The first field contains the login name.

- The second field contains the password for the users in an encrypted form. The password can be assigned to users by the superuser or by the users themselves if they use the passwd utility. The encrypted passwords consist of 13 characters. Passwords consist of numbers (0-9) and both uppercase (A-Z) and lowercase (a-z) alphabets. For user accounts without a password, this field has an NP entry representing no password. This field is blank if a user account is created without a password and the user is yet to login for the first time. The user is prompted to provide a password when the user logs in for the first time.

- The third field stores the number of days between the default date, January 1, 1970, and the day when the password was last changed.

- The fourth field mentions the minimum number of days required between password changes.

- The fifth field mentions the maximum number of days a password is valid. After this, a user is forced to change the password.

- The sixth field mentions the number of days the user is warned before the password expires. A warning message appears during logon indicating the number of days remaining before the password expires.

- The seventh field states the number of days the account can be inactive before the password must be changed. Beyond this date, the account is locked.

- The eighth field gives the expiration date for the account, beyond which the user cannot log on to the system.

- The ninth field is for future use and is not currently used. The root owns the /etc/shadow file.

MANAGING USERS

User management activities can be performed with the command line or with the Solaris Management Console (SMC).

ADDING USERS WITH THE useradd COMMAND

The useradd command can be used to add users to the system. You also can invoke this command to change the default settings. You can display the default user settings on your system and change these settings as required.

Table 11.2 describes the various options of the useradd command.

TABLE 11.2   VARIOUS useradd OPTIONS AND THEIR DESCRIPTIONS

Options	Description
-D	Changes the default values.
-o	Creates a user account with an existing user ID.
-u	Specifies the user ID.
-g	Specifies the user's primary group.
-G	Specifies one or more secondary groups of which the user might be a member. To specify the number of secondary groups, use a comma-separated list.
-s	Specifies the type of shell to be allocated to the user.
-d	Specifies the user's /home directory.
-m	Creates the user's home directory. If this option is not used, an entry is made in the /etc/passwd file but the directory is not created.

continues

TABLE 11.2 CONTINUED

Options	Description
-c	Enters a description about the user. This information is stored in the user's /etc/passwd entry.
-e	Sets the number of days after which the user account expires.
-f	Specifies the days of inactivity.

To add a user by using the useradd command from the command line, perform the following steps:

1. Display the default values for group, base_dir, skel_dir, shell, inactive, and expire. When used with the -g, -b, -f, or -e options, the -d option sets the default values for the specified fields.

   ```
   # useradd -d
   ```

Listing 11.1 displays the output for the useradd command.

LISTING 11.1   Useradd COMMAND OUTPUT

```
    group=other,1   project=,3
    basedir=/home
    skel=/etc/skel
    shell=/bin/sh
    inactive=0
    expire=
    auths=
    profiles=
roles=
```

2. The next step is to modify the default settings for each individual user. However, specifying different defaults for each user can become a tedious task. An alternative is to change defaults to match your requirements. For example, if you want to change the user group to sys, and the user password to expire every 20 days, change the base directory to /export/home, and not lock the user account even if the password expires, issue the following command:

   ```
   #useradd -D -g sys -e15 -f0 -s/bin/ksh
   #useradd -D
   group=sys,3
   project=,3
   basedir=/export/home
   skel=/etc/skel
   shell=/bin/sh
   inactive=0
   expire=
   auths=
   profiles=
   roles=
   ```

When you add a new user to your system, the new user will have the defaults that you have set. For example, to add a new user Alberto, a system architect in the organization, issue the following command:

```
# useradd -c "system architect" -m Alberto
```

The –m flag creates the user's home directory if it does not already exist.

Note that if the user account specified with the useradd command already exists—either the user ID or the user name is duplicated—, an error message is displayed.

ASSIGNING PASSWORDS

Every user should be provided with a password. The passwords are either assigned by the superuser or by the users themselves if they use the passwd command. Following is the syntax of the passwd command:

```
# passwd <username>
```

After typing this, the user is prompted to enter a password. If the user is already assigned a password and wants to change it, he or she is prompted to enter the existing password and then enter the new password twice.

You also can lock a user account to block its access to the system by using the -l option of the passwd command.

```
# passwd  -l  alberto
```

The locked account is identified with an *LK* entry in the encrypted password field of the /etc/shadow file. Listing 11.2 displays the output for the /etc/shadow file.

LISTING 11.2   OUTPUT FOR THE /etc/shadow FILE

```
root:6hOO6cqyNU6Ew:11629::::::
daemon:NP:6445::::::
bin:NP:6445::::::
sys:NP:6445::::::
adm:NP:6445::::::
lp:NP:6445::::::
uucp:NP:6445::::::
nuucp:NP:6445::::::
listen:*LK*:::::::
nobody:NP:6445::::::
noaccess:NP:6445::::::
nobody4:NP:6445::::::
oracle:xEdFEiMpNjqog:11509::::::
Alberto:*LK*:::::::
```

Specify the maximum number of days a password is valid before it must be changed by using the -x option. Define the minimum number of days between password changes for a user by using the -n option. You can warn the user about the password expiration with the -w option.

```
# passwd  -x60  -n30  Alberto
```

The preceding command allows user Alberto to change his password every 60 days and retain the password without changing it for at least 30 days after the password expiration date.

NOTE

The default values for the MAXWEEKS, MINWEEKS, WARNWEEKS, and PASSLENGTH variables are specified in the /etc/default/passwd file. The passwd command changes these default values for the users and modifies the /etc/shadow file accordingly.

Table 11.3 shows the various options of the passwd command along with their descriptions.

TABLE 11.3   OPTIONS FOR THE passwd COMMAND AND THEIR DESCRIPTIONS

Option	Description
-n	Sets the minimum number of days between password changes.
-x	Sets the maximum number of days between password changes.
-w	Sets the number of days the user will be warned before the expiration date.
-l	Disables the password-aging feature.
-s	Prints a single line of information on the account listed.
-a	Lists the password status of all the accounts. This option should be used along with the -s option.

MODIFYING A USER ACCOUNT

The usermod command is used to edit the user account details from the command line. For example, the following syntax modifies the default shell for the user Alberto from the Bourne shell to the korn shell and changes his home directory to /home/alberto:

```
# usermod   -s  /bin/ksh   -d  /home/alberto alberto
```

DELETING A USER ACCOUNT

The userdel command is used to delete a user account from the command line. The userdel command, used with the -r option, deletes the specified user account along with its home directory. The following syntax deletes user Jenny's account along with her home directory:

```
#userdel -r jenny
```

Deleting a user account along with the user's home directory does not remove all files owned by that user. Some files owned by the deleted user might be present in some location other than the user's home directory. Those files will still have the deleted user as their owner. The system administrator should manually find those files owned by the deleted user account (by using the find command) and remove them or change ownership.

MANAGING GROUPS

A group is a collection of users who share files and other system resources or users who are assigned similar responsibilities. Groups are useful in situations where you require many users to access a set of files and directories. For example, you can place all the files related to a project named "Net2Asia" in a directory and assign all the project team members who require access to that directory to a group. Therefore, it becomes easier to assign access permissions to a group related to a specific directory. This prevents access to the directory by non-members of the group.

Each group has a name, a GID, and a list of users who belong to that group. A GID is a unique number that identifies the group internally on a system. A user may belong to two types of groups:

- **Primary group**—The OS associates all files and directories created by the user with this group. Each user must belong to a primary group.

- **Secondary groups**—Specifies one or more groups to which a user belongs. If the primary user of a group requires access to a set of files and directories owned by another group, this user can be added to the second group. For this user, it would be a secondary group. Similarly, this user can be added to other groups that also become the user's secondary groups. Users may belong to a maximum of 15 secondary groups.

The groups command followed by the username lists all the user's groups.

```
# groups hemz
staff prod mac
```

Table 11.4 lists the default groups in Solaris, along with their group IDs and members.

TABLE 11.4   DEFAULT GROUPS IN SOLARIS, ALONG WITH THEIR GROUP IDS AND MEMBER LISTS

Group	Group ID	Members
Root	0	root
Other	1	
Bin	2	root, bin, daemon
Sys	3	root, bin, sys, adm
Adm	4	root, adm, daemon
Uucp	5	root, uucp
Mail	6	root
Tty	7	root, tty, adm
Lp	8	root, lp, adm
Nuucp	9	root, nuucp

continues

TABLE 11.4   CONTINUED

Group	Group ID	Members
Staff	10	
Daemon	12	root, daemon
Sysadmin	14	
Nobody	60001	
Noaccess	60002	
Nogroup	65534	

GROUP ACCOUNTS DATABASE

The /etc/group file stores the group information. The /etc/group file has four colon-separated fields.

- The first field contains the group name, which ranges from 1 to 6 characters.
- The second field contains the encrypted password associated with the group. If the group has no password, this field is blank. The users cannot change groups at will because they are prompted for the group password if they issue the newgrp command to change groups.
- The third field specifies the group ID.
- The fourth field contains a comma-separated list of users of that group.

ADDING A GROUP

You can create a group from the command line by using the groupadd command. The groupadd command adds the appropriate entry to the /etc/group file as displayed in Listing 11.3.

LISTING 11.3   OUTPUT OF THE /etc/group FILE

```
# more /etc/group
root::0:root,jamesm
other::1:
bin::2:root,bin,daemon
sys::3:root,bin,sys,adm
adm::4:root,adm,daemon
uucp::5:root,uucp
mail::6:root
tty::7:root,tty,adm
lp::8:root,lp,adm
nuucp::9:root,nuucp
staff::10:muskanw,linda,anuj,sallyg,samuelb,nicholasd,charlesc,davidy,jamesm
daemon::12:root,daemon
sysadmin::14:james
```

```
nobody::60001:
noaccess::60002:
nogroup::65534:
newhire::102:
class::300:jamesm
group1::301:user3,user4
class3::303:
#
```

For example, the following syntax creates a new group called team.

```
# groupadd team
```

To add users to this group, use the useradd command with the -g option. The following syntax adds new users timf, kenb, jamesm, and bend to the group team:

```
# useradd  -g  team timf kenb jamesm bend
```

Assign the group id for the group by using the groupadd command with the -g option. The -o option assigns the same gid for more than one group.

If you view the contents of the /etc/group file as displayed in Listing 11.4, you will see the listing of the team members you created along with corresponding group members.

LISTING 11.4   CONTENTS OF THE /etc/group FILE

```
# more /etc/group
root::0:root,jamesm
other::1:
bin::2:root,bin,daemon
sys::3:root,bin,sys,adm
adm::4:root,adm,daemon
uucp::5:root,uucp
mail::6:root
tty::7:root,tty,adm
lp::8:root,lp,adm
nuucp::9:root,nuucp
staff::10:muskanw,linda,anuj,sallyg,samuelb,nicholasd,charlesc,davidy,jamesm
daemon::12:root,daemon
sysadmin::14:james
nobody::60001:
noaccess::60002:
nogroup::65534:
team::101:timf,kenb,jamesm,bend
newhire::102:
class::300:jamesm
group1::301:user3,user4
class3::303:
#
```

DELETING A GROUP

You can delete a group if it is no longer needed. The groupdel command deletes a group from the command line. It deletes the appropriate entry from the /etc/group file. For example, the following syntax deletes the group team:

```
# groupdel team
```

MODIFYING A GROUP DEFINITION

The groupmod command modifies a group definition from the command line. The -g option, when used with groupmod, specifies a new groupid for the group team.

The following syntax changes the group ID of the team group to 105.

```
# groupmod  -g  105 team


.....
noaccess::60002:
nogroup::65534:
team::105:timf,kenb,jamesm,bend
newhire::102:
class::300:jamesm
.....
```

You can modify the name of a group by using the -n option. The following syntax changes the group name team to myteam.

```
# groupmod  -n  team myteam
.......
noaccess::60002:
nogroup::65534:
myteam::105:timf,kenb,jamesm,bend
newhire::102:
class::300:jamesm
.......
```

USER MONITOR COMMANDS

Information requests from users pose great security threats to the system because the system must evaluate the type of user before providing the requested data. To protect the data that is sent out to the user, Unix provides user monitor commands that are used to gather information about the user. These commands indicate whether any user is gathering more than a fair share of resources. In addition, these tools help avoid potential performance problems by justifying the need for more CPU, memory, or disk resources to accommodate the growing needs of your user community. The rest of this section defines the different user monitor commands.

THE uptime COMMAND

The uptime command shows the current time, the number of days the machine has been up, the number of users logged in to the system, and the system load average during the past 1, 5, and 15 minutes. This command indicates whether any user is monopolizing the machine's resources.

```
# uptime
  3:33pm  up 11 day(s),  4:27,  5 users,  load average: 0.07, 0.04, 0.04
#
```

THE w COMMAND

The command w provides the uptime information and indicates all active users, the terminal ports the users are using, the names of hosts the user is logged in to, the time when the user logged in, host idle time, the aggregate CPU time of all processes on that terminal port (JCPU), the CPU time of the active process listed in the next field (PCPU), and the commands users are currently running. The idle time gives a good indication of who may be good candidates for being logged out. The following syntax displays a sample output for the w command:

```
# w
  3:30pm  up 11 day(s),  4:25,  5 users,  load average: 0.01, 0.02, 0.03
User      tty            login@  idle  JCPU   PCPU  what
root      console        26Feb0211days 93:57     21  /usr/dt/bin/dtexec -open 0 -t
tpr
root      pts/5          Wed10am 3days  3:53            tail -f kjs_1_CCS0
root      pts/6          1Mar02  5days                  bash
root      pts/3          26Feb02 8days                  tail -f kjs_1_CCS0
root      pts/4          26Feb0211days                  -sh
root      pts/10         Thu12pm 2days  2:55  /usr/bin/../java/bin/../jre/bin/
root      pts/8          Thu12pm 2days  2:19            tail -f kjs_1_CCS0
root      pts/9          2:00pm  11                     w
#
```

NOTE

The JCPU time defines the currently running background jobs attached to tty, but it does not define past background jobs. The PCPU time is the time used by the current process that is named in the what field.

THE ps -ef COMMAND

The ps -ef command gives a lot of information about all running system processes. Pay attention to the time column because this is the cumulative process execution time for the listed process. Any large number indicates processes are running amok, especially if the parent process ID is 1. You might use the kill -9 out_of_control_process_id command to tax the system less. If the procedure should not be killed, then you have the option to use the renice command. The following code displays a sample output for the ps -ef command:

➜ To know more about renice and priocntl commands, **see** "Process Management," **p.277**.

```
# ps -ef | more
     UID   PID  PPID  C    STIME TTY      TIME CMD
     root     0     0  0   Feb 26 ?       0:01 sched
     root     1     0  0   Feb 26 ?       0:12 /etc/init -
     root     2     0  0   Feb 26 ?       0:00 pageout
     root     3     0  1   Feb 26 ?     125:06 fsflush
     root   848   812  0   Feb 26 ?       4:47 mibiisa -r -p 32816
     root   377   376  0   Feb 26 ?       0:04 /usr/SunONE/programs/SunONEWebtop
102/program/sportald.bin -p -c /usr/SunONE/pro
```

```
   root   256    1   0   Feb 26 ?      0:00  /usr/lib/lpsched
   root    60    1   0   Feb 26 ?      0:00  /usr/lib/devfsadm/devfseventd
   root    62    1   0   Feb 26 ?      0:00  /usr/lib/devfsadm/devfsadmd
   root    73    1   0   Feb 26 ?      0:01  /usr/lib/picl/picld
   root   158    1   0   Feb 26 ?      0:00  /usr/lib/inet/in.ndpd
   root   175    1   0   Feb 26 ?      0:00  /usr/sbin/keyserv
   root   269    1   0   Feb 26 ?      0:00  /usr/lib/power/powerd
   root   211    1   0   Feb 26 ?      0:00  /usr/lib/nfs/lockd
   root   234    1   0   Feb 26 ?      0:09  /usr/sbin/cron
   root   228    1   0   Feb 26 ?      0:06  /usr/sbin/syslogd
   root   199    1   0   Feb 26 ?      0:04  /usr/sbin/inetd -s
   root   218    1   0   Feb 26 ?      0:00  /usr/lib/autofs/automountd
   root   172    1   0   Feb 26 ?      0:00  /usr/sbin/rpcbind
 daemon   213    1   0   Feb 26 ?      0:00  /usr/lib/nfs/statd
```

THE prstat COMMAND

The prstat command examines the active processes and provides a statistical report on them. You can use the output of this command to check the % cpu and time columns to identify users who are exploiting the system a bit too much. The size parameter, indicating the process size in pages, can identify users who may be causing memory-to-disk swapping to occur too often. Possibly this information shows that the system needs more memory. The prstat command is displayed in the following syntax:

```
   # prstat
     PID USERNAME  SIZE    RSS STATE  PRI NICE      TIME  CPU PROCESS/NLWP
   12580 root     1552K  1152K cpu3    59    0   0:00.00 0.1% prstat/1
     848 root     3512K  3072K sleep   50    0   0:00.00 0.0% mibiisa/12
   12126 root      304K   304K sleep   48    0   0:00.00 0.0% sh/1
     362 root       20M  8536K sleep   58    0   0:01.30 0.0% lbsd.bin/6
     291 root     2664K  1992K sleep   58    0   0:00.01 0.0% vold/6
     278 root     1016K   664K sleep   59    0   0:00.00 0.0% utmpd/1
     281 root     1592K   696K sleep   20    0   0:00.00 0.0% cimomboot/1
     303 root     2584K   992K sleep   58    0   0:00.00 0.0% nsrexecd/1
     250 root     2528K  1760K sleep   53    0   0:00.00 0.0% nscd/9
     213 daemon   2608K  1808K sleep   50    0   0:00.00 0.0% statd/3
     172 root     2472K  1280K sleep   58    0   0:00.00 0.0% rpcbind/1
     218 root     2976K  1896K sleep   59    0   0:00.00 0.0% automountd/5
     199 root     2720K  1976K sleep   58    0   0:00.04 0.0% inetd/1
     228 root     3584K  2024K sleep   59    0   0:00.01 0.0% syslogd/14
     234 root     1944K  1056K sleep   51    0   0:00.08 0.0% cron/1
     211 root     2016K  1280K sleep   30    0   0:00.00 0.0% lockd/1
     269 root     1368K   880K sleep   50    0   0:00.00 0.0% powerd/3
     175 root     2792K  1312K sleep   50    0   0:00.00 0.0% keyserv/5
     158 root     1888K   760K sleep   59    0   0:00.00 0.0% in.ndpd/1
      73 root     2200K  1792K sleep   12    0   0:00.00 0.0% picld/4
      62 root     2360K  1200K sleep   35    0   0:00.00 0.0% devfsadm/5
      60 root     1304K   856K sleep   51    0   0:00.00 0.0% devfseventd/8
   Total: 126 processes, 467 lwps, load averages: 0.00, 0.02, 0.03
   #
```

THE fuser COMMAND

The fuser command indicates which local process is using the local or remote file systems. Running fuser -u command lists all the usernames and processes that currently use the specified filename. Either the user can be asked to stop tying up the resource, or the offending process can be killed. If a file system—rather than a file—is the resource being tied up, `fuser -cku filesystem_name` kills each task controlling a file residing on the file system. After the command completes, the file system can be unmounted. The `fuser` command is displayed in the following syntax:

```
# fuser -uc /export/home1
/export/home1:      72440(oracle)     67610(oracle)    227630(oracle)
➡227610(oracle)    227590(oracle)    227570(oracle)    227550(oracle)
#
```

THE df AND du COMMANDS

The `df` and `du` commands display the disk usage data. For overly full file systems, `du -s /filesystem/*` displays a grand total of used blocks for each component directory on the file system. You can continue chaining down the largest identified directories until finding something that can be moved, archived, or eliminated. Using `find` with its size parameter automates the same result. The following syntax displays the result of issuing the `df` command:

```
# df
/                   (/dev/dsk/c0t0d0s0 ): 4665158 blocks    391361 files
/usr                (/dev/dsk/c0t0d0s3 ): 1541966 blocks    364959 files
/proc               (/proc            ):       0 blocks      3080 files
/dev/fd             (fd               ):       0 blocks         0 files
/etc/mnttab         (mnttab           ):       0 blocks         0 files
/var                (/dev/dsk/c0t0d0s5 ): 2758004 blocks    365685 files
/var/run            (swap             ): 6997312 blocks    222290 files
/tmp                (swap             ): 6997312 blocks    222290 files
/opt                (/dev/dsk/c0t0d0s4 ): 2918518 blocks    385943 files
/export/home0       (/dev/dsk/c0t3d0s7 ):17398406 blocks   2080418 files
/export/home1       (/dev/dsk/c0t1d0s7 ): 2736216 blocks   2123089 files
/export/home2       (/dev/dsk/c0t2d0s7 ):30801810 blocks   2116365 files
#
# du -s /export/home1
32090284            /export/home1
#
```

THE last COMMAND

The `last` command shows which users are logging on from where and for how long. This command is usually used in conjunction with `acctcom` or `lastcomm`. Acctcom and lastcomm identify system usage by username and tty port. They give administrators insight into what the system is being used for and how much CPU time and memory is being spent on which user tasks. The output indicates when your system is the busiest and why it is busy. To enable these commands, system accounting needs to be turned on and adequate space should be open for raw accounting files to appear and grow. The following syntax shows the result of issuing the `last` command:

```
# last
root       pts/9       172.17.69.42      Sat Mar  9 14:00    still logged in
root       pts/9       172.17.24.63      Fri Mar  8 20:26 - 20:29  (00:03)
root       pts/9       172.17.69.42      Fri Mar  8 16:22 - 17:27  (01:05)
root       pts/9       172.17.69.42      Fri Mar  8 14:25 - 14:27  (00:02)
root       pts/12      172.17.69.42      Fri Mar  8 10:58 - 11:52  (00:54)
```

```
root      pts/9      172.17.69.42     Fri Mar  8 10:57 - 11:52  (00:55)
root      pts/9      172.17.69.42     Thu Mar  7 19:48 - 19:52  (00:03)
root      pts/12     172.17.69.42     Thu Mar  7 19:03 - 19:43  (00:39)
team      pts/13     172.17.24.77     Thu Mar  7 18:32 - 18:37  (00:04)
root      pts/12     172.17.24.62     Thu Mar  7 16:47 - 17:05  (00:18)
root      ftp        172.17.24.62     Thu Mar  7 16:44 - 17:02  (00:17)
root      pts/9      172.17.69.42     Thu Mar  7 14:58 - 19:42  (04:44)
root      ftp        172.17.24.62     Thu Mar  7 14:19 - 14:30  (00:11)
root      pts/16     172.17.26.107    Thu Mar  7 13:01 - 13:02  (00:00)
root      pts/8      172.17.24.99     Thu Mar  7 12:56   still logged in
root      pts/10     172.17.24.99     Thu Mar  7 12:54   still logged in
root      ftp        172.17.24.62     Thu Mar  7 12:50 - 12:53  (00:03)
root      pts/10     172.17.69.42     Thu Mar  7 10:52 - 11:08  (00:15)
root      pts/10     172.17.24.61     Thu Mar  7 10:45 - 10:48  (00:02)
root      pts/10     172.17.24.63     Thu Mar  7 10:16 - 10:17  (00:00)
root      pts/10     172.17.24.62     Wed Mar  6 20:02 - 20:11  (00:09)
root      ftp        172.17.24.62     Wed Mar  6 20:01 - 20:12  (00:10)
```

USER LIMITING COMMANDS

Disk quotas specify how much disk space a user can use. Using disk quotas you can evenly distribute disk space amongst all users. You can begin restricting disk usage by running the following command:

```
#quotaon /user_filesystem
```

The preceding command enables users residing on `user_filesystem` to be reined in. You can define how much disk space each user can legally use by using the `edquota` command. The general form of this command is

```
edquota [-p previously_defined_quota_username] username
```

The `repquota` option gives a summary of all users in the password file for the specified file system.

```
#repquota /appuser_filesystem
```

The quota command reports a specified username's disk usage and limits. If the `-v` option is omitted, only the specified usernames exceeding their limits appear in the output. Again, disk usage and limits are expressed. An example of the `quota` command and its output follows. In this example, user Alberto has exceeded the total kilobyte usage allowed and has 2.8 days left to reduce his usage. That username could create 23 more files before signaling an inode coverage (assuming enough space exists).

```
# quota -v Alberto
Disk quotas for Alberto (uid 1011):
Filesystem   usage  quota limit  timeleft  files  quota  limit     timeleft
/appuser     34512  30000 35720  2.8 days  427    450    750
```

USING SMC TO MANAGE USERS AND GROUPS

To start SMC, type `/usr/bin/smc` at the shell prompt. Any user can view information with SMC, but only users with root privileges can edit information. The Management Tools: Solaris Management Console 2.1 window is displayed in Figure 11.1.

Figure 11.1
Management Tools:
Solaris Management
Console window.

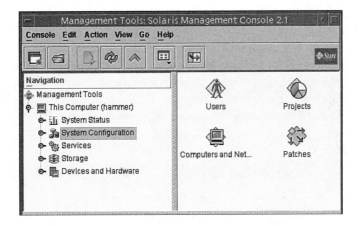

Managing Users and Groups Using SMC

You can use SMC to add, delete, and modify user accounts. The SMC combines the options to perform all these tasks in a single interface. SMC also provides tools to administer groups of users. Just as with the administration tasks performed on a single user, you can add, modify, and delete groups.

Adding Users

To add a user, perform the following steps.

1. Expand the System Configuration option in the Navigation pane as shown in Figure 11.2.

Figure 11.2
System Configuration
option.

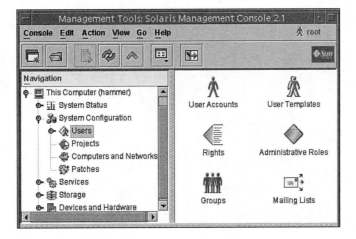

2. Double-click Users to access the User Accounts option. This is where you will add the user's account information.

11

3. Select the Action menu option and then the Add User submenu. Note that you can add users with the wizard or the template. If you choose to use the wizard, Solaris guides you through the steps to add users and define user settings. The template contains pre-defined settings for the user. If you choose the Template option to add users, the settings specified in the template file are defined for the user. The advantage of using the template file is that it provides a fast way to add new users who have common properties. This example uses the Wizard to add users. Select the With Wizard option.

4. The Add User Wizard displays (see Figure 11.3). Specify the user details.

Figure 11.3
Add User Wizard window.

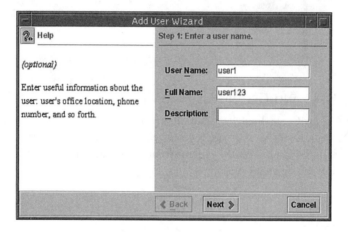

You can see the added user in the right window pane of the Management Tools window (see Figure 11.4) .

Figure 11.4
Added user.

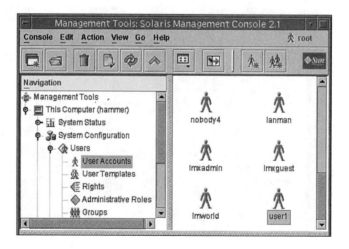

CUSTOMIZING USER TEMPLATES

The User Templates enable you to specify a set of common properties for users. If certain properties for several users are similar, it is advisable to create the User Template. This will help you while creating users.

1. To create the template, select User Templates from the Navigation panel.
2. Select Action, Add User Template.
3. Specify the name of the template in the Add User Template dialog box.
4. Set password options and sharing options. You can set the other options if required.

MODIFYING USERS

You can modify most of the user's properties using the User Properties dialog box. This dialog box enables you to modify general user information, as shown in Figure 11.5.

Figure 11.5
User Properties dialog box.

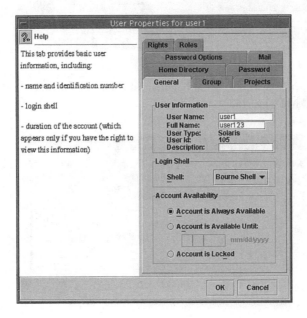

You can also perform other administration tasks, such as specifing privileges to the users to access applications, changing users' passwords, changing users' project memberships, and so on.

DELETING USERS

If you no longer need a user account, you can delete it from the list of users.

1. To delete, select the specific user, right-click, and select the Delete option as displayed in Figure 11.6.

Figure 11.6
Deleting a user.

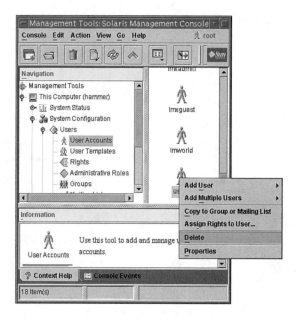

2. You are shown a Warning dialog box that asks you to confirm the deletion of the user, as displayed in Figure 11.7.

Figure 11.7
Warning dialog box.

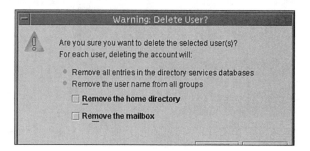

ADDING A GROUP

Before adding a group, you must keep in mind the following guidelines:

- Within a domain, the group name should be unique.
- The group name can contain letters, numerals, underscores, and hyphen.
- The name of the group must begin with a letter and can contain at least 2 to 32 letters.

To add a group, perform the following steps:

1. Select Groups in the Navigation pane.
2. Access the Action menu, Add Group option, as displayed in Figure 11.8.

Figure 11.8
Adding a group.

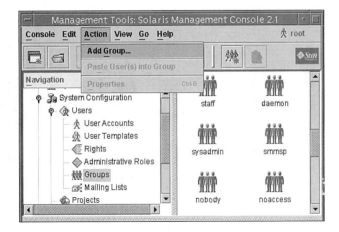

3. The Add Group dialog box appears, as shown in Figure 11.9. Specify the name of the group in the Group Name field.

Figure 11.9
Add Group dialog box.

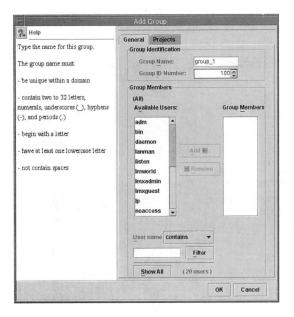

4. Select the users from the Available Users list box and click the Add button. This will add all users you want as the members of the group in the Group Members list box.

You can see the result of adding a group in the right pane of the Management Tools window, as shown in Figure 11.10.

Figure 11.10
Result of adding a group in the Management Tools window.

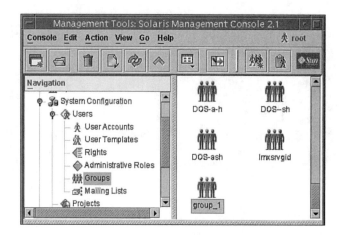

MODIFYING THE GROUP

The Properties dialog box enables you to modify the group properties. It also enables you to add and remove users from a group. In addition, it enables you to define the primary projects for a particular role or group, as shown in Figure 11.11.

Figure 11.11
Modifying the properties of a group.

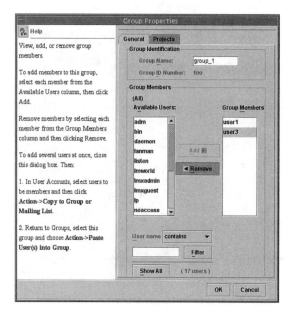

DELETING A GROUP

You can delete a group if it is no longer needed.

1. Select the group you want to delete and then right-click and select the Delete option.

2. The Warning dialog box (see Figure 11.12) warns you of all the group information you will lose by deleting the group.

Figure 11.12
Warning dialog box.

SUMMARY

Solaris enables you to use many administration tools in concert with certain add-on packages to administer your user base. There are three types of users who access the Solaris system: guest, application, and System Administrators or superusers. Each user accessing the Solaris system is given a UID. Any task performed on the Solaris system by a specific user account is owned by that UID. All local user account information is stored in the /etc/passwd file and /etc/shadow file.

Collections of users who share files and other system resources and share similar responsibilities form a group. Each group has a name and a GID. The GID is the unique number that identifies a group. The group user account information is stored in the /etc/group file.

The user and group administration tasks in Solaris include adding, deleting, and modifying user account information. You can perform these administration tasks by using either the command line utility or the Solaris Management Console (SMC). The commands to add, modify, and delete users with the command line utility are useradd, usermod, and userdel, respectively. The commands to add, modify, and delete groups are groupadd, groupmod, and groupdel, respectively.

CHAPTER 12

DISK AND STORAGE ADMINISTRATION

In this chapter

Introducing Disk and Storage Administration   204

Disk Slices   205

Adding and Configuring a New Disk   210

Volume Manager   212

SVM   213

Summary   216

Introducing Disk and Storage Administration

Organizations require data to be available 24×7. Taking a system offline to perform traditional maintenance is not a viable option anymore. Solaris OE provides disk and storage management solutions designed to meet the demands of Solaris users. These solutions provide high data availability and reliability, enhanced system and I/O performance, and simple large system and disk administration. Disk administration requires relevant skills and experience for effective management of the system disks.

This chapter details the disk administration tasks, such as adding and configuring new disks and formatting and repairing the disk drives. The chapter also details the storage management solutions provided by Solaris, such as Solaris Volume Manager (SVM).

Before detailing the administration tasks, let us review some of the basic disk terminology.

The hardware components of a disk are the platters, spindle, tracks, cylinders, sector, and disk controller, and the software components are the disk label and device drivers.

Figure 12.1 illustrates the parts that make up a hard disk.

Figure 12.1
Hard disk.

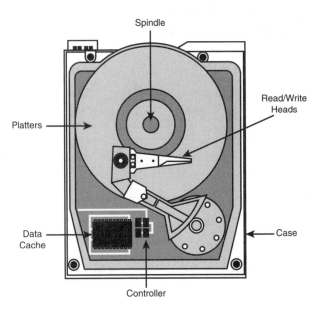

Each disk component has specific functionality that enables data storage activities. The following list describes the basic terminology that defines these components.

- **Platters**—Platters are disks mounted inside a fixed disk drive. Most disk drives use more than one platter mounted on a disk drive to provide more data storage surfaces in a smaller area.

- **Read/Write Head**—Bits of information are stored on and retrieved from computer disk drives using a magnetic read/write head. This information is arranged on concentric tracks, nominally circular in shape. Normal operation of a disk drive requires access to many different tracks. The faster the read/write head can be moved between tracks, the faster information can be stored or retrieved.

- **Spindle**—The spindle is the center shaft of a drive on which the hard disk platters are mounted.

- **Tracks**—Tracks are concentric circles around the central spindle on either side of each platter. When a disk undergoes a low-level format, it is divided into tracks and sectors.

- **Cylinders**—Cylinders are tracks that are placed physically above each other on the platters and then grouped together. Cylinders are further subdivided into sectors.

- **Sector**—A sector is the minimum segment of track length that can be assigned to store information. Sectors are grouped into logical blocks that function as the smallest data unit permitted.

- **Disk controller**—A disk controller is a chip or circuit that translates computer data and commands into low-level commands understood by the hard drive circuitry.

- **Data Cache**—A temporary storage area for frequently accessed or recently accessed data. Cache is used to speed up data transfer to and from a disk.

- **Disk label**—Every disk stores information such as disk controller, geometry, and slices in an area marked for storing this information. The information that is stored is called the *disk label*. Another term used to describe the disk label is *VTOC* (Volume Table of Contents). To label a disk means to write slice information onto the disk. You usually label a disk after changing its slices.

- **Device drivers**—The device driver is a program that controls hardware devices, such as printer, disk drive, and keyboard. Every device must have a driver program. Most drivers are loaded into memory at system boot time.

12

DISK SLICES

A disk slice is a physical subset of a disk that is composed of a single range of contiguous blocks. It can be used either as a raw device or it can hold a disk-based file system.

On SPARC-based systems, Solaris defines eight disk slices. Solaris assigns these eight disk slices, numbered 0 through 7, a set of different tasks.

→ To know more about the eight disk slices, **see** "Understanding the Solaris File System" **p.127**.

Locating a file system in a multiple disk arrangement is made easier if you label each slice with a logical disk name. When you access a disk slice, specify the disk subdirectory to which the disk slice is linked, followed by the controller, disk, and slice specifications. There are two types of disk subdirectories, /dev/dsk and /dev/rdsk. The /dev/dsk subdirectory is the block device interface that includes a buffer from which large blocks of data are read simultaneously. The /dev/rdsk is a raw device interface that transfers data without the use of buffers. Figure 12.2 displays the order in which a disk slice is accessed.

Figure 12.2
Order in which to
access the disk.

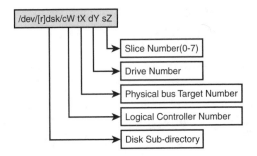

As shown in Figure 12.2, a disk is addressed in the following order:

- **cW**—This stands for the bus controller number W, which refers to the logical controller number of the device interface. For example, a system with one SCSI interface would use c0.

- **tX**—This is the SCSI target ID connected to the controller.

- **dY**—This represents the drive or unit number of the device connected to the target controller tX. The target controller is connected to the bus controller cW.

- **sZ**—This represents the slice or partition number of the device you are addressing.

The disk and file administration commands use the block and raw device interfaces. The use of these interfaces depends upon how data is read from a device.

Format UTILITY

Solaris OE provides an important tool that helps administer the disk: the format utility. This utility can be used to perform the following tasks:

- Display slice information
- Format a disk drive
- Repair a disk drive

> **NOTE**
>
> You must be a superuser to use the format utility. Also, you must make a backup of all data before using this utility to preserve all information.

DISPLAYING SLICE INFORMATION

To view the slice information, become a superuser and enter the format utility by using the format command.

```
# format
```

The format utility searches for the disks in the system and displays a list of available disks, as shown in Listing 12.1.

LISTING 12.1 A LIST OF AVAILABLE LISTS

```
AVAILABLE DISK SELECTIONS:
       0. c0t0d0 <SUN18G cyl 7506 alt 2 hd 19 sec 248>
          /pci@1f,4000/scsi@3/sd@0,0
       1. c0t1d0 <SUN18G cyl 7506 alt 2 hd 19 sec 248>
          /pci@1f,4000/scsi@3/sd@1,0
       2. c0t2d0 <SUN18G cyl 7506 alt 2 hd 19 sec 248>
          /pci@1f,4000/scsi@3/sd@2,0
       3. c0t3d0 <SUN18G cyl 7506 alt 2 hd 19 sec 248>
          /pci@1f,4000/scsi@3/sd@3,0
```

You can select the disk for which you want to display the slice information by specifying the slice number. For example, to display the slice information for c0t3d0, specify the corresponding slice number at the prompt as shown in Listing 12.2.

LISTING 12.2 SLICE INFORMATION FOR A SELECTED DISK

```
Specify disk (enter the number): 3
selecting c0t3d0
[disk formatted]
Warning: Current Disk has mounted partitions.

FORMAT MENU:
        disk       - select a disk
        type       - select (define) a disk type
        partition  - select (define) a partition table
        current    - describe the current disk
        format     - format and analyze the disk
        repair     - repair a defective sector
        label      - write label to the disk
        analyze    - surface analysis
        defect     - defect list management
        backup     - search for backup labels
        verify     - read and display labels
        save       - save new disk/partition definitions
        inquiry    - show vendor, product and revision
        volname    - set 8-character volume name
        !<cmd>     - execute <cmd>, then return
        quit
```

Select a partition by typing **partition** at the format prompt. The partition menu displays (see Listing 12.3) .

LISTING 12.3 PARTITION MENU

```
PARTITION MENU:
        0          - change '0' partition
        1          - change '1' partition
        2          - change '2' partition
        3          - change '3' partition
        4          - change '4' partition
        5          - change '5' partition
```

continues

LISTING 12.3   CONTINUED

```
6       - change '6' partition
7       - change '7' partition
select  - select a predefined table
modify  - modify a predefined partition table
name    - name the current table
print   - display the current table
label   - write partition map and label to the disk
!<cmd>  - execute <cmd>, then return
quit
```

NOTE

If you want to format a specific disk, enter **format** at the `format` prompt.

To display the slice information for the current disk, type **print** at the `partition` prompt. The output for the `print` command is displayed in Listing 12.4.

LISTING 12.4   *Print* COMMAND OUTPUT

```
Total disk cylinders available: 7506 + 2 (reserved cylinders)

Part      Tag    Flag    Cylinders        Size            Blocks
  0 unassigned   wm     0                0          (0/0/0)              0
  1 unassigned   wm     0                0          (0/0/0)              0
  2     backup   wm     0 - 7505     16.86GB        (7506/0/0) 35368272
  3 unassigned   wm     0                0          (0/0/0)              0
  4 unassigned   wm     0                0          (0/0/0)              0
  5 unassigned   wm     0                0          (0/0/0)              0
  6 unassigned   wm     0                0          (0/0/0)              0
  7       home   wm     0 - 7505     16.86GB        (7506/0/0) 35368272
```

Exit the `format` utility by typing **q** at the `partition` prompt and **q** at the `format` prompt.

REPAIRING A DISK

Hard disk corruption can occur because of power or system failures. These failures may not necessarily corrupt the hard disk. However, it may cause damage to the disk label. If it is the disk label that is damaged, you can configure the disk label either manually or automatically. While configuring, you must provide the correct disk type information. The `format` utility should be able to recognize this information. If format recognizes the disk type, the next step is to search for a backup label to label the disk. Labeling the disk with the backup label labels the disk with the correct partitioning information such as disk type and disk geometry.

Figure 12.3 displays a flowchart that depicts the process of recovering a corrupted disk label.

To recover a corrupted disk label, access the disk in the single-user mode and use the `format` utility to relabel the disk. Note that the `format` utility automatically configures any unlabeled disk. After configuring the unlabeled disk, select the disk you want to recover from the list of disks displayed.

Figure 12.3
Flowchart depicts the recovery of a corrupted disk label.

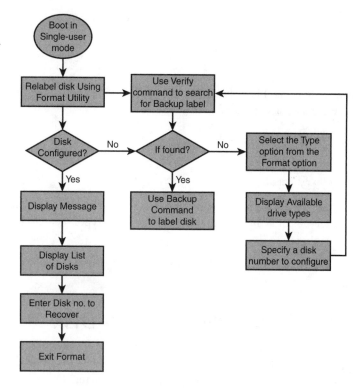

However, if the disk was not configured successfully, search for the backup label by using the Verify command as displayed in Listing 12.5.

LISTING 12.5   OUTPUT OF THE *verify* COMMAND

```
format> Verify
Warning: Could not read primary label.
Warning: Check the current partitioning and 'label' the disk or
use the 'backup' command.
Backup label contents:
Volume name = <          >
ascii name  = <SUN18G cyl 7506 alt 2 hd 19 sec 248>
pcyl        = 7508
ncyl        = 7506
acyl        =    2
nhead       =   19
nsect       =  248
Part      Tag    Flag    Cylinders       Size            Blocks
  0 unassigned    wm     0               0          (0/0/0)           0
  1 unassigned    wm     0               0          (0/0/0)           0
  2     backup    wm     0 - 7505        16.86GB    (7506/0/0) 35368272
  3 unassigned    wm     0               0          (0/0/0)           0
  4 unassigned    wm     0               0          (0/0/0)           0
  5 unassigned    wm     0               0          (0/0/0)           0
  6 unassigned    wm     0               0          (0/0/0)           0
```

continues

12

LISTING 12.5 CONTINUED

```
    7      home    wm     0 - 7505      16.86GB    (7506/0/0) 35368272
format>
```

If the `format` utility was able to find a backup label and the contents of this label appear satisfactory, use the `backup` command to label the disk.

```
format> backup
Disk has a primary label, still continue? y

Searching for backup labels...found.
Restoring primary label
```

However, if the `format` utility is unable to configure the disk automatically, specify the disk type using the `type` command. From the Available Disk Types menu, select the disk type you want to configure.

On successful configuration of the disk, exit the `format` utility.

```
format> q
```

ADDING AND CONFIGURING A NEW DISK

Before adding and configuring a new disk, install the boot block on the system. The boot block is a program located at a fixed point of a hard disk. It loads when the system is turned on or reboots and controls the next phase of loading the actual OS. You can install a boot block on a system disk by using the `installboot` command as displayed in the following command. To install, you have to be the superuser.

```
# /usr/sbin/installboot /usr/platform/'uname -i'/lib/fs/ufs/bootblk
➥/dev/rdsk/cwtxdys0
```

In this command, the OBP program loads the `bootblk` primary boot program from the boot-device or the diag-device. If the `bootblk` is not present or needs to be regenerated, it can be installed by running the `installboot` command. This can be done after booting from a CD-ROM or the network. A copy of the `bootblk` is available at `/usr/platform/'arch -k'/lib/fs/ufs/bootblk`.

Verify whether the boot blocks are installed by rebooting the system to run level 3.

The next step is to create the `/reconfigure` file that will cause the system to reconfigure itself when the system is booted using the following command.

```
# touch /reconfigure
```

Shut down the system by using the following command. In the command, the `-i0` option brings the system down to init state 0 (zero), which is the power-down state. The `-g40` option informs users of the number of seconds left before the system shuts down. Finally, the `-y` option specifies that the command should run without user intervention. You may also use the `init 0` command.

```
# shutdown -i0 -g40 -y
```

The ok or > prompt displays when the system shuts down. Switch off the power to the system and all external peripherals. Connect the disk to the system and ensure that all physical connections are made.

NOTE

Ensure that the disk you are adding has a unique target number.

Turn on the power to all external peripherals and the system. The system boots and displays the login prompt. Use the format utility to automatically configure the disk and then label the disk. Verify the disk label and then quit the format utility.

cfgadm UTILITY

The cfgadm utility is used to perform hot swap procedures. The two types of hot swap procedures are basic and full. Basic hot swap performs the hardware connection process automatically, but it requires manual intervention for the software connection process. Full hot swap performs both hardware and software connections automatically. Using the cfgadm utility, you can enable and disable full and basic hot swap procedures for the I/O slots in a server. When working with the I/O slots, you must know the attachment point ID for each slot. To list the I/O slots in a server with a PCI bus, use the following command:

```
# cfgadm pci
```

You can also determine the configuration information of the disks by using the -al option with the cfgadm utility. Listing 12.6 provides the configuration information about the disks.

LISTING 12.6   DISK CONFIGURATION INFORMATION

```
#cfgadm -al

Ap_Id                        Type        Receptacle   Occupant     Condition
c0                           scsi-bus    connected    configured   unknown
c0::dsk/c0t0d0               disk        connected    configured   unknown
c0::dsk/c0t1d0               disk        connected    configured   unknown
c0::dsk/c0t2d0               disk        connected    configured   unknown
c0::dsk/c0t3d0               disk        connected    configured   unknown
c0::lus0                     unknown     connected    configured   unknown
c1                           scsi-bus    connected    configured   unknown
c1::dsk/c1t6d0               CD-ROM      connected    configured   unknown
c1::lus1                     unknown     connected    configured   unknown
c1::rmt/0                    tape        connected    configured   unknown
#
```

A situation may arise when you configure a disk by using the cfgadm command, and when you view the status of the disk, the disk might be unavailable or might not show up in the listing. In this case, you need to unconfigure the disk and then reconfigure it. To unconfigure an online disk, use the -c option followed by the unconfigure command and the name of the disk, as displayed in Listing 12.6.

> **LISTING 12.7 UNCONFIGURING A DISK**
>
> ```
> #cfgadm -c unconfigure c0::dsk/c0t3d0
>
> Ap_Id                    Type         Receptacle   Occupant     Condition
> c0                       scsi-bus     connected    configured   unknown
> c0::dsk/c0t0d0           disk         connected    configured   unknown
> c0::dsk/c0t1d0           disk         connected    configured   unknown
> c0::dsk/c0t2d0           disk         connected    configured   unknown
> c0::dsk/c0t3d0           unavailable  connected    unconfigured unknown
> c0::lus0                 unknown      connected    configured   unknown
> c1                       scsi-bus     connected    configured   unknown
> c1::dsk/c1t6d0           CD-ROM       connected    configured   unknown
> c1::lus1                 unknown      connected    configured   unknown
> c1::rmt/0                tape         connected    configured   unknown
> #
> ```

RAID LEVELS

RAID (Redundant Array of Independent Disks) enables you to combine a set of disks into one large virtual device. This device provides fault tolerance, redundancy, and/or performance improvement, depending on the type of the RAID system deployed. There are 6 RAID levels ranging from 0–7. Different RAID levels offer dramatic differences in performance, data availability, and data integrity, depending on the specific I/O environment. The RAID levels Solaris supports are RAID 0, 1, and 5.

- RAID 0 stripes data across multiple disk arrays without any redundant information. Although, it reduces redundancy, striping reduces the level of data availability. When a disk array fails, all the blocks of data stored in the array are corrupted.

- RAID 1 maintains duplicate sets of data in different disks. This RAID level provides the highest level of data availability because copies of all data are maintained in separate disks. However, this is a little expensive to implement and maintain because it requires twice the desired disk space.

- RAID 5 distributes data and parity information across disks. It provides a high level of data availability. Even if an underlying disk fails, RAID level 5 can withstand the failure. If used with hot spares, it can stand multiple failures. In the RAID 5 model, every stripe has one area that contains a parity stripe and others that contain data. The parity is spread over all the disks in the array, reducing the write time for large independent writes. This is possible because the writes do not have to wait until a single parity disk can accept the data. This RAID level provides the highest read and lowest write data transaction rate.

VOLUME MANAGER

To administer mass storage, there are products such as Solstice Disk AdminSuite and Veritas Volume Manager available to administer and manage your volumes. With the advent of Solaris 9 OE, a new volume management tool called the Solaris Volume Manager (SVM) is incorporated within the Solaris OE. The SVM has all the capabilities of Sun Solstice Disk AdminSuite. The SVM comes with a friendly user interface and enhanced features, such as soft portioning, which enables you to have more than eight partitions per disk. This feature was not available with Solstice Disk AdminSuite.

SVM

SVM helps you manage a large number of disks and the data on those disks. You can use SVM to increase storage capacity and data availability. SVM also helps improve I/O performance. It uses virtual disks to manage physical disks and their associated data. This virtual disk is called a volume, which is functionally similar to a physical disk. SVM converts I/O requests directed at a volume into I/O requests to the underlying member disks. An easy way to build volumes is to use the GUI built into the SMC software. The Enhanced Storage tool within the SMC software presents you with a view of all the existing volumes. You can easily build any kind of SVM volumes or components, such as state database replicas, hot spare pools, and disk sets, by following the steps in the SVM wizard. The volumes that can be created are RAID 0, RAID 1, and RAID 5. You can build the following components or volumes by using the SVM wizard:

- A state database replica is the database that stores information on the disk about the state of your SVM configuration. Note that SVM cannot operate until you have created the state database replicas.
- The hot spare pool is a collection of slices reserved to be automatically substituted in case of slice failure.
- Disk sets are a set of disk drives that can be shared by multiple hosts. They provide data redundancy and availability and a separate namespace for easier administration.
- RAID 0, RAID 1, and RAID 5 are a set of physical slices that appear as a single logical device to the system.

CONFIGURING SVM

A poorly designed SVM configuration can degrade performance. To ensure optimum performance of the disks, ensure the following conditions are true while configuring the SVM:

- Ensure that a slice that is defined and activated as a volume is not used for any other purpose.
- Place drives in a volume on separate drive paths.
- Back up the system files, /etc/lvm/mddb.cf and /etc/lvm/md.cf, on a regular basis. Editing or deleting these files may cause critical problems. For example, the device may no longer be available for use.
- Do not mount file systems on a volume underlying a slice. If a slice is used for a volume of any kind, you must not mount that slice as a file system. If possible, unmount any physical device you intend to use as a volume before you activate it. For example, if you

create a transactional volume for a UFS, specify the transactional volume name as the device to mount in the /etc/vfstab file.

> **NOTE**
>
> You can view the SVM configuration either from the Enhanced Storage tool within the SMC or use the metastat command from the command line.

To configure SVM, use the metastat -p command that creates the /etc/lvm/md.tab file. This file contains all parameters that the metainit and metahs commands use. These commands help in setting up several similar environments or re-creating the configuration after a system failure.

```
# metastat -p > /etc/lvm/md.tab
```

INITIALIZING SVM FROM A CONFIGURATION FILE

The need to initialize SVM arises when you have no SVM configuration or you have completely lost your existing SVM configuration. In such situations, you have the option of re-creating the SVM from a saved configuration file. The files you can use to recover the SVM configuration are md.cf(4) and md.tab(4) .

> **NOTE**
>
> The md.cf file does not maintain information on active hot spare pools. Therefore, if a hot spare pool is in use when the SVM configuration is lost, those volumes that are hot-spared may be corrupted.

To initialize SVM from a configuration file, perform the following steps:

1. Re-create state database replicas and then create or update the /etc/lvm/md.tab file.
2. Modify the md.tab file, depending on whether you are creating a new SVM configuration or recovering from the last known SVM configuration.
   - If you are creating a new SVM configuration based on a copy of md.tab, then copy the saved file to /etc/lvm/md.tab.
   - If you are attempting to recover the SVM configuration, copy the md.cf file to the md.tab file.
3. Edit the new md.tab file so that
   - All mirrors are one-way mirrors. If the submirrors of a mirror are not the same size, be sure to use the smallest submirror for this one-way mirror. Otherwise data could be lost.
   - RAID 5 volumes must be specified with the -k option to prevent reinitialization of the device.
4. Verify the syntax of the md.tab file entries. Use the metainit command to perform the syntax check. The -n option verifies the syntax of the command line or

/etc/lvm/md.tab entry without setting up the metadevice. When used with the -a option, it verifies all devices without initializing them. The -a option activates all metadevices defined in the /etc/lvm/md.tab file.

```
# metainit -n -a
```

5. Re-create the volumes and hot spare pools from the md.tab file by using the -a option with the metainit command:

```
# metainit -a
```

6. Run the metattach command to convert the one-way mirrors into multi-way mirrors.

7. Validate the data on the volumes.

ACCESSING THE SVM

To access and administer SVM, you must have root access. You can also administer SVM from the SMC if you have equivalent privileges assigned through the User Profile feature of the SMC. However, note that only root has the privilege to access the SVM command line interface.

The SVM graphical user interface is part of the SMC. To access it, perform the following steps:

1. Start SMC on the host system using the following command:

```
% /usr/sbin/smc
```

2. Access the This Computer option and then the Storage option within the expanded menu.

3. Double-click Enhanced Storage to load the SVM tools.

INCREASING THE NUMBER OF DEFAULT VOLUMES

In a storage device, you can increase the storage space by adding volumes. This helps improve performance and increase data availability. You can add volumes using the Enhanced Storage tool in the SMC or the command line. After you increase the number of volumes, you have the option of increasing the size of the file systems mounted within a volume.

The default volumes in the SVM configuration are

- 4 disk sets
- 128 volumes per disk set
- 8192 block state database replicas

You can increase the number of disk sets and the volumes per disk set. Note that after the increase, decreasing the default values can make the existing disk sets or the volumes unusable or unavailable.

12

To increase the number of disk sets, modify the md_nsets field in the md.conf file. After the modification, save your changes and perform a reconfiguration reboot to build the volume names by using the following command:

```
ok boot -r
```

The default volumes per disk set can be increased up to 8192. To increase the volumes, edit the /kernel/drv/md.conf file and change the value of the nmd field. Build the volume names by performing the reconfiguration reboot.

EXPANDING THE FILE SYSTEMS

When you increase the volumes, you must also increase the file systems in these volumes to recognize the added space. You can expand the file system to the size of the volume that contains the file system. You can manually grow the file system using the growfs command.

```
# growfs -M /dev/md/rdsk/d10
```

NOTE

> You cannot write to the volume while the growfs command is running.

SUN STOREDGE (VERITAS) VOLUME MANAGER

A software-based RAID tool, the Sun StorEdge (Veritas) Volume Manager provides easy-to-use, online disk storage management for large computing environments. This volume manager is ideal for enterprise computing environments and data-dependent organizations that require constant and consistent access to mission-critical data. Sun StorEdge (Veritas) Volume Manager provides disk usage analysis, RAID techniques, and the dynamic reconfiguration of disk storage while a system is online. This helps to ensure continuous data availability, ease of use, and data protection. It also provides centralized management and helps enhance system and application performance.

SUMMARY

Managing disks is a critical component of the overall system administration. A disk is composed of hardware components, such as platters, spindle, tracks, cylinders, sector, shaft, and disk controller, and software components, such as disk labels and device drivers.

A disk slice is a group of cylinders used by a file system. Eight disk slices are assigned to file systems. You can locate a file system in a disk slice by using a logical disk name. The file system in a disk is read in a specific logical order that includes slice number, drive number, physical bus target number, logical controller number, and disk subdirectory. The reading of data in the defined order is important because the use of the block and raw device interfaces by the disk and file administration commands depends upon how data is read from a device.

Solaris OE uses the format utility to perform certain administration tasks on a disk. For example, the format utility can be used to display slice information, format a disk drive, and repair a disk drive.

To install a new disk in the system, first install the boot block program to enable the loading of the actual OS. You use the `installboot` command to install the boot block program. The next step is to add and configure the disk. To do that, create the `/reconfigure` file that is read when the system is booting. Shut down the system and connect the disk to the system. Ensure all connections are made. Turn on the power and reboot the system. If you want to perform hot swap procedures, use the `cfgadm` utility.

Included with the Solaris 9 OE is a new Volume Management tool called the SVM. This tool has all the features of Sun Solstice Disk AdminSuite. It helps manage large numbers of disks, increase storage capacity, and improve I/O performance. SVM enables you to create volumes such as state database replicas, hot spare pools, and disk sets.

12

## CHAPTER 13

MANAGING SERIAL DEVICES

In this chapter

Modems and Terminals   220

Managing Modems and Terminals   221

Connecting Modems and Terminals   231

Troubleshooting Modems and Terminals   235

Summary   236

MODEMS AND TERMINALS

Central to the system administrator's responsibilities is enabling users to access distributed and shared system and network resources, such as file systems, applications, terminals, modems, printers, and so on. This chapter looks at the administration of the two network resources: terminals and modems.

In network computing, a *terminal* is a device that acts as the source and destination of data and controls the communication channel. A *modem* is a DCE (Data Communication Equipment) that uses RS-232C interface to exchange data with other computers over the network. DCE is an industry standard technology that provides the interface to enable communication in a distributed computing environment.

RS-232C is an industry standard ("C" refers to current version) defined by the Electronic Industry Association (EIA), which describes the physical interface and protocols for low-speed serial data communication between computers and related devices. RS-232C is the interface that a computer uses to exchange data with modems and other serial devices.

A port is a channel of communication between a device, such as modem, and the Operating System (OS). A port consists of software components such as device driver. It also contains hardware components. Ports when referred to as hardware entity consist of pins and connectors. To explain further, a port can be described as a receptacle with a slot for cables and connectors to which serial devices such as terminals or modems are plugged with cables. Some of the commonly used ports are serial, parallel, small computer systems interface (SCSI), ethernet, Universal Serial Bus (USB), FireWire, audio, and composite.

A serial port transfers information in bits over a single line by using a standard communication protocol. Examples of serial port devices include modems, alphanumeric terminals, and plotters. Generally RS-232-C or RS-423 standards are used in their design.

It is possible to connect several serial port devices to a single computer by using an adapter board. This board provides additional serial ports that help you connect more devices to your computer.

Modems and terminals are connected to the serial ports of a computer. Serial ports provide a standard connector and protocol to let you attach devices, such as modems, to your computer and to enable communications between them.

The name *serial* comes from the fact that a serial port serializes data. That is, it takes a byte of data and transmits the 8 bits in the byte one at a time.

This chapter describes everything you need to know about modems, terminals, and ports, including the method to connect asynchronous modems and terminals to a SPARC workstation/server. However, before describing the steps to connect modems and terminals, it's important to look into the methods to manage and administer these devices. There are certain administrative tools, utilities, and commands that you must understand to be able to perform tasks such as installing, configuring, and connecting modems and terminals.

13

MANAGING MODEMS AND TERMINALS

Different versions of Unix provide several processes and interfaces for administration. For example, HP-UX uses sam, Linux uses wvdial, and so on. The following tools were introduced with Solaris to administer and manage modems and terminals.

- **Service Access Facility (SAF)**—SAF, introduced with Solaris 2.3, is a tool that provides a common interface for the management of different physical resources such as modems, terminals, and other network devices. This helps in the uniform management of the physical resources from a common location.

- **Solaris Management Console (SMC)** —As stated in the earlier chapters, SMC provides a suite of GUI-based system administration tools. It can be used to perform administration tasks on modems and terminals such as configuring and setting up modems and terminals, viewing serial port properties, initializing ports without configuring them, and removing port services.

The following sections describe in detail the different ways to use SAF and SMC to administer modems, terminals, ports, and services.

SAF

Solaris comes with a central access facility known as SAF. Any discussion of device administration under Solaris is incomplete if it doesn't cover SAF. It is important for system administrators to have a good understanding of SAF if they are going to perform device administration tasks.

SAF consists of a group of daemons and administrative commands, which enable you to administer system and network resources through tty devices and local-area networks (LANs). You can use SAF to administer port monitors. This facilitates users to log in from a terminal or modem and use network resources. SAF uses the service access controller (SAC) daemon to monitor ports. Primary components of SAF are SAC, port monitors, and port services (see Figure 13.1). In the SAF hierarchy of components, SAC is at the highest level. SAC is a program that is used to manage port monitors, which serve as the next commander-in-control. Port monitors are used to manage the ports to which the devices, modems, and terminals are connected. They also manage the associated port services.

13

Figure 13.1
SAF hierarchy.

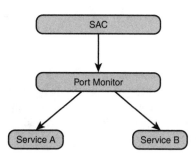

In the following section, you learn about the various commands each of these SAF components use to administer and manage modems and terminals.

SAC

When a system enters init level 2 during the boot phase, the SAC program is automatically invoked based on the entry in the /etc/inittab file. This entry for SAC is automatically included in the /etc/inittab file when Solaris is installed. This file contains the following entry supporting SAC:

```
sc:234:respawn:/usr/lib/saf/sac -t 300
```

In the preceding entry, the -t option defines the time frame within which SAC checks the status of the port monitors. The time frame is measured in seconds. In this example, the time frame defined is 300 seconds.

When the SAC program is invoked, it initiates all the port monitors that the system administrator has created and configured. When SAC is generated, it locates two files: /etc/saf/_sysconfig and /etc/saf/_sactab. The /etc/saf/_sysconfig file is a SAC-specific configuration file. SAC uses this file to customize its own environment governing all the services it controls. The services can be any TCP- or UDP-based services. When SAC is invoked by init(), it reads and interprets the /etc/saf/_sysconfig file prior to the invocation of any service defined in the /etc/saf/_sactab file.

After customizing its environment, SAC fetches the /etc/saf/_sactab file. This file is the administrative file that contains entries related to the port monitor defined by the system administrator. SAC uses this file to determine the type of port monitor to invoke. Listing 13.1 displays the entries in the /etc/saf/_sactab file.

LISTING 13.1   OUTPUT OF THE /etc/saf/_sactab FILE

```
# VERSION=1
cgmon:ttymon::0:/usr/lib/saf/ttymon #
```

Table 13.1 describes each option of the preceding entry in the /etc/saf/_sactab file.

TABLE 13.1   OPTIONS IN THE /etc/saf/_sactab FILE

Options	Decription
VERSION = 1	Specifies the version of SAF.
cgmon	Indicates the name of the port monitor.
ttymon	Indicates the type of port monitor. There are two types of port monitors: ttymon and listen. The ttymon port monitor is used to install, configure, and monitor the tty port services. The listen port monitor uses TCP/IP and helps to provide port services, such as printing and other network services.

13

Options	Decription
::	Indicates the status of the port monitor. Two options can be used to indicate the status: option d and option x. If the status is disabled, option d can be used to start the port monitor. If flagged x, only the system administrator can start the port monitor manually.
0	Specifies the number of times the port monitor should be restarted in case it fails to start. The default count value is zero.
/usr/lib/saf/ttymon	Specifies the pathname for the port monitor.

PORT MONITOR

The SAC invokes the port monitor during system startup. Port monitors are used to administer port activities, such as setting the line speed on incoming phone connections, reinitializing a port when the service terminates, and binding an appropriate network address. Port monitors are also used to monitor port activities, where they monitor incoming port requests, restrict access to systems, and create utmpx entries.

> **NOTE**
> The utmpx database contains user access and accounting information for commands such as who, write, and login.

When a service request is received at a port, the port monitor determines which service request is being made from the port. Port monitors can restrict access to a system without interfering with the currently running services. To be able to do this, the port monitor should be able to maintain two states: enable and disable. The state of the port monitors is defined by the ISTATE variable. SAC creates two environment variables: ISTATE and pmtag. ISTATE is used to indicate to the port monitor what its initial internal state should be. ISTATE is set to enabled or disabled to indicate whether the port monitor is to start in the enabled or disabled mode. The pmtag variable defines the identity of the port monitor. In addition, port monitors are used to create UTMP entries.

There are two types of port monitors: ttymon and listen. The ttymon port monitor provides access to the login services. The listen port monitor provides access to network services, such as printing. Note that the Solaris OE does not support listen by default.

The sacadm command is used to configure the listen port monitor. Each instance of listen can provide multiple services. These services are specified in the port monitor's administrative file. The pmadm and nlsadmin commands are used to configure the administrative file.

For more information on setting up a port listener service, view man pages for pmadm and nlsadmin commands.

Port monitors are administered and managed with the sacadm command. This command is used to perform the following tasks:

13

- Create and remove port monitors.
- Check the status of the port monitor.
- Enable and disable the port monitor.

To create a port monitor, use the following command:

```
#sacadm -a -p<pmtag> -t<type> -c"<pm_cmd>" -v ver ➥
[-fd|x]\[-n<count>][-y"comment"]
```

The options used with the sacadm command are described in Table 13.2.

TABLE 13.2 OPTIONS USED WITH THE sacadm COMMAND

Options	Description
-a	Adds or creates a port monitor.
-p <pmtag>	Defines the name of the port monitor.
-t <type>	Specifies the port monitor type to create (ttymon or listen).
-c "<pm_cmd>"	Specifies the command to run associated port monitors.
-v ver	Specifies the version of the port monitor. If you want to find out the version of either ttymon or listen, use the relevant administration command, ttyadm or nlsadmin, and pass -V option as an argument to -v. For example, you can invoke the nlsadmin command to determine the version of the listen port monitor by using the command #sacadm -a...-v'nlsadmin -V'.
-f[d|x]	Specifies the relevant state of the port monitor.
-n <count>	Defines the number of times to restart a failing port monitor.
-v (ver)	Specifies the version number of the port monitor.

When the port monitor is created, a directory called /etc/saf/<pmtag> is created. As described in Table 13.1, <pmtag> is the tag name specified for the port monitor. For example, if you create a port with a tag name PM1, the directory called /etc/saf/PM1 is created. This directory maintains port-specific files, /etc/saf/PM1/_config and /etc/saf/PM1/_pmtab. The functionalities of these two files are similar to the SAC files. The /etc/saf/PM1/_config is used to customize the port monitor's environment.

The /etc/saf/<pmtag>/_pmtab file is the port monitor administrative file that contains port monitor-specific configuration instructions for the services the port monitor provides. The port monitor uses the /etc/saf/<pmtag>/_pmtab file to bring up the associated port services. This file can be modified by the pmadm command to create, delete, or modify the port services. Use the pmadm command to modify the /etc/saf/<pmtag>/_pmtab file. You can use this command to create new ports, delete the existing ones, and modify port information as required.

You can check the status of the port monitor by using the following command:

```
# sacadm -t<type> -|
```

The -t option obtains a listing of all port monitors of the same type.

```
# sacadm -l -p<pmtag> -l
```

To obtain information about a specific port monitor, use the -p option with the sacadm command. If you created a port monitor named zsmon, you would need to enter the following command to check its status:

```
# sacadm -l -p zsmon
PMTAG          PMTYPE        FLGS RCNT STATUS    COMMAND
zsmon          ttymon         -    0   ENABLED   /usr/lib/saf/ttymon
```

Notice that the status field indicates that the port monitor is enabled. If you check the status immediately after the port monitor is created, the status field may indicate that it is starting.

The port monitor can be in one of the following states:

- **Started**—This is a default state. The port monitor is automatically started as soon as it is added. To start a port monitor, use the sacadm -s -p <pmtag> command. The -s option specifies the start port monitor status flag.

- **Enabled**—In this state, the port monitor accepts requests for service by default when it is added. To enable a port monitor, use the command sacadm -e -p <pmtag>. The -e option specifies the enabled status.

- **Stopped**—Just as the port monitor is enabled when it is added, in the same manner, it is stopped if removed. To remove a port monitor, use the -r option in conjunction with the sacadm command.

- **Disabled**—In this state, the port monitor stops accepting new requests for services when it is removed. However, note that it continues to run existing services. The port monitor is disabled when you use the -d option with the sacadm command.

- **Starting**—This is a transitional state when the port monitor is in the process of starting.

- **Stopping**—This again is a transitional stage when the port monitor is in the process of shutting down. When the port monitor enters the stopping state, no further service requests are accepted. Also, any attempt to re-enable the port monitor is ignored. In this state, the port monitor gives up control of all the ports it controls.

- **Not Running**—In this inactive state, the port monitor is killed and all port services associated with port monitor are inactive.

TTYMON

The port monitor ttymon is used to monitor port services that include requests such as login or access to printers and files. When a login request is generated during the port initialization phase, the port monitor sets the parameters that are required to establish communication between the operating system and the requesting device. Next, it transfers the control to the processes that will provide the requested service.

13

NOTE

> In earlier Unix versions, the utilities `getty` and `uugetty` were used to monitor port services.

Let us look at the complete port initialization phase and the role of ttymon in the same in more detail. Figure 13.2 illustrates the port initialization process and the working of ttymon.

Figure 13.2
The role of the ttymon daemon in the port initialization phase.

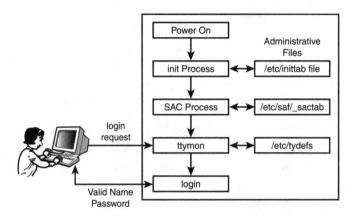

As shown in the figure, when the system boots, the init program is started. This program refers the `/etc/inittab` file. The init program starts the SAC process that is listed in the `/etc/inittab` file. The SAC process automatically starts the port monitors designated in the administrative file `/etc/saf/_sactab`.

In this example, SAC starts ttymon. After it is started, ttymon monitors the serial port lines for service requests such as login requests. When there is a request from the user terminal, the serial port driver passes the request to the operating system. The ttymon port monitor notes the serial port activity and attempts to establish a communications link. It also determines what baud rate, hand-shaking protocol, and line discipline are required to communicate with the user terminal. It then initializes the baud rate and line disciplines. The values used for initialization are taken from the appropriate entry in the `/etc/ttydefs` file.

NOTE

> The `/etc/ttydefs` is an administrative file that contains information that ttymon uses to set up speed and terminal settings for a tty port.

Next, ttymon writes the prompt and waits for user input. If the user indicates that the speed is inappropriate by pressing the Break key, ttymon tries the next speed and writes the prompt again. If autobaud, a feature of ttymon, is enabled for a port, ttymon tries to determine the baud rate on the port automatically. The autobaud feature allows `ttymon` to automatically determine the line speed suitable to the connected terminal. Note that users must press the Return key before ttymon can recognize the baud rate and print the prompt. After initializing the relevant parameters for communication with the user terminal, ttymon passes these parameters to the login program and transfers control to it.

LISTEN

The listen process "listens" for network service requests, accepts requests when they arrive, and starts services in response to the requests. The listen monitoring process is invoked and controlled by SAC. This port monitor runs on any transport provider, such as TCP/IP. The listen port monitor supports two classes of service: a class of general services, such as RFS and network printing; and terminal login services for terminals trying to access the system by connecting directly to the network.

Like ttymon, listen can support and monitor multiple ports, with each assigned a network service to care for. After it is invoked, the listen port monitor initializes port services as defined in its /etc/saf/<pmtag>/_pmtab file. It then monitors the ports for service connection requests. After a request is received on a listen port, the associated service is invoked and the user is connected to it.

PORT SERVICE

As discussed earlier, the port service provides relevant service to devices, modems, and terminals that are attached to the port. For example, you can set up a serial port to provide dial-in, dial-out, and dial-in/dial-out services to a modem. The dial-in service allows remote systems to access your local machine, but it does not allow the local machine to access the remote computers. When the dial-out service is configured in a specific local machine, users using the local machine can access remote systems. However, the dial-out service prevents the remote systems from accessing this local machine. The dial-in/dial-out service provides bi-directional capabilities where the modem can be used to dial both in and out.

To gain access to the port services, the port monitor is used. The port service closely interacts with the system-level services, such as printer service and network service. This service monitors and controls the applications using the physical ports, such as tty and TCP/IP. The tty port monitor enables users to use dial-out utilities such as UUCP and cu. TCP/IP provides services such as printing and NFS services across the network.

The port service is the lowest administrative service in the SAF hierarchy. Being the lowest, this service does not have any administrative files associated with it. You use the pmadm command to perform administrative tasks on the port service. This command can be used to create, modify, enable, disable, and remove a port service.

NOTE

> You should create the port monitor before you create and manage the associated port services.

Before the port service is created, the following two resources should be available:

- tty ports
- a suitable record in the /etc/ttydefs file

To obtain a list of all tty ports that are currently in use, use the command `pmadm -l -t ttymon`.

```
#pmadm -l -t ttymon
PMTAG          PMTYPE         SVCTAG        FLGS ID        <PMSPECIFIC>
zsmon          ttymon         ttyb          u    root      /dev/term/b I - /usr/
bin/login - 9600 ldterm,ttcompat ttyb login:  - tvi925 y  #
```

Next, list the contents of the `/etc/ttydefs` file by entering the command `sttydefs -l`, and examine its contents for the record and label that match your terminal needs. If you do not find one, then you ought to add the desired entry to the database yourself by using the `sttydefs` command.

To create a port service, use the `pmadm` command with the `-a` option. The following command creates a port service:

```
# pmadm -a -p<pmtag> -s<svctag> -m"pmspecific" \
-v ver[-fx|u] -y"comment"
```

In the preceding command, `-p<pmtag>` specifies the port monitor tag, and `-s<svctag>` specifies the port service tag. The port-specific information that needs to be passed as an argument to the `pmadm` command is specified by the `-m"pmspecific"` option. The `-v <ver>` option specifies the version of the port monitor. Note that both the output for `-m` and `-v` options is port monitor-specific. Depending on the type of the port monitor, either ttymon or nlsadmin can be used in command substitution mode. Next, the `-f` option specifies the status in which the port service will be started. This service can either be started in the disabled state or a UTMP service can be created for the service. The UTMP service holds user accounting information for commands such as `who`, `write`, and `login`.

You have the option to list and check the status of all port monitor services or a specific port monitor service. The following command checks the status of all the port monitor services:

```
# pmadm -| -p<pmtag>
```

To check the status of a specific port monitor service, specify the service tag along with the port monitor tag.

```
# pmadm -| -p<pmtag> -s<svctag>
```

To enable, disable, or remove a port service, use the following command. This command enables the port service. It uses the `-e` option in conjunction with the `pmadm` command to enable the port service.

```
#pmadm -p<pmtag> -s<svctag> -e
```

Use the `-d` option with the `pmadm` command to disable a port service.

```
#pmadm -p<pmtag> -s<svctag> -d
```

The `-r` option used with the `pmadm` command removes a port service.

```
#pmadm -p<pmtag> -s<svctag> -r
```

SMC

SMC provides a common user interface for configuring and managing serial ports. You can configure a serial port to provide a terminal or modem service. A modem can provide three types of services: dial in, dial out, or dial in/dial out. However, note that to be able to configure the serial ports, you need appropriate access rights. Usually, users with primary or system administrator authorization levels can perform these tasks.

Implement the following steps to configure a serial port for a dial-in modem:

1. Start SMC, if it is not already running.

2. Select the Devices and Hardware item in the Navigation pane. This item contains the serial ports option.

3. Double-click the Serial Ports option to see a list of existing ports. Figure 13.3 displays two serial ports, a and b.

Figure 13.3
Serial ports a and b displayed in SMC.

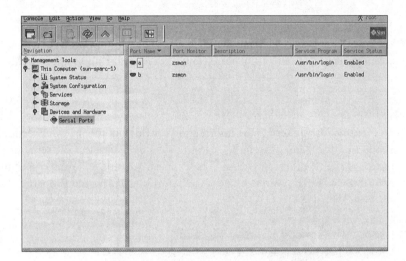

4. To configure a port for the dial-in only modem, select the port in the right pane. Next, click Action, Configure, and Modem (Dial in) option. Notice that the Configure submenu contains the options to configure the serial port for terminal and other modem services (see Figure 13.4).

Figure 13.4
Configure submenu.

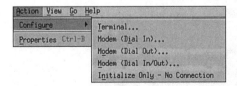

13

5. The Configure Serial Port a: Modem—Dial In Only dialog box appears. This dialog box enables you to enable or disable the service. In addition, it enables you to select the line speed that will be used to communicate over the serial port (see Figure 13.5) .

Figure 13.5
Configure Serial Port
a: Modem–Dial In
Only.

Note that if you no longer require the services of a port, you can remove it by right-clicking the relevant port and selecting the Delete Port Service option. When you delete a port service, the relevant entry of the port service is removed from the port monitor's administrative file.

INITIALIZING AND DISABLING PORTS

You can modify the serial port information provided in the previous section by using the Properties dialog box as well. To access this dialog box, select the serial port in the right pane and click Action, Properties. The Properties dialog box can be used to set some basic and advanced serial port information. Figure 13.6 displays the Properties dialog box with the Basic tab page open.

Figure 13.6
Properties dialog box.

This dialog box provides the option to enable or disable the port service. It also gives you the option to set the line speed, terminal type, and the login prompt. The terminal type defines the terminal you want to access through this serial port. For example, you could specify the terminal type to be vt100, ANSI, or tvi925. Note that no matter which terminal type you specify, it should be listed in the file /etc/termcap. This file defines the escape sequence by which terminals can be controlled.

> **NOTE**
>
> An escape sequence is a series of special characters that can send commands to a device. Generally, escape sequences are specified starting with an escape character. An example of an escape sequence can be the audible bell, with code `bl`. This escape sequence usually appears as `bl=^G`. The sequence tells that the bell sound is obtained by printing the CTRL-G character.

The Advanced page in the Properties dialog box (see Figure 13.7) is used to set advanced serial port information. The Carrier Detection section in this page specifies the carrier type, which can be either hardware or software.

Figure 13.7
Advanced page in the Properties dialog box.

The default port monitor entered in the Port Monitor field is zsmon.

When the Connect on Service check box is selected, it specifies whether the port's associated service will be started immediately after the port monitor receives a request for the service.

When Bidirectional is checked, the serial port is enabled to send information in both directions: input and output.

The Initialize Only Connection Check Box window, when selected, specifies that the port is initialized but not configured.

Now that you have learned about the different utilities to administer modems and terminals, it's time to look at how to set up and establish connections for the two devices.

CONNECTING MODEMS AND TERMINALS

Most Unix platforms offer powerful serial connections that support both modem and terminal services, such as remote login and file transfer services. A properly wired and configured serial interface is a basic requirement that is common to both types of services.

13

The standard interface used to perform external modems/terminal connections is RS232C/D. It defines the interface between DTE and DCE. In practical terms, and for the purposes of this section, this means that it defines the physical interface between a computer that is the Data Terminal Equipment (the DTE) and the modem that is the Data Communication Equipment (the DCE). It also defines the connection between two DTEs.

NOTE

The RS232C/D standard interface in now known as EIA/TIA 232.

The RS232C/D interface defines the standards for how data is transferred over the wire, the connector type, the number of pins supported and what each pin stands for, and the handshake mechanism. To specify the data transfer within the wire, RS232C/D defines what voltage level represents which logical level. For example, RS232C/D also specifies what type of connector will be used for the connection. DB25 is the default connector specified for the RS232C/D interface. DB9 is a new connector that has been defined for modem usage. Used for serial applications such as mouse, modem, and null modem, the DB9 connector has nine pins arranged in two rows, one on top of the other. The top row has five pins and the lower row has four pins. Figure 13.8 displays the DB9 connector.

Figure 13.8
The DB9 connector.

The DB25 connector is used for parallel, serial, or SCSI applications, such as, nullmodem, printer, scanner, and removable storage drive. The DB25 connector has 25 pins arranged in two rows one on top of the other. The top row has 13 pins and the lower row has 12 pins. Figure 13.9 displays the DB25 connector.

Figure 13.9
The DB25 connector.

Last but not least, the handshake mechanism specified by the RS232C/D defines the exchange of data between DTE and DCE or DTE and DTE. The most common requirement is for flow control to match the rate of data transmission to the rate at which it can be processed at the receiving end. For example, the modem indicates to a computer when it is able to accept more data.

The handshake mechanism is enabled and disabled by the XON and XOFF controls. These controls specify the stopping and starting of data transmission between the computer and the terminal. The stty command is used to set them. The options that can be used with the stty command are ixon and ixoff. For example, to enable the transmission of data between devices, use the following command:

stty *ixon*

These commands can also be set in the /etc/inittab or /etc/gettydefs files.

However, there are certain disadvantages to using the XON and XOFF controls. These controls cannot be used for transferring binary data, and they are unreliable on noisy communication lines. As an alternative to these controls, you can use the RTS (Ready-to-Send) and CTS (Clear-to-Send) controls. When the computer is ready to transmit data, it enables the RTS circuit. It then waits for the modem to give permission by enabling the CTS circuit. This usage of the RTS/CTS circuit pair applies to the half-duplex mode of communications. In full-duplex communications, RTS and CTS circuits are used to control the flow of data between the DTE and the DCE devices. The DTE drops its RTS circuit to request the DCE to stop sending data on DTE's receive circuit. Likewise, the DCE drops the CTS to request the DTE to stop sending data on the transmit circuit.

Let us now look at how the physical connections between DTE to DCE and DTE to DTE are established.

Figures 13.10 and 13.11 illustrate the two types of connections.

Figure 13.10
Connection between
DTE and DCE.

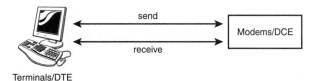

In Figure 13.10, the modem connects to the terminal, where data is exchanged between the two devices asynchronously. Should two DTE's need connection without the modems, a Null Modem adaptor would be required. This adaptor swaps wires between pins in such a way that each DTE device appears to be a DCE device to the other. Figure 13.11 illustrates the connection of two DTEs where the null modem acts as the interface between the two.

Figure 13.11
Connection between
two DTEs.

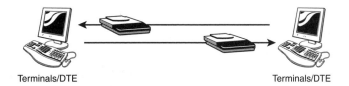

Understanding the connection between DTE and DCE is fairly easy. The connection between DTE and DCE is implemented using a straightforward concept where the pins in the DTE and DCE ports transmit the data between the two devices over a cable.

If you look again at the DTE-to-DCE connection (refer to Figure 13.10), the receive circuit of the modem acknowledges the send circuit from a computer. This forms an Rx- (Receive Data) to-Rx or Tx- (Transmit Data) to-Tx connection. However, it may actually make one wonder how is it possible to connect two DTEs. If the two DTEs were to be connected under the same concept, then in all likelihood there would be data collision. To take care of this situation, the cables are cross-wired as shown in Figure 13.11. This cross-wired cable is also known as the *Null Modem* cable. This means that the receive circuit of one terminal is cross-wired with the transmit circuit of the second terminal. This forms Rx-to-Tx and Tx-to-Rx connections.

Now that you have learned how to make physical connections between devices, the next step is to configure them. The following steps provide the method to configure and set up a modem.

1. The first step to configure the modem is to verify that no active port monitor services are running. To check whether any port services are active, issue the command `pmadm -p zsmon -l` (see Figure 13.12). Notice that the service ttyb is enabled. Remove the service by using the `pmadm -p zsmon -r -s ttyb` command.

Figure 13.12
Verifying active port services.

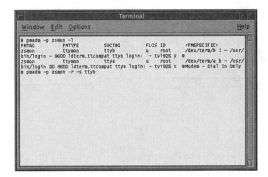

When used with the -r option, the `pmadm` command removes the port service tag defined with the -s option. In this example, the service tag ttyb is removed. You can verify all active port services by issuing the `pmadm -l -p zsmon` command.

2. The next step is to establish connection with the modem by using either the `tip` or the `cu` command. The `tip` command is used to establish connection with the remote host.
   `tip -38400 /dev/cua/a`

3. You can check to see whether the modem responds to commands by using AT commands. The AT commands refer to modem connection commands and are specific to the modem manufacturer. Refer to the documentation from the modem manufacturer for further information.

4. Check whether the modem can provide both dial-in and dial-out services by verifying the `/etc/ttydefs`, `/etc/uucp/dialers`, and `/etc/uucp/devices`. Add the following entries to the file `/etc/ttydefs`. These are the serial port characteristics presented by the answering side.

```
115200:115200 hupcl:115200 hupcl::76800
76800:76800 hupcl:76800 hupcl::57600
57600:57600 hupcl:57600 hupcl::38400
38400:38400 hupcl:38400 hupcl::19200
19200:19200 hupcl:19200 hupcl::9600
9600:9600 hupcl:9600 hupcl::4800
```

5. After establishing the port connections, configure the modem using SMC as specified in the section, "SMC." If you do not have SMC, you also can use the command line to configure the modem. To configure from the command line, edit the `pm_script` file. Specify the baud rate usage, service name usage, and the port monitor type in this file.

```
ttydefs=9600m
mport=/dev/term/b
service=ttyb
pmadm -a -pzsmon -s $ service…
```

6. Change the file permission for execution by issuing the following command:

```
chmod 755 pm_script
```

7. Finally, use the `pmadm` command to verify whether the port monitor you configured is enabled.

TROUBLESHOOTING MODEMS AND TERMINALS

This section describes troubleshooting tips to manage modem or terminal malfunctioning.

Some typical problems that usually occur with modems and terminals can be related to login failures, terminal problems, serial connection problems, and so on. The possible causes for login failures include the following factors:

- Incorrect login credentials provided by the user.
- Problems with the terminal, such as incorrect terminal configuration, being shut off, or having no power.
- Serial cable is loose or unplugged.

To troubleshoot login problems, check the configuration of the terminal or the modem. Determine the relevant ttylabel to communicate with the modem or the terminal.

Another possible cause could be problems occurring in the terminal server. If the terminal checks out, continue to search for the source of the problem on the terminal or the modem server. Use the `pmadm` command to verify that a port monitor has been configured to service the terminal or modem and that it has the correct ttylabel associated with it.

```
$ pmadm -l -t ttymon
```

13

Examine /etc/ttydefs and double check the label definition against the terminal configuration. Use sacadm to check the port monitor's status. Use pmadm to check the service associated with the port the terminal uses.

Problems in the serial connection can also cause failure in the modems and terminals. Check the SAC to check for problems with the serial connection. If the SAC starts the tty port monitor and pmadm reports that the service for the terminal's port is enabled, and if the terminal's configuration matches the port monitor's, then continue to search for the problem by checking the serial connection. A serial connection comprises serial ports, cables, and terminals. Test each of these parts by using it with two other parts that are known to be reliable.

SUMMARY

Among the resources system administrators have to manage are terminals and modems. To manage these resources, Solaris provides two tools: SAF and SAC. SAF recognizes a three-level hierarchy of processes: SAC (service access controller), port monitors, and port services. At the top of the hierarchy is SAC, which is responsible for invoking the port monitors. Next in the hierarchy is the port monitor used to monitor the port services. The two types of port monitors are ttymon and listen. Whereas ttymon administers service requests received via the serial (or tty) ports, listen administers across-the-network services.

After SAF is set up appropriately, the administrator can provide all kinds of services, including dial-in, dial-out, and bi-directional services. As described earlier in the chapter, you can use the SMC or the command line to set up these services.

13

CHAPTER **14**

MANAGING PRINTING

In this chapter

Solaris Printing Services   238

LP Print Service   240

Solaris Print Manager   246

Using lp Commands for Printer Administration   249

Summary   257

SOLARIS PRINTING SERVICES

Since the days of the printing press, governments and business organizations have used printed documents to communicate, record information, and to conduct business transactions. The advent of the information age and the resultant move toward a paperless office has not eliminated the need for printed material. Instead, the information age has spawned new office equipment in the form of the printer. In the networking scenario existing today, printers are important resources supported by any OS that is used to manage a network.

Solaris provides a wide range of printing services that are used to establish, administer, and customize printing facilities on a network. To implement these services, Solaris provides components such as the Print Manager and the LP Print Service. You will be introduced to these components in the course of the chapter. Before learning about the various Solaris printing service components, however, it is important to acquire a bird's eye view of how a typical Solaris printing environment operates.

On a network, printers can be installed as local printers, shared printers, or network printers. Local printers do not service computers on the network other than the computers to which they are physically attached. Shared printers are local printers that are shared with other computers on the network. Computers that share the services of their printer with other computers are called *print servers*. Network printers do not depend on a print server to provide printing services. Instead, they are directly attached to the network and are provided with IP addresses and names, which give them network identities just like any other computers on the network. However, network printers continue to use a print server for tasks such as queuing, filtering, and printer administration. Computers that utilize the services of a print server or a network printer are termed *print clients*.

The Solaris OS installed on the client and the server provides print services that manage the printing features on the client and the server. Now, consider a scenario where the printing needs of a small Solaris network are serviced by a print server. When a user working from a client initiates the print process by issuing a print command, the print service on the client interprets the command as a print request. The client print service processes the command to identify the print server servicing the network. After identifying the print server, the client print service directs the print request to the server. Now, the server print service redirects the print request to the printer to produce the printed document.

To implement such an environment, Solaris provides two important components that form the crux of its print services: the Print Manager and LP Print Service. The Print Manager is a GUI administration utility that provides easy print service administration on any Solaris server or workstation. Although printing service administration can be managed with the Print Manager, the utility itself runs as a GUI front end for the LP Print Service component, which manages printing services by using a host of commands and programs. Before delving into the intricacies of the Print Manager and the LP Print Service components, let us analyze certain requirements that must be complied within the design of a Solaris printing environment.

14

PRINTER ENVIRONMENT DESIGN CONSIDERATIONS

On large corporate networks where the number of users requiring printing services is high, the printer is an important network resource. Before installing printers on such networks it is essential to take into account certain design considerations. Consider a scenario where the various departments in an organization are located on different floors of a building. You need to ensure that each floor has a printer dedicated to the printing needs of a particular department. Therefore, multiple print servers might be required for the network, with each print server managing print requests for its department or floor. The advantage you can derive in implementing multiple print servers is that the servers act as backups, providing print support when any print server is unable to process requests. However, some users need to have local printers installed with their computers. For example, human resource executives might need to use the printer more frequently than other users in the organization.

Apart from the printing requirements specific to each organization or the departments in the organization, it is essential to implement certain system requirements for a print server. The print server performs the vital role of accepting and redirecting print requests from a large number of clients on a network. Therefore, the performance of the print server determines the efficiency of the printing services available on the system. Some of the system requirements for a print server include hard disk, memory, disk space for handling print requests, and page swap features.

Estimating the optimum hard disk space that will be required on a print server is an important system requirement. The print server hard disks need to manage many print requests, as well as print requests of varying sizes. For example, certain print requests, such as image files or large documents, might contain large-sized data to be printed. The hard disk space on a print server that is used to queue and process print requests is called *spooling space*. In the Solaris file system, spooling space is determined by the size of the /var/spool/lp directory. The print requests received by the print server are stored and redirected for printing from the /var/spool/lp directory.

If the /var directory requires more space than what is available on the hard disk, you can utilize additional disk space available on other computers by mounting the remote computer file systems. You need to allocate approximately 600MB for the /var directory if you anticipate large numbers of print requests or large-sized print requests. However, the size of the directory depends on the types of print requests that are fired on a network. For example, the print server servicing the software solutions department of an organization needs to manage large numbers of print requests or large-sized print requests. Employees in that department print code, design documents, and other documents essential in developing software solutions. On the other hand, print requests in the client services department of the organization will be confined to requests for printing small-sized documents related to client details or client complaints. Print servers servicing print requests in such scenarios can contain a spool directory sized at 20MB to 25MB.

14

NOTE

> Although it is possible to mount the /var directory from remote computer file systems, to get better performance from the print server you need to create the spooling directory on the server's local hard disk. It is easier to process print requests from the /var file on the local hard disk than to perform the same operation from a remote /var directory mounted over the network.

In addition to setting the hardware requirements for a print server, you can configure certain vital information related to the print server. This enables client print services to identify print servers easily. For example, you can set the printer name, description, type, and the printer port at the time of installing the printer on the print server. Clients can use this information, also known as *printer definitions*, to identify the printer easily, thereby increasing the efficiency of print services provided to the user. To set the printer definitions, you can use the Print Manager or the LP Print Service commands. Although Print Manager can be used to set printer definitions, some of the options, such as fault recovery information, cannot be set with the Print Manager. On the other hand, LP Print Services commands enable you to define all printer definitions on the print server.

→ For more information about LP commands, **see** "lp commands," **p.241**.

LP PRINT SERVICE

At the very heart of the Solaris Print Service lies a set of commands, utilities, and programs collectively known as the LP Print Service. Apart from several command line utilities, the LP Print Service includes the Print Manager, which provides a GUI to manage print and spooling services. Some of the tasks the LP Print Service performs include scheduling local requests and client print requests, filtering data contained in a request, activating print programs, tracking print jobs, and firing alerts to notify users about problems or the need for new printer accessories. To implement these features, the LP Print Service provides vital components such as the following:

- User commands
- Administrative commands
- Configuration files
- LP daemons and filters
- Terminfo database
- LP activity logs
- Client request staging component
- Client request redirection component
- Spooling directory

You will learn about these components in the following sections.

1p COMMANDS

1p commands, which initiate and manage the print services, form the most basic component of the LP Print Service. 1p commands form a part of the command line utilities provided by Solaris. 1p commands are classified into user commands and administrative commands. Users working from a client computer send print requests with user commands. Administrative commands are used on both the client and the server to manage printers and printing requests. The following list provides a brief description of the 1p commands.

- **1p**—Submits a print request to a local printer, network printer, or a print server. This command is a user command that the print service software on the client computer uses to post a request to the server.

- **1padmin**—Manages the LP Print Service by performing administrative tasks, such as adding, removing, or changing printers, setting default destinations for print clients, and defining alerts for printer errors or for mounting printer wheels. This command can be described as the most important administrative command that is used for administering the LP Print Service.

- **disable**—Deactivates a printer and restricts the processing of print requests. This command is an administration command that is specified on a print server to disable printers. Printers might need to be disabled to enable printer maintenance work.

- **enable**—Activates the printer and allows it to process print requests. This command is an administration command that can be used on a print server to reactivate a printer after it has been disabled.

- **accept**—Queues print requests the server receives that are submitted for processing from clients. This command is used as an administrative command on a print server.

- **reject**—Terminates print requests submitted by a client. The command is used on a print server to reject print requests that the server has yet to process. You can use this command to restrict the print server from processing print requests when the printer is unavailable for servicing the requests.

- **1pstat**—Displays the status of a print request submitted by the user. You can use this command to obtain the status of all print requests submitted to the server.

- **cancel**—Cancels a print request submitted by a user. You need to specify an identification number called the request ID with the cancel command to successfully terminate a print request. You also can use the command to cancel all print requests submitted by a particular user or the print request that is being processed currently by the printer.

- **1pfilter**—Manages filters on a print server. Filters are used to convert the contents of a file submitted as a print request into a format that is compatible with the file format the printer uses.

14

- **lpmove**—Transfers print requests destined for a particular printer to another printer. This administration command transfers the destination printer specified by the lp command when submitting a print request.

- **lpshed**—Activates the scheduler component of the LP Print Service on a client or print server. The command is also used to restart the scheduler if it has been turned off temporarily.

- **lpshut**—Terminates the LP Print Service scheduler. An administrator can use this administration command to terminate the service on a print server.

- **lpusers**—Assigns priority levels for print requests submitted by a particular user. This administration command can be used on a print server to set priorities for print requests.

CONFIGURATION FILES

Configuration files provide vital information the client uses to identify the print server and to submit print requests. In addition, configuration files contain information on the printer that processes the print request. The files are located in the /etc/lp directory. The following list describes each configuration file:

- **printers**—Provides configuration information about the local printer attached to the computer. Configuration information includes information on the printer type and the alert information for each printer type.

- **fd**—Provides information about the filters that are used to format print requests.

- **classes**—Provides information on the printer classes that are used to define and identify the printer.

- **filter.table**—Provides a filter lookup table that contains filter entries related to a particular printer.

- **forms**—Provides information on the directory location where files related to forms need to be stored.

- **interfaces**—Provides information on interfaces that act as intermediaries between the print service software and the printer hardware device.

- **pwheels**—Provides information related to printer wheels, printer cartridges, or other printer accessories.

- **logs**—Provides information on the printer logs that record printer activities.

THE SCHEDULER

To manage and oversee the print process, LP Print Service provides a program run by the lpsched deamon. This program, called the scheduler, can be described as the software equivalent of a system administrator who oversees the printing process.

14

To describe the role of a scheduler, you need to start from the point when the scheduler receives the print request from a user. On receipt of the request, the scheduler first checks for information on the default printer, and the filters, forms, and printer classes associated with the printer. The scheduler also checks for configuration information related to the printer. Next, the scheduler queues the request and directs the request to the printer whenever the printer is available for processing the request.

INTERFACE AND FILTER FILES

Apart from administration components, such as the scheduler, the LP Print Service provides programs that enable printing support across hardware or software platforms. The Interface program provided by the LP Print Service is one such program that acts as a bridge between the hardware devices and the software components dealing with the printing process on a computer. The /usr/lib/lp/model directory stores the program files for the Interface component. The component initializes the connection between the computer and the printer by using information from the terminfo database. The Interface program also initializes the port.

The filter utility enables print clients to use printers—without respect to the printer type—by providing formatting features for the print requests the clients submit. The program is located in the /usr/lib/lp directory. Filters that need to format print requests into the PostScript format are the most commonly used filter files. If you need to create filters for other printer formats, you need to create the filter and store the files in a subdirectory under the /usr/lib/lp directory.

THE terminfo DATABASE

The terminfo database stores information about the capabilities of hardware devices that produce output. Printers and terminals are some examples of such hardware devices. The database contains information on the character sequences that affect the output displayed.

Typically, programs that involve display of output on computer monitors use the information provided by the terminfo database. Some examples of such programs include vi or ls. The terminfo database file is stored in the path specified by the TERMINFO environmental variable. The default path for the database is /usr/share/lib/terminfo.

LOG FILES

The print process involves a number of activities, from the print request submitted by the user to the actual completion of the print process. The log files act as the activity recording mechanism, which can be used to track the print process, troubleshoot printing problems, or to enhance the printer performance. LP Print Service provides two types of log files: current requests log files and request history log files.

14

The current request log files, also called the *print queue logs*, involve two separate sets of files stored in the /var/spool/lp/tmp/<*systemname*> directory and the /var/spool/lp/requests/<*systemname*> directory. The user uses the log file in the /var/spool/lp/tmp/<*systemname*> directory to verify the status of the request submitted. The printer or the print server uses the /var/spool/lp/tmp/<*systemname*> directory to process the request. Print queue log files are maintained only when the request is in queue. After the print server has processed the request, the contents of the log files are transferred to the request history log files.

Request history log files, located in the /var/lp/logs directory, are typically used to resolve printer problems. Two types of log files are stored in the /var/lp/logs directory: lpsched and requests. The /var/lp/logs/requests log file provides information on completed print requests. The /var/lp/logs/lpsched log file is used to obtain information on the local print requests users have submitted.

THE PRINTING PROCESS

Now that you are conversant with the components of the LP Print Service, you can analyze how all these components come into play during the actual print process. The first thing to look at is a local print process. When a user submits a print request with an lp command, the command directs the request to the scheduler. The scheduler (lpsched daemon) first stores the request in the spooling directory. Next, the scheduler verifies information on the printer type, print content in the request, and the default printer information for the print request. Next, the scheduler identifies whether any filters are associated with the printer. After the filtering process is completed, the scheduler activates the interface program and transfers the request to the interface. Now, the interface verifies whether there are any hardware faults and whether the printer is ready to print the content. Next, the interface program transfers the request to the printer, which completes the process by printing the required content.

In a typical printing environment, local printers are not very commonly used. A shared printer, also called a *remote printer*, usually services print requests on a network. The remote printing process differs slightly from the local print process. Here, the lp command submits the print request directly to an lpd deamon on a print server. In turn, the lpd daemon directs the request to an inetd daemon that is listening for network requests. The inetd deamon activates the scheduler, which performs tasks that are similar to those performed by an lpsched daemon in a local print process. The scheduler spools, filters, and directs the request to an interface program, which communicates the request to the hardware device that provides the printed output. Figures 14.1 and 14.2 show you how the Solaris printing process is implemented.

14

Figure 14.1
Solaris local printing process.

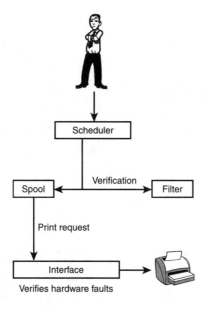

Figure 14.2
Solaris remote printing process.

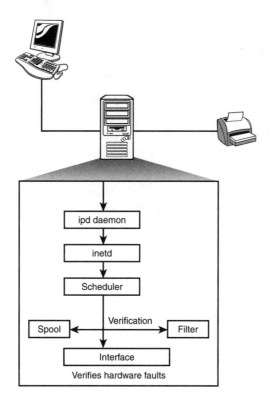

14

SOLARIS PRINT MANAGER

The power of administering the Solaris print environment lies in the various lp commands, which offer greater flexibility and control over a number of aspects of the print service administration. For example, the lp command that enables a user to submit print requests can be used with six options, with each option providing a specific feature for making a print request. The hitch in using lp commands is that the vast number of options and parameters that must be specified makes it difficult to use for administration tasks.

To provide ease in administering print services, a user-friendly GUI front-end for lp commands, called the Print Manager, has been added to LP Print Service. The Print Manager is a Java-based printer administration component that provides options to perform the most common printer administration tasks, such as configuring print clients, servers, network printers, and upgrading configuration information from previous versions of Solaris. On the Solaris OS, the Print Manager exists as a package called the SUNWppm.

When administering the print environment on a Solaris network, it is possible to manage printer configuration information from a centralized location using a name service such as NIS, NIS+, and LDAP. The configuration information includes information related to all the shared printers on the network. Information of all shared printers on the network are made available to all print clients. Name Services, when used in conjunction with Print Manager, enables printers to be shared over the network.

A name service can be described as a central repository containing information on the computer name, IP address, usernames, passwords, user rights and permissions, and user groups.

This central repository enables information on the computers in a network to be shared throughout the network. In addition, name services also store configuration information on peripheral devices, such as scanners or printers servicing the network. The Print Manager can make use of this information on a name service to administer printing services for a network from a centralized location.

You can install different types of name services on Solaris. Some of the name services that can be configured on Solaris include Lightweight Directory Access Protocol (LDAP), Naming Information Service (NIS), and NIS+.

Regardless of the type of name service, the printer configuration information is stored in the printers database of the /etc/nsswitch.conf file. In the database, entries point to locations where the configuration information is stored. For example, when NIS is the name service being used on a network, the printers database entry contains the path $HOME/.printers, which is the default location for the printer configuration file. At the time of submitting requests, print clients can use the name service to identify printer configuration information.

Before moving into the printer administration features provided by Print Manager, you need to learn about certain preinstallation steps for Print Manager. To work with Print Manager, you need to have an X Windows environment or install the xhosts client software. Permissions that are required to administer printers are available to superusers. Therefore, you need to log in as a superuser to use Print Manager.

14

After you have taken care of permissions and software prerequisites, you need to perform certain configuration tasks on the name service you have installed. This is required to enable smooth coordination between the name service and Print Manager during the printer administration process. Each name service has a different configuration requirement. For example, if NIS+ is used as the name service, you need to add the computer using the service into the NIS+ admin group. This step is required to enable a user working from the computer to modify the printers table in the printers database. As the first step, you need to log on as a superuser and determine the admin group that permits printers table modification. Next, you need to use the `nisgrpadm` command to add the computer to the admin group. The following syntax shows you how to add a computer to an admin group with the `nisgrpadm` command.

```
# niscat -o printers.org_dir.testdomain.com
# nisgrpadm -a admin.testdomain.com testcomputer
```

In the syntax, the `niscat` command is used to determine the admin group, which has permissions to administer the printers table. When used with the -o option, the `niscat` command takes the network domain name as a parameter. The name corresponds to an object stored in the printers table. The command displays admin groups as an output. The group names can be used as an argument to the `nisgrpadm` command. Option -a used with the `nisgrpadm` command enables the addition of computers to a group specified as the first parameter to the `nisgrpadm` command. The name of the computer, which needs to be added, must be specified as the second parameter.

LDAP name services require a different set of configuration steps before being put to use for printing services. You need to determine the printer administrator's Distinguished Name (DN) and password. In addition, you must identify the LDAP server with a computer name or IP address. When you have completed configuring your name services, you can start using the Print Manager.

You can use several methods to launch Print Manager, the simplest of which is to use the Tools option of the Common Development Environment (CDE) Workspace menu and select the Printer Administrator option in the Workspace menu. An alternative method of launching Print Manager is to use the Applications menu in the CDE front panel. You need to:

1. Open the Application menu from the CDE front panel. The Application Manager is launched and the System_Admin window is displayed.
2. Click the Printer Administration icon in the System_Admin window to launch the Print Manager.

Alternatively, you can launch the Print Manager from the command prompt by typing the following command:

```
# /usr/sadm/admin/bin/printmgr &
```

You also can launch Print Manager on a remote print server by using the `xhosts` utility. You need to launch `xhosts` from the command prompt on your computer and connect to the

14

remote print server. Next, change the DISPLAY environmental variable by setting the display number value of your computer to the variable. Export the DISPLAY variable value before entering the printmgr command that launches the Print Manager on the remote computer. The commands that must be entered to work with a remote Print Manager are listed in the following syntax.

```
#xhost printer1
#DISPLAY=localcomputername:1
#export DISPLAY
#/usr/sadm/admin/bin/printmgr &
```

After entering the commands as specified in the syntax, the Print Manager is displayed with the Select Naming Services window. You need to select the name service of your choice before proceeding to use Print Manager.

CONFIGURING PRINT SERVER AND PRINT CLIENT

To start administering printers with Print Manager, you need to configure print servers and clients. As mentioned earlier, computers that share their local printers with other computers on the network are termed *print servers*. Computers that use a shared printer attached to a print server for their printing requirements are called *print clients*. To configure a print server and a print client, you need to perform the following steps:

1. Launch the Print Manager on the print server and select the New Attached Printer from the Printer menu in the Print Manager.

2. Complete the information requested by the fields in the New Attached Printer window.

3. Confirm that the printer has been attached to the computer by verifying whether the Print Manager window displays the name of the new printer.

4. To verify whether the printer is accessible to all computers on the network, you need to add access to the printer from client computers by using the Add Access window of Print Manager on a client. Launch Print Manager on the client computer and open the Add Access window from the Printer menu on Print Manager.

5. Provide the information requested by the various options in the Add Access window.

6. Click OK to close the Add Access window and exit Print Manager.

After configuring the print server and client, you can test the configuration by using the lp command to submit print requests from the client.

MIGRATING CONFIGURATION INFORMATION

With the widespread popularity of the Solaris OS, a number of networks ranging from corporate to university networks have a Solaris operating environment already in place. In such scenarios, it is essential to use the existing printer configuration information and migrate the information to the new Solaris 9 printing environment. To migrate printer configuration information from a Solaris 2.5.1 operating environment to the Solaris 9 environment, you need to transfer the printer configuration information from the /etc/lp/printers directory to the /etc/printers.conf file by using the conv_lp command. The following syntax shows you how the conv_lp command is used for migrating printer configuration information.

```
# /usr/lib/print/conv_lp
```

The conv_lp command is also used to migrate printer configuration information on SunOS 5.5.x to Solaris 9. Some networks use lpd-based print servers to service their printing needs. To migrate printer configuration information from lpd-based print servers, you need to perform certain migration tasks. First, you need to transfer the /etc/printcap file from the lpd-based print server to the /etc directory of a Solaris 9 computer. Next, you need to use the conv_lpd command to convert the file into a printer.conf file as shown in the following syntax.

```
# /usr/lib/print/conv_lpd
```

PRINTER ADMINISTRATION USING lp COMMANDS

Using the Print Manager to administer the Solaris print environment has certain limitations. For example, you cannot set certain printer definitions, such as fault recovery options or printer classes, with the Print Manager. When compared to the range of options provided by lp commands, you can see that Print Manager offers limited printer administration features. Typically, system administrators managing Solaris operating environments use lp commands for printer administration rather than Print Manager. lp commands are used for configuring printers, setting printer definitions, administering print requests, scheduling print jobs, and verifying printer status.

CONFIGURING PRINTERS

Although Print Manager provides printer configuration features, a set of lp commands can perform the same operations. Apart from attaching local printers to a print server, lp commands also can be used to configure network printers. First, see how you can attach a new printer to a computer. You need to use a set of commands that are discussed in the following syntax:

```
# chown lp /dev/term/b
# chmod 600 /dev/term/b
# lpadmin -p printer1 -v /dev/term/b
# lpadmin -p printer1 -T PS
# lpadmin -p printer1 -I postscript
# cd /etc/lp/fd
# for filter in *.fd;do
  name='basename $filter.fd'
  lpfilter -f $name -F $filter
  done
# accept printer1
# enable printer1
# lpadmin -p printer1 -D "printer1 Hrdept ps"
# lpstat -p printer1
```

In the code, the chown and chmod commands are used to obtain permission for accessing printer ports. Next, the lpadmin command is used with the -v option to define a name and a

14

port for the printer. The -T option is used to define the printer type. The -I argument is specified with the lpadmin command configures the content type of a print request. Next, the lpfilter command is used to define a filter for the printer. You can define multiple filters by executing the lpfilter command within a for loop as specified in the syntax. You need to complete the configuration by accepting and enabling the printer configuration that you have set. In the syntax, the accept and enable commands are used to perform these steps. Before using the lpstat command to verify the status of the printer, you need to describe the printer by using the lpadmin command with the -D option.

To configure network printers, you need to perform certain tasks in addition to the steps performed for configuring local printers. Network printers have additional requirements, such as protocol name, printer name, destination name, and timeout value. Before delving into the configuration steps for a network printer, it's helpful to analyze each feature and its role in configuring network printers.

To start with, you need to understand certain new terms associated with network printers. For example, the term *printer-host device* refers to the vendor-supplied hardware device that provides networking capabilities to a printer. The device is installed with vendor-specific software that enables network connectivity between the printer and the print server. A combination of the printer-host device and the printer forms the network printer. A printer node is used to connect a non-network printer to the network. It is typically a host connected to the network. Network-capable printers can also be *printer nodes*. Each printer node is assigned a name and an IP address to uniquely identify the printer on the network.

Printer names are assigned to a printer node when the node is configured. One unique feature of printer names is that multiple printer names can be assigned to a single printer node. Apart from uniquely identifying the printer node, printer names are used in lp commands to refer to the printer node. In addition to the printer name, a destination printer name, defined by the vendor, is also assigned to the printer node. The printer node software uses the destination printer name to identify and link the printer with its port.

A network printer uses specific protocols to communicate with the computers on the network. Typically, printers use Transmission Control Protocol (TCP) or the Berkeley Software Design (BSD) Printer Protocol for establishing network connectivity. Another network printer-specific term that is commonly used in printer configuration is timeout value. When a client computer is unable to connect to the printer, the attempt to reconnect occurs after a time interval that is called the *timeout value*. The value is incremented with every unsuccessful connection attempt. If the client is unable to establish connection after a number of attempts, the user is notified with a message that the attempt to connect has failed.

Now that you are conversant with the terms used in network printer configuration, the following section discusses the lp commands that are used for printer configuration tasks. The following syntax shows you how to configure a network printer.

```
lpadmin -p printer1 -v /dev/null
lpadmin -p printer1 -m netstandard
lpadmin -p printer1 -o dest=nimquat:9100 -o protocol=tcp -o timeout=5
lpadmin -p printer1 -I postscript -T PS
```

14

```
cd /etc/lp/fd
for filter in *.fd;do
    name='basename $filter.fd'
    lpfilter -f $name -F $filter
    done
accept printer1
output
enable printer1
output
lpadmin -p printer1 -D "printer1 Hrdept ps"
lpstat -p printer1
```

In the code, the -v option is used with the lpadmin command to define the printer-host device to a null value. Next, the -m option is used to activate the vendor-specific interface script associated with the printer. The protocol name, destination name, and the timeout values are defined using the -o option of the lpadmin command in the next line of the code. The -I and the -T options of the lpadmin command are used to define the content type and the printer type respectively. The lpfilter command specified within a for loop is used to define multiple print filters for the printer. The accept and the enable commands are used to accept and enable printer1 as a network printer. Before verifying the status of printer1 using the lpstat command, the –D option of the lpadmin command is used to describe printer1.

DELETING PRINTERS

There are scenarios where printer configurations must be deleted and re-created. For example, you might need to reconfigure the print server into a newer and much more powerful computer. In such scenarios, you need to delete printer configurations on the print server and on all client computers configured to use the print server. If a naming service is configured with print server information, you need to delete the printer configuration in the naming service.

Primarily, the lpadmin and lpsystem commands with their respective options are used to delete printer access. When deleting printer configurations, you need to follow a certain order in applying the lpadmin and the lpsystem commands. Typically, you remove the printer configurations on all client computers before you delete the printer from the print server. Ensure that you use the superuser or lp logins while working on the clients where printer configuration is deleted. The following list provides the steps that must be followed to delete printer configurations from print servers and clients:

1. To delete the configuration information related to a printer, use the -x option of the lpadmin command. Next, you need to delete the print server configuration from the client. Ensure that the client is not configured with other printers connected to the print server. If multiple printers connected to the print server are configured on the client, you need to use the lpadmin -x command to delete the printer configuration before you delete the print server configuration from the client. To delete the print server configuration, use the lpsystem command with the -r option. The following syntax shows you how to delete printer and print server configurations from a client:

14

```
# lpadmin -x printer1
# lpadmin -x printer2
# lpsystem -r testprintserver
```

2. After removing printer and printer configuration information from all client computers, you can start deleting the printer configurations on the server. You need to log on as superuser or lp on the server to acquire adequate permissions for the delete operation. The first step is to reject any future print request from being processed. You can implement this restriction by using the reject command. You need to reject print requests for all printers connected to the server by using separate reject commands for each printer. Next, terminate all print requests that the printer is currently processing. You need to use the disable command to perform this task. Finally, you need to use the lpadmin and the lpsystem commands to delete the printer and the print client configurations on the print server. The following syntax shows you how print configuration on a server can be removed:

```
# reject printer11
# reject printer11
# disable printer11
# disable printer12
# lpadmin -x printer11
# lpadmin -x printer12
# lpsystem -r testclient1, testclient2
```

NOTE

Printer configuration information on print clients and servers is deleted from the /etc/lp/printers directory. Print server information stored in the /etc/lp/Systems file on print clients is deleted when print server information is deleted from a client computer. Similarly, client information on the print server is deleted from the /etc/lp/Systems file on the print server.

SETTING PRINTER DEFINITIONS

In addition to configuring printers, you need to add printer definitions that describe the printers' names, default destinations, banner pages, alerts, and fault recovery mechanisms. You also can organize printers into groups called classes by setting definitions for printer classes. These definitions enable print clients to identify the printers on the network and to introduce ease in administering printers. One of the most common printer definitions that can be set is the printer description. The lpadmin command is specified with the -D option defines a description for the printer as shown in the following syntax.

```
# lpadmin -p printer1 -D "printer1 Hrdept ps"
```

The -p option in the command specifies the name of the printer and is followed by the -D command, which takes the description of the printer as a parameter. You need to specify special characters such as *, ?, !, ^, /, or \ within single quotes to distinguish the characters from the rest of the description. The printer description provides general information on the printer, such as the location, contact user name, or other information specific to the use of the printer.

DEFAULT PRINTER NAME

As mentioned earlier, some printer definitions ease printer administration by setting default values. A typical example of such a definition is the default printer definition. You can define a particular printer as the default printer for a particular computer. After setting this definition, you need not specify the printer name in the lp commands. This eases the monotony of typing the printer name for every lp command. The default printer name is stored in a number of resources, such as PRINTER, LPDEST, or the _default environment variable in the .printers file. You can set the default printer name by assigning the printer name to these environmental variables. Alternatively, you can use the lpadmin command with the -d option to set the default printer name. The following syntax shows you how to use the lpadmin command to set the default printer name.

```
# lpadmin -d printer1
```

The default printer information set by using the lpadmin command is stored in the /etc/lp/ default file. After you set the default printer name, when a user submits a print request without specifying the printer name, LP Print Service checks for the printer name in the environmental variables. LP Print Service follows a certain file order to check for the printer name. The LPDEST variable is first verified for the existence of a default printer name. If the printer name is not defined in LPDEST, the PRINTER variable, followed by the /etc/lp/default file, is verified for the default printer name configuration.

PRINTER CLASSES

One of the best ways to optimize printer usage on a network is to organize printers into groups by defining printer classes. Users can specify the class name rather than the individual printer name when submitting print requests. When a print request is directed to a printer class, any printer in the printer class that is free to handle print requests processes the submitted request. This way, all printers in the printer class are optimally utilized. When you define printer class names, the naming rules stipulated while defining printer names also apply to class names. For example, you might need to ensure that class names do not exceed 14 alphanumeric characters and do not contain symbols, such as *, ?, !, ^, /, or \.

You can group printers based on several considerations. For example, printers can be grouped based on performance capacity, type, location, or their use by a single department. To understand how printer class definitions can enhance printer usage efficiencies, consider a scenario where an organization needs to define printer classes for the local printers on its network. The organization has a set of PostScript printers on each floor of its head office, in addition to five printers in its billing department. The organization has the choice of defining a printer class consisting of PostScript printers. On the other hand, a class consisting of all the printers used in the billing department can be created.

As with other printer definitions, the lpadmin command is used to define printer classes. You need to use the -c option to define a new printer class and to add a printer to an existing class. The following code snippet shows you how a printer class can be defined:

```
# lpadmin -p printer1 -c testclass
```

14

DEFINING ALERTS

A printer might not successfully complete all print requests. There are situations when the printer needs to notify the user about unsuccessful print jobs. The reasons for failed print jobs are many. For example, print jobs can get disrupted if the paper runs out or if the printer is offline. You can set default printer notification messages by defining fault alerts. As with any other printer definition, you can set fault alerts by using the `lpadmin` command with the `-A` option. Alternatively, you can use the Print Manager to set fault alerts. However, the Print Manager provides only three options to set fault alerts: message to the computer, email to the user who has logged on as root, or no notification.

Although Print Manager provides an easy method for defining fault alerts, only limited fault alert settings can be defined in comparison to the options provided by the `lpadmin` command. In addition to the options provided by Print Manager, the `lpadmin` command used with the `-A` option can define fault alerts to be generated from programs, or to turn off the notification feature for certain problems that you are already aware.

You can supply a variety of parameters for the `-A` option to notify users in different modes. For example, you can send email to a user who has logged on as root with a predefined fault alert. To send email, you need to specify the parameter `'mail<username>'`. Similarly, to display fault alerts on a user terminal, you need to supply the parameter `'write<username>'`. In certain situations, fault alerts are displayed on the user terminal until the problem is resolved. To turn off repeated fault alerts, you need to specify the `quiet` parameter with the `-A` option. When this parameter is specified, the user is notified of the problem only once. To turn off the alert mechanism completely, you need to specify the `none` parameter. Apart from these parameters, you also can specify a command filename that runs fault alert programs to notify users. In the following example, a fault alert is defined using the `lpadmin` command:

```
# lpadmin -p printer1 -A 'mail donna' -W 10
# lpadmin -p printer1 -A 'write donna' -W 10
# lpadmin -p printer1 -A quiet -W 10
# lpadmin -p printer1 -A none
```

In the code, note that the `-W` option is used after the `-A` option. The `-W` option is used to specify a time interval between fault alerts when alerts are repeatedly fired from the printer.

NOTE

The fault alerts defined by using Print Manager or the `lpadmin` command are stored in the `/etc/lp/printers/<printername>/alert.sh` file.

BANNER PAGE DEFINITIONS

In a typical printing environment where multiple print jobs are executed simultaneously, the possibility of confusing or misplacing printouts is high. To avoid such problems, LP Print Services print a banner page before printing a document. Banner pages specify the identity of the user who submitted the print request, the time the request was submitted, and a print request ID that uniquely identifies the print request. In addition, banner pages can also be defined with a title that further identifies a particular printout.

Banner pages are printed by default for all printers. Although banner pages are essential in printing environments with large numbers of users, banner pages are not always necessary. For example, printouts on networks with small numbers of users do not need banner pages. Printouts of bills, checks, or other special materials are some other cases where banner pages are unnecessary. To manipulate banner page settings, you can use the -o option of the lpadmin command apart from the options that you can set with Print Manager. Table 14.1 describes the various parameters that can be supplied with the -o option.

TABLE 14.1   PARAMETERS USED WITH THE –O OPTION.

Parameter	Description
-o banner=always	Sets the banner page on for all printouts.
-o banner=optional	Defines banner page settings as optional.
-o nobanner	Sets the banner page off for a particular print request.
-o banner=never	Sets the banner page off for all print requests.

The banner page settings are stored in the /etc/lp/printers/<printername>/configuration file. The following code snippet shows you how the banner page settings can be defined with lpadmin and the -o option.

```
#lpadmin -p printer1 -o banner=always
#lpadmin -p printer1 -o banner=optional
#lpadmin -p printer1 -o nobanner
#lpadmin -p printer1 -o banner=never
```

To set banner pages on for all printouts, you can also use the -o banner parameter in addition to the -o banner=always parameter.

FAULT RECOVERY DEFINITIONS

In situations where a complete printer failure occurs, you can define printer recovery options. These options enable completion of the print job from the point where the printer failure occurred. You can define different types of fault recovery options to complete the disrupted print requests. For example, the printer can restart the print job from the beginning of the document or from the top of the page that was last being printed at the time of the disruption. To determine the layout of the page being printed, printers use print filters that provide this information in the form of control sequences. On the occurrence of a printer failure, you need to redefine the print filter before restarting any printing activity. You will learn more about filters later in the chapter.

You use the -F option of the lpadmin command to set fault recovery definitions. You can supply three different parameters for the -F option based on your choice of fault recovery.

14

To restart the print job from the beginning of the document, you need to use the `beginning` parameter. If you consider restarting the print job as a waste of time and paper, you can specify the `continue` parameter. This option continues the print job from the point where it was disrupted. The print job restarts at the top of a new page. Before using this parameter, you need to redefine print filters. When a `continue` parameter is specified, the printing restarts immediately after the printer problem is resolved.

To control printer restart after a problem is resolved, you can specify the `wait` parameter. This parameter is similar to the `continue` parameter wherein the print job is continued from the point where it was last stopped. However, you need to use the `enable` command to reactivate the printer before the fault recovery definitions are processed. The following syntax shows you how you can use the `-F` option of the `lpadmin` command to define fault recovery options.

```
# lpadmin -p printer1 -F beginning
# lpadmin -p printer1 -F continue
# lpadmin -p printer1 -F wait
```

ADMINISTERING PRINT REQUESTS

Monitoring and managing print requests is an important task performed by a Solaris administrator. Apart from accepting or rejecting requests, the administrator can control printer availability, cancel a request, manipulate the priority for a request, or transfer a request to another printer. To start with, you can use the `lp` command with a host of options to submit print requests. For example, to print the contents of multiple files, you need to use the `-d` option followed by the name of the printer and the file names separated with commas. The following syntax provides some simple examples of print request submissions that use the `lp` command.

```
# lp -d printer11 testfile1, testfile2, testfile3
# lp /usr/testuser/testfile1
```

After submitting the request, the `lpsched` daemon redirects the request present in the spool directory to the specified destination printer. Typically, this process is automatic. However, there are situations where the scheduler might not work automatically. In such scenarios, you need to start the scheduler manually. To perform this task, you need to log on to the print server as superuser or `lp` and use the `/usr/lib/lp/lpsched` command. To shut down the scheduler, you need to use the `lpshut` command. The following syntax shows you how to shut down and restart the scheduler.

```
# /usr/lib/lp/lpshut
# /urs/lib/lp/lpsched
```

Certain scenarios demand that the printer stop printing the requests in a queue. For example, when recovering from a printer failure, requests in the queue are not processed immediately. In such cases, you need to enable a printer before continuing with the recovery process. For accomplishing this task, you can use the `enable` command. The `disable` command restricts the printer from processing requests in the queue. Although the printer does not execute queued requests, the requests remain in the queue until the printer processes each request. To clear the queue and to restrict any further requests from being queued, you must use the reject command. In contrast, when queued requests need to be processed, you need to use the accept command. The following syntax shows you how to enable, disable, accept, and reject requests:

```
# disable -r "printer recovering from failure" testprinter1
# enable printer11
# reject -r "printer being transferred
# accept printer11
```

In the syntax, observe that the -r option is used with the disable and the reject commands to provide information to the user on the reasons for the action.

Sometimes, a print request needs to be executed immediately regardless of its position in the queue. In such situations, you need to change the request priority by using the lp command. In addition to setting the new priority level, you need to specify the request ID to identify the request whose priority must be modified. You can use the -i option to specify the request ID. To specify the new priority level, use the –H option. The following syntax shows you how to set the new priority level for a request:

```
# lp -i printer11-64 -H 0
# lp -i printer11-46-H 39
```

In the syntax, observe that the priority levels of 0 and 39 have been specified. A priority level of 0 indicates the highest possible priority level that can be specified. A priority level of 39 is the lowest possible priority level that you can set for a request.

SUMMARY

In a world that is moving toward a paperless office, printed material continues to be used for business dealings and transactions. This has bestowed the printer with an important position on any network. Therefore, all operating systems provide printing features that cater to the users' needs. Solaris provides wide-ranging printing services managed by the LP Print Service and the Print Manager.

Before designing the Solaris printing environment on a network, you need to take into account certain requirements. You need to determine the type of printer and the optimum hardware requirements that need to be installed on the network.

Printing services on Solaris are powered by the LP Print Service. The service contains components, such as lp commands, configuration files, the scheduler, and the terminfo database. Although lp commands provide the underlying command line utility for administering print services, Print Manager provides a GUI front end for the commands. However, lp commands are far more powerful and flexible. Apart from configuring printers, lp commands can be used to set printer definitions and to administer print requests in a Solaris print environment.

14

## CHAPTER 15

BACKUP AND RECOVERY

In this chapter

Introducing Backup   260

Solaris Backup Mechanisms   261

Creating and Restoring Backups   266

Summary   275

15

INTRODUCING BACKUP

In any computing environment preserving data is the vital insurance against data loss. With data mushrooming everywhere, backing up becomes an imperative task. If crucial information is not backed up, there is a high probability of losing it. Maintaining a spare copy of your business data is a precautionary measure that has been reiterated time and again. Implementing data backups is similar to keeping spare tires for your car to cope with situations when your car tire punctures.

Solaris OE comes with several built-in backup utilities to perform backups and recoveries. In addition, several third parties offer software that can do the same thing. However, before discussing the backup concepts and the various built-in utilities provided with Solaris OE, this chapter looks in detail at the various causes for data loss and the preventive measures you can take to prevent such losses.

The cause for data loss can be attributed to several factors, such as operating system crash, accidental deletion of files, natural disasters, and so on. The following section describes the common factors that contribute to the loss of data in businesses.

Figure 15.1 depicts the statistics for the prime causes that lead to data loss.

Figure 15.1
Various causes for
data loss.

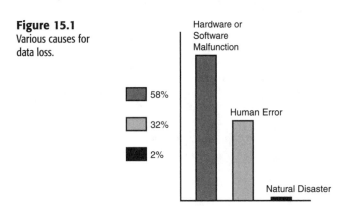

Operating system crashes are an unpleasant reality for the millions of people who count on their servers and workstations everyday. The quest for a crash-proof operating system is a constant effort by system developers. However, there is no crash-proof system that can assure its users 100% reliability.

Human error is another cause for data loss. Mistakes made by the administrator, such as accidental deletions or modifications of important configuration files, can result in the downtime of business-critical services. For example, configuration files could be a routes file created and stored in /etc/rc2.d directory. These configuration files define routes for a relatively complex network environment or any other system or application file. An accidental deletion or modification of this file would hamper the accessibility to and from other systems residing in other subnet networks. However, accidental modification of configuration files can be prevented if you are careful while handling such files and also if you have maintained a backup of the same.

Although uncommon, natural disasters—such as earthquakes, floods, fire, and other unforeseen accidents—can also cause data loss. These can result in the complete destruction of data centers. Natural disasters can cause tremendous loss of data for companies that do not have a defined and sophisticated backup technology. However, there are also companies that manage to come out of unforeseen natural calamities relatively unscathed. These companies have archived data at a safe location outside the disaster area. Redundant data centers are maintained to combat natural disasters, such as earthquakes, floods, fire, and unnatural disasters such as war. Hot sites are also used to capture recent data. They are connected to the main data center by a dedicated WAN link.

A diligent and conscientious effort to plan a backup mechanism and design backup strategies using these utilities can ensure the safety of your data.

SOLARIS BACKUP MECHANISMS

Whether an organization is large or small, data is of utmost importance. Therefore, it becomes imperative for system administrators to lay down an effective planned procedure for data backup and recovery. Planning helps identify your backup requirements and also streamlines the backup process. Realistic expectations and good planning must consider current and future needs.

In contrast to companies dealing with small volumes of online data, organizations working with large online data volumes have a much more challenging task of planning data backup. Consider a scenario where hundreds of servers in a data center span multiple subnets. Each server has its customized build and runs different applications. In this case, one backup server is not sufficient to back up data from all the servers. In such a scenario, it is advisable to use one backup server per subnet to avoid network congestion caused by online backup. Moreover, you may also want to run a separate backup LAN. This ensures that backups are made all the time without causing network congestion. This is especially true in LANs that run other network-based services, such as SMTP, HTTP, FTP, SSH, and so on.

However, note that using one backup server per subnet can result in increased cost overheads and that managing all backup servers centrally can become a daunting task. Larger volumes of backup data require backup media in higher numbers. For example, if you are using a 4GB DAT tape to take backups, and if you need to back up 100GB of data, you need a minimum of 25 tapes. It would be better to use a higher capacity backup storage media, such as a 24GB DAT tape or higher. Managing your tapes and servers efficiently requires planned efforts from the system and network administrators. Before planning your backup, answer the following questions:

- What needs to be backed up and how often?
- What volume of data requires backing up based on the present and future needs?
- What type of backup will be used under what circumstances?

15

- What devices will be used for backup?
- How do you determine the number of devices that will be used for a specific type of backup?
- What is the time available for each backup and when does the backup need to be scheduled?
- What are the utilities to back up?

BACKUP FREQUENCY AND COMPONENTS

File systems are one of the most important components of the Solaris OE. As discussed in Chapter 8, "Understanding the Solaris File System," file systems are the building blocks in Solaris. Back up the file systems and the files and directories within them. For example, the root file system, which is the first file system to be mounted by the kernel, contains the kernel and the device drivers. Although small, this file system contains the most critical system information files. A corrupted root file system generally produces an unbootable system. Therefore, it is important to back up the root file system at regular intervals. Please note that this time interval depends on your site needs. You may back up once a day or even once a month.

The /var subdirectory contained in the root also requires regular backup because it stores frequently modified files, such as user mails. In addition, the /var directory contains system log and message files that are constantly modified. These log files provide you with a complete audit trail of events.

The other file system that you would be interested in backing up is the /export/home directory, where the user home directory resides. Similar to the /var/mail directory, the /export/home file system contains volatile data. It stores the directories and subdirectories of all users in the standalone system. This file system needs to be backed up on a daily basis. For example, imagine that XYZ, Inc., has its head office located in Los Angeles and has a branch office in Sydney, Australia. Users in the branch office and the head office work on a project and at the end of the day upload their work to the FTP server located in the head office, where the data is collected and compiled. Users in the head office evaluate the work done every morning and upload the evaluated data to the FTP server in the evening. This mode of working ensures work is carried on around the clock. The target directory for copying files can be /export/home/pub/ftp/proj/user1. Similarly, there is a directory for each user under /export/home/ftp/pub/proj where the users upload their files at the end of the day. This means that the data is dynamically updated every day. In this case, you should back up data on a daily basis.

The /usr directory contains Solaris built-in commands in /usr/bin and /usr/sbin. The files and directories in this file system contain fairly static content. Some administrators might keep locally compiled programs in /usr/local, but that might happen occasionally. Therefore, backing up this file system once a week or once a month is sufficient.

BACKUP MEDIA

Choosing a backup device depends on many factors, such as amount of data to back up, how critical the data is for you, how can you ensure easy access to the data to minimize restoration time, what cost would be involved in implementing your backup policy and procedure, and so on.

15

NOTE

> Whatever media you choose for backup, it is recommended that these media be kept in a safe place outside the territory of the actual data.

Solaris supports various backup devices, such as floppy disks, tape drives, CDs, Zip drives, optical drives, DAT drives, and storage arrays. You can make your choice of a backup device based on your needs.

FLOPPY DISKS

If you are looking at backing up small volumes, up to 1.44MB of information, you may choose to back the data up on a floppy disk. Floppy disks are portable and cost effective. However, with the availability of better storage media, such as DAT drives, Zip drives, and Optical drives, in recent years, floppy disks are no longer a viable means of backup. Only a small quantity of data can be backed up in a single floppy and floppy disks are vulnerable to corruption.

ZIP DISKS

The key factor that increases the popularity of Zip disks is their larger storage capacity in contrast to the storage capacity provided by floppy disks. Unlike a floppy disk, which has a defined number of sectors per track, Zip disks have variable numbers of sectors per track to make the optimum use of the disk space. Also, the magnetic coating used on the Zip disk is of a higher quality than that of the floppy disk. This reduces the size of the read/write head, which in turn provides thousands of tracks per inch on the track surface. In a floppy disk, the number of tracks is significantly less.

TAPE DRIVES

In the past, backup practices required an operator to remain on premises to change tapes as they became full. Today the need for a tape system operator has been virtually eliminated by high-capacity tapes and automated tape changer systems. Tape drives allow you to schedule and automate the backup procedure. This can help you save tremendous amounts of time in performing regular backups.

In addition, tape drives are cost effective, reliable, and portable. Tapes have a cost per megabyte of less than one cent. If you are under a tight budget control, then perhaps tape drives could serve your needs.

Tape drives meet nearly every backup need. The different types of available tape drives are given in Table 15.1.

15

TABLE 15.1   DIFFERENT TYPES OF TAPE DRIVES

Type Drive	Description
1/2-inch reel tape	The 1/2 inch reel tape has a maximum capacity of 140MB uncompressed. It speeds through both 1600 and 6250bpi tapes at up to 780kb/sec.
2.5GB 1/4-inch cartridge (QIC) tape	Quarter-inch cartridge (QIC) technology is one of the oldest tape technologies. Available in 60MB, 150MB, 250MB, 525MB and larger sizes, these drives are designed to read both higher- and lower-capacity cartridges. Although reliable, this tape technology is expensive and has the slowest transfer rates compared to all other tape technologies.
Digital Data Storage (DDS) 3 4mm cartridge tape (DAT)	DATs (digital audio tapes) are small in size and that is why they are easier to use and store. However, these tapes wear quickly as compared to QIC. Also, the 4mm tape drives are not always compatible. Tapes from one drive might not be readable in another drive.
14GB 8mm cartridge tape	Originally developed by Exabyte, 8mm tape drives offer storage capabilities between 2.2GB and 100GB per cartridge. These tape cartridges are only slightly larger than DAT tapes. These tape drives are reliable but are more expensive than 4mm units.
Digital Linear Tapes (DLT)™ 7000 1/2-inch cartridge tape	Quantum DLT™ 7000 half-inch cartridge tape drives provide data storage and restore features for storage applications. The tape drive provides a data transfer rate of 5Mb/sec. It has a capacity of 35GBs.

OPTICAL DRIVES

Optical disk solutions are ideal for any application that requires millisecond access to large documents, graphic files, and databases. Storage capacity in optical drives ranges from 2.6GB for a single drive to 156GB with the 60-disk jukebox. The multifunction drive writes to both erasable and WORM disks, for flexibility in storing all types of documents.

NOTE   WORM is an acronym for write once, read many, generally refers to optical disks. This means data can be written once to the disk and can be read any number of times.

Optical platters, with an archival life of 40 years, can be erased and rewritten continuously with no degradation in quality. And considering that you can increase storage capacity by 2.6GB for the cost of a single platter, optical storage is cost effective as well.

STORAGE ARRAYS USING SUN STOREDGE

As discussed in Chapter 12, " Disk and Storage Administration," Sun StorEdge is a device that provides storage solutions for online transactions. This storage device has the capacity to store up to 169TB on a single server. Because it has such high storage capacity, additional cache is used to increase the storage server's performance. You can upgrade from 512MB of cache space to 2GB.

Full redundancy ensures that there is no system downtime. For example, two RAID controllers are used to provide a dual-fiber channel interface where each controller accesses a separate array of disk drives. If a controller fails, the other controller takes over and provides access to all drives accessed by the failed controller in addition to its own drives. In addition, each of these controllers has its own cache that provides up to 2GB of memory to provide quick access to frequently accessed data.

> **NOTE**
>
> A RAID controller is an electronic device that provides the interface between the host computer and the array of disks. The RAID controller makes the array of disks look like one virtual disk.

TYPES OF BACKUP

Do you typically need to store an entire file system or just one file? An answer to this question will help you decide on the type of backup you want to perform. There are three types of backup you can perform in Solaris: full, incremental, and snapshot.

A full backup allows you to copy an entire file system or a directory. This means that if you wanted to back up the complete root (/) file system, you must use the full backup mechanism. Making full backups ensures that all your data is in a single location. Because full backups include all data, you don't have to search through several tapes to find the file(s) you need to restore. If you want to restore the entire file system, you can find all current information on the last backup tape on which a full backup was performed. However, imagine having to do a full backup of large volumes of file systems on a more occasional basis. This method offers excellent protection of your file system, but remember that it can be time consuming. Most full backups are done during non-business hours to avoid the network congestion, but many large organizations have far too much data to back up in such a short time period. Therefore, for those situations where there is just too much data and too little time, incremental backups may be the answer.

Incremental backups contain only the data that was created or most recently changed since the last backup. These backups are used frequently, perhaps even on a daily basis, to supplement a full backup. As compared to a full backup, this method of backup is faster. Imagine, for example, that you are making full backups of your data on every Friday and on one Thursday night your system crashes. It is quite apparent that you have lost one week's data. However, if you were performing incremental backups, you would just end up losing a few hours of data. Another advantage to this type of backup is that you can make good use of the

15

media you use to store your incremental backups. Because only a small amount of data is being stored, less storage space is being occupied. However, the flip side to performing an incremental backup is that this kind of backup can make restoring a comparatively difficult task. Restoring has to be sequential, where the last thing backed up is restored first.

NOTE

Labeling your tapes with backup level information is a good practice.

The third backup type is snapshot, which stores a temporary image of file systems. Rather than copy the original blocks of data, the snapshot creates a copy of the metadata structures. Essentially, it stores pointers to all the data blocks. This type of backup is reliable because it allows you to take a copy of the data that is continuously changing. Snapshots are instantaneous. As soon as you issue the `fssnap` command, the temporary image of the file system is stored.

Because snapshots can be taken quickly and consume very little overhead, they can be used extensively without great concern for system performance or disk use. The drawback to snapshot backup is that users of the file systems notice a slight pause when the UFS is first created. This pause increases with the increase in the size of the file system that needs to be captured. Note that performance is affected only when the file system is written to. There is no impact to the file system when it is read.

NOTE

Check the `/var/adm/messages` file for possible snapshot errors.

CREATING AND RESTORING BACKUPS

Solaris OE has several built-in command line backup utilities, such as `cp`, `tar`, `cpio`, and so on. The most widely used by system administrators is `ufsdump`, for a number of reasons:

- Your backup can span multiple tapes, if need be.
- There is no constraint in terms of file types.
- Permissions, ownership, and timestamps can be restored, and backups can be performed incrementally.

However, there are some disadvantages:

- Each file system has to be dumped individually.
- `ufsdump` cannot dump file systems that are mounted over NFS.

CAUTION

When copying files, ensure that the file systems are in the inactive mode. This ensures a consistent output of the `ufsdump` and the correct and complete restoration of the file systems.

The following command displays the syntax of the `ufsdump` utility:

```
/usr/sbin/ufsdump [ options ] [ arguments ] files_to_dump
```

In the syntax, the options that can be used are the following:

- **0 to 9**—Specifies the dump levels. 0 is a full backup and all subsequent backups are incremental backups. Note that the lower the dump level, the more complete the backup. As the dump level increases, backups contain files that are new and modified from the last lower dump level. For example, dump level 1 contains all files modified after the last 0 level dump.

- **u**—Updates the dump record file /etc/dumpdates for each file system dumped successfully. Each line in /etc/dumpdates shows the file system backed up, the level of the last backup, and the day, date, and time of the backup.

- **f**—Specifies the device to which the files are written. You must specify the device name as an argument to this option.

- **v**—Verifies the contents of the media with the source after each dump.

The `arguments` parameter specified in the `ufsdump` syntax define the arguments that each option takes. Each option is associated with a related argument. However, note that arguments are required only if an option specifies an argument. For example, in the following syntax, the argument specified with option f is dump_file. This argument specifies the file on which to dump data.

```
/usr/sbin/ufsdump f <dump_file>
```

The last parameter in the `ufsdump` syntax is `files_to_dump`. This argument specifies the destination of the backup. This destination could be a local or remote tape/drive or the standard output. For a local tape or disk drive, you specify the device on your system with a device abbreviation. To specify the remote tape or disk, use the following syntax:

```
host:device.ufsdump
```

The preceding command writes to the remote device when the root on the local host has access to the remote system. While writing to the remote, include the name of the local host in the /.rhosts file if you run `ufsdump` as root. The /.rhosts file contains entries of all systems that access it. This file is stored in the remote system. Also, if you want a specific user to be able to access the remote system, enter the following command:

```
user@host:device.ufsdump
```

Note that the name of the user must be included in the /.rhosts file.

The command format for using the `ufsdump` command to perform a remote backup is as follows:

```
ufsdump options remote_host_name:tape_device file_system
```

For example, to perform a full backup of the /var file system on system1 to the remote tape device on Saturn, you use the following command:

```
# ufsdump 0uf saturn:/dev/rmt/0 /var
```

15

Now look at how the `ufsdump` utility works. When you use this utility to back up files, it first scans the target file system to be backed up and then builds the table of contents that contains directory and file information. This table of contents is built in memory. It then writes this table of contents to the backup device. Note that when writing to the backup device, the utility builds a single backup file that can span across multiple devices.

Next, the utility makes a second pass on the file system, reads the contents of the file system, and writes the contents to the backup media. Before writing to the backup media, the utility needs to know the block size of the media and also a checkpoint that indicates the end of media. This way it can determine when the media is full during the dump process.

To determine the end of media, the utility writes a sequence of fixed-size records. If a record is only partially written, `ufsdump` assumes that it has reached the physical end of media. However, if the device is unable to notify `ufsdump` that a record has been partially written, an error is generated when `ufsdump` attempts to write to the media.

To restore complete file systems or individual files from removable media to a working directory, use the `ufsrestore` utility.

The syntax used for the `ufsrestore` utility is as follows:

```
ufsrestore [options][arguments][filename…]
```

The options, `i`, `r`, `R`, `x`, `h`, `t`, are used with the `ufsrestore` utility.

- Option `i` runs the `ufsrestore` utility in an interactive mode. This option allows you to scan the media on which you have backed up your data and select the files and directories you want to restore.

- Whereas option `r` is used restore the entire file contents to the current working directory, option `R` is used to resume restoring. If a full restore process is interrupted, option `R` prompts for the volume from which to resume restoring and then starts the restore process.

- Option `x` enables you to extract and restore files specified in the filename argument, which contains the names of files and directories to be restored. Note that when specified, this option will restore all files and directories. If you would like to limit the restoration to specific files and directories, use the `h` option. The `h` option turns off directory expansion and extracts only the files you specify.

- Option `t` is used to build a table of contents that lists the complete file names in the media. It checks the files specified in the filename argument against the media. If the file is present, it lists the full file name and the inode number. Otherwise, it indicates that the file is not found in the dump.

OTHER BACKUP UTILITIES

As mentioned earlier, Solaris also comes with several other built-in backup utilities, such as `tar`, `mt`, `dd`, `cpio`, `pax`, and `volcopy`. Although each utility is used to back up data, they have distinctive characteristics. For example, `tar` (short for tape archive) is used to make tape archives where multiple files are stored in a directory hierarchy. On the other hand, mt (magnetic tape) can be used to find out the status information about the tape drive. The following sections detail each of these utilities.

tar

The tar utility is used to create or restore tape archives. This utility can be used to make offline tape copies of directories and files. You can also use this utility to save files to a floppy disk.

> **NOTE**
>
> The tar utility is one of the main ways by which software is packaged on the Internet.

The syntax for archiving files using the tar command is as follows:

```
tar options device-name filename
```

The different options that are used with the tar utility are the following:

- **c**—Creates the a new tar archive and writes the files specified by one or more file parameters to the beginning of the archive. For example, to create a new tar archive called emp, use the command tar c emp. To create several files, such as emp, dept, and prod, as well as archives in a single tar archive, list the filenames by specifying tar c emp, dept, prod.

- **f**—Creates a tar archive in a disk file rather than a tape. For example, the command tar cf emp.tar emp, creates a new archive in the file emp.tar and includes in it all the files in the directory emp.

- **t**—Displays the list of files in the order in which they appear in the archive. To list the contents of the archive you wrote to a tape, issue the command tar -t.

- **u**—Updates the names of files at the end of an archive if they are not already present in the archive or if they have not been modified since the last write to the archive.

- **v**—Lists the files it adds to an archive by specifiying the v flag, which stands for verbose, with the tar command. This option gives more information about the tape entries, including file sizes, the time when the file was last modified, UID, GID, and permissions.

- **x**—Extracts the contents of a tar archive. You have the option of selectively listing a single file or a list of files.

mt

You can control a tape drive by using the mt (magnetic tape) command. To display the tape drive status, use the following command:

```
example> mt -f /dev/rmt/0 status
Exabyte EXB-8200 8mm tape drive:
sense key(0x0)= NO Additional Sense residual= 0  retries= 0
file no= 0    block no= 0
```

In the preceding command, the tape used is blank.

A quick way to scan a system and locate the status of all tape drives is as follows:

```
mt -f /dev/rmt/$drive status
```

The mt command also enables you to fast forward, fast backward, rewind, and eject the tape. If you use the mt command to fast forward, you can fast forward n number of archive files. The option used for fast forwarding is fsf. For example, in the following command, the tape is fast-forwarded and the pointer is placed after the three archived files:

```
example> mt -f /dev/rmt/0 fsf 3
```

Fast backward is the opposite of fast forward, where you skip preceding archive files. To fast backward, use the nbsf option with the mt command. The following example fast backwards 3 archive files:

```
example> mt -f /dev/rmt/0 nbsf 3
```

To completely rewind the tape, use the rew option as follows:

```
example> mt -f /dev/rmt/0 rew
```

If you want to erase the data in the tape, use the erase option.

```
example> mt -f /dev/rmt/0 erase
```

dd

The dd command converts and copies a file. It reads the standard input, does the specified conversions, and copies this data to the standard output. The quantity of data read by the dd command in one operation is referred to as a *block size*. The input and output block size can also be specified to take advantage of the raw physical I/O. This block size is specified in bytes. The operands ibs=n and obs=n specify the input and output block sizes, respectively, where n refers to the number of bytes. The default size in bytes is 512.

CAUTION

> When copying files, ensure that the block sizes of the media and destination file systems are the same.

The following example uses the dd command to copy content of tape 0h to tape 01:

```
# dd if=/dev/rmt/0h  of=/dev/rmt/1h
```

cpio

This command copies files into and out of archived storage and directories. These files are copied into the raw device rather than the block device, because writing to a block is done asynchronously, so there is no way to know when the end-of-media is reached during the write process. The three cpio commands are cpio -o, cpio -i, and cpio -p.

- The cpio -o command reads the standard input for a list of file path names and copies these files to standard output. The output is in the form of a cpio archive.

- The `cpio -i` command reads an archive from the standard input and conditionally extracts the files contained in it and places them into the current directory tree.

- The `cpio -p` command reads the standard input file for file path names and copies these files into the destination directory tree.

For example, the `ls . | cpio -o > myarchive` command reads a list of files from the standard input and writes a new archive to the standard output, `myarchive`. Such a list might be produced by the `ls` or `find` commands.

pax

Portable archive interchange (`pax`) is used to retrieve information on the members of archive files. There are four modes of operation for the `pax` command: list, read, write, and copy.

Table 15.2 lists the four modes of operation and the corresponding syntax.

TABLE 15.2   FOUR MODES OF OPERATION OF THE *pax* COMMAND

Mode of Operation	Syntax
List	pax
Read	pax -r
Write	pax -w
Copy	pax -r -w

The list mode writes the archive file members along with their path names, extended attributes (if any), and file hierarchy of directories.

The read mode reads the archive file details from the standard input, which includes the archive file member names and their path names. The write mode writes this information to the standard output.

The copy mode copies the file operands to the destination directory. The following list provides examples for all modes of operations for the `pax` command.

- To archive the current directory to device, use the following syntax:
  ```
  # pax -w -f /dev/rdiskette
  ```

- To list archives from the preceding pax, use the following syntax:
  ```
  # pax -l -f /dev/rdiskette
  ```

- To extract one file from the archive, use the following syntax:
  ```
  # pax -r -f /dev/rdiskette /var/log/authlog
  /var/log/authlog
  ```

15

volcopy

Whereas the cpio command is used to move files in one file system to another, the volcopy command is used to make a literal copy or an image copy of the entire file system. Note that cpio and volcopy perform two different tasks, and you should be careful in choosing the relevant command that is more suitable for your situation.

The syntax for volcopy is as follows:

```
volcopy [ -F FSType ] [ -V ] [ generic_options ] [ -o FSType-specific_options ]
operands
```

The -f option specifies the file system type.

> **NOTE**
> The volcopy options are not identical for the different types of file systems on a system. For example, there are separate versions of volcopy for the vxfs and ufs file system types.

The -v option validates the command line but does not execute the command.

The syntax next specifies an argument. These options are mostly supported by the file system-specific command modules. The options available are -a and -s. The -a options prompt the operator to respond whether the copy should be made or not. It waits for 10 seconds for the operator to respond before starting to copy. The -s option invokes the del-if-wrong verification sequence.

For example, you can use the volcopy command to transfer the contents of the old /export/home file system to the new /export/home file system on a separate disk that was recently added to your system.

```
# volcopy -F ufs /export/home  /dev/rdsk/c0t1d0s3 - /dev/rdsk/c0t3d0s3  -
```

Because a file system type has not been specified on the command line, volcopy gets the file system type from /etc/vfstab. If the file system type is not defined in /etc/vfstab, it must be specified on the command line as an argument to the -f option.

The arguments take the following values:

- **fsname**—The mounted name of the file system being copied (such as /home2).
- **src_dev**—The disk partition or tape (such as /dev/rdsk/c0b0t1d0s4 or /dev/rmt/c0s0) from which you are copying the file system. It must be a character special device.

> **NOTE**
> Character special devices are devices or files that support other devices on the system, such as terminals and printers.

- **volname1**—The name (up to six characters long) of the physical volume from which you are copying the file system. (For example: home2, representing /home2, or -, representing the existing volume name.)

15

- **dest_dev**—The disk partition or tape (such as `/dev/rdsk/c0b0t2d0s3` or `/dev/rmt/c0s0`) to which you are copying the file system.

- **volname2**—The name (up to six characters long) of the physical volume to which you are copying the file system. (For example: `bhome2`, representing `backup of home2`, or `-` representing the existing media volume name.)

For example, to make a backup copy of the `/home2` file system, you might enter the following:

```
# volcopy /home2 /dev/rdsk/c0b0t1d0s4 home2 /dev/rdsk/c0b0t2d0s3 bhome2
```

THIRD PARTY BACKUP UTILITIES

In addition to the built-in backup utilities available in Solaris 9 OE, you can use third-party utilities such as Veritas Net Backup and AMANDA to back up data. The following sections discuss the features supported by these utilities.

VERITAS NET BACKUP

The VOS Initiative is the collaboration of Veritas, Oracle, and Sun to integrate the leading server and OS platform, database, and data availability solutions. The solutions provided by Veritas offer offline storage for basic protection of data and a range of other backup and recovery products. Veritas software solutions are scalable, and protect and access mission-critical data in your Solaris environment. The products like Veritas Volume Manager and Veritas Volume Replicator offer disk, online storage, and data management solutions for Solaris OE.

Veritas NetBackup for Solaris offers seamless backup and data protection. The key specifications of the Veritas NetBackup software are

- Multihosted drives
- Media Manager Configuration Analyzer
- Multiplexing with the FlashBackup feature
- Improved caching of migrated files

The Veritas NetBackup software also supports Veritas NetBackup server/client authentication and standardized automated integration between Veritas Storage Manager and Veritas NetBackup software.

The key benefits provided by the utility are

- Transparent access to migrated data for virtually unlimited disk storage space
- Multi-tier migration hierarchy to enable high-performance copy, purge, cache, and migration
- Extensive robotics-device and media support
- Graphical user interface to reduce the time needed to perform backup operations

15

AMANDA

The Advanced Maryland Automated Network Disk Archiver (AMANDA) is a public domain utility developed at the University of Maryland. It is an advanced, free backup utility, and has a large user community. You can use AMANDA to set up a single master backup server for backing up multiple hosts to a single backup drive. AMANDA uses native dump, GNUtar, and can be used to back up a large number of workstations running multiple versions of Unix.

AMANDA uses a holding disk on the tape server machine, does several dumps in parallel into files in the holding disk, and has an independent process that takes data out of the holding disk. In AMANDA, a dump cycle is defined for each area to control the maximum time between full dumps. AMANDA uses the dump cycle information, statistics about past dump performance, and estimates on the size of dumps for this run to decide the backup level. This enables you to use AMANDA for balancing the dumps so the total run time is consistent over days.

The salient features of AMANDA are as follows:

- Designed to handle large numbers of clients and data
- Simple to install and maintain
- Scalability
- Code that is is portable to a large number of Unix platforms
- Use of standard backup software, such as vendor provided dump or GNU tar, to perform actual client dumping
- Support for backing up Windows-based hosts via SAMBA
- Reduced network traffic and client CPU load because software compression is enabled
- Configuration options that are available for controlling almost all aspects of the backup operation and that provide several scheduling methods.

You can use AMANDA for performing periodic archival backup, such as taking full dumps to a vault away from the primary site. Some database areas change completely between each backup operation. You can implement single-restore operations that make it possible to perform full dumps for such database areas.

Using AMANDA makes it convenient to support multiple configurations on the same tape server machine. If there are multiple tape drives, you can enable multiple configurations to run simultaneously on the same tape server.

AMANDA also has a simple tape management system that protects AMANDA from overwriting tapes that still have valid dump images. AMANDA also restricts overwrite from tapes that are not allocated to the configuration. AMANDA permits images to be overwritten when a client is down for an extended period or if not enough tapes are allocated. Prior to the overwrite, AMANDA issues several warnings. AMANDA also can be instructed not to reuse specific tapes. AMANDA emails an activity report after each run. You can also direct AMANDA to send a report to a printer or generate sticky tape labels.

AMANDA does not have a graphical interface. To administer the utility, you need to edit a single text file. User-controlled file recovery is also not supported for security reasons. To make searching online dump catalogs easier when recovering individual files, use an FTP-like restore utility.

Locations of additional software used on the clients, such as GNU, `tar`, and SAMBA, are built into the AMANDA programs during configuration. This requires additional software to be installed in the same place on the AMANDA build machine and on all the clients.

SUMMARY

Data is critical to any organization and therefore ensuring its safety is very important. Data can be secured by backing it up on a regular basis. For large organizations where there is a large volume of data, the backup procedure has to be well planned and laid out. You must first know what to back up, and you should plan for the volume of data that is to be backed up, the devices that will be used to perform the backups, the type of backup, and so on.

In Solaris, you back up file systems and the files and directories within them. The root file system contains the most critical data. It contains the kernel and device drivers. You must back up the root file system at regular intervals. Directories such as /var and /export contain volatile data. These directories should be backed up as frequently as on a daily basis. Based upon the amount of data to back up, you can back up your data onto floppy disks, zip disks, tapes, optical disks, or Sun StorEdge storage arrays.

You can perform three types of backup: full, incremental, and snapshot. A full backup enables you to back up an entire file system. This backup type ensures that your data is found on a single location. Although it is one of the safest modes of backup, making a full backup for large file systems on a daily basis can be strenuous and time consuming. In this case, incremental backups can be used. Incremental backups make a copy of the data that was modified after the last backup. These backups can be performed on a daily basis. The third backup type is snapshot, which takes an image snapshot of your data.

Several utilities are available in Solaris to back up and restore your data. The most commonly used backup and restore utilities are `ufsdump` and `ufsrestore`, respectively. The other built-in backup utilities are `tar`, `mt`, `dd`, `cpio`, `pax`, and `volcopy`. There are several third-party backup solutions, among which the most common are Veritas NetBackup and AMANDA.

## CHAPTER 16

PROCESS MANAGEMENT

In this chapter

Processes—An Overview   278

The CDE Process Manager   283

Process Scheduling   286

Summary   292

PROCESSES—AN OVERVIEW

A process is an instance of a running program. It can be any task that has an address space, executes its own piece of code, and has a unique process ID (PID). When a system executes multiple processes, the execution time for processes such as commands or programs may vary. Some programs may take a long time to complete execution; others may execute almost instantaneously. To avoid unnecessary delays, Solaris supports multitasking, which involves running multiple processes at a single instance. This chapter looks at what processes are and how to manage these processes in a Solaris environment.

A process can create another process called a *child process*. Any process that creates the child process is called the *parent process*. This creation of new processes from existing parent processes is called *forking* (after the C function called fork()). Most processes in the system are created by fork system calls. A system call causes the current process to be split into two processes: a parent process and a child process. The child process continues to execute on the CPU until it completes. On completion, the child process returns to the system any resources that it used during its execution. While the child process is running, the parent process either waits for the child process to complete or continues to execute. If the parent process continues to execute, it periodically checks for the completion of the child process.

Running multiple processes has an impact on system performance because the processes consume system resources, such as memory and processor time, and some processes may even cause the system to hang. Managing processes becomes important in a multi-user environment such as Solaris. Managing processes involves monitoring the processes, finding the resource usage, finding the parent processes that have created child processes, assigning priority for processes, and terminating processes.

MONITORING PROCESSES

A process undergoes many changes during its lifetime. For example, if a parent process waits for the child process to complete execution, the parent process puts itself in sleep state. Such a change from run state to sleep state is known as a *context switch*. During its lifetime a process can exist in four states: Init, Run, Sleep, and Zombie. Init is the first genuine user process the system creates. All other processes on the system are created by forking the Init process. If the process is in the Run state, it means that the process is running on the CPU. In the Sleep state, the process waits for a child process to complete, or waits for a resource. Zombie is the phase in which the child process terminates and is not removed from the system until the parent process acknowledges the death of the child process. In this case, the child process is said to be in a Zombie state.

THE ps COMMAND

To view the state of a process, use the ps and pgrep commands. The ps command, without any options, lists the process ID (PID), associated terminal (TTY), the cumulative execution time (TIME), and the command that generated the process (CMD)(see Listing 16.1) .

LISTING 16.1 *ps* COMMAND OUTPUT

```
$ ps
   PID TTY       TIME CMD
  6213 pts/5    0:00 sh
  6233 pts/5    0:00 ps
```

The ps -a command lists the most frequently requested processes. It displays only the processes that are associated with the terminal from which the ps command is issued. To list all the processes currently running on a system, use the -A option with the ps command.

The ps -el command displays a full listing of all the processes running on the system (see Listing 16.2).

LISTING 16.2 *ps-el* COMMAND OUTPUT

```
$ps -el
 F S    UID   PID  PPID  C PRI NI    ADDR      SZ  WCHAN TTY     TIME CMD
19 T      0     0     0  0   0 SY       ?       0      ?       0:15 sched
 8 S      0     1     0  0  40 20       ?     151    ? ?       0:00 init
19 S      0     2     0  0   0 SY       ?       0    ? ?       0:00 pageout
19 S      0     3     0  0   0 SY       ?       0    ? ?      10:43 fsflush
 8 S      0   314     1  0  40 20       ?     222    ? ?       0:00 sac
 8 S      0   229     1  0  40 20       ?     130    ? ?       0:00 utmpd
 8 S      0   180     1  0  40 20       ?     596    ? ?       0:01 automoun
 8 S      0    52     1  0  40 20       ?     283    ? ?       0:00 sysevent
 8 S      0    59     1  0  40 20       ?     338    ? ?       0:01 picld
 8 S      0   111     1  0  40 20       ?     208    ? ?       0:02 in.route
 8 S      0   118     1  0  40 20       ?     242    ? ?       0:00 in.ndpd
 8 S      0   156     1  0  40 20       ?     311    ? ?       0:00 inetd
 8 S      0   188     1  0  40 20       ?     417    ? ?       0:00 syslogd
 8 S      0   133     1  0  40 20       ?     308    ? ?       0:00 rpcbind
 8 S      0   170     1  0  40 20       ?     289    ? ?       0:00 lockd
 8 S     25   420     1  0  40 20       ?     535    ? ?       0:00 sendmail
 8 S      1   169     1  0  40 20       ?     318    ? ?       0:00 statd
 8 S      0   218     1  0  40 20       ?     176    ? ?       0:00 powerd
 8 S      0   195     1  0  40 20       ?     284    ? ?       0:00 cron
 8 S      0   210     1  0  40 20       ?     387    ? ?       0:01 nscd
 8 S      0  4972  4971  0  80 30       ?     520    ? ?       0:00 dtscreen
```

The following are the fields displayed in the output for the ps -el command shown in Listing 16.2.

- F—Flags associated with the process.
- S—The state of the process.
- UID—The user ID.
- PID—Each process has an associated ID. You can use this ID to determine the state of a specific process.
- PPID—The parent process ID.
- C—Processor utilization.

■ PRI—The set scheduling parameters for a process.

■ NI—The nice value displays the assigned priority to the process.

NOTE

For further information on the fields, view man pages for the ps command.

■ ADDR—The memory address of the process.

■ SZ—The total number of pages in the process, in virtual memory, including all mapped files and devices.

■ WCHAN—The address of an event for which the process is sleeping.

■ TTY—The terminal from which the process originated. System processes have a ? in this field.

■ TIME—The processor utilization time.

■ CMD—The command that has spawned the process.

THE pgrep COMMAND

The pgrep command displays a list of the process IDs of active processes on the system that match the pattern specified in the command line. The pgrep command functionally combines the ps command with the grep command. The syntax for the pgrep command is as follows:

```
pgrep [-option] pattern
```

Table 16.1 describes the options of the pgrep command.

TABLE 16.1   THE OPTIONS FOR THE pgrep COMMAND AND THEIR DESCRIPTIONS

Options	Description
-g pgrplist	Matches the processes with the process group ID.
-G gidlist	Matches the active processes with the group ID(s) specified in the command line. For example, if you are searching for processes running with the group ID sysman, specify the command pgrep −G sysman.
-d delim	Specifies a delimiter for separating PIDs.
-n	Matches the most recent process.
-P ppidlist	The processes are matched with the parent process ID in the listing.
-s sidlist	The processes are matched with the session ID in the list.
-t termlist	Matches the terminal on which the process is running.
-u euidlist	Matches processes with the effective used ID in the list. The effective uid is the uid of the executable file when the SUID of the file is set.
-U uidlist	Matches processes with the real uid in the list. The real uid is the uid that the user uses when starting a task or a process.

Options	Description
-v	Matches all processes except those that meet the specified criteria in the command line.
-f	Matches pattern against full arguments rather than the name of the exe cutable file.
-x	Matches the processes that exactly match the specified pattern.

The following example displays the process ID for the process sh:

```
$ pgrep sh
3
8027
307
765
762
6488
7970
8147
8150
```

The following command displays the process ID of all those processes matching the in pattern:

```
$ pgrep in*
1
59
111
118
156
```

The pgrep command with the -l option displays the name of the processes, which contains the string in along with their PIDs.

```
$ pgrep -l in
    1 init
  111 in.routed
  118 in.ndpd
  156 inetd
  133 rpcbind
```

The following command displays the processes owned by user James:

```
$ pgrep -u james
1459
1464
$
```

You can combine options. In the following example, both the -l and the -u options are used together with the pgrep command to display the names of all the processes run by user James, along with his process ID.

```
$ pgrep -l -u james
 1459 sh
 1464 csh
```

The -d option is used to specify a delimiter for separating PIDs when more than one process ID is tested in the output of the pgrep command. The following example uses delimiters for the listed processes for the user James.

```
$ pgrep -d";" -u james
951; 1042; 1051
```

NOTE

> You can specify more than one user ID by using a comma (,) as a field separator.

TERMINATING PROCESSES

Use the kill and the pkill commands to terminate a process. These commands send the appropriate signal to the intended processes to terminate them. A signal notifies a process that an event has occurred. The event could be raised because of issues with the hardware or software, a change in the system date, a change in the system state, and so forth. An inter-process communication takes place because one process sends a signal to another process to instruct the latter to act in a certain manner.

THE kill COMMAND

The kill command enables the user to kill the process. Only a superuser can kill a process owned by others. The kill command sends a signal to a process, which is used to terminate it. The syntax for the kill command is

```
# kill <signal> <process ID>
```

To kill a process, you should know its process ID. To find the process ID, you may use the following command:

```
ps -ef | grep <process name>
```

Even though many signals are available, signal 15 and 9 are the ones that are generally used with the kill command. Signal 15 sends the SIGTERM signal to the specified process. The SIGTERM signal is referred to as a "gentle signal," which allows the process to rectify itself. Unlike the SIGTERM signal, the SIGKILL (signal 9) is a "sure kill" signal. The processes that are not responding to the SIGTERM signal can be killed with the SIGKILL signal.

Some processes still exist even after a SIGTERM signal. A process might still be alive for the following reasons:

- The process is hung.
- The process is waiting for some other process to execute.
- The process is in the state of Zombie. Note that the process in the Zombie state is not alive and does not use any resources or accomplish any work. However, it is not allowed to die until the parent process acknowledges the exit call.

- The process is waiting for some unavailable resources. The resources may be network resources or access to a device.

NOTE

> The `kill` command, without any signal, issues the SIGTERM (signal 15), by default.

The following syntax sends signal 15 to the process with a process ID of 1305.

```
# kill 1305
```

The following example illustrates using the `kill` command to send signal 9 to kill three different processes:

```
$ kill -9 3012 3019 3510
$ 3510 killed
$ 3019 killed
$ 3012 killed
```

Any number preceded by a minus (-) sign in the `<PID>` field represents a process group ID. In the following example, the –9 signal is sent to the process with PID 1039 and all the processes with the process group 117.

```
#kill -9 1039 -117
```

THE pkill COMMAND

The `pkill` command terminates the displayed processes that match the pattern specified. The pattern is a regular expression that is used to specify processes based on the program name. The `pkill` command sends the SIGTERM (signal 15) to the matching processes. The command syntax for the `pkill` command is as follows:

```
pkill [-option] pattern.
```

For example, to terminate the most recently created Admintool, type the following:

```
# pkill -n admintool
```

The `pkill` command takes any signal other than signal 15 (SIGKILL). The following command sends a SIGKILL signal to the processes owned by user Romando:

```
# pkill -9 -u romando
```

THE CDE PROCESS MANAGER

CDE provides a Process Manager utility to manage processes. You can use Process Manager to change the priority of the processes and to kill them. To kill a process, select a process in the window and click the Kill option in the Process menu. You also can use the Ctrl+C keyboard combination to kill the selected process.

You also can use Process Manager to send signals to a process. For example, to send a sure kill signal to a process, perform the following steps:

1. Select the process from the Process menu.

2. Click the Signal option. The Signal dialog box is displayed.

3. Type **9** in the Signal text box, and press Enter to kill the process.

Process Manager enables you to sort the processes by any of the displayed fields. For example, you click the CPU% option to sort the processes by the amount of CPU time they consume.

Process Manager also enables you to save a list of processes to a log file. It offers a filter option that you use to display all process entries that match the specified criterion.

Figure 16.1 shows the Process Manager window.

Figure 16.1
The CDE Process
Manager window.

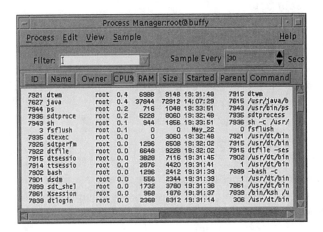

The Process Manager presents a list of all processes on a system. The following are the fields displayed in the Process Manager window:

- **ID**—The process ID
- **Name**—The name of the process
- **Owner**—The owner of the process
- **CPU%**—The CPU time consumed
- **RAM**—The physical memory used
- **Size**— The total virtual memory size of the process, including all mapped files and devices.
- **Started**—The date the process was started
- **Parent**—The parent process ID
- **Command**—The full command string

With the Process Manager, you can sort the processes on the system on the basis of any of the items in the above list. For example, if you click the CPU% option, the process list is displayed on the basis of the CPU usage.

To save a sample of the process listing in a log file, open the Sample submenu of the Process Manager and select the Log File option. This displays the Process Manager—Log File dialog box as shown in Figure 16.2. Specify the location of the log file.

Figure 16.2
The Process Manager–Log File dialog box.

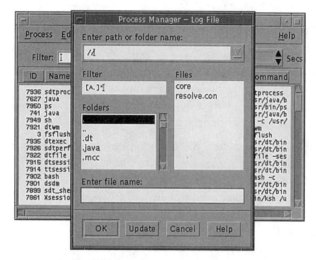

To save a log file of a single sample, choose Sample, Save. The Save As window is displayed. Specify the log file location and click Save, which creates the process log.

With the Process Manager, filter processes that match specified text. Type some text in the Filter text box in the Process Manager and press Return. This displays the process entries that match the typed text. Figure 16.3 shows the processes containing /usr/sbin in their process entries.

Figure 16.3
The process entries that match
/usr/sbin criteria specified in the filter text box.

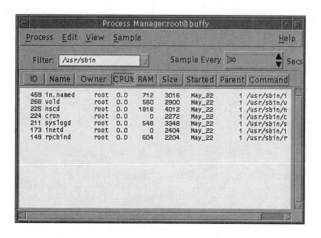

Empty the filter text box and press Enter to redisplay all the processes on the system.

To kill a process, select the process from the listing and select Process, Kill. You also send signals to a process, similar to the signals sent from the command line. For example, to send signal 9 (sure kill) for killing a process, select the process from the Process Manager, click the Signal option, which displays an Action:Signal window where you specify 9 in the Signal text box and press Enter to kill the process.

PROCESS SCHEDULING

Solaris OE offers commands that let you take extra advantage of your existing computer resources. For example, use the crontab and at commands for automatic execution of system events at a scheduled time. The crontab command can schedule multiple system events, whereas the at command schedules a single system event. These commands schedule processes to run when you are not present to start them manually.

In addition to scheduling processes, you can use the nice and the renice commands to alter the priority in which these processes are executed. Before delving into the way to use these commands for changing the priorities of the processes, it's a good idea to look at how you can use the crontab and at commands to schedule processes.

THE crontab COMMAND

The cron daemon schedules events by referring to the crontab files. The crontab files are stored in the /var/spool/cron/crontab directory. The crontab files contain commands that are executed at the scheduled time, which is also specified in the crontab file. Each line corresponds to a command. Each crontab command represents a scheduled task, which is known as a cron job. Any user who has permissions to schedule events has his or her own crontab file.

The crontab file contains six fields. Table 16.2 lists the fields of the crontab file and their descriptions.

TABLE 16.2 THE FIELDS OF THE crontab FILE AND THEIR DESCRIPTIONS

Field No	Field	Values	Description
1	Minute	0-59	Minute of the hour
2	Hour	0-23	Hour of the day
3	Day	1-31	Day of the month
4	Month	1-12	Month of the year
5	Weekday	0-6	Day of the week(0=Sunday)
6	Command	NA	The command to execute

A cron daemon reads this file and schedules the system events accordingly.

By default, the /var/spool/cron/crontabs directory contains the crontab files for system accounts. The default crontab files are adm for accounting, lp for printing, root for administrative tasks, sys for performance collection, and uucp for general Unix-to-Unix Copy (uucp) cleanup.

The /etc/default/cron file alters the functionality of the cron utility. To log the activities of the cron command, ensure the presence of the following entry:

```
CRONLOG=YES
```

This entry logs the activity of cron in the /var/cron/log file. To disable logging, modify this entry as follows:

```
CRONLOG=NO
```

16

Reboot the system to bring the changes into effect.

You can control users' access to the crontab command by using the /etc/cron.d/cron.allow and the /etc.cron.d/cron.deny files. The /etc/cron.d/cron.allow file consists of a list of users who are allowed to use the crontab command. This file does not exist by default. A user's access to the crontab command is confirmed after a search for this file. If the file does not exist, the /etc/cron.d/cron.deny file, which contains a list of users whose access to the crontab command is prohibited, is searched.

By default, the cron.deny file prohibits crontab use by the following system users:

- daemon
- bin
- smtp
- nuucp
- listen
- nobody
- noaccess

If both the files cron.allow and cron.deny do not exist, all users are denied access to crontab except the superuser.

To create a crontab file, use the -e option of the crontab command followed by the file name. For example, the following syntax creates the crontab file for the user Harris:

```
# crontab -e harris
```

The crontab command with the -e option is also used to edit an existing crontab file.

The -1 option lists a crontab file. The following example displays the lp crontab file used for printing.

```
# crontab -1 lp
```

The -r option is used to delete the crontab file. The following example deletes the crontab file for user Harris.

```
# crontab -r harris
```

CAUTION

> If you have accidentally typed the crontab command without any arguments, exit with Ctrl+C. Exiting with Ctrl+D removes all entries in your crontab file.

16 THE at COMMAND

The at command schedules a single system event only once, unlike the crontab command, which can schedule multiple system events repetitively at specified periods. The at command enables users to create, display, and remove their own at jobs.

To schedule at jobs, type **at** followed by the time. After you type this, a prompt <at> is displayed. Specify the command or script that has to execute at the specified time. The time is mentioned in minutes, hours, days, and months.

The following example shows how to remove the files from the home directory of user Jency at 9.55 p.m. on August 2.

```
$ at 9:55PM
at> rm /export/home/jency
at> rm /albert
at> mkdir / albert1
at> <EOT>
commands will be executed using /sbin/sh
job 996807300.a at Thu Aug  2 21:55:00 2001
$
```

NOTE

> Type Ctrl+C to exit the at prompt.

Each at job is given a job ID and has a suffix of .a, which identifies it is an at job. When more than one job is scheduled for execution, it is queued as per the time schedule. To display this queue, use the atq command.

```
# atq
 Rank     Execution Date    Owner    Job          Queue   Job Name
 1st   Aug  2, 2001 21:55   root   996807300.a     a      stdin
 2nd   Aug 15, 2001 12:00   root   997894800.a     a      stdin
#
```

Table 16.3 describes the options of the at command.

Options	Description
-m	Sends mail to the user after execution of the job.
-r	Removes at jobs.
-l	Displays information about the execution time.

TABLE 16.3   THE at COMMAND OPTIONS AND THEIR DESCRIPTIONS

To display an at job you should know its job ID. The -l option is used for this. Type **at -l**, followed by the job ID with the at command to display the at job.

```
$ at -l <job ID>
```

The at -l command, without any arguments, displays the status information for all the at jobs created by the user who executes the at -l command.

```
$ at -l
user = root      996807300.a     Thu Aug  2 21:55:00 2001
user = root      997894800.a     Wed Aug 15 12:00:00 2001
$
```

The at -r command followed by the job ID removes the at job with the specified job ID.

```
# at -r <job id>
```

nice AND renice COMMAND

Commands or processes normally run with equal priority unless specified otherwise. Also, these commands or processes with equal priorities share the CPU resources at an equal level. In some environments, large numbers of processes may be running on a system simultaneously. In this case, it is important to make sure that the system resources are used wisely. You can use the nice command to alter the access priority of processes to system resources.

Every process has a nice number along with the execution priority. Although the system uses the execution priority to determine the order of execution, the system uses the nice number to determine the priority of a process compared to other processes. Every process starts with a nice number that it inherits from the parent process.

The nice number for a process can range from 0 to +40 with 0 indicating the highest priority and 40 indicating the lowest priority. To change the priority order of a process by using the nice command, change the process's nice number. For example, to increase the priority of a process by 10 units, decrease the nice number by 10. The higher the value of nice, the lower is its execution priority.

Both the standard version and the /usr/bin/nice version of the nice command in Solaris use the following syntax:

```
/usr/bin/nice -[+ | -n] command_name
```

In the /usr/bin version of the nice command, the value to add or subtract from the nice number is preceded by a hyphen. For example, to decrease the nice number from 30 to 24, use the following syntax. Note that if no number is specified, the `nice` number is increased by 10 by default, which decreases the priority value by 10 units.

```
/usr/bin/nice --6 command_name
```

Similarly, to increase the `nice` number from 24 to 30, use the following syntax:

```
/usr/bin/nice -6 command_name
```

You can also change the priority of a process while the process is running. Solaris OE provides the `renice` command, which you use to change the priority of an executing process. The `renice` command takes the PID of the process as the operand. The command uses the following syntax:

```
renice [-n priority_change] PID
```

The -n option in the preceding syntax defines the number of units by which to increase or decrease the priority of the running process. By default, all the processes running on the system are assigned a `nice` value equal to 20. Note that after altering the priority of the running process, the new `nice` value is 20 +/- the priority change. This value can range from 0 through 39. PID is the process ID for which the priority has to be changed.

For example, to decrease the priority of the process for PID 324 by 5 during runtime, use the following command:

```
renice -n 5 -p 324
```

In the preceding command, the new `nice` value for the process will be 15.

You also can use the `renice` command to change the priority of processes belonging to a particular user. For example, to increase the execution priority of processes belonging to the user David by 8 units, use the following command:

```
renice -n -8 -u David
```

THE `priocntl` COMMAND

The Solaris OE provides the `priocntl` command, which you use to change the scheduling behavior of a process. The command displays or sets the priority of the processes. You can also use the `priocntl` command to display the current configuration information of the process scheduler.

Table 16.4 describes the options of the `priocntl` command.

TABLE 16.4 THE `priocntl` COMMAND OPTIONS AND THEIR DESCRIPTIONS

Options	Description
-l	Lists currently loaded scheduling classes.
-d	Displays the scheduling parameters of a process.
-e	Creates a process.
-p	Changes the priority of an existing process.

The `priocntl -l` command displays a list of the currently loaded scheduling classes. A sample output of the command follows.

```
# priocntl -l
CONFIGURED CLASSES
==================
SYS (System Class)
TS (Time Sharing)
        Configured TS User Priority Range: -60 through 60
IA (Interactive)
        Configured IA User Priority Range: -60 through 60
#
```

The `priocntl -l` command displays the scheduling parameters of a process. A sample output of the command follows.

```
# priocntl -d -i pid 1
TIME SHARING PROCESSES:
    PID     TSUPRILIM     TSUPRI
     1          0                     0
```

The `priocntl -l` command creates a process. For example, the following command starts the `find` command with a priority of 10.

```
# priocntl -e -c TS -p 10 find / -name core -print
```

In the preceding command, the `-e` option executes the command. The `-c` option specifies the class in which the command executes.

TRUSS

Solaris OE offers the truss utility that you use to track processes running on a system. The truss utility is similar to the trace utility of Solaris 4.x. The truss utility reports the following information about processes:

- System calls made by a process, including arguments and return values
- Signals received by the process
- Machine faults encountered by the process

You use the truss utility to debug problems with processes. Although truss is not a debugging utility, it helps you identify problems a process encounters.

You can use the truss utility to track any executable command or a currently running process by using the PID value of the process. The truss utility tracks the child processes until the process exits. The truss utility uses the following syntax to track processes that are running on the system:

```
truss -aef -p PID
```

where PID is the process ID of a currently running process.

To use truss with an executable command, use the following syntax:

```
truss -aef <command>
```

Table 16.5 shows the commonly used options of the truss command and their descriptions. For a complete list of options, refer to the man pages for the truss command.

TABLE 16.5 THE truss COMMAND OPTIONS AND THEIR DESCRIPTIONS

Option	Description
-a	Displays the arguments to each exec() system call.
-c	Displays a summary of all the system calls made by a process.
-e	Displays the environment of a running process.
-f	Follows all child processes created by the fork and vfork system calls.
-o	Saves the output of the command to a specified file.
-p	Attaches the truss command to a currently running process.

By default, the truss utility dumps the output to the stderr file. You can save the output of the truss utility by using the -o option with the truss command. For example, to save the output of the truss command to the trussoutput.out file use the following command:

```
truss -aef -o /tmp/trussoutput.out -p PID
```

SUMMARY

The multitasking, multiprocessing, and multithreading design of Solaris enables it to provide enhanced performance for key enterprise applications along with stability and accuracy. A process is a running instance of a program. For example, a browser window running on your workstation is a process of the browser program.

Most processes in the system are created by fork system calls. The fork system call makes a copy (child process) of the calling process (parent process) in a new address space in the virtual memory. The child process continues to execute on the CPU until it completes. On completion, the child process returns the resources to the system. A process during its lifetime can exist in any of the following states: Init, Run, Sleep, and Zombie.

Processes running on a system affect the performance of the system because processes consume system resources, such as CPU time and memory. Therefore, it is important that you manage the processes running on the system. Managing the processes running on the system involves monitoring processes, determining processor usage, changing process priorities, and terminating processes.

## CHAPTER 17

ADMINISTERING REMOTE SYSTEMS

In this chapter

Remote Login Services   294

Transferring Files Across Remote Systems   304

Summary   307

REMOTE LOGIN SERVICES

A remote system can be defined as a server or a terminal that needs to be accessed over the network from a different location. Such a feature is required for users who want to perform an operation on different systems from any location on the network.

In a typical business environment, a network may consist of different systems where more than one user may access each system. For example, a typical network at a company's IS department may host a set of systems to maintain vital information. More than one user may access each system to prepare reports, or to execute specific commands to perform various tasks. Designing such complex network architecture and providing remote system accessibility to different users is a challenging task.

Administering these remote systems is the next challenge, especially in a network that hosts a large number of systems. Administering individual systems becomes increasingly difficult as the number of systems grows larger. Therefore, a technique must be adopted to manage remote systems.

Allowing users to administer different systems from various locations involves a high security risk. Vital information becomes vulnerable as gaining access to data becomes easier to users. A strict login authentication is implemented to ensure valid access to remote systems. A user must log in to a remote system to carry out activities. After login, the user gains access to the remote system and is allowed to perform tasks, such as copying files and executing commands.

Solaris provides various tools, such as `rlogin`, `rsh`, `rcp`, and `ftp` to access and administer remote systems. These tools allow administrators and users to log in to remote systems, execute commands remotely, and transfer files between systems. Remote access is backed up by a strong authentication technology that ensures guaranteed security to remote systems.

> **NOTE**
>
> To administer remote systems over an insecure network such as the Internet, you should use a remote login service such as SSH to avoid security compromises. `rlogin`, `rcp`, and `rsh` do not provide a strong authentication or encryption mechanism. These services must be disabled on business-critical systems.

This chapter explains the commands that are used to perform the most common tasks on remote systems. This chapter also explains the parameters supplied with the commands in detail.

THE TELNET UTILITY

Telnet is a TCP/IP protocol that provides connectivity to computers on TCP/IP networks. Telnet uses TCP to establish communication between computers.

Applications that are developed to use these protocols possess the capability to emulate a remote terminal on local systems. Terminal emulation makes the remote connection transparent to the user. The remote terminal is emulated for the user to provide a similar working environment to that on the local system. The commands that are typed by the user are transmitted to the remote system and the results are transmitted back to the user's system.

The Telnet utility uses the Telnet protocol and is used to establish a communication link with a remote system on the network. The `telnet` command invokes the command mode of the utility and expects the user to type the commands associated with the utility. The Telnet utility first initiates connection with the remote system and enables the user to type commands in the input mode. The input mode can be of three types, depending on the mode supported by the remote system:

- Line mode
- Character-at-a-time
- Old line-by-line

In the line mode, the local system processes the characters under the control of the remote system. The input on the local system is transmitted to the remote system and the changes that take effect on the remote system are transmitted to the local system to be displayed to the user. In the character-at-a-time mode, the characters typed locally are immediately transmitted to the remote system. The remote system independently processes the input and replies to the local system with the output. Old line-by-line mode uses local echo for all text typed locally. The input is displayed on the local system until the end of line is encountered. Only complete lines are transmitted to the remote system.

Table 17.1 provides an overview of commands that can be used in Telnet.

TABLE 17.1   COMMANDS USED IN TELNET

Command	Description
`open –l<username>@<destination>`	Opens connection with a remote system.
`Close/quit`	Close the open session and exit Telnet.
`EOF`	Similar to the `close` command. This can be used only in the command mode.
`Mode <type>`	Specify the input mode for the session.
`Status`	Show the current status of Telnet, which includes the peer connection and the input mode.

THE `rlogin` COMMAND

The `rlogin` command is used to log in to a remote system, just as you do with the Telnet utility. This command initiates a connection to the remote system, which remains transparent to the user throughout the session. The command screen of the remote terminal is emulated locally, enabling the user to perform tasks similar to the tasks performed on a local system. The `rlogin` command provides features such as additional command-line options, session suspension, and the passing of environment variables. These features make it more effective than other remote administration tools, such as Telnet.

The syntax for `rlogin` is:

```
rlogin [-8EL] [-e] [-l username] hostname
```

The parameters in the syntax are explained in Table 17.2.

TABLE 17.2   PARAMETERS IN THE `rlogin` COMMAND

Parameter	Description
-8	Pass 8-bit data, rather than 7-bit, over the network.
-E	Do not accept an escape sequence character'.
-L	Session to be run in "litout" mode.
-e	Specify an escape character.
-l	Username on the remote system.

When someone logs in to a remote system, the domain name of the system needs to be determined and appended to the system name. If the domain name is not provided, the remote system is considered to be a part of the same domain as the local system. The login ID is optional. If the login ID is not provided with the command, the current login ID is used to log in at the remote system.

NOTE

You can terminate remote sessions with the ^d combination to return to the local system prompt.

While you use a typical remote administration tool, such as Telnet, the session should be terminated to return to the local system console.

You can use the escape sequence provided by the `rlogin` command to avoid logging in again. An escape sequence is a character that, when typed, enables the user to return to the local system console without logging off from the remote system. The user can toggle back to the remote system consoles by using the `fg` command. For example:

```
[tom@serv2.solaris.com]$ ~^Z
[1]+ Stopped rlogin solaris.com
[tom@serv1.solaris.com]$ fg
[tom@serv2.solaris.com]$
```

In the preceding example, user Tom from the remote system `serv2.solaris.com` types the `^Z` command to return to the local system console, `serv1.solaris.com`. Now, typing the `fg` command on the local system console toggles user Tom to `serv2.solaris.com`. The `fg` command foregrounds the remote session and returns to the remote terminal. This enables the user to toggle between the sessions without terminating either login session.

The rlogin command passes the terminal information of the local system to the remote session. The terminal information is exported to the remote session in the form of environment variables. For instance, the value in the TERM variable that defines the screen interpretation of the local system's input and output is exported to the remote session after rlogin establishes the connection with the remote system.

The administrator can configure the system to disallow remote logins by ensuring that the nologin file is available in the /etc directory. The nologin file contains the message that is displayed when a user tries to log on to a machine that is in the process of shutting down. Using this file, the administrator can also leave messages for the remote login users about the system status or why the access is denied to remote users. The nologin file, however, does not affect the local logins and the users who have already logged in to the system.

LOGIN AUTHENTICATION

Systems on the network can be configured to authenticate remote logins if similar login rights need to be provided to users within a peer group. This enables users within the peer group to log in from any system within the trusted network. For example, if users from the same department need to use different systems with their single login IDs, each system on the network can be configured to authenticate remote logins independently.

Login for a remote system can be authenticated either by the remote system or the network environment (see Figure 17.1). When the login is authenticated by the remote system, the user validation is performed against the information registered with the remote system. The user and the system details are stored in the /etc/hosts.equiv or $HOME/.rhosts file. The /etc/hosts.equiv or $HOME/.rhosts file is read during the authentication process to validate the remote login. When the network environment has authenticated the login, the trusted systems and users are automatically logged in because they are already known to the trusting network environment.

When the remote system performs the authentication, the information in the local files is used to validate the login if the username and user's system name are registered in either of the following:

- The /etc/hosts.equiv file
- The $HOME/.rhosts file

NOTE

When the remote system performs user authentication, the trusted user is never asked for a password. Therefore, the trusted user's password is never transmitted over the network. This feature of rlogin is not supported by Telnet.

Figure 17.1
Authenticating remote logins.

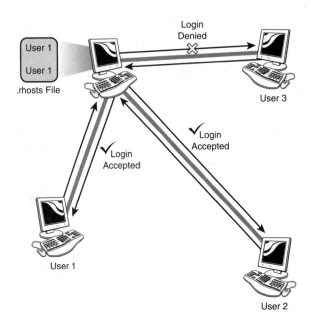

THE hosts.equiv FILE

The entries in the /etc/hosts.equiv file are controlled by the local system administrator. The entries consist of names of the trusted systems. Users attempting to log in from these trusted systems are allowed to access the system without further probe. If there are no entries for a specific system, the user attempting to log in from the system is prompted to enter a valid login name and password to access the remote system. The entries in the hosts.equiv file are as follows:

```
+serv1.solaris.com tom
+serv2.solaris.com
-serv3.solaris.com
```

The entries in the hosts.equiv file determine whether a user from a remote host should be allowed to access the local system with the identity of a local user. In the preceding example, the first entry includes the username Tom at the end of the system name. This ensures that Tom will be allowed to log in without a password being requested, if he attempts to log in from the system, serv1.solaris.com. A plus symbol (+) before the system name means that all systems in the netgroup are trusted. A minus symbol (–) before the system name means that none of the systems in the netgroup are trusted.

The hosts.equiv file needs to be configured to ensure that network security is not breached. As mentioned earlier, a single plus sign before a domain name means that all systems in the netgroup are trusted. This might include systems open to public use or kiosks. Only trusted hosts must be included in the file and if necessary, specific usernames can be configured with the system name to ensure that no other user is allowed to log in without being asked for a password. This file should not include any system that belongs to an entirely different network, which might host dynamic ports to which mobile computers can be connected. Either the hosts.equiv file must be configured to counter all these security issues or the file should be completely removed from the system.

THE .rhosts FILE

The .rhosts file is similar to the hosts.equiv file. The /etc/hosts.equiv file applies to the entire system, whereas individual users can maintain their own .rhosts files in their home directories. The .rhosts file is stored in the user's home directory. It should be noted that the .rhosts file needs to be stored at the top level of the user's home directory and not under any subdirectory. The purpose of maintaining an .rhosts file is similar to that of the hosts.equiv file.

Validation of login primarily depends on the entry made in the hosts.equiv file. When a user attempts to log in at a remote system, the login is validated with the information available in the /etc/hosts.equiv file first. If the file is not found in the remote system or the file does not contain any entry in the name of the remote user, the .rhosts file in the user's home directory is searched for an entry to permit the user to log in. If the .rhosts file does not contain any entry, the user is asked to type a valid password. This information is transmitted over the network and validated by Solaris before the user is permitted to log in at the remote system.

Typical entries in the .rhosts file record the system name and a corresponding username. Each login request from a user is validated against the system from which the login is requested. If only a system name is specified, with no accompanying username, the login name of the remote user is assumed to be the requested login ID. The content of the .rhosts file is similar to the following content:

```
serv1.solaris.com tom
serv2.solaris.com
```

In this example, the first entry that includes the name of the user as Tom ensures that only Tom's login from the system serv1.solaris.com is authorized to attempt a remote login. Others are asked for a valid password during their rlogin attempts. The second entry does not include any username, which would mean that any user from the system serv2.solaris.com can log in without being asked for a password.

Using the .rhosts file for remote login authentication poses a security problem. This file can be created by any user and saved under the home directory. The hosts.equiv file is created and maintained only by the system administrator and the control to modify the file is available only with the administrator. This ensures that invalid entries are avoided and a specific person uses the hosts.equiv file responsibly. On the other hand, any user can create an .rhosts file to authenticate remote logins to his or her system and can modify it whenever required without the knowledge of the system administrator.

17

CAUTION

> If the .rhosts file has a ++ entry, all users are trusted from all systems. This mean that there is no security authentication process to validate remote logins. Therefore, ++ entries should be avoided in an .rhosts file.

You can counter the security problem posed by the .rhosts file by revoking permissions for users to modify the file's content after the system administrator finalizes the entries. The system administrator can change the permission for this file to 000, which disallows any modification to the file, even by the superuser. The .rhosts file is primarily required to allow remote users to perform network backups and other remote services. However, if the .rhosts file is not required to perform these operations, the file can be completely removed from the user's home directory.

NOTE

> Both the hosts.equiv and .rhosts files should contain the actual system name and not a nickname. These files do not exist by default. They need to be explicitly created to provide remote login authentication.

POST LOGIN SEQUENCE

When the user attempts to log in to a remote system, the user's home directory is obtained from the /etc/passwd file of the remote system. If the home directory is found, the user's environment initialization scripts are executed. For example, if you are using the "C" shell, the user's environment variables are placed in the .cshrc and .login files. If the home directory is not found, a message is displayed to notify the user that the home directory is not found and that the root directory in the remote system is assigned as the home directory. However, each user must have a home directory; it is not advisable that all users are allowed to access the root file system. A sample message is shown in the following example:

```
Unable to find home directory, logging in with /
```

The login prompt displays the directory name from where the user had attempted to log in to the remote system. The name of the system in the prompt is changed to the name of the remote system. For example, if user Tom logs in from a system named serv1 and the current working directory on the local system is /home/tom, the initial login prompt looks like the following if the user's default shell is the "C" shell:

```
serv1(/home/tom):
```

If Tom logs in to a remote system named serv2, the directory path in the login prompt remains unchanged, but the name of the system changes, as shown below:

```
serv2(/home/tom)
```

When Tom logs in to serv2, the home directory of the user in the local system is mounted in parallel to the remote user's home directory. The file system is illustrated in Figure 17.2.

Figure 17.2
The directory path in the login prompt.

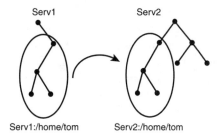

THE SOLARIS SECURE SHELL

Though `rlogin` provides remote login facility to users, it does not implement a secure method of accessing remote systems.

It is imperative to consider a different tool that will provide more control over the network security, especially when the network hosts systems containing vital information that require high levels of security.

Solaris provides Secure Shell as a remote login tool. Similar to the `rlogin` command, Secure Shell provides remote login facility for users on a trusted network. Secure Shell uses strong user authentication methods to provide users a secured access to remote systems on a network. The users are authenticated using password, or session keys (public/private keys) using public key cryptography or a combination of both, depending on the protocol version you are using.

→ For more information on SSH, **see** "Enhanced Security Features," **p.441**.

Transmission over the network is encrypted. This prevents information from being intercepted by intruders. Secure Shell also provides commands that enable users to log in and transfer files over the network both from and to remote systems. Only valid users are allowed to run commands on remote systems.

Secure Shell uses version 2 of Secure Shell Protocol for communication. Version 2 was improved to counter all the basic security design flaws that the earlier version of the protocol exposed.

Authentication methods used in Secure Shell are password-based and key-based. Password-based authentication requires the user to provide a password whenever a login attempt is made. The password is validated and the user gains access to the remote system only if the password is correct. Key-based authentication is based on public key technology. Each user creates a pair of public and private keys. The Secure Shell requires two levels of authentication: user authentication and the host authentication. The default mode of authentication is password-based. If a very high level of security needs to be observed on the network, a pair of public and private keys are created with the `ssh-keygen` command.

→ For more information on the login methods used in SSH, **see** "Enhanced Security Features," **p.441**.

CREATING THE KEY PAIR

The ssh-keygen command is used to create a set of public and private keys, unique for a specific user. These keys are later used for authentication. After the connection is established, a combination of both private and public keys is used to encrypt and decrypt the information communicated between these systems. The keys created by the ssh-keygen command are unique to each user, and each key is also provided with a unique key fingerprint and a passphrase, which make interception and decryption almost impossible.

The following sequence of steps illustrates the procedure to create a private and public key pair for the user Tom from the system named local.

1. Initiate the ssh-keygen command.

   ```
   local(/home/tom): ssh-keygen
   Generating public/private rsa key pair.
   Enter file in which to save the key(/home/tom/.ssh/id_rsa):
   ```

2. Provide the path to the file that will hold the key. By default, the location where the keys are stored is the home directory of the user on the local system. The default name assigned to the file in which the private key is stored is id_rsa, but you can change it when prompted. However, the user may choose to retain the default name by pressing Return. The public key file is named with a .pub extension.

   ```
   Enter file in which to save the key(/home/tom/.ssh/id_rsa): <Return>
   ```

3. Provide a passphrase, which is used to encrypt the private key. This passphrase is not displayed on the screen when the user types. It is a good practice to ensure that the passphrase is a combination of letters, numbers, and special characters.

   ```
   Enter passphrase(empty for no passphrase):
   ```

4. The passphrase must be re-entered for confirmation. The ssh-keygen command creates a key fingerprint and displays it on the screen. A message that the user identification and the public key are saved in the specified location is displayed to confirm the creation of the key pair.

   ```
   Enter same passphrase again:
   Your identification has been saved in /home/tom/.ssh/id_rsa.
   Your public key has been saved in /home/tom/.ssh/id_rsh.pub.
   The key fingerprint is:
   0e:fb:3d:57:71:73:bf:58:b8:eb:f3:a3:aa:df:e0:d1 tom@local
   ```

5. The public key should be copied to the user's home directory and appended to

   ```
   $HOME/.ssh/authorized_keys.
   ```

USING ssh TO LOG IN

Users can use ssh to access remote systems securely. The user can log in by identifying the system to be accessed and passing the name of the system as a parameter to the ssh command. Follow these steps to use ssh to log in to a remote system:

1. The name of the remote system should be mentioned with the ssh command. For example, if the name of the local system is local and the remote system is remote, the command is:

```
local% ssh <remote host>
```

2. If the user is attempting a remote login for the first time on the remote system, the command prompts a question about the authenticity of the remote system. The user should respond to the question by typing yes to continue. The same message displayed during subsequent login attempts means that the remote host has changed its host key, usually due to reinstallation, or that there might be a breach in security.

```
The authenticity of the host 'remote' cant be established.
RSA key finger print in md5 is: 04:9f:bd:fc:3d:3e:d2:e7:49:fd:6e:18:4f:9c:26
Are you sure you want to continue connecting(yes/no)?
```

3. A prompt asks for the Secure Shell passphrase created with the public and private keys and the user login.

```
Enter passphrase for key '/home/tom/.ssh/id_rsa':
tom@remote password:
Last login: Fri May 3 11:12:12 2002 from local
Remote%
```

NOTE

> You can change the passphrase by using the –p option with the ssh-keygen command.

CONFIGURING AGENT DAEMON TO AUTOMATE REMOTE LOGIN

Remote login through the ssh command can automate user logins to the remote system with no password. The agent daemon for Secure Shell ensures that no prompts request the passphrase and password entry during login attempts. To do this, the user must use the ssh-agent command at the beginning of the login session and store the private key with the agent. Keys of multiple accounts maintained on different systems can also be added to the agent. The agent needs to be started after it is configured. Follow these steps to start the agent daemon:

1. Initiate the agent daemon. When the agent daemon is initiated, the process ID is displayed as an acknowledgement.

```
local% eval 'ssh-agent'
Agent pid 9890
local%
```

2. Add the user's private key to the agent daemon by using the ssh-add command. This ensures that the passphrase and the password are not asked for during subsequent login attempts.

```
local% ssh-add
Enter passphrase for /home/tom/.ssh/id_rsa:
Identity added: /home/tom/.ssh/id_rsa(/home/tom/.ssh/id_rsa)
local%
```

3. Use the `ssh` command to initiate a Secure Shell session.

```
local% ssh remote
```

The `ssh-agent` daemon can be configured to run automatically. The `ssh-agent` daemon (`ssh-agent`) can be configured to automatically start using the `.dtprofile` script. This script is stored under the user's home directory. The following code needs to be added to the end of the script:

```
if [ "$SSH_AUTH_SOCK" = "" -a -x /usr/bin/ssh-agent ]; ↪then     eval
'/usr/bin/ssh-agent'
fi
```

The `ssh-agent` daemon needs to be shut down when the user exits the session. You can automate this by adding the following code in the script stored in `$HOME/.dt/sessions/ses-sionexit`:

```
if [ "$SSH_AGENT_PID" != "" -a -x /usr/bin/ssh-agent ]; then
/usr/bin/ssh-agent -kfi
```

USING SECURE SHELL TO COPY FILES

Secure Shell provides a built-in command, `scp`, to copy files in a secure way between networked systems. The `scp` command requires a password from the user to initiate file transfer. The `scp` command encrypts the file to be transferred to ensure safe transmission. Even if the transmission is intercepted, the file cannot be read because it is encrypted by `scp`.

To encrypt the file being transferred, the `scp` command requires the passphrase for the private key. The command also displays the progress meter that indicates the file name, the percentage of the file that has been transferred at any given point in time as a series of asterisks, the quantity of data transferred in kilobytes, and the estimated time of arrival (ETA) of the encrypted file. The syntax for using the `scp` command is as follows:

```
scp <filename> <username>@<remote destination>
```

TRANSFERRING FILES ACROSS REMOTE SYSTEMS

Imagine that a user on the network maintains a set of very important files on a particular system that needs to be transferred over the network to different systems. There may be other situations in which users may want to transfer files to a local server on the network as part of a backup mechanism to maintain a mirror copy of all files on the local system. In all such cases, a user requires a mechanism that provides access to remote systems on the network. File transfer is one of the important reasons for accessing a remote system. There may be other reasons, such as an unattended command execution over the network or monitoring the performance of a remote system. Solaris provides tools that will enable users to execute commands as well as transfer files across remote systems on the network.

Solaris provides the `rsh` command, which is used to execute a `shell` command on a remote system. This command requires either user-to-user or system-to-system authentication to be configured on the network. Implementing user-to-user or system-to-system authentication requires the `.rhosts` or the `hosts.equiv` file to be configured. These files provide the information necessary to access remote systems. The `rsh` command does not prompt the user for a login name or a password. If the remote access is not configured to allow automatic remote login, the `rsh` command returns an error message.

The `rsh` command can be used only to execute an unattended command on the remote system. This means that the command executed on the remote system should require no user interaction. Commands that require user input hang on execution through `rsh`. This results in an error in execution and program termination on the remote system. `rsh` can also be run on silent mode. In the silent mode, the command does not display any output on the terminal's screen. All results are redirected to `/dev/null` to avoid onscreen display.

Apart from the program execution on the remote systems, specific tools are available with Solaris that enable file transfer. The `rcp`, `scp` and `ftp` are some of the utilities provided by Solaris for transferring files across network. A closer analysis of these tools will reveal both similarities and differences among them.

REMOTE COPY

The `rlogin` and the `rsh` commands permit the user to effectively log in and access the remote system. These utilities do require additional system access configurations, such as `.rhosts` and `hosts.equiv` files. There are various other r services in Solaris that depend on the system access configuration. The remote copy (`rcp`) command is one of those r services. The `rcp` command is used to copy files and directories across remote systems on a trusted network.

Solaris enhances the remote access feature of `rlogin` and `rsh` by introducing the `rcp` command, which can access remote files more quickly. Similar to `rsh`, `rcp` does not prompt for any login name or password. Therefore, an authentication method needs to be configured in place before the `rcp` command can be used to transfer files over the network. If an authentication method is not configured, the `rcp` command returns an error message and ceases execution.

The `rcp` command can be used to perform the following operations:

- Copy files and directories from a local system to a remote system.
- Copy files and directories from a remote system to a local system.
- Copy files and directories between remote systems on the network.

You can also perform a remote copy by using the `rcp` command. When you use the `rcp` command to perform a remote copy, the command uses the Solaris Automounter to copy files. However, the `cp` command needs to work within the virtual file system created by the Automounter, and the operations are relative to the user's home directory. The `rcp` command operates beyond these constraints and does not require an Automounter to understand the remote system's file system. The syntax to use the `rcp` command is as follows:

```
rcp [-pr] <source filename/directory> <destination filename/directory>
```

You should note two important things in the preceding syntax:

- The -p option retains the access control list, modification time, and access time of the files and directories being copied.
- The -r option is used to perform a recursive copy on directories. This option is used to copy the directories with the subdirectories and the complete directory tree structure.

The rcp command requires that the user already enjoy permission to access the remote system and copy files from and into the system. In simple terms, the user must posses read and write permissions on the target system. The user should also know the source or target location on the remote system. If the exact location is not known, the user may log in to the remote system with the rlogin command and check the path to the location by navigating the remote file system. You can run the rcp command almost immediately without logging out from the remote system.

CAUTION

> The cp and the rcp commands overwrite existing files without serving a warning message. Users must provide destination file names with extra caution to ensure that an existing file is not accidentally overwritten during the remote copy operation.

For example, imagine that a user wants to copy the file Javacls.class from /home/tom on the remote system named serv1 to the home directory on the local system. The command to perform this operation is as follows:

```
local(home/tom): rcp serv2:/home/tom/Javacls.class
```

THE ftp COMMAND

The ftp command implements the File Transfer Protocol. The ftp command enables a user to log in to remote systems, in a manner similar to that used with the rlogin and rsh commands. The ftp command is similar to remote copy, but is superior because it includes other operations that users can perform over the remote file system.

The ftp command requires that systems be configured for TCP/IP and have the FTP service running. However, it does not require the remote system to be running Solaris or a Unix-based operating system, as rcp would expect. The ftp command requires user authentication for accessing remote systems. The username and the password of authorized user can be stored in the /etc/passwd file or equivalent network information service map or table. The user can also be authenticated through an anonymous FTP account at the remote system.

Table 17.3 describes commonly used ftp commands.

TABLE 17.3   FTP COMMANDS

FTP Command	Description
ftp	Invoke the command interpreter and the ftp interface.
Open	Log in and access the remote system. This command establishes connection with the remote system.
Bye	Terminates the ftp command interpreter.
Close	Closes the session and logs the user out.
Help	Provides a short description of all the commands supplied with the ftp utility.
Ls	Displays the contents of the remote working directory.
Cd	Changes the working directory on the remote system.
lcd	Changes the working directory in the local system.
get/mget	Copies files from the working directory on the remote system to the working directory on the local system.
put/mput	Copies files from the working directory on the local system to the working directory on the remote system.
delete/mdelete	Deletes files from the working directory on the remote system.
Mkdir	Creates a directory on the remote system.
Rmdir	Removes a directory on the remote system.

SUMMARY

Solaris provides various tools to access and administer remote systems on the network. These tools include telnet, rlogin, rsh, rcp, ssh, and ftp. The rlogin command is a remote login tool that enables users to log in to remote systems. Authentication of remote login can be automated by configuring .rhosts or hosts.equiv files on the remote systems. Though these files provide easy access to remote systems, they pose serious problems in controlling network security. The rsh command provides a better solution to the remote login through the enhanced security feature that use private and public key authentication. These keys are used to encrypt transmission over the network, thereby enhancing security.

The file transfer facility in Solaris is provided by the rcp, scp, and ftp utilities. The rcp command augments rsh and rlogin to provide a tool to transfer files and folders across remote systems. The rcp command provides options to copy recursively, which comes in handy when you need to copy subdirectories and nested directories. The ftp command uses the File Transfer Protocol and requires that the destination system be configured to use TCP/IP and be running the FTP service.

## CHAPTER 18

ADMINISTERING TCP/IP

In this chapter

TCP/IP—An Overview 310

Configuring Routers 316

DHCP 316

Introducing Internet Protocol version 6 (IPv6) 328

Troubleshooting Solaris Networks 330

Summary 333

TCP/IP—AN OVERVIEW

TCP/IP is a protocol suite that enables the connection of different networks designed by different vendors into a network. It was designed to create a network of networks and deliver services such as remote logon, email, file transfer, and so on. Being a standard suite of protocols, TCP/IP is used across various operating systems and networks. TCP/IP is a standard protocol for the Internet. TCP/IP protocol can be used to connect several computers to constitute a Local Area Network (LAN), with several LANS connecting together to form Metropolitan Area Networks (MANs) or Wide Area Networks (WANs). You can also connect LANs directly to the Internet. TCP/IP works over almost all network media, such as ethernet, FDDI, token ring, X.25, and ATM.

The OSI (Open System Interconnection) model defines a networking framework for implementing protocols in seven layers: Physical, Data link, Network, Transport, Presentation, Session, and Application. However, the TCP/IP protocol suite does not directly equate to the layers defined in the OSI model. TCP/IP either combines several layers of the OSI model to form a single layer or does not use a particular layer from the OSI model layer.

Figure 18.1 depicts a comparison between TCP/IP protocol stack and seven layers defined in the OSI model.

Figure 18.1
Comparison between TCP

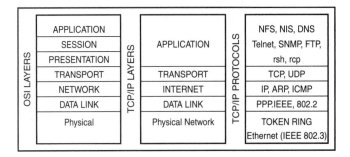

This chapter defines how to set up, administer, and expand a local area network (LAN) that will run the Solaris implementation of TCP/IP.

Notice that the architectural model in Figure 18.1, which represents the Solaris implementation of TCP/IP, contains the layers of the OSI model. Also, notice that this model combines the top three layers of the OSI model—Application, Session, and Presentation—to form a single layer called Application.

The Application layer specifies the Internet services and network applications. The services defined by this layer work in tandem with the Transport layer to send and receive data. The Transport layer ensures that the data packets arrive in a defined sequence and without any errors. In case of errors, this layer retransmits the data packets. The layer below the Transport is the Internet layer. This layer accepts and delivers data packets sent by the Transport layer to the Data Link layer. The Data Link layer identifies the hardware network protocol type of the packet. The bottom layer is the Physical layer, which specifies the characteristics of the communications media.

COMPONENTS OF SOLARIS NETWORK

Before setting up a LAN, you need to understand what the components are that make up a Solaris LAN (see Figure 18.2). Because a LAN is specific to a limited geographic location, it may contain two or more computers attached to a network media. The network media is usually the cable or wire used to connect the computers in the network.

Figure 18.2
Solaris LAN.

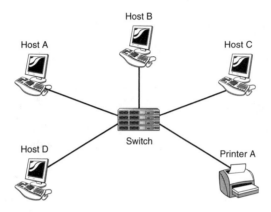

The computers on the network use ports to communicate with each other. As discussed in Chapter 13, "Managing Serial Devices," the serial ports in a computer are used to attach a modem and a terminal and establish a PPP and UUCP connection. PPP and UUCP provide WAN (wide area network) services because they can use telephone lines as their network media.

> **NOTE**
>
> The Point to Point Protocol (PPP) provides connectivity to hosts that need to access the Internet. PPP operates from the Data Link layer of the OSI model. The TCP/IP packets supplied by the Transport and Internet layers are placed in a PPP server. Packets are then transmitted over the network from the server. PPP is an enhancement of the Serial Line Internet Protocol (SLIP) and offers improved error tracking features that were not implemented in SLIP. From the point of view of real-world applications, systems use PPP to connect to their Internet Service Providers (ISPs) .

> **NOTE**
>
> To implement file copy between systems, you can use the Unix-to-Unix Copy (UUCP) utility. UUCP is also used as a protocol. File copy can be implemented between systems located in the local network or on external networks. You need to use modems or telephone connections to implement file copy between systems located on different networks. Although UUCP enables file copy operations, utilities such as FTP are more commonly used.

18

The hardware in a computer that enables you to connect it to a network is known as a network interface. Many computers contain an onboard NIC (network interface card). If you need additional NICs you may need to purchase them separately. Note that each LAN media has its own associated network interface.

PLANNING A NETWORK

You must plan your network topology based upon your organizational requirements. The factors that will help you decide on the topology to use, along with hardware and software requirements, are:

- The geographical locations that would be covered by your LANs, MANs, and WANs.
- The line speed you need for client-server connections.
- The line speed you need for server-to-server connections.
- The applications that will run over the network. Some applications require more bandwidth than usual applications, such as database servers or ERP servers.

> **NOTE**
>
> ERP servers are servers running ERP applications, such as Oracle Financials, SAP, JD Edwards, and so on.

- Determine how many users will be using such applications. Also, estimate the number of concurrently logged in users.
- The number of servers that will be participating in the network.
- What other services your networks will be providing, such as email, Web hosting, directory services, Remote Access Server (RAS), and FTP.
- The type of security model you want to implement on your Internet and intranet hosts.
- Your organization's budgets for IT infrastructure.

After you have identified these factors, you can decide upon the networking medium, such as ethernet cable or optical fiber, and your NIC speeds (such as 10Mbps, 100Mbps, or Gigabit Lan cards). Understanding these factors helps you do sizing of your servers and workstations. You can decide what topology to implement, how you will divide your network into segments, and so on.

Note that the number of host machines that your network can support depends purely upon the organizational requirements. These requirements define the geographical boundaries within which your network has to be set up. For example, you may have to set up a few standalone machines in the single floor of a building, or this network may span across a set of buildings located in the same area. Based on these considerations, you need to decide on the number of host machines. If you have to set up 5,000 hosts across buildings, then you may have to divide your network into subnets.

After you decide on these logistics for your network, you can determine the size of your network and design a physical layout. Note that the size of your network determines the network class and the IP addressing scheme. The IP addressing scheme for your network is based on the network class you choose. There are three classes: Class A, Class B, and Class C. Each class uses a 32-bit IP address space. Figure 18.3 defines the three network classes.

Figure 18.3
Network classes.

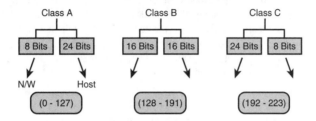

Each class is divided into network address and host address.

- Class A uses 8 bits for the network address and 24 bits for the host address. The first byte of a Class A value ranges between 0 to 127. An example of a Class A IP address would be 92.7.7.5. In this example, 92 represents the network address and the remaining three, 7, 7, and 5, represent the host address.

- Class B, on the other hand, distributes an equal number of bytes as 16 and 16 bit for the network and host address. The total number of bytes an IPv4 address contains is 32 bit. Class B address distributes 16 bit to network addresses and 16 bit to host addresses. The value for the network address ranges from 128 to 191. An example of a class B address could be 128.156.60.87, where the values 128 and 156 are used by the network address and the values 60 and 87 are used by the host address.

- Class C uses 24 bits for the network address and 8 bits as the host address. The values for the network address range from 192 to 223. An example of a Class C IP address is 192.200.201.23, where the network address uses the first three bits, 192, 200, and 201, and the host address uses the last bit, 23.

NOTE

The value of the host address for each class can range from 1 to 254.

The next step is to get your Domain name registered with an internet governing body such as Internet Corporation for Assigned Names and Numbers (ICANN).

NOTE

Internet domain name system (DNS) is used to maintain a directory to store domain names and their corresponding client machines registered to companies or individuals. This domain name is used to host your organization's Web site and to set up your organization's Internet mail.

NOTE

The classful IP addressing scheme resulted in wasted IP addresses. For example, you can use a class B address block to assign IP addresses for more than 254 hosts, which blocks 65535 host addresses. Although the current rate of IP address usage might not require such large volumes of IP addresses, the exponential rate at which the Internet is growing could overtake the maximum number of IP addresses allowed by the classful IP addressing scheme. To avoid IP address wastage and to cater to the potential shortage of IP addresses, a new addressing scheme called Classless Inter Domain Routing (CIDR) was devised. CIDR has been standardized and documented in RFC 1519, released by the Internet Engineering Task Force (IETF). CIDR proposes the creation of a new IP addressing entity called *supernets*. Each supernet is an extension of a subnet mask and enables you to specify multiple subnets within a single subnet mask.

For example, if 20 hosts within a subnet with the IP address 172.17.65.0 must be allocated IP addresses, the subnet mask is represented as 172.17.65.0 /20. This indicates that hosts are assigned IP addresses between 172.17.65.0 and 172.17.65.19. In this way, you can avoid wastage of IP addresses and overcome address space shortage for some time. However, the IPv6 addressing scheme with its 128-bit addresses provides a better remedy to address space shortage than CIDR.

After you receive the network number, you can formulate an IP addressing scheme for the network. Also, assign host names for your host machines. Note that the host names should be unique for each machine.

Next, create a list that contains the host names and IP addresses of all machines in your network, which you can use to build network databases. One of the databases in the network database is the host database, which contains the TCP/IP operation information in your network. This network database is used by a naming service. A naming service maintains network databases in several servers. The naming service maintains machine information such as IP address, host names, ethernet address, and so on.

The Solaris OE supports five types of naming services: NIS (Network Information Service), NIS+, LDAP (Lightweight directory Access Protocol) , DNS (Domain Name Service), and the local directory. You can use one of these naming services for your network.

After your planning and designing stage, you are ready to configure TCP/IP on your network.

CONFIGURING TCP/IP

Each host participating in a network needs to have a valid TCP/IP address, a subnet mask that identifies the network subnet to which the host belongs, and a default gateway, used by the host to communicate with other hosts not on the local network. A default gateway is usually a router.

During the installation process you are prompted to specify the TCP/IP address for the host subnet mask and the default gateway. However, if you decide to change the IP address or subnet mask at some point, you can do so.

There are two ways to assign IP addresses to your host. You can use the ifconfig command to assign static TCP/IP addresses, or you can configure your host to be a DHCP client so that IP addresses are configured dynamically without the administrator's intervention. Of course, you need to have a configured and running DHCP server on your network.

Imagine that during the installation program you had specified the following configuration:

- TCP/IP 172.17.20.50
- Subnet mask 255.255.255.128

Now that these configurations are no longer required, you want your host to have a new TCP/IP address as 206.163.204.201, with a subnet mask as 255.255.255.0

You can use the following command to do so.

```
# ifconfig hme0 10.0.1.138 netmask 255.255.248.0
```

Verify whether the IP addresses have changed using the following command:

```
# ifconfig -a
```

In the preceding command, hme0 is the device name for the interface. Whenever you add a new interface card you can check for the device name in the device's directory. Common device names for NICs are hme, qfe, and so on. If the device name is hme, the first instance will have the device name hme0, the next instance will be hme1, and so on.

The TCP/IP address that you specify with the ifconfig command is not retained during the next bootup. Therefore, to make your settings permanent you need to specify your new configurations in various network configuration files.

Hosts can be set up to obtain TCP/IP configuration information from the local configuration files or from a DHCP server. These files contain the host name information, the IP address, the netmask, the default gateway, and the primary and secondary domain servers.

The steps to configure TCP/IP in your Solaris network are as follows:

1. To configure TCP/IP you must have the superuser access. Log in as the supersuser and then change to the /etc directory.

2. Open the file /etc/nodename using the editor of your choice, such as vi or ed and type the host name of the machine. The file /etc/nodename stores the host name of the local machine.

3. Next, define the network interfaces on the local host by creating an entry in the /etc/hostname.interface file. The interface in the filename is replaced by the name of the primary network interface. Note that the Solaris installation program creates this file. Enter the host name or the IP address associated with the interface in this file. For example, if the host name is host1, enter this name in the file.

4. Specify the IP address assigned to the network in the /etc/inet/hosts file. This file contains the host names and the IP addresses of the primary network interface.

18

5. The next step is to specify the domain in which the host resides. The domain can be specified in the `/etc/defaultdomain` file.

6. If you want to expand your network, you can do that by setting up a new network and connecting it to the existing one. You then have to set up a machine that is to act as the router, thus creating an internetwork. Specify the router name in the `/etc/default-router` file. This can either be a physical router or you can configure one of your Solaris hosts to work as a router. The name of the default router and its IP address is specified in the `/etc/inet/hosts` file. This file should contain an entry for each router connected to the network.

7. Type the network number and the netmask in the file `/etc/inet/netmasks`.

As described earlier in this section, a router is a device that connects two or more networks to form an internetwork, especially in a TCP/IP network. Solaris systems also function as routers. Now it's time to look at the method to configure a Solaris system to work as a router.

CONFIGURING ROUTERS

Routers transfer packets of data from one network to another. A machine can be configured as a router or a host when the `/etc/rc2.d/S69inet` script runs during the system boot time. This script is used to determine whether the machine is a router or a host.

A machine can be configured as a router or a host when the `/etc/rc2.d/S69inet` script runs during the system boot time. These protocols keep a record of the routers in the network. They broadcast router information to the hosts in the network.

Note that one of the requirements for setting up a router is that the machine must have at least two network interfaces. Also, because the router provides an interface between two or more networks, the host names and IP addresses assigned to the routers should be unique.

The following steps detail the method to configure routers.

1. You must have the superuser privileges on the machine that needs to be configured as a router.

2. For each network interface installed, create the file `/etc/hostname.<interface>` and include the host names for each interface. Also, include the host name and the IP address of each interface into `/etc/inet/hosts`.

Note that if the router is connected to any subnetted network, edit `/etc/inet/netmasks` and type the local network number and the associated netmask number.

DHCP

Manually assigning IP addresses to all the machines in the network can be a very strenuous task. Imagine a situation in which you have a network with 1000 hosts and your task as an administrator is to set the IP address to each machine manually. There are two main disadvantages to this. The first is that the whole process of assigning IP addresses to so many machines in the network can be very time consuming. Second, this process is bound to suffer from errors. To eliminate the possibility of errors and also to reduce the time involved in assigning IP addresses, use the Dynamic Host Configuration Protocol (DHCP). This protocol generates IP addresses dynamically for the hosts in a network.

If you plan to set up a network running DHCP, the first step is to gather network information such as network and system services, routers, and switches. If the network you are planning must also support remote clients, the remote client information and the IP addresses of the routers on the remote network should also be obtained.

After you obtain all the required information, you need to decide on the naming service that will store this information. If you are looking at storing information for an enterprise environment, then you can use the standard NIS+ naming service. For storing information about a single server, you can use files.

You can use Solaris OE to configure both DHCP server and the client. This protocol enables a DHCP server to dynamically assign IP address to DHCP clients. This in turn allows for centralized network administration. Without DHCP, the clients have to be configured individually and the IP addresses have to be assigned manually. The following sections define the steps to configure DHCP servers and clients.

CONFIGURING A DHCP SERVER

Solaris 9 OE comes with two built-in utilities, which help in configuring a DHCP server. You can use the DHCP Manager, which is a GUI based tool or the dhcpconfig command line utility for DHCP server configuration. You will learn how to work with each of these tools in this section.

To configure the first DHCP server on your network, you must do the following:

- Ensure that the machine where you choose to set up the DHCP server runs Solaris 2.6, 7, 8, or 9. Note that if you intend to support a large number of clients, then you must install Solaris 8 7/01 or Solaris 9.

- Enable access for the DHCP server machine to all the networks that have clients that use DHCP, either directly on the network or through a BOOTP relay agent.

- Enable routing on the DHCP server.

- Configure the Netmasks table in the DHCP server, which reflects your network topology.

- Set up the lease policy to indicate the lease time and also determine whether clients can renew their leases.

- Provide the IP address of a router the clients can use. If you use DHCP Manager, you can specify that clients should find routers themselves with the router discovery protocol. Discovery enables a client to adapt easily to router changes in the network.

To use the `dhcpconfig` command line utility to configure the DHCP server, perform the following steps:

1. Type the following command:

```
# /usr/sbin/dhcpconfig -D -r datastore -p location
# dhcpconfig -D -r SUNWbinfiles -p /var/dhcp -l 14400 -d xyz.com
    -a  206.163.204.201 -h dns -y xyz.com
```

The preceding command configures DHCP service by using the binary files data store in domain xyz.com for a period of 4 hours (14400 sec).

The data store for DHCP data can be a text file, binary files, or a NIS+ container.

location is the data-store-dependent location where you want to store the DHCP data. For SUNWfiles and SUNWbinfiles, this must be a Unix-absolute path name. For SUNWnisplus, this must be a fully specified NIS+ directory.

2. Use the following command to add one or more networks to the DHCP service. Type the command on the DHCP server system.

```
# /usr/sbin/dhcpconfig -N <network-address>
```

In the preceding syntax, *<network-address>* is the IP address of the network you want to add to the DHCP service.

Use the following command to manage DHCP network tables:`

```
# pntadm -A <ip-address> options  network-address
```

The command used to maintain the network tables of DHCP is `pntadm`. This command is used to add or remove networks under DHCP management. It is also used to add, delete, or modify IP address records in network tables.

The `-A` *<ip-address>* option is used to add a client entry with host name or client IP address to the DHCP network table.

After you have performed the configuration steps, reboot the system for the configuration to take affect.

To configure a DHCP server using DHCP Manager, perform the following steps:

1. Specify the following command in the Terminal:

```
# /usr/sadm/admin/bin/dhcpmgr &
```

2. The Choose Server Configuration window is displayed. Select the Configure as DHCP Server option and click OK.

3. The DHCP Configuration Wizard is activated. You need to specify a data store location. Select the Text Files option.

Figure 18.4
The Choose Server
Configuration window.

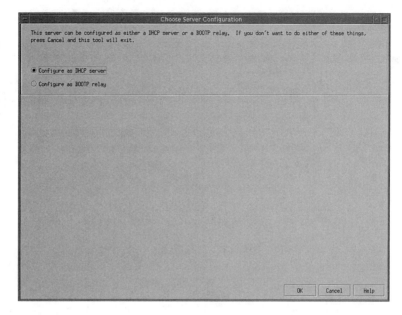

Figure 18.5
DHCP Configuration
Wizard–Choosing a
data store location.

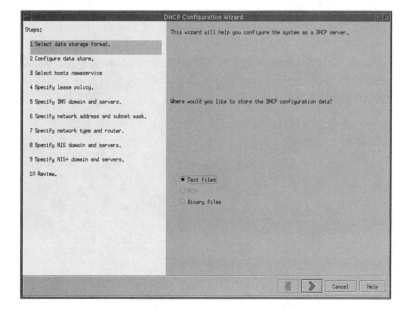

4. You need to specify the path where the text file data store must be located. The default path displayed in the Wizard is /var/dhcp. Retain the default settings.

Figure 18.6
DHCP Configuration Wizard—Specify the data store path.

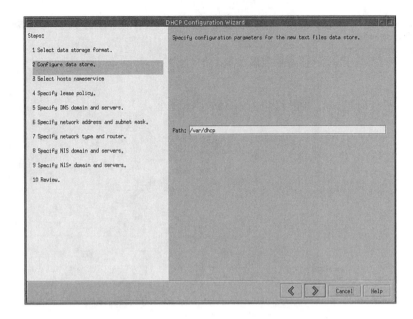

5. You need to select a nameservice that stores host records. In this example, the /etc/hosts option is selected. After selecting a nameservice, move to the next step.

Figure 18.7
DHCP Configuration Wizard—Selecting a nameservice.

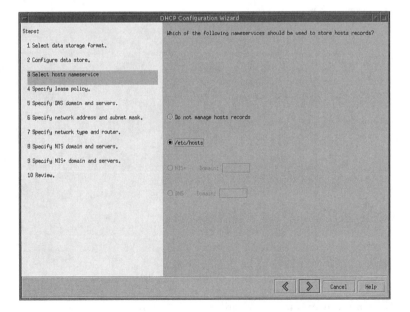

6. You need to specify the lease time for using the IP addresses assigned by the DHCP server. Specify the lease as 15 days.

Figure 18.8
DHCP Configuration
Wizard–Specifying a
lease time for IP
address assignments.

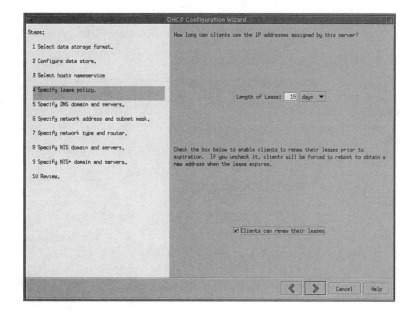

7. You need to specify the domain name and the DNS Server address. In this example, DNS Domain name is specified as `sales.dept.xyz.com`, and the DNS Server IP address as `172.17.65.196`.

18

Figure 18.9
DHCP Configuration
Wizard–Specifying
the DNS domain
name and DNS Server
IP address.

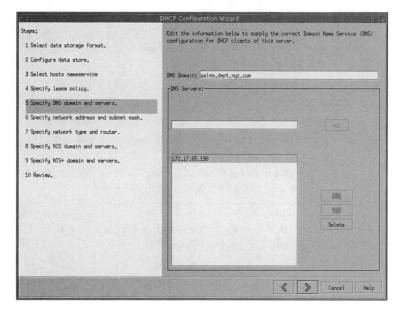

8. You need to specify the network IP address and the subnet mask of the network, which will be serviced by the DHCP server. In this example, the network address is specified as 172.17.65.0 and the subnet mask as 255.255.255.0.

Figure 18.10
DHCP Configuration
Wizard–Specifying
the network address
and subnet mask.

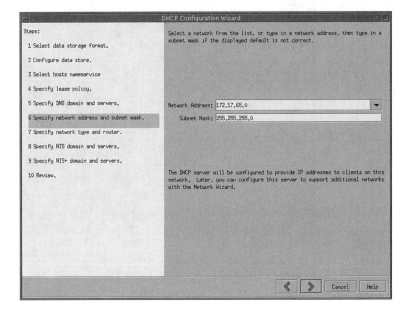

9. You need to specify the network type and routing method that must be used for the DHCP Server. In this example, the Local-Area (LAN) option and the Use Router Discovery Protocol option is selected. After selecting the options, move to the next step.

10. If NIS is used as the naming service, provide NIS information by specifying the NIS domain name and the IP address of the NIS Server. In this example, us.sales.dpt.xyz.com is specified as the NIS Domain and 172.17.65.234 as the NIS Server IP address.

NOTE

If NIS+ is used as the naming service, you need to perform the step similar to step 10. In this case, you can skip the NIS configuration step.

11. Review the DHCP Configuration information displayed in the DHCP Configuration Wizard window before clicking Finish.

Figure 18.11
DHCP Configuration Wizard–Specifying the network type and routing information.

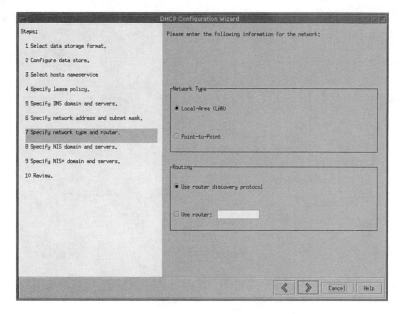

Figure 18.12
DHCP Configuration Wizard–NIS domain name and IP address.

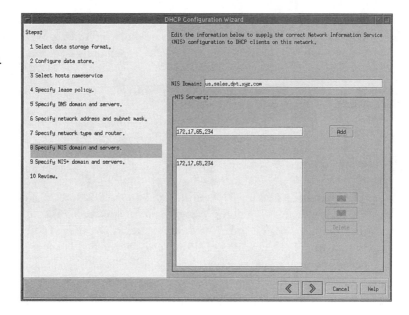

Figure 18.13
DHCP Configuration
Wizard–Review con-
figuration information.

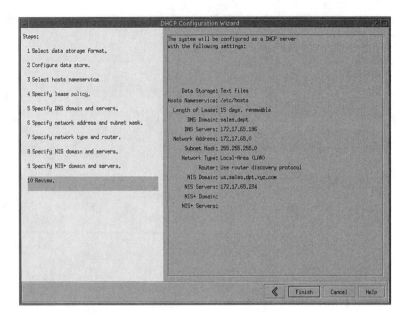

12. You need to provide a list of client IP addresses that the DHCP server can allocate dynamically. To do so, you need to activate the Start Address Wizard by clicking the Yes button in the Start Address Wizard confirmation message window.

Figure 18.14
Start Address Wizard
Confirmation
Message window.

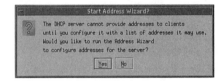

13. The Start Address Wizard is launched and the Add Address to Network window is displayed. In the first step of the Wizard, you need to specify the number of IP addresses that must be allocated and add a comment describing the purpose of the IP addresses. In this example, the number of IP addresses is specified as 100 and the description as Addresses for US sales domain.

14. The DHCP Server name, que, and network address, 172.17.65.0, are displayed. In addition, the root name used to generate client names is displayed as que. Retain the settings.

Figure 18.15
Add Addresses to Network–Number of IP addresses and a description.

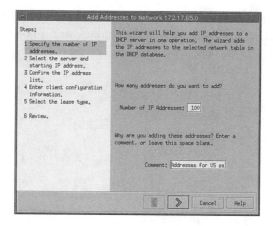

Figure 18.16
Add Addresses to Network–DHCP server name, network address, and root name.

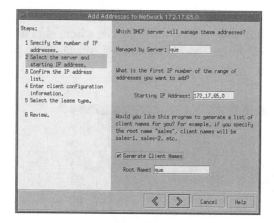

15. The IP address list is displayed. Accept the IP address list by clicking Next.

Figure 18.17
Add Addresses to Network–IP address list confirmation.

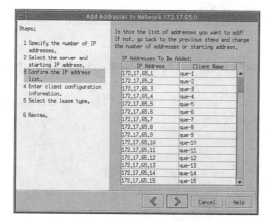

16. The client configuration information can be viewed and modified in this step. By clicking the View button in the Configuration Macro group, you can open the View Macro window to access the client configuration options. Retain the settings and close the View Macro button by clicking OK.

Figure 18.18
Add Addresses to Network—Client configuration information.

17. You need to select an IP address lease type. You can select either the Dynamic Lease Type or the Permanent Lease Type. In this example the Dynamic Lease Type option is selected.

18

Figure 18.19
Add Addresses to Network—Selecting the lease type.

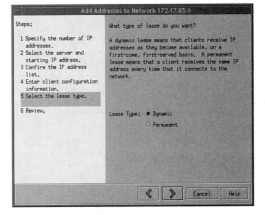

18. You can review the Address list options you have configured before clicking the Finish button.

19. The address list is added to the DHCP Server. This completes DHCP server configuration using the DHCP Manager.

Figure 18.20
Add Addresses to
Network–Review
address list configura-
tion settings.

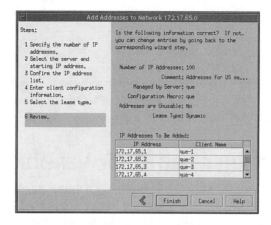

Figure 18.21
Address list added to
DHCP Manager.

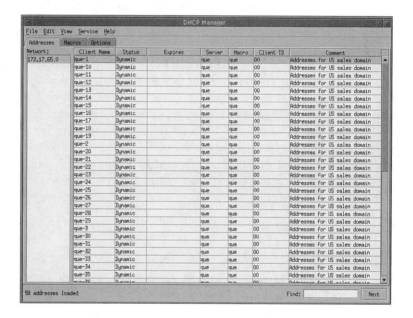

Configuring the DHCP Client

A DHCP client is automatically enabled on your system if you choose to use DHCP to configure the IP address, subnet mask, and default gateway during the Solaris operating system installation. However, if the DHCP client is not enabled during Solaris installation then perform the following steps to enable it.

1. Access the Solaris client using your superuser access privileges.

2. If this system uses preconfiguration rather than interactive configuration, edit the sysidcfg file to add the DHCP subkey to the network_interface keyword.

3. Unconfigure and shut down the system by typing the following command:

   `# sys uncofig`

4. Reboot the system after it has completely shut down.

When prompted to use DHCP to configure network interfaces, specify Yes. If you precon-figured the system by using a `sysidcfg` file, insert the `network_interface` keyword, and specify `dhcp` as a dependent keyword.

INTRODUCING INTERNET PROTOCOL VERSION 6 (IPv6)

Although the Internet continues to expand, the current Internet Protocol (IP) version 4 (IPv4) can support a limited number of addresses. The increase in the number of hosts that are currently participating in forming the Internet has started causing a shortage as far as IP addresses are concerned. The fear of eventually consuming the entire IPv4 address space initiated the call for a new IP architectural model, which could fuel the need for future net-work growths.

IPv6, the next version of Internet Protocol, has been designed and developed so that it can help networks expand. The potential for increased address space is something around four billion times the size of the IPv4 address space. IPv6 is often referred to as "next generation Internet protocol" or IPng. IPv6 is designed to support high-performance networks such as Gigabit Ethernet, ATM, and OC-12, but that does not imply that IPv6 does not support narrow bandwidth networks. Some of the benefits that IPv6 offers over IPv4 is the support for increased address space. IPv4 has a defined address space of 32 bits, whereas IPv6 has increased address space of 128 bits, which means that you can have a higher number of addresses for your nodes.

IPv6 facilitates auto-configuration of addresses, which reduces a lot of administrative tasks.

IPv6 ADDRESSING

Ipv6 addresses are 128 bits long. A single interface can have multiple address. IPv6 supports three types of addresses: unicast, anycase, and multicast:

■ **Unicast**—This type of address is specified for a single interface. If an interface on a sys-tem has been assigned a unicast address xyz, a packet destined to this machine is deliv-ered to its interface using the unicast address.

■ **Anycast**—This type of address is specified for a set of interfaces. These interfaces can reside on the same host or also may belong to different hosts. A packet destined for this address is delivered to one of the interfaces in the set.

■ **Multicast**—Like anycast, this type of address is also defined for a set of interfaces. The only difference is that a packet destined for this address is delivered to all the interfaces in the set.

NOTE

> There are no broadcast addresses in Ipv6, their function being superseded by multicast addresses.

ENABLING IPv6 ADDRESSES ON YOUR HOST

There are two ways you can configure your IPv6 addresses on Solaris OE. The first approach is to use auto configuration so that your IPv6 address are configured automatically, which is recommended. The second approach is to statically assign IPv6 addresses.

Before you start configuring, ensure that IPv6 daemons are running on your host.

- `in.ndpd`—Daemon for IPv6 configuration.
- `in.ripngd`—Routing daemon for IPv6 addresses.
- `inetd`—Internet service daemon.

NOTE

> Check for the `in.ripngd` daemon if your machine is acting as a router.

USING AUTO CONFIGURATION TO ASSIGN IP ADDRESSES

Using auto configuration to assign IPv6 addresses is the easiest approach you can follow.

You have to specify support for IPv6 during the installation of Solaris OE. The installation program creates a file in the `/etc` directory called `/etc/hostname6.interface`. If this file is not already present, then you can create one by using the `touch` command. The interface name is replaced by the actual device name, such as le0, hme0, and so on.

```
# touch /etc/hostname6.hme0
```

After the autoconfiguration process is complete, IPv6 nodes discover each other by using IPv6 Neighbor Discovery Protocol (NDP). The `in.ndpd` daemon implements NDP. After the hosts are discovered, the communication between the hosts can commence. The in.ndpd daemon implements features such as router discovery, prefix discovery, address autoconfiguration, and address resolution. In addition, `in.ndpd` provides neighbor unreachability detection and duplicate address detection features.

NOTE

> The configuration file for the `in.ndpd` daemon is `/etc/inet/ndpd.conf`.

An IPv6 host generates its own link-local address and stores this as an entry in the `ndpd.conf` file. However, information on the link-local addresses of other hosts on the network is not available. Therefore, the `in.ndpd` daemon starts the neighbor discovery process, an IP mechanism, which enables hosts to locate other hosts that reside on an attached link. You can view this address by using the `ifconfig(1M)` command.

```
# ifconfig -a hme0
```

18

NOTE

in.ndpd provides both the host and router autoconfiguration components of Neighbor Discovery for IPv6 and Address Autoconfiguration for IPv6.

ASSIGNING IPv6 ADDRESSES STATICALLY

To define a static IP address on your host interface, you would be required to make an entry in your /etc/hostname6.interface file. Let us suppose you have interface hme0 on your host, which is already running IPv4 service. Instead of removing the IPv4 address you can configure a logical interface hme0:1, and you can assign your IPv6 address to this logical interface. Rename the etc/hostname6.interface file to /etc/hostname6.hme0. Then put a one-line entry in this file, the format for which is

```
addif <hostname>/mask up
```

where addif creates a logical interface, hme0:1, which will be assigned the static IPv6 address you want to specify. If you follow these steps, your physical interface will continue to have the IPv4 address and your logical interface will have the IPv6 address.

Suppose the hostname of your node is titan, and you want to specify 6ffe:40f0:3:5:a00:30ff::6. The entry would look like this in the /etc/hostname6.hme0:

```
 addif titan/64 up
```

After this you would be required to add a static entry in the /etc/inet/ipnodes file, where you would specify the IP address and hostname. This file is equivalent to the /etc/hosts file, which is used in the IPv4 address scheme.

The entry in /etc/inet/ipnodes will look like this:

```
6ffe:40f0:3:5:a00:30ff::6 titan
```

NOTE

The default route would be taken up by the neighbor discovery process. The process of identifying availability of directly connected neighboring routers is called *neighbor discovery process*. The process is implemented using router solicitation and advertisement ICMP messages.

TROUBLESHOOTING SOLARIS NETWORKS

Problems in a network can be caused by different factors. You must follow a sequence of activities to trace the problem. Several command line utilities are available in Solaris, such as ping, ifconfig, snoop, and netstat, that help you monitor and diagnose the fault in your Solaris network activity.

The most common problem is that you are not able to access a remote machine. The most basic test that you should do is to find out whether that machine is reachable or not. You can use the ping command to check whether the remote host is available on the network. The syntax used for pinging is as follows:

```
/usr/sbin/ping host
```

If you suspect that a machine is up and running but may be losing packets, use the ping -s command to determine exactly where the problem lies. If packet loss errors are indicated in the output of the command, it means that the host has dropped packets.

In case ping fails, you can physically go to the machine to verify the status of the network by using the ifconfig and netstat commands. The following command displays the current status of the DHCP client using the ifconfig command:

```
# ifconfig interface
#netstat -rn
```

NOTE

Check the main pages for various other options supported by the netstat command.

If you suspect there is a problem with DHCP server or a client, use the following command:

```
# ifconfig interface dhcp status
```

The current status normally contains information that indicates whether an IP address is bound to a client or not. In addition, it displays the number of requests sent, received, and declined.

The following ifconfig command displays the configuration of the interface qfe0.

```
# ifconfig qfe0
qfe0: flags=1000843<UP,BROADCAST,RUNNING,MULTICAST,IPv4>
➥ mtu 1500 index 3 inet 172.16.32.100 netmask ffffff00
➥ broadcast 172.16.32.255 ether 8:0:20:f9:12:25
```

The output indicates the following:

- The interface is configured UP and is capable of broadcasting.

- The mtu field indicates that the interface has a maximum transfer rate of 1500.

- The IP address is the 32-bit network address of the host you are using. The netmask determines the number of bits and the specific bits in the host address space that represent the subnet number and the host number. The broadcast field displays the IP broadcast address of the interface qfe0.

- The last field provides the machine address of the host. In this example, it is ethernet.

If you want to see the status of all interfaces, rather than a specific interface, use the -a option with the ifconfig command.

```
# ifconfig -a
lo0: flags=1000849<UP,LOOPBACK,RUNNING,MULTICAST,IPv4> mtu 8232 index 1
        inet 127.0.0.1 netmask ff000000
hme0: flags=1000843<UP,BROADCAST,RUNNING,MULTICAST,IPv4> mtu 1500 index 2
```

```
            inet 172.17.22.31 netmask ffffff80 broadcast 172.17.22.127
            ether 8:0:20:f9:12:25
qfe0: flags=1000843<UP,BROADCAST,RUNNING,MULTICAST,IPv4> mtu 1500 index 3
            inet 172.16.32.100 netmask ffffff00 broadcast 172.16.32.255
            ether 8:0:20:f9:12:25
qfe1: flags=1000843<UP,BROADCAST,RUNNING,MULTICAST,IPv4> mtu 1500 index 4
            inet 172.16.64.100 netmask ffffff00 broadcast 172.16.64.255
            ether 8:0:20:f9:12:25
qfe2: flags=1000843<UP,BROADCAST,RUNNING,MULTICAST,IPv4> mtu 1500 index 5
            inet 172.16.96.100 netmask ffffff00 broadcast 172.16.96.255
            ether 8:0:20:f9:12:25
qfe3: flags=1000843<UP,BROADCAST,RUNNING,MULTICAST,IPv4> mtu 1500 index 6
            inet 172.16.128.100 netmask ffffff00 broadcast 172.16.128.255
            ether 8:0:20:f9:12:25
```

Another command that can be used to check the status of the network is the `netstat` command. This command is useful in tracking down network malfunctions. When used, this command generates network status and protocol statistics.

When used with the -s option, the `netstat` command displays the following protocol statistics:

```
# netstat -s
RAWIP
        rawipInDatagrams    =   244      rawipInErrors       =     0
        rawipInCksumErrs    =     0      rawipOutDatagrams   =   830
        rawipOutErrors      =     0

UDP
        udpInDatagrams      = 61002      udpInErrors         =     0
        udpOutDatagrams     = 17378      udpOutErrors        =     0
```

To display the network interface status, use the following command:

```
# netstat -i
Name  Mtu   Net/Dest      Address       Ipkts  Ierrs Opkts  Oerrs Collis Queue
lo0   8232  loopback      localhost     16803  0     16803  0     0      0
hme0  1500  sun           sun           99479  0     32192  0     215    0
qfe0  1500  router-qfe0   router-qfe0   13740  0     12982  80    368    0
qfe1  1500  router-qfe1   router-qfe1   676    5     6565   6     71     0
qfe2  1500  router-qfe2   router-qfe2   0      0     0      0     0      0
qfe3  1500  router-qfe3   router-qfe3   0      0     3584   0     0      0
```

You can use this command to determine the number of packets a machine has transmitted and received in the network. The `Ipkts` field in the command output indicates the input packet count and the `Opkts` indicates the output packet count. In case there are any errors in the transmission or receipt of packets, the same is indicated in the `Ierrs` and `Oerrs` fields, respectively.

Using the `snoop` command is another way to watch packets flow in and out of their destinations. The `snoop` command takes a snapshot of all the packets received and transmitted in the local subnet. This makes `snoop` a very valuable troubleshooting tool, because it can capture data packets from the network. If the patterns of network traffic are as expected, then any application errors due to network problems can be ruled out. Alternatively, when testing a packet filtering firewall, it is important to use snoop to determine whether certain types of traffic are being allowed through the firewall that shouldn't be.

SUMMARY

TCP/IP is designed to deliver network services, such as remote logon, email, file transfer, and so on. This protocol suite is used across various operating systems and networks. The architectural model of TCP/IP resembles that of the OSI model, except that the Application layer in the TCP/IP architectural model combines the three layers: Application, Session, and Presentation.

When planning your network topology, you must keep in mind factors such as the geographical locations covered by your network, the line speed for your network connections, applications running over your network, the number of users, and so on. After deciding on the logistics of your network, you can determine the size of your network, which helps in determining the network class and the IP addressing scheme.

Note that all hosts in a network must have a valid IP address, a subnet mask, and a default gateway. You can provide this information during the installation process. However, you can change the IP address or subnet mask later as well. You can assign IP addresses to your host in two ways: by using the ifconfig command or DHCP.

With expanding networks, the current Internet Protocol (IP) version 4 (IPv4) can support only a limited number of addresses. IPv6, the next version, is designed to help networks expand.

It is important to constantly monitor your network. If there are any problems, you should follow a sequence of defined activities to trace the problem. Solaris provides several command line utilities, such as ping, ifconfig, snoop, and netstat, to trace network problems. These utilities monitor and diagnose the fault in your Solaris network activities.

18

CONFIGURING NETWORK AND NAMING SERVICES

19 DNS   337

20 Network Information Service (NIS)   355

21 Network Information Service + (NIS+ and FNS)   371

22 Lightweight Directory Access Protocol (LDAP)   389

CHAPTER **19**

DNS

In this chapter

Naming Services—An Overview   338

DNS   347

Summary   353

19

NAMING SERVICES—AN OVERVIEW

Imagine a situation where you go to a library and find that there is no catalog you can use to browse through the list of available books. If you are looking for a specific book, it will be difficult for you to browse through every shelf in the library and locate the book you need. In fact, you may end up walking up and down the aisles and may or may not find what you're looking for. However, if the library has a catalog, your task becomes much easier. In the world of networking, the concept of naming services is similar to the catalog in the library. Naming services store system information in a central location in the network that's similar to the library catalog. This enables machines to identify each other in a network, which helps facilitate network communication. Users, machines, and applications use this information to communicate with each other across the network. The information may include hostnames and addresses, usernames, passwords, access permissions, group memberships, printers, and so on.

The Solaris operating environment supports five naming services: Domain Name Service (DNS), Network Information Service (NIS), Network Information Service Plus (NIS+), Federated Naming Service (FNS) , and Lightweight Directory Access Protocol (LDAP). Note that LDAP is a directory service. Directory services and naming services provide the same functions. The difference is in the additional functionalities that directory services provide. These additional functionalities include multiple application compatibility, flexible access control, and ease of configuration and administration.

→ To learn more about the features of Directory Services, **see** "Lightweight Directory Access Protocol" **p.389**.

Before getting into the details of DNS, let us first understand in detail the concept of naming services.

A naming service is a mechanism that associates names to objects. Note that searches for objects in a network are based on the objects' names.

A naming service is used primarily to map user-friendly names to objects such as addresses, identifiers, or objects used by computer programs. For example, DNS is a naming service that is used to map hostnames to IP addresses.

The basic components that constitute naming services are names, binding, references and addresses, context, naming system, and namespace.

- **Names**—For a naming service to be able to look up an object, you supply a name to that object. The convention you follow to name objects depends on the naming service you use. For example, suppose you are using DNS as your naming service and you want to add an object, which is a subdomain called purchase, to an existing domain called mydomain.com. You follow a specific naming convention to name this object. In this case, the name of the new object will be suffixed to the existing domain name. The new object name will be purchase.mydomain.com.

- **Binding**—Binding is a process of associating names to objects. For example, by using the `hostname` command to specify a hostname "mymachine" to a system, you bind a name to an object.

- **Reference and address**—The object names are stored in a name service database. There might be a situation where some objects cannot be stored in the name service directly. In such a case, these objects are stored as references or pointers to an object stored in the name service database. A reference is a piece of information that specifies how an object is to be accessed. Imagine, for example, that you have a printer object. This object might contain information such as the state of a printer, print queue length, and so on. The printer object reference will contain information describing how the printer is to be accessed, the print server name/IP address, and the protocol used to access the printer.

- **Context**—A context can be described as a collection of name-to-object bindings. Contexts are associated with a particular type of naming convention and provide a lookup or resolution service that refers to an object. Contexts also provide functionality for binding and unbinding names. A name in one context object can be bound to another context object. For example, a DNS domain such as com, edu, and gov is a context. A DNS domain name relative to another domain name is a sub-context. For example, in the name mydomain.com, mydomain is the sub-context and com is the context.

- **Naming System**—The same type of contexts connected together performing similar operations form a naming system. A system that implements DNS is a naming system.

- **Namespace**—A set of names in a naming service is called a namespace. A DNS namespace comprises DNS domains.

Now that you have the basic concepts of naming services, you can understand the need for a naming service and the reason for its evolution. In a network, for hosts to communicate with each other, it is important that they maintain the system information of all other hosts in the network. System information includes IP addresses, security information, ethernet interfaces, users, and groups, network services, and so on.

Consider an example of a small network that consists of three hosts: host1, host2, and host3. To enable communication between these hosts, host1 stores the IP addresses of host2 and host3, and similarly the remaining hosts store the hostname and IP address information of each other host (see Figure 19.1). This information is maintained in the files `/etc/hosts` or `/etc/inet/ipnodes`. These files store IP addresses and hostnames of all hosts in a network, including loopback addresses. All hosts on a network maintain a similar copy of the host file. Every time the hostname or the IP address of a particular host changes, or if new hosts are added to the network, that information has to be updated in the host file of every machine. On a medium or large network, this task becomes time consuming and almost unmanageable.

19

Figure 19.1
A small network.

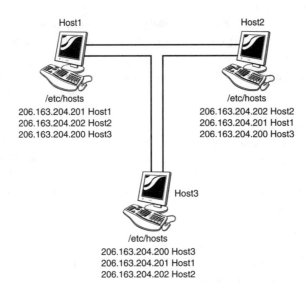

Host1

/etc/hosts
206.163.204.201 Host1
206.163.204.202 Host2
206.163.204.200 Host3

Host2

/etc/hosts
206.163.204.202 Host2
206.163.204.201 Host1
206.163.204.200 Host3

Host3

/etc/hosts
206.163.204.200 Host3
206.163.204.201 Host1
206.163.204.202 Host2

The concept of naming services is an answer to this problem. All the hosts in your network are registered with your local name server. Every time you modify the IP address or host-name of a host or add new hosts to the network, the modifications are updated in your local name server database.

The name server provides lookup services to the clients that query it. This eliminates the need to update the hosts file on every machine in case of any change in the network information.

Naming services associate network names with objects. This feature enables translation of complex network names or IP addresses into user-friendly names.

For example, assume that XYZ, Inc., has an intranet site. This company wants to connect its network to the Internet. The Internet Service Provider (ISP) provides the network number 172.17.0.0 and a domain name xyz.com for the company's network. XYZ, Inc., has four main divisions: Corporate, Technical, Sales, and Marketing. Therefore, XYZ, Inc., has one main net and four subnets. Each subnet needs its own network number. Figure 19.2 describes the domain structure of XYZ, Inc.

Although each division can be uniquely identified by its network number, it would be more convenient if these divisions had some logical network name rather than numbers, which are difficult to remember.

If you follow the DNS naming convention, the top-level domain for XYZ, Inc., is xyz.com; the Corp network is named corp.xyz.com; Tech is named as tech.corp.com, and so on. All communication can be done with names rather than physical addresses. XYZ.com is the top-level domain. The subdomains are corp.xyz.com, tech.xyz.com, and so on.

Figure 19.2
Naming services.

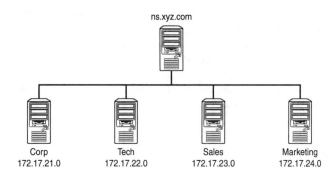

Each subdomain has its own name server, which clients within that domain query for host lookups. If a client named ws1.corp.xyz.com wants to query another client ws1.tech.xyz.com, it forwards its query to the name server in its domain ns.corp.xyz.com (see Figure 19.3). The name server forwards the query to the name server ns.tech.xyz.com of the client ws1.tech.xyz.com. The second name server then further forwards the query to ws1.tech.xyz.com. The client, ws1.tech.xyz.com, then returns the requested information to the requestor, ws1.corp.xyz.com. Figure 19.3 describes how hosts are searched in the xyz.com domain using domain name service.

Figure 19.3
Naming services hierarchy.

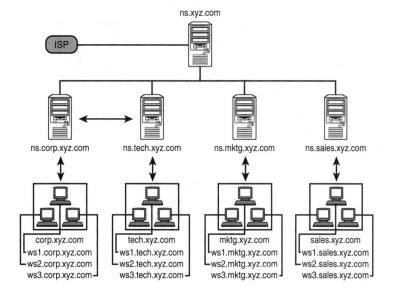

If the client ws1.tech.xyz.com requests information about a client that is not listed in the database of the name server, the name server then forwards request to the next name server, which is the primary domain server that lies next in the hierarchy as shown in Figure 19.3.

In this example, the primary domain server for XYZ Inc. is `ns.xyz.com`. If the primary domain server also does not recognize the hostname, or if the hostname lies beyond its Authoritative Zone, it forwards the request to the root server or the Domain Name server of the Internet Service Provider (ISP).

If the requested information is found, the root server sends the requested information to the requestor. Otherwise, the root server sends back a `Non-existent domain` message.

Now that you understand the basic concepts of naming services, it's time to look briefly at the different naming services supported by Solaris OE.

SOLARIS NAMING SERVICES

The different types of naming services in the Solaris operating environment have their own distinctive namespaces, architecture, data storage specifications, transport protocols, and so on. The following list provides an overview of each of these naming services.

- **DNS**—The Domain Name Service was designed for TCP/IP networks. Its purpose is to resolve the hostnames to the IP addresses. The hostnames and the IP addresses are maintained in the database files. DNS provides a functionality that is similar to the hostname resolution provided by `/etc/hosts` or `/etc/inet/ipnodes` files in UNIX.

  There are three types of DNS servers: master, slave, and caching name servers. The database files are stored in the master server.

→ For more information on the function of these servers, **see** "Name Resolution Process," **p.348**.

- **NIS**—The Network Information Service provides centralized control over a variety of network information. The NIS environment uses a client/server model. There are three types of hosts in the NIS environment: master, slave, and client. Note that the NIS namespace information is stored in NIS maps. These maps are stored in the master server and duplicate maps are stored in the slave servers.

→ To know more about NIS, **see** "Network Information Service (NIS)," **p.355**.

- **NIS+**—Although this naming service is similar to NIS, it has many more new features. NIS+ is designed to conform to organizational requirements. Similar to NIS, NIS+ also uses a client/server model to store information. This information is stored in 16 standard NIS+ tables in the NIS+ namespace. NIS+ uses a security system that allows only authorized clients to access this namespace. It uses its authentication mechanism to verify whether the requestor is a valid user on the network.

- **FNS**—The Federated Naming Service provides a set of common names that can be used over different naming services. Using the FNS conventions, you can name organizations, machines, users, and network services. In addition, FNS extends support for other naming services, such as DNS, NIS, and NIS+.

→ To know more about NIS+ and FNS, **see**, "Network Information Service+ (FNS and NIS+)," **p.371**.

- **LDAP**—LDAP (Lightweight Directory Access Protocol) is a directory service that provides a way to name, manage, and access collections of directory entries.

Table 19.1 summarizes the naming services supported by Solaris 9 OE.

→ To know more about LDAP, **see** "Lightweight Directory Access Portocol (LDAP)," **p.389**.

TABLE 19.1   SOLARIS NAMING SERVICES

	DNS	**LDAP**	**NIS**	**NIS+**	**FNS**
Architecture	Hierarchical Zone Master/ Slave Servers	Hierarchical Master/Replica	Flat Master/Slave	Hierarchical	Hierarchical
Transport Protocol	TCP/IP	TCP/IP	TCP/IP	TCP/IP	TCP/IP
Security Specs.	SSL, DNSSEC	SSL	None	DES authentication	None
Data Storage	Usually text database	Usually text database	Maps – bi-columned	Tables–Multi- columned	Maps

NAME SWITCH FILE (nsswitch.conf)

Most networks use one or more naming services. The nsswitch.conf file is used to coordinate the services. The nsswitch.conf file controls how a client machine obtains network information. The client can obtain information from one or more of switch's sources. For example, NIS can obtain hosts information from the NIS maps and the password information from the /etc files. The contents of the nsswitch.conf file include network information, such as host, password, and group.

During the installation process, Solaris OS automatically loads an nsswitch.conf file in the /etc directory. Based on the type of naming service you selected during installation, one of the four types of nsswitch.conf files are loaded: nsswitch.nisplus, nsswitch.nis, nss-witch.files, or nsswitch.ldap. During installation, the corresponding template file is copied to nsswitch.conf. For example, if you choose NIS as the naming service, the installation process copies the nsswitch.nis to nsswitch.conf.

The following list provides a brief description of each of these files.

- **/etc/nsswitch.nisplus**—This file specifies NIS+ as the primary source for all information. However, this information excludes passwd, group, automount, and aliases. Listing 19.1 displays the contents of the nsswitch.nisplus file. Note that if you need to use both DNS and NIS+ as the name server lookup, uncomment the line # hosts: nisplus dns [NOTFOUND=return] files and comment the line hosts: nisplus [NOTFOUND=return] files. You must also set up the /etc/resolv.conf file for DNS name server lookup.

→ For an explanation of this file, **see** "Name Resolution Process," **p.348**.

LISTING 19.1 */etc/nsswitch.nisplus* **FILE**

```
# /etc/nsswitch.nisplus:
#
#
# An example file that could be copied over to /etc/nsswitch.conf;
# it uses NIS+ (NIS Version 3) in conjunction with files.
#
# "hosts:" and "services:" in this file are used only if the
# /etc/netconfig file has a "-" for nametoaddr_libs of "inet"
# transports.
# the following two lines obviate the "+" entry in /etc/passwd
# and /etc/group.
passwd: files nisplus
group: files nisplus
# consult /etc "files" only if nisplus is down.
hosts: nisplus [NOTFOUND=return] files
# Uncomment the following line, and comment out the above, to use
# both DNS and NIS+. You must also set up the /etc/resolv.conf
# file for DNS name server lookup. See resolv.conf(4).
# hosts: nisplus dns [NOTFOUND=return] files
services: nisplus [NOTFOUND=return] files
networks: nisplus [NOTFOUND=return] files
protocols: nisplus [NOTFOUND=return] files
rpc: nisplus [NOTFOUND=return] files
ethers: nisplus [NOTFOUND=return] files
netmasks: nisplus [NOTFOUND=return] files
bootparams: nisplus [NOTFOUND=return] files
publickey: nisplus
netgroup: nisplus
automount: files nisplus
aliases: files nisplus
sendmailvars: files nisplus
```

■ **/etc/nsswitch.nis**—The nsswitch.nis configuration file is almost identical to the
NIS+ configuration file, except that it specifies NIS maps as the namespace in place of
NIS+ tables. Listing 19.2 displays the /etc/nsswitch.nis file.

LISTING 19.2 */etc/nsswitch.nis* **FILE**

```
# /etc/nsswitch.nis:
#
# An example file that could be copied over to /etc/nsswitch.conf;
# it uses NIS (YP) in conjunction with files.
#
# "hosts:" and "services:" in this file are used only if the
# /etc/netconfig file has a "-" for nametoaddr_libs of "inet"
# transports.
#
# the following two lines obviate the "+" entry in /etc/passwd
# and /etc/group.
passwd: files nis
group: files nis
# consult /etc "files" only if nis is down.
hosts: nis [NOTFOUND=return] files
networks: nis [NOTFOUND=return] files
```

```
protocols: nis [NOTFOUND=return] files
rpc: nis [NOTFOUND=return] files
ethers: nis [NOTFOUND=return] files
netmasks: nis [NOTFOUND=return] files
bootparams: nis [NOTFOUND=return] files
publickey: nis [NOTFOUND=return] files
netgroup: nis
automount: files nis
aliases: files nis
# for efficient getservbyname() avoid nis
services: files nis
sendmailvars: files
```

■ **/etc/nsswitch.files**—The nsswitch.files configuration file specifies local /etc files as the only source of information for the machine. There is no files source for netgroup, so the client does not use that entry in the switch file. Listing 19.3 displays the contents of /etc/nsswitch.files.

NOTE

> A netgroup defines a network-wide group of hosts and users. A netgroup is used to restrict access to shared NFS file systems and remote login and shell access.

LISTING 19.3 */etc/nsswitch.files*

```
# /etc/nsswitch.files:
#
# An example file that could be copied over to /etc/nsswitch.conf;
# it does not use any naming service.
#
# "hosts:" and "services:" in this file are used only if the
# /etc/netconfig file has a "-" for nametoaddr_libs of "inet"
# transports.
passwd: files
group: files
hosts: files
networks: files
protocols: files
rpc: files
ethers: files
netmasks: files
bootparams: files
publickey: files
# At present there isn't a 'files' backend for netgroup;
# the system will figure it out pretty quickly, and will notuse
# netgroups at all.
netgroup: files
automount: files
aliases: files
services: files
sendmailvars: files
```

19

■ **/etc/nsswitch.ldap**—The nsswitch.ldap configuration file specifies the LDAP directory as the primary source of information for the machine. Listing 19.4 displays the contents of the /etc/nsswitch.ldap file.

LISTING 19.4 */etc/nsswitch.files*

```
# /etc/nsswitch.ldap:
#
# An example file that could be copied over to /etc/nsswitch.conf; it
# uses LDAP in conjunction with files.
#
# "hosts:" and "services:" in this file are used only if the
# /etc/netconfig file has a "-" for nametoaddr_libs of "inet" transports.

# the following two lines obviate the "+" entry in /etc/passwd and /etc/group.
passwd:     files ldap
group:      files ldap

# consult /etc "files" only if ldap is down.
hosts:      ldap [NOTFOUND=return] files
ipnodes:    files
# Uncomment the following line and comment out the above to resolve
# both IPv4 and IPv6 addresses from the ipnodes databases. Note that
# IPv4 addresses are searched in all of the ipnodes databases before
# searching the hosts databases. Before turning this option on, consult
# the Network Administration Guide for more details on using IPv6.
#ipnodes:    ldap [NOTFOUND=return] files
# /etc/nsswitch.ldap:
#
# An example file that could be copied over to /etc/nsswitch.conf; it
# uses LDAP in conjunction with files.
#
# "hosts:" and "services:" in this file are used only if the
# /etc/netconfig file has a "-" for nametoaddr_libs of "inet" transports.

# the following two lines obviate the "+" entry in /etc/passwd and /etc/group.
passwd:     files ldap
group:      files ldap

# consult /etc "files" only if ldap is down.
hosts:      ldap [NOTFOUND=return] files
ipnodes:    files
# Uncomment the following line and comment out the above to resolve
# both IPv4 and IPv6 addresses from the ipnodes databases. Note that
# IPv4 addresses are searched in all of the ipnodes databases before
# searching the hosts databases. Before turning this option on, consult
# the Network Administration Guide for more details on using IPv6.
#ipnodes:    ldap [NOTFOUND=return] files
```

These alternate template files contain the default switch configurations used by the NIS+ and NIS services, local files, and LDAP. No default file is provided for DNS, but you can edit any of these files to use DNS.

DNS

DNS is an Application layer protocol that is used as a standard naming service for the Internet. This naming service was designed for name-to-address resolution for TCP/IP networks. This naming service uses the hostname as an index to locate IP addresses in the database.

A DNS domain contains name servers that are used to maintain information about the domain. The DNS environment has three types of name servers: master server, slave server, and a cache server.

The master server maintains a database that contains files similar to the /etc files. These files contain the IP addresses of machines in a particular domain. The slave servers act as backup servers and contain the same information as the master server.

The cache server is used to manage queries. However, it does not maintain any authoritative records or the address records for subzones. It maintains only those records that you require to locate the name servers of a delegated subzone.

To implement the DNS services, the in.named deamon provides DNS services.

The in.named daemon is a public domain TCP/IP program (the Berkeley Internet Name Domain—BIND) that is included with Solaris OE.

NOTE

The in.named daemon implements the Internet domain name service.

To run properly in the recursive mode, the in.named daemon needs a configuration file, /etc/named.conf, and four data files. The four data files are named.ca, hosts, hosts.rev, and named.local. The configuration file contains a list of domain names and the data files contain the host information. Table 19.1 displays the four data files along with their descriptions.

19

TABLE 19.2   DATA FILES AND THEIR DESCRIPTIONS

Data Files	Descriptions
/etc/named.conf	Contains a list of domain names and data file names. This file specifies the type of server on which it is running. Note that the /etc/named.conf file replaces the named.boot file and is the main configuration file of in.named.
/etc/resolv.conf	If the /etc/resolv.conf file exists, the local resolver routines either use a local name resolution database maintained by a local named daemon (a process) to resolve Internet names and addresses, or they use the domain protocol to request name resolution services from a remote domain name server host.

continues

TABLE 19.2   CONTINUED

Data Files	Descriptions
/var/named/named.ca	Establishes the names of root name servers responsible for the "." domain and lists their addresses.
/var/named/hosts	Contains data about every machine in a zone. If a zone covers more than one domain, all machines in all the domains covered by the zone are listed in the zone's host file.
/var/named/hosts.rev	Specifies a zone in the in.addr.arpa domain. The in.addr.arpa domain allows reverse mapping. The name hosts.rev is a generic name, which indicates the file's purpose and content. If you have more than one zone, each zone must have its own hosts.rev file and each zone hosts.rev file must have a unique name. For example, if your DNS domain is divided into xyz.com and sales.xyz.com zones, you could name one hosts.rev file as xyz.rev and the other as sales.rev.
/var/named/named.local	Specifies the address of the local loopback interface or local host (127.0.01) .

DNS domains are identified by the domain names.

The resolv.conf file resides on every DNS client (including DNS servers) and designates the servers that the client queries for DNS information.

The DNS client uses the resolv.conf to resolve users' queries. There are two types of DNS clients: Client Only and Client-Server. Client Only clients use the resolver to resolve queries, whereas the Client-Server uses the in.named daemon.

→ For more information on DNS clients, **see** "Setting Up DNS Clients," **p.349**.

NAME RESOLUTION PROCESS

To understand the name resolution process in DNS, imagine a domain where Client A wants to communicate with the Client B in the network (see Figure 19.4). Client A sends a request to a DNS server that in turn looks up the hostname in its database. If the master server finds the requested IP address in its database, the target client is in the authoritative domain of the master server. If the master server is unable to find the IP address, Client B is outside the authoritative domain of the master server. Figure 19.4 depicts the name resolution process.

When a client application requires the IP address of a host or the hostname corresponding to an IP address, the following process takes place:

1. The client system checks the /etc/nsswitch.conf file to determine the name-resolution order.

2. If specified in the nsswitch.conf file, the client system checks the /etc/inet/hosts file for IP addresses and hostname mapping.

Figure 19.4
Name-to-address resolution.

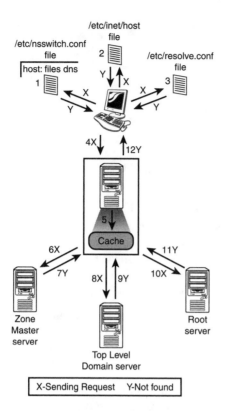

3. If no entry is found in these files, the client system uses the resolv.conf file to determine the name of the DNS servers to be used for name resolution.

4. The resolver sends a query to the local DNS server.

5. The DNS server checks its cache to determine whether the query was resolved recently.

6. If the DNS server does not find the requested information in its cache, it directs the request to the parent domain.

7. In case of non-availability of the information with the parent domain, the request is forwarded to a higher server (or the root domain).

8. If the root server is able to resolve the client request, the request is directed to the relevant DNS server. Otherwise, the root DNS server sends a not found message to the client.

SETTING UP DNS CLIENTS

To set up the DNS client, create the /etc/resolv.conf and /etc/nsswitch.conf files. The resolv.conf file for the client contains entries for the domain name and loopback name server. Each entry contains the IP addresses of the master, slave, or cache-only servers. Listing 19.5 displays a sample resolv.conf file.

LISTING 19.5   SAMPLE *resolv.conf* FILE

```
; Sample resolv.conf file for the machine buffy
domain dom1.com
; try local name server
nameserver 10.0.0.1
; if local name server down, try these servers
nameserver 192.168.16.6
nameserver 192.168.16.7
; sort the addresses returned by gethostbyname(3c)
sortlist
130.155.160.0/255.255.240.0
130.155.0.0
```

In Listing 19.5, the first entry lists the domain name in the form *<domain dom1.com>*. The second entry identifies the loopback name server in the form. The entries following the second entry list the IP addresses of name servers, such as master, slave, or cache-only name servers. The resolver accesses these servers for resolving queries. Note that the resolver queries the name servers in the order they are listed until it finds the information it needs. The fifth entry defines the sort order of the addresses returned by gethostbyname.

After making the appropriate entries in the /etc/resolv.conf file, modify the /etc/nss-witch.conf file.

SETTING UP DNS SERVERS

To set up DNS servers, log in as the superuser and set up the server as a DNS client. Note that setting up the DNS client involves setting up the server's resolv.conf and nsswitch.conf files. The next step is to set up the boot and the data files. Specify the master record for the zone. The master record has three fields. The first field designates the master server. The second field identifies the zone for the master server, and the third field identifies the hosts file. Listing 19.6 displays the contents of the master server boot file. Notice the line that describes master, dom1.com, and db.com. In this line, master is the server, dom1.com is the zone, and db.com is the name of the hosts file.

The next line in this listing specifies the master record for the zone's reverse map. This record designates the server as a master server for the zones reverse address map, that is, the reverse address domain for dom1.com. The record also tells the server where to find the authoritative hosts file. This record has three fields. The first field designates the server as master, the second field identifies the zone, and the third field identifies the hosts.rev file. The reverse address domain for a zone contains the zone's IP address in reverse order, followed by in-addr.arpa. For example, suppose that the dom1.com zone's IP address is 123.321.21. In that case, the reverse address domain would be 21.321.123.in-addr.arpa. Thus, the second-to-last line in the boot file (see Listing 19.6) specifies that the server is the master server for the reverse address domain of the dom1.com zone by using authoritative data from the file doc.rev.

NOTE

The process of mapping IP addresses to DNS names is called *reverse address mapping*. The zone that implements reverse address mapping is known as a *reverse zone*. A domain or a subdomain that functions as a reverse zone is known as *reverse domain*.

The next step specifies the master record for the reverse address of the local loopback interface or host. The first field designates the server as master, the second field identifies the loopback host reverse address, and the third field identifies the hosts file.

LISTING 19.6   CONTENTS OF THE MASTER SERVER BOOT FILE

```
; /etc/named.conf file on the dnsmastr
;
; files required by in.named are located here
directory /var/named
; here are the names of the master files
cache . named.ca
master dom1.com db.doc
master 21.321.123.in-addr.arpa doc.rev
master 0.0.127.in-addr.arpa named.local
```

SETTING UP SLAVE SERVERS

A slave server is like a backup server to the master server; it maintains a copy of the data stored in the master server. The purpose of the slave server is to share the network load and also to act as the backup server in case the master server fails. Note that in case of any change in the host's information, you need to update the data in only the master server. The slave server frequently queries the master server for updates and then updates its database.

To specify that a server is to be the slave server for a given zone, create slave records in the server's /etc/named.conf file. The slave records can specify the loopback host and the zone's reverse address domain. There are three fields in the slave record. The first field designates the server as a slave. The second field identifies the zone server. The third field identifies the IP address of the master of the zone that the slave server uses to obtain information. The following syntax shows how to define a slave server for a zone:

```
slave dom1.com 129.146.168.119 192.146.168.38 dom1.com.bakup
slave 4.0.32.128.in-addr.arpa 129.146.168.119
```

You can also include optional fields, such as IP addresses of additional slave servers and the name of a backup hosts file in the /etc/named.conf after you create the required fields.

The additional slave servers provide sources that the slave server can use to obtain data. The slave server uses the backup host file to load data. It then checks with the master server to ensure that the data that it has loaded is current.

If you want to add an additional slave server, set up the server as a DNS client and the set up the following files:

19

- boot file
- named.ca
- hosts
- hosts.rev
- named.local

ADDING AND DELETING CLIENTS

When you add or delete clients, ensure that you make the changes in the data files stored in the master server. When you add or delete records in the data files stored in the master server, make sure that you inform in.named in the master server that it should reread the data files and update its database. You must also increment the Start of Authority (SOA) resource record when you make any modifications to the data in the DNS database file. For example, if the current SOA number in the data file is 200 and you add a record to the data file, you must change the SOA number to 201. If you fail to increment the SOA, the domain's slave server will not update the copy in the master server database. This will make the data stored in the master server and the slave server out of sync.

To add a client, set the new machine up as a DNS client and then add records for the new machine to the appropriate hosts and hosts.rev files. Perform the following steps to set up additional clients.

1. Create an /etc/resolv.conf file on *new_machine* and add an address record for the *new_machine* in the host file of the master server.
   new_machine IN A 192.168.112

2. In addition to the address record, you can add optional records, such as Alias (CNAME), Mail exchange (MX), Well known services (WKS), and Host information (HINFO) to the host file of the master server.

3. The hosts.rev files must have a pointer (PTR) record for each machine in the subdomain. Add a PTR record for the host machine to the hosts.rev file.

4. Increment the SOA serial number in the master server's hosts and hosts.rev files.

5. Finally, reload the server's data. To reload, either reboot the server or type the following command. This command forces the in.named file to reread the named.conf file and reload the database.
   # kill -HUP 'cat /etc/named.pid'

To remove a client, you must remove the following:

- dns from the hosts line of the machine's nsswitch.conf file.
- The machine's /etc/resolv.conf file.
- Records for the machine from the master server's hosts and hosts.rev files.
- CNAME records pointing to the machine from the hosts file (if applicable).

Note that if the client is a mail host or the host for any other necessary process or service, ensure that you set up some other machine to perform those services.

SUMMARY

When designing a network, it is important to dedicate at least one directory system that will locate hosts on the network. Additional naming services may be required to support directory services for Internet domains. Naming services provide a mechanism to associate names to objects. Solaris 9 supports five naming services: DNS, NIS, NIS+, FNS, and LDAP. Designed for TCP/IP networks, DNS resolves hostnames to IP addresses. NIS/NIS+ is a comprehensive network resource management system for both authorizing access to resources and hosts and handling client/server authentication. LDAP is a directory service that enables you to consolidate information by replacing application-specific databases.

19

## CHAPTER 20

NETWORK INFORMATION SERVICE (NIS)

In this chapter

Introducing NIS   356

Planning the NIS Domain   359

Summary   368

INTRODUCING NIS

Developed in 1985 by Sun Microsystems, Network Information Service (NIS), initially known as Yellow Pages (YP), was the first Unix-based naming service. Now that you've read about DNS in Chapter 19, "DNS" you might wonder what the need was for NIS when DNS was already present. Is it just yet another naming service?

NIS was developed independently of DNS and has a different focus than DNS. The idea of NIS is to enable easier network management by storing information about machine names, users, network, and network services in a centralized location. This also enables a strong central authentication mechanism for your network. On the other hand, DNS is a distributed system and focuses on making communication simpler by mapping hostnames to IP addresses as discussed in Chapter 19. However, for business critical networks, NIS+ or LDAP is an appropriate solution as compared to NIS for security reasons.

NIS ARCHITECTURE

An NIS environment consists of three types of hosts: a master server, slave servers, and clients logically bound in a domain (see Figure 20.1). The master server is the server that contains NIS maps. The NIS maps are databases that specify the system information, such as usernames, group names, passwords, and hostnames. The NIS maps stored in the master server can be updated when required. These maps are intended to replace the Unix **/etc** files and other configuration files, such as **etc/inet/ipnodes**, **/etc/inet/protocols**, and so on.

Figure 20.1
NIS Architecture

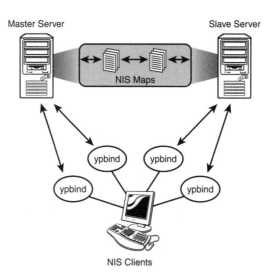

Apart from the master server, an NIS Domain may also consist of one or more slave servers. A slave server acts as the backup server; it contains the copies of the NIS maps contained by the master server. The existence of slave servers also allows the system administrator to distribute the load answering NIS requests across servers.

NIS clients are machines that request network information by using RPC within their domain from the NIS maps on the servers—master or slave. Because the master and slave servers contain the same information, the NIS client does not care which server services its requests. The distinction between master and slave server applies only when you make updates to the NIS maps. Note that whenever the master server's maps are updated, it propagates the updates among the slave servers.

→ To learn more about the steps to propagate the maps in the slave servers, see "Propagating NIS Maps," **p.368**.

NIS DATABASES, DAEMONS, AND UTILITIES

NIS provides a simple network lookup service consisting of databases, daemons, and utilities. This section describes each of these elements.

The NIS database contains files that are usually in the **/var/yp** directory. These files are known as the database maps (dbm) files. Note that the dbm files served by the NIS server are the NIS maps that contain user and system information. Each master server in an NIS domain has a set of NIS maps.

The NIS daemons are **ypserv**, **ypbind**, **ypxfr**, **rpc.yppasswdd**, and **rpc.ypupdated**.

- The **ypserv** daemon is a server process, which is typically activated at system startup from the startup script **/etc/init.d/rpc**. This daemon runs on both master and slave servers, so it can accept and answer client queries by looking up the NIS maps.

> **NOTE**
>
> An alternative way to start the NIS processes is by using the command **ypstart** from the command line. The **ypstop** command is used to stop the NIS services.

- **ypbind**—A binding process that runs on all machines in the domain requesting NIS services. This daemon locates a valid server in the NIS domain and relies on this server for all its queries.
- **ypxfr**—Downloads the current version of the NIS map.
- **rpc.yppasswdd**—Runs on the master server and allows users to update information in the password file.
- **rpc.ypupdated**—Updates the information in NIS maps.

The NIS service is administered by several command line utilities. These utilities are:

- **makedbm**—Generates NIS maps. It converts source text files to the NIS maps in the ndbm format.
- **ypcat**—Lists the values in the NIS map.
- **ypinit**—Sets up the NIS system.
- **yppmatch**—Prints value of one or more keys from an NIS map specified by **mname**. The **mname** option specifies either a map name or a map nickname.

20

- **yppush**—Copies the new values from the NIS maps in the master server to the NIS maps in the slave server.

- **ypset**—Specifies the NIS server process to use the **ypbind** process. The **ypbind** process creates and maintains binding to an NIS server. The **ypbind** process is discussed in more detail in the following section.

- **ypwhich**—Determines which server is the master for an NIS map, or which server supplies the NIS services.

- **ypxfr**—Transfers the NIS map from a server to the local host.

HOW NIS WORKS

In the NIS domain, the function of the NIS server is to process the requests of the NIS clients. NIS clients request information by using the binding process. This process works in two modes: broadcast and server list.

In the broadcast mode, the client broadcasts by initiating the **ypbind** process to locate an NIS server in the domain. Note that this process cannot go beyond the subnet and therefore it becomes important to have at least one server in the same subnet as the client. This server could be the master or a slave server. The **ypbind** process binds the client request to the first server that responds to the broadcast. It then tells the client about the server that responded to the broadcast. The client then directly sends its request to the server. Figure 20.2 illustrates how the broadcast mode works.

Figure 20.2
NIS binding in the broadcast mode.

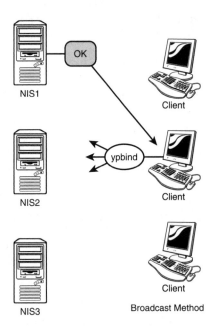

NIS1

Client

ypbind

NIS2

Client

NIS3

Client

Broadcast Method

In the server list mode, when a program running on the NIS client needs a request to be serviced, it asks the **ypbind** for the name of the server (see Figure 20.3). The **ypbind** process queries the **/var/yp/binding/domain/ypservers** list for the names of all the NIS servers in the domain. It initiates binding to the first server that it finds in the list that responds to the request. The **ypbind** daemon then tells the client to contact the server directly for processing its queries. The **ypserv** daemon consults the appropriate NIS map in the server to process the queries at the server end. It then sends the requested information back to the client.

Figure 20.3
NIS binding in the server list mode.

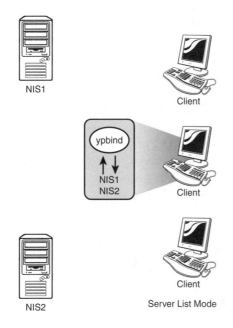

PLANNING THE NIS DOMAIN

Whether your network is large or small, you must plan the layout of your NIS domain before setting it up. The following recommendations are general tips that you can use while designing your NIS domain environment. You should tailor these tips to benefit your site requirements.

20

- Determine the number of domains you need. This number depends on how complex your network is. If your network has some 1000-odd machines, you have a large network. In this case, it is advisable to have more than one NIS domain.

- Choose a name for the domain that will be used when you set up the master server. A domain name should be less than 255 characters long, and it is better to keep it short— 10-30 characters is good. The domain name you choose is at your discretion. However, you should choose a domain name that corresponds to the location or the types of systems it contains. The domain name that you choose can correspond with the Internet domain name. For example, if you are setting up a domain for the Purchase department, you can name your domain **purch.company.com**. The **domainname** command is used to set the domain name on an NIS system. An alternative method is to edit the file **/etc/defaultdomain** directly to specify your domain name. This domain name is assigned at the system startup in the domain file **/var/yp/ypdomain**. Note that the domain names are case sensitive: finance and Finance are different domains.

- Determine the hosts in the network that will serve and use the NIS services. The hosts that will perform the task of serving requests are the servers. As described earlier, each NIS domain in your network will have one master server. Note that you can always change the host that acts as the master server at a later date. The host that you choose as the master server should be a stable and reliable system. This server stores the original database maps for the domain and this is the only server where changes to the NIS database are made. Also, the systems that access the master server should be able to rely on uninterrupted service. In addition, the NIS master server should be easily accessible to the slave and client hosts in your NIS network.

- In addition to the master server, determine the hosts that will act as the slaves for the master server. Once again, the number of slave servers you choose depends on the size of the network and the number of domains over which your network extends. If your domain spreads across networks, it is advisable to have at least two slave servers in case of network or system failures. Also, a number of hosts in a large network accessing the master server can overload it. Additional slave servers are required to balance the load on the master server. Similar to the master servers, the slave servers should be accessible to both the master server and the client server.

- The hosts that will use the services of NIS are the clients. Determine all such clients in your network. Depending upon your network requirements, you can set all hosts in your network as clients.

- Verify whether the data in the **/etc** files is correct. Note that the **/etc** files contain all user and group information and these files are used to populate the NIS maps.

CONFIGURING NIS

After you have planned your domain, you are ready to configure NIS. The first step in configuring NIS is to set up the master server. You use the shell script **/usr/sbin/ypinit** to configure the master server. This script is discussed in more detail later in the chapter. After configuring the master server, start the NIS services on the master server.

If you choose to have slave servers in your domain, then the next step is to configure the slave servers and start the NIS services on the slave server as well.

Finally, set up the client servers. The steps to perform each of these tasks are detailed in the following sections.

PREPARING THE MASTER SERVER

Before you configure the NIS master server, you need to perform certain tasks to prepare for the setup.

You must ensure that the source files used for preparing the NIS maps are stored in a directory different from the /etc directory. The NIS maps contain the replicated data from the source text files. As stated in Chapter 19, the NIS source text files are stored in the /etc directory. For security reasons, it becomes crucial to store these files in a different directory. The /etc directory contains the /etc/passwd and /etc/shadow files. Because these files contain the root password, creating NIS maps using these source files can endanger the system's security. With the NIS maps accessible to every client in the network, unauthorized users can access the root password. Therefore, it is recommended that you store the source input text file in a directory of your choice. When storing the source input text files in another directory, delete the root password entry from the file.

This consideration is especially important when you are creating the password map for the NIS domain. This password map is created from the password file stored in the /etc/password file. When creating a password map, remove the root password entry from this file and store it in the directory of your choice. You can then use this file as the input source for creating the password map.

To relocate the source files to a different directory, make the following modifications to the Makefile. The function of the Makefile is to create the appropriate NIS maps for each of the databases listed under **all**. After the data passes through **makedbm**, it is collected in two files: *mapname*.**dir** and *mapname*.**pag**. Both these files are stored in the /**var**/**yp**/*domainname* directory on the master server. The following command changes the directory to where the Makefile is stored and uses the **vi** editor to open the Makefile.

```
master#cd /var/yp
master#vi Makefile
all: passwd group hosts ipnodes ethers networks rpc services protocols \
        netgroup bootparams aliases publickey netid netmasks c2secure \
        timezone auto.master auto.home \
        auth.attr exec.attr prof.attr user.attr audit.user
```

In the Makefile, edit the line **DIR = /etc**. Assign a different directory of your choice to **DIR**. For example, if you want to store the file in the /**var**/**security** directory, edit the line to

> **NOTE**
>
> If the security directory does not exist, use the **mkdir** command to create the directory. Use the **chmod** command to set the default permission of directory to 700. This is to ensure that only root has access to the source file.

20

```
DIR = /var/security/etc
```

The next step is to copy the input data from the /**etc** directory to the /**var**/**security** directory. The following command copies the most commonly used source file's password, group, hosts, ethers, networks, protocols, RPC, and services to the /**var**/**yp** directory. Table 20.1 lists the contents of each file.

```
master#cd /etc
master#mkdir /var/security/etc
master#cp passwd group hosts ethers aliases protocols rpc services
➥/var/security/etc
```

TABLE 20.1 SOURCE FILES AND THEIR DESCRIPTIONS

Source Files	Descriptions
/etc/passwd	Contains user account information.
/etc/group	Specifies group definitions.
/etc/hosts	Maps hostnames and IP addresses.
/etc/ethers	Maps hostnames and ethernet addresses.
/etc/aliases	Specifies mail alias definitions.
/etc/protocols	Maps text names to protocol numbers.
/etc/rpc	Lists ID numbers for RPC services
/etc/services	Lists port numbers for network services.

Next, remove all information from the files that should not be distributed across the network. For example, the root password information should be removed from the **passwd** and **group** files. The Makefile builds **passwd** maps from the **/PWDIR/passwd**, **/PWDIR/shadow**, and **/PWDIR/security/passwd.adjunct** files, as appropriate. Note that you must change the directory path, **PWDIR = /etc**, which is the default password entry in the Makefile and which points to the file where you have copied the password file. The following syntax changes the entry of the directory path to **/var/yp**.

PWDIR = /var/yp

In addition to the password file, the four Role Back Access Control (RBAC) databases contain user and group information that should not be distributed across the network. The four RBAC database files are **user_attr**, **auth_attr**, **exec_attr**, and **prof_attr**. These files store data that include information on roles, authorizations, profiles, and security attributes. Copy these databases to a directory of your choice and modify the RBACDIR entry in the Makefile from **RBACDIR = /etc/security** to **RBACDIR = /Dir 1** where *Dir 1* is the name of the directory that you choose for storing the RBAC databases.

Unlike the source files mentioned previously, the **/etc/mail/aliases** cannot be moved from their source location. In this case, you must check the aliases file for completeness, to see whether this file contains all the aliases in the domain. The aliases file contains all the mail addresses or aliases the mail program recognizes for the local host.

The next step is to check to make sure that all the files are clean and do not contain any extra comments or lines. You can use a **sed** or **awk** script to do the cleaning. Although Makefile does some cleaning, it is a good practice to check each file manually and make sure there are no extraneous lines. Also, make sure that the data in all the files is formatted as necessary.

20

To set up the NIS master server, perform the following steps:

1. Log in as root. Provide a name for your NIS domain in which you will set up the hosts by using the **domainname** command. For example, if you are creating a domain for the marketing department, name the domain to correspond to the name of the department. Issue the following command to name the domain **mktg.company.com**.

   ```
   # domainname mktg.company.com
   ```

2. After the domain is created, populate the domain file stored in the **/etc** directory with the domain name.

   ```
   # echo mktg.company.com
   > /etc/defaultdomain
   ```

3. Edit the **/etc/hosts** or **/etc/inet/ipnodes** file to add the name and IP address of each of the NIS servers.

4. Copy the contents of the **nsswitch.file** to the **nsswitch.conf** file.

   ```
   # cp /etc/nsswitch.file /etc/nsswitch.conf
   ```

5. To build new maps on the master server, type

   ```
   # /usr/sbin/ypinit -m
   ```

6. The **ypinit** command prompts for a list of other machines to become NIS slave servers. Type the name of the server you are working on along with the names of your NIS slave servers and press Ctrl+D.

7. The **ypinit** command asks whether you want the procedure to terminate at the first nonfatal error or continue despite nonfatal errors. Type **y**.

   When you enter y, **ypinit** exits upon encountering the nonfatal error that can be fixed manually at a later time. A nonfatal error can appear when some of the map files are not present. This an error that doesn't affect the functionality of NIS. You might need to add maps manually if they were not created automatically.

8. After **ypinit** has constructed the list of servers, it invokes **make**. The **make** command cleans any remaining comment lines from the files you designated and runs **makedbm** on them. The **makedbm** command creates the appropriate maps and establishes the name of the master server for each map.

   ```
   # make
   ```

   In case the map being pushed corresponds to a domain other than the one returned by the command **domainname** on the master server, ensure it is pushed to the correct domain by starting **make** in the **ypinit** shell script with a proper identification of the variable DOM, as follows. The **make** command pushes the password map to the correct target domain.

   ```
   # make DOM=domainname password
   ```

9. Use the following command to make sure the new master maps are there. All the NIS maps are stored in the /var/yp/solaris.com directory.

   ```
   # ypcat -k hosts
   ```

10. To enable NIS as the naming service, type the following:

    ```
    # cp /etc/nsswitch.nis /etc/nsswitch.conf
    ```

20

This replaces the current switch file with the default NIS-oriented switch file. You can edit this file as necessary.

After configuring, start the NIS daemons on the master server and begin service.

SETTING UP NIS SLAVE SERVERS

Because the slave servers play the role of backup servers for the master servers, they store the same information as the master server. Therefore, the NIS maps that you store in the slave servers are copies of the master server. After the master server is set up, all you need to do is copy the NIS maps from the master server to the slave server.

Before setting up the slave server, ensure that the domain name of the slave server is the same as the master server. To do so, run the **domainname** command on each slave server. After you are sure that the domain names of both the slave servers and the master server are same, perform the following tasks to configure the slave server:

1. Populate the names and IP addresses of all the NIS servers in the **/etc/hosts** or **/etc/inet/ipnodes** file.

2. Next, initialize the slave server as a client by running the **ypinit** shell script.

   ```
   # /usr/sbin/ypinit -c
   ```

   When this command is issued, it prompts you to enter a list of servers in your domain. You can start by typing the name of the local slave server you are working on, then give the name of the master server followed by other servers (if any) in the domain. After you are finished adding the names of the servers, press Ctrl-D.

3. Determine whether **ypbind** is running by issuing the following command. Note that if the command displays a list, it means that **ypbind** is running:

   ```
   # ps -ef | grep ypbind
   ```

4. If **ypbind** is running, stop it by typing

   ```
   # /usr/lib/netsvc/yp/ypstop
   ```

   and then restart it by typing

   ```
   # /usr/lib/netsvc/yp/ypstart
   ```

5. To initialize the local machine as a slave, type the following:

   ```
   # /usr/sbin/ypinit -s master
   ```

   Where *master* is the machine name of the existing NIS master server.

   The next step is to start the NIS service on a slave server. You can do so by rebooting the slave server. Alternatively, you can use the following commands to start the services.

   To start the services, stop the **yp** processes using the following command:

   ```
   # /usr/lib/netsvc/yp/ypstop
   ```

   Now run the **ypbind** and start the services by using the following command:

   ```
   # /usr/lib/netsvc/yp/ypstart
   ```

ADDING SLAVE SERVERS

If you have a domain with a large number of hosts, it is advisable to include more than one slave server. The greater the number of hosts in a domain, the greater the number of requests. This increases the load on the master server. Adding more than one slave server to the domain helps in reducing the load on the master server. In addition, with the load being shared among servers, the response time for processing queries decreases largely.

For example, imagine a domain called domcp. This domain has a master server mascp and a slave server called slacp_1. This domain has more than 700 clients. With many clients requesting query processing, the load on the master server has increased. The slave server slacp shares some load from the master server. However, you can add another slave server, slacp_2, which will share the load further and help to increase performance of the servers in the domain.

To add a new slave server to the domain, perform the following steps:

1. Change the directory path to the NIS domain directory by issuing the command **cd /var/yp** at the command prompt.

2. Next, specify the name of the NIS domain to which the slave server is to be added and the name of the slave server host by entering the **makedbm** command.

    ```
    (makedbm -u domcp/ypservers ; echo slacp_2) | makedbm - tservers
    ```

    In this command, the slave server slacp_2 is added to the **ypservers** map. This command lists the contents of the current **ypservers** map, appends the name of the new slave server, and then creates a new map called **tservers**.

3. Verify that the new map contains the names of all the slave servers by entering this command:

    ```
    makedbm -u tservers
    ```

4. Replace the old **ypservers** map files with the new ones by entering the following two commands:

    ```
    mv tservers.pag domcp/ypservers.pag
    mv tservers.dir domcp/ypservers.dir
    ```

SETTING UP NIS CLIENTS

There are two methods to configure a machine to use NIS as its naming service. You can either issue the **ypinit -c** command or use the broadcast method. Both these methods are described as follows:

- **ypinit -c**—When you issue the **ypinit -c** command, it prompts you to enter the list of servers from which the client will obtain the naming service information. The servers you enter can be located anywhere in the domain. It is recommended that you enter the name of the server closest (in network terms) to the local machine that you are setting up as the client, followed by the other servers in the domain.

20

■ **Broadcast**—The broadcast method is an old method of setting up the NIS client. In this method, you first log in as the superuser, set the domain name, and run **ypbind**.

```
# domainname doc.com
# ypbind -broadcast
```

The **ypbind** command looks for an NIS server in the domain. It binds to the first server that responds to the broadcast message. If there is no NIS server on the client's local subnet, it fails to bind and the client machine is unable to obtain namespace data from the NIS service.

ADDING USERS TO THE NIS DOMAIN

Now that you have servers and clients ready, you can add new users to the NIS domain. Adding a new user to an NIS domain is similar to adding to a standalone machine, except for a few extra steps. This section details the procedure to add users to the NIS domain. To add users, you must have superuser privileges.

The steps to create a new user in an NIS domain are as follows:

1. Create a new user named Bill by using the **useradd** command. This command creates an entry for the user Bill in the /etc/passwd and /etc/shadow files in the NIS master server.

   ```
   # useradd Bill
   ```

2. Next, assign the initial password for the user Bill, which he will use to log in to the system the first time. To create a new password, run the **passwd** command for the user ID Bill.

   ```
   # passwd Bill
   ```

3. When the preceding command is run, you are prompted to enter the new password. The password that you assign in this case is billpassword.

4. After creating the user and the initial password, copy the user information stored in the files in the /etc directory to the password and shadow files stored in the directory of your choice. The line that is to be copied from the /etc/passwd and the /etc/shadow files looks something like this:

   ```
   Bill:x:1295:325:User Bill:/home/baruch:/bin/csh:
   ```

5. Delete the source information from the /etc directory in the master server by using the **userdel** command.

   ```
   userdel Bill
   ```

6. Update the NIS passwd maps by running **make** in the directory containing the source file. If the source file is in /var/yp, run the following commands:

   ```
   # cd /var/yp
   #/usr/ccd/bin/make passwd
   ```

7. Inform the user about the initial password you created to enable the user to log in the first time. The user can change this password by using the **passwd** command. However, before the users are allowed to change the password, you need to start the **rpc.yppasswd**

daemon. This helps update the password file. The commands for starting the daemon are present in the **/usr/lib/netsvc/yp/ypstart** file.

You can use these steps to create multiple users for the NIS domain. Note that for administrative purposes, you can assign these users to be a part of a specific group called Netgroups. For example, you can assign administrative privileges to groups of users in a specific Netgroup that enable them to access machines in a specific domain. Each Netgroup contains its own identity.

The NIS maps use the Netgroup name rather than a specific username or machine name. This is especially helpful when you want to set specific functions for the users in the Netgroup. For example, suppose there is a Netgroup called Nadmin and you would like to give administrative privileges to all the users in this group. In this case, you need not give individual permission to each member of the group. Instead, all you need to do is add the Netgroup entry in the **/etc/passwd** file and then propagate this file to the NIS Netgroup map in the master server.

A sample Netgroup file follows:

```
% cat /etc/netgroup
  root-users       (,tim,), (,jay,), (,jana,)
  trusted-machines      (sw001,,), (sw002,,), (sw003,,)
```

Note that the file contains **name** and **ID** fields. The **name** indicates the name of the Netgroup, and the **ID** indicates the users or machines who belong to this Netgroup. Use the following syntax to add members to the Netgroup:

```
([-|machine], [-|user], [domain])
```

Where *machine* is a machine name and *user* is a user ID. The machine and user element of each member's entry are required, but a dash (-) indicates a null. There is no necessary relationship between the machine and user elements in an entry. If you add a new NIS user or machine to your network, be sure to add them to appropriate Netgroups in the Netgroup input file. Then use the **make** and **yppush** commands to create the Netgroup maps and push them to all your NIS servers.

CREATING NIS MAPS

You can create maps by using an existing text file or the standard input. The existing text files could be files created with an editor located on the master server. These files can be taken as the source input files for the NIS map.

Suppose you have an existing file called **mapsc** located in the **/var/yp** directory. You should use this file to create the NIS map and locate this file in the directory of your choice. To create the map, change the directory to the location where the existing file is stored and then run the **makedbm** command.

```
cd /var/yp
makedbm mapsc.asc yourchoice/mapsc
```

Another method to create a map file is via the standard input. Add the entries to the map file using the keyboard as follows:

```
cd /var/yp
makedbm -____ - homedomain/mymapkey1 key2value2 key3value3
```

PROPAGATING NIS MAPS

You propagate maps to the slave servers by copying the maps from the master server to all the slave servers. There are two advantages to this:

- You can avoid updating the individual maps on each slave server.
- The master server and the slave server maintain the same copies of the NIS maps, which enables any server to respond to client queries.

To propagate maps, you can issue the **yppush** command, run the **ypupdate** daemon, or restart the master server by one of the following methods:

- Issue the **yppush** command on the master server. This prompts the slave servers to copy the latest NIS maps from the master server. The syntax used to issue this command is

  ```
  /usr/sbin/yppush [-v] [-d Domain] Mapname
  ```

  In the preceding syntax, there are two flags: **-v** and **-d**. The **-v** option displays the in-progress messages as each server is called and displays one message for each server's response. The **ypserv** daemon on each slave server runs the **ypxfr** command to get the updated map. The following example copies the Netgroup map from the Sales domain onto each slave server in the network:

  ```
  /usr/sbin/yppush -v -d Sales netgroup
  ```

- Another method to propagate the latest maps in the slave servers is to run the **ypupdated** daemon in the master server. If this daemon is running, then the maps are propagated at regular intervals in the slave servers. This daemon consults the **ypservers** map in the **/var/yp** directory to determine which maps need to be updated. The syntaxes used to start and stop this daemon are as follows:

  ```
  startsrc -s ypupdated
  stopsrc -s ypupdated
  ```

- In addition to using the **yppush** command and the **ypupdated** daemon, if you stop and restart NIS on the master server, all the maps propagate to the slave servers.

SUMMARY

Formerly known as Yellow Pages (YP), NIS was the first Unix-based naming service that made network management an easy task by storing network information in a centralized location. The NIS environment consists of three types of hosts: master, slave, and client. The master server contains the NIS maps that store user and system information. The client servers access the maps in the master server for relevant information. The slave servers act as the backup servers for the master server. They store the same information as the master server. The slave servers serve two purposes. If the master server goes down, the slave server acts as the master server and handles all client requests. Also, the slave servers share the load from the master server. In a large network, the number of queries generated by the clients can overload the master server. The slave servers are used to share the load from the master server. The number of slave servers in a network depends on the size of the network. If you have a large network, you may choose to have more than one slave server.

To configure a master server, use the shell script **/usr/sbin/ypinit** to configure the master server. After configuring the master server, start the NIS services on the master server. If you choose to have slave servers in your domain, then the next step is to configure the slave servers and start the NIS services on the slave server as well. You can configure a machine to use NIS as its naming service by either issuing the **ypinit -c** command or using the broadcast method.

The master server contains the NIS maps. These are databases that specify the system information, such as usernames, group names, passwords, and hostnames. You can create NIS maps by using an existing text file or the standard input. You propagate maps to the slave servers by copying the maps from the master server to all the slave servers.

20

## CHAPTER 21

NETWORK INFORMATION SERVICE PLUS AND FEDERATED NAMING SYSTEM (NIS+ AND FNS)

In this chapter

Getting Started with NIS+   372

Configuring the Master and Slave Servers   381

Federated Naming Service (FNS)   386

Summary   387

GETTING STARTED WITH NIS+

Network Information Service Plus (NIS+), like NIS, is a naming service that enables you to store information, such as machine names, the address of each machine in a network, user information, security information, and information about the available network services. Though both NIS and NIS+ are naming services, which helps you centrally administer network resources, NIS+ was specifically designed to replace NIS. When NIS was designed, it was intended to cater to small client-server computing networks. Later, as the number and requirements of clients and servers in distributed networks increased, many new issues cropped up. NIS+ was designed to address these issues.

NIS+ is the default naming service for Solaris. It stores relevant information about all machines and the network services in a network in a centralized location so that each machine on a network can access the information. This collection of network information is referred to as the *NIS+ namespace*.

The NIS+ namespace is hierarchical in structure, unlike NIS, which has a flat structure. Therefore, data is stored in different levels in NIS+. Additionally, it can be divided into logical units called *domains*. These domains can then be associated with an organization's logical hierarchy. Thus, the NIS+ namespace is flexible and caters to the needs of large organizations that have various departments. In other words, the hierarchical structure of NIS+ can be rearranged as necessary to meet the structural needs of an organization.

The NIS+ namespace consists of three types of objects, collectively referred to as NIS+ objects. They are as follows:

- Directory objects
- Table objects
- Group objects

The directory objects make up the backbone of the NIS+ namespace. An NIS+ directory object contains other directories, tables, and groups. The topmost directory object is referred to as the *root* directory, which in turn comprises one or more directory objects. The directory object available under the root object is referred to as the *child* directory, and the root directory, in this case, can also be referred to as the *parent* directory.

All domain-level directories of NIS+ contain three sub-directories: groups_dir, org_dir, and ctx_dir. The groups_dir directory stores information about an NIS+ group, and the org_dir directory stores the NIS+ tables. The ctx_dir directory is optional and is present only if you are using the Federated Naming System (FNS) .

→ For more detail on FNS, **see** "Federated Naming Service," **p.386**.

Another NIS+ object is the table object. A table object consists of rows and columns that store information about machines, users, and network services.

In addition to the directory and the table objects, NIS+ also provides objects referred to as *group* objects that consist of a list of members in a specific group. A group can be a collection of either users or machines. Each group has a specific name for identification purposes. The access rights assigned to a group are applicable to all the members of that group.

NIS+ follows a client/server model to search for and retrieve information stored in the NIS+ namespace. The client/server model of NIS+ consists of domains and subdomains. A set of servers is associated with each domain. The principal server in the set of servers is referred to as the *master* server and the backup servers are referred to as *replica* servers. Replica servers are also called *slave* servers.

Figure 21.1 depicts the NIS+ client/server model with a master server and replicas.

Figure 21.1
The NIS+ client/server model.

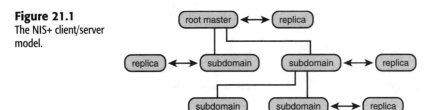

A copy of the NIS+ table is maintained in both the master server and the replica servers. All modifications to the information in the master server are automatically updated to all the replica servers.

Thus, data is updated faster and effectively, unlike in NIS, which has to update an entire map every time it is modified.

DIFFERENCE BETWEEN NIS AND NIS+

NIS+ may sound like an enhancement to NIS, but it is not so. As stated earlier, NIS+ is a replacement for NIS. Many new features have been incorporated in NIS+ and the basic commands differ from the NIS commands. Some of the differences between NIS and NIS+ are given in Table 21.1.

TABLE 21.1 DIFFERENCES BETWEEN NIS AND NIS+	
NIS	**NIS+**
NIS domains are flat and do not have a hierarchical structure.	NIS+ domains can be flat or have a hierarchical structure.
NIS has no specialized authentication features.	NIS+ namespace have enhanced security features, such as the Data Encryption System (DES) authentication that can restrict access to specified components in the namespace.

21

continues

TABLE 21.1 CONTINUED

NIS	NIS+
The usernames and machine names can be . the same	All usernames and machine names must be unique.
Data or information is stored in structures referred to as *maps*.	Data or information is stored in structures referred to as *tables*.
Data retrieved from search operations is maintained in duplicate maps.	Data in NIS+ tables can be searched by column name in a table.
NIS maps are stored on the server in /var/ yp/*domainname*.	NIS+ tables are stored on the server in /var/nis/data.
There is only one source for network information.	There are several sources for network information, such as NIS and DNS.
Data updating is delayed because of batch propagation.	Data updating is faster because of dynamic updates.
The maximum size of an NIS record is 1024 bytes.	There is no restriction to the size of an NIS+ record.

You need to know the significance of some of the differences between NIS and NIS+ for a smooth transition from NIS to NIS+. It is best to design the NIS+ namespace considering the following differences between NIS and NIS+:

■ Structure of the domain

■ Security

■ Data management

STRUCTURE OF THE NIS+ DOMAIN

As stated earlier, NIS+ follows a hierarchical structure made up of domains and subdomains. Each domain and subdomain can be associated with the logical hierarchical structure of any organization. For example, consider a university with various departments, such as Computer Science, Sociology, and Literature. Each department can be treated as a subdomain to the domain University. This hierarchical structure of NIS+ can help manage information stored in each domain or subdomain independently and effectively.

You can also have subdomains below a specific subdomain. For example, in English.Literature.University.edu, the Literature subdomain under the domain University has a subdomain English. Clients in one domain can access data or information in other domains if they have the appropriate permissions.

Thus NIS+ can be used both in simple and smaller networks and complex and larger networks.

21

SECURITY

Unlike the NIS environment, where clients are not authenticated, NIS+ implements an authentication mechanism by assigning credentials. These credentials are used to authenticate users. They are in the form of `UID@domainname`. Based upon the type of access rights, the user is allowed to read, write, or modify the NIS+ tables.

> **NOTE**
>
> NIS+ implements two types of credentials: user and workstation.

The mechanism that defines the credentials essentially creates private/public key pairs and stores these key pairs in a secure area. This mechanism is called Public Key Cryptography (PKC).

During the authentication process, only the public key is passed between the sender and the receiver. The public key is a key that is known to everyone involved in a transaction. Any user can use this key to encrypt data. However, a private key is specific to a user or the recipient of a message. Only recipients for whom a message is intended can decrypt messages by using their respective private keys. Now suppose Stacy sends an important message to James. Stacy uses the public key to encrypt the data. To decrypt this data, James uses his private key. This mechanism is a secure way for the transfer of messages because you do not have to transfer secret keys over a channel. In addition, only the recipient of a message can decrypt messages. Note that it is impossible to deduce the private key by using a public key.

The following steps describe the NIS+ security process:

1. The client sends a request along with its credential information to the NIS+ server.
2. The NIS+ server evaluates this credential information to validate the client. The server also determines the client's class: Owner, Group, World, or Nobody.
3. Based on the credential information, the server grants access rights to the clients.
4. If the access rights granted to the sender's class match the type of operation, the operation is performed.

Figure 21.2 illustrates the NIS+ security process.

DATA MANAGEMENT

NIS+ stores data in multicolumn tables. Each column in the NIS+ table can be searched, linked, or edited if the clients have the appropriate access rights. There are 16 predefined NIS+ tables, referred to as the *system tables*. These tables store information such as the host-names and addresses of machines in a network, password information for users in a specific domain, networks in a domain, ethernet addresses of machines in a domain, and the list of protocols used in a domain. Most of this information is stored when you set up a network or assign a user group to a domain. The 16 system tables of NIS+ are as follows:

- `auto_home`—Stores the location of home directories of all users in a particular domain.
- `auto_master`—Lists all the Automounter maps in a domain.

Figure 21.2
The NIS+ security
process.

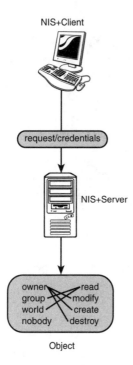

NIS+Client

request/credentials

NIS+Server

owner — read
group — modify
world — create
nobody — destroy

Object

- **bootparams**—Lists the names of all diskless clients in a domain and the locations of boot files that they need during the booting phase.
- **cred**—Stores the credentials of clients in a domain.
- **ethers**—Lists the ethernet address of every machine in a domain.
- **group**—Stores the name, ID, password, and members of a group in a specific domain.
- **hosts**—Lists the name and address of every machine in a domain.
- **mail_aliases**—Lists the mail aliases of all users in a particular domain.
- **netgroup**—Lists the netgroups to which a machine or user is associated in a domain.
- **netmasks**—Stores the list of networks and their netmasks in a domain.
- **networks**—Lists the names of networks in a domain.
- **passwd**—Stores the password information of all users in a domain.
- **protocols**—Lists the IP protocols used in a domain.
- **RPC**—Stores the number of the RPC services running in a domain.
- **services**—Lists the IP services and their port numbers in a domain.
- **timezone**—Lists the timezone of each machine in a domain.

NIS+ tables are similar to NIS maps. However, there are two major differences between the two. They are as follows:

21

- NIS+ tables are multicolumn, whereas NIS maps are made up of two columns. The first column is referred to as the key and the other column stores the actual information.

- Any column in the NIS+ table can be searched, unlike NIS maps, where only the key column may be searched.

Each NIS+ table can be accessed and modified at the table level, entry level, and column level.

Note that a table stores information about the names and addresses of machines and users who belong to the same domain as that of the table. In other words, a table stores information about the domain to which it belongs. Thus, if a user of one domain needs to access the information in another domain, the entire path of the other domain has to be specified.

You also can create links to search information stored in tables of other domains. To create a link, you must use the `nisln` command. Links are used to search remote tables. This means that links do not search information in local tables. Instead, they start searching information in remote tables. Following is the syntax for the `nisln` command.

```
nisln source_obj target_obj
```

In the preceding syntax,

- `source_obj` is the name of the source object.
- `target_obj` is the name of the target object.

Transition from NIS to NIS+

The transition process from NIS to NIS+ requires prior planning and designing before the actual implementation. While upgrading or moving from NIS to NIS+, you need to keep in mind a few important points. These points help make the transition phase easier and more effective. Some of the most important points include the following:

- Determine which version of the Solaris operating system and the NIS+ service is currently running before implementing the transition.

- Simplify the steps involved in the transition by using a flat namespace and not modifying the domain names or directory structures.

- Plan as necessary to reduce the time your network uses both NIS and NIS+ services.

- Both the administrators and users must have a sound knowledge of NIS+ and its features.

- Design the NIS+ namespace based on organizational requirements before starting the transition phase.

- Ensure that the same patches are running on all servers and clients.

- Inform users about the transition phase in advance.

- Ensure that your users are aware of the NIS+ features before they start using NIS+ services.

21

- Create scripts for faster transition of clients to NIS+ services.
- Verify the correctness of the NIS+ setup at the end of the implementation phase.

PREPARING THE NIS+ NAMESPACE

Designing the NIS+ namespace is one of the first things that you need to perform while configuring NIS+.

Because the namespace is a repository of a whole lot of network information, such as that of machines, users, and network services, designing the namespace plays a significant role in the transition phase.

To design a namespace, you must be clear with the requirements or needs of the organization that will make use of the namespace. The hierarchy in which the network information has to be stored, the security features that have to be incorporated, and the budget involved must be clear before you can design the namespace.

During the design of the namespace, the hierarchical structure of the NIS+ domain must be used effectively. Design the namespace to specify different levels, and make sure each level can act independently of the other. You can ensure this by assigning administration and security policies to each domain.

Though NIS+ was designed to handle any number of domains, having too many levels leads to administration problems. In addition, you need to ensure that each NIS+ domain has at least one server. It is always recommended that you add a master server to each domain first and then add one or more replicas to each domain. One important function of replicas is to process client requests when the master server is temporarily unavailable.

Ensure that all the servers are more powerful than their clients. This will have a major impact on the performance of NIS+ service.

Prepare a diagrammatic sketch that depicts the namespace with the root domain, clients, servers, replicas, the connections between them, and the different levels in the hierarchy. This will do a lot of good while you are setting up the NIS+ environment.

While designing the namespace, you also can choose names for your domains. It is advisable to have short and descriptive names for easy identification.

Because NIS+ tables can be connected through paths and links, it is necessary to decide whether you will be using NIS or NIS+ clients in the NIS+ namespace. If you use an NIS client in the NIS+ namespace, NIS clients use paths or links to search information.

Note that in a network supporting NIS and NIS+, the NIS+ tables must provide access to requests sent by the NIS client software. If access is not provided to these requests, the requests are classified as unauthenticated.

Finally, ensure that machine names and usernames are unique.

POPULATING THE NIS+ TABLES

All 16 predefined tables of NIS+ are stored in the org_dir directory. Prior to the creation of any table, you must ensure that the org_dir directory is available in the specific domain. You can create the org_dir directory by using any of the methods described in the following sections.

USING THE nisserver SCRIPT

The nisserver script can be used to create the default tables with their default access rights. This script is typically used to set up a new domain. NIS+ scripts are a group of commands that can be executed as a batch. In other words, if NIS+ scripts are used, you need not type each command individually. The nisserver script creates the groups_dir and org_dir directories with the 16 NIS+ system tables. You can use the following syntax for executing the nisserver script:

```
/usr/lib/nis/nisserver -r -d domain_name
```

In the syntax,

- -r is used to set up a master server for a domain.
- -d is used to specify the NIS+ domain.
- domain_name is used to specify the domain's name.

USING THE nismkdir COMMAND

The nismkdir command is typically used to create sub-directories within a domain. You also can create replicated directories with this command. Unlike the nisserver script, the nismkdir command creates the org_dir directory only and not the system tables. Use the following syntax to create a directory within a domain:

```
nismkdir dir_name.domain_name
```

In the syntax,

- dir_name is the name of the new directory.
- domain_name is the name of the domain that holds the new directory.

USING THE nistbladm UTILITY

The nistbladm command can be used to create, modify, or delete NIS+ tables. It is mainly used to administer tables and their entries. A client can create, modify, or delete tables with this command only if the appropriate access rights are granted for the client. For example, if a client does not have the right to delete tables in the org_dir directory, then the request for deletion of a table is turned down.

Following is the syntax that is used to create a table.

```
%%nistbladm -c table_type column_name table_name
```

21

In the syntax,

- `table_type` is the type of the table.
- `column_name` is the name of the columns in the newly created table.
- `table_name` is the name of the domain in which the table has to be created.

Each column can have three associated attributes, namely `searchable`, `encrypted`, and `case insensitive`. These attributes can be associated to a column during table creation with the `nistbladm` command. For example, if you need to create a Students table with two columns, such as `student_id` and `student_name` in the University domain, and associate both the columns to the searchable attribute, you can use the following syntax:

```
%%nistbladm -c Students student_id=S student_name=S Students.University.com
```

In the syntax,

- `Students` is the type of the table.
- `student_id` and `student_name` are the two columns in the `Students` table.
- `S` is the searchable attribute.
- `University.com` is the name of the domain.

NOTE

> You need to assign S, I, and C, respectively, for the column's searchable, case insensitive, and encrypted attributes.

USING THE nissetup UTILITY

The `nissetup` utility is used to create the `org_dir` and `groups_dir` directories and all the NIS+ system tables. The following syntax is used to create the directories and system tables within a root directory:

```
rootdir# /usr/lib/nis/nissetup
```

In the syntax, `rootdir` specifies the root directory.

THE nispopulate SCRIPT AND nisaddent UTILITY

After creating the directories and the system tables, you need to populate the tables. You can populate the NIS+ tables from NIS maps, ASCII files, or manually. The following list provides the method to populate the NIS+ maps using the three methods:

- Populating NIS+ Tables from NIS maps

    As stated earlier, NIS maps store information about a network. If you are updating the existing NIS service to NIS+, you can transfer all the data stored in NIS maps to the NIS+ tables with the `nispopulate` script or the `nisaddent` utility.

You can use the following syntax of the `nispopulate` script to populate NIS+ tables from NIS maps.

`/usr/lib/nis/nispopulate -Y -y nis_domain -h yp_server -d nis+_domain`

In the syntax,

- `-Y` specifies that data is populated from NIS maps to NIS+ tables.
- `-y` specifies the NIS domain.
- `nis_domain` specifies the name of the NIS domain.
- `-h` specifies the name of the NIS server.
- `yp_server` is the name of the server that runs the YP compatibility mode. In this mode, the NIS+ server handles NIS (YP) requests as well as NIS+ requests.
- `-d` specifies the NIS+ domain.
- `nis+_domain` specifies the name of the NIS+ domain.

■ Populating NIS+ tables from ASCII files

If your network is not using any other network information service, and all information is stored in ASCII files, you can transfer the data from the ASCII files to the NIS+ tables. The `nispopulate` script or the `nisaddent` utility can be used for this purpose.

You can use the following syntax of the `nispopulate` script to populate NIS+ tables from ASCII files.

`/usr/lib/nis/nispopulate -F -p file_path -l passwd table_name`

In the syntax,

- `-F` specifies that data is transferred from files.
- `-p` specifies the directory that contains the files.
- `file_path` specifies the entire path of the file.
- `-l` specifies the network password used to populate the NIS+ table.
- `passwd` specifies the encrypted network password that has to be used.
- `table_name` specifies the name of the NIS+ table.

■ Populating NIS+ tables manually

Populating NIS+ tables manually is done when no network information is available. In other words, when a network is set up for the first time, all information about the network has to be keyed in manually. The data can either be entered directly to the NIS+ tables or written to an ASCII file and then transferred to the NIS+ tables.

CONFIGURING THE MASTER AND SLAVE SERVERS

NIS+ provides a set of commands for configuring the master NIS+ server and the NIS+ slave servers, which are also referred to as NIS+ clients. In addition to the commands, you also can use the NIS+ scripts for easy and effective configuration.

An NIS+ server also can be treated as an NIS+ client. Before you set up a machine as a server, you must initialize it as an NIS+ client. This is true for all servers except for the root master server. Therefore, each server forms a part of a domain in addition to acting as a backbone of a domain.

SETTING UP THE MASTER NIS+ SERVER

The first step in establishing the NIS+ domain is setting up the master NIS+ server. Setting up the master server is one of the key steps to configuring the root domain. To configure the root domain, you need to do the following:

1. Create the root domain.
2. Set up and initialize the root master server.
3. Create the root domain admin group.

To create the root domain, you need to first modify the value of the superuser's PATH variable to /usr/lib/nis. If you use DES authentication, you need to specify the length of the Diffie-Hellman key also. After specifying values to the PATH variable and the Diffie-Hellman key, you can set up the master server.

→ To know more about the Diffie-Hellman key, **see** "Network File System (NFS)" **p.151**.

To set up the master NIS+ server, you need to use the nisserver script. Before running the nisserver script, check whether the /etc/passwd file has an entry for the root domain. In addition, you need to have the name of the domain that has to be created and the password of the machine that will be set up as the root master server. The nisserver script is used to build the root domain. The command used to run this script is as follows:

```
master-server#nisserver -r -d domain_name
```

In the syntax,

- master-server is the name of the machine that has to be set as the root master server.
- -r specifies that a root master must be configured.
- -d specifies the name of the NIS+ domain.
- domain_name is the name of your NIS+ domain.

> **NOTE** All domain names end with a period.

After setting up the master NIS+ server, you can specify a group of users who can access and change the information stored in the newly created domain. This group of users is collectively referred to as the NIS+ group. The default NIS+ group is admin.domain_name.

The nisserver script runs the nisinit command automatically to initialize the root master server. After initializing, the nissetup is executed to create standard directories and tables. At each stage where the user input is required, the nisserver script first prompts the user to key in the required information and later verify the information for correctness. After the standard directories and tables—including the `org_dir` directory—are created, the `nisserver` script prompts the user to enter the login password. The specified password is written to `/etc/rootkey` and a message stating that the specified domain has been configured is displayed. The final step in setting up the root master server is to populate the newly created tables with the `nispopulate` or `nisaddnet` commands.

SETTING UP THE NIS+ SLAVE SERVER/CLIENT

After populating the system tables of the root master server from either NIS maps or ASCII files, you can start setting up the NIS+ clients. The `nisclient` script can be used to set up the NIS+ client. Ensure that the root domain is already created and that the root master server is configured before you run the `nisclient` script. Check to see whether the required information, such as the domain name, password of the machine that will be set up as the client, network password, the Diffie-Hellman key length, and the IP address of the root master server, is available to run the `nisclient` script.

To set up the NIS+ client, you need to do the following:

1. Access the root directory on the master server.
2. Check whether the specific NIS+ client has an entry in the NIS+ host table.
3. Run the `nisclient` script.

The command used to run the `nisclient` script on the master server is as follows:

```
root-master#nisclient -d domain_name -c client_name
```

In the syntax,

- `root-master` specifies the name of the root master server.
- `-d` specifies the name of the NIS+ domain.
- `-c` specifies the name of the NIS+ client.
- `domain_name` is the name of your NIS+ domain.
- `client_name` is the name of the client.

4. Log in to the client machine and access the root directory.
5. Run the `nisclient` script to initialize the NIS+ client.

The command used to run the nisclient on the client machine is as follows:

```
client_name#nisclient -i -h master_system -a ip_add -d domain_name
```

In the syntax,

- `client_name` is the name of the new NIS+ client.
- `-i` is used to initialize an NIS+ client.
- `-h` specifies the name of the NIS+ host.
- `master_system` is the name of the NIS+ master server.

21

- `ip_add` is the IP address of the NIS+ master server.
- `-d` specifies the name of the NIS+ domain.
- `domain_name` is the name of the NIS+ domain.

The `nisclient` script, similar to the `nisserver` script, prompts the user to enter information, such as the IP address of the root master server, the network password, and the root password of the client machine. You can add any number of clients to the same domain or to a different domain by repeating the setup procedure. If you add clients to a different domain, ensure that the names of the domain and the master server are changed appropriately.

CONFIGURING THE ROOT DOMAIN

Configuring the root domain involves preparing the root master server and creating the root domain. Just as with the root master server and the clients, you can also configure the root domain by using the NIS+ scripts. Before configuring the root domain, ensure that you have the necessary information, such as the name of the root domain and the admin group of the root domain, user ID and password, network password, password of the machine that will be the root master server, and the user ID of the administrator whose credentials will be added to the root domain. All the machine names must be unique and must not have a dot in their names.

The following is the sequence of steps performed to configure the root domain:

1. Log on to the machine that will act as the root master server and check the domain name of the root master server. You can use the `domainname` command to check whether the name of the root master server follows the correct naming conventions, such as the requirement that all domain names be unique and have a dot in their names. The syntax for logging on to the root master server as superuser is as follows:

   ```
   rootmastername % su
   ```

   Following is the syntax used to check the name of a domain:

   ```
   # domainname
   ```

2. Ensure that the root master server uses the correct version of the `nsswitch.conf` file, which is the switch configuration file of the root master server. To check for the nsswitch.com file, use the following command:

   ```
   # more/etc/nsswitch.conf
   ```

3. Remove all files from `/var/nis`. This is done to ensure that all the previous NIS+ processes and data are removed from the current machine. To remove all the previous NIS+ files, use the following command:

   ```
   # rm -rf /var/nis/*
   ```

4. Identify and name the admin groups that will be associated with the root domain. Following is the command used to name the admin group:

   ```
   # NIS_GROUP=group_name.domain_name
   ```

21

5. Identify and define the `org_dir` and `groups_dir` directories of the root domain.

6. Using the `nisinit` command, create a root directory and initialize the root master server. Following is the syntax used to initialize the root master server:

   `#nisinit -r`

7. Using the `rpc.nisd` command as follows, start the NIS+ daemon and set the security level of the server to zero:

   `# rpc.nisd -S 0`

8. Ensure that the root directory object exists and the NIS+ daemon is running.

9. Create the sub-directories and tables for the root domain with the following command:

   `# /usr/lib/nis/nissetup [-Y]`

10. Assign DES credentials for the root master server so that it can process its own requests. To do so, use the following command:

    `#nisaddcred des`

11. Create the group of users who are authorized to access and modify the information in the root master server, and then add the root master to the root domain's admin group. To create the default admin group, use the following command:

    `# nisgrpadm -c admin.domain_name`

    After creating the admin group, you need to assign full access rights to the root directory. There are four types of access rights in NIS+: Read, Modify, Destroy, and Create. If you have Read access, you can view contents of an object. To change the contents of an object, you must have Modify access rights. To delete an object, you must have Destroy rights to the object. The highest level of right is Create. This access right allows you to create objects such as tables within a directory.

    To assign full access rights, use the following command:

    `# nischmod g+rmcd domain_name`

12. Using the information in the `cred` table, update the keys of the `org_dir` and `groups_dir` directories of the root master server in addition to updating the keys of the root directory. To do so, issue the following commands:

    `# /usr/lib/nis/nisupdkeys domain_name`
    `# /usr/lib/nis/nisupdkeys org_dir.domain_name`
    `# /usr/lib/nis/nisupdkeys groups_dir.domain_name`

13. Restart the NIS+ daemon and set the security level of the server to two. Use the following command to restart the NIS+ daemon:

    `# rpc.nisd [-Y]`

14. Add local access rights and DES credentials to the root domain. All users except root trying to access NIS+ need local credentials. These credentials are required to convert the local identification of the OS into an NIS+ principal name. You can add the local credentials with the following command:

    `# nisaddcred -p 121 -P admin.domain_name local`

21

15. Assign credentials for administrators to the root domain and add the administrators to the admin group of the root domain. Use the following command to add other administrators to the admin group:

```
# nisgrpadm -a admin.domain_name
```

16. Assign required space for NIS+ tables.

FEDERATED NAMING SERVICE (FNS)

Federated Naming Service (FNS) is a naming service that provides a set of common names that can be used over different naming services. Using the FNS conventions, you can name organizations, machines, users, and network services. In addition, FNS extends support for other naming services, such as DNS, NIS, and NIS+.

FNS lists the various namespaces available, types of namespaces, structure of the namespaces, and the conventions followed by these namespaces. However, it does not specify the various names the naming services use.

The FNS Application Programming Interface (API) that provides the defined set of names and policies is specified by X/Open Federated Naming (XFN). XFN is a public, open interface supported by various vendors.

Two popular terms associated with FNS are *composite names* and *contexts*. A composite name is a name that is used to identify a list of names of components from other naming systems. FNS defines the syntax for creating composite names. However, the syntax for creating each component identified by the composite name is defined by the associated naming service.

A context contains a list of bindings that associate each name to an object. It also lists each object's address or reference. Using contexts, you can bind names and attributes to objects. You can also search, modify, or retrieve attributes associated with objects.

ADVANTAGES OF USING FNS

Some of the most important advantages of FNS include the following:

- Using FNS, you can create consistent names that can be used across other naming services.
- Because FNS provides a common interface for accessing various naming services, there is no need to modify names used by existing naming services.
- Developers can learn and work with just one naming service, rather than confusing themselves with various naming services.
- FNS policies can be used for naming global-, enterprise-, and application-level services.

ADMINISTERING FNS

Administration of FNS service varies according to the naming service used. The type of naming service used has an impact on the users' access rights to the contexts and subcontexts. Table 21.3 lists the naming services and identifies the relevant administration feature of FNS for each one.

TABLE 21.3 NAMING SERVICES AND THE ASSOCIATED FNS ADMINISTRATION FEATURES	
Naming service	**FNS administration**
NIS+	FNS system administration tasks can be performed by authorized users only. If a set or a group of people is required to perform FNS system administration tasks using NIS+, you can create an NIS+ group and assign that group privileges required to perform administration tasks. You can add users to this group. All members belonging to this group can perform system administration functions.
NIS	Only users who have the relevant access on the NIS master server can modify the contexts and subcontexts. Clients who have root access on the master server perform all administration functions associated with the FNS service.

A named FNS object can have one or more attributes associated with it. Each attribute of an object has a unique identifier used for identification purposes. In addition, an attribute also has a set of values associated with it. You can use the `fnattr` command to add, delete, and modify an attribute. You also can use the `fnattr` command to list attributes.

Following is the syntax used for using the `fnattr` command to add an attribute:

```
fnattr -a [-s] comp_name attr_name attr_values
```

In the preceding syntax,

- `-a` creates a new attribute.
- `-s` removes existing attribute values and creates new values.
- `comp_name` specifies the composite_name, an FNx1S named object.
- `attr_name` is the attribute name.
- `attr_values` is the attribute value.

NOTE

> You can use `-m` and `-d`, respectively, with the `fnattr` command to modify or delete an attribute. To list attributes, use `-l` with the `fnattr` command.

21

SUMMARY

Network Information Service + (NIS+), like NIS, is a naming service that allows you to store information, such as machine names, addresses for each machine in a network, user information, security information, and information about the available network services. It is the default naming service for Solaris. The NIS+ namespace is hierarchical in nature. Hence, it can be divided into logical units called *domains*. Differences between NIS and NIS+ must be considered for a smooth transition from NIS to NIS+. Using the NIS+ scripts, you can set up the master NIS+ server, NIS+ client, and configure the root domain. All the 16 predefined system tables of NIS+ are used to store information about users, machines, and network services. Note that it is preferable to use NIS+ rather than NIS. Also, NIS+ is more secure than NIS.

Federated Naming Service (FNS) is a naming service that provides a set of common names that can be used over different naming services. Using the FNS conventions, you can name organizations, machines, users, and network services. In addition, FNS extends support for other naming services, such as DNS, NIS, and NIS+.

## CHAPTER 22

LIGHTWEIGHT DIRECTORY ACCESS PROTOCOL (LDAP)

In this chapter

Directory Services—An Overview   390

Setting up LDAP   393

Summary   401

22

DIRECTORY SERVICES—AN OVERVIEW

We all know that a directory is an index that helps people find information. The directories that are more familiar to us are probably paper-based resources, such as the telephone book. In the context of the Internet, directories are repositories of network names and other information, essential for navigating loosely structured data like you find on the Web.

Directory services help users or computers search through the directory list. These services enable you to search through a structured repository of information. Directory services can be local or global. Local directory services have a restricted context and are local to the context where they are running, whereas global directory services span over intranets and the Internet. One of the most common directory services is the Domain Name System (DNS). DNS requires users to know the domain name they need. Therefore, for applications such as email, directories need to include more specific entries such as people names or geographical locale. With the growing global address space, it becomes all the more important to have a service that caters to the requirements of organizations spread over wide geographic distances.

LDAP

Lightweight Directory Access Protocol(LDAP) is quickly gaining acceptance as the directory service structure for the Internet. It was designed to run over the TCP/IP network, making it an ideal solution for the Internet. LDAP has many features, such as providing network information services, including encryption support, access control lists, fast read access, and more.

Solaris 9 supports LDAP in conjunction with the iPlanet™ Directory Server 5.1 and other LDAP directory servers. LDAP in Solaris 9 provides many features, including simplified configuration of the directory service using the `idsconfig` command, a security model that supports strong authentication, an easy method to populate the directory server using `ldapaddent`, and so on. The commands `idsconfig` and `ldapaddent` are explained in greater detail later in the chapter.

NOTE

> LDAP does not support pre-Solaris 8 clients. Also, an LDAP server cannot be its own client. You cannot run instances of the iPlanet directory server and client on the same host.

LDAP MODELS

You can provide directory services in a variety of ways, depending on the kind of information you want stored in your repository, where the information is to be placed, and how the information is to be queried.

LDAP is implemented on four basic models. These models define the information that can be stored in a directory and also the functions used to access this information.

- **Information model**—This model defines what kind of information can be stored in an LDAP directory. This model refers to the entries, which are the most basic components of a directory. Each entry has a set of attributes associated with it and each attribute has an attribute type and one or more values associated with it.

- **Naming model**—This model defines how information in a directory can be organized and data in the directory can be referred to. In this model you can give a unique name to any entry in the directory. LDAP uses Distinguished Names (DNs) to refer to entries within a directory or multiple directories.

- **Function model**—This model describes the way LDAP functions. It defines how you can use the LDAP protocol to access and update the information in directories. This model also defines who can access the LDAP directories.

- **Security model**—This model defines how the information stored in the directories can be protected from unauthorized access or modification. LDAP uses Simple Authentication and Security Layer (SASL) to support multiple authentication methods. In simple authentication, when an LDAP client sends a request to the server for a specific entry, it sends a Distinguished Name (DN) for that entry and an unencrypted password. The server looks up the entry in the directory corresponding to the DN provided by the client and validates whether the password matches the value stored in the userpassword attribute. If the password supplied by the client matches the password stored in the userpassword attribute, the client is authenticated; otherwise an error code is returned to the client. LDAP uses Secure Sockets Layer(SSL)/Transport Layer Security (TLS) protocol to encrypt all the data flowing between a client and a server. LDAP over SSL, also known as Secure LDAP (LDAPS), enables secure LDAP client access and authentication facilities.

NOTE

The process of authenticating the user to the directory is called *binding*.

LDAP Directory Information Tree

The LDAP directory is organized in a tree-like structure. This is known as the *Directory Information Tree* (DIT). DIT provides containers for storing different types of information. LDAP enables directory entries to be arranged in a hierarchical structure reflecting geographical and organizational boundaries (see Figure 22.1) .

There are no pre-defined rules to arrange a directory structure. It can be arranged in any manner that meets your organizational requirements.

The DIT is divided into subtrees known as *containers*. Each container contains a specific information type. The directory's top-level domain is referred to as the *root*. It is also known as the *base distinguished name* (base DN). It is up to you to choose the format of your base DN. However, the general norm is if the root domain of your company is .com, then the domain component would be represented as DC=com.

Figure 22.1
LDAP directory tree.

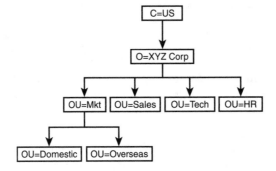

In Figure 22.2, notice that the top-level domain has the format DC=com. Beneath this base DN, you have a single entry that corresponds to the rest of your DNS domain name. For example, the top-level domains in this example are DC=com and dc=que. If que.com were to merge with prenhall.com and mac.com, then the top-level domain would look like the one shown in Figure 22.3.

Figure 22.2
Top-level domain.

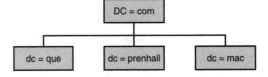

Figure 22.3
Adding domain components.

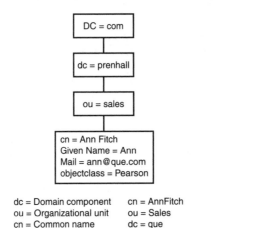

LDAP's information model and namespace are based on entries. Each entry is uniquely identified in a directory by a distinguished name and is associated by a set of attributes. The primary attribute for any entry is objectclass, which defines the type of entry. For example, the objectclass person represents an individual in the organization. LDAP follows the concept of fully qualified domain names (FQDNs) because of its hierarchical namespace.

SETTING UP LDAP

The LDAP setup contains a master server that stores the LDAP directory, one or more replica servers, and client machines. The server that contains the LDAP directory and provides the directory service to other hosts in the domain is called the *master server*. The LDAP clients are machines that access information from DITs stored in the master server.

In addition to the master server and client machines, the LDAP domain may also contain replica servers. The replica servers can be compared with the slave servers in an NIS environment and replica servers in the NIS+ environment. Like their counterparts in the NIS and NIS+ environments, these replica servers act as backup servers in case of any unforeseen situation. In addition, they help in sharing the network load and thus improve performance by making several copies of data and storing them close to the users and applications that use them. The data in these replica servers are updated automatically. The replica servers are synchronized with the master server. In case of any updates in the master server, the same is reflected in the replica servers.

The following sections look at the steps to set up an LDAP master server, replica server, and the client machines.

SETTING UP THE IPLANET 5.1 DIRECTORY SERVER

During the setup process for the server, you are prompted for information such as port number, the user and group under which you will run the administrative server and the directory server, the location in which the directory server and the administrative domain are to be stored, and so on. You must plan out how you are going to configure the basic parameters before beginning the configuration process. Note that the parameters listed are based on the type of configuration you decide to perform. The different types of configuration are express, typical, and custom. These configurations are discussed later in this chapter in the sections titled "Express Configuration," "Typical Configuration," and "Custom Configuration." The following list provides the basic parameters that are to be configured during the setup process.

- When prompted to select a port number, choose a unique number. This number can range from 1 to 65535. However, you should be aware of some reserved port numbers before you choose your port numbers. Note that the Internet Assigned Numbers Authority (IANA) reserves port numbers 1 to 1024 for various services. The standard LDAP Directory Server (LDAP) port number is 389, and the port 636 is reserved for LDAP over SSL (LDAPS).

- Decide on the user and group under which you will run the administrative server and the directory server. Create user accounts for all iPlanet servers, in case the directory server is not running as root. The type of user and group for the administrative server depends on the port number. If you are using the default port number, run the administrative server as root. If the port number is over 1024, create user accounts for all iPlanet servers.

- Next, you are asked to define the authentication entities. Note that the following list of entities depends upon the type of configuration you are performing.

  - The Directory Manager password must be at least eight characters long.
  - The administrative server user and password should be the same as the configuration directory administrator ID and password.
  - The configuration directory administrator should not be the same as the directory manager.

  The configuration directory administrator is the one who uses the iPlanet console to manage the iPlanet servers. The configuration directory is an instance of the directory server that stores configuration information. The information is stored in the o=NetscapeRoot directory tree. To ease the upgrade process, it is recommended that you install the directory server dedicated to the support of the o=NetscapeRoot directory.

- In addition to selecting the location of the directory server, choose the location for the user directory. Just as the configuration directory server is the directory server used for the iPlanet server administration, the user directory is the directory server containing entries for users and groups in your enterprise.

- The user directory and the configuration directory should be placed in two separate server instances. The user directory is expected to receive overwhelming directory traffic and needs to devote a large number of computing resources to the user directory. On the other hand, the configuration directory will experience less network traffic. Therefore, it can be installed on a machine with low-end resources.

The following sections list the steps to configure the iPlanet 5.1 Directory Server. Note that it is important to set up the iPlanet server before configuring it for use with LDAP clients.

You can configure the iPlanet server using one of the configuration processes: express, typical, or custom.

EXPRESS CONFIGURATION

If you are looking to test the deployment of the directory service in your network environment, you may choose the Express configuration type. Implementing the directory server in a production environment with the Express configuration is not recommended. The iPlanet directory server is installed with minimal components.

To perform the Express configuration, log in as root. Execute the following command to run the directory server.

```
# /usr/sbin/directoryserver setup
```

Next, choose Express when prompted to select the type of configuration. Note that the default configuration type is Typical. After selecting the configuration type, enter the relevant identity to run the server as a user directory and the configuration directory.

TYPICAL CONFIGURATION

If you are installing the directory server for the first time, you use this method to configure the directory server. To use this method, run the Directory Server program by using the setup command as mentioned in the Express configuration setup steps. Next, select the following default entries when prompted:

- iPlanet Servers
- Directory Suite and Administration Services
- Directory Suite Components
- Administration Components
- Configuration Directory
- Server used for user data
- Directory Server Port
- Directory Server Identifier

Next, enter the relevant values for the following:

- **Configuration Directory Administrator ID and Password**—This enables you to log in to the console with full privileges.
- **Directory Suffix**—This should be a unique name.
- **Directory Manager DN**—This is used to manage the contents of your directory, providing you with unlimited privileges.
- **Directory Manager Password**—Enter an 8-character password.
- **Administration Domain**—Should be a unique string describing the organization administering the domain.
- **Administration Port Number**—Should be a unique value. Note that the port numbers can range from 1 to 65535. However, the port numbers from 1 to 1024 are assigned by the Internet Assigned Numbers Authority. The only two port numbers that you use between 1 and 1024 are 389 and 636. These two port numbers are used for directory services.

NOTE

> iPlanet Directory Server 5.1 must run as root, using either port 389 or 636.

After setting the iPlanet server you can configure the server for use with LDAP clients. Run the idsconfig command. This command is used to set up an iPlanet Directory Server that is to be populated with data and serve LDAP clients. The following list of client attributes can be set with the idsconfig.

The command to configure an iPlanet server for use with LDAP clients is

```
# /usr/lib/ldap/idsconfig
```

22

If you are setting up the server for the first time, you will be prompted to answer several questions. The default answer to these questions is No [n]. If you need help to clarify any question, type **h**.

Listing 22.1 displays the configuration steps for the iPlanet Directory Server.

LISTING 22.1 CONFIGURATION STEPS

```
It is strongly recommended that you BACKUP the directory server
before running idsconfig.sh.
Hit Ctrl-C at any time before the final confirmation to exit.
Do you wish to continue with server setup (y/n/h)? [n] Y
Enter the iPlanet Directory Server's (iPlanet Directory Server)
hostname to setup: IPDSERVER
Enter the port number for iPlanet Directory Server (h=help): [389]
Enter the directory manager DN: [cn=Directory Manager]
Enter passwd for cn=Directory Manager :
Enter the domainname to be served (h=help): [west.example.com]
Enter LDAP Base DN (h=help): [dc=west,dc=example,dc=com]
Enter the profile name (h=help): [default]
Default server list (h=help): [192.168.0.0]
Preferred server list (h=help):
Choose desired search scope (one, sub, h=help): [one]
The following are the supported credential levels:
1 anonymous
2 proxy
3 proxy anonymous
Choose Credential level [h=help]: [1] 2
The following are the supported Authentication Methods:
1 none
2 simple
3 sasl/DIGEST-MD5
4 tls:simple
5 tls:sasl/DIGEST-MD5
Choose Authentication Method (h=help): [1] 2
Current authenticationMethod: simple
Do you want to add another Authentication Method? N
Do you want the clients to follow referrals (y/n/h)? [n] Y
Do you want to modify the server timelimit value (y/n/h)? [n] Y
Enter the time limit for iPlanet Directory Server (current=3600): [-1]
Do you want to modify the server sizelimit value (y/n/h)? [n] Y
Enter the size limit for iPlanet Directory Server (current=2000): [-1]
Do you want to store passwords in "crypt" format (y/n/h)? [n] Y
Do you want to setup a Service Authentication Methods (y/n/h)? [n]
Client search time limit in seconds (h=help): [30]
Profile Time To Live in seconds (h=help): [43200]
Bind time limit in seconds (h=help): [10] 2
Do you wish to setup Service Search Descriptors (y/n/h)?  [n]
Summary of Configuration
1 Domain to serve : west.example.com
2 Base DN to setup : dc=west,dc=example,dc=com
3 Profile name to create : default
4 Default Server List : 192.168.0.0
5 Preferred Server List :
6 Default Search Scope : one
7 Credential Level : proxy
```

```
 8 Authentication Method : simple
 9 Enable Follow Referrals : TRUE
10 iPlanet Directory Server Time Limit : -1
11 iPlanet Directory Server Size Limit : -1
12 Enable crypt password storage : TRUE
13 Service Auth Method pam_ldap :
14 Service Auth Method keyserv :
15 Service Auth Method passwd-cmd:
16 Search Time Limit : 30
17 Profile Time to Live : 43200
18 Bind Limit : 2
19 Service Search Descriptors Menu
Enter config value to change: (1-19 0=commit changes) [0]
Enter DN for proxy agent:[cn=proxyagent,ou=profile,dc=west,dc=example,dc=com]
Enter passwd for proxyagent:
Re-enter passwd:
WARNING: About to start committing changes. (y=continue, n=EXIT) Y
1. Changed timelimit to -1 in cn=config.
2. Changed sizelimit to -1 in cn=config.
3. Changed passwordstoragescheme to "crypt" in cn=config.
4. Schema attributes have been updated.
5. Schema objectclass definitions have been added.
6. Created DN component dc=west.
7. NisDomainObject added to dc=west,dc=example,dc=com.
8. Top level "ou" containers complete.
9. Nis maps: auto_home auto_direct auto_master auto_shared processed.
10. ACI for dc=west,dc=example,dc=com modified to disable self modify.
11. Add of VLV Access Control Information (ACI).
12. Proxy Agent cn=proxyagent,ou=profile,dc=west,dc=example,dc=com added.
13. Give cn=proxyagent,ou=profile,dc=west,dc=example,dc=com read permission for
password.
14. Generated client profile and loaded on server.
15. Processing eq,pres indexes:
ipHostNumber (eq,pres) Finished indexing.
uidNumber (eq,pres) Finished indexing.
ipNetworkNumber (eq,pres) Finished indexing.
gidnumber (eq,pres) Finished indexing.
oncrpcnumber (eq,pres) Finished indexing.
16. Processing eq,pres,sub indexes:
membernisnetgroup (eq,pres,sub) Finished indexing.
nisnetgrouptriple (eq,pres,sub) Finished indexing.
17. Processing VLV indexes:
getgrent vlv_index Entry created
gethostent vlv_index Entry created
getnetent vlv_index Entry created
getpwent vlv_index Entry created
getrpcent vlv_index Entry created
getspent vlv_index Entry created
idsconfig.sh: Setup of iPlanet Directory Server server ipdserver is complete.
Note: idsconfig has created entries for VLV indexes. Use
```

The next step is to populate the directory servers with the data from the standard input. For example, if you need to populate the directory servers with user passwords, use the ldapadd-dent command to read the input file /etc/passwd and place the data into the containers associated with the service. The following syntax populates the directory container with user password data:

```
# ldapaddent -D "cn=directory manager" -f /etc/passwd passwd
```

The -D option used with the ldapaddent command creates an entry that has write permission to the base DN. The -f option specifies the input file from which data can be read. In the preceding example, the input file is the password file.

You can add additional client profiles by using the genprofile option with the ldapclient command. The ldapclient command is used to initialize LDAP clients and restore network service environment on them. It also is used to list the contents of the LDAP client cache. When used with the genprofile command, the ldapclient writes an LDAP Data Interchange Format (LDIF) formatted configuration profile. The directory server uses LDIF to specify directory entries in text format. LDIF is commonly used to build a directory database or to add large numbers of entries to the directory all at once. The client can download the profile you create by using ldapclient init. To add additional profiles by using the genprofile option with ldapclient, enter the following command in the command line:

```
# ldapclient genprofile -a profileName=myprofile \
-a defaultSearchBase=dc=west,dc=example,dc=com \
-a "defaultServerList=192.168.0.0 192.168.0.1:386" \
myprofile.ldif
```

Next, upload the new profile to the server with the following command.

```
# ldapadd -h 192.168.0.0 --D "cn=directory manager" --f
myprofile.ldif
```

You can add printer entries into the LDAP directory by using either the Printmgr configuration tool or the lpset -n command. The lpset command sets printing configuration information in the system configuration databases. When used with the -n option, the lpset command creates or updates configuration information for the directories in the LDAP server or NIS+ tables.

Note that the printer objects added to the directory only define the connection parameter—required by print system clients—of printers. Local print server configuration data is still held in files. A typical printer entry would look like the following:

```
printer-uri=printer1,ou=printers,dc=sales,dc=xyz,dc=com
objectclass=top
objectclass=printServ

objectclass=enterprizeprinter
printer-name=printer1
ENT-printer-bsdaddr=printserver1.xyz.com,printer1,Unix
ENT-printer-kvp=description=QMS LaserJet
printer-uri=printer1
```

SETTING UP LDAP CLIENTS

LDAP clients use the `ldap_cachemgr` daemon to download the latest client profile from the directory. The LDAP client profile is a collection of configuration information an LDAP client uses to access the LDAP naming service information on supporting LDAP servers to provide LDAP naming services. The `ldap_cachemgr` daemon accesses configuration information running as root and updates the configuration information from the server to the client. Note that `ldap_cachemgr` must run on the client at all times to enable clients to refresh information. To access the information stored in the LDAP repository, clients can first establish their identity with the directory server. This identity can be either anonymous or it can be an object recognized by the LDAP server. Based on the client's identity and the server's access control information (ACI), the LDAP server allows the client to read or write directory information.

To simplify LDAP client setup, and avoid having to re-enter the same information for each and every client, create a single client profile on the directory server. This way, a single profile defines the configuration for all clients configured to use it. Any subsequent change to the profile attributes is propagated to the clients at a rate defined by the refresh interval.

For a Solaris client to use LDAP as a naming service, the following conditions need to be met:

- The client's domain name must be served by the LDAP server.
- The `nsswitch.conf` file needs to point to LDAP for the required services.
- The client needs to be configured with all the given parameters that define its behavior and `ldap_cachemgr` needs to be running on the client. At least one server for which a client is configured must be up and running.

INITIALIZING A CLIENT

You can initialize a client manually or use profiles or proxy credentials. To initialize the client with profiles, run the `ldapclient` with `init`.

```
# ldapclient init -a profileName=new -a \
```

The proxy credentials use proxy values with the `ldapclient` for initializing the client.

```
# ldapclient init -a
proxyDn=cn=proxyagent,ou=profile,dc=west,dc=example,dc=com -a
domainname=west.example.com -a profilename=pit1 -a
proxypassword=test1234 192.168.0.0
System successfully configured
```

The `-a proxyDn` and `-a proxypassword` are required if the profile to be used is set up for proxy. Because the credentials are not stored in the profile saved on the server, you need to supply the information when you initialize the client. This method is more secure than the older method of storing the proxy credentials on the server. The proxy info is used to create the `/var/ldap/ldap_client_cred`, and the rest of the information is put in `/var/ldap/ldap_client_file`.

Note that superuser can perform manual client configurations. However, many of the checks are bypassed during the process, so it is relatively easy to misconfigure your system. In addition, you must change settings on every machine, rather than in one central place, as is done when using profiles.

To initialize a client manually, use the `ldapclient manual` command.

```
# ldapclient manual --a domainName=dc=west.example.com \
--a credentialLevel=proxy --a defaultSearchBase=dc=west,
dc=example, dc=com \
--a proxyDN=cn=proxyagent,ou=profile,dc=west,dc=example,dc=com \
--a proxyPassword=testtest 192.168.0.0
```

Next, use the `ldapclient list` to verify the initialization.

```
NS_LDAP_FILE_VERSION= 2.0
NS_LDAP_BINDDN= cn=proxyagent,ou=profile,dc=west,dc=example,dc=com
NS_LDAP_BINDPASSWD= {NS1}4a3788e8c053424f
NS_LDAP_SERVERS= 192.168.0.0
NS_LDAP_SEARCH_BASEDN= dc=west,dc=example,dc=com
NS_LDAP_CREDENTIAL_LEVEL= proxy
```

To un-initialize a client, use `ldapclient uninit`.

```
# ldapclient uninit
System successfully recovered
```

The `ldapclient uninit` command restores the client name service to what it was prior to the most recent init, modify, or manual operation. In other words, it performs an "undo" on the last step taken. For example, if the client was configured to use profile1 and was then changed to use profile2, using the `ldapclient uninit` command would revert the client back to using profile1.

FINDING A DIRECTORY ENTRY

If you are looking for a particular directory entry, use the `ldapsearch` command to find the directory entry. The `ldapsearch` command connects to the LDAP directory server, binds to the directory server, and performs the directory search.

For example, the following command performs a subtree search for a commonName "ann joan." The command looks for the commonName and telephoneNumber values. If the values are found, the output is printed on the screen.

```
# ldapsearch "cn=ann joan" cn telephoneNumber
```

Listing 22.2 shows the output for the search.

LISTING 22.2   *Ldapsearch* OUTPUT

```
cn=Ann Joan, ou=Mkt, ou=Seattle, ou=People, o=XYZ, c=US
cn=Ann Joan
  .

  .
telephoneNumber=+1 918 813 6449
```

ADDING A DIRECTORY ENTRY

Use the ldapadd command to add an entry to the LDAP. The following example shows how to add entries. Create a file /tmp/addentry and specify the information that you want to add.

Suppose the file, /tmp/addentry, contains a new entry for the user Ann Joans as listed in Listing 22.3.

LISTING 22.3   ENTRY FOR A USER IN THE /tmp/addentry FILE

```
dn: cn=Ann Joans, o=XYZ, c=US
objectClass: person
cn: Ann Joans
cn: Annette Joans
sn: Joans
title: system analyst
mail: ajones@corp.xyz.us.com
uid: ajones
```

Issue the following command at the command line to add this entry:

```
# ldapadd -f /tmp/addentry
```

The above entry adds a new entry for Ann Joans, which uses the information in the file.

DELETING A DIRECTORY ENTRY

Delete an entry from the LDAP directory by using the ldapdelete command. Suppose you want to delete the record for Ann Joans. The file /tmp/notrequired contains the information for Ann Joans.

```
dn: cn=Ann Joans, o=XYZ, c=US
changetype: delete
```

Using the command ldapdelete removes Ann Joans' entry.

```
example% ldapdelete -f /tmp/notrequired
```

SUMMARY

A directory is like a database where you can include information and retrieve it later over the network. However, this directory is specialized. It is designed for reading more than writing. It also enables you to perform simple updates. Directory services, such as Lightweight Directory Access Protocol (LDAP), are used to perform read, search, and update operations over the network with maximum performance.

LDAP is both an information model and a protocol for querying and manipulating it. The LDAP protocol itself is designed to run directly over the TCP/IP stack. LDAP provides both local and global directory services. Solaris 9 supports LDAP in conjunction with the iPlanet Directory Server 5.1 and other LDAP Directory Servers. LDAP is quickly gaining

22

in support and popularity because of its features, and it may be expected to replace many other network information and directory services in the near future. LDAPS, the secure LDAP, is also the best choice for security-minded installations.

PART **VI**

ADVANCED SOLARIS ADMINISTRATION

23   Mailing Service   405

24   Implementing Security   421

25   Enhanced Security Features   441

26   Performance Monitoring   489

## CHAPTER 23

MAILING SERVICE

In this chapter

Email   406

Implementing a Mail System   411

Administering the Mail Services   417

Summary   419

EMAIL

Electronic mail (email) has evolved into the most powerful means of communication for most of us today. Email is the term given to an electronic mail or message, usually a simple text message that a user types on a computer system for delivery to another user on a local or a remote computer. This message is then transmitted over a network to the user for whom it is intended.

As the Internet has become available to more and more people, the email facilities available to users have evolved from proprietary mail systems to the current trend of intranets. Proprietary mail systems used to be available to users within a company's network. With the evolution of the Internet, mail systems were able to connect to the Internet for transferring messages outside the local network. They now use a software interface that converts the local messages into a recognized standard form that is suitable for transfer over the Internet.

Email speeds up your day-to-day transactions. It provides a fast and economical way to transfer messages. Messages can easily be sent at any time to a single recipient or a group of people across the globe. Incoming messages can be stored at the mail server when the recipient is away from his desk and can be collected later. However, if your organization has Web mail services enabled, then users can access their mail whenever they want and from wherever they are. This is beneficial for people who are on the move most of the time. In addition, email messages require no paper or resources other than storage space on a computer disk drive.

Setting up and administering an electronic mail service are tasks that are critical to the operation of your network. As an administrator, your tasks may include setting up a mail service or expanding the existing mail service. This chapter details the concept you need to understand to set up mailing services, as well as how to implement them.

COMPONENTS OF A MAIL SYSTEM

Let us first look at the various components that are required to establish a mail service. There are both hardware and software components. The hardware components include the mail gateway, mail hosts, mail servers, and mail clients. Figure 23.1 displays a typical electronic mail configuration.

- **Mail gateway**—The mail gateway handles communication between networks, whether they use different protocols or the same protocol. For example, you can set up a mail gateway to connect a network running Systems Network Architecture (SNA) with another network running TCP/IP.

- **Mail host**—The mail host is a server that is responsible for delivering and receiving all email for your host and the network. To designate a system as the mail host, add the word `mailhost` to the right of the IP address in the local `/etc/inet/hosts` file or the hosts file in the naming service.

- **Mail server**—A mail server maintains the users' mailboxes. The mailboxes are files that contain users' mail. Mailboxes can be stored in a local mail server or a remote mail server. On Solaris systems, mail is usually stored in the `/var/mail` directory.

EMAIL | 407

■ **Mail client**—A mail client is any system that can access mail from the server. You can configure your mail clients to read mail directly from the mail server and have them stored on the mail server only, or you can configure the client to download your mail from the server and store it on your workstation.

Figure 23.1
Mail configuration.

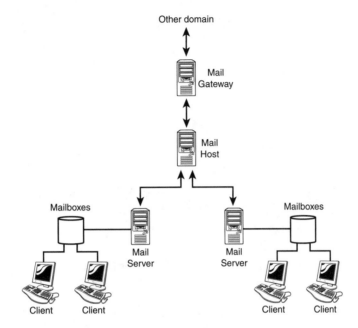

Other domain

The software components of a mail service are the mail user agent, mail transfer agent, and mail delivery agent.

■ **Mail user agent**—A program that acts as an interface between the user and the mail transfer agent. Examples of a mail user agent in Solaris are `/usr/bin/mail`, `/usr/bin/mailx`, `$OPENWINHOME/bin/mailtoolm`, and `/usr/dt/bin/dtmail`.

■ **Mail transfer agent**—A program that routes mail messages and resolves mail addresses. It is also called the mail transport agent (MTA). MTA accepts messages from the mail user agent and sends them to the destination addresses. Sendmail is the MTA on Solaris systems.

■ **Local delivery agent**—A program that delivers mail to the Unix file system mailbox formats (on Unix systems). Examples of local delivery agents include uucp and mail.local.

INTERACTIONS BETWEEN MAIL PROGRAMS

Mail services are provided by a combination of theprograms, which interact as shown in Figure 23.2.

Figure 23.2
Interaction between
mail programs.

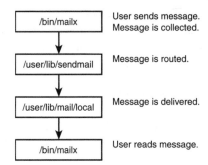

The `/usr/bin/mailx` is a user agent that sends and receives the mail message. The message is passed to the `sendmail` daemon, which uses the configuration file `/etc/mail/sendmail.cf` to parse the addresses in the message. This way, it determines the network name syntax, aliases, forwarding addresses, and so on. The sendmail program is a mail transport agent that uses the configuration file `sendmail.cf` to provide aliasing and forwarding services. It also enables automatic routing to network gateways.

→ For more information on `sendmail` **see** "sendmail," **p.410**.

> **NOTE**
>
> The `sendmail.cf` file is a configuration file that contains the operational details for `sendmail`. For more information, you may want to visit the Sendmail Consortium at `http://www.sendmail.org`.

The `sendmail` daemon transfers the message to the destination. The `/usr/lib/mail.local` program is a program on the local system that delivers the mail to the recipient's mailbox directory. The user can use the mail, Mail, or mailx programs to read and write messages. For example, if you have to read mail sent to user root, you issue any of the following commands:

- `mail -u root`
- `Mail -u root`
- `mailx -f root`

The `-f` option used with `mailx` is used to read messages from a file rather than from a mailbox. If no file is specified, the mbox is used. All user mail files are stored in the `/var/mail` directory. All root mails reside in the `/var/mail/root` file.

MAIL TRANSFER PROTOCOLS

Email messages can be transferred over many protocols. Some of the most popular protocols include the following:

- Simple Mail Transfer Protocol (SMTP)
- Post Office Protocol (POP)
- Internet Message Access Protocol (IMAP)

The following sections describe these protocols.

SMTP

SMTP is a widely used upper-layer protocol in the Internet Protocol stack. As is evident from its name, it is a protocol that specifies how mail is to be transmitted between two users.

The SMTP provides mechanisms for the transmission of mail directly from the sender's host to the receiver's host. The two hosts have to be connected to the same transport service, such as TCP/IP.

The MTA uses TCP/IP to carry out the exchange of mail. The main task of the MTA is to receive and deliver mail. It receives messages from the sender's host, reads the destination address, and delivers the mail to the specified destinations.

Users do not have to deal with the MTA. It is the system administrator who is responsible for the task of setting up and administering the MTA. The SMTP protocol describes how two MTAs communicate with each other over a TCP connection.

SMTP uses the concept of *spooling*. Spooling enables mail to be sent from a local application to the SMTP application. The SMTP application stores the mail on the disk or in memory. The mail is put in a queue after it arrives at the spool. A server checks to see whether any messages are in the queue and then attempts to deliver them. If the user or host is not available for delivery, the server retries later. If, for some reason, the mail cannot be delivered, (for example, if the mail server does not recognize the recipient), it will be discarded or sent back to the sender. This process is known as an end-to-end delivery system, because the server attempts to contact the destination and keeps the mail in the spool until it has been delivered.

POP

POP (Post Office Protocol) defines a set of rules for storing and accessing your mail on a central server. When you access messages, they are usually downloaded to your local computer and deleted from the server. Note that POP cannot be used to send mail—you have to use SMTP for that.

POP is useful when the user connects to the server through a dial-up connection to the Internet or an intranet. When a client has to use the service, it establishes a TCP connection with the server. After establishing a connection with the server, the client receives mail from the server. It then disconnects from the server to read incoming messages and compose responses offline. It might then re-establish a connection with the server so that it can send the responses. This procedure helps reduce the time for which a client application is connected to the server.

Consider a situation where a relatively small node in the Internet, such as a workstation, may not have adequate resources to keep an SMTP server and mail delivery system running continuously. In addition, it may prove expensive to keep a personal computer interconnected to an IP-based network for long hours. Handling and managing mails on these smaller nodes becomes a difficult proposition. POP solves this problem. POP can be termed as a store-and-forward mail system. The mail server receives mail and keeps it until the client application asks for the mail. The mail server usually deletes the mail after transferring it to the client's computer.

IMAP

IMAP is a client-server mail protocol in which the mail server keeps all mail that it receives at all times. Unlike POP, the client can read and manipulate mail only while connected to the mail server. An IMAP client-server connection remains active while messages are read or composed. IMAP is not preferable in a dial-in situation because the user has to remain connected to the Internet to perform any functions with the mailbox. IMAP also consumes more bandwidth and is more sensitive to network latency than POP.

Sendmail

The sendmail version 8.12 software is included within the Solaris 9 OE. Sendmail acts as an interface between mail reading programs, such as mail, mailx, and mailtool, and mail delivery programs, such as Unix-to-Unix copy program (UUCP) or mail.local. Sendmail controls email messages that are sent by the users. It deciphers the addresses of the recipients. Sendmail then decides on an appropriate delivery program and rewrites the addresses in a format that the delivery mechanism understands. It formats the mail headers as required and sends the message to the mail program for delivery to the recipient.

SENDMAIL CONFIGURATION FILE

A configuration file controls the manner in which sendmail performs its tasks. The choice of delivery mechanism to be used, address rewriting rules, and the mail header format are all specified in the configuration file.

Each system has a default sendmail.cf file installed in the /etc/mail directory. There is no need to edit or change the default configuration file for most mail servers or mail clients. However, mail hosts, mail gateways, and relay hosts need customized configuration files.

Which configuration file you use on a system depends on the role the system plays in your mail service. For mail clients or mail servers, you do not need to do anything to set up or edit the default configuration file. To set up a mail host, relay host, or gateway, copy the main.cf file and rename it sendmail.cf in the /etc/mail directory. Then, edit the sendmail.cf file to set the relay mailer and relay host parameters needed for your mail configuration.

HOW SENDMAIL WORKS

Sendmail processes and delivers incoming mail the same way it processes the outgoing mail. The only difference is the source of the mail. It receives incoming mail from other hosts via a mail server.

Sendmail processes and delivers mail messages in the following manner:

1. Sendmail collects a message from a program such as mailx or mailtool. It also collects the recipient address to determine aliases, forwarding addresses, or expanded address lists.

2. Next, the program generates two files. One of the files is an envelope that contains the header and a list of recipients. The other file contains the message body. Sendmail stores the header in memory and the message body in a temporary file.

3. Then sendmail expands and validates recipient addresses, aliases, and recipient lists. Sendmail matches the recipient address with an entry in the alias database and appends the new address to the recipient list.

> **NOTE**
>
> When a new address is appended to the recipient list, the old address is retained in the list and a flag is set that tells the delivery phase to ignore the old name. In this way, the recipient list is kept free from duplicates, preventing alias loops.

4. After the validation, messages are forwarded to the local recipients. The message is sent in two parts: a message header and a message body, separated from each other by a blank line.

   A sample "from" header might be `From: Ann Joan <ajoan@study.com>`.

5. If a mailer returns a status that indicates it cannot handle the message immediately, sendmail puts the message in the mail queue and tries again to deliver it the next time the mail queue is processed.

6. If a message contains an invalid recipient name or if the destination mailer refuses to accept the message because of errors generated during processing, the message is returned to the sender.

IMPLEMENTING A MAIL SYSTEM

You can configure your mail system in several modes. The most basic mode is a local network environment, where two or more workstations are connected to one mail host. This local network environment is not connected to the outside world. You can configure mail for a more complex network environment, such as a two-domain configuration attached to a mail gateway. You can decide on the type of mail configuration you want to set up based upon your requirements.

Regardless of the mode in which you configure your mailing service, you need the following elements:

- A mailbox to store or spool mail for each user.
- A `sendmail.cf` configuration on each system running `sendmail`.
- Alias files with an alias for each user to point to the place where mail is stored (when required) and a `postmaster` alias for the person who administers mail services.

23

The four modes in which you can configure your mail system are local mail only, local mail in remote mode, local mail and a remote connection, and two domains and a gateway.

As said earlier, the local mode is the simplest mode. Figure 23.3 displays a local mail configuration, in which three workstations are attached to one mail host. All three workstations act as mail servers and store mail.

Figure 23.3
Local mail configuration.

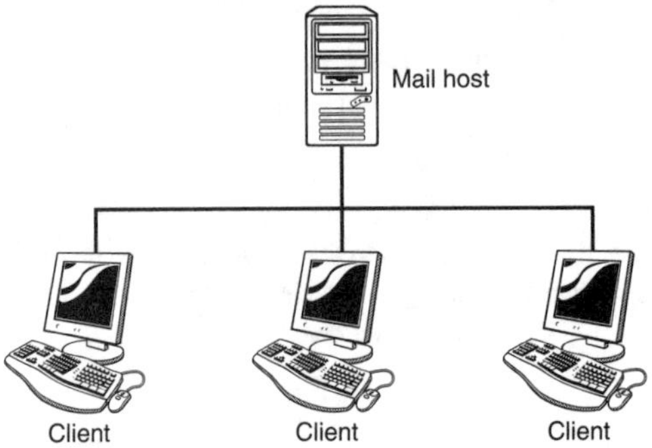

To set up this kind of mail configuration, you need to

- Assign at least one machine as the mail host.
- Ensure that each client system using the mailing service contains the sendmail configuration file: `/etc/mail/sendmail.cf`.
- Ensure that there is enough mailbox space in each client.
- Make certain that the `/etc/mail/aliases` file exists on any system that has a local mailbox. The `/etc/mail/aliases` file contains the mail forwarding information.

The local mail mode can be configured in remote mode as well, so that mail clients can mount their mailboxes from one mail server that provides mail spooling for client mailboxes. This server can also be the mail host. This configuration makes it easy to back up the mailboxes for each client. For this mode, you require all the elements discussed in the local mode. In addition, you need to have entries in each mail client's `/etc/vfstab` file or `/etc/auto_direct` to mount the `/var/mail` directory.

Another mode in which mail service can be configured is the local mail with a remote connection mode. In this mode, one server acts as the mail server, mail host, and mail gateway to the outside world. Figure 23.4 displays the local mail configuration with a remote connection.

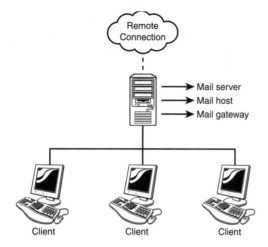

Figure 23.4
Local mail configuration with a remote connection.

To set up this type of a mail configuration, ensure all the elements discussed in the local and remote mode are present. In addition, a sample configuration file for main systems called `main.cf` must exist in the mail gateway. The path in which the file can be found is `/usr/lib/mail/cf/main.cf`. Note that the main.cf file is automatically created at the time of installation.

The mail configuration shown in figure 23.5 has two domains and a mail gateway. In this set up, it is quite possible that each domain has different mail servers, hosts, and gateways. In such a case, a name service is used to administer and distribute mail.

This mail configuration contains all elements mentioned earlier for all three modes of configuration, in addition to the following elements:

- Customize `sendmail.cf` by adding special rules.
- Add an alias entry for each user to point to the location where the mail is stored. In the NIS+ environment, add an entry to the `mail_aliases.org_dir` file, and in NIS add the entry to the aliases map.

The following subsections detail the steps to set up a mail system for a networking environment.

SETTING UP A MAIL SYSTEM

Consider a scenario where you as an administrator are given the task to set up mail service for your organization. You will need to select the systems in the network that should act as the mail host, mail server, and the mail client. If your company requirements state that the mail service must connect to the Internet as well, you will need a mail gateway.

The following sections detail the steps to set up a mail gateway, mail host, mail server, and mail clients.

Figure 23.5
Two domains and a
mail gateway.

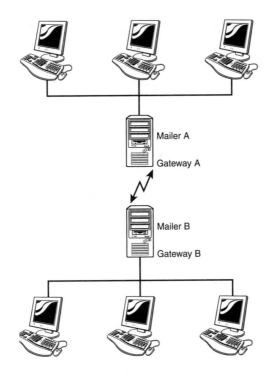

Mailer A

Gateway A

Mailer B

Gateway B

SETTING UP A MAIL GATEWAY

A mail gateway should be a system that is connected either as a router to the Internet or is attached to ethernet and phone lines. Perform the following steps to set up a mail gateway:

1. To set up the mail systems, you must assume the role of a superuser.

2. Stop `sendmail` by issuing the following command:
   `# /etc/init.d/sendmail stop`

3. Copy and rename the `main.cf` configuration file, as follows:.
   `# cp /etc/mail/main.cf /etc/mail/sendmail.cf`

4. Run the `check-hostname` script to verify that `sendmail` can identify the fully qualified hostname for this server:
   `# /usr/lib/mail/sh/check-hostname`

   If this script is not able to identify the fully qualified hostname, add the fully qualified hostname as the first alias for the host in `/etc/hosts`.

5. Ensure that your name service is started.

6. Restart `sendmail` and test your mail configuration.

➔ To learn more about the steps to test mail configuration, **see** "Testing the Mail Configuration," **p.417**.

SETTING UP A MAIL HOST

As described earlier in this chapter, a mail host is a machine that you designate as the main mail machine on your network. A mail host helps to resolve email addresses and reroutes mail within your domain.

Follow these steps to set up a mail host:

1. Become the superuser on the mail host system or assume an equivalent role. Stop `sendmail` with the `stop` command and verify the hostname configuration.

2. If you are using NIS or NIS+, update the `/etc/hosts` `file` by adding the word `mailhost` and `mailhost.`*`domain`* after the IP address and system name of the mail host system. This designates the system as a mail host.

   `IP_address mailhost` `mailhost mailhost.`*`domain`* `loghost`

3. Select the configuration file and copy and rename the file.

   `# cp /etc/mail/main.cf /etc/mail/sendmail.cf`

4. Restart `sendmail` and test your mail configuration.

SETTING UP A MAIL SERVER

While setting up the mail server, ensure that the mail server has sufficient spooling space for client mailboxes. For this task, check the `/etc/dfs/dfstab` file to ensure that the `/var` directory is exported.

The steps to set up a mail server are as follows:

1. Assume the role of a superuser. Stop `sendmail` by using the `stop` command.

2. To check whether the `/var/mail` directory is available for remote access, use the `share` command.

   `# share`

   If the `/var/mail` directory is not listed, add the following command line to `/etc/dfs/dfstab`:

   `share -F nfs -o rw /var/mail`

3. Next, make the file system available for mounting by using the `shareall` command:

   `# shareall`

4. The next step is to start the name service . Depending upon the name service you are using, issue one of the following commands. If you are running DNS, use the `nslookup` command.

   `# nslookup` *`hostname`*

   If NIS is the naming service used in your network environment, use the `ypwhich` command. This command returns the name of the NIS server that supplies the NIS name services to an NIS client:

   `ypwhich`

23

For the NIS+ naming service, the `nisls` command is used. This command lists the contents of a NIS+ directory:

```
nisls
```

Use the command `ldaplist` if you are using LDAP as your naming service. The `ldaplist` command lists the naming information from an LDAP directory:

```
ldaplist
```

5. Finally, restart `sendmail` by issuing the following command:

```
# /etc/init.d/sendmail start
```

The preceding steps will get your mail server up and running. The next task is to set up the mail client. The following section details the steps to perform mail client setup.

SETTING UP A MAIL CLIENT

To set up a mail client, you essentially need to ensure that the `/var/mail` directory exists on the client. This directory is usually created during the installation process.

You need to perform the following steps to set up a mail client with a mailbox on the mail server:

1. If the `sendmail` daemon is running, stop the daemon.

2. Ensure that the `/var/mail` mount point exists on the mail client's system. Also, ensure that the `/var/mail` directory is empty when it is mounted from the server by issuing the following command:

```
ls -l /var/mail
```

3. Mount the `/var/mail` directory from the mail server. This directory can be mounted either automatically or at boot time. To mount the directory automatically, add the following entry in the `/etc/auto_direct` file:

```
/var/mail -rw,hard,actimeo=0 server:/var/mail
```

To mount at boot time, add the following entry to the `/etc/vfstab` file.

```
server:/var/mail - /var/mail nfs - no rw,hard,actimeo=0
```

The client's mailbox is automatically mounted any time the system is rebooted. If you are not rebooting the system, type the following command to mount the client mailbox:

```
mountall
```

4. If you are using a name service, edit the `/etc/hosts` and add the following entry for the mail server.

```
# cat /etc/hosts
#
# Internet host table
#
..
IP_address     mailhost  mailhost  mailhost.example.com
```

5. Add an entry for the client to one of the alias files.

6. Restart `sendmail`:

```
# /etc/init.d/sendmail start
```

TESTING THE MAIL CONFIGURATION

To ensure that mail messages can be sent and received after all the systems are set up, test the setup. Start by sending test messages from each system by typing **/usr/lib/sendmail -v** *recipient email address* **</dev/null>** and press Return. This command sends a null message to the specified recipient and displays messages while it runs. If you have to set up a UUCP connection on your phone line to another host, send mail to someone at that host and have that person send mail back or call you when the message is received.

Ask someone to send mail to you over the UUCP connection. The sendmail program cannot tell whether the message gets through because it hands the message to UUCP for delivery.

Send a message to the postmaster on different systems and make sure that it comes to your postmaster's mailbox.

ADMINISTERING MAIL SERVICES

To ensure smooth operation of your mail services, you must constantly monitor the mail services. There may be situations when heavy load on the network or on the mail host results in slow network performance. You need to take appropriate measures to ensure that the mail service functions properly under such conditions. As an administrator for mail services, your tasks include

- Examining systems that are down and where mail is backing up.
- Checking the mail queues to see whether mail is flowing out in and out.
- Administering the alias database.
- Setting up forward files.
- Fixing mailing list problems for owners.
- Analyzing the postmaster mail to check for problems in the mailing service.

MAIL QUEUE

During temporary failure conditions or during heavy loads on the network, the `sendmail` program queues the messages in the mail server instead of delivering to the client immediately. When the system is up, the mail queue is processed automatically. Despite the automatic processing of the queue, there may be times when you may have to intervene, because when the host restarts, the performance of `sendmail` may have come down. That is when you may want to view the queue directory and see a list of messages queued. You can then force these messages to be processed. To view the number of messages in the queue and also to see how quickly they are being cleared, issue the following command. This command displays the contents of the queue, which includes queue ID, size of message, the date when the message entered the queue status, and the sender and recipient of the message.

```
# /usr/bin/mailq | more
```

In the output to the command, if you see there are messages that are not being cleared automatically, you can force the processing of the messages by using the following command:

```
# /usr/bin/sendmail -q -v
```

The option -q in the preceding command defines the process must save messages in the queue at given time intervals. The -v option is for verbose mode.

Note that if you want only a particular message to be processed, use the following command:

```
# /usr/bin/sendmail -qRstring
```

In the preceding command, replace string with the recipient's name or the hostname. You can also use a queue ID rather than a recipient name or the hostname as follows:

```
# /usr/bin/sendmail -qInnn
```

MAIL ALIASES

Mail users can be assigned an alternate name, also known as the alias name. This ensures that when mail is sent, it is delivered to the correct destination rather than a central address. For example, imagine there are two mail users in your network called Steve Quinn. You assign aliases to both users to ensure that when a message is sent, it is delivered to the relevant user. You must assign a unique alias name for each Steve Quinn. For example, you can assign the alias steveq@abc for one of them and stevequ@abc for the other.

Notice that both Steve Quinns have been given a unique alias.

You create an aliasby adding the alias name in the /etc/aliases file as displayed in the following syntax:

```
cat /etc/mailaliases
jim: jim@host.domain.com
```

You can configure an NIS alias map by entering a map name, using the following syntax:

```
nis:mail.aliases@nis_domain
```

To add aliases to an NIS+ table, add the following entry in it:

```
aliasadm -a steve steve.quinn@abc "Steve Quinn"
```

The preceding command can be broken down as follows:

- The aliasadm command manages the entries in the NIS+ tables.
- The -a option used with the aliasadm command is used to add the alias entry into the table.
- steve is the short form of the alias name.
- steve.quinn is the expanded alias name.
- "Steve Quinn" is the name for the alias.

SUMMARY

Electronic mail (email) has gained popularity, in both corporate and personal domains, over the years. As an administrator, one of your most critical tasks is to set up and maintain this mail system.

A mail system is composed of both hardware and software components. The hardware components include the mail gateway, mail hosts, mail servers, and mail clients. The mail gateway handles communication between networks that use protocols, such as SMTP, POP, or IMAP. The mail host delivers and receives the mail messages for the hosts in your network. Mail servers maintain the mail messages. The mail clients access these mail messages from the mail servers. Different software components, such as mail user agent, mail transfer agent, and mail delivery agent, enable the messaging between servers. An example of the mail transfer agent is `sendmail`. This agent is used to provide aliasing and forwarding services on most Unix systems, including Solaris.

## CHAPTER 24

IMPLEMENTING SECURITY

In this chapter

Solaris 9 and Security Considerations   422

Securing Your Open Boot Prom (OBP)   423

File System Security   426

Monitoring User LogIn   432

Summary   439

SOLARIS 9 AND SECURITY CONSIDERATIONS

With the rise in attacks on corporate networks and theft of business data, it has become increasingly important to secure business systems. Solaris 9 provides a dependable, easy-to-configure, and flexible platform for securing business-critical data and applications.

Implementing security at your site requires careful planning. Planning and implementing security in a network is not an easy task. The capabilities, technical skills, and tools available to people attempting unauthorized entry into networks and network-based systems have grown with the capabilities of applications and platforms to stop such unauthorized attempts. Attempts at hacking, for destructive or experimental purposes, have grown more frequent in recent years. As a result, you need to secure your computing environment to the maximum possible degree to safeguard it from hackers.

This chapter describes methods of setting up security at various levels of the operating environment. It defines security measures for controlling the firmware-level access (OBP or OK prompt) control for SPARC systems, controlling user login at the OS level, monitoring users who access the systems either from the console or from a remote location on the network, or securing an entire site or a portal running on Sun SPARC-based servers that use Solaris OE.

Securing an individual workstation requires that you ensure the following:

- Only individuals with authorized access to the system can use it.
- Individuals who have access to the system can access only their own data or the data that is made available to them by others.
- Information is not available to anyone without the permission of the owner.
- Resources on the workstation, such as a CD-ROM drive, disk space, and network bandwidth, are available only to the authorized users.

Different categories of people might try to gain unauthorized access to your computing environment. Here are some of them:

- Individuals testing their skills at gaining unauthorized entry into a system. Although these people make such attempts just for fun, they often cause serious damage.
- Users who misuse the resources of a computer or a network. An example of such a misuse is email bombing and spamming.
- People who steal data stored in a system and use it for personal gain. Although the person may steal data and sell it for money, the attack can also involve modifying or damaging the data to discredit the organization. These categories of people pose the highest degree of risk to a system or to an organization as a whole.

Although most modern applications and operating environments provide some levels of protection against unauthorized access, they often have some flaws in their design or implementation. Such flaws are identified almost as soon as the software is available in the market and are then exploited by hackers and other unauthorized users to gain entry into the system.

SECURING YOUR OPENBOOT PROM (OBP)

Let us first examine what happens when you boot a SPARC workstation or a server. After the machine is turned on, or after a reset, the system firmware (in PROM) executes the power-on self test (POST). When these tests have completed successfully, the non-volatile storage (EEPROM) is checked to determine whether the auto-boot flag is set to True. If the auto-boot flag is not set to True, the system drops to firmware or the ok prompt. If the auto-boot flag is set to be True, then the OS starts loading from the specified device, such as disk, Internet or CD-ROM.

NOTE

> OpenBoot version 4.x is the current version of OpenBoot.

OBP security is the first level of security for SPARC based-systems. For example, you can configure the OBP to prompt the user for a password to proceed with the boot process. You can specify one of the following security levels to prevent unauthorized access to the OBP:

- **None**—This security level does not require the user to enter any password to access OBP. All Sun SPARC systems are shipped with the OBP security level set to None. However, this level allows any user to change all the OBP variables and execute any OBP command. You should change the security level from None to Command or Full when you first set up the system for use.

- **Command**— This security level prevents a user from making any changes to the OBP variables and executing any commands. To make any changes, the user must enter a password. However, the system allows the user to execute the boot and go commands without a password. This means that the user can boot the system from the default device and continue operating the system after pressing the Stop+A key.

    The following example shows you how to set the OpenBoot security level to Command and specify a password while at the OpenBoot prompt.

    ```
    ok setenv security-mode command
    security-mode =      command
    ok setenv security-password ********
    security-password =
    ```

    Another example that shows how to change the OBP security to command while at the OBP prompt is as follows:

    ```
    ok password
    ok New password (only first 8 characters are used):********
    ok Retype new password:********
    ok
    ```

- **Full**— In addition to providing all the security features of the Command security level, this security level requires the user to enter a password to boot the system. However, the user can still execute the go command without the password. The following example shows how to set the OpenBoot security level to full and specify a password from the shell:

```
# eeprom security-mode=full
Changing PROM password
New password: ********
Retype new password: ********
```

PASSWORD RECOVERY PROCEDURE

There may be situations where any of the following might occur:

- The administrator forgets the root password.
- The /etc/shadow file is corrupted.
- The file permissions change where the Read permissions are revoked.
- Someone hacks into the system and changes the root password and takes control over the system.

These situations may make it impossible for you to log in to the system. To combat them, you need to use your system administrator skills to get the server/workstation back in your control. The following procedure provides the steps to recover the root password. These steps are performed from the ok prompt.

1. Determine the device name for the partition from the /etc directory.
2. Insert the Solaris OE CD into the system CD-ROM drive.
3. If a prompt is displayed, enter **sync** to empty the file system cache. However, if the prompt is not displayed, halt the system to bring it to the ok prompt by using the Stop+A key.
4. Enter **boot cdrom -s** when the system displays the ok prompt.
5. When the system displays the # prompt, enter the following command to mount the disk that has the root partition. In the following example, c0t0d0s0 is the disk that contains the root partition.

   mount/dev/dsk/c0t0d0s0 /a

   The system may display the following error message:

   ```
   mount: the state of /dev/dsk/c0t30s0 is not okay and
          it was attempted to be mounted read/write
   mount: please run fsck and try again
   ```

6. This error indicates that you need to run fsck to repair the file system. Enter the following command to run fsck:

   fsck /dev/rdsk/c0t0d0s0

7. Enter **cd/a/etc** to change to the directory with the root password.
8. Enter **cp shadow shadow.RECOVER** to create a backup of the /etc/shadow file.
9. Use the vi command to edit the root password entry in the /etc/shadow file. The initial entry in the /etc/shadow is as follows:

   ```
   # cat /etc/shadow

   root:DstKf4z/3nqYE:6445::::::
   ```

Change this entry to:

```
# cat /etc/shadow
root:::::::::
```

10. Save the file.

11. Enter **cd/** to change to the root directory.

12. Enter **umount/a** to unmount the file system.

13. Enter **sync** to empty the file system cache.

14. Enter **init 0** to halt the system.

15. Remove the Solaris OE CD-ROM from the system's CD-ROM drive.

Enter **boot** at the ok prompt to boot the system. Log in as root. You will be asked to enter a new password for root (see Figure 24.1) .

Figure 24.1
Password_msg_popup
dialog box.

PREVENTING UNAUTHORIZED OBP PASSWORD CHANGES

When you set the security levels as Command or Full for the OBP, the system prompts the user for a password to execute a command. In this case, an unauthorized user may try to guess the OBP password. You can track the number of such attempts by using the following command:

```
# eeprom security-#badlogins
security-#badlogins=3
```

You can add the preceding command to an initialization script to track the number of attempts to guess the password every time OBP is accessed. To reset the counter, use the following commands:

```
# eeprom security-#badlogins=0
security-#badlogins=0
```

However, you can prevent a user from dropping to the OBP level while the Solaris OE is running. As mentioned earlier, a user can use the Stop+A key combination to drop to the OBP. The steps to prevent a user from dropping to OBP by using the <Stop+A> key combination while the OS is running is as follows:

1. Open the /etc/default/kbd file.

2. Locate the following line:
   ```
   #KEYBOARD_ABORT=enable
   ```

3. Change the line to:

```
KEYBOARD_ABORT=disable
```

Changing this line prevents a user from accessing the OBP while the Solaris OE is running. However, a user can still drop to the OBP level by using any of the following methods:

- Send a break code or power-cycle the console terminal on a system where a terminal is attached to the serial port of the console.

- Execute the `init 0` command to halt the system and access OBP.

- Run the `eeprom` program to access OBP.

You can prevent a user from dropping to the OBP while the OS is running by disabling the <Stop+A> key. You can set the OBP security level to Command or Full, depending on whether you want to give OBP access to other users.

FILE SYSTEM SECURITY

As discussed in Chapter 8, "Understanding the Solaris File System," you can specify access permissions for each file or directory in a file system. In addition, every file or directory is owned by a particular user. Specifying the access permissions enables the user or the group to control the access to its files and directories.

Controlling access through permissions is critical to the security of files and directories. Although setting file permissions is a basic administration task, administrators often do not pay the required amount of attention to it. Consider a situation where an administrator needs to change the permission of some files and subdirectories within a directory. Some administrators may adopt a shortcut approach to change the permissions recursively rather than specify required permissions for individual files and directories. This weakens the file system security for that particular directory as a whole.

You can use certain commands to implement file security permissions while allowing applications to access the required files and directories. This section discusses the different factors you need to consider when you implement file security measures on a system running Solaris OE. You will also learn how to execute commands to implement file security permissions.

UNDERSTANDING FILE SYSTEM PERMISSION LEVELS

The Solaris OE file system permissions depend on two concepts: the identity of the user accessing a file or a directory and the permissions granted to the user. The user can be either an individual user or a group of users. After you specify the user or group that has the permission to access a file or a directory, you specify the permission level for that particular user or group.

You can specify three primary permissions for a file or a directory in the Solaris file system. These three permissions are Read, Write, and Execute. In addition, you can specify special permissions, such as SetUID, SetGID, and Sticky Bit, for files and directories.

Table 24.1 describes the different permissions for files and directories.

TABLE 24.1   FILE SYSTEM PERMISSION LEVELS

Permission	Description
Read-File	The user can read the contents of the file.
Read-Directory	The user can view the files that reside in a directory.
Write-File	The user can write to a file. This means that the user can add, modify, or delete a file's contents. However, the user cannot delete the file altogether if its directory does not have write permissions.
Write-Directory	The user can create, remove, and delete files that reside in a directory. However, the user cannot overwrite a file unless the file permissions allow it.
Execute–File	The user can execute the file if the file is an executable program.
Execute-Directory	Execute permission on a directory is required if you need to change directory and list the contents of the directory with the `ls` command. You can also create, edit, rename, access, and delete files or sub-directories within the directory. The Execute permission is also required to execute a program or shell script within a directory.
SetUID-File	Applies only if the file is an executable. The executable assumes the privileges of the file's owner, regardless of who is running the program.
SetGID-File	Applies only if the file is an executable. The executable assumes the privileges of the file's group, regardless of who is running the program. This means that the executable has access to all files and directories owned by that group.
SetGID-Directory	The files and directories created within the directory inherit its group ID and not the group ID of the user creating the files or directories.
Sticky Bit-Directory	The user can delete or rename files within the directory. This permission assumes the following: The directory is writable The user owns the file The user owns the directory The file is writable for the user The user is root This permission prevents users from deleting files owned by other users in such places as `/tmp` and `/var/tmp`.

METHODS FOR SETTING FILE AND DIRECTORY PERMISSIONS

You can use the `ls` command to view the permissions specified for a file or a directory. The following example shows the output of the `ls` command:

```
% ls -la test
-rwxrwxrwx    1 stacy guest    896    May 2 14:10     test
```

The output of the ls command is in the -rwxrwxrwx format. This is called the *symbolic method* of representing file system permissions. The -rwxrwxrwx+ permission field indicates the Read, Write, and Execute permissions specified for different users. Figure 24.2 provides information about this permission field.

Figure 24.2
ls command permission field descriptions.

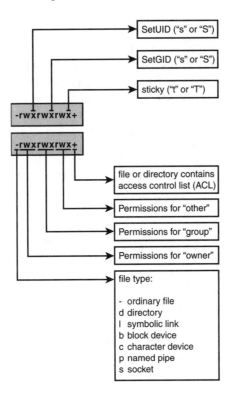

You can also use an alternative numerical method to specify file permissions.

The numerical method of indicating permissions uses a four-digit code to specify permissions. This method of notation can indicate Read, Write, Execute, SetUID, SetGID, and Sticky Bit permissions for a user, group, or others.

The numbers used for different types of permissions for users, groups, and others are

- Execute—1
- Write—2
- Read—4

If you need to combine permissions, you just add up the values of the numbers. For example:

- Read and Write—4+2=6
- Read, Write, and Execute—4+2+1=7

A three-digit code represents the permissions for the user, group, and others. For example, 654 – 6 is the user permission (Read and Write); 5 is the group permission (Read and Execute); 4 is the others permission (Read only) .

In a four-digit code, the first digit represents the permission for sticky bit, SetUID, and SetGID permissions. The numbers used for Sticky Bit, SetUID, and SetGID are:

- Sticky bit—1
- SetGID—2
- SetUID—4

As with the other permissions, you can add the permission numbers to indicate a combination of permissions. For example, with 5654 – sticky and SetUID, user can read and write, group can read and execute, and other can only read.

NOTE

> The numeric permission number 0 (zero) means that no permissions are specified for a user. The user cannot read, write, or execute a particular file or directory.

USING chmod AND chown TO SET FILES AND DIRECTORY PERMISSIONS

In the previous sections, you learned that there are two ways you can set file and directory permissions: numeric and symbolic. You can also use the chmod command to set or modify file permissions. To change the owner of the file you use the chown command.

You can use the chmod command to change permissions either numerically or symbolically. The syntax for the chmod command is as follows:

```
chmod nnnn filenames
```

In this syntax, nnnn is the numerical combination of permissions. The filenames parameter specifies a list of files and directories. This parameter can also refer to a single file or directory.

The following example shows how to set Read and Execute permissions for the file address for a user and a group, but no permissions for others:

```
chmod 550 address
```

The syntax to set the permissions symbolically with the chmod command is as follows:

```
chmod symbol-list filenames
```

In the preceding syntax, symbol-list indicates three different characters: a who symbol, an operator symbol, and a what symbol.

The who symbol represents the user category and can be one of the following symbols:

- **u**—user
- **g**—group
- **o**—other
- **a**—all

The operator symbol represents the operation on the permissions and can be one of the following symbols:

- **+**—add permissions
- **-**—remove permissions
- **=**—assign permissions

The what symbol represents the permission and can be one of the following symbols:

- **r**—read
- **w**—write
- **x**—execute
- **s**—SetUID or SetGID
- **t**—sticky bit
- **u, g, o**—Remove existing permissions from user, group, or other

You can use a comma to separate multiple permissions in a single chmod command. These symbols can be used with the chmod command as follows:

- To add Read, Write, and Execute permissions for a group for the file address:
  ```
  chmod g+rwx address
  ```
- To specify Read and Write permissions for a user and remove Execute permissions for others for the file address:

  ```
  chmod u=rw,o-x address
  ```

THE chown COMMAND

With the chown command, you can modify the owner of files and directories. For example, imagine that a user, Jim, owns certain application log files on a system. Now Jim has been assigned to other tasks and the task of monitoring application log files is assigned to Mary, a user on this system. To assign the ownership of the application log files to Mary, use the chown command.

Perform the following steps to change the owner of the files:

1. Check the files for which ownership has to be changed:
   ```
   #ls -l
   -r--------  1 jim      staff       75490876 May 24 15:45 app1.log
   -r--------  1 jim      staff       89955675 May 24 15:45 app2.log
   ```

2. Use the `chown` command to change the user:

```
bash-2.05# chown mary app1.log
bash-2.05# chown mary app2.log
```

3. List the files again to see whether the ownership has changed:

```
bash-2.05# ls -l
total 10
-r--------   1 mary        staff            75490876 May 24 15:45 app1.log
-r--------   1 mary        staff            89955675 May 24 15:45 app2.log
```

You can use the `chgrp` command to change the group ownership while retaining the original user ownership:

```
chgrpnew-group filename
```

If Mary's group has changed from staff to sys, change the group ownership of files as well. Use the following command to do so:

```
# chgrp sys app1.log app2.log
```

Now use the `ls` command to view the file listing.

```
bash-2.05# ls -l
total 10
-r--------   1 mary        sys              75490876 May 24 15:45 app1.log
-r--------   1 mary        sys              89955675 May 24 15:45 app2.log
```

Note that the group has changed to sys from staff.

You must ensure that file permissions are assigned very carefully because improper permissions can weaken the security of the system. Most determined intruders would be aware of the `chmod` and `chown` commands and if a weak permissions assignment is identified, it stands every risk of being exploited for unauthorized modification or accessing data stored in the file.

UMASK

The `umask` value specifies which permissions are set by default in a file or a directory when it is created. You can set both numeric and symbolic values to `umask`.

Each Solaris system has a default `umask` value that is assigned to all files or directories when they are created. However, a user can use the `umask` command to determine and change the `umask` value assigned to a file. To maintain the integrity and privacy of data, you should ensure that the file's owner has the highest level of permissions, and the group and the other has a much lower level of permissions or none at all.

Let us see how a numeric value is assigned to `umask`. Take the example of a system that assigns `umask` 102 to all files created. The 1 means that user does not have Execute permissions; the 0 means that no permissions are denied for the group; the 2 means that the other does not have Write permissions.

You can also determine the meaning of a `umask` value by subtracting it from 777. For example, subtract `umask` 102 from 777. The resulting permission is 675. The 6 means that the user has Read and Write permissions (4+2); 7 means that the group has Read, Write, and

Execute permissions (4+2+1); 5 means that the other has Read and Execute permissions (4+1) .

You can also set a symbolic value for umask. The syntax is similar to the symbolic syntax of the chmod command. For example, you can represent umask 102 as follows:

```
umask u+rw,g+rwx,o+rx
```

DEFAULT FILE PERMISSIONS AND umask

When a file is created with vi, ed, cp, or touch commands or with shell redirection, you can determine the permissions for the file by subtracting the umask value from 666. For example:

```
% umask
0102
% touch almeda
% ls -ld almeda
-rw-r----- 1 stacy   guest  2 May 2 19:15 almeda
%
```

DEFAULT DIRECTORY PERMISSIONS AND umask

When a directory is created with commands such as mkdir, you can determine the permissions for the file by subtracting the umask value from 777. For example:

```
% umask
0102
% mkdir utils
% ls -la utils
-rwxr-x--- 3 stacy   guest  2 May 2 19:15 utils
%
```

In the preceding example, you can determine the permissions for the file by subtracting the umask value of 102 from 777. This results in the value 675, which indicates the permissions for the file. You can set UMASK from the /etc/default/login file.

MONITORING USER LOGIN

Monitoring user logins is a vital system security process. Monitoring the successful and failed login attempts enables the system administrator to keep a track of people trying to access the Solaris system. Solaris provides various commands such as last, who, and finger to monitor login attempts, and trace recently logged in and logged off users.

Some users might try to log in to the system without valid authorization and try to access confidential data. The system administrator can monitor such users with the help of the various log files, such as the loginlog and wtmpx files.

Consider a database server in your production environment that is accessed by a web-based application. This server has a database that contains the employee details owned by HR. Only system administrators at the site have the permissions to access the server from console or to log in from a remote terminal as a superuser. For a server containing such critical data, it is important to monitor the activities on the system. The task of monitoring includes maintaining a clear audit log of who logged in to the server and at what time. In addition, it is important to monitor unsuccessful login attempts, because there may be people who are attempting to break into the system. You can use the log file to identify the problem areas and take the necessary measures to secure the system.

To enable Solaris 9 to log the unsuccessful login attempts, you need to create an empty file named `loginlog` under the `/var/adm` directory. The `/var/adm/loginlog` file should be accessible only by root. The system logs failed login attempts in this file after five unsuccessful attempts. You can view this file to monitor the repeatedly unsuccessful login attempts. This file enables the system administrator to trace the user who tries to hack in to the system.

The `loginlog` file contains the login name, terminal details, and the date and time of the failed login attempt.

Listing 24.1 displays a sample listing of the `/var/adm/loginlog` file.

LISTING 24.1   SAMPLE LISTING OF THE `/var/adm/loginlog` FILE

```
hemz:/dev/pts/7:Wed May 22 03:40:08 2002
romando:/dev/pts/7: Wed May 22 03:42:22 2002
root:/dev/pts/7: Wed May 22 03:44:31 2002
```

You can also use the `logins` command to monitor the login details on a Solaris system. The `logins` command enables you to list the login information of all users. You can use this command to verify the validity of a user in the system. For example, if an application user is performing some tasks limited to the members of the sysadmin group, you can use the `logins` command to verify whether the user belongs to the sysadmin group or has appropriate privileges to perform those activities.

The `logins` command, without any arguments, displays the following information:

- user(or)system login name
- user id(UID)
- Primary group name
- Primary group id

Table 24.2 lists the options you can use with the `logins` command and their descriptions.

TABLE 24.2   FLAGS USED WITH THE `logins` COMMAND

Flags	Description
-m	Displays all groups of which an account is a member.
-g group	Displays the accounts that belong to the mentioned group.
-d	Displays the accounts with identical UIDs.
-l	Displays the specified login account.

continues

TABLE 24.2 CONTINUED

Flags	Description
-a	Displays the number of days until the account password expires due to inactivity and the date the password expires.
-o	Converts the output to a format that uses colon-delimited fields.
-p	Displays accounts without any assigned password.
-s	Displays administrative accounts.
-t	Sorts the output by the account name rather than by UID.
-u	Displays non-administrative accounts.
-x	Displays extended information, such as the user's home directory, default login shell, and password aging.

You can also use the `logins` command to list the users who do not have passwords. You must ensure all users have passwords to restrict unauthorized access to the system. The accounts that do not have a password make it viable for hackers to log in to the system. Another command to monitor the currently logged on users is the `who` command. You use this command to monitor how long a user has been logged on to the system. You can also use this command to ensure that only the users who are scheduled to work at a particular time are actually logged on to the system. The `who` command displays the following information about the currently logged on users:

- Users currently logged in
- Login device name
- Date and time of login along with the remote system name

You may want to perform random checks to monitor the tasks that users are performing on the system. The `whodo` command is used to display the user sessions. This command displays the UID, terminal information, the process name, and the PID. Listing 24.2 displays the output of the `whodo` command.

LISTING 24.2 OUTPUT OF THE *whodo* COMMAND

```
bash-2.05# whodo | more
Tue May 28 18:23:21 IST 2002
buffy

pts/1      root      18:08
    pts/1        5564     0:00 bash
    pts/1        5584     0:00 man
    pts/1        5599     0:00 sh
    pts/1        5600     0:00 more

console    test1     18:42
```

```
    ?          2689    0:00  Xsession
    ?          2700    0:00  fbconsole
    ?          2737    0:00  dsdm
  pts/6        2738    0:00  sdt_shell
  pts/6        2740    0:00  sh
  pts/6        2755    0:03  dtsession
    ?          2757    0:00  dtwm
    ?          2761    0:00  sdtperfmeter
    ?          2758    0:00  dtfile
    ?          2785    0:00  dtfile
    ?          2810    0:00  dtexec
    ?          2811    0:00  dtscreen
  pts/6        2754    0:00  ttsession
```

USING syslog

In addition to `loginlog`, Solaris also uses `syslog` to log system activity messages. You can use `syslog` to monitor user activities and login attempts.

The `syslog` daemon, `syslogd`, provides the `syslog` service on a Solaris system. `syslogd` is installed by default. However, you need to configure it to specify the messages you want to be logged.

The `syslog` system messages are categorized according to the system component that generates the messages. `syslog` categorizes these components as facilities and prioritizes messages from these facilities. Depending on how you configure `syslog`, it logs messages from various facilities. Table 24.3 describes the various facilities of `syslog`.

TABLE 24.3 *syslog* FACILITIES AND THEIR DESCRIPTIONS

Facility	Description
Auth	Generated by authorization programs such as login and su.
Cron	Generated by cron and at.
Daemon	Generated by system and network daemons.
Kern	Generated by kernel.
Lpr	Generated by the printing system.
mail	Generated by mail system.
mark	Generated by `syslog` for time stamps.
news	Generated by the news system.
user	Generated by the user applications.
uucp	Generated by the UUCP system.
Local0...7	Reserved for local use.

24

In addition to the facilities, `syslog` uses priority levels to categorize and log messages. Table 24.4 lists the priority levels `syslog` uses.

TABLE 24.4 `syslog` PRIORITIES AND THEIR DESCRIPTIONS

Priority	Description
debug	Debug messages
info	Informational messages
notice	Notices for various users
warning	Warning messages
Err	System error messages
crit	Critical system failure messages, such as printer failure
alert	System alerts requiring immediate attention
emerg	Emergency messages, such as system shutdown

Before you start using syslog, you need to specify the system facilities and their priorities that you want to store in the syslog. The `syslog` then logs the system messages generated by the facilities in a log file. You can specify different files to log messages from different facilities. You need to specify the files in which you want to store system messages in the `/etc/syslog.conf` file.

In addition, you can specify the hosts where these messages will be logged. These messages can be logged at a central loghost or the localhost.

> **NOTE**
>
> You may need to create log files manually for different facilities if they do not already exist. To prevent unauthorized access, you should ensure that only root has Read and Write permissions for these files.

For example, to log all debug messages from the auth facility to a specified log file, you need to enter the following line in the `/etc/syslog.conf` file:

```
auth.debug          /var/logs/auth.log
```

An example `/etc/syslog.conf` file is shown in Listing 24.3.

LISTING 24.3 `etc/syslog.conf` FILE

```
#
# syslog configuration file (local hosts)
#
# output to console
*.err;mail,kern.notice;daemon,auth.debug;user.info    /dev/console
# output to local file "messages" for automatic log file analysis
*.err;auth,daemon,mark,kern.debug;mail,user.notice    /var/adm/messages
# output to local files for archiving messages of potential interest
```

```
auth.debug      /var/adm/auth.log
daemon.debug  /var/adm/daemon.log
lpr.debug     /var/adm/lpr.log
mail.debug      /var/adm/mail.log
# forward to loghost
mark.debug;*.debug    @loghost
# end of /etc/syslog.conf
#
# syslog configuration file (loghost)
#
# output to console
*.err;mail,kern.notice;daemon,auth.debug;user.info/dev/console
# output to local file "messages" for automatic log file
analysis (logsurfer)
*.err;auth,daemon,mark,kern.debug;mail,user.notice/var/log/messages
# output to local files for archiving messages of potential interest
auth.debug          /var/log/auth.log
daemon.debug          /var/log/daemon.log
lpr.debug           /var/log/lpr.log
mail.debug          /var/log/mail.log
news.debug          /var/log/news.log
uucp.debug          /var/log/uucp.log
user.debug          /var/log/user.log
# end of /etc/syslog.conf
```

MONITORING SUPERUSER ACCOUNT USAGE

The superuser or the root account is the most important account in a Solaris system. This account is based on the "all or nothing" model. This model implies that:

- The superuser can access all the files, execute all the commands, and perform all the activities on the system.

- Most of the administrative tasks, such as adding users, deleting users, installing packages and patches, and so on require superuser access.

A superuser has the power to perform the following tasks, among others:

- Add new users and remove existing users in a Solaris system.
- Change file permissions.
- Add and remove hosts and change the permissions granted to a host.
- Install software and patches.
- Perform archive backups in the system.
- Access and modify system log files.
- Use the su command to log in as any user.

LOG FILES USED TO MONITOR USAGE OF THE SUPERUSER ACCOUNT

As discussed in the last section, the superuser has access to all the files, and has the permissions to perform all the processes on the Solaris machine.

You can monitor the superuser logins by viewing the /var/adm/sulog file. This file records all the successful and unsuccessful attempts to use the su command. However, note that this file does not show root logins that do not use su. In addition, this file logs the port from which the command was issued, the name of the user, and the switched identity. You can enable the /var/adm/sulog file by editing the /etc/default/su file. To enable the /var/adm/sulog file you need to

1. Log in as the superuser.
2. Open the /etc/default/su file and uncomment the following line:
   SULOG=/var/adm/sulog

You can also specify whether su login attempts should be displayed in the console. This enables you to monitor all su login attempts and when they occur. To display all the successful and unsuccessful su login attempts at the system console, you need to

1. Edit the /etc/default/su file.
2. Uncomment the following line:
   CONSOLE=/dev/console

After you edit the /etc/default/su file, you can view the /var/adm/sulog any time. The /var/adm/sulog file contains the following fields:

- Date
- Time
- Attempts both successful and unsuccessful
- Port
- User who executes the su command

The sulog variable records all su attempts:

```
bash-2.05# more /var/adm/sulog
SU 05/21 14:13 + ??? root-uucp
SU 05/23 14:44 + pts/2 root-root
SU 05/23 14:44 + pts/2 root-test1
SU 05/23 14:44 - pts/2 root-root
SU 05/23 14:47 + pts/2 root-root
bash-2.05#
```

You can also use the last command to trace the users who have logged on or logged off from the system. The syntax of the command is as follows:

```
last root
bash-2.05# last
root     pts/9      radhika-d190.ltb Thu May 23 17:57 - 17:58  (00:00)
root     console    :0               Thu May 23 14:33   still logged in
root     pts/2      arminderk-d190.l Thu May 23 14:32   still logged in
root     console    :0               Thu May 23 08:51 - 09:01  (00:09)
```

```
root       pts/1         chetan.ltb.in.ni Wed May 22 19:15 - 09:49  (14:33)
root       dtremote      tanujj-d190.ltb. Wed May 22 18:36 - 19:13  (00:37)
test       pts/4         172.17.68.80     Wed May 22 17:28 - 17:30  (00:01)
root       pts/3         ksb-sun-prx.ltb. Wed May 22 17:20 - 18:45  (01:25)
root       pts/1         ksb-sun-prx.ltb. Wed May 22 17:00 - 19:13  (02:13)
reboot     system boot                    Wed May 22 16:59
root       pts/7         ksb-sun-prx.ltb. Wed May 22 16:37 - 16:58  (00:21)
root       pts/6         ksb-sun-prx.ltb. Wed May 22 16:21 - 16:58  (00:37)
root       dtremote      tanujj-d190.ltb. Wed May 22 12:38 - 12:41  (00:02)
root       pts/2         ksb-sun-prx.ltb. Wed May 22 12:37 - 16:51  (04:13)
root       dtremote      tanujj-d190.ltb. Wed May 22 12:13 - 12:15  (00:01)
root       pts/8         ksb-sun-prx.ltb. Wed May 22 12:12 - 12:15  (00:03)
root       pts/8         ksb-sun-prx.ltb. Wed May 22 12:12 - 12:12  (00:00)
root       pts/8         ksb-sun-prx.ltb. Wed May 22 12:11 - 12:11  (00:00)
root       pts/8         ksb-sun-prx.ltb. Wed May 22 12:11 - 12:11  (00:00)
root       pts/8         ksb-sun-prx.ltb. Wed May 22 12:10 - 12:11  (00:00)
root       pts/2         ksb-sun-prx.ltb. Wed May 22 12:06 - 12:16  (00:09)
```

SUMMARY

Solaris 9 provides ways and means to protect your network and data from unauthorized access and other threats, so that your system can be available 24×7. Solaris 9 includes security features that provide firewall protection, file access control, and monitoring methods. Solaris 9 enables you to implement security checks at various levels from login level to file level. In addition, Solaris 9 enables you to preempt security violations by authorized users by allowing you to monitor activities of all the users, including the superuser. These security features of Solaris 9 enable a system administrator to maintain a flexible, user-friendly, robust, and yet completely secure system.

## CHAPTER 25

ENHANCED SECURITY FEATURES

In this chapter

Solaris Security Features—An Overview   442

SSH   442

Understanding, Planning, and Implementing SEAM   445

Using Kerberos with Solaris 9   451

GSS-API   455

Role-Based Access Control (RBAC)   456

ASET   468

TCP Wrappers   471

IPSec   472

Internet Key Exchange (IKE)   476

Firewalls   480

Summary   488

SOLARIS SECURITY FEATURES—AN OVERVIEW

In the previous chapter, you learned about implementing security at the system level. You learned how to monitor incorrect logins, set up permissions to secure file systems, secure OpenBoot PROM, monitor logged-in users, recover lost passwords, and so on. In addition to these security features, you can implement various advanced security features for the Solaris 9 environment, such as securing networks by encrypting data over the network by using various encryption algorithms, implementing RBAC, Kerberos, and Secure Shell (SSH).

This chapter provides information on the various security protocols, mechanisms, and products that are available for Solaris 9. Although the list of technologies covered in this chapter is far from exhaustive, the information will go a long way toward helping you protect your network, its services, applications, and data from unauthorized access and attack.

SSH

SSH (Secure Shell) is a tool that enables secure remote login over insecure networks. Unlike Telnet and `rlogin`, SSH provides an encrypted terminal session. SSH has a strong authentication mechanism for both the server and client that uses public-key cryptography.

Some of the key features of SSH include the following:

- Provides different types of user authentication methods
- Allows secure passage through firewalls
- Allows secure file transfers
- Forwards X Windows (X11) connections automatically

In the previous versions of Solaris, you needed to install SSH as a separate package. However, in Solaris 9, SSH is included within the operating environment.

> **NOTE**
>
> Solaris 9 Secure Shell supports both SSH1 and SSH2 protocols, SSH2 being the more recent version of SSH protocols.

An SSH daemon is started at boot. The SSH daemon (`sshd`) is initiated from the `/etc/init.d` directory. When an SSH session is started, the `sshd` daemon is forked for each incoming connection from clients. After the local host and the remote host authenticate each other with the help of the `sshd` daemon, you can execute commands remotely and transfer data as required.

SSH AUTHENTICATION

You need a password and/or a public/private key pair for SSH authentication. When you log in to a remote host, you need to provide the appropriate password. For further security, you can create a public/private key pair. You use the private key stored on the local host to encrypt outgoing data, and the remote host uses the supplied public key to decrypt the incoming data. This assumes that the remote host has access to your public key.

To create a public/private key pair in Solaris 9, perform the following steps:

1. To start the key generation program, enter the following commands:

```
myLocalHost % ssh-keygen
Generating public/private rsa key pair.
Enter file in which to save the key(/home/davidS/.ssh/id_rsa):
```

2. Press Return to accept the default file name, id_rsa, or enter an alternate file name.

3. Specify a passphrase of 10 to 30 characters to encrypt the private key. A null entry means that no passphrase is used to encrypt the private key.

CAUTION

If you do not provide a passphrase, anyone can copy and use your keys, therefore it is strongly recommended that you provide a passphrase.

```
Enter passphrase(empty for no passphrase): passphrase
```

NOTE

You can use the ssh-keygen with the –p option to change the passphrase.

4. Re-enter the passphrase to confirm it.

```
Enter same passphrase again: passphrase
Your identification has been saved in /home/davidS/.ssh/id_rsa.
Your public key has been saved in /home/davidS/.ssh/id_rsa.pub.
The key fingerprint is:
0e:fb:3d:57:71:73:bf:58:b8:eb:f3:a3:aa:df:e0:d1 DavidS@host1myLocalHost
```

5. Copy the public key to the home directory on the remote host and append it to $HOME/.ssh/authorized_keys.

To log in to a remote host with ssh:

1. Use ssh and connect to the remote host.

```
myLocalHost % ssh <RemoteHost>
```

NOTE

The first time you run ssh to connect to a remote host, the following prompt is displayed:

```
The authenticity of host 'myRemoteHost' can't be established.
RSA key fingerprint in md5 is:
04:9f:bd:fc:3d:3e:d2:e7:49:fd:6e:18:4f:9c:26
Are you sure you want to continue connecting(yes/no)?
```

This prompt is normal. Enter **yes** to continue. However, if this prompt is displayed on subsequent instances of running ssh, it is possible that the security of your system has been compromised—check that the system you are connecting to is indeed the system you want to connect to.

2. Enter the passphrase and the account password.

```
Enter passphrase for key '/home/stacy/.ssh/id_rsa': Return
stacy@myRemoteHost's password: Return
Last login: Mon May 06 14:32:05 2002 from myLocalHost
myRemoteHost%
```

3. Transact with the remote host.

4. Enter **exit** to close the remote session.

```
myRemoteHost% exit
myRemoteHost% logout
Connection to myRemoteHost closed
myLocalHost%
```

You also can connect to a remote host without specifying a password or passphrase. To do this, you need to use the ssh agent daemon.

To use the ssh agent to log in to a remote host with no password, implement the following steps:

1. Enter the following command to start the agent daemon manually:

```
myLocalHost% eval 'ssh-agent'
Agent pid 9236
myLocalHost%
```

The ssh-agent starts the agent daemon and displays the process ID of the agent daemon.

2. Enter the following command to add the private key to the agent daemon:

```
myLocalHost% ssh-add
Enter passphrase for /home/davidS/.ssh/id_rsa:
Identity added: /home/davidS/.ssh/id_rsa(/home/davidS/.ssh/id_rsa)
myLocalHost%
```

3. Start an ssh connection to the remote host.

```
myLocalHost% ssh myRemoteHost
```

You can use the scp command to copy files between a local host and a remote host or even between two remote hosts in a secure way. The scp command is similar to the rcp command, except that the scp command prompts for a password and encrypts the transmitted information on the fly for added security. This ensures a higher degree of security for files residing on a system because the file transfer is encrypted with the selected encryption algorithm.

To copy files with scp, follow these steps:

1. Enter the scp command and specify the source file you want to copy. In addition, specify the username at the remote host and the directory within which the source file resides.

```
myLocalHost% scp file.1 davidS@remotehost:~
```

2. Enter the ssh passphrase.

```
Enter passphrase for key '/home/davidS/.ssh/id_rsa': Return
copythisfile.1      48% |*******              |   640 KB 0:14 ETA
copythisfile.1
```

After you enter the passphrase, the progress meter indicates the percentage of the file transferred. Note that a series of asterisks graphically indicates the percentage, the data already transferred, and the time remaining for the rest of the data to be transferred.

UNDERSTANDING, PLANNING, AND IMPLEMENTING SEAM

Sun Enterprise Authentication Mechanism (SEAM) provided by the Solaris 9 OE was first introduced as part of the Solaris Easy Access Server (SEAS) in Solaris 2.6 and 7. In version 8 of Solaris, the SEAM client was added to the OS. In addition, the SEAM KDC and remote application components were added to SEAM in Solaris 8. In Solaris 9, the client and KDC components are the only features supported by the SEAM utility. SEAM has client/server architecture. It provides user authentication and data integrity over networks. Based on the industry standard network authentication system Kerberos Version 5, SEAM provides interoperability in heterogeneous networks. If you have used Kerberos Version 5, you will find SEAM very similar. In fact, SEAM and Kerberos are so similar that they can be used interchangeably.

You can use SEAM to securely access remote systems to execute commands and exchange data. SEAM also provides authorization services, which means that the administrator can allow or restrict access to services and machines. In addition, individual users can restrict access to their accounts. SEAM also provides the user the advantage of signing on just once per session. After the user is authenticated by the system, all subsequent commands and transactions can be carried out securely without any prompting for a password.

HOW SEAM WORKS

The authentication process in SEAM is based on the concept of a *ticket*. A ticket contains information that enables the system to identify you every time authentication is required. For example, when you log in to another system, you begin a SEAM session by requesting a ticket-granting ticket (TGT) from the key distribution center (KDC) of that system. A ticket-granting ticket is needed to obtain other tickets for specific services. The KDC sends an encrypted TGT back to your system, which uses the system password to decrypt it (see Figure 25.1).

After you get a TGT, you do not need to give any password or any details whenever authentication is required. The TGT provides the required information to the authentication processes as and when required behind the scenes. Every time you make a request or execute a command, the TGT requests a ticket for that operation from the KDC (see Figure 25.2). However, the TGT has a specified life and allows network operations only as long as it lasts. The life of a TGT depends on the life specified in the system's KDC.

25

Figure 25.1
Requesting a TGT from the KDC of that system.

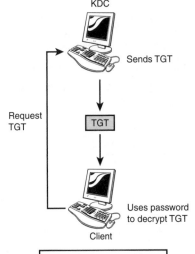

KDC

Sends TGT

Request TGT

TGT

Uses password to decrypt TGT

Client

TGT - Ticket-granting ticket
KDC - Key distribution Centre

25

Figure 25.2
TGT provides the required information to the authentication processes.

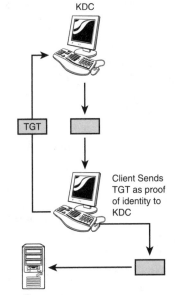

KDC

TGT

Client Sends TGT as proof of identity to KDC

Server allows access

TGT - Ticket-granting ticket
KDC - Key distribution Centre

After the KDC of the server-side system grants a TGT to your client, you do not need to log in manually or provide any password for any operation. The one-time sign-in advantage of SEAM means that all authentication processes take place in the background.

When you need to make a request or execute a command on a remote server, your system sends the TGT to the KDC for authentication. After authentication, the KDC sends a ticket for the particular operation to the client. In turn, the client sends the ticket to the server, which grants access to the client.

The KDC uses the concept of a *principal* to assign an identity and subsequently identify a client. A principal is a unique identity and can be a user or a service, such as NFS.

A principal name is divided into three parts: the primary, the instance, and the realm. For example, davidS/guest@solaris.admin.com is a typical SEAM principal. In this example, davidS is the primary and can be a username, a service, or the word host. The instance is guest, which is optional for a user principal. With a service principal, the instance is required and should be a fully qualified hostname. solaris.admin.com is the realm of the principal.

REALMS

One of the main features of SEAM is that it permits authentication across realms. Realms are hierarchical or non-hierarchical logical networks that define a group of systems in the same master KDC. Figure 25.3 illustrates how realms relate to one another.

Figure 25.3
How realms relate.

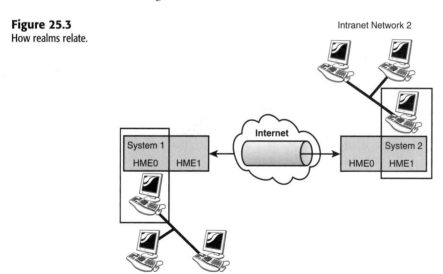

Each realm has at least one master KDC server and a slave KDC server. The slave KDC server is essentially a backup for the network, and takes over if the master KDC fails. This means that any modifications or updates to the master KDC need to be propagated to the slave KDC also. The master KDC server contains the principal database, and the slave server has the copy of the principal database. Both these types of servers are used to issue tickets for authentication. Figure 25.4 displays what a realm may contain.

Figure 25.4
Components of a realm.

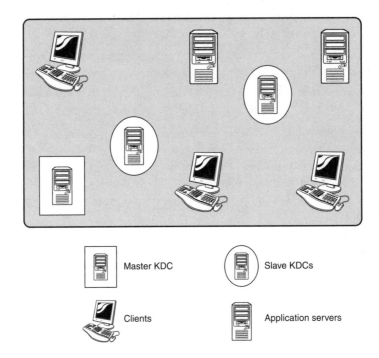

Master KDC

Slave KDCs

Clients

Application servers

INSTALLING SEAM

You need to consider various variables before you install SEAM on a network. First of all, you need to decide whether SEAM will satisfy your requirements. After the initial installation, you will find it more and more difficult to change the SEAM configuration as new clients are added to the network. Therefore, it is better to plan according to the long-term requirements of the network.

Before you install SEAM, you need to consider the following:

- Defining the names, number, sizes, and hierarchy of realms in the network.
- Assigning ports for the KDC and System Admin services.
- Setting up slave KDCs.
- Synchronizing the internal clock on all hosts in the network (using the Network Time Protocol (NTP), for example).
- Propagating the databases on the master KDC.

After you install the SEAM software, you need to configure the KDC servers. You need to configure at least one master KDC server and one slave KDC server. The KDC master and slave servers provide the service that issues accept requests for clients and also issues tickets to clients.

The following procedures provide the steps required to configure a master KDC server, a slave KDC server, and a SEAM client.

To configure a master KDC server, you first need to install the master KDC software on the Solaris OE. In addition, DNS is also required so that the principals can be assigned a domain name.

To configure a master KDC server:

1. Log in as the superuser on the master KDC server.
2. Access the Kerberos configuration file, /etc/krb5/krb5.conf.
3. Edit the realm names and the server names in the krb.conf file to the required realm and server names.
4. Access the KDC configuration file, /etc/krb5/kdc.conf, and edit the realm name.
5. Use the kdb5_util command to create the KDC database.
6. Access the Kerberos access control list, kadm5.acl, and populate it with all principals permitted to administer the KDC. For example, you can add the following lines in the /etc/krb5/kadm5.acl file:

```
# vi /etc/krb5/kadm5.acl
kadmin/admin@<your KERBEROS REALM> *
username@<your KERBEROS REALM> *
krbadm@< your KERBEROS REALM> *
*/*@<your KERBEROS REALM> *
```

7. Start kadmin.local.
8. Add administration principals to the KDC database.
9. Create a keytab file for kadmin and quit kadmin.local. The Kerberos administration daemon (kadmind) uses a keytab file to determine what type of access control it should provide to administrators.
10. Start the Kerberos daemons.
11. Start kadmin.
12. Create the master KDC host principal.
13. Add the master KDC's host principal to the master KDC's keytab file and quit kadmin.
14. Add an entry for each KDC to the propagation configuration file, kpropd.acl.

→ To learn more about how to create a master KDC, add master KDCs, and add an entry for each master KDS, **see** http://docs.sun.com.

To configure a slave KDC server, you need to ensure that the master KDC server is configured and the slave KDC software is installed on kdc3.

To configure a slave KDC server, follow these steps:

1. Become the superuser on the master KDC server.

2. On the master KDC, start `kadmin` and log on with an administrative principal existing in the KDC database.

3. Add slave KDC hosts to the list of principals in the database and quit `kadmin`.

4. Edit the Kerberos configuration file, `krb5.conf`, and add an entry for each KDC slave.

5. Add an entry for each slave KDC to the database propagation configuration file, `kpropd.acl`.

6. Copy the KDC administration files from the master KDC to each slave KDC server.

7. Add the host principal to the keytab file of each slave KDC.

8. Add the slave KDC names to the cron job on the master KDC server.

9. Take a backup of the database and propagate it on the master KDC server.

10. Create a stash file on each slave KDC server.

11. Start the KDC daemon on each KDC slave server.

After you configure the master and slave KDC servers, you need to configure the SEAM clients. A SEAM client is any host, excluding the KDC servers, on the network that needs to use the SEAM services. You need to install the SEAM client software on the system before you can configure the SEAM client. (It is usually installed by default.)

To configure a SEAM client, follow these steps:

1. Edit the Kerberos configuration file, `/etc/krb/krb5.conf`, and change the realm and server names.

2. Create a user principal in the KDC database.

3. Create a root principal.

4. Create an entry in the `/etc/krb5/warn.conf` file to warn users about Kerberos ticket expiration limits if desired.

After you configure the master and slave KDC servers and the SEAM client, you can start sending requests to the KDC server to execute commands on remote servers. On exit, Kerberos deletes the tickets. However, if required, you can also create, view, and delete tickets.

To create a ticket when the existing ticket has expired, follow these steps:

1. Enter the `kinit` command.
   ```
   # /usr/bin/kinit
   ```

2. Enter your password when `kinit` prompts you for it. You can use various options with the `kinit` command to create a ticket that suits your requirements. For example, you can use the ñ1 option to specify a time limit for the ticket, or the `-f` option to forward the ticket to yourself.

To view a ticket, enter the `klist` command with the -f option.

```
# /usr/bin/klist -f
```

Table 25.1 shows the most important symbols and the attributes they represent for a ticket.

TABLE 25.1   SYMBOLS AND ATTRIBUTES FOR A TICKET

Symbols	Attributes
f	Forwardable
F	Forwarded
d	Postdateable
D	Postdated
R	Renewable

To destroy tickets on a system, use the `kdestroy` command.

```
# /usr/bin/kdestroy
```

NOTE

The `kdestroy` command destroys all your tickets on the system. This command is useful when you need to leave your system unattended and do not want an unauthorized person to steal the tickets.

USING KERBEROS WITH SOLARIS 9

Kerberos is a network authentication system developed at the Massachusetts Institute of Technology (MIT). Solaris OE versions 2.6, 7, and 8 have used Kerberos to secure network applications. Kerberos Version 5 is built into Solaris 9.

Kerberos enables administrators and users to conduct remote sessions securely. Strong authentication and encrypted data transfers enable network resources to be shared freely, without fear of unauthorized access to data and resources.

The Kerberos security architecture consists of the following concepts:

- A Key Distribution Center (KDC)
- A ticket
- A principal

When a client running Kerberos needs to connect to remote hosts and execute a command or transfer files, it sends a request to the Kerberos KDC, which issues a ticket after authenticating the identity. A ticket contains electronic information that identifies the client uniquely. In a Kerberos environment, any entity that has a unique identity is called a *principal*. A principal may be a username, a fully qualified domain name of the host, or a service, such as NFS.

In a typical setup, the KDC server also runs the Kerberos Administration daemon, which controls commands such as adding and deleting principals from the Kerberos database. The KDC server, the admin system, and the Kerberos database are all usually kept on one machine.

When you initialize the Kerberos database for the first time, you need to run the `kdb5_util` command, which gives you the option of creating a stash file. The stash file is a duplicate of the master key that is generated from the master password that you enter while creating the KDC database. Although keeping a local stash file may compromise system security, it can be retained if the system is reasonably secure. The stash file allows you the convenience of not having to provide a password manually every time the `krb5kdc` process is started.

The configuration information for the KDC and the Kerberos administration daemons resides in the `/etc/krb5/kdc.conf` file. This file describes the locations of various files and ports that the KDC and the administration daemon will use. Although changing the parameters in the `kdc.conf` file does not result in any enhancement in security, you can adjust some parameters to enhance security. Table 25.2 briefly describes some of the important adjustable parameters in the `kdc.conf` file.

TABLE 25.2 ADJUSTABLE PARAMETERS IN THE *kdc.conf* FILE

Parameter	Description
kdc_ports	Defines the ports on which the KDC listens to receive requests. The standard port for Kerberos V5 is 88, although Solaris 9 listens on port 750 for compatibility with earlier versions of Kerberos.
max_life	Defines the maximum life of a ticket issued by the Kerberos KDC. The default life of a ticket is 8 hours.
supported_enctypes	Defines the encryption types supported by the KDC. Currently, SEAM supports only des-cbc-crc:normal encryption types.
dict_file	Defines the location of a dictionary file, which contains strings not allowed as passwords. You can modify the parameter to specify trivial passwords that the system will reject.

NOTE

You can find a complete list of the parameters in the `kdc.conf` file in the `kdc.conf(4)` man page at `http://docs.sun.com`.

SETTING ADMINISTRATIVE ACCESS CONTROLS

You can specify precise functions and access rights to each administrator in the Kerberos environment. You can specify different access rights to the system by using the ACL file, which resides in the /etc/krb5 directory. The syntax for the ACL file allows wildcard assignment of the principal names, saving you the trouble of listing each administrator in the ACL file. You can modify the privileges for each administrator in the ACL file, allowing them only the permitted access level. For example, you can specify a parameter that enables an administrator to modify the principals or policies in the KDC database.

After the ACL files are set up, you need to add the actual administrator principals to the database. You should take care to assign two separate principals to each administrative user. This means that the administrator will use the /admin principal only when executing administrator commands. This prevents possible misuse of the administrator login when the user leaves a workstation unattended.

SYNCHRONIZING SERVER CLOCKS

It is essential that you synchronize the internal clocks of all the nodes in the Kerberos environment. This allows the clients and the servers in the network to authenticate a request within a specified time limit. For example, if a client has its internal clock set outside the configured time limit of the other machines in the network, it will be impossible for the client to acquire a TGT from a server.

You should also ensure that the clock synchronization operation is handled in a secure manner. The safest way to synchronize the internal clocks is by using the Network Time Protocol (NTP). Solaris 9 comes installed with the NTP client and server software. However, the NTP infrastructure also needs to be secured before you synchronize the internal clocks.

KERBEROS OPTIONS

All Kerberos applications use the information in the /etc/krb5/krb5.conf file to determine the server and realm with which they are communicating. The krb5.conf file contains an appdefaults section that defines parameters controlling Kerberos client tools. Although the various Kerberos applications use the same options, the options may be tailored to meet the requirements for each client. The following true/false options are the same for all Kerberos client applications:

- **renewable [true/false]**—Renews a TGT that has not yet expired. Setting the value to True means that the TGT can be renewed by the user to the maximum lifetime the system allows.

- **forwardable [true/false]** —The system can issue forwardable TGTs to users. Setting the value to True means that the local TGT can be forwarded to Kerberized network services and can be used to access Kerberos services without re-authentication.

- **forward [true/false]**—The system can forward a copy of the TGT to the remote server after authenticating it.

- **encrypt [true/false]**—The system encrypts all data passing between the client and the remote server.

KERBEROS CLIENT APPLICATIONS

As mentioned earlier, the different Kerberos client applications use the options set in the `krb5.conf` file. The following list discusses the configuration of the different client applications in the Kerberos environment.

- **kinit**—Each principal is authenticated by a Kerberos system that uses an authentication ticket. To obtain this ticket, you need to use the `kinit` command. This command provides an initial ticket-granting ticket and puts it in the ticket cache. To run the `kinit` utility in an interactive mode, you need to use the u command without specifying options. In this case, `kinit` prompts you to enter the principal name and password. The `kinit` command uses the details you provide to authenticate your login with the Kerberos server. On authentication, an initial ticket-granting ticket is retrieved and stored in the default file location on the ticket cache. By default the `/tmp/krb5cc_uid` file maintains initial ticket-granting tickets. The tickets are maintained in the ticket cache for a specified time before being deleted. To know more about `kinit` command view the `kinit` main page.

- **telnet**—The Kerberos telnet client is controlled by various command line arguments. A user can use the -F and -f commands for the telnet client to forward a copy of the TGT that is used for authentication to a remote server. However, the telnet client continues to be connected to the remote server even after the ticket expires. To prevent this from becoming a threat to the system security, it is recommended that you reinitialize the telnet connection by manually disconnecting and requesting a fresh ticket for connecting to the remote server.

- **rlogin/rsh**—The rlogin and rsh clients in a Kerberos environment respond to the same commands as the non-Kerberized versions. However, they are similar to the Kerberos telnet client in the respect that they remain connected to the remote server even after the ticket expires. To prevent this from becoming a threat to the security of your system, remember to reinitialize the connection periodically.

- **rcp**—You can use the Kerberos rcp client to securely transfer data between systems. However, ensure that your system already has the TGT installed before you use the rcp encryption feature. To transfer encrypted data, you need to use the -x command line option in rcp; otherwise the data transfer will be non-Kerberized and insecure.

- **login**—The Kerberos login client (`login.krb5`) is different from the standard login daemon in Solaris OE. The Kerberos login client is forked from a successful authentication by the Kerberized telnet or rlogin daemons.

- **ftp**—The ftp client in the Kerberos environment uses GSS-API and the Kerberos V5 mechanism for securing data transmission. The ftp client takes only the -f and -m Kerberos-related command line options. You can set three protection levels for the Kerberos ftp client: clear, safe, and private, where clear is the lowest level of security with no encryption and private is the highest level of security.

GSS-API

Generic Security Standard Application Programming Interface (GSS-API) enables programmers to write applications that are not tailored for any particular security or transport protocol but use the security services provided by different security technologies. This generic nature enables the application to be portable and work with any security protocol. For example, you can use GSS-API to ensure secure data transfer between different applications within a network, regardless of the platform, security mechanism, or transport protocol.

Rather than enhance the security of a system, GSS-API provides a way to create applications that are independent of any particular security mechanism. You can consider GSS-API as a framework providing security services. By nature, GSS-API applications can support a range of security mechanisms and technologies, such as Kerberos or public key technologies.

GSS-API provides the following services:

- Creates a contextual relationship between two applications. This security context means that the applications that share a security context recognize each other and data transfer can take place between them.
- Applies different protection mechanisms to the data being transferred as required.
- Provides services such as data conversion, error-checking, and identity validation.

The preceding services provided by GSS-API mean that all applications created according to GSS-API provide integrity in data transfer. Even if data is received from a recognized application, the data could be corrupted. GSS-API allows a Message Integrity Tag (MIT) to be attached to transmitted data, which alerts you to any corruption of the data over transmission. In addition, if the underlying security mechanism enables data encryption, GSS-API enhances the security of the data transmission by making it harder for an unauthorized user to read it.

The current version of GSS-API works only with Kerberos V5. However, if you use the Remote Procedure Call (RPC) protocol to create the networking applications, you can use the RPCSEC_GSS layer on top of the GSS-API. RPCSEC_GSS provides all the functionalities of GSS-API, tailored to RPC.

25

ROLE-BASED ACCESS CONTROL (RBAC)

Role-Based Access Control (RBAC) is a solution for the concerns raised by the possibility of misuse of the root account. RBAC is based on the principle that no user should get more permission than is required to perform that person's job. In other words, it is a distributed privilege model. You can use RBAC to create separate roles for people with different needs and requirements from the system or set of systems over a network. You can retain the root access for only special cases, and create separate roles that permit access to only selected areas of the system. You can then allot these roles to users and administrators based on the requirements of their profiles.

In an RBAC environment, all users can log in to the system and assume special identities that enable them to run administration tools and utilities depending on their authorization levels. The RBAC model is based on the following three concepts:

- **Role**—An identity that is specified for users only.
- **Authorization**—Permission granted to a role or a user to perform a certain class of actions that the system policies otherwise do not permit.
- **Rights profile**—A packaged set of authorizations that you can assign to a role or a user. A rights profile may contain authorizations and supplementary rights profiles.

By default, the root user has access to all rights and authorizations, including the right to grant rights profiles to other users and administrators. However, there are certain applications, called privileged applications, which override the system settings. In addition, privileged applications check for authorizations or for specific UIDs or GIDs.

You create a role in almost the same way as you do a normal user account. You need to specify various details, such as group and password. All users with a particular role share the same home directory, operate in the same environment, and can access the same files. A system stores all the role information in four databases: **passwd**, **shadow**, **user_attrib**, and **audit_user**. However, a user cannot log in to a role directly. To start using the permissions in a role, a user first needs to log in with his or her user ID and password. When the user assumes the role, the attributes of the role replace the attributes of the user's profile.

Although Solaris is not shipped with predefined roles, you can assign a user one of the following rights profiles:

- **Primary administrator**—Can create roles that can perform administrative tasks, grant rights to others, edit administrative rights.
- **System administrator**—Can create roles that can perform most tasks, such as creating a new user and adding and installing packages, patches, and so on.
- **Operator**—Can create a role that can perform simple administrative tasks, such as backing up and restoring data.

RIGHTS PROFILES IN RBAC

Each rights profile in the RBAC environment has a help file associated with it, which is stored in the `/usr/lib/help/profiles/locale/C` directory. Some typical rights profiles in RBAC are the following:

- **All Rights**—This profile uses the wildcard to include all commands with no security attributes. Typically, the authorizations specified in rights profiles may not be enough to fulfill the requirements of the user. You add the wildcard command, *, at the end of explicitly stated commands in the rights profile.

- **Primary Administrator** —This profile is generally assigned to the most powerful role on the system. This effectively means that the role has control of the root. This profile carries the `solaris.*` authorization, which enables the user to execute all commands on the system. You should take care when assigning this profile to a role because this profile gives the user complete control over the system.

- **System Administrator** —This profile is meant specifically for the system administrator and does not enable you to add wildcard commands. This profile can carry authorizations that allow the user to execute discrete administration tasks, such as printer management, cron management, maintenance and repair, media backup, and software installation. In addition, the All Rights profile can be assigned as a supplementary right to this profile. Tasks associated with system security are not included in this profile.

- **Operator** —This profile carries authorizations only for general tasks, such as media backups and printer maintenance. If required, you can add the All Rights profile to the Operator profile.

- **Basic Solaris user rights profile** —This profile is assigned by default to all users on a system. It provides basic administration authorizations, such as read-only permissions for general resources and read and write permissions for personal resources.

SETTING UP RBAC

You can use SMC to set up RBAC to install a role, create a new rights profile, and add the rights profile to the role.

To install a role:

1. Log in as root and launch SMC.
2. Select the Users icon and double-click the Administrative Roles icon (Figure 25.5).
3. From the Actions menu, select the Add Administrative Roles option (Figure 25.6).

Figure 25.5
The Administrative
Roles icon in SMC.

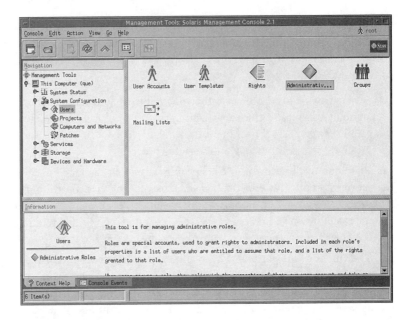

Figure 25.6
The Add
Administrative Roles
option in the Actions
menu.

25

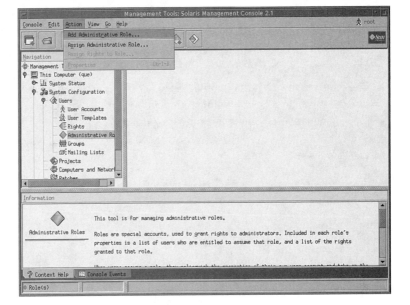

4. In the Step 1: Enter a Role Name dialog box, enter the abbreviated form of the role name and other identification information as shown in Figure 25.7 and click Next.

Figure 25.7
The Add Administrative Roles window in SMC.

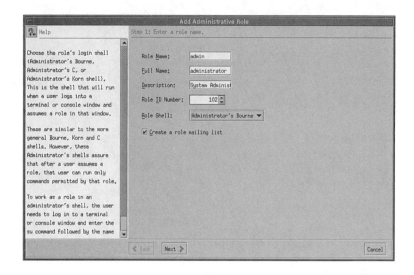

5. You can select a role shell from the choice of shells provided by the Role Shell drop-down. The choices include Bourne, C, and Korn Shells (Figure 25.8).

Figure 25.8
Choice of role shells from the Role Shell drop-down.

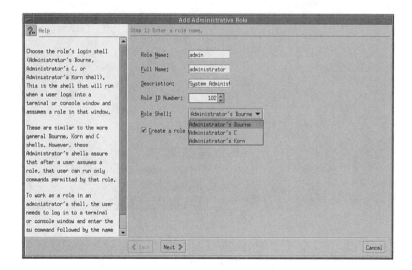

6. In the Step 2: Enter a Role Password dialog box, enter the role password, re-enter password for conformation, and click Next (Figure 25.9).

7. In the Step 3: Enter Role Rights dialog box, from the Available Rights column, select the rights profiles you want to add to the role and click Next (Figure 25.10) .

Figure 25.9
Setting role passwords.

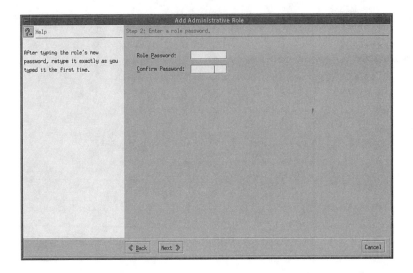

Figure 25.10
Setting role rights.

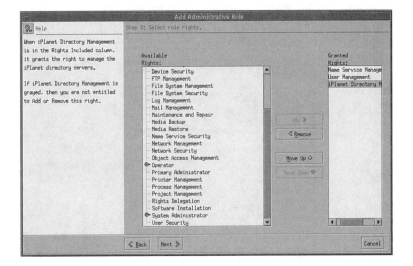

8. In the Step 4: Enter Home Directory dialog box, specify the server and the path for the home directory and click Next (Figure 25.11).

9. In the Step 5: Assign Users to This Role dialog box, enter the login names of the users you want to assign to this role and click Next (Figure 25.12).

Figure 25.11
Configuring home directory settings.

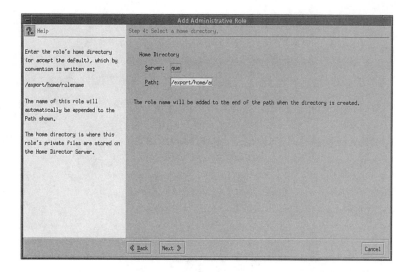

Figure 25.12
Assigning users to a role.

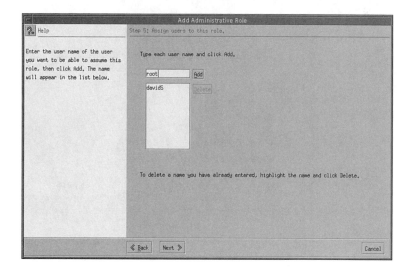

25

10. In the Review dialog box, check if the information is entered correctly and click Finish (Figure 25.13) .

11. The admin role is displayed in the View pane of Administrative Role (Figure 25.14) .

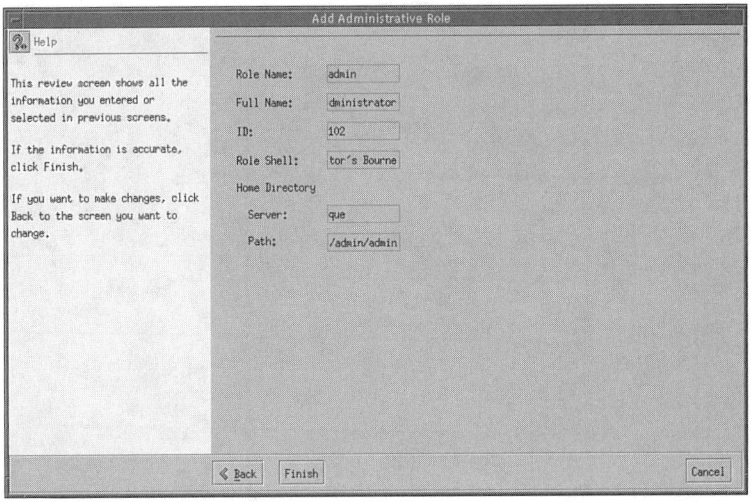

Figure 25.13
Reviewing the configuration settings.

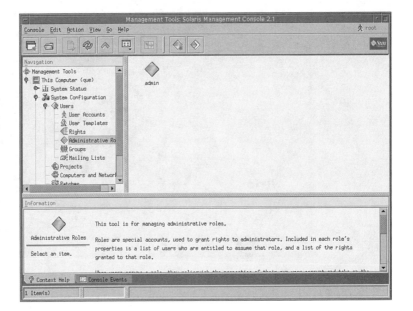

Figure 25.14
The newly created admin role.

The following procedure provides the steps to create a new rights profile called Name Admin. This profile sets EUID-0 for all commands in the /etc/init.d directory. This profile can be assigned to the System Administrator or Operator to start and stop system daemons.

To create a new rights profile, follow these steps:

1. In the SMC, select This Computer, System Configuration, Users, Rights icon (Figure 25.15).

Figure 25.15
The contents of the Rights icon displayed in the View pane.

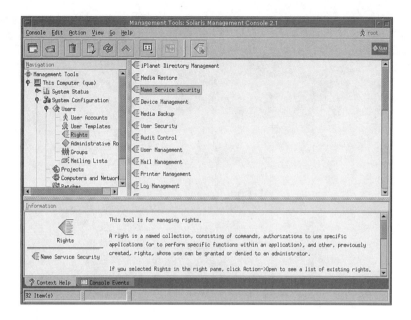

2. From the Action menu, select Add Right. The Add Right dialog box is displayed (Figure 25.16).

Figure 25.16
The Add Right option in the Actions menu.

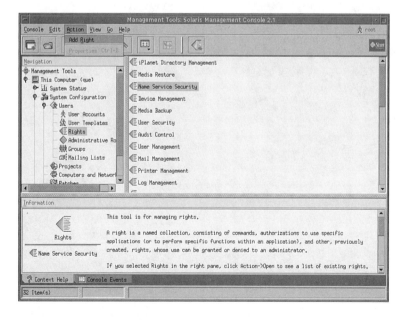

3. In the General tab, enter the name of the profile. In this example the profile is specified as Name Admin, the description as Name Service Administrator, and the name of the help file for the profile as usr/lib/profiles/name_admin.html.

Figure 25.17
Profile description in
the General tab.

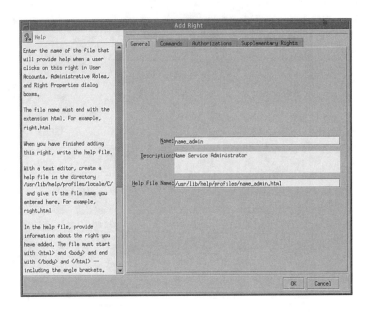

25

4. Click the Commands tab. The command assignment fields are displayed, as shown in
   Figure 25.18.

Figure 25.18
The Commands tab in
the Right Properties
dialog box.

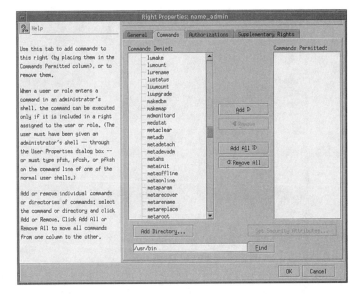

5. Click the Add Directory button, enter **/etc/init.d** in the displayed dialog box (Figure
   25.19), and click OK.

Figure 25.19
Specifying the directory location for the profile.

6. You need to specify the /etc/init.d directory and click the Add button between the two columns. The /etc/init.d directory and its contents are now added to the new profile in the right column (Figure 25.20).

Figure 25.20
Adding the required commands.

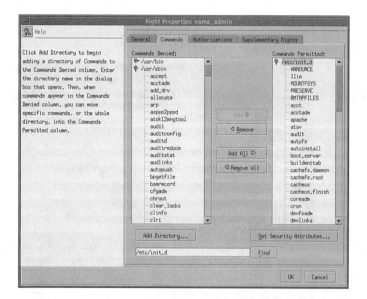

7. Select the /etc/init.d directory and click the Set Security Attributes button. The Set Security Attributes dialog box is displayed.

8. Select the Effective radio button.

9. Select the user from the User text box and group from the Group text box. Click Apply, and then click Close (Figure 25.21) .

10. In the Add Right dialog box, click OK. The name_admin profile is now available in the Rights tool of the Solaris Management Console (Figure 25.22) .

Figure 25.21
Selecting ownership attributes.

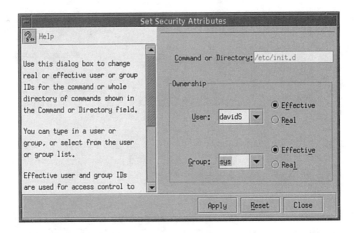

Figure 25.22
Completed profile settings displayed in the Rights View pane.

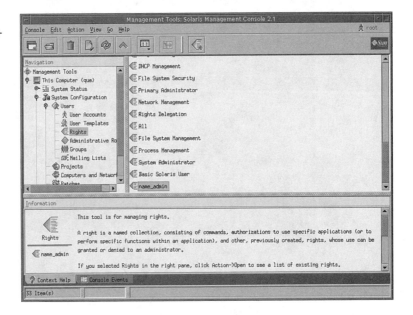

To add a rights profile to an existing role, follow these steps:

1. In the navigation pane of the SMC, click the Administrative Role icon. The Roles View pane on the right of the window displays the available existing roles. The admin role that you created is displayed (Figure 25.23) .

2. Double-click the admin role. The Role Properties dialog box is displayed.

3. Click the Rights tab. The rights selection fields are displayed (Figure 25.4).

Figure 25.23
The admin role is displayed in the Roles View pane.

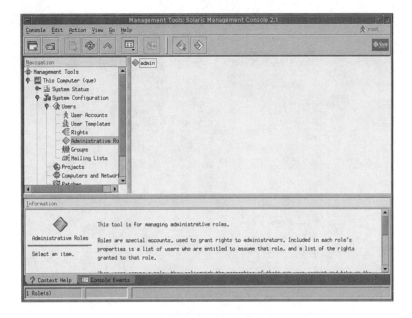

Figure 25.24
The rights for the admin role displayed in the Rights tab.

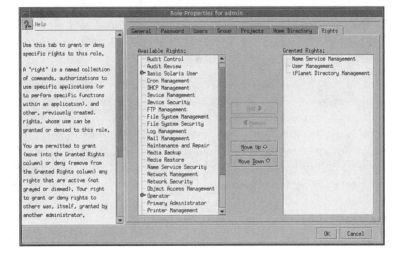

4. In the Available rights column, double-click on the profile you want to specify. In this example, FTP management is selected (Figure 25.25). The profile is assigned to the admin role. In the Role Properties dialog box, click OK.

Figure 25.25
Assigning profiles to the admin role.

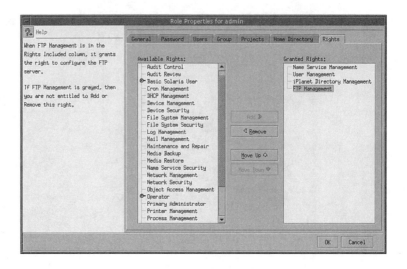

ASET

Solaris 9 has a built-in security administration tool called the Automated Security Enhancement Tool (ASET), which automates the tasks to monitor and control system security. This tool is especially helpful in tightening the file system security. You can specify three different security levels. At each higher level, the file system security is raised and access to the system is further restricted.

ASET uses the master files of the system for its configuration. All ASET files, master files, and reports reside in the /etc/aset directory. When you install the highest security level of ASET on a system, the automated tools analyze the system and attempt to correct all weak points in the system security. If the tools cannot fix the weaknesses, ASET reports the problem for further action manually. However, ASET utilizes system resources heavily and interferes with normal system activity when it is running. Therefore, ASET should typically be set up to run once every day or two, mostly at times when the load of the system is low.

ASET SECURITY LEVELS

You can specify three different security levels in ASET: low, medium, and high.

The low-level security ensures that standard release values are set for all system files. At this level, ASET performs security checks and reports security weakness. However, ASET does not take any automated corrective action to overcome any limitations it may detect. At the medium level, ASET restricts system access and modifies some settings of system files and parameters restricting system access to reduce the risks of security attacks. ASET reports all modifications it makes to the system settings. In addition, it reports weak points in security. At this level, ASET does not affect system services. With high-level security, ASET modifies the parameter settings for system files to the minimum access permission level.

A report is generated whenever ASET makes a modification to the system file or parameter settings. This report contains detailed information about the exact modification or weakness in the system security. You need to know the different tasks in ASET to properly understand the reports these tasks generate. You use the taskstat utility to determine the ASET tasks that are completed or are still running.

Table 25.3 provides a brief description of the various tasks of ASET.

TABLE 25.3 ASET TASKS

ASET Task	Description
Tuning the system file permissions.	This task sets the security levels that you set for system files. This task is run when you install ASET.
Checking system files	This task validates each system file and compares it with the description of that file in the master file, which is created when ASET first runs this task. This task examines system files on various parameters, such as owner, group, permissions, size, and checksum.
Checking users and groups	This task ensures that user accounts and groups are assigned in the passwd and group files. This task checks for various violations, such as duplicate names and IDs, entries in incorrect formats, and invalid logins. It also checks for NIS and NIS+ password files.
Checking system configuration files	This task ensures that ASET checks various system tables for different system configuration files, such as /etc/default/login and /.rhosts.
Checking environment variables	This task ensures that the PAST and UMASK environments are set correctly for root and other users. This task checks the /.ptrofile, /.login, and /.cshrc files.

CONFIGURING ASET

In most cases, the default configuration of ASET suffices and you do not need to configure or administer ASET. However, you can modify parameters in the configuration files to enhance the operation and security provided by ASET. You can modify the following configuration files to control the behavior of ASET tasks:

- /usr/aset/asetenv
- /usr/aset/masters/tune.low
- /usr/aset/masters/tune.med
- /usr/aset/masters/tune.high

The `asetenv` file is the environment file in ASET and contains a list of variables that influence the behavior of ASET tasks. The `asetenv` file has two sections: a section with configurable parameters and another with internal environment variables. You can modify the parameters in the configurable section to:

- **Choose the ASET tasks to be run**—All tasks in the ASET environment have a specific function and cover a specific area of the system security. Although it is recommended that you run all ASET tasks, you can choose which tasks to run.

- **Specify the directories for the checklist tasks**—The checklist environment variables verify the file attributes in the selected directories. You can specify the directories the task checks and the level of security that the task uses to check the directory. In the low security level, the `CKLISTPATH_LOW` variable specifies the directories to be checked. Similarly, the variables `CKLISTPATH_MED` and `CKLISTPATH_HIGH` function for the medium and high level security, respectively.

- **Schedule execution of ASET tasks**—You can schedule ASET tasks to run at scheduled times and for a specified period. When you start ASET, you can either start tasks interactively or use the ASET `-p` option to specify a schedule for them.

- **Specify an aliases file**—You use the `UID_ALIASES` variable to specify an aliases file that lists the shared user IDs on the system.

- **Extend checks to NIS+ tables**—You use the `YPCHECK` variable to specify whether ASET should check the system configuration file tables. Setting a false value for `YPCHECK` disables NIS+ table checking. For example, consider the situation when ASET checks the `passwd` file. When you set `YPCHECK` to True, the task checks the local `passwd` file and the NIS+ `passwd` file for the domain of the system. When set to False, the task checks only the local `passwd` file.

ASET uses three tune files to allow or restrict access to critical system files. These files are `tune.low`, `tune.med`, and `tune.high`. The `tune.low` file represents the lowest level of security, and `tune.high` represents the highest level of security. All three master tune files reside in the `/usr/aset/masters` directory.

To run ASET interactively:

1. Log in as root.

2. Use the `aset` command to run ASET interactively.
   ```
   # /usr/aset/aset -1 level -d pathname
   ```
   Here, `level` specifies the level of security and takes the values low, medium, and high. The `pathname` argument specifies the working directory for ASET.

3. Verify that ASET is running by looking at the ASET execution log displayed on the screen.

To run ASET periodically, follow these steps:

1. Use the PERIODIC_SCHEDULE variable to specify the time when you want ASET to run.

2. Specify the asset command as an entry in the crontab file.

   ```
   # /usr/asset/asset -p
   ```

   Here, -p inserts a line in the crontab file that starts ASET at the time scheduled by the PERIODIC_SCHEDULE variable in the /usr/aset/asetenv file.

3. View the crontab entry to verify the time when ASET will run.

   ```
   # crontab -1 root
   ```

TCP WRAPPERS

Most Unix systems use a daemon called inetd (or on Solaris, in.inetd) to respond to the incoming TCP/IP connections. The inetd daemon lies dormant until a request comes in. After a connection is established, the daemon starts the appropriate service and lies dormant again until the next request comes in. However, the standard inetd daemon does not provide access control.

You can use TCP wrappers to solve the restrictions of the inetd daemon. TCP wrappers are intermediate entities that lie between the client and the server. TCP wrappers act as servers until the client sending the request is authenticatedFor example, consider the following example where a client attempts to FTP a server.

Client---->FTP client---->inetd daemon---->FTP---->transfer files

In a case of a TCP wrapped server:

Client---->FTP client---->inetd daemon -> tcpd daemon---->FTP---->transfer files

In this way, the TCP wrappers prevent the a server's network services from being exposed to possible attacks and attempts to gain unauthorized entry. TCP wrappers intercept and filter all requests that come in for network services such as FINGER, FTP, TELNET, RLOGIN, and RSH.

TCP wrappers provide both access control and logging services to a system. They enable or restrict access, depending on the source and destination of the request. Assuming the access control lists enable a particular connection request, the TCP wrapper initiates a filter program before the requested server process is started. In addition, TCP wrappers log all successful and unsuccessful connection requests. All messages relating to connections are logged via the syslogd daemon.

To control access to TCP services when you use TCP wrappers, enable TCP wrappers by adding the following line in the /etc/default/inetd file.

ENABLE_TCPWRAPPERS=YES

After enabling TCP wrappers, kill and restart the inetd daemon. Finally, configure TCP wrappers by following these steps:

25

1. To enable users to log in over TCP connections, you need to log in as root.

2. Open the etc/default/inetd file to modify the following line:
   ENABLE_CONNECTION_LOGGING=YES

3. Finally, you need to kill the inetd deamon before restarting it.

USING TCP WRAPPERS TO PREVENT IP SPOOFING ATTACKS AND FOR EARLY WARNING

To validate a connection's authenticity, TCP wrappers check the IP addresses of each incoming request against the IP addresses permitted in the configuration files. However, it is possible for an unauthorized person to fake an IP address. To prevent such access, TCP wrappers look up the hostname for each IP address and then perform a reverse lookup by identifying the IP address for the hostname. The connection is denied access if the two IP addresses do not match. In some cases where the host does not allow reverse lookups, the connection is denied even though the host may be valid. This TCP wrapper mode is called PARANOID. It is an optional mode that you can disable at compile time.

You also can use TCP wrappers to give you an early warning of an attack on your system. To do this, you need to enable those network services that are not configured on your system. Then you need to set the configuration files to deny access to all requests for these newly configured services. When a client requests these services, the tpcd daemon denies the request but logs it. This allows you to look up the IP address that is trying to request access into the system. Although the remote system may move on to more sophisticated methods of attack, trapping the IP address may give you time to harden your system or reduce exposure by shutting down non-essential network services.

To further ensure security, you should make periodic backups of your system and store them in a safe location. It is quite easy for skilled attackers to sneak into the system, make changes to the system files, and then access the system in any way they want. Ensuring that the system files retain the original rules helps maintain the security of the system.

IPSEC

The TCP/IP family of protocols is used to transfer data over the Internet. However, unauthorized people can intercept the data packets in TCP/IP transmissions. The IP Security Architecture (IPSec) protocol suite was designed by the Internet Engineering Task Force (IETF) to overcome the security threats in TCP/IP networks.

IPSec is essentially a set of extensions to the IP protocol. IPSec supports authentication, integrity, access control, and confidentiality of data packets at the network layer. IPSec is an ideal network security measure because of the various advantages it offers. For example, if an organization implements security at the IP level by using the IPSec suite, it ensures security for all applications, whether or not those applications have a built-in network security mechanism. The primary advantages of IPSec are as follows:

- In IPSec, encryption and authentication take place in the TCP/IP stack. This eliminates the need to modify applications to have a security mechanism.

- IPSec is interoperable with products from different vendors.

- IPSec operates at Layer 3 of the OSI reference model. When you implement IPSec in end systems, upper-layer software is not impacted. This eliminates the need for any upgrades to the infrastructure.

- IPSec is transparent to the application, eliminating the need for manual commands.

IPSec Modes

You can use IPSec to encrypt either the data transfer from one system to another or the data passing through a specific portion of a network. You can deploy IPSec in the following two modes:

- **Tunnel mode**—You use the tunnel mode of IPSec to encrypt both the header and the data of a packet. The tunnel mode also protects the IP tunnel through which the packet is transmitted.

   You typically use the tunnel mode when at least one end of the communication channel is a router or firewall. The tunnel mode encrypts the IP tunnel, even in a case where there are multiple routes for the data to reach a destination. The tunnel mode uses two IP headers for each data packet: the inner IP header and outer IP header. Whereas the inner IP header specifies the final destination, the outer IP header specifies the immediate IPSec destination. The Authentication Header (AH) or Encapsulated Security Payload (ESP) headers appear between these two IP headers.

   In the tunnel mode, ESP protects only the inner IP header and the higher-layer protocol. However, AH protects the inner IP header, some portions of the outer IP header, and the higher-layer protocol.

- **Transport mode**—You use the transport mode of IPSec to transmit data between two systems. In the transport mode, IPSec encrypts only the data portion of the data packet and leaves the header portion untouched. The AH or ESP security protocol header lies between the IP header and the transport layer protocols, such as TCP or UDP. Whereas the transport mode ESP protects only higher-layer protocols, the transport mode AH protects some part of the IP header and also the higher-layer protocol. The transport mode does not require any extra IP header and is faster than the tunnel mode.

IPSec Security Protocols

IPSec provides network security by using the Authentication Header (AH) and the Encapsulated Security Payload (ESP) protocols. The AH protocol uses strong cryptographic checksums to provide authentication for packets. For example, if you send a packet with AH, a checksum operation at the receiving end confirms whether the packet has been tampered with. If the checksum operation is successful, it means that the recipient confirms that the packet originated from an expected peer and not an impersonator.

25

When you send a packet, the system applies a hash function to it and a Message Digest (MD) is created. The MD builds an AH, which is attached to the data packet. AH wraps the entire packet and ensures that it reaches the correct recipient without tampering. The recipient computes another hash function by hashing the packets. The recipient system then compares the two hash functions for authenticity. If the hash functions do not match, it means that the packet was tampered with in transit.

Table 25.4 describes the various fields in AH.

TABLE 25.4 AH FIELDS

Field	Description
Next Header	Indicates the higher-layer protocol, which can be IP, TCP, or UDP.
Length	Indicates the length of the AH protocol header. The length of the AH header varies depending upon the hash algorithm used.
Security Parameter Index (SPI)	Identifies the AH security association, which is a security standard for data transmission, with the help of the destination IP address.
Sequence number	Represents the anti-replay sequence number.
Authentication data	Contains the integrity check value.

In IPSec, AH does not encrypt the data packets. AH simply wraps the clear text during transmission. To encrypt the data packets, IPSec uses ESP. ESP provides authentication, integrity, replay protection, and confidentiality of the data during transmission.

ESP uses encryption algorithms to provide a confidentiality guarantee for data packets during transmission. If a data packet with ESP is received and successfully decrypted, it means that the packet was not intercepted in transmission. The level of protection of the data packet depends on the strength of the encryption algorithm. By default, ESP uses the 56-bit Data Encryption Standard (DES).

ESP includes both a header and a trailer. Apart from encrypting data packets, ESP also encrypts a part of the header and trailer. Table 25.5 describes the fields of an ESP header.

TABLE 25.5 ESP HEADER FIELDS

Field	Description
Security Parameter Index (SPI)	Identifies the AH security association with the help of the destination IP address.
Sequence number	Represents the anti-replay sequence number.

Table 25.6 describes the fields of an ESP trailer.

TABLE 25.6 ESP TRAILER FIELDS

Field	Description
Padding	Ensures that data to be encrypted is in multiples of the cryptographic block size. Also ensures that the next header comprises 32 bits.
Pad length	Specifies the size of the padding field.
Next Header	Indicates the higher-layer protocol, which can be IP, TCP, or UDP.
Authentication data	Contains the integrity check value.

Both AH and ESP provide a service called Security Association (SA). SA is a security standard for network traffic between two computers and specifies how data should be protected during transmission.

Now, have a look at how communication happens between two systems that use IPsec. The communication is completed in two phases. In the first phase the packet is transmitted from the system and in the second phase the packet is received from a system.

When a packet is transmitted from a system, the IPSec completes a number of tasks. This is the phase one process and is called the outbound process. The following list describes the steps in the outbound process.

1. IP determines the destination addresses for the outbound packet and routes the packet.
2. If ESP must be applied, the packet is protected with ESP. If ESP is not required, the packet is checked to see whether AH is required.
3. If AH is required, the packet is protected with AH.
4. If AH is not required, the packet is checked to see whether it should be encapsulated for ESP tunnel-mode. If the tunnel mode is adopted for transmission, the packet is further protected within the IP datagram.
5. The packet is transmitted to the destination computer.

On receipt of the packet from the other system, an inbound process takes place. The following list describes the steps in the inbound process:

1. The existence of AH in the packet is verified. If AH is present, AH is processed and the packet is marked as AH protected.
2. If AH is not present in the packet, the existence of ESP is verified. If ESP is present, it is processed and the packet is marked as ESP-protected.
3. The destination address is verified and delivered to the user.

To secure traffic between systems, you need to specify IPsec parameters in the following files:

- The /etc/inet/ipnodes file contains the IP addresses and host names for the other system.

- The /etc/inet/ipsecinit file contains the IP security policy.

- The /etc/inet/secret/ipseckeys file contains a pair of security associations between the two systems.

The following syntax depicts how to add security association between two hosts:

```
add ah spi random-number dst local-system authalg an_algorithm_name \
    authkey random-hex-string-of-algorithm-specified-length
add ah spi random-number dst remote-system authalg an_algorithm_name \
    authkey random-hex-string-of-algorithm-specified-length
```

After you have made relevant edits to the files, reboot each system.

When the systems reboot, the /etc/inet/secret/ipseckeys file is read. Note that when you change the keys, ensure that they are changed in both systems. Safeguard the key files from unauthorized access and copying. After you configure IPsec, use ping and traceroute to see that everything works as it should.

INTERNET KEY EXCHANGE (IKE)

25

Internet Key Exchange (IKE) is a key management protocol that is used in conjunction with the IPSec standard. It is not mandatory to implement IPSec with IKE. However, IKE enhances IPsec by providing additional features.

IKE is a hybrid protocol, which implements Oakley and Skeme key exchanges inside the Internet Security Association and Key Management Protocol (ISAKMP) framework. The ISAKMP defines a mechanism of implementing the key exchange protocol, which defines how to derive the authenticated keying material, whereas Skeme provides for secure and fast key refreshment.

NOTE

> Keying material is the data, such as keys and certificates, that is required to establish and maintain cryptographic keying relationships.

IKE negotiates IPSec security associations automatically, which enables IPSec communication to be more secure and cost effective. Some of the advantages of implementing IPSec in conjunction with IKE include the following:

- You do not need to manually specify any of the IPsec security parameter in crypto maps, neither at the initiator node nor at the destination node.

NOTE

> Crypto maps are designed to combine the information required to establish general security associations. The initiator node is the host that initiates a connection, and the destination node is the host to which the initiator node requests the connection.

- You can modify encryption keys even during an IPSec session.
- Allows peers to be authenticated dynamically.

THE `in.iked` DAEMON

Automated key management is required to establish security associations. In Solaris, the `in.iked` daemon uses the IKE protocol to perform this task. The daemon implements IKE authentication and encryption. To implement authentication, `in.iked` uses pre-shared keys or signatures in the AH. The signatures used by `in.iked` include DSS, RSA, or RSA encryption. The `in.ked` daemon also uses cipher-based signatures, such as DES, Blowfish, or 3DES, and hash-based signatures, such as HMAC-MD5 and HMAC-SHA-1, to implement authentication.

To implement encryption, `in.iked` uses the Diffie-Hellman key derivations. Diffie-Hellman is an encryption algorithm that uses a 768-, 1024-, or 1536-bit public key to encrypt data. However, `in.iked` manages the encryption of authentication data alone. If you use the `/etc/inet/ike/config` file to configure the daemon, it is started at boot and waits for any IKE request from network users. The `in.iked` daemon uses the `ikeadm` and `ikecert` utilities to implement IKE administration and diagnosis. You will learn about these utilities in the later part of this section. Currently, IKE can be implemented for IPv4 only.

NOTE

> The `/etc/inet/ike/config` file contains a site's rules for matching inbound IKE requests and preparing outbound IKE requests.

25

Take a scenario where two hosts, host A and host B, communicate with each other. If a packet must be sent from A to B, the existence of computer B's public key is verified in computer A's pre-shared key database. When the key is found, A uses B's public key to encrypt the packet and transmits the packet to B. On receipt, B uses its private key to decrypt the packet.

The `in.iked` daemon performs this key exchange in two phases. During phase 1 exchange, which is also called main mode, hosts or users use the public-key encryption methods to authenticate each other. After authentication, an ISAKMP security association (SA) is established. This SA acts as a secured tunnel for IKE that is used to negotiate keying material for IP packets. Only one SA is required because ISAKMP SA is bi-directional. Figure 25.26 describes phase 1 of the `in.iked` daemon's key exchange process.

You can implement IKE by using the `in.iked` daemon. IKE provides flexibility to administrators in how they want the keying material to be negotiated. To provide a negotiation specification, you can edit the `/etc/inet/ike/config` file. The configurable parameters in this file can be described as follows:

- The encryption algorithm that you want to use for IKE negotiation.
- The authentication mechanism that you want to use.
- The perfect forward secrecy that you want to use.

Figure 25.26
Phase 1 of the
`in.iked` key
exchange process.

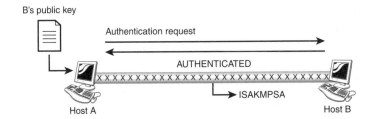

The two types of authentication methods, which are implemented in phase 1 IKE exchange process, are pre-shared keys and public key certificates.

> **NOTE**
>
> To know more about these two kinds of authentication methods, you can refer to PKI material available on the Web or PKI product documentation provided by vendors such as Entrust, iPlanet, or VeriSign.

During phase 2 of the IKE exchange process, which is also called quick mode, IKE creates and manages the IPSec SA between hosts running the IKE daemon. The tunnel created in the phase 1 exchange is used to protect the transmitted keying material. The IKE daemon uses the `/dev/random` device to generate keys. The keys generated are dynamic in nature. This means that when you use a randomly generated key to transmit a packet, and when the connection is refreshed, the next packet is assigned with a different key. The rate at which the connection can be refreshed is configurable.

ADMINISTERING IKE

Solaris provides various utilities to administer IKE. Some of these utilities, such as `in.iked`, `ikeadm`, and `ikecert` are described in the following list.

- **`in.iked`**—This is the Internet Key Exchange daemon. For hosts to be able to use IKE, this daemon should be running on all hosts. The daemon is started automatically when the system is booted, if the `/etc/inet/ike/config` file is available. You can also start the daemon from the command line by using the following command.

  `# /usr/lib/inet/in.iked`

- **`ikeadm`**—This command is used for viewing and modifying IKE policy. The command retrieves and alters `in.iked` configuration files. You can activate the `ikeadm` interactive mode if you use the `ikeadm` command without specifying arguments. The options available for the `ikeadm` interactive mode are specified in the following listing.

LISTING 25.1 *ikeadm* **OPTIONS**

```
# ikeadm
ikeadm> help
Valid commands and objects:
        get     debug|priv|stats|p1|rule|preshared [identifier]
        set     debug|priv level
```

```
add    rule|preshared {definition}|filename
del    p1|rule|preshared identifier
dump   p1|rule|preshared
flush  p1
read   rule|preshared [filename]
write  rule|preshared filename
help   [get|set|add|del|dump|flush|read|write|help]
exit   exit the program
quit   exit the program
ikeadm>
```

- **ikecert** —This command line utility helps you manage certificates. You can manipulate local public key certificate databases. For usage and supported arguments, refer to the ikecert man page.

IKE Configuration Files

Configuration files play an important part in implementing key exchange when you use IKE. You learned about the /etc/inet/ike/config file in the previous sections. Apart from this file, the other important IKE configuration files and directories that help you administer IKE are the following:

- **/etc/inet/ike/publickeys**—This directory contains the public part of the public-private key pair apart from the certificates. The default permission assigned to this directory is 0755. You need to use the ikecert certdb command to populate this directory.

- **/etc/inet/ike/ike.privatekeys** —As the name suggests, this directory contains the private key files that are part of a public-private key pair. The default permission for this directory is 0700. All private keys have corresponding public keys in the public key database. You need to use the ikecert certlocal command to populate this directory.

- **/etc/inet/ike/crl** —This directory contains the certification revocation list. Each file in this directory corresponds to a public certificate file in the /etc/inet/publickeys directory.

IKE configuration can be performed in different ways, depending on your requirements. You can configure IKE using

- Pre-shared keys
- Self-signed certificates
- Self-signed public certificates
- Public keys signed by a CA

For more information on setting up IKE, view the Sun documentation site at http://docs.sun.com.

25

FIREWALLS

Firewalls are among the most important tools in strengthening network security. A firewall performs two tasks. First, the firewall acts as a gateway for all the data traffic between two networks. Second, the firewall restricts network access for users without proper authentication and authorization. Typically, to access a network that is secured with a firewall, external users need to provide IDs and passwords to authenticate themselves.

You should consider the use of a firewall as a mandatory security feature for your network to protect it from attacks from external networks, such as the Internet. A firewall is effective even when there are multiple networks within a network. In this case, the firewall does not allow data transfer between two networks unless the firewall itself is the origin or the destination address.

There are many firewalls available, such as CheckPoint , Gaunlet, and SunScreen. There are also many free open source firewalls and firewall toolkits. Each firewall has its own advantages and disadvantages. You choose a product depending on your needs and organizational requirements. The following section discusses SunScreen Lite , which is available for free from Sun Microsystems. Readers who are new to firewalls may like to start with SunScreen because of its simple installation, configuration, and administration features.

SunScreen Lite is the lighter version of core SunScreen software. SunScreen Lite is a firewall for protecting individual servers and small work groups. If you have the Solaris 9 Software 2 of 2 CD-ROM, you can install SunScreen from the following location on the CD-ROM:

```
# cd /cdrom/cdrom0/Solaris_9/EA/products/SunScreen_3.1_Lite/
```

You can also download the SunScreen Lite software from
`http://www.sun.com/software/securenet/lite/download.html`.

SunScreen Lite provides various advantages for implementing security for the network at the host level. SunScreen Lite

- Provides basic packet filtering for networks.
- Can be used in virtual private networks (VPNs) and for secondary machines in a centralized management group.
- Provides remote administration facility through a Web browser.
- Uses Simple Key management for Internet Protocols (SKIP) for encryption, authentication, and access control.

For instructions on installing SunScreen Lite for a network, refer to the complete SunScreen Lite installation manual, available at
`http://docs.sun.com:80/ab2/coll.557.2/SSCRNLITEINST/`.

NOTE

> SunScreen Lite does not have a full set of features for network security and is not recommended for complete network security. For example, some of the disadvantages of SunScreen Lite are that it
>
> ■ Cannot support more than ten unregistered IP addresses that can be translated to registered addresses when you use network address translation (NAT).
>
> ■ Does not support stealth-mode operation.
>
> ■ Cannot support more than two routing interfaces.
>
> ■ Does not support proxies.
>
> For enterprise-level protection, it is recommended that you use the full version of SunScreen or another enterprise-class firewall.

The following sections look at four aspects of SunScreen:

■ SunScreen administration

■ SunScreen security considerations

■ SunScreen security policy

■ SunScreen proxies

SunScreen Administration

There are two basic components in SunScreen: a Screen and an Administration Station. You install a Screen at each location in the network that provides direct public access. A Screen protects a location from the external network by making it transparent and by routing the IP address. You use routers to do the routing. You can configure a multi-homed system to act as a router by enabling IP forwarding. Sunscreen protects your network from external attacks by enforcing security policies and denying access to connections initiated from anonymous or unknown hosts or networks. A Screen also provides filtering to all traffic going in and out of the network. You install the Administration Station to administer one or more Screens locally or remotely.

The number of Screens and Administration Stations in a network depends on the network topology and security requirement. For example, with a small network that requires local administration of Screens, you can install both the Screen and the Administration Station on a single machine. For a larger network, you can install multiple Screens on different machines, with the Administration Station on a separate machine for remote administration.

In Figure 25.27, a Screen separates the internal network from the external network (the Internet) and routes the traffic passing between the two networks. A remote Administration Station on the internal network administers the Screen, and another remote Administration Station on the external network administers the entire network from a remote location. Both Administration Stations are configured to use SKIP encryption to communicate with the Screen.

However, in a network with local administration, you do not need to encrypt the communication between the Administration Station and the Screens because they are all on the same host. Figure 25.27 describes how the Administration Station and the Screen are set up within in a network.

Figure 25.27
The Screen configuration.

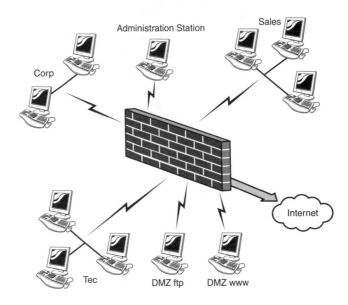

SETTING UP THE SUNSCREEN SCREEN

When you install a Screen on a network location, you must take care to place it so that all traffic between the internal and external network passes through the Screen. In addition, you must ensure that there is only a single path for the traffic to flow through. Multiple paths for traffic mean that some traffic can bypass the Screen and compromise the network security. Figure 25.28 shows how a Screen divides a network into several sub-networks.

Figure 25.28
The Screen divides a network into several sub-networks.

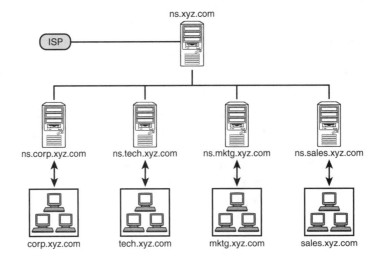

Even when a Screen separates the internal network from the external network (Internet), you can specify areas within the internal network as demilitarized zones (DMZs). You can set up public access services on each DMZ. This allows your network to function and provide access to external entities. The Screen ensures that the network continues to function even if the security of one or more DMZs is compromised.

SECURITY CONSIDERATIONS

When you install SunScreen, it divides each portion of your network into distinct areas, each of which can be considered as a network within a network. Each network uses a different interface to screen itself from the others, and you can specify filtering rules for each interface.

You can specify both routing-mode and stealth-mode filtering with SunScreen. In the routing mode, each network has a different interface with a unique IP address. Each network uses TCP to access the proxy servers.

In the stealth mode, each network is partitioned and you cannot subnet a network to another existing network. In the stealth mode, network interfaces do not have IP addresses, and they bridge the mac layer. In addition, you need to configure one interface as an administration interface to allow remote administration of all Screens.

Figure 25.29 describes a single network that is divided into multiple areas. In this figure, Network A is screened from the other networks. Connectivity between Network A and the rest of the networks is provided over the Internet.

25

Figure 25.29
Connectivity between networks is established.

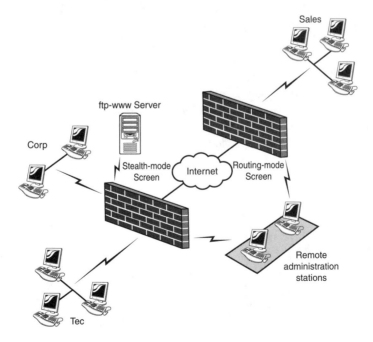

You use three graphical user interfaces (GUIs) in SunScreen and SunScreen SKIP:

- SunScreen installation wizard
- SunScreen administration GUI
- SunScreen SKIP skiptool GUI

You use the installation wizard to configure the network interface Screen in the routing mode or in stealth mode. After installation, you use the administration GUI to administer the Screen either on the local machine or from a remote system, which may be located in another network. The administration GUI enables you to administer both single Screens and Screens installed on high availability (HA) clusters locally or remotely.

NOTE

An HA cluster is a set of systems with identical configuration and data. They are used to provide a failover mechanism to enhance reliability.

SunScreen Security Policy

A primary aspect governing the installation and configuration of a firewall is the security policy, which defines the use of various means to secure a network. When you install the SunScreen software on a network, a security policy called Initial is installed by default. This policy takes into account various data objects in the network. Data objects include entities such as addresses, services, interface certificates, filtering rules, and administration access rules.

The SunScreen security policy allows the Screens in a network to implement dynamic packet filtering. Dynamic packet filtering enables a Screen to filter the traffic based on security policy rules. The security policy defines a series of policy rules that specify which services are to be allowed through the Screen, what is to be done with packets for services that are not allowed, and what is to be done when packets are dropped. You can organize the policy rules in sequence to specify priorities. For example, the security policy defines whether a Screen should allow packets to pass based on the information contained in each data packet and the state retained from previous events.

Using SunScreen with Network Address Translation

You can combine the advantages of a firewall and network address translation (NAT) to enhance your network's security. When you set up NAT with SunScreen, NAT modifies the address fields in the data packets as they pass through the Screens. In addition, NAT also modifies the checksum and sequence number fields in the packets.

You can use NAT to make a Screen translate one set of addresses to another set. For example, you can use NAT to hide the internal topology of a network by translating the private addresses within the network to a set of registered public addresses. To an external entity, it appears that all traffic originates from the public address, and not from the private addresses. In fact, most companies manage to get only one or two usable addresses registered. NAT enables these companies to optimize the registered addresses and route all traffic through these addresses.

SunScreen and Logging

Logging traffic through SunScreen enables you to identify possible attacks on your network's security. In addition, logging can also help to indicate a problem with the configuration or the administration of the network.

When you install SunScreen on a network, each Screen logs all the incoming and outgoing traffic through it. However, in an HA cluster only the active Screen logs the incoming and outgoing traffic. The passive Screens log only the incoming traffic that is specifically routed to it.

You can configure SunScreen to log packets when they match or do not match a particular rule. The rule you specify controls whether a packet should be dropped or logged and what information should be recorded.

SunScreen and Proxies

You use proxies on a firewall to filter specific content in the incoming or outgoing traffic and to provide authentication. For example, you can specify the proxy to block all traffic with VB Script attachments, a common source of virus infections.

You can set up proxies for FTP, HTTP, SMTP, and Telnet protocols in a SunScreen environment. You do not need to install any additional software to set up these proxies. You can specify a security policy and activate it to apply to all proxies on your firewall. Because proxies share common objects and policy rules, you can specify filtering rules, as well as valid and invalid sources and destinations of packets for all proxies on your firewall. However, each proxy has different filtering capabilities and requirements and may or may not follow all the rules you specify in the security policy.

Logging In to SunScreen Lite

After you install SunScreen on a machine, you need to monitor the logs for signs of any unauthorized entry. However, before you start using the firewall, you need to specify the depth of logging. For example, if you choose to log a large number of variables, you may not have enough time to scan the logs for intrusion attempts. Conversely, choosing too little to log may not give you enough information to warn you against an intrusion attempt.

Choosing the appropriate level of logging is an iterative task. You need to specify a logging policy, check whether it needs your requirements, and update it if modifications are required. Table 25.7 describes the four different types of logging that you can specify for SunScreen Lite.

25

TABLE 25.7 SUNSCREEN LITE LOGGING TYPES

Log Type	Description
LOG_NONE	SunScreen does not log anything.
LOG_SUMMARY	SunScreen logs only the first 40 bytes of a data packet.
LOG_DETAIL	SunScreen logs the entire data packet.
LOG_SESSION	SunScreen logs the source and destination addresses and ports, amount of data transferred in each direction, and the session length.

To display the log of SunScreen Lite, use the following commands:

```
ssadm log get > /tmp/sunscreen.log
# ssadm logdump -i /tmp/sunscreen.log
```

If you want to display only the packets that were dropped, use the following command:

```
# ssadm logdump -i /tmp/sunscreen.log logwhy 256
```

In the preceding command, the logwhy option enables you to configure the logs to filter the packet descriptions. Table 25.8 describes the most commonly used why codes.

TABLE 25.8 COMMONLY USED why CODES

Number	Log Error Message	Description
1	Passed Packet Logged	The packet was passed by a rule that specified that the packet should be logged.
256	Denied or No Pass Rule Found	The packet was dropped because it did not match any rule.
257	No Connection	The packet was dropped because of missing state information.
260	Invalid Port	The packet was dropped because of invalid port number specification.
272	Bad Source Address	The source address of the packet was invalid for the network interface.

Often the log size can increase to unmanageable levels because the log includes variables that you do not need to monitor. For example, if you have a Microsoft Windows system on the same subnet as the firewall host, the firewall logs will display multiple NetBIOS packets. You can hide these packets by using the following command:

```
edit> add ADDRESS dmz-bc HOST abc.abc.abc.abc COMMENT "DMZ broadcast address"
edit> insert rule 6 netbios * dmz-bc DENY COMMENT "Silently drop netbios"
```

You can also specify a rule that drops the denied packets without logging them. To specify such a rule, you first need to create a group that includes all the services that the logs are to silently deny. For this, use the following command:

```
edit> add service not-logged GROUP netbios
edit> replace rule 7 not-logged * * DENY COMMENT "Deny without logging"
```

Finally, you need to add a "tripwire rule" to the logs to alert you in case of an intrusion attempt. For example, consider a network where the SunScreen host machine is in a DMZ and provides access to both the internal and the external networks. The network is configured such that there is no Telnet traffic from any system in the DMZ to the host. You can add a rule to identify any Telnet traffic originating from any system and directed toward the host. If any unauthorized user tries to Telnet the host, the rule alerts the Administration Station. To specify a tripwire rule for Telnet, use the following command:

```
edit> delete screen nsgweb
edit> add screen nsgweb CDP SNMP abc.abc.abc.abc
edit> insert rule 7 telnet dmz nsgweb DENY LOG DETAIL SNMP COMMENT[ic:ccc}
"tripwire rule for telnet"
edit> list rules
```

DISABLING AND UNINSTALLING SUNSCREEN

Sometimes SunScreen is not installed properly and you may need to disable the software to diagnose the problems in the network. To disable the SunScreen software, use the following commands:

```
# mv /etc/opt/SUNWicg/SunScreen/.active /etc/opt/SUNWicg/SunScreen/.not-active
# init 6
```

When you run the `disable` command for SunScreen, the Solaris OE passes the data packets directly from the network interface to the IP stack. You can scan the system logs when the system is in this state to identify any misconfiguration or missing rule. After the system diagnosis is complete, you can enable SunScreen by renaming the `.not-active` file to `.active` and rebooting the system.

To uninstall the SunScreen software from your system, you run the uninstall program by using the following command:

```
# cd /var/sadm/prod
# java uninstall_SunScreen_3_1 -nodisplay
```

If you want to remove the SunScreen configuration files and log files also, you need to delete the directories in which these files are stored. To delete these directories, use the following command:

```
# rm -rf /etc/opt/SUNWicg /etc/skip /var/opt/SUNWicg
```

FIREWALL-1

FireWall-1 is a scalable firewall that enables you to integrate and centrally manage all elements of network security. FireWall-1 is based on the concept of a single security policy for the entire enterprise and all access nodes use the same rules to filter traffic passing through the network. It is available from CheckPoint Technologies at `http://www.checkpoint.com`.

SUMMARY

Corporate networks and data centers have to contend with the threat of attacks on networks, theft of data, and damage to critical services and applications on a 24×7 basis. Although you can secure a network by using advanced security mechanisms and products, measures to overcome such security problems are also available as free and/or open source software.

The challenge for the system administrator is to always keep a step ahead of the attempts to compromise system and network security and the integrity of stored data. In this chapter, you learned how to implement various security protocols and mechanisms to secure Solaris 9 systems.

25

CHAPTER **26**

PERFORMANCE MONITORING

In this chapter

An Overview of Performance Monitoring   490

Monitoring CPU Usage   490

Monitoring Virtual Memory   493

Monitoring Disk Utilization   499

Monitoring Network Activity   501

Using sar to Monitor Systems   505

Using the Solaris Management Console (SMC) for Performance Monitoring   508

Summary   513

AN OVERVIEW OF PERFORMANCE MONITORING

Monitoring system performance is one of the important tasks an administrator performs. A system's performance state includes issues such as CPU usage, virtual memory performance, hard disk utilization, and network activity. By monitoring performance, you can identify bottlenecks or problem areas that must be handled immediately. Performance monitoring also enables you to avoid potential problems, which can lead to downtime.

When analyzing system performance, administrators typically look out for issues such as high load on the system, CPU overrun, virtual memory shortage, swap space, and lack of disk space. Solaris 9 OE provides several performance monitoring tools, which help in analyzing performance statistics of various system components. This chapter deals with the performance monitoring tools in Solaris.

MONITORING CPU USAGE

By monitoring CPU usage, you can identify the reasons for a system's slow performance. You can monitor CPU usage by using CPU counters, such as Idle, System, User, Nice, and so on. Solaris provides commands, such as mpstat and prstat, that you can use to obtain performance reports related to CPU usage. Performance reports generated by these commands provide information on processor faults, interrupts, context switches, locks, and the current state of a process. This section discusses the commands, methods of using these commands, and the output provided by these commands.

THE mpstat COMMAND

The mpstat command provides performance reports on processor activity. Reports are presented in the form of rows and columns, with the first column providing processor activity information for a period, known as an *interval*, that extends from boot up to a specific time. For subsequent intervals, all events occurring for each second in an interval are recorded and generated as a table.

You can use a variety of options with the mpstat command to obtain the required statistical information. Table 26.1 describes the various options used with mpstat.

TABLE 26.1 OPTIONS USED WITH THE *mpstat* COMMAND

Options	Description
-a	This option is used to obtain aggregate information on a set of processors in a CPU. By default, the output provided when you use this option is sorted by the unique CPU ID of each processor in the system.
-p	This option is used to identify the processor set membership in a CPU. By default, the report is sorted by the CPU number.
-P <set>	This option is used to retrieve information on the processor set specified with the <set> parameter.

26

Options	Description
Interval	This option is used to specify the time interval between each performance report. You need to specify this option in terms of seconds.
Count	This option is used to indicate that only count reports must be generated.

The syntax for using this command, as well as a sample command output with the -p option, is described in Listing 26.1:

LISTING 26.1 THE *mpstat* COMMAND OUTPUT

```
mpstat [-a] [-p | -P processor_set] [interval [count]]
# mpstat 3 5
CPU minf mjf xcal  intr ithr  csw icsw migr smtx  srw syscl  usr sys  wt idl
  0    1   0    0   288  188  306    1    0    0    0   197    0   0    0 100
  0    3  16    0   406  306  379   18    0    0    0  2471    5  10   19  66
  0    1   0    0   318  218  335   17    0    0    0  2240    3   9    0  87
  0    0   0    0   319  219  333   16    0    0    0  2220    4  11    0  86
  0    0  19    0   387  287  406   15    0    0    0  1803    4   6   29  61
#
```

In the command output, observe that the rows of the table are specified under specific columns, with each column indicating a particular performance condition. The mpstat utility reports the following issues:

- **CPU**—Indicates the CPU number for which performance statistics are generated.
- **minf**—Indicates that a minor fault has occurred during an interval.
- **mjf**—Indicates that a major fault has occurred during an interval.
- **xcal**—Provides information on the inter-processor cross-calls that have occurred during an interval.
- **intr**—Provides information on the processor interrupts that have occurred during an interval.
- **ithr**—Provides information on interrupts by representing interrupts as threads. This information does not count the CPU clock thread.
- **csw**—Provides information on the context switches that have occurred during an interval.
- **icsw**—Provides information on any involuntary context switches that occurred during an interval.
- **migr**—Provides information on any switch by a thread to another process. This event, known as *thread migration*, is recorded and reported in the table.
- **smtx**—Provides the number of times the CPU failed to acquire mutexes (lock not acquired on first try).

26

- **srw**—Records the number of times the CPU failed to obtain a read/write lock on the first try.

- **syscl**—Provides information on the number of system calls.

- **usr/sys/wt/idl**—Records the CPU percentages for user time, system time, wait time, and idle time.

THE prstat COMMAND

The prstat command provides a performance report on the active processes running in a system. You can format the output by grouping or ordering it based on an output mode. Performance reports can be organized based on a number of factors, such as the processor ID or user ID. A variety of options can be used with the prstat command. You can use multiple options separated by commas with the command. Table 26.2 describes the commonly used prstat command options.

TABLE 26.2   OPTIONS USED WITH THE prstat COMMAND

Options	Description
-a	This option generates reports with information on processes being used by specific users.
-k <tasklist>	This option generates reports for processes whose task IDs have been specified as a parameter.
-C psrsetlist	This option generates reports for a set of processors indicated by the processor set names in the <psrsetlist> parameter. The report provides information on the average load on each processor set.
-p pidlist	This option generates reports on processes indicated by a PID list. This list must be specified as comma-separated parameters for the option.
-P cpulist	This option generates reports on the recently executed processes in the CPU. Each CPU is specified by a comma-separated CPU ID list as parameters for the option
-u euidlist	This option is used to generate reports for processes identified with a particular user. The users are identified by an effective user ID, also known as an *euid*. The list of euids must be specified as a parameter for the option.
-U uidlist	This option is used to generate reports for processes identified with a particular user. The users are identified with a real user id (uid). The list of uids is specified as parameters for the option.

The prstat command provides a tabular output with columns describing the process ID, username, virtual memory size, state of a process, priority for the process, and so on. Listing 26.2 provides an example for using the prstat command:

26

LISTING 26.2   THE *prstat* COMMAND OUTPUT

```
  PID USERNAME   SIZE   RSS STATE   PRI NICE     TIME  CPU PROCESS/NLWP
 2346 root     1836K 1508K sleep    60    0  0:00:03 8.6% ls/1
 2345 root     2380K 1392K sleep    59    0  0:00:00 0.5% truss/2
  682 root       74M   23M sleep    59    0  0:07:38 0.3% java/33
 2349 root     4404K 4020K cpu0     59    0  0:00:00 0.1% prstat/1
 2317 root     2456K 1512K sleep    59    0  0:00:00 0.0% bash/1
  231 root     4092K 1660K sleep    59    0  0:00:00 0.0% nscd/25
  721 root     3092K 1012K sleep    59    0  0:00:00 0.0% remotedprovider/4
  716 root     3044K  128K sleep    59    0  0:00:00 0.0% remotedprovider/4
  258 root     1096K  324K sleep    59    0  0:00:00 0.0% utmpd/1
  275 root     2612K  860K sleep    59    0  0:00:00 0.0% vold/3
  245 root     1344K    0K sleep    59    0  0:00:00 0.0% powerd/2
  720 root     4184K  128K sleep    59    0  0:00:00 0.0% remotedprovider/4
  217 root     3148K  584K sleep    59    0  0:00:00 0.0% syslogd/11
  199 root     2156K    0K sleep    59    0  0:00:00 0.0% lockd/2
  202 daemon   2444K    0K sleep    59    0  0:00:00 0.0% statd/1
  PID USERNAME   SIZE   RSS STATE   PRI NICE     TIME  CPU PROCESS/NLWP
 2346 root     1836K 1508K run      45    0  0:00:03 8.9% ls/1
 2345 root     2380K 1392K sleep    59    0  0:00:00 0.5% truss/2
  682 root       74M   23M sleep    59    0  0:07:38 0.2% java/33
 2349 root     4404K 4020K cpu0     59    0  0:00:00 0.1% prstat/1
 2317 root     2456K 1512K sleep    59    0  0:00:00 0.0% bash/1
  231 root     4092K 1660K sleep    59    0  0:00:00 0.0% nscd/25
  721 root     3092K 1012K sleep    59    0  0:00:00 0.0% remotedprovider/4
  716 root     3044K  128K sleep    59    0  0:00:00 0.0% remotedprovider/4
  258 root     1096K  324K sleep    59    0  0:00:00 0.0% utmpd/1
  275 root     2612K  860K sleep    59    0  0:00:00 0.0% vold/3
  245 root     1344K    0K sleep    59    0  0:00:00 0.0% powerd/2
  720 root     4184K  128K sleep    59    0  0:00:00 0.0% remotedprovider/4
  217 root     3148K  584K sleep    59    0  0:00:00 0.0% syslogd/11
  199 root     2156K    0K sleep    59    0  0:00:00 0.0% lockd/2
```

26

MONITORING VIRTUAL MEMORY

It is always good to have as much virtual memory as possible. This helps in fast execution of programs and processes. Sometimes administrators might face the problem of systems going into a hang state, system performance degradation, or slow execution of applications. In such scenarios, checking the virtual memory statistics is recommended. There might be a severe RAM shortage or too much paging or swapping taking place.

NOTE

Paging ensures that the required data is made available to the executing program as quickly as possible. The operating system copies a certain number of pages from the storage device to the main memory (RAM). When the executing program requests a page that is not in the main memory, the operating system replaces one of the pages currently residing in the main memory with the requested page.

NOTE

> When an executing program requires more execution space than what is available in the main memory, the OS copies as much data as possible from the main memory to the disk. When the executing program requires data that is not available on the main memory, the leftover data (or the required segment of data) is copied into the main memory and the not-required segment of data is copied to disk. This process is called *swapping*.

You can use the vmstat, swap, and pmap commands to monitor virtual memory in Solaris. By monitoring virtual memory, you can identify performance bottlenecks. The following sections discuss the usage of virtual memory monitoring commands provided by Solaris OE.

THE vmstat COMMAND

The vmstat command generates reports on the state of virtual memory in a system. The information includes statistics on a number of system events related to virtual memory, such as paging, device interrupts, system calls, and CPU load. To obtain the required performance information, you need to use a number of options with the vmstat command. Table 26.3 describes some of the options used with the command.

TABLE 26.3   OPTIONS USED WITH THE *vmstat* COMMAND

Options	Description
time interval	This option is used to display virtual memory information between time intervals. The time interval is indicated as an integer that signifies the number of seconds between the intervals.
-s	This option is used to generate a report on the system events that have occurred from the last time the system was booted.
-S	This option is used to display information on the page swapping that has happened in the system. The output from this command provides the average number of processes swapped as indicated by the integer under the si field. In addition, the number of whole processes that were swapped is indicated under the si field.
-I	This option is used to indicate the number of interrupts that have occurred for each processor.

The output for the vmstat command includes information on processes, memory, page faults, and CPU usage. The following list describes the output obtained for the vmstat command.

- **memory**—The output for memory includes information on the available swap space and the free space in virtual memory indicated by the free list. Typically, information on the usage of real and virtual memory on the system can be analyzed from memory output.
- **page**—Information on the page faults and paging activity is provided by this output head. Some of the other output information includes major faults, minor faults, page in

and page out size in KB, potential memory requirements for recently swapped-in processes, and the number of pages scanned by the page daemon.

- **procs**—Information provided under this head includes the number of kernel threads in the dispatch queue and blocked threads awaiting resource allocation. The procs head also includes information on the number of swapped-out processes waiting for other processes to end execution.

- **disk**—The disks head provides information on the number of disk operations occurring per second.

- **cpu**—CPU usage time is indicated under this head. This includes information on the user time, system time, and idle time when the CPU was used.

- **faults**—Interrupts occurring for each second are provided as information under this head. In addition, information on the number of system calls and CPU context switches are also reported.

Listing 26.3 provides examples for using the vmstat command with its various options.

LISTING 26.3   THE *vmstat* COMMAND OUTPUT

```
# vmstat 5
 kthr      memory            page              disk          faults      cpu
 r b w   swap  free   re  mf pi po fr de sr cd f0 s0 --   in   sy   cs us sy id
 0 0 0 625084 39976    0   1  1  1  1  0  1  0  0  0  0  289  218  310  0  0 100
 0 0 0 606944 50360    0   2 66  0  0  0  0 18  0  0  0  353 2475  471  5  9 86
 0 0 0 606920 50280    0   0  0  0  0  0  0  0  0  0  0  318 2325  421  4  9 87
 0 0 0 606920 50168    0   0 121 0  0  0  0 48  0  0  0  414 2316  497  5 11 84
 0 0 0 606912 50064    0   0 204 0  0  0  0 79  0  0  0  476 1999  576  6  6 87
 0 1 0 606900 50124    4  42 212 0  0  0  0 122 0  0  0  567 2897  553  6 13 81
 0 0 0 606084 49208    1   0 140 0  0  0  0 41  0  0  0  405 1506  462  3  6 91
 0 0 0 606076 48472    1   0 164 0  0  0  0 51  0  0  0  421 1966  498  5  7 87
 0 0 0 606076 50628    0   0 200 0  0  0  0 65  0  0  0  452 2477  551  6 11 83
#
```

→   For information on tunable parameters, **see** "Solaris Tunable Parameters," **p.559**.

THE swap COMMAND

The swap command is used to monitor the swap area of the virtual memory. You can also use this command to add or delete swap area. For monitoring performance, the -1 and the -s options are commonly used with this command.

The -1 option provides information on the status of the swap areas in the form of a list. The output for this command is provided under fields, such as path, dev, swaplow, blocks, and free. The following list describes these fields.

- **path**—This field provides the pathname for the swap area on the hard disk.

- **dev**—This field provides device numbers for major and minor devices. If the device is not a block special device, zeros are provided in the output.

26

- **swaplow**—This field provides the swaplow value for the swap area. The value is provided in terms of 512-byte blocks.

- **blocks**—This field provides the swaplen value for the swap area. The swaplen value is indicated in terms of 512-byte blocks.

- **free**—This field provides information on the unallocated blocks in the swap area. The number of 512-byte blocks unallocated in the swap area is indicated under this field.

The -s option generates a summary of total swap space usage under various heads, such as allocated, used, available, and reserved. Table 26.4 describes the output fields in detail.

TABLE 26.4   OUTPUT FIELDS FOR THE *swap* -s **COMMAND**

Fields	Description
Allocated	This field provides summary information on the total amount of swap space that is allocated in the swap area. The information under this field is displayed as byte value.
Used	This field provides summary information on the swap space in use. This includes space that is allocated or reserved.
Available	This field provides information on the total swap space that is available for future allocation.
Reserved	This field provides information on swap space that is not allocated to any resource but that a resource has reserved for future use.

Listing 26.4 provides an example of swap command usage with the -l and -s options.

LISTING 26.4   THE *swap* **COMMAND OUTPUT**

```
# swap -s
total: 62580k bytes allocated + 7996k reserved = 70576k used, 617136k available
# swap -l
swapfile            dev  swaplo blocks    free
/dev/dsk/c0d0s4     102,4      8 1207576 1108704
```

THE pmap COMMAND

The pmap command is used to generate information on the memory address space used by a process. The output for this command includes information on the virtual address, virtual mapping size, and other information related to the mapping between a process and a memory address on the hard disk. To obtain this information, you can use a number of options with the pmap command. Table 26.5 describes the options used with the command.

TABLE 26.5 OPTIONS USED WITH THE *pmap* COMMAND

Options	Description
-a	This option is used to print information on the anonymous and swap memory areas reserved for process mapping.
-F	This option is used to enforce a takeover of a mapped memory area that another process is currently using.
-r	This option is used to print information on a process's reserved memory addresses.
-s	This option is used to print the HAT page size for a process.
-x	This option is used to print information related to the size of a process map, apart from information on the amount of physical memory, anonymous memory, and locked memory.

The output for a `pmap` command is provided in a single line with values specified under a number of fields. The fields displayed in the output provide vital information on a process mapping. The following list describes some of these fields in detail:

- **Virtual Address**—This field displays the virtual address assigned to a process-memory address mapping in ascending order.

- **Virtual Mapping Size**—This field displays the virtual size of a process-memory address mapping.

- **Resident Physical Memory**—This field displays information on the size of the physical address allocated to a mapping.

- **Anonymous Memory**—This field displays information on the size of the anonymous memory allocated to a process mapping. By default, this field is not included in the output unless you use the -a option with the `pmap` command.

- **Mapping Name**—This field displays information on the mapping name. The names displayed in this field are based on the mapped file name, anonymous memory, or shared memory area.

- **Locked**—This field provides information on the number of pages locked by a process mapping.

Listing 26.5 provides an example of using the `pmap` command:

LISTING 26.5 THE *pmap* COMMAND OUTPUT

```
#pmap <pid>
bash-2.05# pmap 1302
1302:   /usr/dt/bin/dtscreen -mode blank
08041000     28K rwx--   [ stack ]
08050000     44K r-x--   /usr/dt/bin/dtscreen
0806A000      4K rwx--   /usr/dt/bin/dtscreen
0806B000     68K rwx--   [ heap ]
```

continues

26

LISTING 26.5   CONTINUED

```
DD4A0000      4K r--s-  dev:102,6 ino:222550
DD4B0000      8K rw---    [ anon ]
DD501000      4K rw---    [ anon ]
DD579000      4K rw---    [ anon ]
DD5F1000      4K rw---    [ anon ]
DD650000      4K rwx--    [ anon ]
DD660000     12K r-x--  /usr/lib/libmp.so.2
DD673000      4K rwx--  /usr/lib/libmp.so.2
DD690000     72K r-x--  /usr/openwin/lib/libICE.so.6
DD6B2000      4K rwx--  /usr/openwin/lib/libICE.so.6
DD6B3000      8K rwx--  /usr/openwin/lib/libICE.so.6
DD6C0000      4K rwx--    [ anon ]
DD6D0000     32K r-x--  /usr/openwin/lib/libSM.so.6
DD6E8000      4K rwx--  /usr/openwin/lib/libSM.so.6
DD6F0000     80K r-x--  /usr/openwin/lib/libXext.so.0
DD714000      4K rwx--  /usr/openwin/lib/libXext.so.0
DD720000     24K r-x--  /usr/lib/libgen.so.1
DD736000      4K rwx--  /usr/lib/libgen.so.1
DD740000      4K r-x--  /usr/lib/libw.so.1
DD750000      4K rwx--    [ anon ]
DD760000    548K r-x--  /usr/lib/libnsl.so.1
DD7F9000     20K rwx--  /usr/lib/libnsl.so.1
DD7FE000     32K rwx--  /usr/lib/libnsl.so.1
DD810000     44K r-x--  /usr/lib/libsocket.so.1
DD82B000      4K rwx--  /usr/lib/libsocket.so. 1
DD830000     36K r-x--  /usr/lib/libCrun.so.1
DD848000      4K rwx--  /usr/lib/libCrun.so.1
DD849000     16K rwx--  /usr/lib/libCrun.so. 1
DD850000    288K r-x--  /usr/openwin/lib/libXt.so.4
DD8A8000     20K rwx--  /usr/openwin/lib/libXt.so.4
DD8B0000      4K rwx--    [ anon ]
DD8C0000    492K r-x--  /usr/openwin/lib/libtt.so.2
DD94C000     12K rwx--  /usr/openwin/lib/libtt.so.2
DD960000    624K r-x--  /usr/lib/libc.so.1
DDA0C000     24K rwx--  /usr/lib/libc.so.1
DDA12000      4K rwx--  /usr/lib/libc.so.1
DDA20000      4K r-x--  /usr/dt/lib/libSDtFwa.so.1
DDA30000      4K rwx--  /usr/dt/lib/libSDtFwa.so.1
DDA40000     52K r-x--  /usr/lib/libm.so.1
DDA5C000      4K rwx--  /usr/lib/libm.so.1
DDA60000      4K rwx--    [ anon ]
DDA70000    508K r-x--  /usr/openwin/lib/libX11.so.4
DDAFF000     16K rwx--  /usr/openwin/lib/libX11.so.4
DDB10000    344K r-x--  /usr/dt/lib/libDtSvc.so.1
DDB76000      8K rwx--  /usr/dt/lib/libDtSvc.so.1
DDB78000      8K rwx--  /usr/dt/lib/libDtSvc.so.1
DDB80000      4K r-x--  /usr/lib/libdl.so.1
DDB90000    292K r-x--  /usr/lib/ld.so.1
DDBE9000     16K rwx--  /usr/lib/ld.so.1
DDBED000      8K rwx--  /usr/lib/ld.so. 1
 total     3876K
bash-2.05#
```

MONITORING DISK UTILIZATION

Hard disk utilization must be monitored periodically to avoid problems related to disk space availability and usage. Solaris provides commands such as `iostat` and `df` to report disk utilization statistics. The following section discusses the use of these commands for monitoring disk utilization performance.

THE `iostat` COMMAND

The `iostat` command provides information on a system's disk I/O. Information related to disk I/O includes utilization, queue lengths, throughput, rate of transactions, and the service time. The output generated by the `iostat` command depends on the options used with the command.

When you specify the time interval as a parameter, the `iostat` command provides output with information on the terminal, disk, and CPU. Every line of output provides information on disk activity within the interval specified with the command. In the output, terminal fields provide information on the number of characters queued in the terminal for input and output. Disk information fields specify the blocks and transactions per second apart from the average service time. The service time is specified in milliseconds. CPU-related fields provide information on whether the disk is idle, awaits I/O, or is used in user mode or system mode. Listing 26.6 is an example of using the iostat command with a time interval parameter:

LISTING 26.6   THE *iostat* COMMAND OUTPUT# IOSTAT 2

```
    tty        cmdk0          fd0           sd0           nfs1          cpu
tin tout kps tps serv  kps tps serv  kps tps serv  kps tps serv  us sy wt id
  0    5   1   0   23    0   0    0    0   0    0    0   0    0    0  0  0 100
  0  118   0   0    0    0   0    0    0   0    0    0   0    0    0  0  0 100
  0   40   0   0    0    0   0    0    0   0    0    0   0    0    0  0  0 100
  0   40   0   0    0    0   0    0    0   0    0    0   0    0    0  0  0 100
```

When used with the `-xtc` option, `iostat` provides disk utilization information for multiple hard disks present in the system. For this option, the fields displayed in the output include `r/s`, `w/s`, and `kr/s`. The following list describes the fields displayed for the `iostat -xtc` command.

- **r/s**—This field provides information on the number of disk reads occurring per second.

- **w/s**—This field provides information on the number of disk writes occurring per second.

- **kr/s**—This field provides information on the size of each read occurring every second. The size is indicated in KB.

- **kw/s**—This field provides information on the size of each write occurring every second. The size is indicated in KB.

- **wait**—This field displays the average number of transactions awaiting servicing.

26

- **actv** —This field displays the average number of transactions being serviced currently.
- **svc_t** —This field displays the average service time. The time value is specified in milliseconds.
- **%w** —This field indicates the time percentage when the transaction queue is occupied.
- **%b** —This field indicates the time percentage when the disk is busy.

Listing 26.7 provides an example for the iostat -xtc command.

LISTING 26.7   THE *iostat -xtc* COMMAND OUTPUT

```
# iostat -xtc
                  extended device statistics            tty       cpu
  device  r/s   w/s   kr/s   kw/s  wait  actv  svc_t  %w  %b  tin tout  us sy wt id
  cmdk0   0.1   0.0   0.5    0.3   0.0   0.0   23.4   0   0    0    5   0  0  0 100
  fd0     0.0   0.0   0.0    0.0   0.0   0.0    0.0   0   0
  sd0     0.0   0.0   0.0    0.0   0.0   0.0    0.0   0   0
  nfs1    0.0   0.0   0.0    0.0   0.0   0.0    0.0   0   0
```

THE df COMMAND

The df command generates information on the free disk space available on a system. The disk space reported by this command takes into account only 90% of the space available on the hard disk. When reporting disk space availability, df divides used disk space value with the available disk space value. To obtain disk space information, you need to use the -k or the -h options with the command.

The -k option provides output with fields, such as kbytes, used, avail, and so on. The following list describes the fields displayed with the df -k option.

- **kbytes**—This field indicates the total size of usable disk space on the hard disk.
- **used**—This field indicates the used space on the hard disk.
- **avail**—This field indicates the disk space available for usage on the hard disk.
- **capacity**—This field indicates the used disk space on the hard disk in terms of percentage.
- **mounted on**—This field indicates the mount point on the hard disk.

Listing 26.8 provides an example of the df -k command:

LISTING 26.8   THE *df -k* COMMAND

```
# df -k
Filesystem            kbytes    used   avail capacity  Mounted on
/dev/dsk/c0d0s0        65143   35318   23311    61%    /
/dev/dsk/c0d0s6      1529622  700503  767935    48%    /usr
/dev/dsk/c0d0p0:boot   10484    1508    8976    15%    /boot
/proc                      0       0       0     0%    /proc
mnttab                     0       0       0     0%    /etc/mnttab
```

```
fd                              0        0        0    0%    /dev/fd
/dev/dsk/c0d0s3             61615    44482    10972   81%    /var
swap                      615092       24   615068    1%    /var/run
swap                      615760      692   615068    1%    /tmp
/dev/dsk/c0d0s5            24239       15    21801    1%    /opt
/dev/dsk/c0d0s7          5023838       21  4973579    1%    /export/home
/dev/dsk/c0d0s1           744966   264607   420762   39%    /usr/openwin
```

When used with the -h option, the df command generates output in a much more user-friendly format. For example, information on disk size values is represented as KB, MB, or GB values rather than bytes. Information generated when you use the -h command includes total space for each file system, space allocated for existing files, space available for use by unprivileged users, and the available disk space allocated for all files in terms of percentage. Listing 26.9 provides an example of the df -h command:

LISTING 26.9   THE *df -h* COMMAND OUTPUT

```
# df -h
Filesystem              size    used   avail  capacity  Mounted on
/dev/dsk/c0d0s0         64M     34M     23M     61%     /
/dev/dsk/c0d0s6        1.5G    684M    750M     48%     /usr
/dev/dsk/c0d0p0:boot   10M     1.5M    8.8M     15%     /boot
/proc                   0K      0K      0K      0%     /proc
mnttab                  0K      0K      0K      0%     /etc/mnttab
fd                      0K      0K      0K      0%     /dev/fd
/dev/dsk/c0d0s3        60M     43M     11M     81%     /var
swap                  601M     24K    601M      1%     /var/run
swap                  601M    692K    601M      1%     /tmp
/dev/dsk/c0d0s5        24M     15K     21M      1%     /opt
/dev/dsk/c0d0s7       4.8G     21K    4.7G      1%     /export/home
/dev/dsk/c0d0s1       728M    258M    411M     39%     /usr/openwin
```

When you compare the output for the df command with the -k and -h options, you can see that the -h options describe disk size values with K or M prefixes.

26

MONITORING NETWORK ACTIVITY

Network activity is an important factor that affects system performance. Monitoring the network activity of a system enables administrators to resolve and avoid problems. Solaris provides a number of commands, such as ifconfig, netstat, snoop, and ping, that help in monitoring network activity. This section discusses the use of these commands for monitoring network activity.

THE ifconfig COMMAND

The ifconfig command is primarily used to assign network addresses to newly installed systems. In addition, the command can be used to redefine the system network address. For monitoring performance, you need to use the -a option with the ifconfig command. This option describes flags, Maximum Transmission Unit (MTU), index, and netmask for each interface in the system. In addition, a host of network addresses, such as the inet address, broadcast address, and ethernet address for a system, are displayed as output.

Listing 26.10 provides an example of the `ifconfig -a` command.

LISTING 26.10   THE *ifconfig -a* COMMAND

```
# ifconfig -a
lo0: flags=1000849<UP,LOOPBACK,RUNNING,MULTICAST,IPv4> mtu 8232 index 1
        inet 127.0.0.1 netmask ff000000
hme0: flags=1000843<UP,BROADCAST,RUNNING,MULTICAST,IPv4> mtu 1500 index 2
        inet 172.17.65.187 netmask ffffff00 broadcast 172.17.65.255
        ether 0:50:da:d0:c4:d4
```

THE netstat COMMAND

To obtain statistical information on network traffic flow, you can use the `netstat` command. This command displays information in different formats based on the options specified with the command. For example, if you use the -r option, you can view the routing table maintained on the system. For monitoring network traffic flow, you need to use the -i or -s options.

The `netstat -i` command displays information on the current status of all interfaces on the system. Some of the fields displayed in the output include Collis (collissions), Ierrs (input errors), and Oerrs (output errors). By using the output in the fields with certain formulas, you can monitor the traffic flow on the system. For example, if the output of Ierrs or Ipkts is greater that 25%, an overloaded network condition is possible because packets are being dropped before reaching their destination. Listing 26.11 provides an example for the `net-stat -i` command.

LISTING 26.11   THE *netstat -i* COMMAND OUTPUT

```
# netstat -i
Name  Mtu  Net/Dest    Address      Ipkts    Ierrs Opkts   Oerrs Collis Queue
lo0   8232 loopback    localhost    1100827  0     1100827 0     0      0

hme0 1500 que          que          449972   0     119903  0     4685   0
```

The `netstat -s` command provides information on the invalid header fields, checksums, or data loss on the packets received by the system. This information is provided as a summary of the output provided by the command. Listing 26.12 provides a sample summary for a `netstat -s` command output.

LISTING 26.12   THE *netstat -s* COMMAND OUTPUT

```
    4275 messages received
        0 messages received with too few bytes
        0 messages received with bad checksum
```

```
    4275 membership queries received
       0 membership queries received with invalid field(s)
       0 membership reports received
       0 membership reports received with invalid field(s)
       0 membership reports received for groups to which we belong
       0 membership reports sent
```

THE ping COMMAND

The ping command is primarily used to check for the reachability of remote hosts. However, you can also detect whether there is network congestion between two hosts. The command transmits ICMP messages to elicit a response from target computers and uses the response to report data loss. The ping command also reports the time taken for sending packets and receiving acknowledgements. This data is called *round trip time*. You need to use the -sRv option to obtain this information. Listing 26.13 provides an example of using the ping command with the -sRv option:

LISTING 26.13   THE *ping -sRv* COMMAND OUTPUT

```
# ping -sRv 172.17.17.157
PING 172.17.17.157: 56 data bytes
64 bytes from 172.17.17.157: icmp_seq=0. time=12. ms
  IP options:  <record route> 172.17.64.1, 172.16.101.25, 172.17.8.1, 172.17.17.
129, ^C
----172.17.17.157 PING Statistics----
88 packets transmitted, 1 packets received, 98% packet loss
round-trip (ms)  min/avg/max = 12/12/12
```

In the output, you can observe that a data loss of 98% has been reported. This indicates that a condition of congestion exists on the network.

THE traceroute COMMAND

The traceroute command is primarily used to identify the route taken by a packet to a destination computer. To monitor network activity, you can use the traceroute command without options. This provides information on the reachability or availability of a target computer. Listing 26.14 shows you how the traceroute command is used:

LISTING 26.14   THE *traceroute* COMMAND OUTPUT

```
# traceroute 172.17.68.116
traceroute to 172.17.68.116 (172.17.68.116), 30 hops max, 40 byte packets
 1  172.17.65.1 (172.17.65.1)  14.300 ms  3.759 ms  0.618 ms
 2  172.17.68.116 (172.17.68.116)  0.549 ms  0.648 ms  0.508 ms
```

In the first column, the hop count is displayed followed by the hop IP address and the time taken to send and receive packets to the hop address.

26

THE nfsstat COMMAND

The nfsstat command is used to retrieve performance information on Network File System (NFS) servers and clients on the network. The -c, -s, and -m options are particularly useful for monitoring NFS performance. A summary of performance statistics can be obtained by using the nfsstat command with these options. The following list describes the options in detail:

- -c—This option provides information on the NFS Remote Procedure Calls (RPCs) that occur on the client computers. In addition, it provides information on the NFS access list maintained on client computers.

- -s—This option displays NFS RPC information on NFS servers. The NFS server's access list information is also displayed when you use this option with the nfsstat command.

- -m—This option displays statistical information on each NFS file system mounted on a computer. A number of fields are displayed in the output with information on the server name, server IP address, mount flags, data read and write statistics, and a packet retransmission count.

Listing 26.15 provides an example of using nfsstat with the -c, -s, and -m options:

LISTING 26.15 THE *nfstat* COMMAND OUTPUT

```
# nfsstat -s

Server rpc:
calls       badcalls    nullrecv    badlen      xdrcall
13035786    38          0           0           38

Server nfs:
calls       badcalls
13035690    550
null            getattr     setattr     root        lookup          readlink    read
284296    2% 4505230 35%33568   0% 0   0%        3089153 24%157057  1% 2735504  21%
wrcache         write       create      remove      rename          link        symlink
0   0%          1774230 14%61417   0% 52958   0% 8306   0%       4631   0%    13388   0%
mkdir           rmdir       readdir     fsstat
1410   0%       677   0%    270178 13% 43600   0%
```

From the output, notice that NFS writes exceed 10%. This means that excessive write operations are occurring on your network share. You might need to reconfigure your NFS settings in a way that your processes are writing to local disks. You can also physically move disks to the machines running the processes or add a NFS accelerator.

If you need to confirm that NFS is causing a bottleneck, run the prstat command. If the process named nfsd remains consistently at the top of the list, it indicates that many system resources are used up in writing NFS data to disk.

THE snoop COMMAND

The snoop command is used to capture packets from the network and display the contents of the captured packets. The snoop command uses the network packet filter and streams buffer modules to efficiently capture packets from the network. Captured packets can be displayed as they are received, or saved to a file that you can view later. You can use the -d, -i, and the -o options to monitor performance with the snoop command.

The -d option enables you to observe the packets captured by a particular interface. However, the -d option scrolls the output over a number of pages. Therefore, you need to use the -i option with the -d option. You need to specify a filename as a parameter for the -i option. This ensures that the output of the -d option is stored in the specified file. To read the contents of a file you need to use the -o option with the snoop command. Listing 26.16 provides an example of the -d, -i, and the -o options:

LISTING 26.16   THE snoop COMMAND OUTPUT

```
# snoop -d hme0
Using device /dev/hme0 (promiscuous mode)
172.17.65.91 -> que          TELNET C port=3898
         que -> 172.17.65.91 TELNET R port=3898 /dev/hme0 (promiscu
           ? -> (multicast)  ETHER Type=0000 (LLC/802.3), size = 52 bytes
         que -> 172.17.65.173 XWIN C port=40691
         que -> 172.17.65.173 XWIN C port=40691
172.17.65.173 -> que         XWIN R port=40691
172.17.65.173 -> que         XWIN R port=40691
         que -> 172.17.65.173 XWIN C port=40691
172.17.65.173 -> que         XWIN R port=40691
         que -> 172.17.65.173 XWIN C port=40691
         que -> 172.17.65.173 XWIN C port=40691
         que -> 172.17.65.173 XWIN C port=40691
172.17.65.173 -> que         XWIN R port=40691
172.17.65.173 -> que         XWIN R port=40691
         que -> 172.17.65.173 XWIN C port=40691
172.17.65.91 -> que          TELNET C port=3898
         que -> 172.17.65.173 XWIN C port=40691
         que -> 172.17.65.173 XWIN C port=40691
172.17.65.173 -> que         XWIN R port=40691
172.17.65.173 -> que         XWIN R port=40691
```

USING sar TO MONITOR SYSTEMS

The System Activity Reporter, also known as sar, is a comprehensive performance monitoring mechanism offered by Solaris. The sar program classifies system activity into distinct groups and provides information on each group. The groups sar monitors include the following:

- Block device
- Buffer activity

- CPU run queue

- CPU usage statistics

- File access

- Kernel memory allocation

- Message and semaphores

- Paging in activity

- Paging out

- System call

- System swapping

- System tables

- TTY device

- Unused memory and disk pages

Before delving into the sar command and its options, you need to configure the sar utility. If you run sar without performing configuration steps, the following error is displayed:

```
# sar -a
sar: can't open /var/adm/sa
No such file or directory
```

The sar utility depends on three other utilities: sadc, sa1, and sa2. The sadc utility collects system activity information and stores it in binary files. The sa1 utility acts as a wrapper for the sadc program. The sa2 utility acts as a wrapper to the sar utility and prints the system activity information stored in the binary files in ASCII format. In effect, if you do not run sa1 and sa2 utilities, sar will not work. Therefore, the sar configuration task primarily involves executing sa1 and sa2 before running the sar command. The simplest method of configuring sa1 and sa2 to execute is to modify the crontab file by using the vi editor or any other editor of your choice. The crontab file contains the path to the sa1 and sa2 executables, commented with a # symbol. To run the sa1 and sa2 utilities on startup, remove the # symbol and save the file.

You also need to add the following commands to the sys crontab file to enable sar:

```
0 * * * 0-6 /usr/lib/sa/sa1
20,40 8-17 * * /usr/lib/sa/sa1
5 18 * * 1-5 /usr/lib/sa/sa2 -s 8:00 -e 18:1 -I 15:01 -I 1200 -A
```

The first line of the crontab file uses sa1 to collect system performance data at the beginning of every hour each day. The second line takes snapshots of the data at the 20th and 40th minute between 8:00 a.m. and 5:00 p.m., Monday through Friday. The last line schedules sa2 to run at 6:05 p.m. each Monday through Friday, and creates an ASCII report from the data collected by sa1.

After these tasks are complete, you can start using the sar command. Listing 26.17 provides an example of the sar command:

LISTING 26.17   THE *sar* COMMAND OUTPUT

```
$ sar
SunOS froggie 5.9 Generic_ sun4u 03/05/02
00:00:00 %usr %sys %wio %idle
01:00:00 0 1 0 99 02:00:00 0 1 0 99 03:00:00 0
➡1 0 99 04:00:00 0 1 0 99 05:00:00 0 1 0 99 06:00:00 0 1 0 99 07:00:00 0 1 0 99
08:00:00 0 1 0 99 08:20:01 2 1 0 97 08:40:00 0 1 0 99 09:00:00
➡6 1 0 93 09:20:00 0 1 0 99 09:40:00 3 1 1 94
Average 1 1 0 99
```

When the -a option is specified, the sar command displays data under fields, such as igest/s, namei/s, and dirbk/s. The iget/s field provides information on the number of requests per second that were made to inodes. The namei/s field provides information on the number of file path search tasks that were executed per second. The dirbk/s field displays information on the directory block reads per second.

The -b option is used to retrieve information on buffer activity. With this option, the sar command displays fields, such as bread/s, lread/s, and so on. Table 26.6 describes the fields displayed in the sar -b command output.

TABLE 26.6   FIELDS DISPLAYED WITH THE *sar -b* COMMAND OUTPUT

Fields	Description
bread/s	This field displays the average number of disk reads to the buffer cache occurring per second.
lread/s	This field displays the average number of logical reads per second that happens from the buffer cache.
%rcache	This field displays a fraction of the logical reads contained in the buffer cache.
bwrit/s	This field displays the average number of physical blocks written from the cache to the hard disk each second.
lwrit/s	This field displays the average number of logical writes to the hard disk occurring every second.
%wcache	This field displays the fraction of logical writes contained in the buffer cache.
pread/s	This field displays the average number of physical reads occurring each second that use character device interfaces.
pwrit/s	This field displays the average number of physical writes that use character device interfaces. The writes occur each second.

26

USING THE SOLARIS MANAGEMENT CONSOLE (SMC) FOR PERFORMANCE MONITORING

The Solaris Management Console (SMC) provides views that enable you to monitor performance statistics for processes running on a system and users working with the system. It also provides a performance summary of processes running on the system. In addition, information on the processes, system information, and a log viewer are provided in SMC. The following steps describe how you can access performance statistics in SMC:

1. Launch SMC and access the System view under the System Status, Performance views (Figure 26.1).

Figure 26.1
The System View in SMC.

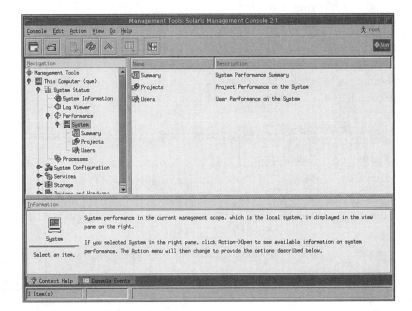

2. Click the Summary view to access a summarized view of information on the performance statistics (Figure 26.2).

3. Click the Projects view to access performance information on the projects running on the system (Figure 26.3).

4. Click the Users view to access performance information on the users working with the system (Figure 26.4).

Figure 26.2
Summarized performance information in the Summary View.

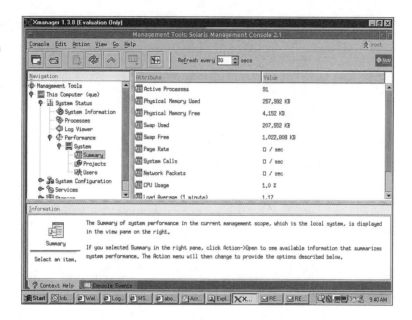

Figure 26.3
Project information displayed in the Projects View.

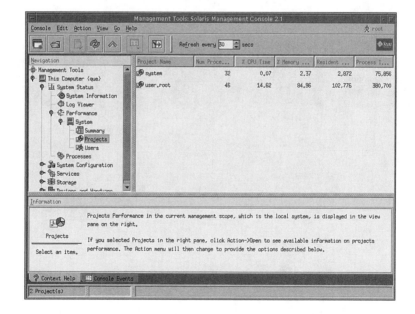

26

Figure 26.4
User information displayed in the User view.

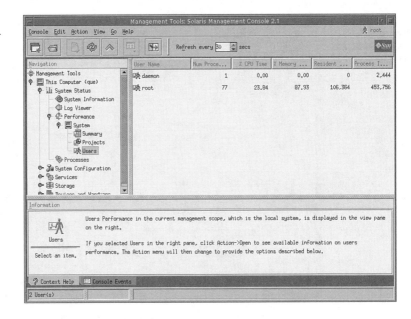

5. Click the System Information view to observe system configuration information on the view pane (Figure 26.5).

Figure 26.5
System configuration information displayed in the System Information view.

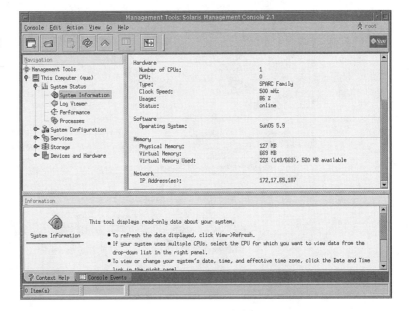

6. Click the Log Viewer view to observe event logs recorded in the Log Viewer view pane (Figure 26.6) .

Figure 26.6
Event logs displayed in
the Log Viewer view.

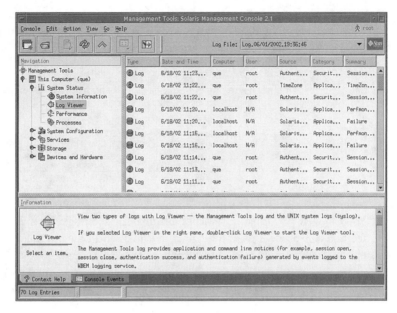

7. To view the performance status of processes running on the system, you need to click
   the Processes view. Performance statistics for processes are displayed in the view pane
   (Figure 26.7) .

Figure 26.7
Process information
displayed in the
Processes view.

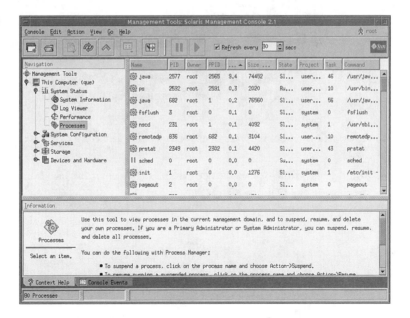

26

In addition to SMC, you can access performance information by using the performance meter utility. This utility displays the current performance statistics in the form of a dynamic graphic window. The following steps describe how you can work with the performance meter:

1. Launch Performance Meter by clicking the Performance Meter button on the xx bar (Figure 26.8).

Figure 26.8
Launching the Performance Meter utility.

2. You can view performance statistics for different devices, such as CPU or disks, or for factors, such as load, page, interrupts, and so on. To view information based on different factors, you need to choose View from the View menu (Figure 26.9).

Figure 26.9
The various views in Performance Meter.

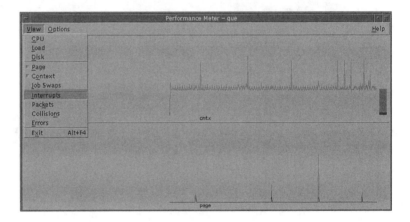

3. Information on interrupts is displayed after the Interrupts view is selected (Figure 26.10).
4. You can also display performance values as strip charts or bar charts by using options specified in the Options menu (Figure 26.11) .

Figure 26.10
Interrupts information
is displayed in
Performance Meter.

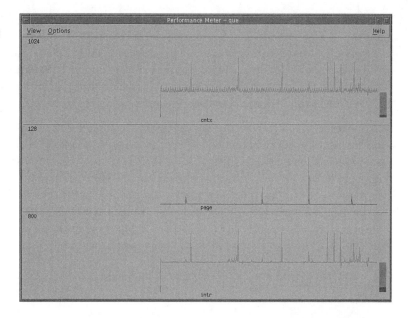

Figure 26.11
Chart display options
in the Options menu.

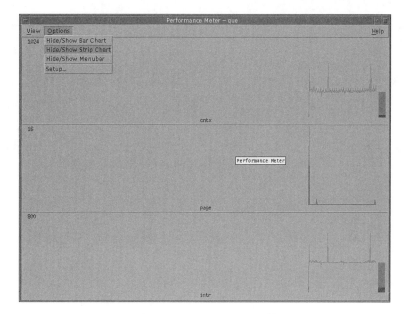

26

SUMMARY

Monitoring system performance is one of the important tasks performed by administrators. Administrators require performance reports detailing statistics on CPU usage, virtual memory, disk utilization, and network activity. To report performance statistics for each of these issues, Solaris provides a number of command line utilities.

You can use the mpstat and prstat commands to monitor CPU utilization. The mpstat command displays performance reports on processor activity. The prstat command reports information on the active processes running on the system. In Solaris, you can use the vmstat, swap, and pmap commands to monitor virtual memory. The vmstat command generates reports on the status of virtual memory. The swap command monitors the swap area in the virtual memory. The pmap command is used to monitor process maps.

Solaris provides commands such as iostat and df to monitor disk utilization. The iostat command provides information on disk I/O happening on a system. The df command reports information on the free disk space available on the system. A host of commands are available in Solaris for network activity monitoring. Commands such as ifconfig, netstat, ping, traceroute, nfstat, and snoop provide information on the state of network interfaces, network congestion, data loss, and transmission time. The sar command can be used to monitor system activity. In addition to the CLI commands, you can use GUI tools such as SMC and Performance Meter to monitor system performance.

26

PART VII

APPENDIXES

A What's New in Solaris 9.0 517

B NVRAM Parameters 525

C Solaris Management Tools 531

D Troubleshooting 537

E Solaris Tunable Parameters 559

F Glossary 567

APPENDIX

What's New in Solaris 9

In this appendix

New Features for System Administrators   518

New Features for Desktop users   523

A number of additions and enhancements have been made to the Solaris 9 Operating Environment (OE). The following sections focus on the additions and enhancements that will be of use to administrators and desktop users.

NEW FEATURES FOR SYSTEM ADMINISTRATORS

A host of new system administration features have been added to the Solaris OE. Enhancements affect system resources, the file system, system performance, and security. Additional features that have been incorporated into Solaris include system administration tools such as FX Scheduler and Resource Manager, installation features, server and client management features, device management features, removable media management features, and language support. Table A.1 details the new system administration features in Solaris 9.

TABLE A.1   NEW SYSTEM ADMINISTRATION FEATURES IN SOLARIS 9

Feature	Description
Resource Manager	This tool enhances management of system resources. Examples of the operations that you can use this tool to perform include allocation of system resources, performance monitoring of resources, and generating resource usage reports.
FX Scheduler	This tool provides a mechanism for fixed scheduling of policy for processes. You can set fixed priorities for processes running on the system with this tool.
Process Debugging	New process debugging commands, such as `pargs` and `preap` have been introduced in Solaris 9. The `pargs` command reports information on environmental variables and arguments associated with current active processes. To terminate processes in Zombie state, you can use the `preap` command.
Enhanced Command Display Options	The `-h` option has been added to commands such as `df`, `du`, and `ls` to enhance output interpretation. The `-h` option displays size values in terms of the power of 1024. This simplifies output, with values displayed in KB, MB, GB, or TB measures.
Integration with iPlanet Directory Server	The iPlanet Directory Server 5.1 has been integrated with the Solaris 9 OE, in the form of the iPlanet Lightweight Directory Access Protocol (LDAP) directory service. In versions before Solaris 9, the directory server was required to be installed separately.

A

Feature	Description
LDAP Naming Services Support	In addition to NIS and NIS+, you can use LDAP as a naming service on Solaris 9 OE. If you are using NIS+ as the naming service, you can migrate to LDAP by using NIS+-to-LDAP migration tools provided with the Solaris 9 OE.
IP Security	To provide enhanced IP security, features such as IPsec and IKE have been added to the Solaris 9 OE. IPsec provides support for IPv4, as well as IPv6. However, the Internet Key Exchange (IKE) is also available for IPv4. Manual IPsec was available in Solaris 8 as well.
File Transfer Enhancements	The File Transfer Protocol (FTP) client utility on Solaris 9 has been enhanced to include features such as passive connect mode, TCP window size management, default transfer mode based on the target system's OS, and restarting failed transfers. The Trivial File Transfer Protocol (TFTP) client features have also been enhanced to include timeout intervals, new options, and management of transfer size. In addition, TFTP clients on Solaris 9 can negotiate the block size of data being transferred. The scp utility is another file transfer feature in Solaris 9. This utility enables encrypted transfer of files between computers that use the Secure Shell (SSH) protocol. You need to provide a username and password to initiate file transfer. The scp utility displays a progress meter indicating the progress of the file transfer task.
IP Over ATM	With Solaris 9, support for data transmission over Asynchronous Transfer Mode (ATM) networks that use IPv6 have been incorporated.
Enhancements to snoop	The snoop utility has been enhanced in Solaris 9 to support decoding of packets from AppleTalk and SCTP clients.
sendmail Enhancements	On Solaris 9, a number of new features have been added to sendmail. These include new command line options, macros, queue features, compile flags, delivery agent flags, and configuration file options. The new sendmail software can also work with IPv6 addresses. Modifications to related utilities, such as makemap and editmap, have also been made in Solaris 9.

continues

TABLE A.1 CONTINUED

Feature	Description
Link Down Notification	The IP Multipathing daemon has been enhanced with a link down notification feature. With this feature, the daemon can identify loss of link with the network.
Mobile IP Support	This feature enables computers to communicate with mobile devices, such as laptops or Personal Digital Assistants (PDAs) running from external networks, also known as *foreign networks*. A server on the foreign network, called the *foreign agent*, manages communication with the mobile device. With Solaris 9, you can configure foreign agents to send periodic advertisement messages. These messages enable you to verify connectivity with the mobile device.
Solaris Volume Manager	Features provided by Solstice DiskSuite have been incorporated into the Solaris OE in the form of the Solaris Volume Manager. This tool provides features such as active disk monitoring, device identification, and multipartition drives, and supports other volume management features, such as RAID and so on.
Solaris Management Console (SMC)	Introduced in Solaris 8, SMC is a comprehensive management console with a Java-based GUI front end. SMC provides a number of features that provide information on system status, performance, logs, processes, and projects running on the system. In addition, you can view information on users, other computers on the network, and scheduled jobs.
Patch Manager	In Solaris 9, you can manage patches for the Solaris OE with the Patch Manager. This feature enables you to add, remove and download patches for Solaris.
Solaris Web-Based Enterprise Management (WBEM) Services	Solaris 9 has incorporated the WBEM service and implements it as the Solaris WBEM service. This feature enables you to manage enterprise computing under a single umbrella.
Log Rotation	With Solaris 9, you can implement a generic log rotation feature that facilitates maintenance of application log files on a rotational basis.
Concurrent Read-Write Access	In contrast to earlier data access methods, the new UFS direct I/O file access feature enables applications to access unbuffered file system data concurrently.
Enhanced Directory Name Look-up Cache (DNLC)	Enhancements to DNLC have been introduced to provide directory name lookups for directories having hundreds of files.

Feature	Description
`fssnap` command	Snapshots of file system contents can be created with this command, which was introduced with Solaris 8 and later versions.
Faster file system creation	The `mkfs` command that is used to create file systemshas been enhanced to perform faster file system creation operations. Performance improvements are especially visible on systems with high-capacity hard disks.
Solaris Live Upgrade enhancements	With Solaris 9, the Live Upgrade feature has been enhanced to include progress reports, priority scheduling, and boot environment naming support.
Enhanced Installation Features	Installation files that were grouped under metaclusters have now been moved into separate or existing packages. Some of these installation files are related to the CacheFS, NFS, Distributed File System (DFS), Telnet server, TFTP server, and NIS-related files. Support for longer package names extending up to 32 characters has been introduced in Solaris 9.
Time Zone additions	The number of time zones supported by Solaris OE has been increased in version 9.
Root Mirror Upgrades	In Solaris 9, you can upgrade existing root mirrors and metadevices created by Solaris Volume Manager in the previous versions of Solaris OE.
Multiple Page Size Support (MPSS)	In Solaris 9, the MPSS feature allows access to multiple virtual memory pages instead of 8KB pages that were allowed for access in the previous versions.
Enhanced Multithreading Library	With Solaris 9, the performance of the multithreading library has been enhanced over `libthread`, which was used in previous Solaris versions.
Internet Key Exchange (IKE) Protocol Support	To implement IPsec, encryption keys need to be exchanged between communicating systems. The IKE protocol enables key exchange. In Solaris 9, IKE is implemented by the in.iked daemon. Currently, IKE support is available only for IPv4 networks.
Secure Shell (SSH)	The Secure Shell feature in Solaris 9 implements a security blanket for users accessing remote systems. This feature protects user sessions from eavesdropping, intermediary attacks, and session hijacking.

continues

A

TABLE A.1 CONTINUED

Feature	Description
Kerberos Key Distribution Center (KDC)	The Kerberos KDC V5 that provides enhanced system security features has been incorporated into the Solaris 9 OE. Examples of the security features provided by KDC include principal administration, principal data base maintenance, ticket issue, principal database replication, and addressless tickets.
LDAP Client Security	With Solaris 9, security for LDAP clients has been enhanced to include features such as SSL, TLS, or CRAM-MD5 encryption.
Encryption Modules	Software modules related to encryption for IPSec and Kerberos utilities have been added to Solaris 9 OE. Previously, you had to install these modules separately.
Support for IPv6 on X Windows	The X Windows System libraries in Solaris 9 provide support for both IPv4 and IPv6 addresses when they are establishing connections between servers and clients.
Xserver Connection Security	Advanced security options have been added to Solaris X Server. These features enable administrators to control transport methods and connections to the server. On Solaris 9, encrypted connections can be implemented between X Servers and clients.
Keyboard Bell Options	On Solaris 9, instead of using the keyboard bell to ring beep sounds, an audio device can play a tone. The Xsun server can be configured to implement this feature. Users can also modify the volume, pitch, and choice of tones.
CD Write Feature	This feature, added in Solaris 9, enables creation of file systems on CD-R or CD-RW devices. The `cdrw` command implements this feature on Solaris 9. Using this command, you can create audio or data CDs, copy CDs, or erase CD-RW content.
Traffic Management	The Sun StorEdge Traffic Manager feature provided by Solaris 9 manages load balancing between multiple system devices such as interfaces or storage devices.
Universal Language Support	Support for 39 languages and 162 locale environments have been added to Solaris 9.
New Chinese Character Set	Introduced in Solaris 8 and upgraded in Solaris 9, the new Chinese character set called GB18030-2000 contains support for approximately 30,000 characters.

A

New Features for Desktop Users

Desktop users constitute an important segment in the Solaris OE user market. With Solaris 9, a number of enhancements and additions have been made to the Solaris OE desktop environment. Table A.2 describes some of these new features.

TABLE A.2 NEW DESKTOP FEATURES IN SOLARIS 9

Feature	Description
Multibyte Character Set Support	With Solaris 9, the Xterm terminal emulator supports multibyte character set locales, such as UTF-8.
Graphical Workspace Manager	To manage workspaces, the Graphical Workspace Manager utility was introduced in Solaris 8. This utility has been further updated in Solaris 9. Graphical Workspace Manager provides a GUI representation of workspaces created on the system. You can use this utility to navigate across workspaces and to work with the applications in each workspace.
Window List	To locate applications across workspaces and to organize a list of currently running applications, you can use the Window List utility. You can also perform common tasks with a collection of windows.
Energy Star Standards Compliance	To comply with the Energy Star standards stipulated by the U.S. government, power management on Solaris systems has been enhanced with the Frame Buffer Power Management (FBPM) extension for the Display Power Management System (DPMS) component.
Multiple Mail Attachments	To add multiple attachments to an email, the functionality of the Mailer Attachment Add dialog box has been modified. The dialog box remains open to enable users add multiple attachments. This new functionality has been added in Solaris 9.
New Non-ISO-1 Print Format	On Solaris 9, non-ISO-1 text files are filtered by the `dltp` utility before being displayed or submitted to the printer.
New Audio Directories	Additional audio files and directories have been added to Solaris 9. These include the `/usr/include/audio` directory that stores application header files, and the `/usr/include/audio/au.h` file that stores audio file formats.
Freeware Utilities	A host of freeware utilities have been provided in Solaris 9. The GNU grep 2.4.2 pattern matcher, GNU tar 1.13 archiver, and GNU wget file retriever are some of the freeware utilities available on Solaris 9.

APPENDIX

NVRAM Parameters

Table B.1 defines the configuration parameters available in the NVRAM.

TABLE B.1 CONFIGURATION VARIABLES

Variables	Description
auto-boot?	The default value of this variable is true. When true, the system boots automatically after power is switched on or is reset.
auto-boot-on-error	This variable controls degraded reboot of the system when subsystem failure occurs.
boot-command	This command is executed if the value of auto-boot is set to true. The default value for the boot-command variable is boot.
boot-device	This variable specifies the device from which to boot. Its default value is disk net.
boot-file	This variable stores the arguments passed to a booted program and typically contains an empty string.
diag-device	This refers to a diagnostic boot source device and typically contains net.
diag-file	This variable refers to the arguments passed to a booted program in diagnostic mode.
diag-switch?	The default value for this variable is false. If the value is set to true, it runs in diagnostic mode.
fcode-debug?	The variable is assigned a default value of false. If true, the variable includes the name fields for plug-in Fcodes.
input-device	The default input device is the keyboard. The typical console input device is keyboard, ttya, or ttyb.
nvramac	This variable contains the content of nvramrc and is typically empty.
oem-banner	This is the custom OEM banner and is enabled by oem-banner?true.
oem-logo	This is the byte array custom OEM logo and is enabled by using oem-logo?true.
oem-logo?	The default value is false. If true, you need to use the custom OEM logo. If not, use the Sun logo.
output-device	The default output device is the screen. The typical output device is screen, ttya, or ttyb.
screen-#columns	The default value of this variable is 80 and represents the number of characters or lines onscreen.
screen-#rows	This represents the number of lines and its default value is 34.
security-#badlogins	This variable contains the number of times an incorrect security password was entered. There is no default value for this variable.

Variables	Description
security-mode	This variable represents the firmware security levels and can contain any of the three options: full, command, or none.
security-password	This variable represents the firmware security password and is never displayed.
use-nvramrc?	The default value is false and if it set to true, the nvramrc commands are executed during system start-up.
local-mac-address?	The default value for this variable is false. However, if set to true, then all network devices use their own MAC addresses.
error-reset-recovery	This is used for recovery after an error-reset trap occurs and can contain three options: none, sync, or boot. The default value for this variable is boot.
watchdog-reboot	If a fault occurs, which the system deems to be potentially dangerous, the system drops to the OBP. If the watchdog-reboot is set to true the system reboots after dropping to the firmware.

B

Table B.2 details OBP configuration variable commands.

TABLE B.2   CONFIGURATION VARIABLE COMMANDS

Commands	Description
Printenv	This command displays the OpenBoot PROM configuration variables stored in the system NVRAM.
setenv *variable-name value*	This command can be used to modify specific nvram parameters. To do so, you need to execute this command at the ok prompt.
set-default *variable*	At the ok prompt, this command resets the value of the specified variable to its default value.
set-defaults	This command resets the value for all the variables to factory defaults.
Password	This command sets the security-password variable.

Table B.3 describes the commands affecting NVRAMAC.

TABLE B.3 COMMANDS AFFECTING NVRAMAC

Command	Description
nvalias alias device-path	This stores the command devalias alias device-path in the script. The alias exists until either nvunalias or set-defaults is executed.
$nvalias	This command is similar to nvalias. However, it picks up the arguments name-string and device-string from the stack.
nvedit	This command edits data, if any, from the previous nvedit session. If not, it edits the content of nvramrc that is transferred into a buffer.
nvquit	This commands removes the content of the buffer without writing it to nvramrc after confirmation.
nvrecover	This command can be used to recover the contents of nvramrc that are lost when you execute the set-defaults command. However, the action of this command will fail if nvedit is executed.
nvrun	This command executes the temporary buffer contents.
nvstore	This command empties the contents of the buffer and copies them into nvramrc.
nvunalias alias	This command can be used to delete the specified alias from nvramrc.
$nvunalias	This command has a function similar to that of nvunalias but it takes its argument, name-string, from the stack.

Table B.4 describes some of the important NVRAM Diagnostic parameters.

TABLE B.4 NVRAM DIAGNOSTIC PARAMETERS

Parameters	Description
diag-passes	The parameter is used to specify the total number of consecutive OpenBoot diagnostic tests.
diag-verbosity	This parameter is used to display a success or failure notification for a device test being performed.
diag-continue?	This parameter is used to stop testing in a routine when an error is encountered within the routine.
diag-level	This parameter is used to determine the level of testing that has been performed.

Parameters	Description
diag-script	This parameter is used to determine the OpenBoot diagnostic tests that run automatically after a reset event activated by the diag-trigger parameter.
diag-trigger	This parameter is used to specify reset events for automating OpenBoot Diagnostic tests.

B

SOLARIS MANAGEMENT TOOLS

In this appendix

Solaris Management Commands   534

The Solaris 9 Operating Environment (OE) provides a number of tools for managing services and other utilities. You can use these tools to manage jobs, log files, hard disks, performance, users, groups, printers, and projects, and to retrieve system information. In the Solaris OE, some of the management tools are grouped under umbrella applications, such as the Solaris Management Console (SMC) or the Print Manager. The following list describes the Solaris management tools grouped under SMC, Print Manager, or existing as standalone applications in the OE.

- **Users and Groups Tool**—The Users view in SMC provides tools to manage user accounts, groups, mailing lists, rights, and administrative roles. Each of these features are represented as views under the Users view in SMC. You also can add new users based on predefined user templates available in the User Templates view.

- **System Information Tool**—This tool is available as the System Information view under the System Status view in SMC. The System Information view displays information on the system hardware, software, memory, and IP address. Information on the host name, model, and ID is also displayed under the Host Information heading in the View pane.

- **Serial Port Tool**—This tool is used to manage serial ports available on the system. The tool is represented as the Serial Ports view under the Devices and Hardware view of SMC. You can use the Serial Ports view to configure ports for dial-in modems, dial-out modems, or terminals.

- **Role-Based Access Control (RBAC) Support**—The RBAC feature is used to grant specific privileges and rights for users in the form of roles. You can create a role and assign a set of privileges to the role. By granting a role to a user, you grant role-based privileges to the user. In SMC, you can use the Administrative Roles view to create roles and assign specific rights to the role. To use RBAC, users are given the choice of login into SMC with or without their assigned roles.

- **Projects Tool**—To manage projects created on the system, you can use the Projects tool. This tool is represented as the Projects view under the Performance view in SMC. The Projects view can be used to create and delete projects. In addition, you can copy or modify project properties with the view.

- **Printer Support**—On Solaris 9, printer support is implemented through the Print Manager. This tool provides a Java-based GUI front-end to a host of `lp` commands. You can use Print Manager to perform printer administration tasks, such as configuring print clients, servers, and network printers, and migrating configuration information to the latest version of Solaris.

- **Performance Tool**—In SMC, the Performance view provides performance reports on projects and users. In addition, you can also view a summarized performance report on processes, CPU usage, physical memory, swap space, and system calls.

- **Patch Tool**—You can manage patches on Solaris 9 by using the Patch tool in SMC. The tool is available as the Patches view under the System Configuration view in SMC. Before using the tool, you need to download and install the PatchPro utility from `http://www.sun.com/PatchPro`.

The Patches view uses the PatchPro utility to add patches to single or multiple systems, delete patches, and modify patch properties. The Patches view is also used to download patches from the Web.

- **Mounts and Shares Tool**—To manage file system mounts and shares on the network, you can use the Mounts and Shares tool that is implemented as a view under the Storage view of SMC. This tool enables you to mount the file system of the remote computer and access shared directories on the computer. The Mounts view under the Mounts and Shares view enables you to list the mounts available on the network. You also can add new mounts, unmount existing mounts, modify mount properties, and sort the mount list displayed in the view. The Shares view under the Mounts and Shares view lists the directory shares available on the system. Apart from adding and deleting shares, you can modify share properties with this view. You can also sort the list of shares displayed in the Share view.

- **Mail Alias Support**—On Solaris 9 OE, you can assign alias names for email IDs by using the `smmaillist` command. Alias names provide user-friendly references for long or difficult-to-remember email addresses. You will learn more about the `smmaillist` command in the following section.

- **Log Viewer**—The Log Viewer view in SMC provides two types of logs: the Management tool log and the Unix system log. You can use the management tool log to track notifications related to sessions, authentication, and other applications running on the system. In addition, you can set logging parameters to modify management log features. Some of the log management tasks that can be performed with the Management tool log include specifying log file parameters, log file subset display, log entry sort, and log backup. You can also view or delete backed-up log entries. In contrast to management tool log, you can only view Unix system log and cannot implement logging features.

- **Job Scheduler**—SMC implements job scheduling features by using the Job Scheduler tool located in the Services view. This tool enables you to create and delete scheduled jobs. You can also view job status and modify job properties with the Job Scheduler. To track events associated with a job, you can enable or disable job logging features in Job Scheduler.

- **Enhanced Disk Tool**—Enhanced Disk tool features are provided by the Enhanced Storage view in SMC. This view enables you to create different RAID level volumes and manage stripes, concatenations, mirrors, and soft partitions in the volumes. The Enhanced Storage view is also used to manage disk sets, hot spare pools, and state database replicas.

- **Diskless Client Support**—Diskless clients are systems that do not have local hard disks and work on disk resources provided by a server. Apart from the disk space on the server, diskless clients also use the server's virtual memory resources. On Solaris, you implement support for diskless clients by using the `smdiskless` and `smosservice` commands. You will learn more about these commands in the following section.

- **Disk Tools**—Disk tools are implemented by using the Disk view under the Storage view in SMC. The Disk view enables you to create disk partitions and list partition information. You also can copy disk layouts onto other disks, create `fdisk` partitions, and change the active `fdisk` partitions. In addition to disk management tasks, the Disk view can be used to access information about hard disks on a Solaris system.

- **Computers and Network Tools**—This tool exists as a view under the System Configuration view of SMC. You can use this tool to manage computers and subnetworks existing on the network. Some of the tasks that can be performed with this tool include addition or deletion of computers, networks, and subnetworks displayed in the view. You also can modify the properties of computers and networks with the view.

- **Autoclient**—AutoClients are Solaris systems that use system resources available on the server for all operations. However, these clients are not diskless clients and must have at least 100MB of free disk space on the local hard disk. AutoClients use this disk space to swap cache entries from the root directory and the `/usr` directory on the server. If the link with the server is not available, AutoClient can continue to function by using the cache entries on its hard disk. Solaris servers provide the AutoClient 3.0.1 utility to support AutoClients.

> **NOTE**
>
> To learn more about these commands, you can refer to `http://docs.sun.com`.

SOLARIS MANAGEMENT COMMANDS

The Solaris 9 OE provides a number of commands that facilitate management tasks. Some of these commands provide the underlying implementation of the views in SMC. Table C.1 describes the Solaris management commands.

TABLE C.1   SOLARIS MANAGEMENT COMMANDS

Command	Description
smrole	This command is used to manage user account information in a role. You can add, delete, or modify user accounts from a role.
smmultiuser	This command is used to manage bulk operations related to user entries in a name service, such as NIS or NIS+. The entries are stored in the `/etc` file system on the local hard disk. You can use input files or clear text piped with the `smmultiuser` command to manage bulk operations.
smuser	This command is used to manage user entries in name services such as NIS or NIS+. You can also manage user entries in the local file system. With this command, you can add, delete, or modify user entries.
smgroup	This command is used to manage group entries in the group database. You can use this command to add, delete, modify, or view a list of group entries.

Command	Description
smserialport	This command is used to manage serial ports on a Solaris system. You can con figure, delete, or modify ports with this command. You can also list existing ports using smserialport.
smosservice	This command is used to manage operating system (OS) services on a Solaris system. Using this command, you can list, add, or delete OS services. You can also manage patch installations on diskless clients.
smdiskless	This command is used to implement support for diskless clients. You can add or delete diskless clients. You can also use this command to view a list of existing diskless clients on the network.
smprofile	This command is used to manage profiles maintained in the prof_attr or exec_attr databases of a name service, such as NIS, NIS+, or a local name service. The command can be used to add, delete, modify, or list profiles.
smexec	This command is used to manage entries for exec_attr databases located in a name service. You can add, delete, or modify database entries by using this command.
smmaillist	This command is used to manage email address alias names maintained in a name service. You can use this command to add, delete, list, or modify email address alias names.

NOTE

To learn more about these commands, you can refer to http://docs.sun.com.

C

TROUBLESHOOTING

In this appendix

Troubleshooting Installation of Software Packages   538

Troubleshooting File System-Related Problems   539

Troubleshooting Printing-Related Problems   550

Troubleshooting System Crash   554

This appendix discusses some of the common problems users face while working with Solaris, as well as their possible solutions. Some of the most common problems faced on Solaris systems relate to installing packages, working with files, printers, and backup.

TROUBLESHOOTING INSTALLATION OF SOFTWARE PACKAGES

Many times while installing or uninstalling packages, you might face certain problems. These problems can be categorized into two groups: Specific Package Installation Errors, and General Package Installation Errors. The Specific Package Installation Errors are errors encountered while installing and administering software packages, whereas the General Package Installation Errors are errors related to general working of the software.

The Specific Package Installation Errors indicate that the software installed on the system doesn't contain all the required files. For example, you might use the pkgadd command line utility to install software from an NFS mounted partition on a server. In this case, you might not have sufficient rights to install the package, or access to some system files may be denied. This causes the Specific Package Installation Errors to be generated for the package.

A possible solution to this problem is to specify a symbolic link target when you install the package on the client system. This symbolic link target is specified in the pkgmap file. This option was not available in the earlier versions of Solaris, where the symbolic link pointed to the source of the package rather than the destination. This caused problems at the time of upgrading or when new patches needed to be installed. These upgrades and patches needed to make changes to the destination links, but their information was not available.

In the current version of Solaris, when a packages need to be upgraded, the pkgadd command by default makes changes to the packages' destination links, rather than the source links. However, the behavior followed by the pkgadd command might not be supported by all the packages. To implement this behavior globally, you need to use the PKG_NONABI_SYM-LINKS environment variable to create a link between the earlier and current symbolic link behaviors.

If the value of the environment variable has been set to true, pkgadd tracks the symbolic link that leads to the package source. An administrator needs to set this variable before installing the package to ensure that the package follows the default behavior of the pkgadd command. In certain cases, the symbolic link behavior for a package might fail while the pgkadd command is being used to install it. In such a case, the following error message would be displayed:

```
unable to create a symbolic link to [path]
```

In the preceding statement, [path] would contain information about where the package has been installed. If you face the preceding error message, you can call the Resolution Center and report the problem along with information about the package you are trying to install. You could also try setting the PKG_NONABI_SYMLINKS environment variable and using the pkgadd command to reinstall the package. You need to implement the following commands to set the environment variable:

```
# PKG_NONABI_SYMLINKS=true
# export PKG_NONABI_SYMLINKS
# pkgadd pkg_name
```

The General Package Installation Errors are problems commonly encountered by users trying to install or remove packages created for the earlier versions of Solaris (mostly for Solaris 5 and earlier versions). While installing or uninstalling these packages, you might be prompted for more information, which might then be ignored. The entire installation might also fail after displaying an error. A possible solution to this problem can be setting the value of the NON_ABISCRIPTS to true, and then trying to reinstall the package that had failed.

TROUBLESHOOTING FILE SYSTEM-RELATED PROBLEMS

You also can face problems relating to accessing files on the local system and over the network. Many of these problems are general in nature and a user can easily solve them without any administrative intervention. Therefore, administrators need to make the users on the network aware of the common causes of the problems and their solutions. Some of the common reasons for files and directories becoming inaccessible are:

- Improper file and directory access permissions.
- Change in network configuration.
- Change in search path or sequence of search.

PROBLEMS RELATED TO FILE ACCESS ON THE LOCAL SYSTEM

One of the most common reasons for users not being able to access files and directories that were accessible earlier is changes in file and directory permissions. This restriction can also be imposed because of changes in file and directory ownership. For example, the ownership of files can be changed if a user makes modifications to the file while logged in as a superuser. Users can also face similar problems if administrators create home directories for them without making them the owners of the directories. This leaves the users without appropriate permissions to create, save, and modify files in the home directory. Users can face similar problems if the group to which they belong is deleted or if the group permission for the file and directory changes. The administrator needs to take the following steps to ensure that users have proper access to files and directories:

- When creating home directories for users, administrators should ensure that users have proper access permissions for the directory.
- Administrators should also restrict access to the individual home directories to the users to which the home directory belongs. This ensures that only the home directory's owner has access to make modifications to the files stored in the home directory.

D

- Administrators should create groups and assign them specific rights and permissions to perform specific tasks. Individual users can then be added to the required user groups based on the user's requirement for accessing certain files or services.

- Administrators also need to ensure that they do not delete group accounts before assigning their users to appropriate groups.

PROBLEMS RELATED TO ACCESSING FILES OVER THE NETWORK

Sometimes, you might encounter an Access Denied error while trying to copy some files from a remote server. A probable reason for this is that the remote server might have imposed restrictions on accessing those files. Or the two systems might not have a trust relationship. Administrators can solve these problems by implementing security policies on the network. They can also ensure that remote users have proper access permissions to access resources and information on remote machines. If specific computers need to access services running on remote machines, or groups of users need to be assigned access to both the machines, administrators can establish a trust relationship between both computers. This ensures that users authenticated on one system are also trusted on the other system. However, secure methods, such as Kerberos or Secure Shell, should be used in these cases.

PROBLEMS RELATED TO SEARCH PATHS

Sometimes files and directories might not be accessible because either the search path has changed or the sequence of search is incorrect. A search path contains the location from where a specific command or file can be accessed. If the command does not exist on the system, or if the path to the file is not included, the file will not be found. The sequence in the search path also determines whether the correct version of the command is displayed. For example, you might have two command files having similar names but stored in separate directories. When the command is executed, the first instance of the file detected is returned and executed. After the command is found, the search does not continue. Therefore, the second version of the command cannot be executed even if it exists in the search path. The echo command is used along with the PATH environment variable to display the search path followed on the system. The syntax of the command is as follows:

```
# echo $PATH
```

You can use the which command to determine whether you are currently using the correct version of another command. The which command is used primarily for locating commands and for displaying the location where the commands exist. The command searches an existing list of commands and determines the appropriate command that should be executed. It is a recommended practice to use the which command only in the C shell. Following is the syntax of the which command:

```
$ which <command name>
```

NOTE

> It is recommended not to execute the `which` command from the Korn or Bourne shell, because when the command is executed from these shells, it retrieves incorrect information from the .cshrc file. An alternative to the `which` command is the `whence` command, which can be used to retrieve the same information in the Korn shell.

The first step in ensuring that you use the correct version of a command is to display the path in which the search will take place. As mentioned previously, you use the `echo $PATH` command to retrieve this information. After the information is displayed, you need to check whether the search path is as per your requirement. If there are multiple versions of the same command stored on the system, you need to ensure that the search path lists the correct directory location for the version you require. The path should be listed before the paths of the other versions to ensure that the correct version is executed.

If the path is incorrect or if the directory is not located in the search path, you need to set the correct path in the PATH environment variable. The location where the information is stored depends on the shell version being used on the system. For example, if you are using the Bourne or Korn shell, then the path information is available in the `$HOME/.profile` file. If you are using the C shell, the path information is stored in the `$HOME/.cshrc` or the `$HOME/.login` files.

After the path information has been set or identified, you need to activate the path before the path can be used for searching. With the C shell, different commands need to be used depending on where the path information is stored. If the information is stored in the .cshrc file, the first command is used; if the information is stored in the .login file, then the second command is used. These commands are as follows:

```
hostname% source .cshrc
hostname% source .login
```

If you are using the Bourne or Korn shell, the PATH environment variable is stored in the .profile file. This file is present in the user's home directory. If this directory is not present, you can use any of the text editors to create it.

The syntax of specifying the path in the .profile is as follows:

```
PATH= /usr/sbin:/usr/bin:/usr/ucb/bin...
Export PATH
```

If you have modified the existing PATH, use the following command to activate the new PATH:

```
. ./.profile
```

Finally, you need to confirm that the path has indeed changed by using the `which` command to display the path information.

USING `fsck` TO AUDIT AND REPAIR FILE SYSTEM INCONSISTENCIES

The `fsck` command is primarily used to check file systems for errors in case the system reboots or shuts down because of a power failure or because it was switched off while the OS was running. In such a case, certain information that the system keeps in its memory cannot be saved on the hard disk. The fsck command reports both fixable and unfixable errors it finds while scanning the file system. The command can also be used to fix some of the encountered errors. When an error that can be fixed is encountered, the command provides the user with a possible solution and prompts for a reply. You can also specify that all suggested solutions should be accepted by using the -y option. This option sets yes as the default reply. However, be careful when using this option because there are situations when you do not want to reply with a yes.

The fsck command uses multiple passes to check the file system. Each pass analyzes a different type of information and displays appropriate messages. Most of the checks, also known as *phases*, analyze different parts of the file system, such as pathnames, connectivity, block sizes, available blocks, and reference counts. The scan begins with initialization and continues for five additional phases. The following list includes the phases and what is checked in each phase:

- **Phase 1**—Performs a check on blocks and their sizes.
- **Phase 2**—Performs a check on pathnames.
- **Phase 3**—Performs a check on connectivity.
- **Phase 4**—Performs a check on reference counts.
- **Phase 5**—Performs a check on cylinder groups.

During each phase, the command keeps displaying appropriate information and error messages regarding any problems found on the system. Because all the error messages display the name of the system's affected sections in abbreviation, you need to know the abbreviations to decipher the error messages. Table D.1 lists abbreviations of all the sections that could contain errors.

TABLE D.1   ABBREVIATIONS FOUND IN fsck ERROR MESSAGES

Abbreviation	Description
MTIME	Contains information about the time when the file was last modified.
DIR	Contains information regarding the directory name where this error was found.
BLK	Contains information regarding the block number where the error was found.
UNREF	Contains information about all unreferenced data found on the system. This information is generally in scrap files that are created if the system shuts down without saving the information that is stored in the memory to the disk.
DUP	Contains information about duplicate block numbers found on the system.
CG	Contains information about the cylinder group that contains the error.

The error messages displayed by the command can also contain information that is variable in nature. For example, the inode numbers can be used to display information regarding errors encountered.

These errors, which are encountered by the system after initialization, give you the option to continue working by ignoring them. However, it is recommended not to do so, because some of these errors can prove fatal for the system. These errors can be the cause of system failure and should be fixed when encountered. When these errors appear, you must immediately stop all activities and shut down the system. If you cannot understand these errors or detect their source, you must immediately report the problem to the administrator. Table D.2 lists some of the most common errors that the system can encounter after initialization.

TABLE D.2   ERRORS ENCOUNTERED BY THE FSCK COMMAND

Errors Encountered	Source
CANNOT WRITE: BLK *block-number* (CONTINUE)	This error is encountered if the system attempts to write to a specific block on the hard disk and the write attempt fails. If the write attempt fails once, the system attempts to write to the disk again. If the attempt fails again, the fsck command lists all the sectors to which the system could not write. If the block exists in the memory and is part of the memory buffer cache, the fatal I/O error message is displayed. A possible cause of the error could be that the system is write-protected. If this is true, remove the write protect and run the fsck command again. If the error continues, you need to report the problem to your local administrator.
CANNOT READ: BLK *block-number* (Continue)	This error is encountered if a read attempt to a specific block address or number fails. The system uses the block-number parameter to specify the block number where the read attempt has failed. The system also alerts the administrator about an imminent hardware failure. If you decide to resume the file check, fsck attempts to again read the block that it was previously unable to read. If it still is not able to read the block, it lists all the sectors that could not be read properly. If the file system check fails again, you should run fsck again to confirm whether the hardware problem still exists. If the system does not contain a hardware problem, the information needs to be reported to the administrator.

continues

TABLE D.2   CONTINUED

Errors Encountered	Source
CANNOT SEEK: BLK *block-number* (CONTINUE)	This error implies that an attemptto access a specific block in the memory or the hard disk was not successful. If the file system check is continued, the fsck command displays all the sectors that could not be accessed. If the block-number belongs to a memory location, the fsck command will display a fatal I/O error and stop execution. You can run the fsck command again to re-examine the system. If the problem continues, you need to contact your administrator to solve the problem.

There are other types of errors that can occur during the initialization stage. In this stage, the fsck command is used to create various tables, and the different files required by the system are opened. The phase also involves configuring the command line options used on the system. The error messages display information relating to the following areas:

- Opening files
- Condition of files
- Incorrect configuration of command line options
- Checks on the size of the file system
- Requests for memory
- Creating new files

All these issues can be classified as initialization errors. These errors can cause the fsck command not to function properly. Table A.3 lists some of the common initialization errors that can occur on a system during the initialization phase.

TABLE D.3   ERRORS ENCOUNTERED DURING THE INITIALIZATION PHASE

Errors Encountered	Source
bad inode number inode-number to ginode	This error is encountered if the specified inode number does not exist. The fsck command displays the error message and then exits. This error usually occurs when a process requires memory, which is not available because other processes might be using it. This error also suggests imminent system failure. Therefore, you should call your administrator and get the system checked.

Errors Encountered	Source
Can't roll the log for device-name. DISCARDING THE LOG MAY DISCARD PENDING TRANSACTIONS DISCARD THE LOG AND CONTINUE?	The fsck command needs to clear the transaction log of a UFS file system before the command can begin scanning the system for errors. This error is mostly encountered if the fsck command is unable to clear the transaction log. If you answer Yes to the prompt to either discard the log file or to continue, then all the log information currently stored in the memory and not to the disk is lost. You will again be prompted to reclaim the blocks in a later stage during scanning. If you do not discard the changes, all the information currently stored in memory is placed in log files. The drawback of this choice is that the file system cannot be mounted again.
Can't open *filename*	This error occurs when the fsck command cannot open a specific file. If the command is running interactively with the file system, the command displays an error and then continues scanning the next file. A possible solution to this problem is to check the file's read and write permissions.
Can't open checklist file: *filename*	This error occurs if the command is unable to open the system checklist file. The fsck command displays the error and stops execution. You can check whether the file exists and whether it provides the appropriate access permission.
Can't stat *file_name* Can't make sense out of name *filename*	During scanning, the fsck command gathers certain information or statistics about the files being checked. This error is encountered if the command is unable to gather statistical information about a specific file. The command displays an appropriate error and continues scanning the next file. You can solve the problem by ensuring that the file exists and provides appropriate access permission.
filename: (NO Write)	This error is encountered if the fsck command is unable to write to a specific file. This error occurs if the -n option is used along with the command, or if the appropriate access permissions are not provided. When the -n option is used, the file system is not writable and only the error messages are displayed. These messages can then be used to diagnose the problem. Another possible reason for the error could be an incorrect file type.
Can't stat root	While scanning the file system, the fsck command also gathers information about the root directory. If the command is not able to gather information about the root directory, the error message is displayed and the command stops functioning. If the command cannot gather the required information, it suggests imminent system failure. Therefore, you should contact your local administrator to get the system checked.

D

In phase 1, when the system is being scanned, the following tasks need to be performed in the inode list:

- Determine the type of inodes available on the file system.
- Test for bad blocks or incorrect inode numbers.
- Test to ensure accurate inode size.
- Test to ensure accurate inode format.
- Configure a zero-link-count table.

The following types of errors generally occur in phase 1:

- **block-number DUP I=inode number**—Each block in the inode contains a unique block number. A warning message regarding a block number is displayed if the specified block number is already in use by another block. If a single inode or different inodes attempt to access multiple block numbers, the system encounters an EXCESSIVE DUP BLKS error message.

- **block-number BAD I=inode-number**—All block numbers used in inodes are assigned from a specific range of values. Therefore, an assigned block number should not be less than the block number assigned to the first data block on the file system and not more than the block number assigned to the last block. If the block number doesn't satisfy either of these conditions, the system encounters an EXCESSIVE DUP BLKS error message.

- **BAD STATE state-number TO BLKERR**—The file system might face an internal error that could cause the state maps used by the `fsck` command to display an incorrect state number. This error causes the system to display the error and then it causes the command to stop executing. The administrator needs to be contacted and informed about the error.

- **BAD MODE: MAKE IT A FILE?**—If there is system damage, the system sets the status of the specified inode as 1. This error message does not indicate that the physical disk has been damaged. However, if the `-y` option is used repeatedly with the `fsck` command and the error message is also displayed, this could lead to physical disk damage. Therefore, it is advisable to use the `-y` option cautiously.

- **EXCESSIVE BAD-BLOCKS I=inode number (CONTINUE)**—This error occurs in cases where there are more than 10 blocks whose block numbers are either more than the last block number specified for a file system or less than the first block number. If the `-o` option is used along with the command, the program stops execution after displaying the error. You can continue execution by typing **y** at the CONTINUE prompt. If this error occurs, you need to use the `fsck` command to run a complete diagnostic of the file system.

- **DUP TABLE OVERFLOW (CONTINUE)**—This error occurs if the space in the internal tables used by the `fsck` command is exhausted. The table stores records of multiple block numbers found in the file system. If the `-o` option is used along with the `fsck` command, the program stops executing after the error message is displayed. You can continue execution by typing the -y option at the CONTINUE prompt. Because a complete diagnostic of the file system is not possible, the error is displayed when duplicate entries for the same block number are found. You can solve this problem by increasing the amount of virtual memory available on the system and by executing the fsck command to rescan the system.

- **EXCESSIVE DUP BLKS I=inode-number (CONTINUE)**—This error occurs when the same block number is assigned to a single inode or to multiple inodes. As is the case with other errors, if the -o option is used with the fsck command, the program stops executing after the error is displayed. Because a complete diagnostic of the file system is not possible, you need to run the fsck command again to check the file system for any more errors.

- **LINK COUNT TABLE OVERFLOW (CONTINUE)**—This error indicates that the internal link table does not contain any more space to store inode values that have a link count of zero. If the -o option is used with the fsck command, the program terminates and needs to be continued manually. The error message is displayed for every entry found containing a zero-link count with the inode. Because a complete diagnostic of the file system is not possible, you need to run the fsck command repeatedly until all the errors in the file system are detected. You can kill some of the unnecessary processes on the system to free some memory and increase the swap space. After the additional memory is available, you can run the fsck command again to complete the scanning of the file system. You can also end the entire process by typing **n** at the CONTINUE prompt.

- **PARTIALLY ALLOCATED INODE I=inode-number (CLEAR)**—This error is encountered if the specified inode values are neither allocated nor unallocated. In such circumstances, if the -o option is used with the fsck command the inode values are emptied. You need to type the **-y** option if you need to deallocate the inode number and specify zero as its value. This might also cause the system to generate the DEALLO-CATED error that is encountered in phase 2 for every pointer to the inode. If you type the value **n**, it indicates that you want to ignore the error condition. However, ignoring the error condition is advisable only if you want to use other measures to solve the problem.

- **PARTIALLY TRUNCATED INODE I=inode-number (SALVAGE)**—This error message is generated if the fsck command detects an inode value that is shorter in size as compared to the number of blocks allocated to it. The error occurs if the system crashes while attempting to truncate a file. The fsck command attempts to truncate the file to a specified file size. You need to type **y** at the SALVAGE prompt to complete the process and type **n** to ignore the error and continue.

- **UNKNOWN FILE TYPE I=inode number (CLEAR)**—The mode value indicates that the specified inode is not a special block inode, pipe, regular inode, special character inode, directory inode, or a symbolic link. If you specify the -o option along with the fsck command, the value contained in the inode is cleared. You can deallocate an inode by zeroing its content. Deallocating an inode might cause an UNALLOCATD

D

error to occur. This error is generally generated in phase 2 for every directory that points to this inode location. You can either type **y** at the CLEAR prompt to deallocate the inode or you can type **n** to ignore the error.

In phase 2 of scanning, all the directory entries that link to the bad inode values detected in phase 1 are deleted. Phase 2 generally returns errors arising from any of the following:

- Out-of-range directory pointers
- Directory integrity checks
- Incorrect inode status and mode
- Entries pointing to bad inode values

The following types of errors generally occur in phase 2:

- **BAD INODE NUMBER FOR '.' I=inode-number OWNER=UID MODE=file-MODE SIZE=file-size MTIME=modification-time DIR=filename (FIX)**—This error is generated if the specified inode number for a directory inode does not match another inode value. You can either fix the inode value by typing **y** when prompted to fix at the FIX prompt. However, if you do not want to fix the inode value and want to leave it as it is, you need to type **n** at the FIX prompt.

- **BAD RETURN STATE state-number FROM DESCEND**—This error is generated if the fsck command encounters an internal error because it has specified an invalid state number. This state number is then passed to the function that handles the file system directory structure. The fsck command displays the error message and stops execution. You need to contact your local administrator to solve the error generated by this command.

- **BAD STATE state-number FOR INODE=inode-number**—This error is generated if an internal error caused by the fsck command causes an unlikely state number to be specified to an inode number. The fsck command stops execution after displaying this error. You need to contact your local administrator to get this error solved.

- **BAD STATE state-number FOR ROOT INODE**—This error is generated if an internal error caused by the fsck command causes an unlikely state number to be specified to the root inode. The fsck command stops executing after displaying this error. You need to contact your local administrator to get this error solved.

- **DIRECTORY TOO SHORT I=inode-number OWNER=UID MODE=file-mode SIZE=file-size MTIME=modification-time DIR=filename (FIX)**—This error indicates the presence of a directory file name whose size is less than the minimum directory size. The error message also displays information about the UID of the owner, the file-mode, the last time the file was modified, and the directory name. You have the option to either fix the directory size or increase it to the minimum directory size, or to ignore the error.

- **DIRECTORY filename: LENGTH file-size NOT MULTIPLE of block-number (ADJUST)**—This error is encountered if a directory filename is detected during scanning whose file size is not a multiple of the block number's directory size. You can solve this problem by rounding up the file size to an appropriate block size, or you can ignore the problem. The `fsck` command displays a warning message and then adjusts the directory size.

- **DIRECTORY CORRUPTED I=inode-number OWNER=UID MODE=file-mode SIZE=file-size MTIME=modification-time DIR=filename (SALVAGE)**—This error is generated if the scan detects an error in the internal state of a directory that needs to be fixed before continuing. You can solve this error by typing **y** at the SALVAGE prompt. This deletes all entries until the next directory boundary, which is generally 512 bytes away. This is an extreme step and should be implemented only if all other measures to solve the problem have failed. You can type **n** at the SALVAGE prompt to indicate that you want to skip to the next directory boundary and continue scanning, but do not want to change the directory information.

- **DUP/BAD I=inode-number OWNER=O MODE=M SIZE=file-size MTIME=modification-time TYPE=filename (REMOVE)**—This error is generated if the system detects bad or duplicate blocks in the root inode during scanning in phase 1. You can empty the current content of the inode and assign other content. You need to type **y** at the REALLOCATE prompt to move all the files and directories found in the root inode to the `lost and found` directory. If the system is not able to reallocate the information, it stops execution after displaying an appropriate message. You need to type **y** at the CONTINUE prompt to ignore the DUPS/BAD errors and continue with the rest of the scanning. However, if the root inode is not correct it can lead to other errors.

- **hard link number IS AN EXTRANEOUS HARD LINK TO A DIRECTORY filename (REMOVE)**—This error is generated if the `fsck` command detects an extraneous hard link to a directory. The `fsck` command ignores all hard links while scanning. You can delete the hard link by typing **y** at the REMOVE prompt.

In the phase 3 of scanning, all the directory entries that were checked in phase 2 are rechecked based on additional criteria. In Phase 3 most of the errors are caused by the following:

- Omitted or misplaced directories
- Directories that have no references in the file system

The following types of errors generally occur in phase 3:

- **DIRECTORY filename LENGTH file-size NOT MULTIPLE of block-number (ADJUST)**—This error is generated if the scan detects a directory whose file size is not a multiple of a specified block number. You have the option of either rounding off the length of the block size by typing **y** at the ADJUST prompt. The `fsck` command displays the error message and stops execution. The other option is to ignore the error and continue scanning.

- **lost+found IS NOT A DIRECTORY (REALLOCATE)**—This error is generated if certain lost+found entries are retrieved during scanning and they do not correspond to actual directory entries. A possible solution to the error can be allocating a directory inode and referencing the lost+found entry to it. You can establish the reference by typing **y** at the REALLOCATE prompt. However, you need to remember that the earlier reference is not automatically deleted. The link is either declared as an unreferenced inode or the link is used in a later phase. If the system is unable to create the directory, it displays an appropriate message and stops executing.

- **NO SPACE LEFT IN lost/found (EXPAND)**—This error is generated if the system attempts to add a new entry to the lost+found directory and finds that no disk space is left. The fsck command can be used to increase the size of the lost+found directory to accommodate additional entries. To expand the directory you need to type **y** at the EXPAND prompt. If the system is unable to increase the directory size, it displays an appropriate error message and exits. You could create some additional space in the lost+found directory by deleting certain unnecessary entries.

In the phase 4 of scanning, all the directory entries acquired after the first three phases of scanning are checked for a different set of errors. In phase 4 most of the errors are caused by the following:

- Files, symbolic links, and directories that have no references
- An omitted or packed lost+found directory
- Files that have no reference anywhere in the file system
- Files, symbolic links, and directories that provide incorrect links
- Inaccurate total count of free-inodes
- Duplicate or bad blocks existing in files and directories

Phase 5 is the final phase or level of scanning. In this phase, the system does a complete scan for all free blocks and inode maps used on the system. In phase 5 most of the errors are caused by the following:

- Incorrect reference to free blocks in the free block maps
- Incorrect reference to free inodes in the used inode maps
- Incorrect reference to used inodes in the used inode maps
- Incorrect total count of used inodes
- Incorrect total count of free blocks

The next section discusses some of the issues relating to troubleshooting printer problems.

TROUBLESHOOTING PRINTING-RELATED PROBLEMS

A printer is also a critical piece of hardware and needs to be maintained properly to get the expected output. You need to check the printer regularly to ensure that it receives the correct input and provides the correct output. There are also certain precautions that you can take for troubleshooting hardware-related problems. The following sections discuss these measures.

PROBLEMS RELATED TO HARDWARE

If the printer does not provide the proper output, you need to check certain things to solve the problem. Some of these steps are very simple and quite often easily overlooked. The first step is to check whether the printer is properly plugged and switched on. Then you need to check whether the printer cable connecting the printer to the system is properly connected to both the printer and the system. You also need to ensure that you use the proper cable and that the cable itself is not defective. For example, if the printer needs to be connected to the serial port you need to ensure that the serial cable is properly connected and forms a live connection between the system and the printer.

Check that all the hardware switches for the port have been correctly set. Problems here are common and difficult to diagnose. You might need to refer to the manufacturer's reference manual to get the correct settings for the printer. Each type of printer has a different setting that is required for it to function correctly. Next, you need to check whether the printer is functional and operational. You can generally test this by using the self-test feature available in most printers. The self-test prints a predefined page and ensures that the printer is functioning correctly. Next, you need to check the baud setting of the system and the printer. The baud settings for both the printer and the system need to be same for the printer to function correctly. If the baud settings are not configured correctly, you might either get incorrect output or no output at all.

PROBLEMS RELATED TO NETWORK CONNECTIONS

After ensuring that the printer is working correctly, the next step is to ensure that the network connection bringing information from the system to the printer is also functioning correctly. Therefore, you need to check the link between the printer server and the printer client installed on the system. One of the methods of checking whether the connection is alive is to print to the print server. If the print server replies, it means that the network connection is working. The message also provides you with information about whether the hostname you specified was translated by either a naming service or the local /etc/hosts file. If the name cannot be resolved by either of them, you can also specify the printer server's IP address.

If an error message is displayed or if the printer could not be accessed, you need to check how NIS or NIS+ have been configured on the network. If neither of these naming services are configured on the network, you need to specify the printer's IP address in the host files of all the client systems and add entries for each client in the /etc/hosts file on the print server.

D

PROBLEMS RELATED TO INCORRECT PRINTER CONFIGURATION

The next step for ensuring that the printer is working correctly is to check the printer configuration. The first step is to ensure that the LP printer service is running. You can check this by using the lpstat command. Following is how the command can be used:

```
# lpstat -r
```

The preceding command shows whether the print service is running. If the scheduler is not running, you can use the following command to start the scheduler.

```
# /usr/lib/lp/lpsched
```

After you have made sure that the print service is running correctly, you need to check whether both the print server and the print client are able to accept requests. The following command is used for this purpose:

```
# lpstat -a
```

The preceding command displays whether the printer would be able to handle print requests. The command also verifies that the LP system can handle requests made for any printer configured on the system. If the printer cannot handle print requests, you can enable this service by using the accept luna command. However, it is important to note that you need to be logged on as a superuser or lp to enable this service on the printer. Following is how the command can be used:

```
# accept luna
```

The next step after ensuring that the printer server and the client can receive and send requests is to ensure that the printer can print the submitted requests. The first step is to ensure that the printer is enabled, and the following command does so:

```
# lpstat -p luna
```

The preceding command displays the printer status and informs you whether it can print. If the printer is disabled, you first need to enable it before you can print anything. The next step in ensuring that the printer is working correctly is to check that the printer is connected to the appropriate serial port. The following command is used to check this:

```
lpstat -t
```

The preceding command checks whether the printer is connected to the proper port and the message device displays the port address. The next task is to assign appropriate access permissions. Before you can assign access permissions, you need to log in as a superuser. Then, you need to change the ownership of the device files that are used to access the port by using the following command:

```
# chown lp device-filename
```

In the preceding command, the user lp is assigned as the owner of the printer device file. Next, you need to change the access permission for the file by using the following command:

```
# chmod 600 device-filename
```

This command restricts the right to access the printer port device file to only the superuser or the lp user accounts. Next, you need to ensure that the printer is configured properly on the print server and the client system. The following command is used for this purpose:

```
# lpstat -p luna -l
```

Then, you need to ensure that the printer is functioning on the print server. If an error occurs on the print server, the printer is stopped and all print tasks are either suspended or deleted.

STEPS TO DELETE A PRINTER AND DENY ACCESS TO REMOTE PRINTERS

If you need to delete a printer available on a remote machine, you also need to delete all the references to the printer from the client machines. If the reference to the deleted remote printer remains on the client machine, users receive an error message if they try to print to the printer. However, it is not necessary to delete the existing printer information if you share another printer on the remote machine with the same share name. To delete all references to the printer, implement the following steps:

1. Log in to the system as a superuser, lp, or a user account with similar privileges or access permission to the printer.

2. Delete information about the printer from all clients who were assigned rights to access the printer. Use the lpadmin command to delete all references to the printer from the specified client. The information is stored in the /etc/lp/printers directory. You can use the following command to perform the task:

   ```
   print client# lpadmin -x printer-name
   ```

3. If there is only one printer available on the printer server, you also need to delete all references to the print server from the client computer. The printer server information is stored in the /etc/lp/System file on the client system. The following command is used to delete all reference to the print server:

   ```
   print client# lpsystem -r print server
   ```

4. Log in to the printer server as a superuser or using a user account with similar rights.

5. Stop the print service running on the server and refuse to service any more print requests. The following command is used to perform the task:

   ```
   print server# reject printer-name
   ```

6. Next, you need to stop or disable the printer. The following command is used for this purpose:

   ```
   print server# disable printer-name
   ```

7. If there are any pending print requests, they need to be redirected to another printer.

8. You then need to delete the printer information from the print server. The printer information is stored in the /etc/lp/printers directory. You need to use the following command to delete the printer from the print server:

   ```
   print server# lpadmin -x printer-name
   ```

D

9. After the printer has been deleted you also need to delete information about all the clients who had the right to access the printer from the print server. However, this step is not required if the clients are provided access to another printer on the same print server. The following command is used to delete the client information:

```
print server# lpsystem -r print client[,print client2…]
```

10. After the printer has been deleted, you need to verify that all the relevant printer information has also been deleted from each of the client machines. You can use the following command to verify the deletion:

```
print client# lpstat -p printer-name -1
```

11. You also need to use the following command to verify that all the printer information has been deleted from the print server.

```
print server# lpstat -p printer-name -1.
```

STEPS TO EXAMINE THE STATUS OF PRINTERS

The printer maintains the status of the different print jobs. If an error occurs on the print server, all print jobs are suspended and the status of the current print job shows an error. Therefore, you need to examine the status of printers to identify the source of the error. You need to perform the following steps to display the printer status:

1. Log on to any of the systems available on the network.

2. Use the lpstat command to display information about the status of a printer available on the network. Following is the syntax of the command:

```
#lpstat [-d] [-p printer-name [-p] [-l]] [-t]
```

The -d option is used to display information about the default printer. You can also specify the printer name by using the -p option. The command displays information about whether the printer is available. You can also display information about multiple printers with the same command. Each printer name should be enclosed within quotes. By default, if no printer name is specified, the status information about all the available printers is displayed. You can also display the characteristics of the current printer by using the -1 command. The same command can also be used to display information of any other printer if the printer name is specified. The -t option is used to provide information about whether the LP print service is available.

TROUBLESHOOTING SYSTEM CRASH

Most systems crash because of either operating system failure or application errors. When an operating system starts, it compares the resources available with the system against the list of registered components in its memory. If the components do not match, the system crashes. Similarly, when an application starts, it searches for resources at a specific location. If the required resources are not found, the application cannot function and therefore might lead to a system crash. For example, if an application attempts to read an unreferenced memory location or attempts to write to a location on the hard disk that is inaccessible, this can cause the system to crash.

D

If an administrator is responsible for repairing the system, you need to provide the information about the cause of the crash so that the problem can easily be identified. In the event of a system crash, you need to note down all the console messages because they offer a rich source of information about why the system crashed. Therefore, before you reboot the system you need to note all the information available on the screen. If the system reboots before you have a chance to note all the error messages and information, you can access the same information from the /var/adm/messages file. This file stores all the error information and diagnostics gathered by the system at the time of the system crash. This file contains information that can be used for diagnosing the cause of the system crash. The information is also beneficial for the administrator for getting the system back online. After you have noted all the information, you need to synchronize the disks and reboot the system. You also need to ensure that the crash dump information that is created when the system crashes is also saved. Because this is a default option, you might only need to ensure that this has taken place.

The following section discusses what type of information you need to gather from a crashed system.

INFORMATION OBTAINED FROM CRASHED SYSTEMS

It would be incorrect to say that all information returned by the system during system crash is important. Therefore, the question that arises is what are the various kinds of information that you need to collect from a crashed system. Following is a list of some of the critical pieces of information that you need to ensure are saved from a crashed system:

- **Reproducing the problem**—It is important to know that the problem can be reproduced at a later stage. Reproducing the problem helps administrators diagnose the reasons why the problem occurred and the preventive measures that can be taken to secure the system against the problem. It also helps them ensure that the problem is solved if it is a bug in the system software.

- **Use of third-party drivers**—If the system uses third-party drivers, the crash could have been caused by multiple drivers trying to gain access to the same memory space on the kernel. This could be a bug in the drivers and would need to be solved before the system can function smoothly.

- **Processes and tasks running on the system**—It is also important to know all the processes and tasks that were running on the system at the time the system crashed. This information also helps to diagnose the cause of the crash and ensure that it does not happen in future.

- **Displayed console messages**—Most of the time, the console messages that are displayed on a crashed system are a rich source of information about why the system crashed.

- **Parameters used or changed on the system**—Another reason why a system might crash is because you might make certain changes to the system settings that are not supported, or you might make a mistake while tuning certain performance parameters. For example, you might increase the shared memory segment, which causes the system to allocate more memory for use by various processes than it actually needs. This causes the system to fall short of its memory requirement and subsequently crash.

- **Time when the problem was first noticed**—Identifying the time period during which the problem has been occurring is also critical for detecting the source of the problem. For example, if the problem was first noticed after the installation of new hardware or software, or when a certain driver was upgraded, the driver or software could be the cause of the problem. Increase in system load, upgrades or changes made to the CPU, and upgrade of memory are other common reasons of system crashes.

STEPS TO DISPLAY THE CURRENT SYSTEM'S CRASH DUMP CONFIGURATION

You can display the core dump information created by the system. The information is stored on the local machine and can be displayed if you use the `dumpadm` command. You use the following steps to display the dump information:

1. Log on to the system as a superuser.
2. At the command prompt type **dumpadm**.
3. The information contains details about where the crash dump information will be stored and whether the saving of crash dump files is enabled.

STEPS TO SCRUTINIZE CRASH DUMP INFORMATION

You can also examine the core dump information and identify the causes that lead to the core dump. Following are the steps you need to follow to accomplish this task:

1. Log on to the system as a superuser.
2. Use the `mbd` utility to scrutinize the dump information. The syntax of the utility is as follows:
   ```
   # /user/bin/mbd [-k] crashdump-file
   ```
3. The crash dump information is displayed.

STEPS TO MODIFY A CRASH DUMP CONFIGURATION

You can modify the way information is stored in the core dump and also the type of information that can be stored in it. You need to perform the following steps to accomplish this task:

1. Log on to the system as a superuser.
2. Execute the `dumpadm` command from the command prompt to display the crash information of the current system.
3. Modify the information in the crash dump file. You can use the following syntax to modify the information:
   ```
   # dumpadm -c content -d dump-device -m nnnk | nnnm| nnn% -n -s
   ➥savecore-dir
   ```

The -c option is used to provide information about the type of data that can be stored in the dump file. You need to specify kernel if only the kernel information needs to be stored. If you want to store all the information in the dump file, you need to specify all. By default, only the kernel information is stored. The -d option is used for specifying where the dump information needs to be stored temporarily when the system crashes.

By default, the information is stored in the swap partition before it is saved to the disk. The -m option is used to specify the minimum amount of disk space that needs to be kept aside for storing the crash information. This value can either be specified in kb, mb, or as a percentage. The savecore command checks for the required amount of disk space before saving the dump information to the disk. If adequate disk space is not available, the information is not saved to the disk and an error message is registered. A -n option can also be used with the dumpadm command to state that the savecore command should not perform the disk space check while the system is booting. You can also use a different directory to store the dump information by using the -s option to specify the path.

STEPS TO RECOVER FROM A FULL CRASH DUMP DIRECTORY

Sometimes, after the savecore command detects that no disk space is available on the disk, you might still want to save certain information that is essentially required for system diagnostics. You need to perform the following steps to save the information:

1. Log on to the system as a superuser.
2. Navigate to the savecore directory, which is by default situated at /var/crash/ <hostname>, and delete all the current information. You can also specify an alternative location to store the dump information while using the savecore command.
3. If you need to specify an alternate location to store the dump information, execute the savecore command manually from the command prompt. Following is the syntax of the command:

```
# savecore [<path to alternative location>]
```

STEPS TO DISABLE OR ENABLE SAVING CRASH DUMP INFORMATION

You can also enable or disable the saving of crash dump information by using the following steps:

1. Log on to the system as a superuser.
2. Use the dumpadm command to enable or disable the saving of crash dump information:

```
# dumpadm -n| -y
```

EXAMINING SYSTEM MESSAGES

System messages are in text format and are displayed on the console device. The message typically contains the message ID, the facility to which it belongs, and the severity level. The system displays all error messages and warnings by using the default error-logging syslogd daemon available in Solaris. The default location where these log files are stored is the /var/adm directory. These log files provide advance warning about imminent system or hardware failure. The /var/adm directory stores all the messages files together. However, the most recent message files are stored in the /var/adm/messages directory and are named message.1, message.2, and message.3 files. After a specific time interval, when a new message file is created, the new file is named message.1, the previous message.1 is renamed message.2, the previous message.2 is renames message.3, and the earlier message.3 file is then deleted.

Because the /var/adm directory stores all the message files and dump information, it soon gets large and consumes a lot of disk space. Therefore, it is advisable to periodically save the old files to different locations and periodically remove unnecessary files. You could also automate the task and schedule it periodically by using cron. You can also display all the recent messages generated because of a system crash or unexpected reboot by using the dmesg command.

D

APPENDIX

SOLARIS TUNABLE PARAMETERS

Solaris 9 can be described as a self-tuning operating environment (OE), which manages OS tuning based on current load requirements. However, you can perform manual tuning operations by manipulating tunable parameters specified in the /etc/system file. The following sections describe some of the important kernel, TCP/IP, and NFS tunable parameters that are used in system tuning. However, unless you clearly understand what you are doing, do not modify any of these parameters. Incorrect settings may result in system crashes or even inability to boot the OS.

Table E.1 describes kernel tunable parameters available in the Solaris 9 Operating Environment.

TABLE E.1   KERNEL TUNABLE PARAMETERS

Parameter	Description
physmem	This parameter modifies the number of physical pages of memory after the OS and firmware are accounted for. You need to change this parameter to test the system under conditions of minimal memory. The value assigned to this parameter must be less than the total memory available on the system. The value does not include memory allocation for data structures and core kernel resources on the system.
lwp_default_stksize	This parameter specifies the default stack size used to allocate stacks for new kernel threads. The value is used in scenarios where a calling program does not specify stack sizes for the kernel thread. You need to modify this parameter in situations when the OS runs out of stack space.
tune_t_fsflush	fsflush is a daemon that runs periodically to flush dirty file system pages, to examine portions of memory, and to write modified pages to their backing store. tune_t_fsflush specifies the number of seconds between fsflush invocations.
autoup	This parameter is used to control the number of memory pages scanned by fsflush. In addition, you can control file system sync operations using this parameter. You need to modify the parameter value to control the number of pages scanned by the fsflush daemon.
maxusers	This parameter defines the number of processes and quota structures on the system, in addition to the total number of concurrently logged in users. The size of the Directory Name Lookup Cache (DNLC) is also defined by this parameter. You need to modify the parameter value to increase or decrease the number of user processes on the system. When you increase this value, remember that you still have the same RAM and processing power.
reserved_procs	This parameter is used to specify the number of reserved system process slots in the process table. When specifying this parameter value, you need to count only processes with the UID of root(0).

E

Parameter	Description
lotsfree	This parameter is used to specify a threshold value for triggering page scanning. You can modify the parameter value to begin a preemptive memory page scan. This helps in coping with sudden increases in page demands from the OS.
desfree	This parameter specifies the desired free memory space on the system. You can modify this parameter value to reduce the available free memory space on systems with large memory capacities.
swapfs_reserve	This parameter defines the memory size reserved for system processes. You can modify this parameter to increase the availability of swap space for system process that are terminating because of system shut down.
swapfs_minfree	This parameter is used to specify the desired amount of free physical memory that the OS must maintain. You can modify this parameter to free memory space for swapping when processes require memory in emergency scenarios.
noexec_user_stack	This parameter is used to define stack space allocations as unusable. If you use this parameter, you may avoid harmful effects of buffer over flows. Modifying this parameter is allowed only in situations where applications use the reserved stack area explicitly for execution.
modedebug	This parameter is used to define values that are displayed during a module load process. You can use the parameter values to test whether a module is loading without errors.
maxphys	This parameter is used to define a threshold value for a physical I/O request that an application can place. If the request is bigger than the threshold value defined by the parameter, the request is chunked into smaller sizes equivalent to the size defined in maxphys. You need to modify this parameter in scenarios where physical I/O must be implemented to and from raw devices.
rlim_fd_max	This parameter is used to define the threshold limit on the number of file descriptors opened by a single process. You must modify this parameter value if a process needs to open a higher number of descriptors than the number allowed by the current threshold value.
ncsize	This parameter defines the number of entries allowed in the Domain Name Lookup Cache (DNLC). If the number of DNLC entries is high, you can modify this parameter value.
rstchown	This parameter is used to identify whether POSIX semantics are being used for chown system calls. If POSIX semantics are not required, you can use this parameter to turn off the feature.

continues

E

TABLE E.1 CONTINUED

Parameter	Description
segkpsize	This parameter specifies the amount of kernel pageable memory available on the system. By modifying this parameter, you can increase or decrease pageable memory allocated to kernel threads. If you need to increase system capacity for managing higher numbers of processes, you need to increase this parameter value.
bufhwm	This parameter specifies the maximum memory space that can be allocated for caching I/O buffers that are used for storing UFS metadata information.
ndquot	This parameter indicates the maximum number of quota structures that can be allocated on UFS. You need to modify this parameter value if the default number of quotas is not enough, which results in an overflow of the dqot table. This situation is indicated by the dquot table full message displayed on the console or written in the message log.

NOTE

> To learn more about these tunable parameters, you can refer to the sun documentation site, at http://docs.sun.com.

Table E.2 describes important TCP/IP tunable parameters available on the Solaris 9 OE.

TABLE E.2 TCP/IP TUNABLE PARAMETERS

Parameter	Description
ip_icmp_err_interval and ip_icmp_err_burst	This parameter specifies the interval between IPv4 and IPv6 ICMP error messages. You specify the number of error messages by using the ip_icmp_err_burst parameter. You can modify the values for both parameters to increase or decrease the rate of ICMP error messages.
ip_forwarding	This parameter is used to specify whether the IPv4 or IPv6 modules on Solaris 9 perform packet forwarding. You can use this parameter to enable or disable IP forwarding.
ip_addrs_per_if	This parameter is used to specify the threshold limit on the number of logical interfaces related to a real interface. You can increase the parameter value if more logical interfaces are needed. However, this change is not recommended because an increase of logical interface numbers have an adverse impact on IP's performance.

Parameter	Description
tcp_deferred_ack_interval	This parameter is used to specify the timeout value for retransmitting a TCP segment if an acknowledgement is not received before the timeout elapses. You need to modify this parameter value to increase timeouts to accommodate late receipt of acknowledgements on slow networks.
tcp_local_dack_interval	This parameter is used to specify a delayed acknowledgement timeout value for systems that are directly connected to each other. You can increase this parameter value to accommodate late receipts of acknowledgements on slow networks.
tcp_deffered_acks_max	This parameter specifies the number of TCP segments that a system can receive before transmitting an acknowledgement for the segments. You can reduce the parameter value to transmit immediate acknowledgements in scenarios where bursty network traffic exists.
tcp_wscale_always	This parameter indicates that the TCP module on the system must transmit SYN segments with the window scale option. You can use this parameter to enable the window scale option setting on SYN segments.
tcp_tstamp_always	This parameter indicates that SYN segments must be transmitted with the timestamp option enabled. In scenarios where TCP sequence number wrapping occurs, or when round trip time (RTT) value estimation is difficult, you need to use this parameter to enable timestamps on TCP segments.
tcp_cwnd_max	This parameter is used to specify the maximum congestion window size for TCP segments transmitted from a system. You can modify this parameter value based on the congestion conditions existing on the network.
tcp_slow_start_initial	This parameter specifies the maximum initial congestion window size. This parameter value can be used to control the implementation of the slow start technique that is used as a remedy for network congestion conditions.

Table E.3 describes the most important NFS tunable parameters available on the Solaris 9 OE.

TABLE E.3 NFS TUNABLE PARAMETERS

Parameter	Description
nfs:nfs_pathconf_disable_cache	This parameter is used to control information provided by the pathconf command. The command provides information related to NFS version 3 file systems. You need to modify this parameter to disable caching of patchconf information.
nfs:nfs_allow_preepoch_time	This parameter controls the display of files with negative timestamps. If you need to access files with negative or futuristic timestamps, you can modify this parameter.
nfs: nfs3_cots_timeo	This parameter is used to specify the default RPC time-out value for NFS mounted files systems that use TCP for connectivity. You need to increase the parameter value on slow networks where higher round trip times might result in frequent timeouts.
nfs:nfs_do_symlink_cache	This parameter is used to control caching of symbolic link file contents on NFS version 2 mounted file systems. You can modify this parameter to enable or disable the caching of symbolic link file contents.
nfs:nfs_dynamic	This parameter is used to control the dynamic retrans mission feature on NFS version 2 mounted file systems. You might need to use this parameter to disable the dynamic retransmission feature on systems located in volatile network traffic environments.
nfs:nfs_lookup_neg_cache	This parameter defines caching of names that were not found after a domain name lookup. Such names are called *negative names*. You need to work with this parameter to filter negative names from DNLC.
nfs:nfs_max_threads	This parameter is used to control the number of kernel threads that perform asynchronous I/O operations. You need to modify this parameter to reduce the number of simultaneous asynchronous I/O operations performed by kernel threads.
nfs:nfs_nra	This parameter controls the number of read-ahead requests submitted by an NFS client. The client queues these requests if a sequential read of a file must be implemented. You need to modify this parameter if an NFS client queues a large number of read-ahead requests.
ns:nrnode	This parameter controls the rnode cache size on an NFS client. This cache provides information about the files in an NFS client. You can modify the parameter value to enable caching of large volumes of file information.

E

Parameter	Description
nfs:nfs_write_error_interval	This parameter defines the time interval between recording the ENOSPC and EDQOT errors on an NFS client. If the volume of messages recorded on the NFSclient is high, you can use this parameter to modify the time interval.

E

GLOSSARY

/etc/inittab   A file that controls the behavior of the init process. The init process refers to the /etc/inittab file and it starts, stops, respawns, and modifies the processes based on that.

/etc/nsswitch.files   A configuration file that specifies local /etc files as the only source of information for the machine.

/etc/nsswitch.ldap   A configuration file that specifies the LDAP directory as the primary source of information for the machine.

/etc/nsswitch.nis   A configuration file that is almost identical to the NIS+ configuration file, except that it specifies NIS maps as the namespace in place of NIS+ tables.

/etc/nsswitch.nisplus   A file that specifies NIS+ as the primary source for all information.

/etc/system   Unix system configuration file.

/swap   A Solaris directory, which contains virtual memory space that improves performance by moving the unused segments of programs (or data) from memory to disk.

aliases   Pseudonyms that are used to represent the corresponding commands for which they are set. The need for aliases arises when you want to set a shortcut for frequently-used commands that are lengthy. An alias defined in a parent shell is available to all its child shells.

anycast   A type of IP address that is specified for a set of interfaces. These interfaces can reside on the same host or also may belong to different hosts. A packet destined for this address is delivered to one of the interfaces in the set.

application software   Programs used for various applications such as database management systems, word processors, text editors, and multimedia utilities.

asynchronous writes   A feature that enables the server to cache client requests in memory. Asynchronous writes improves the server's response time because the client need not wait for the server to commit the changes to disk.

at   A command that schedules a single system event.

Authenticaion Header (AH)   A protocol that uses strong cryptographic checksums to provide authentication for packets. For example, if you send a packet with AH, a checksum operation at the receiving end confirms whether the packet has been tampered with. If the checksum operation is successful, it means that the recipient confirms that the packet originated from an expected peer and not an impersonator.

Automated Security Enhancement Tool (ASET)   A built-in security administration tool that automates the tasks to monitor and control system security. This tool is especially helpful in tightening the file system security.

Automounter   A utility that provides mounting facilities for all users. You do not need the superuser facility if you are using Automounter to mount files. Automounter mounts files only on an as-needed basis. After a user finishes viewing a file, it is unmounted automatically.

background processes   Processes that run in the background while the user continues to work with other tasks. These processes are time-consuming and are not interactive in nature.

backup servers   The replica servers are referred to as *backup servers*. Replica servers are also called the *slave servers*.

banner page definitions   A test page that specifies the identity of the user who submitted the print request, the time the request was submitted, and a print request ID that uniquely identifies the print request. In addition, banner pages can also be defined with a title that further identifies a particular printout.

bash   An enhancement to the Bourne shell. The bash shell is the default shell for most Linux systems. The term bash is an acronym for Bourne Again Shell.

basic hot swap procedure   A procedure that performs a hardware connection process automatically but requires manual intervention for a software connection process.

binding   Binding is a process of associating names to objects.

boot block   A part of the disk label that contains a loader used to boot the operating system.

Boot PROM VERSIONS   The resident firmware on SPARC systems that is soldered with the system motherboard. The various versions of Boot PROM are 1.x, 2.x, and 3.x. The current version used by SPARC systems is 3.x. Some older systems still use Version 2.x. Version 1.x is not supported any longer.

bootblk   A primary boot program that is loaded from the boot device or the diag device. If the bootblk is not present or needs to be regenerated, you can install it by running the

installboot command This can be done after booting from a CD-ROM or the network. A copy of the `bootblk` is available at `/usr/platform/'arch -k'/lib/fs/ufs/bootblk`.

bootblk The primary boot program, which finds and executes the secondary boot program `ufsboot`.

Bourne shell The default shell for Solaris. The Bourne shell is the original command processor developed at AT&T and named after its developer, Stephen R. Bourne. This shell is officially distributed with all Unix systems. The Bourne shell is the fastest Unix command processor available and is available on all Unix systems. The "sh" is the executable file for the Bourne shell and is located in the /bin directory.

C shell A command processor, developed by William Joy and others at the University of California at Berkeley. It got its name from its programming language, which resembles the C programming language in syntax. The C shell was developed to provide a programming interface similar to the C programming language. However, it was not appropriate for writing sophisticated shell scripts. The C shell's executable file is named csh.

cache file system (cachefs) A file system that is used to access data from the file system cache that is stored on the local system. The cachefs file system is useful if you have a remote file system or CD-ROM where access speed can be considerably improved.

cache directory The directory where the cache resides.

cachefs_maxthreads A parameter that specifies the maximum number of asynchronous I/O daemons that can be run per CacheFS mount. Asynchronous I/O daemons are used for only asynchronous I/O requests issued against file systems.

cachefs_readahead A parameter that defines the number of blocks that are to be read asynchronously ahead of the current read block. The default value this parameter specifies for the number of blocks is 1. The minimum value is 0 and the maximum value is 10.

CDE application manager A container where other CDE applications are located. You can use the objects in the application manager to perform system actions.

CDE A user-friendly desktop environment that maintains a consistent look across all Unix platforms. Users can use CDE to customize their workstations. It has an extended Front Panel that can be used to manage files and print jobs, send mail, administer network services, and provide online help.

chgrp A command that is used to change the group ownership while the original user ownership is still retained.

chmod command A command line utility to set permissions and other attributes to the file.

chown A command that is used to modify ownership of files and directories.

Class A An IPv4 address class that uses 8 bits for the network address and 24 bits for the host address. The first byte of a Class A value ranges from 0 to 127. An example of a Class A IP address would be 92.7.7.5. In this example, 92 represents the network address, and the remaining three, 7, 7, and 5, represent the host address.

F

Class B   An IPv4 address class that distributes an equal number of bytes as 16 bit for the network and host address. The total number of bytes in an IPv4 address is 32 bits. Class B address assigns 16 bit to network address and 16 bit to host address. The value for the network address ranges from 128 to 191. An example of a class B address is 128.156.60.87, where the values 128 and 156 are used by the network address and the values 60 and 87 are used by the host address.

Class C   An IPv4 address class that assigns 24 bits to the network address and 8 bits to the host address. The values for the network address range from 192 to 223. An example of a Class C IP address is 192.200.201.23, where the network address uses the first three bits, 192, 200, and 201, and the host address uses the last bit, 23.

Classless Inter Domain Routing (CIDR)   An addressing scheme that proposes the creation of a new IP addressing entity called *supernets*. Each supernet is an extension of a subnet mask and enables you to specify multiple subnets within a single subnet mask. CIDR has been standardized and documented in RFC 1519, released by the Internet Engineering Task Force (IETF).

command alias   Alternative names for commonly used commands. These aliases are abbreviations of the actual commands. You can also have a combination of commands denoted by one alias.

command history   A history of all the commands that you have used, which enables you to check your command history not only for the current but also for the previous session.

Command Line Interface (CLI)   A character-based user interface that displays a prompt that accepts commands from a user. CLI requires users to enter commands and instructions for executing the commands to work with a CLI-based utility or application.

Common Desktop Environment (CDE)   An advanced Motif-based desktop with an easy-to-use interface. CDE delivers a consistent look and feel across various Unix platforms.

Common Information Model   An object-oriented information model that is used to describe managed resources. CIM objects are used to represent managed resources, such as disks, CPUs, and the operating system (OS).

controllers   A hardware device that manages data transfer between a host and peripheral devices such as keyboards, monitors, printers, and hard disk drives.

`cpio`   A command that copies files into and out of archived storage and directories.

crash dump   A collection of files created by the `savecore` command that is activated in the event of a system crash. Crash dump files are stored in the `/var/crash/<systemname>` directory and they contain files such as `unix.<dumpsequencenum>` and `vmcore.<dumpsequencenum>`. The crash dump files contain crash dump information for each crash uniquely identified by a dump sequence number specified in the file extension.

`cron` **job**   A scheduled task activated by a `crontab` command.

`crontab`   A command that schedules multiple system events.

Custom JumpStart An installation method you can run using a command line interface (CLI). By using this method, you can install many systems simultaneously. This method requires you to have knowledge of shell scripting and the JumpStart system. You can write scripts to perform installation tasks. You can also create profiles for all the systems on which you want to install or upgrade Solaris.

cylinders Tracks that are placed physically above each other on the platters and then grouped together. Cylinders are further subdivided into sectors.

data block The storage unit of data in the Solaris file system. The default size of a data block in a Solaris file system is 8192 bytes. After a block is full, the file is allotted another block. The addresses of these blocks are stored as an array in the Inode.

DCE A DCE (Data Communication Equipment) uses RS-232C interface to exchange data with other computers over the network. DCE is an industry-standard technology that provides the interface to enable communication in a distributed computing environment.

dd A command that reads the standard input, does the specified conversions, and copies this data to the standard output.

default router A router that provides default packet routing services for the hosts on the network.

device driver A program that controls hardware devices, such as a printer, disk drive, and keyboard. Every device must have a driver program. Most drivers are loaded into memory at system boot time.

df A command that generates information on the free disk space available on a system.

DHCP (Dynamic Host Configuration Protocol) A protocol that enables dynamic client IP address configuration from a server.

dhcpconfig A utility that is used to configure and manage Dynamic Host Configuration Protocol(DHCP) or Boot Protocol (BOOTP) services on a host.

Directory Information Tree (DIT) An organized method of providing containers for storing different types of information.

directory service A service that helps users or computers to search through the directory list. These services enable you to search through a structured repository of information.

disk controller A chip or circuit that translates computer data and commands into low-level commands understood by the hard drive circuitry.

disk label Every disk stores information such as disk controller, geometry, and slices in an area marked for storing this information. The information that is stored is called the *disk label*.

disk quota An individual user's share of hard disk space. A disk quota helps in imposing a restriction on the hard disk space a user can use. The two kinds of limits that can be imposed are a soft limit and a hard limit.

F

disk slice   A physical subset of a disk that is composed of a single range of contiguous blocks. It can be used as a raw device or it can hold a disk-based file system.

display card   A hardware device that enables transmission of signals between the CPU and the monitor on a host.

DNS cache server   A DNS server that is used to manage queries. It does not maintain any authoritative records or the address records for subzones. The server maintains only those records that you require to locate the name servers of a delegated subzone.

domain name   The name given to a domain, which typically encompasses a group of hosts. You need to decide whether your system uses the domain name service or not. If a domain name service is used, determine the type of name service for the environment.

Domain Naming Service (DNS)   An Application layer protocol that is used as a standard naming service for the Internet. This naming service was designed for name-to-address resolution for TCP/IP networks. This naming service uses the hostname as an index to locate IP addresses in the database.

dynamic failover   A feature that enables read-only resources, such as man pages and shared binaries.

Dynamic Host Control Protocol (DHCP)   An Application layer protocol that is used to configure IP addresses for hosts dynamically, without the administrator's intervention.

eeprom   A command used to set the security modes from the OS prompt, but only if you have root (superuser) privileges.

ethernet card   A hardware device that implements physical data transfer between hosts on a network.

factory JumpStart   An installation method that installs software components based on your system's configuration. You are not prompted for any information. The installation procedure starts as soon as you insert the Solaris 9 DVD or the Solaris 1 of 2 CD.

Federated Naming Service (FNS)   A name service that provides a set of common names that can be used over different naming services. Using the FNS conventions, you can name organizations, machines, users, and network services. In addition, FNS extends support for other naming services, such as DNS, NIS, and NIS+.

fg   Moves a background job in the current environment into the foreground.

file system   One of the basic building blocks of an operating system. A file system can be a structure of directories used to organize and store files. It can also be a logical grouping of files and directories in a partition.

file systems   A file management system adopted by an OS that enables organization and maintenance of files and folders on the hard disk.

File Transfer Protocol (FTP)   A protocol operating from the Application layer of the TCP/IP reference model. FTP is used to transfer files between hosts. The protocol provides user authentication features that enable you to query for the username and password of users who need to transfer files from a remote host to their system.

fileheader_cache_size   A parameter that defines the size of the in-memory cache of file header information in 512-byte units. The parameter value indicates the number of such headers retained after other system internal data for a file has been released.

Finger   A command line utility used to display information such as username, terminal type, login time, idle time, and so on, about currently logged in local and remote users.

Firewalls   A tool that strengthens network security by acting as a gateway for all the data traffic between two networks. The firewall restricts network access for users without proper authentication and authorization. Typically, to access a network that is secured with a firewall, external users need to provide IDs and passwords to authenticate themselves.

Fixed-Priority (FX) scheduler   A process scheduler that provides a scheduling policy to prioritize processes that require user attention.

floppy disks   Portable and cost effective storage media that hold small volumes of data. You can store up to 1.44MB of information on a floppy disk.

forking   The task of creating new processes from existing parent processes. Forking is named after the C function called fork().

format utility   A tool provided in Solaris OE that helps administer the disk. This utility can be used to display slice information, format a disk drive, and repair a disk drive.

Forth monitor mode   A monitor type used in the newer models of SPARC, such as the SunFire. This monitor type displays an ok prompt and also supports the restricted monitor. Several OpenBoot commands can be issued at the ok prompt to perform functions, such as hardware testing and initialization, boot from various resources, and determining hardware configuration of the system.

Front Panel   A GUI desktop element that contains the main panel and several subpanels. The large rectangular window in the bottom of the display is the main panel.

fsck   A command that is used to check the integrity of the cached file system. It reports any inconsistencies in the file systems. If it finds any inconsistencies, fschk prompts for permissions to repair the relevant file system.

ftp   A command that uses the File Transfer Protocol to transfer files from a remote computer to the local computer. The ftp command requires the remote system to be configured with the FTP service.

full backup   A backup method that enables you to copy an entire file system or a directory.

full host swap procedure   A hot swap procedure that performs both hardware and software connections automatically.

F

Generic Security Standard Application Programming Interface (GSS-API) An API that enables programmers to write applications that are not tailored for any particular security or transport protocol but use the security services provided by different security technologies.

genunix A core image file that contains the Solaris kernel. The genunix image file is a platform-independent image file that is present in the Solaris kernel.

GID A unique number that identifies a group.

GNOME A GUI front-end that provides user-friendly applications, easy access to global information, and an easy-to-use desktop. It is designed to help users locate information and launch applications easily.

Graphical User Interface (GUI) A graphical representation of the commands and features an application supports. By representing commonly used commands as menu items or buttons, GUI transforms a complex command line utility into a user-friendly software program.

group A collection of users who share files and other system resources or users who are assigned similar responsibilities.

halt A command used to halt currently processing tasks and to write pending information to the hard disk before shutting down the processor.

High Sierra File System (HSFS) The standard file system for CD-ROMs.

ICMP Router Discovery (RDISC) A method of routing packets. ICMP Router Discovery uses ICMP messages to verify the availability of neighboring routers that are located in the path to the destination computer. Based on the reply to the ICMP router discovery messages, a router determines the best possible route for a packet.

idsconfig A command that is used to set up an iPlanet Directory Server that is to be populated with data and serve LDAP clients.

ifconfig A command that assigns static TCP/IP addresses to hosts. The command is also used to assign network addresses to newly installed systems.

ikeadm A command that is used for viewing and modifying IKE policy. The command retrieves and alters in.iked configuration files. You can activate the ikeadm interactive mode if you use the ikeadm command without specifying arguments.

ikecert A command line utility that helps you manage certificates. You can use this command to manipulate local public key certificate databases.

in.iked daemon A daemon that uses IKE protocol to automate key management for establishing security associations.

in.named A public domain TCP/IP program (the Berkeley Internet Name Domain—BIND) that is included with Solaris OE. The in.named daemon implements the Internet domain name service.

in.ndpd daemon   A daemon that performs router discovery, prefix discovery, address auto-configuration, and address resolution.

in.ripngd   A routing daemon that routes packets destined for IPv6 addresses.

Incremental backups   A backup method that contains only the data that was created or changed since the last backup. These backups are used frequently, perhaps even on a daily basis, to supplement a full backup.

inetd   A daemon that is used to respond to the incoming TCP/IP connections. The inetd daemon lies dormant until a request comes in. After a connection is established, the daemon starts the appropriate service and lies dormant again until the next request comes in. However, the inetd daemon is ineffective in restricting requests from an external entity to access systems resources.

init Phase   A phase of system startup where the init process starts other processes by reading the information stored in the /etc/inittab file. The init process reads the /etc/default/init file to set the environment variables and then searches for the init default entry in the /etc/inittab file. The init default signifies the initial run level of the system. If it does not exist in /etc/inittab, the init process prompts the user to enter a run level from the system console.

init   The program that executes the run control scripts used to set up the various system services.

Inode Block   A kernel structure that contains a pointer to the disk blocks that store data. This pointer points to information such as file type, permission type, owner and group information, file size, file modification time, and so on.

Input/Output Redirection   The technique of instructing programs to obtain the input from a file other than the standard input device is called input redirection. Programs are instructed to send the output to a file rather than to the standard output, which is the Visual Display Unit. This is called *output redirection*.

interactive processing   An interactive dialog with the shell through which communication between a system and the user is implemented.

Internet Key Exchange (IKE)   A tool that automates the key management for the IP Security Architecture (IPsec). This way an administrator need not be concerned about manual key management because the IKE protocol dynamically generates and manages keys for IPsec.

Internet Message Access Protocol (IMAP)   A client-server mail protocol in which the mail server stores mail that it receives at all times. To retrieve mail, a user must connect to the server and download the mail.

Internet Security Association and Key Management Protocol (ISAKMP) framework   A framework that defines a mechanism of implementing the key exchange protocol to derive the authenticated keying material.

F

iostat   A command that provides information on the disk I/O of a system.

IP address   A host naming convention that identifies each host on the network with a unique 32-bit or 128-bit number. The numbers are separated into four components separated by dots. The components of an IP address represent the network, domain, default gateway, and host ID.

IP Security Architecture (IPSec)   A protocol suite was designed by the Internet Engineering Task Force (IETF) to overcome the security threats in TCP/IP networks. IPSec is essentially a set of extensions to the IP protocol. IPSec supports authentication, integrity, access control, and confidentiality of data packets at the Network layer.

IPv4   A set of standards that defines rules for routing packets over a network. IPv4 also defines an addressing scheme that uniquely identifies hosts on a network. The next version of IPv4 was termed IPng (IP next generation), but later named IPv6.

IPv6 Neighbor Discovery Protocol (NDP)   A protocol that is used to verify the Link layer addresses of neighboring routers. The protocol is also used to track the reachability and availability of neighboring routers.

IPv6   The latest version of IP standards. IPv6 proposes a number of enhancements to the IPv4 standards. Some of the features defined in IPv6 include a 128-bit addressing scheme, fewer fields in the IP header, and incorporation of features such as IPSec and Mobile IP into the IP packet structure.

kdc_ports   A variable that defines the ports on which the KDC listens to receive requests. The standard port for Kerberos V5 is 88, although Solaris 9 listens on port 750 for compatibility with earlier versions of Kerberos.

Kerberos   A centralized server for local and remote management of users and security policies.

Kerberos   A network authentication protocol developed by Massachusetts Institute of Technology (MIT). Kerberos uses secret-key-based cryptography to implement authentication services for clients and servers communicating over a network.

kernel   The core component of an OS, which manages memory, disk space allocation, processes, and tasks performed by applications running in the OS. On OS startup, the kernel is the first component that is loaded into memory.

Key Distribution Center (KDC)   A utility that manages distribution of security keys in an electrical data format between computers on a network. Community Security (COMSEC) has developed KDC.

kill   A command that enables the user to kill the process.

kinit   A command that is used to obtain an authentication ticket that enables each principal to be authenticated by a Kerberos system. The kinit command provides an initial ticket-granting ticket and puts it in the ticket cache.

Korn Shell   A shell developed by David Korn. This shell is a product of AT&T, and it combines the best features of both the Bourne and the C shells. The name of the executable filename is ksh.

last   A command that traces the users who have logged in or logged out of the system.

ldap_cachemgr   The ldap_cachemgr daemon is a process that provides an up-to-date configuration cache for LDAP naming services. It is started during multi-user boot.

ldapadd   A command that is used to add an entry to the LDAP database.

ldapclient   A utility that is used to initialize LDAP clients and restore the network service environment to them.

ldapsearch   A command that connects clients to the LDAP directory server, binds to the directory server, and performs the directory search.

Lightweight Directory Access Protocol (LDAP)   A protocol that provides directory and naming services for clients on a network.

Links   A special feature of all Unix-based operating systems. A link is a reference entry in a directory to a file stored in another directory. There might be several links—references—to a file. Links eliminate redundancy because you do not need to store multiple copies of a file.

listen port monitor   A port monitor that provides port services, such as printing and other network services. Use the sacadm command to configure it.

listen process   A process that "listens" for network service requests, accepts requests when they arrive, and starts services in response to the requests.

live upgrade   An upgrade method that is used for upgrading a running version of Solaris without halting your system in most cases. This method saves downtime for production servers.

local delivery agent   A program that delivers mail to the Unix file system mailbox formats (on Unix systems). Examples of local delivery agents include UUCP and mail.local.

local printers   Printers that do not service computers on the network other than the computers to which they are physically attached.

Lockd   A daemon that supports record-locking operations on NFS files. Three options can be used with record locking: -g, -t, and nthreads.

Login Manager   A tool that displays the login screen, authenticates users, and passes control to the Session Manager. Login Manager accept requests from the hosts on the network to display a login screen on a particular terminal, which can either be a local or a network terminal. For local login, the Login Manager starts an X server automatically and displays a login screen.

Loginlog   After five unsuccessful login attempts, all the attempts are logged in the file /var/adm/loginlog. This file contains one record for each failed attempt. Each record contains the login name, tty specification, and time.

logins   A command that is used to monitor the login details on a Solaris system. The logins command enables you to list the login information of all users. You can use this command to verify the validity of a user in the system.

lp commands   Commands that initiate and manage the print services. lp commands are classified into user commands and administrative commands. Users working from a client computer send print requests with user commands. Administrative commands are used on both the client and the server to manage printers and printing requests.

LP Print Service   A set of commands, utilities, and programs that provide printing services in the Solaris OE.

lpsched deamon   A daemon that runs the scheduler utility to manage and oversee the print process.

lpset   A command that sets printing configuration information in the system configuration databases.

mail client   A client system that can access mail from the server. You can configure your mail clients to read mail directly from the mail server and have it stored on the mail server only, or you can configure the client to download mail from the server and store it on the client system.

mail gateway   A gateway that handles communication between networks, whether they use different protocols or the same protocol. For example, you can set up a mail gateway to connect a network running Systems Network Architecture (SNA) with another network running TCP/IP.

mail host   A server that is responsible for delivering and receiving all email for your host and the network. To designate a system as the mail host, add the word mailhost to the right of the IP address in the local /etc/inet/hosts file or the hosts file in the naming service.

mail server   A server that maintains the users' mailboxes. The mailboxes are files that contain users' mail. Mailboxes can be stored in a local mail server or a remote mail server. On Solaris systems, mail is usually stored in the /var/mail directory.

mail transfer agent   A program that routes mail messages and resolves mail addresses. It is also called the mail transport agent (MTA). MTA accepts messages from the mail user agent and sends them to the destination addresses. Sendmail is the MTA on Solaris systems.

mail user agent   A program that acts as an interface between the user and the mail transfer agent. Examples of a mail user agent in Solaris are /usr/bin/mail, /usr/bin/mailx, $OPENWINHOME/bin/mailtoolm, and /usr/dt/bin/dtmail.

mailx   A user agent that sends and receives mail messages.

makedbm   A utility that generates NIS maps. It converts source text files to the NIS maps in ndbm file format.

master server   The principal server in the set of servers.

maxblocks parameter   A parameter that defines the maximum number of caches that is allowed to be claimed within the front file system. The parameter value is relative to the total number of blocks in the front file system.

maxfiles parameter   A parameter that sets the maximum percentage of available inodes that CacheFS can claim. minfiles are defined in terms of the percentage of the total number of inodes in the front file system, which CacheFS can use without limitation.

minblocks parameter   A parameter that sets the minimum number of blocks available to CacheFS.

mkdir   A command that creates a directory on the remote system.

Modular Debugger (mdb)   An enhanced debugging utility that provides debugging support to the Solaris kernel.

Motif Window Manager (mwm)   The industry-standard GUI, which conforms to the IEEE 1295 standard.

mount point   A directory where the system is mounted.

Mountd   An RPC server that enables remote systems to mount file systems.

mpstat   A command that provides performance reports on processor activity.

mt (magnetic tape)   A command that controls a tape drive.

multicast—A type of IP address that is defined for a set of interfaces. A packet destined for this address is delivered to all the interfaces in the set.

multitasking   A processing technique that enables users to perform several tasks at a time. Some tasks execute in the background while the user continues to work in the foreground. The non-interactive tasks are usually executed in the background.

multithreading   The capability of a program or an OS process to manage multiple requests by the same user without having to have multiple copies of the programming running in the computer.

multiuser   A login environment where multiple users can log in and simultaneously use the system. They can work on the same application or file concurrently.

name server   A server that provides lookup services to the clients that query it.

name service   A service that maintains information on machine addresses, usernames, passwords, network printers, and file access permissions related to all hosts and users on the network. A name service runs on a Server that manages such common information for all hosts on the network, thereby providing a centralized information center for the network.

namespace   A set of names in a naming service.

naming service   A mechanism that associates names to objects. A naming service is used primarily to map user-friendly names to objects such as addresses, identifiers, or objects used by computer programs. For example, DNS is a naming service that is used to map hostnames to IP addresses.

F

netstat   A command that identifies network malfunctions. When used, this command generates network status and protocol statistics.

netstat   A command that is used to obtain statistical information on network traffic flow.

Network File System (NFS)   A file system protocol that enables users to share file systems across heterogeneous hosts on the network.

Network Information Service (NIS) maps   Databases that specify the system information, such as usernames, group names, passwords, and hostnames.

network printers   Printers that are directly attached to the network and are provided with IP addresses and names, which give them network identities just like any other computers on the network. Network printers do not depend on a print server to provide printing services. However, network printers continue to use a print server for tasks such as queuing, filtering, and printer administration.

Network Time Protocol (NTP)   The Network Time Protocol (NTP) provides a mechanism to synchronize time on computers across networks.

New Fixed-Priority (FX) scheduling class   A new FX scheduler class that provides a scheduling policy for processes that require user or application control of scheduling priorities.

NFS   The default Solaris file system for sharing file systems among remote systems.

Nfsd   A daemon that handles requests for other file systems. The current version of Nfsd on Solaris 9 does not generate multiple copies to manage client requests.

nfsstat   A command that is used to retrieve performance information on Network File System (NFS) servers and clients on the network.

NIS clients—Machines that request network information from the NIS maps on the servers—master or slave—by using Remote Procedure Calls (RPCs). .

NIS   A naming service that enables easier network management by storing information about machine names, users, network, and network services in a centralized location.

NIS+ namespace   A repository of information, such as machine names, users, and network services in a network.

NIS+   A naming service that is designed to conform to organizational requirements. Similar to NIS, NIS+ also uses a client/server model to store information. This information is stored in 16 standard NIS+ tables in the NIS+ namespace. NIS+ uses a security system that allows only authorized clients to access this namespace. It uses its authentication mechanism to verify whether the requestor is a valid user on the network.

nisaddent   A command that is used for populating the NIS+ tables with information.

nismkdir   A command that is typically used to create subdirectories within a domain. You can also use this command to create replicated directories.

nismkdir A command that is used to create subdirectories within a domain. You can also use this command to create replicated directories. Unlike the `nisserver` script, the `nismkdir` command creates the `org_dir` directory only and not the system tables.

nispopulate A command that is used for populating the NIS+ tables with information. It provides the same function as the `nisaddent` utility.

nissetup A command that is used to create the `org_dir` and `groups_dir` directories and all the system tables of NIS+.

nissetup A command that is used to create the `org_dir` and `groups_dir` directories and all the system tables of NIS+.

nistbladm A command that is used to create, modify, or delete NIS+ tables.

nistbladm A command that is used to create, modify, or delete NIS+ tables. It is mainly used to administer tables and their entries.

NVRAM A removable chip with a unique host ID. The uniqueness of the host ID is important in software licensing and hence, whenever a new motherboard is installed, this chip must be retained to maintain the uniqueness of the host ID. The NVRAM chip also has the ethernet address, time-of-day clock, and an EEPROM section. The EEPROM section stores the system's configuration parameters.

Open Boot PROM A trademark of Sun Microsystems, Inc.

package instance name The file name for the package. For example, SUNWypr is the package instance name for NIS Server.

package A set of independent products that is licensed as a single product. When a product is developed, vendors define packages in the license certificate and not in the software product. This allows vendors to change the components of a package until the time they ship the license.

PARANOID A TCP wrapper mode that denies connection to a valid host if the host does not allow reverse lookups.

parent process Any process that creates a child process.

Patch Manager A patch management tool introduced in Solaris 9 that allows you to install, add, and remove patches. You can download patches from SunSolve Online service.

patches Files that are used to fix any defects (bugs) in the system source code. The patches contain the files that replace or update existing files that prevent the proper execution of the software. A patch is a collection of files and directories that contains the actual program used to fix the bugs, along with some other files and directories related to the patch.

PC File System (PCFS) The standard file system for DOS-formatted disks.

performance meter A GUI tool that provides a graphical representation of the CPU and hard disk performance.

pgrep   A command that displays a list of the process IDs of active processes on the system that match the pattern specified in the command line. The pgrep command functionally combines the ps command with the grep command.

ping   A command that is primarily used to check for the availability of remote hosts. However, ping can also detect whether there is network congestion between two hosts. The command transmits ICMP messages to elicit a response from target computers and uses the response to report data loss. The ping command also reports the time taken for sending packets and receiving acknowledgements.

ping   A command that is primarily used to check for the availability of remote hosts.

pipes   A mechanism that enables simple programs to be connected to perform more complex functions. This helps minimize the need to develop new programs.

pkill   A command that is used to terminate the processes that match the pattern specified with the command.

platters   Disks mounted inside a fixed disk drive. Most disk drives use more than one platter mounted on a disk drive to provide more data storage surfaces in a smaller area.

pmap   A command that is used to generate information on the memory address space a process uses.

pntadm   A command that is used to add or remove networks under DHCP management. It is also used to add, delete, or modify IP address records in network tables.

Point to Point Protocol (PPP)   A protocol that provides connectivity to hosts that need to access the Internet. PPP operates from the Data Link layer of the OSI model.

POP (Post Office Protocol)   A protocol that defines a set of rules for storing and accessing your mail on a central server.

port   A channel of communication between a device, such as a modem, and the Operating System (OS). A port comprises software components, such as device drivers, and hardware components. A port, when referred to as a hardware entity, can be described as a receptacle with a slot into which the cables and connectors for serial devices such as terminals or modems are plugged.

port monitor   A utility that is used to administer port activities, such as setting the line speed on incoming phone connections, reinitializing a port when the service terminates, and binding an appropriate network address. Port monitors are also used to monitor port activities, where they monitor incoming port requests, restrict access to systems, and create utmpx entries.

port service   A service that enables hardware devices such as modems and terminals to work with a port. For example, you can set up a serial port to provide dial-in, dial-out, and dial-in/dial-out services to a modem.

F

Portable archive interchange (pax)   A utility that is used to retrieve information on the members of archive files.

Portable Operating System Interface (POSIX)   An IEEE standard designed to facilitate application portability. POSIX is an attempt by a consortium of vendors to create a single standard version of Unix.

Power On Self Test (POST)   A hardware device that conducts a series of tests on other hardware devices on the computer, such as RAM, keyboard, and disk drives. POST conducts these tests to verify whether all peripheral devices are available and functioning before continuing with system bootup.

poweroff   A command used to halt currently processing tasks and to write pending information to the hard disk before shutting down the processor. In addition, the poweroff command also turns off system power if the poweroff feature is supported by the host hardware.

primary group   A group that the OS uses to associate all files and directories created by the user. Each user must belong to a primary group.

print clients   Computers that utilize the services of a print server or a network printer.

Print Manager   A Java-based printer administration utility that provides options to perform the most common printer administration tasks, such as configuring print clients, servers, and network printers, and upgrading configuration information from previous versions of Solaris. On the Solaris OS, the Print Manager exists as a package called the SUNWppm.

print server   A computer that shares the services of its printer with other computers. A print server performs the vital role of accepting and redirecting print requests from a large number of clients on a network. Therefore, the performance of the print server determines the efficiency of the printing services available on the system. Some of the system requirements for a print server include hard disk, memory, disk space for handling print requests, and page swap features.

printer classes   Printers organized into groups to optimize printer usage. Users can specify the class name rather than the individual printer name when submitting print requests. When a print request is directed to a printer class, any printer in the printer class that is free to handle print requests processes the submitted request.

priocntl   A command that is used to change the scheduling behavior of a process.

process   An executing instance of a program that is performing a particular task.

process file system (procfs)   A depiction of the kernel state and system memory through processes represented as directories. Only the kernel and the debugging system utilities use the proc file system. It does not physically exist on the disk.

process ID (PID)   An identifier assigned to each process running on Solaris. The root process is assigned a PID of 0.

Programmable Read-Only Memory (PROM) A memory chip that provides a read-only data store facility. In contrast to other memory devices, PROM is located within the computer and continues to store information across system boots. By default, PROM does not contain information. You need to use a PROM programmer device to record information into a PROM device.

programming language constructs Features that enable a shell to be used as a programming language. These features can be used to build shell scripts that perform complex operations.

protocols A set of standards or specifications that stipulate methods for establishing, maintaining, or terminating communication between computers.

proxy server configuration A configuration process that is performed during the installation procedure to configure the proxy server. Note that this choice appears only if you are using the Solaris WebStart program. When this choice appears, you need to specify whether your system is directly connected to the Internet or you will be using a proxy server to connect to the Internet. If you choose to use the proxy server, then you have to specify the hostname of your proxy server and the port number. Note that unless a port is assigned a specific number, the port number is normally 80.

prstat A command that provides a performance report on the active processes running in a system.

ps A command that is used to view a process's state.

RAID (Redundant Array of Independent Disks) A feature that makes it possible to combine a set of disks into one large virtual device. This device provides fault tolerance, redundancy, and/or performance improvement depending on the type of the RAID system deployed. There are 6 RAID levels, ranging from 0nd]7. Different RAID levels offer dramatic differences in performance, data availability, and data integrity, depending on the specific I/O environment.

RAID controllers An electronic device that provides the interface between the host computer and the array of disks. The RAID controller makes the array of disks look like one virtual disk.

rcp A command that provides options to copy recursively, which comes in handy when you need to copy subdirectories and nested directories.

reboot A command used to restart the kernel. In effect, the reboot command performs shutdown of a host.

Reduced Instruction Set Computer (RISC) A processor architecture that is based on the fact that a complex instruction in a conventional computer can be reduced to a series of simpler operations, requiring a simpler architecture and a more compact and faster microprocessor.

remote system A server or a terminal that is accessed over the network from a different location.

renice A command that is used to change the priority of an executing process.

replacement_timeout A parameter that controls the time between successive cache reconstructions made by the replacement daemon (`cachefs_replacement`). If the kernel makes no replacement requests within this time limit, the daemon times out and reconstructs the list.

Request to Send (RTS) and Clear to Send (CTS) Circuits that are used to control the flow of data between the DTE and the DCE devices. The DTE drops its RTS circuit to request the DCE to stop sending data on DTE's receive circuit. Likewise, the DCE drops the CTS to request the DTE to stop sending data on the transmit circuit.

resolv.conf A configuration file of the DNS resolver library, which resides on every DNS client (including DNS servers) and designates the servers that the client queries for DNS information.

respawn A keyword in the `action` field of the `initab` file that starts a process and restarts it when it dies.

Restricted Monitor Mode The default prompt in older SPARC systems. The restricted monitor has a > prompt. You can use the restricted monitor to boot the OS with options, which resumes execution of a halted program.

restricted shell A shell that is used to restrict the users' activities on the system. This shell allows you to assign a guest login privilege, which has read-only access to a single directory.

reverse address map A process of mapping IP addresses to DNS names.

reverse domain A domain or a subdomain that functions as a reverse zone.

reverse zone The zone that implements reverse address mapping.

rlogin A command that is used to log in to a remote system.

rmdir A command that removes a directory on the remote system.

Role-Based Access Control (RBAC) A distributed privilege model that addresses the concerns raised by the possibility of misuse of the root account. RBAC is based on the principle that no user should get more permission than is required to perform that person's job. You can use RBAC to create separate roles for people with different needs and requirements for the system or the set of systems over a network.

router A computer or a device that identifies the destination of a packet from the packet header and determines the shortest possible route to the destination. A router determines the route to the destination by using ICMP messages to verify the availability of other routers.

Routing Information Protocol (RIP)   An Internet Layer protocol that enables routers to determine a route for a packet by communicating with other routers by means of request and reply messages. These messages enable routers to identify the availability of other routers on the path to the destination computer. RIP is based on the distance-vector algorithm.

rpc.yppasswdd   A daemon that runs on the master server and allows users to update information in the password file.

rpc.ypupdated   A daemon that updates the information in NIS maps.

rsh   A command that is used to execute a `shell` command on a remote system. This command requires either user-to-user or system-to-system authentication to be configured on the network.

run level   A system state defined by a set of system services or processes. It is a software configuration, which consists of a selected group of processes. Solaris has eight run levels, with each level having a defined set of services, processes, and resources available to the users.

sa2   A utility that acts as a wrapper to the `sar` utility and prints the system activity information stored on the binary files in ASCII format.

SAC   SAC is a program that is spawned by init upon system startup when multiuser mode is entered. The SAC program invokes and controls all port monitors, without respect to type, which have been created and configured by the system administrator.

sadc   A utility that collects system activity information and stores it in binary files.

sa1   A utility that acts as a wrapper for the `sadc` program.

sar   A comprehensive performance monitoring mechanism. The `sar` is also known as the system activity reporter.

scheduler   A program run by the `lpsched` daemon that receives the print request from a user and checks for information on the default printer, filters, forms, and printer classes associated with the printer. The scheduler checks for configuration information related to the printer. The scheduler also queues the request and directs the request to the printer whenever the printer is available for processing the request.

scp   A command that is used to copy files between a local host and a remote host or even between two remote hosts in a secure way.

sector   The minimum segment of track length that can be assigned to store information. Sectors are grouped into logical blocks that function as the smallest data unit permitted.

secure shell   A shell that uses strong user authentication methods to provide users a secured access to remote systems on a network.

security   New and enhanced security features in Solaris 9 enable administrators to implement secured management of systems locally as well as remotely. Examples of security management features in Solaris 9 are Internet Key Exchange (IKE) Protocol, Solaris Secure Shell, and Kerberos.

`sendmail.cf` A configuration file that contains the operational details for `sendmail`.

Service Access Facility (SAF) A tool that provides a common interface for the management of different physical resources such as modems, terminals, and other network devices. SAF helps in the uniform management of the physical resources from a common location.

Session Manager A tool that starts, maintains, and tracks the user sessions.

session A group of settings, applications, and resources that are present on a user's desktop. The session manager, which exists as an executable file `Xsession` in the location `/usr/dt/bin`, controls the user sessions.

shared printers Local printers that are shared with other computers on the network.

shell An intermediary between the user and the system kernel. It interprets the commands that are typed at the terminal and translates them into system calls that are performed by the kernel or other programs. The shell thus acts as a cover around the kernel and eliminates the need for a direct interaction with the kernel by the user.

shell scripts The file that stores a frequently used set of shell commands. The file can later be used to execute the stored commands with a single command.

shell variables Variables containing data that can be used to control the shell's behavior, as well as other programs and utilities. For example, the `PATH` variable stores the pathnames of all the directories to be searched for an executable file.

shells A utility that interfaces between the OS and the user. It is used as a command execution tool that runs executables located in the OS in response to user commands.

`shutdown` A command used to change the state of a host from a multiuser environment to a single user environment where users can work only with the console.

`SIGKILL` A signal that is referred to as a "sure kill" signal.

`SIGTERM` A signal that allows the process to rectify itself. The `SIGTERM` signal is referred to as a "gentle signal."

Simple Mail Transfer Protocol (SMTP) A widely used upper-layer protocol in the Internet Protocol stack. SMTP is a protocol that specifies how mail is to be transmitted between two users.

SMC (Solaris Management console) A graphical user interface that enables the administrator to perform system administration effectively by avoiding the complexities of the command line. SMC is used for managing patches, managing hosts, administering users and groups, editing and updating user information, and setting up printer, modems, terminals, and other devices.

snapshot backup A backup method that stores a temporary image of file systems.

F

snoop A command that is used to capture packets from the network and display the contents of the captured packet.

software group Collection of software displayed as a choice to the user during Solaris 9 installation. The choices of software groups are Entire Plus OEM, Entire, Developer, End User, and Core.

Solaris 9 Resource Manager A resource management utility that provides features, such as allocating and monitoring of computing resources and fair share scheduling.

Solaris Management Console (SMC) A powerful new suite of GUI-based system administration tools, which can be used to perform efficient system administration tasks.

Solaris Secure Shell A secured tunnel that allows data transfer, data access, and interactive user sessions in encrypted and compressed format. This feature provides fast and secure data transaction. With the introduction of the Secure Shell (SSH), users no longer need to bother about accessing data over an unsecured network.

Solaris SunInstall An installation program that is run using a command line interface. This installation program guides you step by step through installing or upgrading to Solaris 9.

Solaris Volume Manager A tool that supports several kinds of management functionality, such as active disk monitoring, common management interface for storage devices, and disk partitioning on a single drive.

SPARC—Scalable Processor Architecture A 32- and 64-bit microprocessor architecture from Sun Microsystems that is based on Reduced Instruction Set Computing (RISC) architecture.

Spindle The center shaft of a drive on which the hard disk platters are mounted.

SSH (Secure Shell) A tool that enables secure remote login over insecure networks. SSH provides encrypted terminal sessions.

ssh-keygen A command that is used to create a set of public and private keys, unique for a specific user. These keys are later used for authentication.

Statd A daemon that works in tandem with the Lockd daemon. It enables lock and recovery functions for the Lock Manager. This daemon is stored in the NFS client and the NFS server.

subnet mask A 32-bit number, written in dotted decimal form, in much the same way an IP address is displayed (for example, 255.255.255.128). Only hosts that are on the same subnet can communicate with others without a router. Computers on different subnets cannot see each other's local broadcasts, and they need to communicate to each other through a router, even though they may be on the same network.

F

Sun Enterprise Authentication Mechanism (SEAM)   A tool that provides user authentication and data integrity over networks. Based on the industry-standard network authentication system Kerberos Version 5, SEAM provides interoperability in heterogeneous networks. SEAM was first introduced in Solaris 2.6 and 7 as the Solaris Easy Access Server (SEAS).

SunScreen Lite   A firewall that protects individual servers and small work groups.

Super Block   A special block located within all partitions within the Unix filing system. The super block contains the basic information about the entire file system. This information includes the size of the file system, the status of the file system, the date and time of the last update, and the pathname of the last mount point.

swap   A command that is used to monitor the swap area of the virtual memory.

swapper process   The parent process for all other processes on the system with a process ID of 0. This process starts the first process init with a process ID of 1.

syslogd   A daemon that runs the syslog service on a Solaris system.

system software   Software that controls the hardware resources of the computer by translating the high-level language instructions to machine-level binary code.

System V File System (S5)   An old type of hard disk file system.

tar   A utility that is used to create or restore tape archives. This utility can be used to make offline tape copies of directories and files. You can also use this utility to save files to a floppy disk.

taskstat   A utility that determines the ASET tasks that are completed or are still running.

TCP Wrappers   Intermediate entities that lie between the client and the server. TCP wrappers act as servers until the client sending the request is authenticated. You can use TCP wrappers to solve the restrictions of the inetd daemon.

Tcsh   An enhancement of the C shell. The Tcsh can be used as an interactive login shell and a shell script command processor. Tcsh stands for Tom's C shell. It is also known as the TC shell.

telnet command   A command that invokes the command mode of the utility and expects the user to type the commands associated with the utility.

Telnet protocol   A TCP/IP protocol that provides connectivity to computers on TCP/IP networks.

template initialization files   Files that store the template of user-level initialization files. The users can customize their environment by copying these template files to their home directories and modifying them.

temporary file system (tmpfs)   A file system that stores all the active processes running in the system. All files in tmpfs are deleted when the system is shut down or re-booted.

F

terminal   A device that acts as the source and destination of data and controls the communication channel.

terminfo database   A database that stores information about the capabilities of hardware devices that produce output. Printers and terminals are some examples of such hardware devices. The database contains information on the character sequences that affect the output displayed.

The OSI (Open System Interconnection) model   A networking model that defines a framework for implementing protocols in seven layers, such as Physical, Data Link, Network, Transport, Presentation, Session, and Application

threshblocks parameter   The threshblocks parameter sets the high water mark for disk usage. It defines the threshold value for the inodes that CacheFS can access after it reaches the usage level specified by the minfiles parameter.

ticket-granting ticket (TGT)   A ticket that is needed to obtain other tickets for specific services.

time sharing   A processing technique where the central processing unit allocates each program a specific amount of time for execution.

time zone   An option where you can specify the time zone settings based on the geographic location, offset from GMT, or a time zone file.

timeout value   When a client computer is unable to connect to the printer, the attempt to reconnect occurs after a time interval that is called the timeout value.

token   A data packet GSS-API used to transfer data.

traceroute   A command that is primarily used to identify the route taken by a packet to a destination computer.

tracks   Concentric circles around the central spindle on either side of each platter. When a disk undergoes a low-level format, it is divided into tracks and sectors.

Transmission Control Protocol/Internet Protocol (TCP/IP)   A standard protocol for the Internet. TCP/IP protocol can be used to connect several computers to constitute a Local Area Network (LAN), with several LANS connecting together to form Metropolitan Area Networks (MANs) or Wide Area Networks (WANs).

trash can   A special File Manager container that contains the objects you have deleted.

truss   A utility that is used to track processes running on a system.

ttymon   A port monitor that is used to install, configure, and monitor the tty port services.

ufsboot   The secondary boot program that loads and transfers control to the kernel.

ufsdump   A utility that backs up all files specified by files_to_dump (normally either a whole file system or files within a file system changed after a certain date) to magnetic tape, floppy disk, or disk file.

F

ufsrestore   A utility that restores complete file systems or individual files from removable media to a working directory.

ulimit   A built-in shell command, which displays the current file size limit. The default value for the maximum file size, set inside the kernel, is 1500 blocks.

umask   A value that specifies the permissions set by default in a file or a directory when it is created. You can set both numeric and symbolic values to umask.

unicast address   A type of IP address that is specified for a single interface. If an interface on a system has been assigned a unicast address xyz, a packet destined for this machine uses the unicast address to be delivered to its interface.

Universal Disk Format file system (UDF)   An industry-standard file system format that was introduced with Solaris 8 for storing information on DVDs. It has the advantages of flexibility in the exchange of information across platforms and access to industry-standard DVD-ROM media containing the UDF file system, as well as improved audio/video quality. UDF does not support re-writeable CDs, DVD-RAM, or incremental recording.

UNIX File System (UFS)   The default file system for the Solaris Operating Environment.

Unix to Unix Copy (UUCP)   A utility that implements file copy between systems. UUCP is also used as a protocol.

unix   A core image file that consists of the Solaris kernel. The unix file, apart from the genunix file, makes up the kernel of the Solaris OS. Platform-specific versions of the unix file are available in the kernel.

user account   A login that is required by every user who needs to access the server/workstation.

user identification number (UID)   A unique identifier that identifies a user. The user with this identifier owns any processes or files created by the user account.

user templates   A template that enables you to specify a set of common properties for users. If certain properties for several users are similar, it is advisable to create a user template.

utmpx   A database that contains user access and accounting information for commands such as who, write, and login.

virtual file systems   Special memory-based systems that provide access to kernel-related information to enable efficient system management.

virtual memory   A portion of the hard disk that is used as a swap space or as a temporary storage area to facilitate effective processing when the amount of RAM or the physical memory does not meet the memory requirement in a system.

Virtual memory   An alternate set of memory addresses apart from the addresses available in the main memory.

F

virtual node   A data structure that represents an open file, directory, or device, which appears in the file system namespace. The virtual node is also called a ynode. A vnode does not render the physical file system it implements.

vmstat   A command that generates reports on the state of virtual memory in a system.

volcopy   A command that is used to make a literal copy or an image copy of the entire file system.

WBEM Services 2.5   An Internet management technology that unifies enterprise computing management. In Solaris 9, the WBEM includes an SNMP adapter that allows system administrators to access system management information.

WebNFS support   A file system that enables file access through the Internet, even through firewalls. The WebNFS implementation reduces the time needed to access a file by providing greater throughput for HyperText Transfer Protocol (HTTP) access to a Web server. In addition, this implementation provides the features to share files without the administration overhead.

WebStart Flash   An installation method that helps you install several systems simultaneously using the same software and configuration. The installation is based on the configuration on the master system that the WebStart Flash installation uses.

WebStart Wizard SDK 3.0.1   A wizard that simplifies the installation tasks and the administration of native Solaris, Java, and the new Java applications. In addition, developers can use this wizard to co-package both Solaris and Microsoft Windows versions of their applications.

WebStart   An installation method that bundles all necessary software components as a single entity, allowing network administrators to use a familiar Web interface to install Solaris.

who   A command that monitors the time duration of a user login session. You can also use this command to ensure that only the users who are scheduled to work at a particular time are actually logged on to the system.

whodo   A command that displays the current user sessions. This command displays the UID, terminal information, process name, and PID.

Window Manager   A program that controls the features of the GUI. The windowing system uses the Window Manager to keep track of the location of each window on the desktop. Operations such as opening, closing, moving, resizing, and positioning of windows and handling windowing sessions are handled by Window Managers. X Windows uses many Window Managers to manage the various desktop environments.

Workspace Manager   A tool that controls the appearance and behavior of the windows in various workspaces.

X Display Manager Control Protocol (XDMCP)   A tool the Login Manager uses to accept or reject network or login requests for remote logins.

X Windows   A windowing system that comprises of a set of software libraries that is used to control and manage a system's graphical capabilities.

X/Open Federated Naming (XFN)   A Federated Naming Service Application Programming Interface (API) that provides a defined set of names and policies. XFN is a public, open interface supported by various vendors.

XFileChooser class   A Java class that enables Java 2 applications to display a file chooser, which enables users to access files on a local disk or on an NFS server through the NFS URL.

Xsun Server   A server that can be used as a display device without keyboard and mouse support. You can use alternative devices, rather than a keyboard or mouse, to use the server.

Xterm Terminal Emulator   A utility that supports multibyte character sets. This feature enables the use of xterm windows in UTF-8 and other multibyte locales. UTF-8 is a standard font format with the new X-term support.

ypbind   A binding process that runs on all machines in the domain requesting NIS services. This daemon locates a valid server in the NIS domain and relies on this server for all its queries.

ypcat   A utility that lists the values in an NIS map.

ypinit   A utility that sets up the NIS system.

yppmatch   A utility that prints the value of one or more keys from an NIS map specified by the mname option. The mname option specifies either a map name or a map nickname.

yppush   A utility that copies the new values from the NIS maps in the master server to the NIS maps in the slave server.

ypserv   A daemon that runs as a server process. Typically, the daemon is activated at system startup from the startup script /etc/init.d/rpc.

ypset   A utility that directs the NIS server process to use the ypbind process. The ypbind process creates and maintains binding to an NIS server.

ypwhich   A utility that determines which server is the master for an NIS map, or which server supplies the NIS services.

ypxfr   A utility that downloads the current version of the NIS map.

ypxfr   A utility that transfers the NIS map from a server to the local host.

zip disks   A storage media that has a variable number of sectors per track to make the optimum use of the disk space.

zsh   zsh is an interactive shell that has many useful features of bash, ksh, and tcsh.

F

INDEX

Symbol

- (minus sign), 298
(pound sign), 118
$ (dollar sign), 118
* (asterisk), 181
/ (forward slash), 118
/ (root) file system, 134
/ directory, 37, 133
? (question mark), 27, 94
[::] option (/etc/saf/_sactab file), 223
[-g] option, shutdown command, 80
[-I init-state] option, shutdown command, 80
[-message] option, shutdown command, 80
[-y] option, shutdown command, 80
\ (backslash), 27, 118
"" (double quotation marks), 27
+ (plus sign), 298
> prompt, 22

Numbers

0 option (/etc/saf/_sactab file), 223
1/2-inch reel tape (tape drive), 264
1 run level, shutdown, 79
2 run level, shutdown, 79
2.5GB 1/4-inch cartridge (QIC), tape drive, 264
4 run level, shutdown, 79
5 run level, shutdown, 79
6 run level, shutdown, 79
-8 option (rlogin command), 296
14GB 8mm cartridge tape (tape drive), 264

A

-a arch options (pkginfo command), 58
-a option
  boot command, 28
  df command, 145
  du command, 146
  ifconfig command, 501
  logins command, 434
  mpstat command, 490
  passwd command, 186
  pmap command, 497
  prstat command, 492
  quot command, 147
  sacadm command, 224
  sar command, 507
  truss command, 292
  volcopy utility, 272
accept command, 250, 257
accept luna command, 552
access
  guest users, 180
  login services, 223
  network services, 223
  remote access, /var/mail directory, 415
  remote hosts, 298
  remote printer access, denying, 553-554
  systems (port monitors), 223
  TCP wrappers, 471
  WebNFS, 163
access Denied error, 540
access priority, processes, 289
access rights, NIS+, 385
accessing
  applications, 91
  groups, 187
  login server, 98
  performance statistics, SMC (Solaris Management Console), 508, 511
  port services, 227
  printer ports, 249
  printers, 92
  remote systems, 302, 306
  SVM (Solaris Volume Manager), 215
  tools, 92
accounts
  daemon accounts, 180
  root accounts, 180. See superusers
  user accounts, 180-181, 185-186
ACL file, 453
ACSII transfer mode (FTP), 63
action keywords, /etc/inittab file, 75
Action menu commands
  Add Administrative Roles, 457
  Add Group, 198

Add Patches, 64
Add Patches to Multiple Systems, 64
Add Right, 463
Add User, Template, 196-197
Add User, Wizard, 196
Configure, Modem (Dial in), 229
Properties, 230

Action, Download Patches command (Patches menu), 63

Action:Signal window, 286

active processes, 192

actv field (iostat command), 500

adaptors, Null Modem, 233

Add Access, command or window, 248

Add Address to Network window, 324

Add Administrative Roles command (Actions menu), 457

Add command (Edit menu), 54

Add Directory button, 464

Add Group
command (Action menu), 198
dialog box, 199

Add Item To Menu (Tools subpanel), 93

Add Patches, command or wizard, 64

Add Patches to Multiple Systems, command or wizard, 64

Add Right
command (Action menu), 463
dialog box, 463-465

Add User, Template
command (Action menu), 196-197
dialog box, 197

Add User, Wizard command (Action menu), 196

Additional Flash Archives panel, 47

Address Manager, personal application (Cards subpanel), 89

addresses
IP addresses
assigning. See DHCP
hosts, 315
LANs, planning, 314
sysidcfg files, 40
TCP wrappers, 472
verifying, 315
IPv6 addresses, enabling, 328-330
mail addresses, storing, 92
network addresses, assigning, 501
translating (SunScreens), 484

addressing disks, 206

adm default group, 187

administration
cfgadm utility, 211-212
disks, 204-205, 210-212
FNS, 387
IKE (Internet Key Exchange), 478-479
mail services, 417-418
printing, lp commands, 249-257
RAID (Redundant Array of Independent Disks), 205-212
remote systems, 294
storage, 204-205, 212
SunScreen, 481-483

Administration Station, SunScreen component, 481

administrative lp commands, 241

Administrative Role icon, 457, 466

administrator access controls, Kerberos, 453

administrators, 456-457

Admintool, 52-53, 60

Admintool:Customize Installation window, 56

Admintool:Delete Software window, 61

Admintool:Set Source Media window, 54

Admintool:Software window, 54

Admintool:Warning dialog box, 60

Advanced Maryland Automated Network Disk Archiver (AMANDA), 274-275

agent daemon, automate remote login, 303-304

agents, 407-408, 444

AH (Authentication Header), 473-474

alert priority (syslog file), 436

alerts, printers, 254

Alias (CNAME), 352

alias command, 122

aliasadm command, 418

aliases, 110
C shell, 123
command alias, 111
creating, 418
default aliases, Korn shells, 122
ifconfig command, 123
mail aliases, 418
master servers, NIC configurations, 362
NIS+ table, 418
removing, 124
shells, 122-124

All (software package), 54

All Rights, rights profiles (RBAC), 457

allocated field, -s option (swap command), 496

allotting inodes, 132

AMANDA (Advanced Maryland Automated Network Disk Archiver) utility, 274-275

Anonymous Memory field (pmap command), 497

Application (software package), 54

Application layer, OSI (Open System Interconnection), 310

Application Manager, 91, 247

Application Programming Interface (API), FNS (Federated Naming Service), 386

application users, 180

applications
    accessing, 91
    client applications (Kerberos), 454-455
    file management applications, storing, 90
    GNOMEs, installing, 105-106
    personal applications, storing, 89
    RDBMSs (Relative Database Management Systems), 11
    Web applications, storing, 89
    Web servers, 11

Applications (Applications subpanel), 91

architecture, 14
    file system, 16-17
    kernel, 15
    NIS (Network Information Service), 356
    RISC (Reduced Instruction Set Computing), 17-18
    shells, 15-16
    SPARC, 17-19

Archive, file management application (Files subpanel), 90

archives
    installing (WebStart Flash), 47
    storing, 270
    tape archives, 269
    WebStart Flash, 46-48

arguments, values (volcopy utility), 272-273

arguments parameter, 267

arrays, storage arrays (Sun StorEdge), 265

ASCII (American Standard Code for Information Interchange) files
    NIS+ tables (populating), 381
    NSF (Network File System), 159

ASET (Automated Security Enhancement Tool), 468-471

asetenv file, 470

Assign Users to This Role dialog box, 460

asterisk (*), 181

at command, 288-289

at jobs, 288

attacks, system attacks (TCP wrappers), 472

attributes
    FNS objects, 387
    NIS+ tables, 380
    tickets, 451
    userpassword, 391

Auth facility (syslog file), 435

authentication
    DH (Diffie-Hellman), 161
    entities, LDAP parameter, 394
    IKE (Internet Key Exchange), 477-478
    login authentication, 297
    NIS+, 373-375
    packets, 473
    RPC (NFS), 161

SEAM (Sun Enterprise Authentication Mechanism), 445-448

Secure Shell, 301, 442-445

system-to-system authentication (remote systems), 304

users, 159, 301, 391

user-to-user authentication (remote systems), 304

Authentication Header (AH), 473-474

Authentication data field, 474-475

authorization, RBAC (Role-Based Access Control), 456

auto configuration, IPv6 addresses, 329-330

Auto transfer mode (FTP), 63

auto-boot parameter, 71

auto-boot?, 27, 526

autobaud, 226

autofs
    automatic mounting, 156
    mounted file systems, 169

automated key management, IKE (Internet Key Exchange), 477

Automated Security Enhancement Tool. See ASET

automatic file-system sharing, 158-159

automatic mounting, 156

automount command, 156-157

autoup (kernel tunable parameter), 560

auto_home (NIS+ system table), 375

auto_master (NIS+ system table), 375

avail field (df command), 500

Available Disk Types menu, 210

available field, -s option (swap command), 496

Available Users list box, 199

B

%b field (iostat command), 500

-B backout directory option, 65-66

-b option (sar command), 507

back file systems, 166, 169

background processing, 16, 110

backslash (\), 118

backups, 260
  components, 262
  creating, 266-275
  /export/home directory, 262
  file systems, 262
  frequency, 262
  full backups, 265
  incremental backups, 265
  LDAP (Lightweight Directory Access Protocol), 393
  media, 263-265
  networks, 261
  planning, 261
  restoring, 266-275
  servers, 261
  snapshot backups, 266
  /usr directory, 262
  /var directory, 262

banner command, 28-29, 44

banner pages, printers, 254-255

BASE command, 172

base directories, file system, 16

base distinguished name (DN), 391

base patch code, 61

bash (Bourne again) shell, 114

basic hot swaps, 211

Berkeley Software Design (BSD) Printer Protocol, network printers, 250

Bidirectional check box, 231

/bin directory, 113

bin default group, 187

Binary transfer mode (FTP), 63

binding directories, 391

binding process, NIS (Network Information Service), 358

BLK error message (fsck command), 542

block size, data, 270

blocks
  boot blocks, 210
  CacheFS (Cache File System), 168
  double indirect blocks, 132
  file system, 129-132
  indirect blocks, 132
  reporting, 147
  super blocks, 143-144

blocks field, -l option (swap command), 496

Bonobo software (GNOMEs), 104

boot, automount, 157

boot –r command, 71

boot –s command, 71

boot <HD name> command, 71

boot blocks, 130, 210

boot cdrom command, 71

boot command, 23, 28, 71

boot devices, device-specifier names, 27

boot environments, Live Upgrade, 48

boot options, reboot command (shutdown), 81

Boot PROM (OpenBoot component), 22-23

boot-command configuration variable (NVRAM parameter), 526

boot-command? (OpenBoot parameter), 27

boot-device configuration variable (NVRAM parameter), 526

boot-device parameter, 26

boot-file configuration variable (NVRAM parameter), 526

boot-file? (OpenBoot parameter), 27

bootblk primary boot program, 70-71

booting
  boot program phase, 71
  init phase, 74-77
  kernel initialization, 71-74
  modes, 71
  OBP, 71
  reconfiguration boots, 71
  SPARC boot process, 70
  systems (OpenBoot), 26-29

bootparams (NIS+ system table), 376

Bourne Again (bash) shell, 114

Bourne shell, 113
  aliases, 122
  initialization files, 116
  which command, 541

boxes. See also check boxes; dialog boxes; list boxes; text boxes

bread/s field (sar command), 507

broadcast mode, NIS (Network Information Service), 358

Browse menu commands, Software, 54

browsers, Hot Java Web Browser, 94

browsing file systems, 156

BSD (Berkeley Software Design) Printer Protocol, network printers, 250

bufhwm (kernel tunable parameter), 562

buttons
Add Directory, 464
Customize, 56
Delete, 60
Exit, 95
Lock, 95
Performance Meter, 512
Select All, 56
Set Security Attributes, 465
Space Meter, 55
StartOver, 87
workspace, 101
Workspace buttons, 95

bwrit/s field (sar command), 507

bye ftp command, 307

C

-c option
Nfsd daemon (NFS), 155
nfsstat command, 504
quot command, 147
tar utility, 269, 272-273, 279-280, 284
truss command, 292
useradd command, 184

-c pm_cmd> option (sacadm command), 224

-C psrsetlist option (prstat command), 492

C shell, 113
aliases, 122-123
environment variables, 119
initialization files, 116

Cache File System. See CacheFS

cache server, DNS (Domain Name Service), 347

Cache-directory options (mount command), 169

cached data, mounting, 166

-cached-filename-or-directory option (cachefs-pack command), 172

CacheFS (Cache File System), 129, 166
blocks, 168
CacheFSpack command, 170-173
cfsadmin command, 166-170
clearing, 170
creating, 167
defining, 166
disk usage, 168
file systems, 166
files, 167-168
inodes, 168
maintenance, 173-175
modified times, 173
parameters, 167-168, 174-175
performance, 174
space, 167-168
troubleshooting, 174

cachefslog command, 175

CacheFSpack command, 170-173

cachefsstat command, 169

cachefswssize command, 175

cachefs_maxthreads parameter (CacheFS), 174

cachefs_readahead parameter (CacheFS), 174

cachelogs directory, 175

Calendar Manager, personal application (Cards subpanel), 89

CANNOT READ: block-number (Continue), fsck command error, 543

CANNOT SEEK: BLK block-number (CONTINUE), fsck command error, 544

CANNOT WRITE: BLK block-number (CONTINUE), fsck command error, 543

capacity field (df command), 500

cards
Creator3D cards, 106
graphics cards, GNOME installation planning, 105

Cards subpanel, 89

Carries Detection option (Properties dialog box), 231

% cd /net/wasp command (troubleshooting NFS), 162

CD file system (ISO 96601), 17

cd ftp command, 307

CD-ROMs
drives, SunInstall, 45
package installation, 59
software requirements (WebStart installation), 38

CD with Volume, software package location, 54

CD without Volume, software package location, 54

CDE (Common Desktop Environment), 87
configuring, 96-101
exiting, 95
Front Panel, 89-95
workspaces, 88
X utilities, 88

CDE Error Log (Tools subpanel), 93

CDE Process Manager, 283-286

CDPATH environment shell variable, 118

cfgadm utility, 211-212

cfsadmin command, 166-170, 173

CG error message (fsck command), 542

cgmon option (/etc/saf/_sactab file), 222

characters, special characters (printer descriptions), 252

check boxes
  Bidirectional, 231
  Connect on Service, 231

checking
  file systems, fsck command, 141-143
  mounted file systems, 142
  unmounted file systems, 143

CheckPoint, 480

CheckPoint Technologies Web site, 487

chgrp command, 431

child directories, directory objects, 372

child processes, 278

chmod command, 249, 429-431

Choose Server Configuration window, 318

chooser screens, 97

chown command, 249, 429-431

Class A (network class), 313

Class B (network class), 313

Class C (network class), 313

classes
  networks, 313
  printers, 252-253
  scheduling classes, 291

Clear-to-Send (CTS) controls, 233

clearing
  CacheFS (Cache File System), 170
  inodes, 148

CLI (command line interface), 22, 38

Client Only (DNS), 348

client profiles, iPlanet 5.1 Directory Service, 398

Client-Server (DNS), 348

client/server models, NIS+, 373

clientname command, 44

clients
  applications (Kerberos), 454-455
  DHCP (Dynamic Host Configuration Protocol), 327-328, 331
  DNS (Domain Name Service), 348-353
  LDAP (Lightweight Directory Access Protocol), 395, 399-401
  mail clients, 416
  NIS (Naming Information Service), 357, 365
  print clients, 238, 248, 252
  SEAM (Sun Enterprise Authentication Mechanism) clients, configuring, 450

clocks, server clocks (Kerberos), 453

clone systems, WebStart Flash, 47-48

close ftp command, 307

close/quit command (Telnet utility), 295

clri command, 148

co-packaged software, WebStart installations, 41

codes, why codes, 486. *See also* **syntax**

color server, 101

columns, /etc/vfstab (Virtual File System Table) file, 137

Command (OBP security level), 423

command history, 111

command line
  automount, 157
  packages, 56, 61

Command Line Interface (CLI), 22, 38

command lines, 52, 64

commands. *See individual commands*

Commands tab, 464

comment fields, users, 182

Common Desktop Environment. *See* **CDE**

common keys, 160-161

Common Open Software Environment (COSE), 87

communication
  computers (Telnet utility), 294
  hosts, 339-340
  IPSec (IP Security Architecture), security protocols, 475

compatibility patches, 61, 66

components
  backups, 262
  disks, 204-205
  email, 406-408
  GNOMEs, 104
  LANs, 311
  LP Print Service, 240
  naming services, 338-339
  OpenBoot, 22
  SunScreen, 481

composite names, FNS (Federated Naming Service), 386

Compress File, file management application (Files subpanel), 90

compression, patches, 64

computers, communication (Telnet utility), 294

configurations
  default configurations, CDE, 96
  directories, LDAP parameter, 394
  email, 406-407
  Express configuration (iPlanet 5.1 Directory Server), 394
  files
    IKE (Internet Key Exchange), 479
    Login Manager, 97
    LP Print Service, 242
    NFS (Network File System), 159

sendmail.cf, 408
sendmailcf. file, 410
Session Manager, 101
storing, 96
Workspace Manager, 102
iPlanet 5.1 Directory
Server, 395-398
LDAP (Lightweight
Directory Access
Protocol), 393
local mail configurations,
412
mail systems, testing, 417
printer configurations, 246
printing, troubleshooting,
552-553
system configurations,
WebStart installations, 41
system-wide configurations,
CDE, 96
user-specific configurations,
CDE, 96
variables, NVRAM parame-
ters, 526-527

**Configure Serial Port a:
Modem—Dial In Only dia-
log box, 229**

**Configure, Modem (Dial in)
command (Action menu),
229**

configuring
ASET (Automated Security
Enhancement Tool),
469-471
CDE (Common Desktop
Environment), 96-101
DHCP (Dynamic Host
Configuration Protocol)
clients, 327-328
servers, 317-326
disk labels, 208
disks, 210-212
disks (information), 211
JumpStart servers, 44-45
KDC (key distribution
server), 448-450
kernels, 72
listen port monitor, 223
mail systems, 411-412
master servers, 382-383
modems, 234-235

NIS domains, 360-364
NVRAM (Non-Volatile
Random Access Memory)
parameters, 24-26
Print Manager, migrating
information, 248-249
printers, 248-252
replica servers, 383-384
root domains (NIS+),
382-386
routers, 316
SEAM clients, 450
serial ports, 228-229
server-related files, 96
ssh-agent daemon, 304
SVM (Solaris Volume
Manager), 213-215
TCP wrappers, 471-472
TCP/IP, 314-316

**Connect on Service check
box, 231**

connections
hardware/software (hot
swaps), 211
modems, 220, 231-235
networks, printing (trou-
bleshooting), 551
POP (Post Office Protocol),
409
serial connections, trou-
bleshooting (monitors/ter-
minals), 236
serial ports, 220
TCP wrappers, 471
terminals, 220, 231-235

**consistency, CacheFS main-
tenance, 173**

Console icon, 94

consoles, patches, 66

**containers, DIT (Directory
Information Tree), 391**

context, FNS, 386

context switch, 278

controls
administrator access con-
trols, Kerberos, 453
CTS (Clear-to-Send) con-
trols, 233

RTS (Ready-to-Send) con-
trols, 233
XOFF, 232-233
XON controls, 232-233

**conversation keys, DES
(Data Encryption System),
160**

conv_lp command, 249

**copy mode of operation (pax
utility), 271**

Core software group, 36

**COSE (Common Open
Software Environment), 87**

**Count option (mpstat com-
mand), 491**

**counters, CPU counters,
490**

cp command, 305

cpio utility, 270

**CPU (mpstat command),
491**

cpu (vmstat command), 495

**CPUs (central processing
units), 490-493**

**crashed systems, informa-
tion, 555-556**

**Create access right (NIS+),
385**

creating
aliases, 418
backups, 266-275
CacheFS (cfsadmin com-
mand), 167
crontab files, 287
file systems, 134
hard links, 133
key pairs, 302
networks (TCP/IP), 310
NIS+ tables, 379-380
packing list files, 171
passwords (NIS domain
users), 366
port services, 228
rights profiles (RBAC),
462-467
roles, 456
Rules file, 44

shared local resources, 154
soft links, 133
sysidcfg file, 40
WebStart Flash installation profile, 47

Creator3D cards, 106

cred (NIS+ system table), 376

credentials, DES (Data Encryption System), 160

crit priority (syslog file), 436

cron daemon, 286

crontab, 286-288, 506

cryptography, Diffie-Hellman (DH), 159

.cshrc file, 116

csw (mpstat command), 491

CTS (Clear-to-Send) controls, 233

current requests log files, LP Print Service, 243-244

Current sessions, 99

custom installs, GNOME, 106

Custom JumpStart installation, 42-45

custom profiles, software (JumpStart installations), 42-43

custom WebStart Flash installations, 47-48

Customize button, 56

Customize Workspace Menu (Tools subpanel), 93

customizing
desktops, 87
environments, 120
Front Panel, 103
shells, 115-117
software packages, 56
User Templates, 197
Workspace Manager, 103

cW, addressing disks, 206

cylinders, hard disks, 129

D

-d delim option (pgrep command, 280

-d option
patch installations, 65
cfsadmin command, 170
du command, 146
ldapaddent command, 398
logins command, 433
patchadd command, 65
priocntl command, 290
snoop command, 505
useradd command, 183
pkginfo command, 58

-d spooldir option (pkgchk command), 59

daemons
accounts, 180
agent daemon, automate remote login, 303-304
cron daemon, 286
default group, 188
in.iked daemon, 477-479
in.named, 347
inetd daemon, 471
IPv6, 329
Kerberos Administration, 452
ldap_cachemgr, 399
lpsched daemon, print requests, 256
NFS (Network File System), 154-155
NIS (Network Information Service), 357
NIS+ daemons, restarting, 385
SAC (service access controller), 221
sendmail daemon, 408-411
SSH (Secure Shell), 442
syslogd, 435, 557
ypupdate daemon, 368

DAT (Digital Data Storage), tape drive, 264

data
block size, 270
cached data, mounting, 166

disk usage data, 193
striping (RAID 0), 212

data blocks, 132

Data Communication Equipment (DCE), 220, 232-233

Data Encryption System (DES), 159-161

data files, DNS (Domain Name Service), 347-348

Data Link layer, OSI (Open System Interconnection), 310

data loss, preventing, 260

data management, NIS+ versus NIS, 375-377

Data Terminal Equipment (DTE), 232-233

database maps (dbm) files, 357

databases
group accounts database, 188
Kerberos databases, initializing, 452
NIS (Network Information Service), 357
RBAC (Role Back Access Control), master servers (NIC configurations), 362
terminfo database, LP Print Service, 243
user account databases, 181-183
utmpx database, 223

dates, sysidcfg files, 40

dbm (database maps) files, 357

DCE (Data Communication Equipment), 220, 232-233

dd utility, 270

debug priority (syslog file), 436

debugging processes, 291

decrypting keys, 161

default aliases, Korn shell, 122

default configuration file (Workspace Manager), 102

default configurations, CDE (Common Desktop Environment), 96

default directory permissions, file systems (umask value), 432

default file permissions, file systems (umask value), 432

default file systems, local/remote, 140

default groups, 187-188

Default option (Personal Printers subpanel), 92

default printer names, 253

default profiles, 115

default prompts, shells, 117

default user settings, 183

default values, Xconfig files, 98

default volumes, SVM (Solaris Volume Manager), 215

definitions
group definitions, 190
printers, 252-256

Delete
button, 60
command (Edit menu), 60, 66
option (SMC), 197, 201

delete/mdelete ftp command, 307

deleting
DNS clients, 352-353
groups, 190, 201
packages, 60-61
patches, 66
print client/server information, 252
printers, 251-252, 553-554
user accounts, 186
users (SMC), 197-198

demandconst option (cfsadmin command), 173

demilitarized zones (DMZs), 483

DES (Data Encryption System), 159-161

desfree (kernel tunable parameter), 561

designing
namespaces (NIS+), 378
printing environments, 239-240

Desktop Controls (Tools subpanel), 93

desktop search paths, 100

Desktop Window Manger (DTWM), 87

desktops, 11
customizing, 87
GNOMEs, 104
locking, 95

Destroy access right (NIS+), 385

/dev/dsk (disk subdirectory), 205

/dev/rdsk (disk subdirectory), 205

dev field, -l option (swap command), 495

Developer software group, 34-36

development platforms, GNOMEs, 104

device names, 315

device to mount column, /etc/vfstab (Virtual File System Table) file, 137

device-specifier names, boot devices, 27

devices. See also serial devices
boot devices, device-specifier names, 27
meta devices, 128
printer-host device, 250
tty devices, SAF (Service Access Facility), 221
virtual devices, disks, 212

devnm command, 147

df command, 144-145, 193, 500-501

DH (Diffie-Hellman), 159-161

DHCP (Dynamic Host Configuration Protocol), 12, 316
DHCP Manager, 318-328, 331
dhcpconfig command, 318, 331
installation planning, 34
networks, 318
planning, 317
servers, configuring, 317-326
sysidcfg files, 40

DHCP Configuration Wizard, 318, 322

DHCP Manager, 318-326

dhcpconfig command, 318

diag-continue? diagnostic parameter (NVRAM), 528

diag-device configuration variable (NVRAM parameter), 526

diag-device (OpenBoot parameter), 27

diag-file configuration variable (NVRAM parameter), 526

diag-file (OpenBoot parameter), 27

diag-level diagnostic parameter (NVRAM), 528

diag-passes diagnostic parameter (NVRAM), 528

diag-script diagnostic parameter (NVRAM), 529

diag-switch? configuration variable (NVRAM parameter), 526

diag-trigger diagnostic parameter (NVRAM), 529

diag-verbosity diagnostic parameter (NVRAM), 528

diagnostic mode, 29

diagnostic parameters, NVRAM, 528

dial-in service, modems, 227

dial-out service, modems, 227

dialog boxes
Add Group, 199
Add Right, 463-465
Add User Template, 197
Admintool:Warning, 60
Assign User to This Role, 460
Configure Serial Port a: Modem—Dial In Only, 229
Enter a Role Name, 458
Enter a Role Password, 459
Enter Home Directory, 460
Enter Role Rights, 459
File Manager, 90
Introduction to the Desktop, 100
Process Manager—Log File, 285
Properties, 200, 230
Review, 461
Role Properties, 466-467
Signal, 284
Style Manager, 93
User Properties, 197
Warning, 198, 201
WebStart Installation Kiosk and Welcome to Solaris, 42

dict_file parameter (/etc/krb5/kdc.conf file), 452

Diffie-Hellman (DH), 159-161

digital Data Storage (DDS), tape drive, 264

Digital Linear Tapes (DLT), tape drive, 264

DIR error message (fsck command), 542

directories. See also subdirectories, 37, 64
/ directory, 133
base directories, file system, 16
/bin directory, 113
cachelogs, 175
child directories, directory objects, 372
configuration directories, LDAP parameter, 394
DN (Distinguished Names), LDAP, 391
entries (LDAP), 391
/etc, 76
/etc/aset directory, 468
/etc/init.d, 442
/etc/krb5 directory, 453
/etc/lp directory, configuration files, 242
/etc/mail directory, 410
/etc/saf/<pmtag> directory, 224
/etc/skel directory, 120
/export/home directory, 262
groups_dir, 380
home directories, 34, 300, 539
inodes, fsck command, 143
local cache directory, 167
lost + found directory, 133
mount point directories, 133-135, 169
NIS+, 372
org_dir, 379-380
owners, file system permissions, 430-431
parent directories, directory objects, 372
root directories, 16, 372
savecore, 557
/sbin directory, 76
security, 361, 391
shared directories, packing files, 172
spool directories, package installation, 59
umask value, 431
user directories, 182, 394
/usr directory, 262

/usr/lib/lp directory, filter (LP Print Service), 243
/usr/lib/lp/model directory, Interface (LP Print Service), 243
/var directory, print environment design, 239-240
/var/adm directory, 433, 558
/var/mail directory, 415-416
/var/spool/cron/crontab directory, 286-287
/var/yp directory, 357

directory entries, LDAP clients, 400-401

Directory Information Tree (DIT), LDAP, 391-392

directory object, 372

Directory Server, 395

directory servers, iPlanet 5.1 Directory Server, 397

directory services, 338, 390-392

disable command, 256, 487

disable state, port monitors, 223

disk (vmstat command), 495

disk administration, 204-210

disk labels, 208

disk quotas, 140, 194

disk sets, building, 213

disk slices, 205-210

disk space
file systems, 139-140
installation planning, 33-34
Live Upgrade, 48
users, 194

disk usage
CacheFS (Cache File System), 168
data, 193
monitoring, file systems, 144-147

disk utilization, performance monitoring, 499-501

disk-based file systems, 17, 128

disks
addressing, 206
booting, 71
components, 204-205
configuring (information), 211
cylinders, 129
disk quota, 140
floppy disks, backups, 263
GNOME installation planning, 105
hardware, 204
PCFS (FAT) disks, sysidcfg file storage, 39
performance (SVM), 213
print servers, printing environment design, 239
repairing, 208-210
subdirectories, 205
unconfiguring, 211
virtual devices, 212
zip disks, backups, 263

displaying
disk slice information, 206-208
fault alerts, printers, 254
file system information, 144-145
login screens, 96
packed file information, 172
screen savers, 95
software packages, 54
su command login attempts, 438
super blocks, 143

displays, login screens, 99

Distinguished Name (DN), 247, 391

DIT (Directory Information Tree), LDAP, 391-392

DLT (Digital Linear Tapes), tape drive, 264

DMZs (demilitarized zones), 483

DN (Distinguished Name), 247, 391

DNS (Domain Name Service), 313-314, 342-343, 390
clients, 348-353
data files, 347-348
implementing, 347
mail servers, 415
name resolution process, 348-349
reverse address mapping, 351
servers, 347, 350-351

documents. See also files; packages; patches

dollar sign ($), 118

Domain Name Service. See DNS

domain names
LANs, planning, 313
remote systems, 296
sysidcfg files, 39

domain structure, NIS+ versus NIS, 374

domainname command, 364, 384

domains
namespaces, 372, 378
NIS domains, 356
    clients, 365
    configuring, 360-364
    maps, 367
    naming, 359
    planning tips, 359
    propagating maps, 368
    slave servers, 364-365
    users, 366-367
root domains, configuring (NIS+), 382-386

double indirect blocks, 132

double quotation marks (""), 27

Download Patches wizard, 63

downloading
patches, 62-64
SunScreen Lite, 480

drives
CD-ROM drives, SunInstall, 45
optical drives, backups, 264
tape drives, 263-264, 270

Drv module (kernels), 72

DTE (Data Terminal Equipment), 232-233

dtksh (desktop kornshell) shell, 114

.dtprofile, 100

DTWM (Desktop Window Manager), 87

du command, 146, 193

dump information, crashed systems, 556-557

dumpadm command, 556-557

DUP error message (fsck command), 542

DVD ROMs, software requirements (WebStart installation), 38

DVD Universal Disk Format (UDF), 17

dY, addressing disks, 206

Dynamic Host Configuration Protocol. See DHCP

dynamic packet filtering, SunScreen, 484

E

-e command, 44

-e option
priocntl command, 290
rlogin command 296
truss command, 292
useradd command, 184

echo command, 540

Edit menu commands
Add, 54
Delete, 60, 66

editors, Hotkey Editor (Tools subpanel), 93

Edquota (disk quotas), 140

edquota command, 194

eeprom, 24-27

EIA (Electronic Industry Association), 220

email, 406-411

emerg priority (syslog file), 436

Empty Trash Can (Trash subpanel), 95

enable command, 250, 256

enable state, port monitors, 223

enabling IPv6 addresses, 329-330

Encapsulated Security Payload (ESP), 473-475

encrypt [true/false] option (Kerberos), 454

encrypted passwords, 182, 188

Encryption, file management application (Files subpanel), 90

encryption
  conversation keys (DES), 160
  files (Secure Shell), 304
  IKE (Internet Key Exchange), 477
  keys, 161
  packets, 474
  SunScreen, 482

End User software group, 34-36

end-to-end delivery system, 409

Enhanced Storage tool, 213-214

Enter a Role Name dialog box, 458

Enter a Role Password dialog box, 459

Enter Home Directory dialog box, 460

Enter Role Rights dialog box, 459

Entire Plus OEM software group, 36

Entire software group, 34-36

entities, authentication entities (LDAP parameter), 394

entries
  adding, 401
  deleting, 401
  directories (LDAP), 391, 400
  Directory Server, 395
  LDAP (Lightweight Directory Access Protocol), 392
  UTMP entries, 223

environment variables
  passing (remote systems), 296
  PKG_NONABI_SYMLINKS, 538
  shells, 117-118
  values (shells), 119

environments
  boot environments, Live Upgrade, 48
  customizing, 120
  local network environments, mail systems, 411
  network environments, login authentication, 297
  user environments, 180-183

EOF command (Telnet utility), 295

erase option (mt utility), 270

Err priority (syslog file), 436

error handling, 15

error-reset-recovery configuration variable (NVRAM parameter), 527

errors
  Access Denied error, 540
  fsck command, 542-544
  General Package Installation Errors, 539

initialization errors, fsck command, 544-545

NFS (Network File System), 161
  phase 1, fsck command, 546-548
  phase 2, fsck command, 548-549
  phase 3, fsck command, 549-550
  phase 4, fsck command, 550
  phase 5, fsck command, 550
  Specific Package Installation Errors, 538-539

escape sequences, 231, 296

ESP (Encapsulated Security Payload), 473-475

/etc/init.d/autofs start command (troubleshooting NFS), 162

/etc/init.d/nfs.server command (troubleshooting NFS), 162

/etc directories, 76

/etc files, NIS domains, 360

/etc/aset directory, 468

/etc/default/cron file, 287

/etc/default/fs ASCII file (NSF), 159

/etc/default/fs file, 140

/etc/dfs/dfstab ASCII file (NSF), 159

/etc/dfs/dfstab file, 158

/etc/dfs/fstypes ASCII file (NSF), 159

/etc/dfs/sharetab ASCII file (NSF), 159

/etc/group file, 188-190

/etc/hosts.equiv file, 299

/etc/inet/ike/config file, 477-479

/etc/inet/ike/crl file, 479

/etc/inet/ike/ike.privatekeys file, 479

/etc/inet/ike/publickeys file, 479

/etc/inet/secret/ipseckeys file, 476

/etc/init.d directory, 442

/etc/inittab file, 75-76, 226

/etc/krb5 directory, 453

/etc/krb5/kdc.conf file, parameters, 452

/etc/lp directory, configuration files, 242

/etc/lvm/md.tab file, 214

/etc/mail directory, 410

/etc/mnttab ASCII file (NSF), 159

/etc/mnttab files, 138

/etc/named.conf data file (DNS), 347

/etc/nsswitch.conf file, 349

/etc/nsswitch.file, 345-346

/etc/nsswitch.ldap file, 346

/etc/nsswitch.nis file, 344-345

/etc/nsswitch.nisplus file, 344

/etc/passwd file, 117, 181

/etc/profile, syntax, 115-116

/etc/resolv.conf data file (DNS), 347-348

/etc/resolv.conf file, 350

/etc/rmtab ASCII file (NSF), 159

/etc/saf/_sactab file, options, 222-223

/etc/saf/<pmtag> directory, 224

/etc/shadow file, 181-182, 185

/etc/skel directory, 120

/etc/skel/local.login, syntax, 121

/etc/skel/local.schrc, syntax, 122

/etc/skel/profile, syntax, 120-121

/etc/syslog file, syntax, 436-437

/etc/system file, 72-74

/etc/ttydefs file, 226-228

/etc/vfstab (Virutal File System Table) file, 136-138, 159, 169

/export/home directory, 37, 262

ethers (NIS+ system table), 376

Exec module (kernels), 72

Execute permissions, file systems (security), 426

Execute-Directory permission (file system security), 427

Execute-File permission (file system security), 427

execution priority, processes, 289

Exit button, 95

export command, 119

exporting variables, shells, 119

Express configuration (iPlanet 5.1 Directory Server), 394

expressions, regular expressions, packing lists, 172

F

F field, ps –el command, 279

-f option
CacheFSpack command, 171-172
df command, 144
ldapaddent command, 398
patchrm command, 66
pgrep command, 281
pmap command, 497
quot command, 147

truss command, 292
useradd command, 184
volcopy utility, 272

-f[d|x] option (sacadm command), 224

F6 function key, 50

facilities, syslog file, 435

Factory Jumpstart installations, 45

fault alerts, printers, 254

fault recovery definitions, printers, 255-256

faults (vmstat command), 495

fcode-debug? configuration variable (NVRAM parameter), 526

Federated Naming Service (FNS), 338, 343, 386-387

fields
AH (Authentication Header), 474
-b option (sar command), 507
comment fields, users, 182
crontab file, 286
ESP (Encapsulated Security Protocol), 474-475
/etc/group file, fields, 188
/etc/inittab file, 75
/etc/passwd file, 181
/etc/shadow file, 182-183
-l option (swap command), 495-496
netstat command, 502
output, 497-500
Process Manager window, 284
ps –el command, 279-280

file handles, file systems, 156

file management, 15, 90

File Manager, 90, 93

file systems, 16, 166
ASET (Automated Security Enhancement Tool), 468
backup component, 262
blocks, 129-132

browsing, 156
CD file systems (ISO 96601), 17
checking, fsck command, 141-143
commands, 147-148
creating, 134
default file systems (local/remote), 140
disk slices, 205
disk space, 139-140
disk usage, monitoring, 144-147
disk-based, 17, 128
/etc/vfstab (Virtual File System Table) file, 136-138
file handles, 156
file size, 139-140
firewalls, 157
fsck command, phases, 142-143
functions, 133-138
inactive modes, 266
information, displaying, 144-145
inodes, clearing, 148
inverted tree structure, 128
links, 132-133
logical device names, 147
memory-based, 129
meta devices, 128
monitoring, 145
mounted, 138, 142-144, 168-170
mounting, 134-136, 154-157, 415
network-based, 17
NFS (Network File System), 39, 129
PCFS (PC file system), 17
permissions, 428-431
repairing, 141-144
requests, 154
root file systems, 133
security, 426-432
slices, 135
states, resetting, 158
SVM (Solaris Volume Manager), adding, 216

troubleshooting
    fsck command, 541-550
    local systems, 539-540
    networks, 540
    search paths, 540-541
types, determining, 147
UDF (DVD Universal Disk Format), 17
UFS (Unix file system), 17
unmounting, 136, 143, 193
URLs, 157
/var file systems, disk space (installation planning), 33
virtual, 17
WebNFS access, 163

fileheader_cache_size parameter (CacheFS), 174

files. *See also* **packages**
ACL files, 453
ASCII files, 159, 381
asetenv file, 470
CacheFS, 167-168, 171
.cshrc, 116
configuration files
    /etc/inet/ike/crl file, 479
    /etc/inet/ike/ike/privatekeys file, 479
    /etc/inet/ike/publickeys file, 479
    IKE (Internet Key Exchange), 479
    Login Manager, 97
    LP Print Service, 242
    Session Manager, 101
    storing, 96
    Workspace Manager, 102
copying, 304, 444-445
crontab file, 287, 506
data files, DNS (Domain Name Service), 347-348
databases maps (dbm) files, 357
encrypting (Secure Shell), 304
/etc files, NIS domains, 360
/etc/default/cron file, 287
/etc/default/fs file, 140
/etc/dfs/dfstab file, 158
/etc/group file, 188-190
/etc/hosts.equiv file, 299

/etc/inet/ike/config file, 477-479
/etc/inet/secret/ipseckeys file, 476
/etc/inittab file, 75-76, 226
/etc/krb5/kdc.conf file, parameters, 452
/etc/lvm/md.tab, 214
/etc/mnttab, 138
/etc/nsswitch conf file, 349
/etc/nsswitch.file, 345-346
/etc/nsswitch.ldap file, 346
/etc/nsswitch.nis file, 344-345
/etc/nsswitch.nisplus file, 344
/etc/passwd file, 117, 181
/etc/resolv.conf file, 350
/etc/saf/_sactab file, options, 222-223
/etc/shadow file, 181-182, 185
/etc/syslog file, syntax, 436-437
/etc/system file, 72-74
/etc/ttydefs file, 226-228
/etc/vfstab (Virtual File System Table), file systems, 136-138, 169
help files, rights profiles (RBAC), 457
hosts.equiv file, 298-299
information, storing, 131
initialization files, shell customization, 115-117
/kernel/drv/md.conf file, 216
.Ksh_env, 116
large files, locating (NFS), 158
log files
    CacheFS (Cache File System), 175
    LP Print Service, 243
    saving (processes), 285
    superusers, 438-439
    user login security, 432
.login, 116
master server boot files, 351
md.cf(4), 214-215
md.tab(4), 214-215

NFS (Network File System) files, 159

nsswitch.conf file, 343-346, 384

owners, file system permissions, 430-431

packing list files, creating, 171

packing, displayed information, 172

patches, 61-66

pkgmap files, symbolic link targets, 538

.profile file, 100, 116

/reconfigure file, 210

restoring (deleting patches), 66

.rhosts file, 299-300

root (/) system files, upgrades, 49

rule files, JumpStart installations, 42

Rules file, creating, 44

sendmail.cf file, 408-410

server-related files, configuring, 96

shash files, 452

source filesmaster servers, 361-362

stderr file, 292

sysidcfg file, 39-40, 44-46

syslog file, 435-437

template initialization files, shells, 120-121

temporary files, file systems, 139

text files, NIS maps (creating), 367

/tmp/addentry file, 401

transferring (remote systems), 301, 304-307

umask value, 431

unpacking (CacheFS), 173

/var/adm/loginlog file, 433

/var/adm/messages file, 555

/var/adm/sulog file, 438

Xaccess file, 98

Xconfig file, 98

Xresources file, 99

Xservers file, 99

Files subpanel, 90

files_to_dump parameter, 267

Filter text box, 285

filtering, 484-485

filters
    LP Print Service, 243
    multiple filters, printers, 250
    print filters, fault recovery definitions, 255

Find File, file management application (Files subpanel), 90

Find Host icon, 94

Find Process (Tools subpanel), 93

Find Web Page, Web application (Links subpanel), 89

FireWall-1, 487

firewalls
    CheckPoint, 480
    Gaunlets, 480
    NFS file systems, mounting, 157
    SunScreen, 480-487
    SunScreen Lite, 480-481, 485-487
    WebNFS access, 163

firmware states, 22

Flash, WebStart Flash installations, 46-48

Flash Archive Retrieval Method screen, 47

Flash Archive Selection screen, 47

Flash Archives Summary panel, 47

floppy disks, backups, 263

fnattr command, 387

FNS (Federated Naming Service), 338, 343, 386-387

folders, Home Folder (file management application), 90

fork system calls, 278

forking, 278

format command, 206

format utility, 206-210

Forth monitor mode, CLI (command line interface), Boot PROM, 22-23

forward [true/false] option (Kerberos), 454

forwardable [true/false] option (Kerberos), 453

forward slash (/), 27, 118

FQDNs (fully qualified domain names), 392

free field, -l option (swap command), 496

front file systems, 166

Front Panel
    Applications subpanel, 91
    Cards subpanel, 89
    customizing, 103
    Exit button, 95
    Files subpanel, 90
    Help subpanel, 94
    Hosts subpanel, 93-94
    Links subpanel, 89
    Lock button, 95
    Mail subpanel, 92
    menu, 102
    Personal Printers subpanel, 92
    Tools subpanel, 92-93
    Trash subpanel, 94-95
    Workspace buttons, 95

Fs module (kernels), 72

FS type column, /etc/vfstab (Virtual File System Table) file, 137

fsck command, 174
    errors, 542-544
    file systems, troubleshooting, 541-550
    initialization errors, 544-545
    logical raw device names, 141
    options, 142
    Phase 1, 142, 546-548
    Phase 2, 143, 548-549
    Phase 3, 143, 549-550

Phase 4, 143, 550
Phase 5, 143, 550
phases, 542

fsck pass column, /etc/vfstab
(Virtual File System Table)
file, 137

fsf option (mt utility), 270

fsname argument value (volcopy utility), 272

fstyp command, 147

Fstype options (mount command), 169

FTP (File Transfer
Protocol), 62-63

ftp client application
(Kerberos), 455

ftp command, file transfer
(remote systems), 306-307

Full (OBP security level),
423

full backups, 265

full hot swaps, 211

fully qualified domain names
(FQDNs), 392

function keys
commands, 93
F6, 50

functions
file systems, 133-138
variables, Xresources files,
99

fuser command, 148, 192

G

-G gidlist option (pgrep
command, 280

-g option
lockd daemon (NFS), 155
groupadd command, 189
groupmod command, 190
logins command, 433
useradd command, 183, 189

-g pgrplist option (pgrep
command, 280

gateways, mail gateways,
406, 414

Gaunlet, 480

GConf software (GNOMEs),
104

General Package Installation
Errors, 539

Generic Security Standard
Application Programming
Interface (GSS-API), 153,
455

genprofile command, 398

get/mget ftp command, 307

GID (group identification),
182, 187

global directory services, 390

GNOME VFS (Virutal File
System) software, 104

GNOMEs, 87, 104-107

graphical user interfaces. *See*
GUIs

graphics cards, GNOME
installation planning, 105

graphics. *See* images

group (NIS+ system table),
376

group accounts database,
188

group identification (GID),
187

group management, 187
groups, 188-190
SMC (Solaris Management
Console), 194, 198-201
user limiting commands,
194
user monitor commands,
190-194

Group Members list box,
199

group objects, 372-373

Group text box, 465

groupadd command,
188-189

groupdel command, 190

grouping printers, 253

groupmod command, 190

groups
accessing, 187
default groups, 187-188
encrypted passwords, 188
GID (group identification)
number, 182
JumpStart installations, 42
LDAP parameter, 393
managing (deleting), 190
names, 198
primary groups, 187
secondary groups, 187
users, 182, 382

groups command, 187

groups_dir directory, 380

growsfs command, 216

GSS-API (Generic Security
Standard Application
Programming Interface),
153, 455

guest users, 180

GUIs (graphical user interfaces)
CDE (Common Desktop
Environment)
configurations, 96-101
Front Panel, 89-95
workspaces, 88
GNOMEs, 104-107
language locales, 107-108
logins, 96
starting, 87
SunScreen, 484
troubleshooting, 88
Unix, 86
WebStart installations, 38,
41-42
Window Manager, 86-88
Workspace Manager,
101-104
X Windows, introduction
and history, 86

H

-h option (df command), 501

halt command, shutdown, 81

handles, file handles (file systems), 156

handling, error or interrupt, 15

handshake mechanism, RS232C/D, 232

Hard Disk, software package location, 54

hard disk utilization, performance monitoring, 499-501

hard disks. *See* disks

hard limits, disk quotas, 140

hard links, 133

hardware
connections, hot swaps, 211
disks, 204
email components, 406
LP Print Services, 243
printing, troubleshooting, 551
required, 38
supported hardware, Sun, 18-19
testing (OpenBoot), 28-29

header fields, ESP (Encapsulated Security Protocol), 474

Help
command, 23
files, rights profiles (RBAC), 457
ftp command, 307
subpanel, 94

Help Manager (Help subpanel), 94

hierarchies, 373-374, 378

High Sierra File System (HSFS), disk-based file system, 129

HINFO (Host information), 352

history, command history, 111

HISTORY environment shell variable, 118

/home file system, 134

home directories
disk space (installation planning), 34
remote systems, 300
troubleshooting, 539

HOME environment shell variable, 117

Home Folder, file management application (Files subpanel), 90

Home sessions, 100

Host information (HINFO), 352

host names, LANs, 314

hosting machines, LANs, 312

hostnames
sysidcfg files, 40
Xaccess files, 98

hosts
communications, 339-340
files, copying between, 444-445
IP addresses, 315
IPv6 addresses, enabling, 329-330
local hosts, network interfaces, 315
mail hosts, 415
NIS (Network Information Service), 356, 360
NIS+ system table, 376
remote hosts, 298, 443-444, 503

Hosts subpanel, 93-94

hosts.equiv file, 298-299

Hot Java Web Browser, 94

hot spare pools, building, 213

hot swaps, 211

Hotkey Editor (Tools subpanel), 93

HP-VUE (Hewlett Packard Visual User Environment), desktops, 87

HSFS (High Sierra File System), disk-based file system, 129

I

-i option
cachefspack command, 172
cpio utility, 271
netstat command, 502
pkginfo command, 58
snoop command, 505

I/O (input/output), 15
performance reports, 499
slots, cfgadm utility, 211
SVM (Solaris Volume Manager), 213

icons
Administrative Role, 457, 466
Admintool, 53
Console, 94
Find Host, 94
Printer Administration, 247
question mark (?), 94
Rights, 462

ID field (Process Manager), 284

identities, LDAP clients, 399

IDs, process IDs, 280-282

idsconfig command, 395

IEEE 1295, Motif Window Manager (mwm), 87

IETF (Internet Engineering Task Force), 472

ifconfig command, 123, 315, 331, 501

IGNORE command, 172

IKE (Internet Key Exchange), 13, 476-479

ikeadm command, IKE (Internet Key Exchange), 478

ikecert command, IKE (Internet Key Exchange), 479

images, Net installation images (SunInstall), 45

IMAP (Internet Message Access Transfer Protocol), 410

implementing
IKE (Internet Key Exchange), 477
mail systems, 411-417

in.iked, 477-479

in.named daemon, 347

inactive modes, file systems, 266

inbound phases, IPSec (IP Security Architecture), 475

incremental backups, 265

indirect blocks, 132

inetd daemon, 471

info priority (syslog file), 436

Information model (LDAP), 391

init 6 command, 79

init command, shutdown, 78-79

init default, action keyword (/etc/inittab file), 76

init phase, 74-77

init state, 74, 278

Initial security policy, SunScreen, 484

Initial sessions, 100

initialization errors, fsck command, 544-545

initialization files
shell customization, 115-117
template initialization files (shells), 120-121

Initialize Only Connection Check Box window, 231

initializing
Kerberos databases, 452
kernels (booting), 71-74
LDAP clients, 399-400

NIS+ master server, 382
serial ports, 230-231
SVM (Solaris Volume Manager), 214-215

inodes
allotting, 132
blocks, 131-132
CacheFS (Cache File System), 168
clearing, 148
directories, fsck command, 143
fsck command, 142
links, 133
number, 131, 543

input-device configuration variable (NVRAM parameter), 526

input/output redirection, 16, 110

inserted tree structure, file systems, 134

Installation Directory text box, 56

installations
applications, GNOMEs, 105-106
archives (WebStart Flash), 47
boot blocks, 210
features, 32-33
GNOMEs, 105-107
JumpStart, 42-45
Live Upgrade, 48-50
packages, 52-60
patches, 64-66
planning, 33-37, 104
principals, 447
Print Manager, 246-247
roles (RBAC), 457-461
SEAM (Sun Enterprise Authentication Mechanism), 448-451
software package installations, troubleshooting, 538-539
SSH (Secure Shell), 442
SunInstall, 45-46

syslogd daemon, 435
WebStart Flash installations, 38-42, 46-48

installboot command, 210

Installer screen (WebStart), 42

integrity, CacheFS maintenance, 174

interactions, email components, 407-408

interactive processing, 16, 110

Interface, LP Print Service, 243

interfaces
modems/terminals, 232
network interfaces
LAN component, 312
local hosts, 315
routers, 316
status, 332
sysidcfg files, 40
RS-232C, 220

Internet Engineering Task Force (IETF), 472

Internet Key Exchange (IKE), 13, 476-479

Internet layer, OSI (Open System Interconnection), 310

Internet Protocol Version 6. See IPv6

Internet Security Association and Key Management Protocol (ISAKMP), 476

interrupt handling, 15

interrupt processing, 29

Interval option (mpstat command), 491

intervals, performance reports, 490

intr (mpstat command), 491

Introduction to the Desktop dialog box, 100

inverted tree structure, 128, 133

iostat command, 499-500

IP addresses
assigning. *See* DHCP
hosts, 315
LANs, planning, 314
networks, 313-314
reverse address mapping, 351
sysidcfg files, 40
TCP wrappers, 472
verifying, 315

IP Security Architecture (IPSec), 472-477

iPlanet 5.1 Directory Server, 393-398

iPlanet Directory Server, 390

IPSec (IP Security Architecture), 472-477

IPv6 (Internet Protocol Version 6), 33
addresses, 328-330
daemons, 329
Neighbor Discovery Protocol (NDP), 329
NFS (Network File System), 154
sysidcfg files, 40

ip_addrs_per_if (TCP/IP tunable parameter), 562

ip_forwarding (TCP/IP tunable parameter), 562

ip_icmp_err-burst (TCP/IP tunable parameter), 562

ip_icmp_err_interval (TCP/IP tunable parameter), 562

ISAKMP (Internet Security Association and Key Management Protocol), 476

ISTATE variable, 223

ithr (mpstat command), 491

J-K

JavaBeans, NFS (Network File System), 154

JCPU time, 191

JumpStart, 42-45

-k <tasklist> option (prstat command), 492

-k option
df command, 145, 500-501
du command, 146

kbytes field (df command), 500

kdb5_util command, 449, 452

KDC (key distribution center)
Kerberos, 451
principals, 447
SEAM (Sun Enterprise Authentication Mechanism), 445
servers, configuring, 447-452

kdc_ports parameter (/etc/krb5/kdc.conf file), 452

KDE (K Desktop Environment), 87

kdestroy command, 451

Kerberos, 451-455

/kernel/drv/md.conf file, 216

kernels
configuring, 72
dump information, modifying, 557
/etc/system file, 72-74
init process (booting), 74
initialization, 71-74
modules, 71-74
parameters, 74
swapper process, 74
system resources, 15
tunable parameters, 560-562
ufsboot secondary boot program, 71

key distribution center (KDC), 445

key pairs, creating, 302

key-based authentication, Secure Shell, 301

keyboard interrupt keys, 29

keyboard shortcuts
Ctrl+C, 283, 288
Ctrl+D, 363
Ctrl-D, 364

keying material, 476

keylogins, DES (Data Encryption System), 160

keys. *See also* function keys
common keys, 160-161
conversation keys, DES (Data Encryption System), 160
decrypting, 161
encrypting, 161
keyboard interrupt keys, 29
pre-shared keys, IKE (Internet Key Exchange), 479
private keys, 161, 375, 443
public keys, 375, 479

keywords
set keyword, kernel parameters, 74
sysidcfg files, 39

keyworks, action keywords (inittab file), 75

kill command, 282-283

killing processes, 283, 286

kinit client application (Kerberos), 454

kinit command, 450

Korn shell, 114-116, 122, 541

kr/s field (iostat command), 499

Ksh_env [period before] file, 116

kw/s field (iostat command), 499

L

-l command, 554

-l option
  at command, 289
  df command, 145
  logins command, 433
  Nfsd daemon (NFS), 155
  passwd command, 186
  pkginfo command, 58
  poweroff command (shut-
    down), 81
  priocntl command, 290
  rlogin command, 296
  swap command, 495

labels, disk labels, 208

LANG environment shell
  variable, 118

language locales, 107-108

Language option (Options
  drop-down list), 87

language supports, disk
  space (installation planning), 34

LANs (local area networks),
  310-314, 221

large files, locating (NFS),
  158

-largefiles option, 158-159

last command, 193-194, 438

layers, OSI (Open System
  Interconnection), 310

lcd ftp command, 307

LDAP (Lightweight
  Directory Access Protocol),
  12, 246, 314, 342-343
  backup, 393
  clients, 395
  configurations, 393
  DIT (Directory
    Information Tree),
    391-392
  features, 390
  iPlanet Directory Server,
    390
  mail servers, 416
  master servers, 393

models, 390-391
replica servers, 393
setting up, 393-401
directory entries, 400-401
identities, 399
initializing, 399-400
configurations, 395-398
Express configuration, 394

LDAP Data Interchange
  Format (LDIF), 398

LDAP Name Service, Print
  Manager installations, 247

ldapadd command, 401

ldapaddent command, 397

ldapclient command, 398

ldapclient manual command,
  400

ldapclient uninit command,
  400

ldapdelete command, 401

ldaplist command, 416

ldapsearch command, 400

ldap_cachemgr daemon, 399

LDIF (LDAP Data
  Interchange Format), 398

Length field, AH
  (Authentication Header),
  474

levels
  ASET (Automated Security
    Enhancement Tool),
    468-469
  permission levels, file sys-
    tem security, 427
  RAID (Redundant Array of
    Independent Disks), 212
  run levels, shutdown, 78-79
  security levels, OBP
    (OpenBoot PROM), 423
  system levels, file size limit,
    139

Lightweight Directory
  Access Protocol. See LDAP

-li option, syntax (ls command), 131-132

limits, hard/soft limits (disk
  quotas), 140

line speed, terminals, 226

linking remote systems, 295

links, 132-133
  files/directories, fsck com-
    mand, 143
  NIS+ tables, 377

Links subpanel, 89

list boxes
  Available Users, 199
  Group Members, 199

LIST command, 172

list mode of operation (pax
  utility), 271

listen port monitor, 223, 227

lists, 171-172

Live Upgrade, 48-50

ln command, links, 133

loading modules (kernels),
  71

local area networks (LANs),
  221, 310-314

local cache directory, 167

local delivery agent, 407

local directory services, 390

local file systems, default file
  systems, 140

local hosts, network interfaces, 315

local logins, 88, 99

local mail configurations,
  412

local mail with remote connection, mail systems, 412

local media, disk space
  (installation planning), 34

local network environments,
  mail systems, 411

local print process, LP Print
  Service, 244

local printers, 238

local processes, 192

local systems
file systems, troubleshooting, 539-540
patches, installing, 64
remote systems, 295-297

local-mac-address? configuration variable (NVRAM parameter), 527

Local0, 7 facility (syslog file), 435

locals
languages, 107-108
sysidcfg files, 40

Lock button, 95

lock manager, NFS (Network File System), 155

Lockd daemon, NFS (Network File System), 155

Locked field (pmap command), 497

locking
desktops, 95
record locking, NFS (Network File System), 155
user accounts, 185

Log File command (Sample menu), 285

log files
CacheFS (Cache File System), 175
LP Print Service, 243
saving (processes), 285
superusers, 438-439
user login security, 432

Log Viewer view, 510

logging
remote hosts, 443-444
SunScreen, 485

logical device names, file systems, 147

logical raw device names, 141

login authentication, 297

login client application (Kerberos), 454

Login Manager (Login Server), 87-88, 96-99

login shells, 182

.login file, 116

logins, 87
chooser screens, 97
exiting, 88
GUI, 96
local logins, 88, 99
names, users, 181-182
network logins, 99
remote logins, 88, 303-304
remote systems, 294-304
screens, 95, 99
server, accessing, 98
services, access, 223
troubleshooting (modems/terminals), 235
user logins, security, 432-439
log files, 432
superusers, 437-439
syslog file, 435-437
validating (remote systems), 299

logins command, 433-434

LOGNAME environment shell variable, 117

LOG_DETAIL, SunScreen Lite, 486

LOG_NONE, SunScreen Lite, 486

LOG_SESSION, SunScreen Lite, 486

LOG_SUMMARY, SunScreen Lite, 486

lost + found directory, 133

lost + found sub-directory, 143

lotsfree (kernel tunable parameter), 561

lp command, printer administration, 241-242
configurations, 249-252
definitions, 252-256
print requests, 256-257

lp default group, 187

LP Print Service, 238-244

lpadmin command, 241, 250-255, 553

LPDEST environment shell variable, 118

lpfilter command, 250

Lpr facility (syslog file), 435

lpsched daemon, print requests, 256

lpset command, 398

lpstat command, 250, 552-554

lpsystem commands, 251

lread/s field (sar command), 507

ls command, 427

ls ftp command, 307

lwp_default_stksize (kernel tunable parameter), 560

lwrit/s field (sar command), 507

M

-m option
at command, 289
fsck command, 142
fsck command, 174
logins command, 433
mount command, 136
nfsstat command, 504
patch installations, 65
patchadd command, 65
useradd command, 183

machine names, NIS+ versus NIS, 374

Mail –u root command, 408

mail addresses, storing, 92

mail aliases, 418

mail clients, 416

mail default group, 187

MAIL environment shell variable, 118

Mail exchange (MX), 352

mail facility (syslog file), 435

mail gateways, 406, 414

mail hosts, 415

Mail Manager (Mail sub-panel), 92

mail queues, 417-418

mail servers, 415-416

mail services
administering, 417-418
email, 406-411
IMAP (Internet Message Access Protocol), 410
POP (Post Office Protocol), 409-410
SMTP (Simple Mail Transfer Protocol), 409-411
proprietary, 406

Mail subpanel, 92

mail systems, 411-417

mail transfer protocols, 408-410

mail user agent, 407

Mailer Compose window, 92

mailx –f root command, 408

mail_aliases (NIS+ system table), 376

main panel (Front Panel), 103

maintaining, CacheFS (Cache File System), 173-175

makedbm utility, NIS (Network Information Service), 357

Makefile, source files (master servers), 361

management
adding, 195-199
Address Manager, personal application (Cards sub-panel), 89
Application Manager, 247
Calendar Manager, personal application (Cards sub-panel), 89

data, NIS+ versus NIS, 375-377
deleting, 197-198, 201
DHCP Manager, 318-326
files, 15
groups, 187-194
modifying, 190-194, 200
Help Manager, 94
lock manager, NFS (Network File System), 155
Login Manager, 87, 96-99
memory, 15
modifying, 197
packages, 52-61
port services, 227-228
power management, sysidcfg files, 40
Print Manager, 238, 246-249
print services, 241
processes, 15
security, 15
Session Manager, 99-101
terminals, 230
User Templates, 183-185, 197
user sessions, 87
users, 183-186, 194
volume management, 55
Window Manager, 86-88
Workspace Manager, 101-104

management commands, 534-535

management tools, 532-534

Management Tools window, 199

MANSECTS environment shell variable, 118

Mapping Name field (pmap command), 497

maps
NIS domains, 367-368
NIS maps, 356, 361, 418
NIS+ tables (populating), 380-381
slave servers, 364
versus NIS+ tables, 376-377

password maps, master servers (NIS configurations), 361

mark facility (syslog file), 435

masks, Netmasks (sysidcfg files), 40

master KDC servers, configuring, 448-449

master records, DNS servers, 350

master servers
boot files, 351
configuring, 382-383
DNS (Domain Name Service), 347
LDAP (Lightweight Directory Access Protocol), 393
loads, 365
NIS (Network Information Service), 356, 360-364
NIS+, 373
restarting, 368
source files, 362

master servers, NIS domains, 360

material, keying, 476

maxblocks parameters (CacheFS), 168

maxfiles parameters (CacheFS), 168

maxphys (kernel tunable parameter), 561

maxusers (kernel tunable parameter), 560

max_life parameter (/etc/krb5/kdc.conf file), 452

MD (Message Digest), 474

md.cf(4) file, 214-215

md.tab(4) file, 214-215

mdb (Module Debugger), 14

measuring performance, 94

media, backups, 263-265

memory
file systems, 129
GNOME installation planning, 105
managing, 15
paging, 493
pmap command, 496-498
swapping, 494-496
virtual memory, performance monitoring, 493-498
vmstat command, 494-495

menus
Available Disk Types, 210
partition menu, 207
Workspace Manager, 102
Workspace menu, adding items, 93

Message Digest (MD), 474

Message Integrity Tag (MIT), 455

messages
system messages, crashed systems, 557
welcome messages, 100

meta devices, 128

metainit command, 214

metastat command, 214

methods
numerical methods, file system permissions (setting), 428
symbolic methods, 428
transfer methods, FTP, 63

mget command, 63

migr (mpstat command), 491

minblocks parameters (CacheFS), 168

minf (mpstat command), 491

minfiles parameters (CacheFS), 168

minus sign (-), 298

mirrors, md.tab file, 214

Misc module (kernels), 72

MIT (Message Integrity Tag), 455

mjf (mpstat command), 491

mkdir ftp command, 307

Mode <type> command (Telnet utility), 295

modedebug (kernel tunable parameter), 561

models
client/server models, NIS+, 373
LDAP models, 390-391

modems
configuring, 234-235
connecting, 220, 231-235
dial-in service, 227
dial-out service, 227
serial devices, 220
port service, 227-228
SAF (Service Access Facility), 221-227
SMC (Solaris Management Console), 228-231
setting up, 234-235
troubleshooting, 235-236

modes
binding process, NIS (Network Information Service), 358
booting, 71
CLI (command line interface), Boot PROM, 22
diagnostic mode, 29
inactive modes, file systems, 266
IPSec (IP Security Architecture), 473
mail systems, configuring, 411-412
multi-user modes, shutdown, 79
single-user mode, shutdown, 80
SunScreen, 483

modes of operation, pax utility, 271

modification times, CacheFS (Cache File System), 173

Modify access right (NIS+), 385

modifying
dump information (crashed systems), 556-557
groups (SMC), 200
shells, 117
user accounts, 186
users (SMC), 197
workspaces, 95, 103

Modular Debugger (mdb), 14

modules, kernels, 71-74

module_info command, hardware testing (OpenBoot), 28

monitoring. *See also* performance monitoring
disk usage, file systems, 144-147
files systems, 145
processes, 278-282
users, 434-435

monitors, port monitors, 221-227

Motif Window Manager (mwm), 87

Mount at boot column, /etc/vfstab (Virtual File System Table) file, 137

mount command, 135-136, 169

Mount options column, /etc/vfstab (Virtual File System Table) file, 137

Mount point column, /etc/vfstab (Virtual File System Table) file, 137

mount point directory, 133-135, 169

mount-point option, 169-170

mountall command, 141

mountd daemon, NFS (Network File System), 154

mounted file systems
CacheFS, 168-170
checking, 142

df command, 144
/etc/mnttab files, 138
information, 138

mounted on field (df command), 500

mounting
automatic mounting, 156
cached data, 166
file systems, 134-136, 154-157, 415
firewalls, 157
URLs, 157
partitions, 156-157
/var/mail directory, 416

mpstat command, 490-492

mt utility, 269-270

MTA, 409

MTIME error message (fsck command), 542

multi-user mode, 71, 79

multiple filters, printers, 250

multiple permissions, chmod command, 430

multiple processes, 278

multiple users, NIS domains, 367

multiple workspaces, 103

multitasking, 10, 278

mwm (Motif Window Manager), 87

MX (Mail Exchange), 352

N

-n <count> option (sacadm command), 224

-n option
poweroff command (shutdown), 81
fsck command, 142
groupmod command, 190
passwd command, 186

Name Database Server, WebStart installations, 40-41

name resolution process, DNS (Domain Name Service), 348-349

name servers, sysidcfg files, 39

Name Services, 39, 246-247, 251

names
composite names, FNS, 386
device names, 315
domain names, 39, 313
groups, 198
host names, LANs, planning, 314
logical device names, file systems, 147
logical raw device names, 141
login names, users, 181-182
package instance names, 57
path names, user directories, 182

names component (naming services), 338

namespaces
designing (NIS+), 378
FNS (Federated Naming Service), 386
NIS+, 372, 378

naming
networks (naming services), 340
NIS, 359-360
printers, 250
run control scripts, 77

Naming Information Service (NIS), 246

naming services, 314, 338-346. *See also* **NIS+**
components, 338-339
coordinating, 343
DNS (Domain Name Service), 342-343, 347-353
FNS (Federated Naming Service), 338, 343, 386-387
host communication, 339-340

LDAP (Lightweight Directory Access Protocol), 342-343
mail clients, 416
mail servers, 415
networks, 339
NIS (Network Information Service), 338, 343
nsswitch.conf file, 343-346

NAT (Network Address Translation), 484

Nautilus software (GNOMEs), 104

Navigation pane, 195

nbsf option (mt utility), 270

ncsize (kernel tunable parameter), 561

NDP (Neighbor Discovery Protocol), 329

ndquot (kernel tunable parameter), 562

neighbor discovery process, 330

Neighbor Discovery Protocol (NDP), 329

Net installation images, SunInstall, 45

netgroups, 298, 345, 376

Netgroups, multiple users (NIS domains), 367

netmasks, 40, 376

netstat command, 331-332, 502-503

Network Address Translation (NAT), 484

Network File System (NFS). *See* **NFS**

Network Information Service (NIS). *See* **NIS**

Network Information Service Plus (NIS+). *See* **NIS+**

Network Time Protocol (NTP), 453

network-based file systems, 17

networking, 12-13, 312

networks

addresses, assigning, 501

backups, 261

classes, 313

creating (TCP/IP), 310

DHCP (adding), 318

disk space (installation planning), 34

environments, login authentication, 297

expanding, 316

file systems, troubleshooting, 540

installation planning, 34

interfaces, 40, 312, 315-316, 332

IP addresses, 313-314

LANs, 310-314, 221

logins, 99

medias, LAN component, 311

namespace design (NIS+), 378

naming services, 339-340

NIS+ system table, 376

packets, 505

performance monitoring, 501-505

printers, 238, 249-250

printing, troubleshooting, 551

remote hosts, 503

remote machines, troubleshooting, 330

services, 223, 340

size, LANs, planning, 313

status, 332

SunScreen, 482-483

tables, DHCP, 318

troubleshooting, 330-333

New Attached Printer, command or window, 248

newfs command, 134, 143

newkey command, 161

news facility (syslog file), 435

Next Header field, 474-475

NFS (Network File System), 12, 129

automatic file-system sharing, 158-159

benefits, 152

CacheFS (Cache File System), 166

daemons, 154-155

evolution, 152-154

features, 152-153

files, 159

GSS-API (Generic Security Standard), 153

IPV6, 154

JavaBeans, 154

lock manager, 155

mounted file systems, 156-157

prstat command, 504

record locking, 155

security, 153, 159-161

sysidcfg file storage, 39

troubleshooting, 161-163

tunable parameters, 564-565

UDP (User Datagram Protocol), 152

WebNFS, 153, 163

Nfsd daemon, NFS (Network File System), 154

Nfsstat –m command (troubleshooting NFS), 163

nfsstat command, options, 504

nfs: nfs3_cots_timeo (NFS tunable parameter), 564

nfs:nfs_allow_preepoch_time (NFS tunable parameter), 564

nfs:nfs_do_symlink_cache (NFS tunable parameter), 564

nfs:nfs_dynamic (NFS tunable parameter), 564

nfs:nfs_lookup_neg_cache (NFS tunable parameter), 564

nfs:nfs_max_threads (NFS tunable parameter), 564

nfs:nfs_nra (NFS tunable parameter), 564

nfs:nfs_pathconf_disable_cache (NFS tunable parameter), 564

nfs:nfs_write_error_interval (NFS tunable parameter), 565

nice command, 289-290

NIS (Network Information Service), 314, 338, 343

alias map, 418

architecture, 356

binding process, modes, 358

clients, 357

daemons, 357

databases, 357

domains, 256

clients, 360, 365

configuring, 360-364

/etc files, 360

hosts, 360

maps, 367

master servers, 360

naming, 359

planning tips, 359

propagating maps, 368

slave servers, 360, 364-365

users, 366-367

hosts, 356

mail servers, 415

maps, 356, 361, 376-377, 380-381

creating, 367

propagating, 368

slave servers, 364

transitioning to NIS+, 377

utilities, 357

versus NIS+, 373-377

NIS (Naming Information Service), 246

NIS+ (Network Information Service Plus), 246, 314, 338, 343

access rights, 385

authentication, 375

client/server models, 373

clients. See NIS+, replica server

daemons, restarting, 385
directories, 372
hierarchies, 374
mail servers, 416
master servers, configuring, 382-383
namespaces, 372, 378
objects, 372
PKC (Public Key Cryptography), 375
replica servers, configuring, 383-384
root domains, configuring, 382-386
tables, 375-381, 418
transitioning from NIS, 377
versus NIS, 373-377
nisaddcred command, 161
nisaddent command, 380-381
niscat command, 247
nisclient syntax, NIS+ replica server, 383-384
nisgrpadm command, 247
nisln command, 377
nismkdir command, 379
nispopulate syntax, 380-381
nisserver syntax, 379, 382
nissetup command, 380
nistbladm command, 379-380
noaccess default group, 188
nobody default group, 188
nodes, printer nodes, 250
noexec_user_stack (kernel tunable parameter), 561
nogroup default group, 188
Non-Volatile Random Access Memory (NVRAM), 22-26
None (OBP security level), 423
notice priority (syslog file), 436
NSF, ASCII files, 159

nslookup command, 415
-Nsservers option, Nfsd daemon (NFS), 155
nsswitch.conf file, 343-346, 384
ns:nrnode (NFS tunable parameter), 564
-Nthreads option, lockd daemon (NFS), 155
NTP (Network Time Protocol), 453
Null Modem adaptor, 233
numbers
    disk slice numbers, 207
    inode number, 131
    port numbers, LDAP parameter, 393
numeric values, umask, 431
numerical methods, file system permissions, 428
nuucp default group, 187
$nvalias command (NVRA-MAC), 528
$nvunalias command (NVRAMAC), 528
nvalias alias device-path command (NVRAMAC), 528
nvedit command (NVRA-MAC), 528
nvquit command (NVRA-MAC), 528
NVRAM (Non-Volatile Random Access Memory)
    commands, 528
    diagnostic parameters, 528
    OpenBoot component, 22-23
    parameters, configuring, 24-26, 526-527
    troubleshooting, 29
nvramac configuration variable (NVRAM parameter), 526
nvrecover command (NVRAMAC), 528

nvrun command (NVRA-MAC), 528
nvstore command (NVRA-MAC), 528
nvunalias command (NVRA-MAC), 528

O

-o fg option (mount command), 136
-o largefiles option (mount command), 136
-o lbg option (mount command), 136
-o nolargefiles option (mount command), 136
-o option
    fsck command, 142, 174
    groupadd command, 189
    logins command, 434
    mount command, 136
    snoop command, 505
    truss command, 292
    useradd command, 183
-o ro option (mount command), 136
-o rw option (mount command), 136
o option (cpio utility), 270
Oakley, 476
objects
    FNS objects, attributes, 387
    NIS+, 372
OBP (Open Boot PROM), 18, 70
    dropping to, 425-426
    password recovery, 424-425
    POST (power on self test), 71
    security levels, 423
    unauthorized password changes, preventing, 425-426
oem-banner configuration variable (NVRAM parameter), 526

oem-logo configuration variable (NVRAM parameter), 526

office, GNOMEs, 104

ok boot cdrom command, 41

ok boot net command, 41

ok prompt, 23, 29

open –l<username>@<destination> command (Telnet utility), 295

Open CD-ROM, file management application (Files subpanel), 90

Open Floppy, file management application (Files subpanel), 90

open ftp command, 307

Open System Interconnection (OSI), 310

OpenBoot, 22-29

OpenBoot PROM. See OBP

Operator, rights profile (RBAC), 456-457

operator symbol, chmod command, 430

/opt directory, 37

/opt file system, 134

optical drives, backups, 264

Option menu commands, Session, FailSafe Session, 88

options
-a option, ifconfig command, 501
at command, 288
boot command, 28
-cached-filename-or-directory option (cachefspack command), 172
CacheFSpack command, 171
cfsadmin command, 167
crontab command, 287
-d option, 65, 170
Default option (Personal Printers subpanel), 92

Delete (SMC), 197, 201

demandconst option (cfsadmin command), 173

df command, 145, 500-501

du command, 146

/etc/saf/_sactab file, 222-223

-F option (df command), 144

fsck command, 142

-g option, 189-190

-i option (cachefspack command), 172

init command, 80

installation planning, 34-37

-k option (df command), 145

Language option (Option drop-down list), 87

-largefiles option, 158-159

-li option, syntax (ls command), 131-132

lockd daemon (NFS), 155

logins command, 433-434

-m option, 65, 174

mount command, 136, 169

mount-point option (cfsadmin command), 170

Mountd daemon (NFS), 154

mpstat command, 490-491

-n option (groupmod command), 190

netstat command, 502

Nfsd daemon (NFS), 155

nfsstat command, 504

-o option, 174, 189

passwd command, 186

patchadd command, 65

patchrm command, 66

pgrep command, 280-281

pkgchk command, 59

pkginfo command, 58

pmap command, 497

poweroff command (shutdown), 81

priocntl command, 290

prstat command, 492

-public option, WebNFS access, 163

quot command, 147

renice command, 290

Return_to Local Host option (Option drop-down list), 87

-R option, patch installations, 65

rloging command, 296

sacadm command, 224

Sessions option (Option drop-down list), 87

snoop command, 505

tar utility, 269

This Computer (SMC), 215

truss command, 292

-u option (cachefspack command), 173

ufsdump utility, 267

ufsrestore utility, 268

User Accounts (SMC), 195

useradd command, 183-184

vmstat command, 494
boot options, reboot command (shutdown), 81

Options option (mount command), 169

org_dir directory, 379-380

OSI (Open System Interconnection), 310

other default group, 187

outbound phases, IPSec (IP Security Architecture), 475

output
cfsadmin –l command, 170
df command, 500-501
/etc/group file, 188
/etc/saf/_sactab file, 222
/etc/shadow file, 185
fields (sar command), 507
iostat command, 499-500
mpstat command, 491
netstat command, 502
nfsstat command, 504
ping command, 503
pmap command, 497-498
print command, 208
prstat command, 493
ps –ef command, 191
ps command, 279
sar command, 507
snoop command, 505

swap command, 496
traceroute command, 503
useradd command, 184
verify command, 209-210
vmstat command, 494-495
w command, 191
whodo command, 434-435

output-device configuration variable (NVRAM parameter), 526

overwriting AMANDA backups, 274

owners, files/directories, 430-431

P

-p <pmtag> option (sacadm command), 224

-P <set> option (mpstat command), 490

-P cpulist option (prstat command), 492

-p option
CacheFSpack command, 171
cpio utility, 271
logins command, 434
mount command, 136
mpstat command, 490
patchadd command, 65
pkginfo command, 58
priocntl command, 290
truss command, 292

-p pidlist option (prstat command), 492

-P ppidlist option (pgrep command, 280

package instance names, 57

packages
deleting, 60-61
installing, 52-60
managing, 52-61
required packages, Live Upgrade, 49
software packages, 54-56, 538-539

spooling, 58, 61
verifying installations, 59
versions, 57

packets, 505
authenticating, 473
encrypting, 474
round trip time, 503
transmitting, 332

packing files/lists, 171-172

Pad length field, ESP (Encapsulated Security Protocol), 475

Padding field, ESP (Encapsulated Security Protocol), 475

page (vmstat command), 494

pages, banner pages (printers), 254-255

paging, 493

panels. *See also* **Front panel; subpanels**
Additional Flash Archives panel, 47
Flash Archives Summary panel, 47
main panel (Front Panel), 103
Product Selection panel, 50
Select, 49
Select Flash Archives panel, 47
Specify Media panel, 47

panes
Navigation pane, 195
Role View pane, 466

parameters
arguments, 267
ASET security configurations, 469-470
auto-boot parameter, 71
boot-device parameter, 26
CacheFS (Cache File System), 167-175
configurations, LDAP (Lightweight Directory Access Protocol), 393
diagnostic parameters, NVRAM, 528

eeprom parameter, 27
/etc/krb5/kdc.conf file, 452
files_to_dump, 267
IPSec (IP Security Architecture), security protocols, 475-476
kernels, 74
NVRAM (Non-Volatile Random Access Memory), 24-26, 526-527
OpenBoot parameters, 26-27
scheduling parameters, processes, 291
tunable parameters, 560-565

parent directories, directory objects, 372

parent processes, 278

partition menu, 207

partitions
disk slices, 207
disk space (installation planning), 33
mounting, 156-157
root (/) file system partition (WebStart), 42
super blocks, 130

passphrases, private keys, 443

passwd (NIS+ system table), 376

passwd command, 185-186, 366

Password configuration variable command (NVRAM parameter), 527

password maps, master servers (NIS configurations), 361

password-based authentication, Secure Shell, 301

passwords
assigning (users), 185-186
creating (NIS domain users), 366
encrypted passwords, 182, 188

/etc/shadow file, 181
recovering (OBP), 424-425
root passwords, sysidcfg files, 40
unauthorized changes, preventing (OBP), 425-426
users, 434

Patch Report Update report, 62

patch revision number, 61

patchadd command, 64-66

patches, 61-66

Patches menu commands, Action, Download Patches, 63

patchrm command, options, 66

PATH environment shell variable, 118

path field, -l option (swap command), 495

path names, user directories, 182

paths
desktop search paths, 100
search paths, file systems (troubleshooting), 540-541

pax utility, 271

PC File System (PCFS), 17, 129

PCFS (FAT) disks, sysidcfg file storage, 39

PCFS (PC File System), 17, 129

pcia-probe-list command, hardware testing (OpenBoot), 28

PCPU time, 191

performance
CacheFS (Cache File System), 174
disks (SVM), 213
measuring, 94
multiple processes, 278

Performance Meter, 93, 512

performance monitoring
CPUs, 490-493
disk utilization, 499-501
networks, 501-505
sar, 505-507
SMC (Solaris Management Console), 508-512
virtual memory, 493-498

performance reports, 490-496

permissions
file systems, 426-431
levels, file system security, 427
multiple permissions, chmod command, 430
remote systems, 306
.rhosts file, 300
symbolic method (file systems), 428

personal applications, storing, 89

Personal Bookmarks, Web application (Links subpanel), 89

Personal Printers subpanel, 92

pgrep command, 278-282

Phase 1, fsck command, 142, 546-548

Phase 2, fsck command, 143, 548-549

Phase 3, fsck command, 143, 549-550

Phase 4, fsck command, 143, 550

Phase 5, fsck command, 143, 550

phases
fsck command, 542
IPSec (IP Security Architecture), security protocols, 475
phase 1, errors (fsck command), 546-548
phase 2, errors (fsck command), 548-549

phase 3, errors (fsck command), 549-550
phase 4, errors (fsck command), 550
phase 5, errors (fsck command), 550

Physical layer, OSI (Open System Interconnection), 311

physmem (kernel tunable parameter), 560

PID (process ID), 278, 291

ping command, 331, 503

pipes, 16, 110

PKC (Public Key Cryptography), 375

pkgadd command, 56-58, 538

pkgchk -v <package name> command, 59

pkgchk command, 59

pkginfo command, 57-58

pkgmap file, symbolic link targets, 538

pkgrm command, 61

PKG_NONABI_SYMLINKS environment variables, 538

pkill command, 283

placeholders, passwords (/etc/shadow file), 181

planning
backups, 261
DHCP (Dynamic Host Configuration Protocol), 317
installations, 33-37, 104
LANs (local area networks), 312-314
NIS domains, 359
security, 422

/platform/'uname -m'/ufs-boot program, 71

platters component (disks), 204

Please Enter Your User Name text box, 87

plus sign (+), 298

pmadm command, 227

pmap command, 496-498

pmtag variable, 223

pntadm command, 318

Point-to-Point Protocol (PPP), LAN component, 311

pointers, inode blocks, 131

POP (Post Office Transfer Protocol), 409-410

port initialization phase, 226

port monitors, 221-227

port numbers, LDAP parameter, 393

port services, 227-228

portable archive interchange (pax utility), 271

ports
    LAN component, 311
    printer ports, accessing, 249
    serial ports, 220, 228-231
    tty ports, 228

POST (power on self test), 29, 70-71

post login sequence, 300

pound sign (#), 118

power management, sysidcfg files, 40

power on self test (POST), 29, 70-71

powerfail, action keyword (/etc/inittab file), 76

poweroff command, shutdown, 81

PPP (Point to Point Protocol), LAN component, 311

pre-shared keys, IKE (Internet Key Exchange), 479

pread/s field (sar command), 507

preparations, pre-installation tasks (WebStart Flash), 46-48

primary, principals, 447

Primary Administrator, rights profile (RBAC), 456-457

primary groups, 187

principals
    KDC, 447
    Kerberos, 452

print clients, 238
    configuring (Print Manager), 248
    information, 252
    troubleshooting, 552

print command, 208

print filters, fault recovery definitions, 255

Print Manager, 92, 238
    Add Access window, 248
    configurations, 246-249
    fault alerts, 254
    installing, 246-247
    launching, 247
    limitations, 249
    Name Services, 246
    print clients configurations, 248
    print server configurations, 248
    printer sharing, 246
    Select Naming Service window, 248

print process, LP Print Service, 244

print queue logs, LP Print Service, 244

print requests, printers, 256-257

print servers, 238
    configuring (Print Manager), 248
    hard disks, spooling space, 239
    information, deleting, 252
    print environment design, 239
    troubleshooting, 552

print services, managing, 241

Printer Administration icon, 247

Printer menu commands, 248

printer-host device, 250

printers
    accessing, 92
    classes, 252
    configuration file (LP Print Service), 242
    configuring, 249-252
    definitions, 240, 252-256
    deleting, 251-252
    descriptions, special characters, 252
    entries, iPlanet 5.1 Directory Service, 398
    grouping, 253
    multiple filters, 250
    naming, 250
    network printers, 250
    nodes, 250
    ports, accessing, 249
    remote printers, access (denying), 553-554
    sharing, 246
    status, 552

printevn command, 24-25

Printevn configuration variable command (NVRAM parameter), 527

printing
    administering, lp commands, 249-257
    configurations, 246
    environment, 238-240
    local printers, 238
    LP Print Service, 240-244
    Name Services, 246
    network printers, 238
    Print Manager, 246-249
    shared printers, 238
    troubleshooting, 244, 550-554

/proc directory, 37

/proc file system, 134

priocntl command, 290-291

priority
processes, 290
syslog file, 436

private keys
authentication (NIS+), 375
DH (Diffie-Hellman)
authentication, 161
pairs, creating, 302
passphrases, 443

privileges, superuser privileges, 79-81

probe-scsi all command, hardware testing (OpenBoot), 28

probe-scsi command, hardware testing (OpenBoot), 28

proccesses, 278-283
running (priority), 290
scheduling, 286-292

process file system (procfs), memory-based file system, 129

process ID (PID), 278-282

Process Manager, 283-286

Process Manager—Log File dialog box, 285

Process menu commands, 283-284

processes
access priority, 289
active processes, 192
at jobs, 288
binding process, NIS
(Network Information
Service), 358
child processes, 278
debugging, 291
execution priority, 289
killing, 283, 286
local processes, 192
managing, 15
monitoring, 278-282
multiple processes, 278
multitasking, 278
name resolution process,
DNS (Domain Name
Service), 348-349

neighbor discovery process,
330
parent processes, 278
priority, 290
Process Manager, 283-285
running system processes,
191
scheduling, 291
sorting, 284-285
states, viewing, 278
swapper process, 74
terminating, 282-283
tracking, 291
user processes, file systems,
148

processing
background processing, 16,
110
interactive processing, 16,
110
interrupt processing, 29

procfs (process file system), memory-based file system, 129

procs (vmstat command), 495

Product Selection panel, 50

.profile file, 100, 116

profiles, 115
client profiles, iPlanet 5.1
Directory Service, 398
custom profiles, JumpStart
software, 42-43
Factory JumpStart installations, 45
JumpStart servers, 44-45
rights profiles, RBAC
(Role-Based Access
Control), 456-457
user profiles, 100
WebStart Flash installations, creating, 47

programming language constructs, 16, 111

programs, boot programs, 70-71

Projects view, 508

PROM versions (OpenBoot), 22

prompts
> prompt, 22
default prompts, shells, 117
ok prompt, 23, 29

Properties
command (Action menu),
230
dialog box, 200, 230
file management application
(Files subpanel), 90

proprietary mail services, 406

protocols. *See also* **LDAP (Lightweight Directory Access Protocol); TCP (Transmission Control Protocol)**
AH (Authentication
Header), 473-474
ESP (Encapsulated Security
Payload), 473-475
IKE (Internet Key
Exchange), 13, 476-479
IPSec (IP Security
Architecture), 472-477
mail transfer protocols,
408-410
network printers, 250
NIS+ system table, 376
Secure Sockets Layer
(SSL)/Transport Layer
Security (TLS), 391
security protocols, IPSec
(IP Security Architecture),
473-476
SSH1, 442
SSH2, 442

proxies, SunScreen, 485

prstat command, 192, 492-493, 504

 # ps –ef | grep Mountd command (troubleshooting NFS), 162

 # ps –ef | grep Nfsd command (troubleshooting NFS), 162

ps command, 117, 278-280

ps -ef command, 191-192

PS1 environment shell variable, 118

PS2 environment shell variable, 118

Public Key Cryptography (PKC), 375

public keys
    authentication (NIS+), 375
    IKE (Internet Key Exchange), 479
    pairs, creating, 302

-public option, WebNFS access, 163

public/private key pairs, SSH authentication, 443

put/mput ftp command, 307

pwrit/s field (sar command), 507

Q

question mark (?), 27, 94

queue email, 417-418

quick mode, authentication (IKE), 478

Quick Reference Section, Patch Report Update report, 62

quot command, options, 147

Quota (disk quotas), 140

quota command, 194

Quotacheck (disk quotas), 140

Quotaoff (disk quotas), 140

Quotaon (disk quotas), 140

R

-r option
    at command, 289
    boot command, 28
    du command, 146
    Mountd daemon (NFS), 154
    netstat command, 502
    patch installations, 65

patchadd command, 65

patchrm command, 66

pkginfo command, 58

pmap command, 497

-R root_path options (pkginfo command), 58

r/s field (iostat command), 499

RAID (Redundant Array of Independent Disks), 212, 265

RAID 0, building, 213

RAID 1, building, 213

RAID 5, building, 213

RBAC (Role-Based Access Control), 456-467

%rcache field (sar command), 507

rc scripts (run control scripts), 76-77, 81

rcp client application (Kerberos), 454

rcp command, 305

RDBMSs (Relative Database Management Systems), 11

re-preinstall command, 42

Read access right (NIS+), 385

read mode of operation (pax utility), 271

Read permissions, file systems, 426

Read-Directory permission (file system security), 427

Read-File permission (file system security), 427

read-only file systems, 166

Ready-to-Send (RTS) controls, 233

realms, 447

reboot command, shutdown, 81

Recommended Paths Section, Patch Report Update report, 62

reconfiguration boots, 71

/reconfigure file, 210

record locking, NFS (Network File System), 155

records, slave records, 351

Reduced Instruction Set Computing (RISC), 17-18

Redundant Array of Independent Disks (RAID), 212, 265

references. *See* links

regular expressions, packing lists, 172

reject command, 257

Relative Database Management Systems (RDBMs), 11

remote access, /var/mail directory, 415

remote copy, file transfer, 305-306

remote file systems, 134, 140

remote hosts
    access, 298
    logging in, 443-444
    networks, 503

remote logins, 88, 303-304

remote machines, troubleshooting, 330

remote mode, mail systems, 412

remote print process, LP Print Service, 244

remote printers, access, 553-554

Remote Procedure Call (RPC), 455

remote servers, troubleshooting, 540

remote sessions, terminating, 296

remote systems
    accessing, 302, 306
    administering, 294

domain names, 296
escape sequences, 296
files, transferring, 301, 304-307
home directories, 300
linking, 295
local systems, 295-297
logins, 294-304
permissions, 306
security, 294
sessions, toggling, 296

remote terminal emulation, 294

renewable [true/false] option (Kerberos), 453

renice command, 289-290

repairing
disks, 208-210
file systems, 141-144

replacement_timeout parameter (CacheFS), 175

replica servers
configuring, 383-384
LDAP, 393
NIS+, 373

reports
ASET (Automated Security Enhancement Tool), 469
Patch Report Update, 62
performance reports, 490-496

Repquota (disk quotas), 140

request history log files, LP Print Service, 243-244

requests
file systems, 154
print requests, definitions, 256-257

reserved_prosc (kernel tunable parameter), 560

reset command, 25

resetting file system states, 158

Resident Physical Memory field (pmap command), 497

resources
sessions, 101
shared local resources, creating, 154
system resources, 15

respawn, action keyword (/etc/inittab file), 76

restoring
backups, 266-268
AMANDA utility, 274-275
cpio utility, 270
dd utility, 270
mt utility, 269-270
pax utility, 271
tar utility, 269
Veritas Net Backup utility, 273
volcopy utility, 272-273
files (deleting patches), 66

restricted monitor mode, CLI (command line interface), 22

restricted shells, limitations, 114

Return_to Local Host option (Options drop-down list), 87

reverse address mapping, 351

reversed field, -s option (swap command), 496

Review dialog box, 461

rew option (mt utility), 270

.rhosts file, 299-300

Rights icon, 462

rights profiles, RBAC (Role-Based Access Control), 456-467

RISC (Reduced Instruction Set Computing), 17-18

rlim_fd_max (kernel tunable parameter), 561

rlogin command, 295-300

rlogin/rsh client application (Kerberos), 454

rmdir ftp command, 307

Role Back Access Control (RBAC) databases, master servers, 362

Role Properties dialog box, 466-467

Role-Based Access Control. See RBAC

roles
creating, 456
information, storing, 456
installing (RBAC), 457-461
RBAC (Role-Based Access Control), 456
rights profiles, creating (RBAC), 466-467

Roles View pane, 466

root (/) file system partitions (WebStart), 42

root access, SVM (Solaris Volume Manager), 215

root accounts. See Superusers

root default group, 187

root directories, 16, 372

root domains, configuring (NIS+), 382-386

root file systems, 133

root menu. See Workspace menu

root passwords, sysidcfg files, 40

round trip time, 503

routers, configuring, 316

routing-mode, SunScreen, 483

RPC (Remote Procedure Call), 161, 376, 455

% rpcinfo –s bee | egrep command (troubleshooting NFS), 162

RS-232C interface, 220

RS232C/D connections, modems/terminals, 232

rsh command, 304

rstchown (kernel tunable parameter), 561

RTS (Ready-to-Send) controls, 233

Rules files, 42-44

run control scripts (rc scripts), 76-77, 81

run levels, 74-75, 78-79

Run state, processes, 278

running processes (priority), 290

running system processes, 191

S

-s option
boot command, 28
du command, 146
logins command, 434
netstat command, 502
nfsstat command, 504
passwd command, 186
pmap command, 497
swap command, 496
useradd command, 183
vmstat command, 494
volcopy utility, 272

s run level, shutdown, 78

-s sidlist option (pgrep command, 280

S5 (System V File System), disk-based file system, 129

SA (Security Association), 475-477

sa1 command (sar), 506

sa2 command (sar), 506

SAC (service access controller), 221-223

sacadm command, 223-224

sadc command (sar), 506

SAF (Service Access Facility), 221-227

Sample menu commands, 285

sar (System Activity Reporter), 505-507

SASL (Simple Authentication and Security Layer), 391

Save As window, 285

Save command (Sample menu), 285

savecore, command or directory, 557

saving
dump information (crashed systems), 557
log files (processes), 285

/sbin directory, 76

Scalable Processor Architecture. See SPARC

sched module (kernels), 72

scheduler
LP Print Service, 242
print requests, 256
shutting down, 256
starting, 256

scheduling, process scheduling, 286-292

scheduling classes, 291

scheduling parameters, processes, 291

scp command, 304, 444-445

Screen, SunScreen, 481-482

screen savers, displaying, 95

screen-#columns configuration variable (NVRAM parameter), 526

screen-#rows configuration variable (NVRAM parameter), 526

screens
chooser screens, 97
Flash Archive Retrieval Method, 47
Flash Archive Selection screen, 47
Installer screen (WebStart), 42
login screens, 95, 99

Select Media screen (WebStart), 42
Welcome screen (WebStart), 42

scripts. See syntax

SEAM (Sun Enterprise Authentication Mechanism), 445-451

search paths
desktop search paths, 100
file systems, troubleshooting, 540-541

SEAS (Solaris Easy Access Server), 445

secondary groups, 187

Secure Shell, 301-304, 442-445. See SSH

Secure Sockets Layer (SSL)/Transport Layer Security (TLS) protocol, 391

security
ASET (Automated Security Enhancement Tool), 468-471
considerations, 422
directories, 361, 391
file systems, 426-432
firewalls, 480-487
GSS-API (Generic Security Standard Application Programming Interface), 455
IKE (Internet Key Exchange), 476-479
IPSec (IP Security Architecture), 472-476
Kerberos, 451-455
levels, OBP (OpenBoot PROM), 423
management, 15
NFS (Network File System), 153, 159, 161
NIS+, versus NIS, 375
OBP (OpenBoot PROM), 423-426
planning, 422
protocols, 473-476

RBAC (Role-Based Access Control), 456-467

remote systems, 294

.rhosts file, 299-300

SEAM (Sun Enterprise Authentication Mechanism), 445-451

SSH (Secure Shell), 442-445

sysidcfg files, 40

TCP wrappers, 471-472

user data requests, 190

user logins, 432-439

users, 422

Security Association (SA), 475-477

Security Parameter Index (SPI) field, 474

security-#badlogins configuration variable (NVRAM parameter), 526

security-mode configuration variable (NVRAM parameter), 527

security-password configuration variable (NVRAM parameter), 527

sekpsize (kernel tunable parameter), 562

Select All button, 56

Select Flash Archives panel, 47

Select Media screen (WebStart), 42

Select Naming Services window, 248

Select panel, 49

self-signed certificates, IKE (Internet Key Exchange), 479

sendmail daemon, 408-411

sendmail.cf file, 408

Sequence number field, 474

sequences, escape sequences, 231

serial connections, troubleshooting (monitors/terminals), 236

serial devices, 220

modems, 231-236

monitors

port service, 227-228

SAF (Service Access Facility), 221-227

SMC (Solaris Management Console), 228-231

terminals

connecting, 231, 233-235

port service, 227-228

SAF (Service Access Facility), 221-227

SMC (Solaris Management Console), 228-231

troubleshooting, 235-236

serial ports, 220, 228-231

server clocks, Kerberos (synchronizing), 453

server list mode, NIS (Network Information Service), 359

server-related files, configuring, 96

servers

backups, 261

color server, 101

DHCP (Dynamic Host Configuration), 317-326, 331

dhcpconfig command, 318

directory servers, iPlanet 5.1 Directory Server, 397

DNS (Domain Name Service), 347, 350-351

iPlanet 5.1 Directory Server, 393-398

JumpStart servers, 43-45

KDC servers, 447-452

Login Server, 98

mail servers, 415-416

master servers

configuring, 382-383

LDAP, 393

loads, 365

NIS (Network Information Service), 356, 360-364

restarting, 368

source files, 362

Name Database Server, WebStart installations, 40-41

name servers, sysidcfg files, 39

namespace design (NIS+), 378

print clients, troubleshooting, 552

print servers, 238

configuring (Print Manager), 248

information (deleting), 252

print environment design, 239

troubleshooting, 552

remote servers, troubleshooting, 540

replica servers, 383-384 393

slave servers

DNS (Domain Name Service), 351-352

NIS (Network Information Service), 356

NIS domains, 360, 364-365

NIS domains (adding), 365

slave records, 351

troubleshooting (terminals/monitors), 235

Web servers, 11

service access controller (SAC), 221-223

Service Access Facility (SAF), 221-227

services. *See also* mail services; naming services

directory services, 338, 390-392

DIT (Directory Information Tree), 390-392

networking services, 12

NIS+ system table, 376
port services, 227-228

Session layer, OSI (Open System Interconnection), 310

Session Manager, 99-101

session suspension (remote systems), 296

Session, FailSafe Session command (Option menu), 88

sessions
Current sessions, 99
Home sessions, 100
Initial sessions, 100
remote sessions, terminating, 296
resources, 101
toggling, 296

Sessions option (Options drop-down list), 87

set command, shell environment variables, 119

set keyword, kernel parameters, 74

Set Security Attributes button, 465

set-default variable configuration variable command (NVRAM parameter), 527

set-defaults configuration variable command (NVRAM parameter), 527

setenv command, 25

setenv variable-name value configuration variable command (NVRAM parameter), 527

SetGID-Directory permission (file system security), 427

SetGID-File permission (file system security), 427

settings, default user settings, 183

SetUID-File permission (file system security), 427

setup command, 395

share command, 154, 158, 415

shareall
command, 415
syntax, 43

shared directories, packing files, 172

shared local resources, creating, 154

shared printers, 238

sharing
automatic file-system sharing, 158-159
printers, 246

shells
aliases, 122-124
background processing, 110
bash (Bourne again) shell, 114
Bourne shell, 113, 116, 541
C shell, 113, 116, 123
command alias, 111
command history, 111
command interpretation, 112
commands, ulimit command, 139
comparing, 114
customizing, 115-117
default prompts, 117
dtksh (desktop kornshell) shell, 114
features, 16
input/output redirection, 110
interactive processing, 110
Korn shell, 114-116, 122, 541
login shells, 182
pipes, 16, 110
programming language constructs, 111
restricted, limitations, 114
scripts, 111-113
system calls, 15
system-defined variables, 119
Tcsh (Tom's C) shell, 114

template initialization files, 120-121
user-defined variables, 119
variables, 111, 117-120
Zsh shell, 114

shortcuts, commands, 122. *See also* keyboard shortcuts

show_devs command, hardware testing (OpenBoot), 28

shutdown, 210
command, 79-80
halt command, 81
init command, 78-79
poweroff command, 81
reboot command, 81
run control scripts, 81
run levels, 78-79
scheduler, 256
super blocks, 130

SIGKILL signal, 282-283

signals, 282-284

SIGTERM signal, 282-283

Simple Authentication and Security Layer (SASL), 391

Simple Mail Transfer Protocol (SMTP), 409

single-user mode, 71, 80

size
block size, data, 270
file size, file systems, 39-140
disk quota, 140
NIS+, versus NIS, 374
ulimit command, 139-140

Skeme, 476

slave KDC servers, 447-450

slave records, 351

slave servers. *See* replica servers
DNS (Domain Name Service), 347, 351-352
NIS (Network Information Service), 356, 360, 364-365
slave records, 351

Sleep state, processes, 278

slices

disk slices, 205-210

disks, format utility, 206-210

file systems, 135

root (/) system files, upgrades, 49

slots, I/O slots, 211

SMC (Solaris Management Console)

downloading, 62

group management, 194, 198-201

monitors, 228-231

patches, 64-66

performance, 508-512

RBAC (Role-Based Access Control), setting up, 457

serial ports, 230-231

SVM access, 215

terminals, 228-231

user management, 194-198

smdiskless management command, 535

smexec management command, 535

smgroup management command, 534

smmaillist management command, 535

smmultiuser management command, 534

smosservice management command, 535

smprofile management command, 535

smrole management command, 534

smserialport management command, 535

SMTP (Simple Mail Transfer Protocol), 409

smtx (mpstat command), 491

smuser management command, 534

snapshot backups, 266

snoop command, 332, 505

SOA (Start of Authority), 352

soft limits, disk quotas, 140

soft links, 133

software

connections, hot swaps, 211

co-packaged software, WebStart installations, 41

custom profiles (JumpStart installations), 42

disk space (installation planning), 33

email components, 407

GNOMEs, 104

groups, disk space (installation planning), 34

Live Upgrade, 49-50

packages, 54-56, 538-539

required, 38

Software command (Browse menu), 54

Solaris 2.6, upgrades, 48

Solaris 7, upgrades, 48-49

Solaris 8, upgrades, 48-49

Solaris Easy Access Server (SEAS), 445

Solaris Management Console. *See* **SMC**

Solaris OE, upgrades, 48

Solaris Volume Manager (SVM), 213-216

Solstice Disk AdminSuite, 212

sorting processes, 284-285

source files, master servers, 361-362

space

CacheFS, 167-168

disk space, users, 194

Space Meter button, 55

SPARC (Scalable Processor Architecture), 17

Factory JumpStart installations, 45

Jumpstart installations, 42

OBP (OpenBoot PROM), 423

OpenBoot, 22

OpenBoot PROM, 18

Sun Fire, 19

SPARC boot process, 70

special characters, printer descriptions, 252

Specific Package Installation Errors, 538-539

Specify Media panel, 47

speed, line speed, terminals, 226

SPI (Security Parameter Index) field, 474

spool directories, package installation, 59

spooled packages, deleting, 61

spooling, 409

mail servers, 415

packages, 58

spooling space, 239

-sRv option (ping command), 503

srw (mpstat command), 492

SSH (Secure Shell), 301-304, 442-445

ssh agents, remote hosts, 444

ssh command, 302-303

ssh-keygen command, 302

SSH1 protocols, 442

SSH2 protocols, 442

staff default group, 188

StarOver button, 87

Start Address Wizard, 324

Start of Authority (SOA) resource, 352

start scripts, run control scripts, 77

starting

GUIs, 87

Live Upgrade, 50

NFS daemons, 154

scheduler, 256

stash files, 452

Statd daemon, NFS (Network File System), 155

state database replicas, building, 213

states
firmware states, 22
port monitors, 223-225
process states, viewing, 278
processes, 278

static IPv6 addresses, enabling, 330

status
networks, 332
port monitors, 225
port services, 228
printing, 552-554
tape drives, 270

status command (Telnet utility), 295

stderr file, 292

stealth-mode, SunScreen, 483

Sticky Bit-Directory permission (file system security), 427

Stop, keyboard interrupt key, 29

stop command, 415

stop scripts, run control scripts, 77

Stop+A, keyboard interrupt key, 29

Stop+D, keyboard interrupt key, 29

Stop+N, keyboard interrupt key, 29

storage, archive storage, 270

storage administration, 204-205, 212

storage arrays (Sun StorEdge), backups, 265

storing
banner page settings, printers, 255
configuration files, 96
default printer names, 253

fault alerts, printers, 254
file information, 131
file management applications, 90
Front Panel customizations, 103
mail addresses, 92
NIS+ tables, 379
patches, 65
personal applications, 89
.rhosts file, 299
role information, 456
run control scripts, 76-77
source files, master servers (NIS configurations), 361
sysidcfg files, 39
Web applications, 89

striping, data (RAID 0), 212

Strmod module (kernels), 72

structures, domain structures, 374

stty command, 232

Style Manager, 93

su command, loging attempts (displaying), 438

subdirectories
disks, 205
lost + found, 143
patches, 64
/var, 262

subpanels
Applications subpanel, 91
Cards, 89
Files, 90
Front panel, 103
Help subpanel, 94
Hosts subpanel, 93-94
Links, 89
Mail subpanel, 92
Personal Printers subpanel, 92
Tools subpanel, 92-93
Trash subpanel, 94-95

Suggestion Box option (Mail subpanel), 92

sulog variable, 438

Sun, supported hardware, 18-19

Sun Enterprise Authentication Mechanism (SEAM), 445-451

Sun Fire, 19

Sun Microsystems, 17

Sun StorEdge, storage array, 265

Sun StorEdge (Vertas) Volume Manager, 216

Sun Web site, 479-480

SunInstall, 45-46

SunOS 5.5.x, Solaris 9, 249

SunScreen, 480-487

SunScreen Lite, 480-481, 485-487

SUNWppm, Print Manager, 246

super blocks, 130, 143-144

Superusers, 180, 437-439
format utility, 206
privileges, 79-81

supported_enctypes parameter (/etc/krb5/kdc.conf file), 452

surrogate super blocks, 130

svc_t field (iostat command), 500

SVM (Solaris Volume Manager), 213-216

/swap directory, 37

swap command, options, 495-496

swapfs_minfree (kernel tunable parameter), 561

swapfs_reserve (kernel tunable parameter), 561

swaplow field, -l option (swap command), 496

swapper process, 74

swapping, 494

symbolic link targets (soft links), 133, 538

symbolic method, 428

symbolic values, umask, 431-432

symbols
chmod command, 429-430
tickets, 451

synchronizing server clocks, Kerberos, 453

syntax
chmod command, 429
clri command, 148
devnm command, 147
df command, 193, 500
disk configuration information, 211
disk slices, 206-207
disk unconfiguration, 211
.dtprofile script, 100
du command, 146
eeprom command, 25-26
/etc/dfs/dfstab file, 158
/etc/inittab file, 75
/etc/mnttab files, 138
/etc/nsswitch nis file, 344-345
/etc/nsswitch nisplus file, 344
/etc/nsswitch.file, 345-346
/etc/profile, 115-116
/etc/resolv.conf file, 350
/etc/saf/_sactab file, 222
/etc/skel/local.cshrc, 122
/etc/skel/local.login, 121
/etc/skel/profile, 120-121
/etc/syslog file, 436-437
/etc/system file, 72-74
/etc/vfstab file (Virtual File System Table), 137
fstyp command, 147
fuser command, 148
init command, 80
iPlanet 5.1 Directory Server configurations, 396-397
large files, locating, 158
last command, 193-194
-li option (ls command), 131-132
master server boot files, 351
misserver syntax, NIS+ master server, 382
mpstat command output, 491

network printer configuration, 250
nfsstat command output, 504
nisclient syntax, NIS+ replica server, 383-384
nispopulate, 380-381
nisserver, 379
output, iostat command, 500
packages, installing, 52-53
packing files, shared directories, 172
partition menu, 207
passwd command, 185
ping command output, 503
pkgchk –v package name> command, 59
pkginfo command, 57
pmap command output, 497-498
print command output, 208
printevn command, 24-25
prstat command, 192, 493
ps command, 279
quot command, 147
reboot command (shutdown), 81
Rules file, creating, 44
run control scripts, 76-77, 81
sar command output, 507
shareall syntax, 43
shells, 16, 111
snoop command output, 505
start scripts, run control scripts, 77
stop scripts, run control scripts, 77
swap command output, 496
sysidcfg file, 40
traceroute command output, 503
verify command output, 209-210
vmstat command output, 495
whodo command, 434-435
Xfailsafe, 88
Xsession.d script, 100

sys default group, 187

Sys module (kernels), 72

sysadmin default group, 188

syscl (mpstat command), 492

sysidcfg file, 39-40, 44-46

sysinit, action keyword (/etc/inittab file), 76

syslog file, 435-437

syslogd daemon, 435, 557

System (software package), 54

system accounting, 15

System Activity Reporter (sar), 505-507

System Administrator, 180, 456-457

system boot, super blocks, 130

System Configuration (SMC), 195

System Information view, 510

system tables, NIS+, 375-376

System V File System (S5), disk-based file system, 129

System view, 508

system-defined variables, shells, 119

system-specific configuration file (Workspace Manager), 102

system-to-system authentication (remote systems), 304

system-wide configurations, CDE, 96

system-wide initialization files, 115

systems. *See also* file systems; remote systems
access (port monitors), 223
attacks, TCP wrappers, 472
booting (OpenBoot), 26-29
calls, 15, 278

clone systems, 47-48

configurations, WebStart installations, 41

end-to-end delivery system, 409

files, root (/) system files, upgrades, 49

levels, file size limit, 139

local systems, 295-297, 539-540

messages, crashed systems, 557

performance. *See* performance monitoring

resources, 15

troubleshooting, 554-558

users, validating, 433

windowing systems. *See* GUIs

System_Admin window, 247

sZ, addressing disks, 206

T

-t <type> option (sacadm command), 224

-t option
lockd daemon (NFS), 155

logins command, 434

command (troubleshooting NFS), 162

-t termilist option (pgrep command), 280

table objects, 372

tables
network tables, DHCP, 318

NIS+, 375, 381
aliases, 418
attributes, 380
creating, 379-380
links, 377
populating, 380
versus NIS maps, 376-377

tabs, Commands, 464

tape archives, 269

tape drives, 263-264, 270

tar command, 64

tar utility, 269

TCP (Transmission Control Protocol), 12
configuring, 314-316

DHCP (Dynamic Host Configuration Protocol), 316-328

IPv6 (Internet Protocol Version 6), 328-330

LANs (local area networks), 310-314

networks, 250, 310, 330-333

OSI (Open System Interconnection), 310

routers, configuring, 316

SMTP (Simple Mail Transfer Protocol), 409

Solaris LAN components, 311

tunable parameters, 562-563

wrappers, 471-472

tcp_cwnd_max (TCP/IP tunable parameter), 563

tcp_deferred_ack_interval (TCP/IP tunable parameter), 563

tcp_deffered_acks_max (TCP/IP tunable parameter), 563

tcp_local_dack_interval (TCP/IP tunable parameter), 563

tcp_slow_start_initial (TCP/IP tunable parameter), 563

tcp_tstamp_always (TCP/IP tunable parameter), 563

tcp_wscale_always (TCP/IP tunable parameter), 563

Tcsh (Tom's C) shell, 114

telnet client application (Kerberos), 454

Telnet utility, 294-295

template initialization files, shells, 120-121

templates, User Templates, 197

temporary file system (tmpfs), memory-based file system, 129

temporary files, file systems, 139

TERM environment shell variable, 118

terminal types, sysidcfg files, 40

Terminal window, 105

terminals
connecting, 220, 231-235

escape sequences, 231

line speed, 226

managing, 230

serial devices, 220
port service, 227-228
SAF (Service Access Facility), 221-227
SMC (Solaris Management Console), 228-231

troubleshooting, 235-236

terminating
processes, 282-283

remote sessions, 296

terminfo database, LP Print Service, 243

TERMINFO environment shell variable, 118

test floppy command, hardware testing (OpenBoot), 28

test memory command, hardware testing (OpenBoot), 28

test net command, hardware testing (OpenBoot), 28

test-all command, hardware testing (OpenBoot), 28

testing
hardware (OpenBoot), 28-29

mail system configurations, 417

print client configurations (Print Manager), 248
print server configurations (Print Manager), 248

text boxes
Filter, 285
Group, 465
Installation Directory, 56
Please Enter Your User Name, 87
Signal, 284
Unresolved Dependencies, 56
User, 465

Text Editor (Applications subpanel), 91

text files, NIS maps, 367

Text Note (Applications subpanel), 91

TGT (ticket-granting ticket), 445

This Computer option (SMC), 215

threshblocks parameters (CacheFS), 168

threshfiles parameters (CacheFS), 168

ticket, attributes, 451

ticket-granting ticket (TGT), 445

tickets
Kerberos, 451
SEAM, 445, 450-451
symbols, 451

time interval option (vmstat command), 494

time stamps, DES (Data Encryption System), 160

time zones, sysidcfg files, 40

timeout values, network printers, 250

times
modified times, CacheFS (Cache File System), 173
sysidcfg files, 40

timezone (NIS+ system table), 376

/tmp directory, 37

/tmp file system, 134

/tmp/addentry file, 401

tmpfs (temporary file system), memory-based file system, 129

toggling sessions, 296

Tom's C shell (tcsh), 114

tools
accessing, 92
Admintool, 52-53, 60
Enhanced Storage tool, 213-214
management tools, 532-534
Users and Groups tool, 532

Tools subpanel, 92-93

Tools, Printer Administrator command (Workspace menu), 247

Tooltalk, 100

touch command, 329

traceroute command, 503

tracking processes, 291

trailer fields, ESP (Encapsulated Security Protocol), 475

transfer methods, FTP, 63

transferring files, remote systems, 301

Transmission Control Protocol. *See* **TCP**

transmitting packets, 332

Transport layer, OSI (Open System Interconnection), 310

Transport mode, IPSec (IP Security Architecture), 473

Trash subpanel, 94-95

tripwire rule, SunScreen Lite, 487

troubleshooting. *See also* **performance monitoring**
CacheFS (Cache File System), 174
commands, 540-541

data loss, 260
DHCP, 331
disk repair, 208, 210
file systems, 141-142
fsck command, 541-550
local systems, 539-540
networks, 540
search paths, 540-541
super block repair, 143-144
GUIs, 88
home directories, 539
modems, 235-236
networks, 330-333
NFS (Network File System), 161-163
NVRAM, 29
patches, 61-66
printing, 244, 254-256, 550-554
remote machines, 330
remote servers, 540
software package installations, 538-539
systems, 554-558
terminals, 235-236

truss command, 291-292

trusted netgroups, 298

trusted users, login authentication, 297

tty default group, 187

tty devices, SAF (Service Access Facility), 221

tty ports, 228

ttymon port monitor, 223-227

tunable parameters, 560-565

tune_t_fsflush (kernel tunable parameter), 560

tuning CacheFS maintenance, 174-175

Tunnel mode, IPSec (IP Security Architecture), 473

tX, addressing disks, 206

type command, 210

types, file systems, 147

typical installs, GNOME, 106

TZ environment shell variable, 118

U

-u euidlist option, 280, 492

-u option
CacheFSpack command, 171-173
logins command, 434
useradd command, 183

-U uidlist option, 280, 492

UDF (DVD Universal Disk Format), 17

UDP (User Datagram Protocol), 152

UFS (Unix file system), 17, 39, 129

ufsboot secondary boot program, 70-71

ufsdump utility, 266-267

ufsrestore utility, options, 268

UID (unique user identification) number, 180-182

ulimit command, 139-140

umask value, 431-432

umount command, 136

umountall command, 136

unalias utility, 124

unattended commands, remote systems, 305

Unbundled Product Patches, Patch Report Update report, 62

unconfigure command, 211

unique group identification (GID) number, 182

unique user identification (UID) number, 180-182

Universal Disk Format File System (UDF), disk-based file system, 129

Unix
Bourne shell, 113
GUI, 86
Window Managers, Motif Window Manager (mwm), 87

Unix file system (UFS), 17, 129

Unix-to-Unix Copy (UUCP), LAN component, 311

unmounting file systems, 136, 143, 193

unpacking files (CacheFS), 173

UNREF error message (fsck command), 542

Unresolved Dependencies text box, 56

unzip command, 64

upgrades, 48-49

uptime command, 190

URLs, NFS file systems, mounting, 157

use-nvramrc? configuration variable (NVRAM parameter), 527

used field, -s option (swap command), 496

used field (df command), 500

User Accounts option (SMC), 195

user agents, /usr/bin/mailx, 408

User and Groups tool, 532

user authentication, Secure Shell, 301

User Datagram Protocol (UDP), 152

user facility (syslog file), 435

user groups, NIS+ master servers, 382

user limiting commands, 194

user lp commands, 241

user management, 183-186, 194-197

user monitor commands, 190-194

user processes, file systems, 148

User Properties dialog box, 197

user sessions, managing, 87

User Templates, customizing, 197

User text box, 465

user-defined variables, 117-119

user-level initialization files, 116

user-specific configurations, 96, 102

user-to-user authentication (remote systems), 304

useradd command, 183-185, 189, 366

userdel command, 186

usermod command, 186

usernames, NIS+ versus NIS, 374

userpassword attribute, 391

users
accounts, 180-185
activities, monitoring, 435
adding, 183-185
application users, 180
authenticating, 159, 391
comment fields, 182
data requests, security, 190
directories, 182, 394
disk space, 194
environments, 180-183
groups, 182
guest users, 180
LDAP parameter, 393
logins, 181-182, 432-439
monitoring, 434
NIS domains, 366-367
passwords, 434
permissions, file system security, 426

profiles, 100
security, 422
Superusers, 180
System Administrators, 180
systems, validating, 433
trusted users, login authentication, 297
UID (unique user identification) number, 182

USF (Universal Disk Format File System), disk-based file system, 129

 # /usr/bin/rpcinfo -u command (troubleshooting NFS), 162-163

% /usr/bin/getent hosts bee command (troubleshooting NFS), 162

% /usr/bin/rpcinfo –u bee command (troubleshooting NFS), 162

% /usr/lib/nis/nisping command (troubleshooting NFS), 162

% /usr/sbin/ping/ bee command (troubleshooting NFS), 162

% /usr/sbin/showmount –e bee command (troubleshooting NFS), 162

/usr directory, 37, 262

/usr file system, 134

/usr/bin/mailx user agent, 408

/usr/lib/lp directory, filter (LP Print Service), 243

/usr/lib/lp/model directory, Interface (LP Print Service), 243

/usr/lib/saf/ttymon option (/etc/saf/_sactab file), 223

/usr/lib/sendmail –v recipient email address </dev/null> command, 417

usr/sys/wt/idl (mpstat command), 492

utilities. *See* **commands**

Utilities, Save Workspace command (Workspace menu), 103

UTMP entries, 223

utmpx database, 223

UUCP (Unix-to-Unix Copy), LAN component, 311

uucp default group, 187

uucp facility (syslog file), 435

V

-v (ver) option (sacadm command), 224

-v option
boot command, 28
fsck command, 142
Mountd daemon (NFS), 154
pgrep command, 281
quot command) 147
volcopy utility, 272

-v version options (pkginfo command), 58

validating
logins (remote systems), 299
system users, 433

values
argument values, volcopy utility, 272-273
default values, Xconfig files, 98
Directory Server, 395
environment variables, shells, 119
timeout values, network printers, 250
umask value, 431-432

/var directory, 37, 239-240

/var file system, 33, 134

/var subdirectory, 262

/var/adm directory, 433, 558

/var/adm/loginlog file, 433

/var/adm/messages file, 555

/var/adm/sulog file, 438

/var/mail directory, 415-416

/var/named/hosts.rev data file (DNS), 348

/var/named/named.ca data file (DNS), 348

/var/named/named.local data file (DNS), 348

/var/spool/cron/crontab directory, 286-287

/var/yp directory, 357

variables. *See also* **environment variables**
configuration variables, NVRAM parameters, 526-527
commands, 527
/etc/system file, 74
ISTATE variable, 223
kernel modules, 74
pmtag variable, 223
shells, 16, 111, 117-120
sulog variable, 438
Xresources files, 99

verifiers, DES (Data Encryption System), 160

verify command, 209-210

verifying
boot block installations, 210
IP addresses, 315
log files, CacheFS (Cache File System), 175
mounted file systems, 135
package installations, 59

Veritas Net Backup utility, 273

Veritas Volume Manager, 212

version, PROM versions (OpenBoot), 22

VERSION = 1 option (/etc/saf/_sactab file), 222

version command, hardware testing (OpenBoot), 28

versions, packages, 57

vi command, 424

View Macro window, 326

View menu commands, 512

viewing
    process states, 278
    queued email, 417

views, 508-510

Virtual Address field (pmap command), 497

virtual devices, disks, 212

virtual disks, 213-216

virtual file systems, 17

Virtual Mapping Size field (pmap command), 497

virtual memory, 493-498

vmstat command, 494-495

vnodes, 132

volcopy utility, 272-273

volume management, software packages, 55

Volume Manager, 212

volumes, 213-216

W

%w field (iostat command), 500

w command, 191

-w option (passwd command), 186

w/s field (iostat command), 499

wait, action keyword (/etc/inittab file), 76

wait field (iostat command), 499

Warning dialog box, 198, 201

warning priority (syslog file), 436

watch-clock command, hardware testing (OpenBoot), 28

watch-net command, hardware testing (OpenBoot), 28

watchdog-reboot configuration variable (NVRAM parameter), 527

watch_aui command, hardware testing (OpenBoot), 28

%wcache field (sar command), 507

Web applications, storing, 89

Web Browser, Web application (Links subpanel), 89

Web servers, 11

Web sites
    CheckPoint Technologies, 487
    Sun, 479-480

WebNFS (Network File System), 153, 163

WebStart Flash
    automating installation, 38-41
    CLI (Command Line Interface), 38
    GUI, 38
    installations, 41-42, 46-48

WebStart Enhanced Installation CD, 33

WebStart Installation Kiosk and Welcome to Solaris dialog box, 42

welcome messages, 100

Welcome screen (WebStart), 42

Well known services (WKS), 352

what symbol, chmod command, 430

which command, 540-541

who command, 434

who symbol, chmod command, 429

whodo command, 434

why codes, 486

wild card patterns, 16

Window Manager, 86-88

Window menu, 102

windowing systems. See GUIs

windows
    Action:Signal, 286
    Add Access window, 248
    Add Address to Network, 324
    Admintool window, 53
    Admintool:Customize Installation window, 56
    Admintool:Delete Software window, 61
    Admintool:Set Source Media, 54
    Admintool:Software window, 54
    Application Manager window, 91
    Choose Server Configuration window, 318
    DHCP Configuration Wizard window, 322
    File Manager window, 93
    Initialize Only Connection Check Box window, 231
    Mailer Compose window, 92
    Management Tools window, 199
    New Attached Printer window, 248
    Process Manager window, 284
    Save As, 285
    Select Naming Service window, 248
    System_Admin window, 247
    Terminal window, 105
    View Macro, 326

wizards
    Add Patches, 64
    Add Patches to Multiple Systems, 64
    Add User Wizard, 196

DHCP Configuration Wizard, 318, 322
Download Patches, 63
Start Address Wizard, 324
SVM Wizard, 213

WKS (Well known services), 352

Workspace buttons, 95, 101

Workspace Manager, 101-104

Workspace menu, 102
adding items, 93
commands
Tools, Printer Administrator, 247
Utilities, Save Workspace, 103

workspaces
CDE, 88
modifying, 95, 103
multiple workspaces, 103
switch, 102

WORM (write once, read many), 264

write mode of operation (pax utility), 271

Write permissions, file systems, 426

Write-Directory permission (file system security), 427

Write-File permission (file system security), 427

X

X Display Manager Control Protocol (XDMCP), 88

-x option
logins command, 434
passwd command, 186
pgrep command, 281
pmap command, 497

X utilities, 88

X Windows, introduction and history, 86

X/Open Federated Naming (XFN), 386

X11 (X Windows), 86

Xaccess files, 98

xcal (mpstat command), 491

Xconfig files, default values, 98

XDMCP (X Display Manager Control Protocol), 88

Xfailsafe script, 88

XFN (X/Open Federated Naming), 386

xhosts utility, 247

XOFF controls, 232-233

XON controls, 232-233

Xresources files, 99

Xservers files, 99

Xsession.d script, 100

-xtc option (iostat command), 499-500

Y-Z

-y option
fsck command, 142
poweroff command (shutdown), 81

Yellow Pages (YP). *See* **NIS (Network Information Service)**

ypbind process, NIS (Network Information Service), 358-359

ypinit –c method, NIS clients, 365

yppush command, 368

ypserv daemon, NIS (Network Information Service), 357

ypupdate daemon, 368

ypwhich command, 415

zip disks, backups, 263

Zombie state, processes, 278

Zsh shell, 114